A HISTORY
OF LATIN
LITERATURE

A HISTORY

OF LATIN

LITERATURE

By

MOSES HADAS

Jay Professor of Greek
Columbia University

Columbia University Press

NEW YORK

COPYRIGHT 1952 COLUMBIA UNIVERSITY PRESS

ISBN 0-231-01848-7

PRINTED IN THE UNITED STATES OF AMERICA

15 14 13

PREFACE

For out of olde feldes, as men seith,
Cometh al this newe corn fro yeer to yere;
And out of olde bokes, in good feith,
Cometh al this newe science that men lere.
—*Parlement of Foules*

SO VARIED AND SPECIALIZED IS THE VOLUME OF knowledge which modern man requires for understanding himself and his world that no one could reasonably desire classical education to be restored to the primacy it held up to two generations ago. But literate persons must always retain a curiosity concerning the important segment of their spiritual history represented by Rome. The proper repository for the spiritual achievement of a people is its literature, and it is for the curious literate, not professional students of antiquity, that this book on Latin literature has been written. Any good library could supply fuller and more professional treatment of every work here mentioned; all that is the author's is the compression and the prejudices (not, it is hoped, the caprices) of a single mind surveying the whole of Latin literature in the middle of the twentieth century. To attempt a greater degree of originality in a summary treatment of a subject which has been elaborated by generations of competent scholars would be arrogant as well as capricious, and in distilling so much of the accumulated body of criticism as suited the scope of this book I have thought it right to appropriate the work of my predecessors. Full documentation is neither possible nor desirable for the newest thin layer on a snowball.

In accordance with the aims of the book, the use of Latin has been avoided except in a very few instances where the sound of the words is significant and the meaning transparent. Titles are given in either language or both, the aim being to facilitate both understanding and recognition. Apportionment of space is inequitable, partly perforce and partly by intention; for the literate reader Lucretius or Vergil need only be fitted into context, whereas fragmentary early writers like Lucilius or neglected later writers like Ammianus Marcellinus require relatively fuller treatment. Quotations have been used rather freely because the general reader cannot be expected to recall or search out central passages, and lyric poets can be explained in no other way. To the translators whose work has been cited grateful acknowledgement is made; their names are recorded in the citations and their books in the Bibliographical Notes. Far the greater number are from the indispensable Loeb Classical Library; for their use cordial thanks are due to the Harvard University Press. Particular thanks are due also to the University of Chicago Press for a long extract from Professor Richard McKeon's Introduction and Professor Hubert McN. Poteat's translations from *Marcus Tullius Cicero: Brutus, On the Nature of Gods, On Divination, On Duties* (1950); to Professor E. A. Havelock for a passage from his *Lyric Genius of Catullus* (Oxford, Blackwell, 1939); to Professor Mark Van Doren for a paragraph from his *The Noble Voice* (New York, Henry Holt, 1946); to Oxford University Press for an extract from F. J. E. Raby's *Christian-Latin Poetry* (1927). Finally, acknowledgement must be made for permission to use passages from my introductions to *The Basic Writings of Cicero* and *The Complete Works of Tacitus* in the Modern Library series; from my essay on "Later Latin Epic and Lucan" in *Classical Weekly,* Vol. XXIX; and from my papers on Seneca, Livy, and Vergil in *American Journal of Philology,* Vols. LX, LXI, and LXIX.

Moses Hadas

Columbia University in the City of New York
December, 1951

CONTENTS

CONTENTS

A HISTORY

OF LATIN

LITERATURE

I

THE NATURE OF LATIN LITERATURE

THE LATIN LITERATURE WHICH WE ARE ABOUT TO consider represents the choicest thought and expression of Europe during several critical and seminal centuries of its history, and up to the present it has been properly regarded, along with the Greek which nourished it, as the backbone of European education. Of the two we may grant at once that in originality, scope, imagination, and taste the Greek is superior. Taken in isolation, moreover, and separated from the historical and cultural development out of which it arose and which it reflects, Latin literature must be pronounced inferior to more than one of its daughter literatures. Nor would the Romans themselves be astonished or disturbed at such a judgment. They were well aware of the superiority of the Greeks in literature, and indeed the more aware as they became more sensitive to literary values; but they were quite complacent in their inferiority. To the Romans litera- ture was never at the center of life but at best an ornament. They them- selves had no doubt that as men and citizens (the two concepts were identical) they were far superior to the frivolous Greeks, who could exaggerate the importance of literature because they were incapable of more substantial achievements, and history seemed to bear them out: What Greek city was able to impose its will upon its neighbors and the world as Rome had done? *Poeticae artis honos non erat; si quis in ea re studebat aut sese ad convivia adplicabat grassator vocaba- tur*—so the Elder Cato in his *Carmen de moribus*—"The art of poetry was not respectable; if a man engaged in it or applied himself to junketings he was called a wanton." There was not even a word for poet: *poeta* and *vates* are not native. The term *scriba* was applied alike to poets and scriveners (*scriba proprio nomine antiqui et librarios et poetas vocabant: Festus 446 L*); a *scriba* who worked with pen and paper was in the same class as a cobbler who worked with awl and leather.

But the claim of Latin literature upon the attention of everyone concerned with European life and letters must remain unchallenged nevertheless, for the literary expression of the achievements and aspirations of Rome has been a paramount factor in shaping the character of Europe. Man's preeminence over brute creation lies in his ability to transmit intellectual achievement, and the symbols of language which are the instrument of transmission are as essentially artificial as they are powerful and persistent. The connotations of language which distinguish a culture are not by nature inherent in the symbol, but have to be acquired by each individual; an individual brought up in isolation from a society would have to learn that society's set of connotations before he could participate in its life. Now the connotations of such symbols as patriotism and propriety, duty, decency, dignity, religion and loyalty, the symbols which are the warp and woof of our life, and more important, the value which we attach to these symbols, were shaped by Rome, and by Rome transmitted to Europe. If it had fallen to Greece to civilize Europe directly instead of through the mediation of Rome, Greece might have done a more effective job; it is quite certain that it would have done a different job. What we call the Near East and sometimes characterize as Levantine has that character—to people who look through Roman spectacles—because there Rome's influence was exerted, if at all, through Greece.

Whether it was by destiny and their own superior moral fibre, as they themselves thought, or by some concatenation of accidents that the Romans achieved their eminence, they were able to impose their own views of the moral duties of the citizen upon all of Europe. Speaking of the legend of the divine birth of Romulus and Remus (and he himself plainly doubts the story) Livy says (*Preface* 7):

If any people ought to be allowed to consecrate their origins and refer them to a divine source, so great is the military glory of the Roman People that when they profess that their Father and the Father of their Founder was none other than Mars, the nations of the earth may well submit to this also with as good a grace as they submit to Rome's dominion.

—*B. O. Foster*

Latin literature was thus able to make Europe submit to its own values because of a unique and important circumstance: for many centuries it remained *the* literature of an unfragmented Europe. If it was not ecumenical it was at least European. Spaniards and Africans and Gauls and Greeks (and indeed very few Romans) wrote it; they all contributed to a single stream, and local patriotisms merged with Roman patriotism, which became identical with European if not ecumenical patriotism. Parochial divagations developed peculiar characteristics, to the point of achieving apparent independence; yet they are divagations nevertheless, and cannot be fully intelligible without reference to their ecumenical source. The very distinctiveness and national color which is their pride is but a burgeoned seed of the national pride which the Romans invented and fostered and which, until the fragmentation, they succeeded in equating with Europeanism.

The interplay of historical forces which set Rome upon the pinnacle whence it could wield this formidable power we cannot analyse. We can only glance briefly at the factors, geographic, ethnologic, political, and social, which shaped Roman character, and then observe how that character left its impress on Roman literature. Italy's harbors are on its western rather than eastern shore. Rome's back was turned on Greece and it looked to the new world in the west. Greek influences reached Rome in a trickle from the south for centuries before they came in a direct stream from Greece itself. The Alps are less of an obstacle to entering than to leaving Italy, and when history raises its curtain Italy was already inhabited by peoples of diverse ethnic origin. On the coast were immigrants from Illyria, Veneti, Picenes, and Messapii. The tough Sabelli and related Umbri and Volsci held the mountainous central regions, from which they tended to expand. In the northwest were the Ligurians, probably of native neolithic stock. North of the Tiber were the Etruscans. Below them were the Latini and the related Falisci and Hernici, and then the Aurunci-Ausones and Oenotri, who were possibly Sicels. The southern coastlands were called Magna Graecia, and were Greek-speaking. In the Po valley Gauls began to settle about 400 B.C. Aside from the Greeks, Gauls, Etruscans, Ligurians, and lesser groups the people of Italy spoke what is called the Italic branch of the Indo-European family of languages. In common usage the term Italic dialects is confined to Oscan and Umbrian, the two chief non-Latin dialects. Of the Latin dialects the language of the city of Rome was only one, and it expanded and effaced its rivals as Roman power grew paramount.

The non-Latin peoples of Italy who contributed largely to the formation of Roman character and the Roman state were the Greeks, the

Etruscans, and the Celts. By far the most advanced culturally were the Greeks. Later legend ascribed the foundation of certain cities to Greek heroes returning from the Trojan war; thus Rome itself was said to have been founded by Aeneas, Lanuvium by Diomede, and Tusculum by Telegonus. The first historical Greek colony in Italy was Cumae, which was founded by the Chalcidians about 740 B.C. and soon became a center of civilization famed for its temple of Apollo and the Grotto of the Sibyl; from it the Etruscans and the Italians alike received their alphabet. Thereafter numerous Greek settlements dotted the southwest shores of Italy and soon became centers of wealth and enlightenment. Their brilliant civilization, which made significant contributions to the culture of the mother country itself, reached its height in the sixth century. Its effects in Italy were far-reaching. It Hellenized the natives of the south, radiated its influence even into Etruria, and brought Italy into the main current of Mediterranean civilization.

The most direct and continuous non-Latin influence in early Rome was that exerted by the Etruscans. The origin of the Etruscans is still a vexed question, in which modern nationalisms play a part. The most convincing view is that they originated in Asia Minor and came to Italy in numbers about 800 B.C., attracted by the copper of Etruria and the iron of Elba. The conquerors formed an aristocracy and established themselves in a number of fortified self-governing cities, ruled at first by kings (*lucumones*), such as Lars Porsenna of Clusium, and later by oligarchies. Their twelve chief cities were joined in a loose confederacy and annually celebrated a communal festival at Voltumna (perhaps Orvieto). The league survived as a religious body to the time of Constantine. Their wealth enabled the Etruscans to develop a luxurious and artistic civilization, as their magnificent tombs, especially those at Caere, amply demonstrate. In the seventh century they imported not only Greek artistic wares in quantity but also Greek artists, and their own craftsmen in gold, silver, and bronze produced works of high merit. Their brilliant tomb paintings illustrate not only the luxurious appointments of their feasts but also their gloomy religious beliefs. They seem to have been preoccupied by death and its terrors; if they did not introduce human sacrifice into Italy they enjoyed massacring their captives and pitting them against one another in gladiatorial combats. Their priests, who seem to have exercised great power, were largely concerned with divination; much of their lore appears to have derived from Hittites, Babylonians, and Chaldaeans. The underworld was a place of torment; the demons depicted in their frescoes inspired Renaissance artists with ideas of Satan, Purgatory, and Hell.

Their superior wealth and organization made expansion inevitable, and they spread northward to the Po, southward to Campania, and westward by the sea. About 535 B.C. they combined with Carthage to break the naval predominance of the Greeks by defeating the Phocaeans in a battle off Alalia. But the Cumaeans defeated them on land in 524 and 506; the Greeks defeated their Carthaginian allies at Himera in 480 B.C., and shortly thereafter Hiero of Syracuse broke the Etruscan naval power in a battle off Cumae. Had it not been for internal dissensions, to which their military decline was due, the Etruscans would doubtless have anticipated the Romans in unifying Italy. But it may well be that without the Etruscan ingredient Rome itself might not have succeeded in that task. The Etruscans themselves had gone farther in transforming a religious league into a nation than the Greeks had done, and Rome itself became a city during the period of Etruscan influence. They probably supplied the name and city plan of Rome, and certainly drained the swamps and made the Forum habitable. The symbol of the city's unity was the Capitoline temple to the Etruscan triad of Jupiter, Juno, and Minerva, and an Etruscan artist, Vulca of Veii, made the cult statue and the sculptural ornaments of the temple. In the religious, political, military, economic, and cultural spheres Rome's debt to the Etruscans was very great. Besides the founding of temples, the Romans learned from the Etruscans their anthropomorphic conceptions of deity and the elaborate practice and political uses of augury. It was under their Etruscan kings that the Romans acquired a centralized government and also the insignia of the magistrates—fasces, the curule chair, the purple toga, the ivory rod, and the golden wreath. Roman military equipment and organization doubtless owed much to the Etruscans. Etruscan urbanization and industry gave an impulse to Roman commerce and made of Rome a commercial city with which Carthage saw fit to conclude a treaty. But even while it was dominated by Etruscan kings Rome itself never became an Etruscan city; there are no Etruscan archaeological remains in Rome from that period.

In Latium, which is the seat of Rome, volcanic activity made settlement impossible until relatively recent times; it is only at the beginning of the Iron Age that the Latins appear, and not till after 700 B.C. that they begin to enter into the life of Italy. Settlements were small, and the only impulse to federation were common religious cults. There was a common cult of Venus at Lavinium and one of Diana at Aricia, on the Aventine at Rome, and near Tusculum. The annual spring festival of Jupiter Latiaris in the Alban hills gradually developed a league which acquired political as well as religious sanctions.

About fifteen miles from the Tiber mouth villages nesting on a group of hills which commanded the surrounding plain and the Tiber ford gradually coalesced to form the city of Rome. The advantages of location near the river and the center of Italy promoted its rise. Of early Rome we know little, for it was not till the end of the third century that the Romans began to write its history, and by then national pride led them to connect their history with that of the Greek world by forging links with Greek mythology. Foundation stories attributed to the Romans a Trojan origin through Aeneas, with a succession of his descendants filling the interval between his traditional date in the twelfth century and the traditional founding of Rome in 753 B.C. In that year Romulus and Remus founded Rome, the previous kings having ruled at Alba Longa. Romulus was succeeded by six kings: Numa Pompilius, Tullus Hostilius, Ancus Marcius, Tarquinius Priscus, Servius Tullius, and Tarquinius Superbus. At least some of these were historical figures, for there were surely kings in Rome, and some were surely Etruscan. The king was advised by a council of elders (senate) who belonged to the patrician clans, which enjoyed special political and religious privileges. The less privileged classes included plebeians and clients. Certain administrative reforms, involving the division of the people into tribes and classes and centuries on a property basis, are attributed to Servius.

The monarchy and the Etruscan yoke ended with the expulsion of Tarquinius Superbus (510 B.C.), and an aristocratic republic under two annually elected consuls was established. Two strands of development control Roman history for the next two and a half centuries: the struggle between plebeian and patrician orders, and the expansion of Rome. Step by step the plebeians were admitted to one magistracy after another, until they attained full political, and eventually social, equality. Step by step Roman power expanded until it covered all Italy except Cisalpine Gaul. To this era later Romans looked back as the formative period of their character. Its heroes were canonized as exemplifying the frugal and austere and selfless virtues. Rome was now a world power, and her next task was the elimination of the Carthaginian rival, which was effected by the Punic wars. Victory left Rome with overseas provinces, and the inexorable course of expansion soon brought her into control of the entire Mediterranean basin. For the first time in history Rome realized the ecumenical ideal: all of western civilization was embraced in one political system.

The achievement was truly astonishing. "Can anyone be so indifferent or idle," wrote Polybius, "as not to care to know by what means and under what kind of polity almost the whole inhabited world was conquered and brought under the dominion of the single city of Rome, and that within a period of not quite fifty-three years?" Polybius attributed Roman success to moral qualities and an excellent constitution. Modern historians may prefer to speak of geographical and economic advantages, superior manpower and superior armaments. But the Romans themselves made no question that all these advantages were the result of the peculiar and indeed unique Roman moral virtues, which justified destiny in assigning them the role of guardian of peace and order to the whole world.

It is well to look at the components of idealized virtue which the Romans cherished from their first recorded history until their dissolution. In his earliest exaltation of Rome Ennius had written (*Annales* 500), *Moribus antiquis res stat Romana virisque*—" 'Tis by virtue of her morals and her men of old that Rome abides." The frequency with which this line is quoted shows that it was accepted as a prime article of faith. At the beginning of the empire, when the doctrine of Rome's mission was canonized and publicized, the greatest writers in prose and poetry referred the doctrine to superhuman authority. Livy (1.16.8) attributed to the deified Romulus the behest: "Go and proclaim to the Romans that it is the will of heaven that my Rome shall be capital of the world. . . . They must know, and they must transmit to posterity the knowledge, that no human resources can avail against Roman arms." Vergil placed a more specific statement of Rome's destiny on the lips of Anchises, Aeneas' father, in an apocalyptic pronouncement from the underworld (*Aeneid* 6.847–

53): "Others, I doubt not, shall beat out the breathing bronze with softer lines; shall from marble draw forth the features of life; shall plead their causes better; with the rod shall trace the paths of heaven and tell the rising of the stars: remember thou, O Roman, to rule the nations with thy sway—these shall be thine arts—to crown Peace with Law, to spare the humbled, and to tame in war the proud." The persistence of the doctrine is shown by the very last historian of pagan Rome. Towards the end of the fourth century Ammianus Marcellinus writes (14.6.3): "At the time when Rome first began to rise into a position of worldwide splendor, destined to live so long as men shall exist, in order that she might grow to a towering stature, Virtue and Fortune, ordinarily at variance, formed a pact of eternal peace."

In literary expression, at least, and there more widely than one would expect, the consciousness of Rome's divine mission and of the responsibility that the charge entailed, is ever recurrent. *Aeneid* differs from *Iliad* and *Odyssey* in that it celebrates an institution, not a man. Aeneas the individual is submerged in the divinely directed founder of the state, and the Romans are called *Aeneadae*—as the Hebrews are called children of Israel. Romans never forget they are Romans. Not only in the theatrical pages of Seneca but in each of the Roman historians characters always strut or stalk (was any other gait possible for the *gens togata?*), always are conscious of an audience, in which posterity as well as contemporaries are included. One gathers the impression that the self-aware Roman spent a good part of his life rehearsing the dramatic utterance with which he would take leave of it. The Roman walked in the limelight, and if his self-consciousness was due in part to a pride which history conspired to justify, a good part was due to the sense of responsibility inherent in being a Roman. To the Romans the prophet's admonition would have been a truism: "You only have I known of all the families of the earth: therefore I will punish you for all your iniquities." Iniquity to the Roman was anything frivolous, capricious, irresponsible, unsystematic, undisciplined. Ebullience and imagination were suspect. The qualities expected of a Roman were gravity, dignity, austerity, integrity, fortitude, and above all disciplined obedience to the *mos maiorum,* the legacy of usages and system and organization inherited from the past.

Emphasis on these traits takes on the character almost of religious apologetics and implies a conscious rivalry with and rejection of a different pattern, perhaps with an admission that an apologetic is called for. The "others" of whom Vergil speaks as being superior in the realms of culture are of course the Greeks. No observer, ancient or modern, could fail to be impressed by the extent of Roman indebtedness to Greece. It could not have been otherwise. Every European culture stands upon the shoulders not only of its own but of its neighbors' past. In the case of Rome a village barbaric by Greek standards suddenly finds itself thrust into the highest place of opulence and power. The suddenly enlarged villagers could not be expected to develop their native porridge into a more elegant cuisine by normal processes of growth when experts in the sophisticated cookery of the Greeks were available to them. They could not be expected to traverse the laborious steps upwards from primitive art when Greek masterpieces were there to shame their crudities and Greek artisans with centuries of tradition behind them were available to multiply copies. Their formless deities were inevitably assimilated to the brilliant anthropomorphic Olympians whose types had been imperishably fixed by Phidias and Praxiteles. So in the face of the overwhelming superiority of what the Greeks had long ago achieved it was impossible for poetry and prose to develop in isolation out of the childish cult chants we shall presently glance at. Roman literature proper begins with a translation from the Greek; the greatest Roman poet starts his career with *Eclogues* that are sometimes little more than translations of Theocritus, continues with the *Georgics,* inspired by Hesiod, and crowns his work and Latin literature with an epic which would be inconceivable without the models of *Iliad* and *Odyssey*. Their greatest lyric poet bases his claim to originality on having been the first to introduce certain Greek measures into Latin poetry. Lucretius' masterpiece is a translation of the "longer catechism" of Epicurus, and Cicero (*To Atticus* 12.52) admits that his philosophical essays were "copies of the Greek to which I contribute only words, of which I have a great plenty." "Captive Greece," said Horace (*Epistles* 2.1.156), "took her fierce conqueror captive and introduced her arts into rude Latium." But not altogether, for Greek love of beauty and Greek love of knowledge for its own sake and Greek eagerness for innovation were not only never naturalized at Rome, but were vehemently opposed by a nationalist party associated with the name of the elder Cato.

If American literature is a different thing from English literature, or, better, if Chaucer's *Troilus and Criseyde* is a different thing than Boccaccio's *Filostrato,* then surely its Roman stamp makes Latin literature a thing different from its Greek models. The Roman claim to originality rests on something more than the rather questionable invention of satire. The various types of Latin literature illustrate various aspects of Romanism as purposefully as the various types of Old Testament literature illustrate aspects of Hebraism. Latin literature is always an answer to some practical need, always edifying, always in the service of the national ideal; when it is not these things it is utterly frivolous. Roman poets are far more interested in natural scenery than are the Greeks, but it is Italian scenery they describe, and love for Italy that they wish to inculcate. Roman authors are far more interested in biography, but they are Roman worthies who stride across the pages of Ennius and Vergil and Livy; to know the careers of these Roman great is a patriotic duty. Cicero undertakes to write philosophic treatises as a patriotic duty—when the turn of politics had prevented him from performing functions more directly useful to the state. Philosophy had been neglected hitherto because it was of no importance in comparison with the practical concerns which engaged Roman attention, and because in view of acknowledged Roman superiority in character philosophy was unnecessary (*Tusculan Disputations* 1.1): "Where among any people has been found a dignity of manners, a firmness, a greatness of soul, uprightness, good faith, or outstanding virtue of every kind, comparable to the qualities of our forefathers?" Cicero's justification of poetry (in the *For Archias*) is very revealing: poetry is useful because it affords statesmen like himself an armory of examples as well as relaxation from real work, and because, by the hope of immortalization which it holds out, it provides an incentive for patriotic heroism.

Paradoxically, this tone seems not unnatural in Latin literature, for Latin literature is itself not natural. It is the most "literary" of literatures. Not only its forms and themes, but its versification and prose rhythms are borrowed. Hence it tends to echo the imitative ring of all classicizing literature, with only authors of authentic genius surmounting the handicap. Its authors were solemnly and serenely aware that they were classics. Horace is the most endearingly affable of all the Romans we know, and yet he too is very sure (*Odes* 3.30) that the monument he has erected is more enduring than bronze and will survive all the corrosions of time. We do not know what proportion of the Roman audience was sufficiently at home in essentially alien metrical systems and mythology to comprehend what the learned (*doctus* is a regular epithet for a poet) authors said. Like the Alexandrians, Roman authors addressed themselves to a specially educated class; the classic Greeks also observed forms rigidly, but their work was appreciated, as Greek drama shows, by a large proportion of the population. It is therefore important to notice that Latin literature at its most representative is far more serious than Alexandrian, and that its authors are moved by an inner compulsion to significant utterance as well as by an appetite to display virtuosity. The sense of the responsibility as well as of the dignity of the literary artist is not the least item in Rome's legacy to its daughter literatures.

The formalism and finish of Latin literature bears a functional relationship to the Latin language. It is a sonorous language, but sober and efficient, and unimaginative, capable of indicating relationships within a sentence with great precision, and not likely to become prolix. It is a perfect instrument for the precise formulation of law, of decrees, of military commands, of tombstone inscriptions. By reason of its verbal economy and the natural assonances of its accidence it tends naturally to fall into memorable *sententiae;* it is as suited to the lapidary as to the chancellery style. The dominance of Latin did not at once efface its rivals in Italy. Greek was spoken in the south almost to modern times; the Etruscans presented a kind of play in their language as late as Cicero's day; and Pompeian *graffiti* show that Oscan was spoken there down to the destruction. Perhaps pronunciation of the kindred Italic dialects affected the vulgar Latin of the empire from which the romance languages evolved, but aside from this their influence on Latin seems to have been slight. Italic dialects play nothing like the part in Latin literature that Hellenic dialects do in Greek.

It may be convenient, before we enter upon consideration of the remains of Latin literature, to set forth the periods into which the literature and the language alike are customarily divided, remembering, of course, that the divisions are approximate and marked for convenience; there are naturally no sharp breaks. (1) The period from the beginnings down to 240 B.C. is pre-literary, and bears less relation to what follows than does English literature before the Norman invasion to that after the invasion. (2) About 240 Plautus, Ennius, and others begin to produce the first formal literature in a literary language which diverges from the vernacular, and about 70 B.C. the Social War had extinguished Rome's rivals and made Latin ready for use by the authors of (3) the Golden Age, whose close is marked by the death of Augustus in A.D. 14. (4) The period from A.D. 14–180 is designated the Silver Age, and is characterized by increasing artificiality, rhetorical straining for effect, and wider divergence between the literary and vernacular language. (5) These same tendencies continue after 180. The written language remains relatively constant, but the spoken language follows its own laws and development. The provinces, indeed, had so far been Romanized by the fourth century, especially by the schools of Gaul in the West (the East persisted in its use of Greek), as to have forgotten their native tongues. With the dissolution of the bonds of empire Latin was the base from which local variations diverged to form the various Romance languages.

II

THE BEGINNINGS

IT IS AN EXAGGERATION TO SAY THAT ROME HAD no literature before the middle of the third century, but it is true that nothing which antedates Livius Andronicus' translation of the *Odyssey* can be of much interest to the student of Latin literature. The crude cult and festival songs and chronicles were doubtless like those of the other Italic peoples, and the slight remains we have fall rather into the province of the linguist and the anthropologist. The specimens we have are a mere handful. From the sixth century there is the inscription containing the word *regei* written up and down the Forum stele under the Lapis Niger. From the fifth century we have the inscription written from right to left on the Praeneste fibula: *Manios me fhefhaked Numasioi = Manius me fecit Numerio.* The fourth-century Duenos bowl, showing Greek influence, which was found on the Quirinal, has the words *Duenos me feced—feced* being a weakened and unreduplicated form of *fhefhaked.* Earlier than the Hannibalic war is a dedication from Tusculum: *M. Fourio C.f. tribunos militare praedad Maurte dedit = M. Furius C.f. tribunus militaris de praeda Marti dedit.* To the same period belong the epitaphs in Saturnian verse of Scipio Barbatus, consul in 298 B.C., and of his son, consul in 259. A nearer approach to literature were the records of official proceedings which needed to be preserved. Of this character were the rosters, enactments, and chronicles of events, kept by priestly colleges or by magistrates. We find mention of *libri pontificum, augurum, saliorum, magistratuum; commentarii pontificum, sacrorum, augurales, consulares; tabulae publicae; acta; monumenta; tabulae censoriae, libri censorii, commentarii censorii; libri lintei* (records written on linen, used by C. Licinius Macer and Q. Aelius Tubero, but apparently of dubious authenticity). Chronicles were originally embodied in priestly calendars and recorded magistracies, political events, dearths, eclipses, prodigies. These data were worked into the *Annales maximi* (so called to distinguish them from records kept by private persons) towards the end of the second century B.C.; for the early period they were probably constructed of whole cloth. For us the

pontifical records survive in the lists of magistrates and of triumphators as preserved in the so-called *Fasti Capitolini*. What has been
preserved of such things, and of treaties and especially of the *Twelve
Tables,* is mostly in a modernized form, but there are some archaic
passages whose meaning is not clear. Speeches in the Senate and
funeral orations must have stimulated the development of oratory.
A very early type of speech is the apologue of the belly and the members which Livy (2.32) says that Menenius Agrippa delivered *prisco
illo dicendi et horrido modo.*

The earliest compositions which may be designated literature are
the *Carmen Saliare* and the *Carmen Arvale*. There were two priestly
colleges of Salii who were concerned with the warlike activities of
the state. By Horace's day their incantations had become unintelligible,
but we know that in the early Empire such personages as Augustus
and Germanicus were included in their litanies by official acts. The
song of the Arval Brethren, connected with tilth, was a similar cult
chant; an extant version inscribed on stone consists of patterned lines,
approaching gibberish, which were to be repeated a prescribed number of times. Aside from work songs and lullabies, of which we have
record, songs must have been sung in early days as they were in
Caedmon's beer hall. Varro records that at banquets boys used to sing
lays celebrating the deeds of great men, and Cato says that the ban-
queters themselves sang such songs. Many legends pertaining to
the exploits of the great houses of Rome may have originated in
this manner. When the credibility of Roman history before the Gallic
invasion came to be questioned Niebuhr maintained that the historical
traditions embodied in the early books of Livy and elsewhere were
based on such balladry, and in his *Lays of Ancient Rome* Macaulay
thought he was providing specimens of what such ballads must have
been like. Such productions as these may be regarded as the germs of
lyric and epic.

From earliest times the Romans appreciated satire and repartee
and enjoyed rhetoric and spectacle. The origin of Roman drama seems
to have been in the ribald exchanges chanted at weddings and triumphs. So upon Caesar's triumphal entry his soldiers are said to
have called out: "City-folk, mind your wives; 'tis the bald wanton we
bring." Such carnival repartee was called Fescennine verse; the ancients derived the name from Fescennium, a town in Etruria, or

fascinum, witchcraft, the songs being supposedly apotropaic. Our fullest ancient account of the beginnings of drama in Rome is a passage in Livy (7.2):

When neither human wisdom nor the help of Heaven was found to mitigate the scourge [364 B.C.], men gave way to superstitious fears, and, amongst other efforts to disarm the wrath of the gods, are said to have instituted scenic entertainments. This was a new departure for a warlike people, whose only exhibitions had been those of the circus; but indeed it began in a small way, as most things do, and even so was imported from abroad. Without any singing, without imitating the action of singers, players who had been brought in from Etruria danced to the strains of the flautist and performed not ungraceful evolutions in the Tuscan fashion. Next the young Romans began to imitate them, at the same time exchanging jests in uncouth verses, and bringing their movements into a certain harmony with the words. And so the amusement was adopted, and frequent use kept it alive. The native professional actors were called *histriones,* from *ister,* the Tuscan word for player; they no longer—as before—alternately threw off rude lines hastily improvised, like the Fescennines, but performed medleys, full of musical measures, to melodies which were now written out to go with the flute, and with appropriate gesticulation.

Livius was the first, some years later, to abandon *saturae* and compose a play with a plot . . . When this type of performance had begun to wean the drama from laughter and informal jest, and the play had gradually developed into art, the young men abandoned the acting of comedies to professionals and revived the ancient practice of fashioning their nonsense into verses and letting fly with them at one another; this was the source of the after-plays which came later to be called *exodia,* and were usually combined with Atellan farces. The Atellan was a species of comedy acquired from the Oscans, and the young men kept it for themselves and would not allow it to be polluted by the professional actors; that is why it is a fixed tradition that performers of Atellan plays are not disfranchised, but serve in the army as though they had no connexion with the stage.

—*B. O. Foster*

Every sentence in this account has been questioned, some seeing in it a reflection of Aristotle's view of the origin of comedy, and some a nationalist insistence that the origin of Roman drama was native. But Livy had a special interest in drama, and whatever proportion or date we assign to the various ingredients he mentions, it is clear that each contributed.

To Livius Andronicus (ca.284–ca.204 B.C.) Livy credits the introduction of the first regular play with a plot, and the ancients (see Horace *Epistles* 2.1.62) and moderns alike regard Livius as the originator of Latin literature. Andronicus was born at Tarentum, and therefore was probably a Greek, and when that city was captured in 272 he was brought to Rome as a captive and upon manumission took the name of his master, Livius Salinator. In Rome he became a schoolmaster, and because there were no Latin books to teach from he undertook the unexampled task of turning the *Odyssey* into Latin. At about this same period other non-Hellenic peoples were turning to translation; the version of the Pentateuch known as the Septuagint was made at about this time. But the Jewish translators in Alexandria, the Babylonian Berossus, and the Egyptians Sesostris and Manetho were translating not from but into Greek; they were content with their own proud past, and wished to bolster the esteem of their own people and win them the approval of the dominant Greek culture. Only the Romans borrowed, and on a wholesale scale. Livius' meter, however, appears to have been native. It was the Saturnian, whose nature has never been satisfactorily explained, for it falls naturally into neither an accentual nor a quantitative pattern. Despite the disparaging remarks of Cicero (*Brutus* 18.71: "The Latin *Odyssey* might well be likened to a statue from the chisel of Daedalus, and the plays of Livius are not worth a second reading") and Horace (*Epistles* 2.1. 69–71: "That Livius' poem should seem correct, beautiful, and all but perfect I find strange"), for scope and originality and actual execution Livius' achievement was remarkable. The forty-six scattered lines which survive of the *Odissia,* including the opening *Virum mihi camena insece versutum,* are impressive; and if we find them unsatisfactory Homer, we may ask what subsequent version is satisfactory Homer.

A more tangible, though hardly more seminal influence, was initiated by Livius' work in the drama. For the Ludi Romani of 240 B.C., by the request of the aedile (but surely at Livius' own suggestion) Livius composed and acted in the first Latin comedy and the first Latin tragedy, and so gave Roman drama its abiding form. Livius' dramatic works were all translated from the Greek, and he had doubtless seen many of them enacted in Greek in Tarentum. Eight titles and forty lines of his tragedies are preserved: *Achilles, Aegisthus,*

Aiax Mastigophorus, Andromeda, Danae, Equus Troianus, Hermiona, Tereus. The *Aiax* is clearly modeled on the extant play of Sophocles; the others are Sophoclean, Euripidean, or post-Euripidean. Stories from the Trojan cycle had a topical interest for the Romans, for they had recently discovered in Sicily the story of their own Trojan origin. The Greek chorus could not be reproduced, and indeed it had fallen out of use even in Greek plays in Livius' day; hence Livius, and after him Naevius, increased the number of monodies, and thus made Roman tragedy more like modern opera than Greek tragedy had been. Livius' tragedies long held the stage; in comedy he was soon supplanted by his successors. His comic fragments and titles—*Gladiolus* ("Swashbuckler"?), *Ludius* ("Gamester"?)—suggest models in the New Comedy. By 207 B.C., when the pontifices ordained that thrice nine maidens should chant an intercessory hymn through the city to expiate evil omens during the Second Punic War, Livius was naturally the poet designated to compose the hymn. Livy tells us (27.37) that the poem was perhaps worthy of praise according to the ideas of those days, but nowadays would seem rough and unpolished. In honor of his having composed this hymn, and because he both wrote plays and acted in them, Festus (492.22) tells us, the guild of writers and actors was permitted to hold meetings and present votive offerings in the temple of Minerva on the Aventine. Livius, then, was not only himself a poet but the cause of poetry in others; through him poetry received official public recognition. One last notice of the life of Livius is that Cato, who was born six years after Livius composed his first play, lived to see him as an old man (Cicero, *On Old Age* 14.50).

More survives from Livius' younger contemporary Gnaeus Naevius (ca.270–ca.201 B.C.), who was a more original poet and gave Latin literature a nationalist direction. He was a Roman citizen and served in the First Punic War (264–241 B.C.). Beginning in 235, he was active as a playwright for some thirty years. His chief production was in comedy, and we have some 130 lines from his *palliatae*, or comedies in Greek dress. Their very titles show a liveliness: *Acontizomenos* ("Speared"), *Agitatoria* ("Derby Day"), *Agrypnuntes* ("The Night-Hawks"), *Appella* ("The Circumcised"), *Tarentilla* ("The Flirt"), of whom a line says, *Alii adnutat, alii adnictat, alium amat, alium tenet,* "To one she nods, at another she winks; one she caresses, another embraces." The *Ariolus* ("Soothsayer"), of which a fragment tells how to entertain guests from Praeneste and Lanuvium, seems to have been a *togata,* or comedy in Roman dress. Aulus Gellius (3.3.15) tells us that Naevius wrote this play and the *Leon* in prison as an apology for his earlier impudence (as we shall see, against the Metelli in particular) and was released in consequence. From the prologue to Terence's *Andria* we know that Naevius practiced *contaminatio,* that is, the fusion of two Greek plays into one in Latin. Of tragedies on Greek models we have some sixty lines and seven titles: *Andromacha, Danae, Equus Troianus, Hector Proficiscens, Hesione, Iphigenia, Lycurgus.* But Naevius' originality and his native note are shown by his two *praetextae,* or plays on historical Roman subjects. There are *Romulus or The Wolf* and *Clastidium,* which dramatizes Marcellus' and Scipio's campaign in Cisalpine Gaul in 222 B.C. Such Roman plays never became popular; the only extant example is the *Octavia* ascribed to Seneca. But Naevius' comedies too have a distinctly Roman touch in their bold and pointed attacks on famous statesmen living in Rome. One passage, almost certainly from a *togata,* tells how Scipio Africanus' father dragged him from the arms of his mistress. His altercation with the Metelli was continuous. "It's fate," he wrote, "that makes Metelli consuls at Rome," and the consul Metellus answered in the line all scholars cite as the example of the Saturnian, *Dabunt malum Metelli Naevio poetae,* "The Metelli will make the poet Naevius rue it." They did, as we have seen, imprison him, and even after his release they were probably responsible for his exile to Utica where he died.

But his dramatic works are by no means the sum of Naevius' contribution to Latin literature. Besides the *Satura,* which can hardly have been the title of a play, and the epitaph, which we shall cite below, Naevius wrote a national epic in the national meter, tracing the legendary origins of Rome (and perhaps also of Carthage), bringing in stories of heroes and gods, and promulgating in Latin verse the connection between Rome and Troy. The *Bellum Punicum* glorified Rome and set forth its final victory in a terrible war. Romans continued to admire it. Its influence on Ennius and Vergil is unmistakable. In 165 B.C. it was divided into seven books by C. Octavius Lampadio, and we know of other early commentators who worked upon it. Cicero (*Brutus* 75), though he gives the palm to Ennius, compares the

Bellum Punicum to a statue by Myron, and not to the primitive carving of a Daedalus.

Livius was a Greek, a freedman, and a schoolmaster, and the term *scriba* applied to him has a banausic ring. In Naevius we have a Roman citizen asserting the dignity of the writer's craft. The precedent was important, for Rome like other stolid societies was inclined to look down upon artists. Naevius' pride is recorded in his epitaph, in which he claims distinction not only as a poet but as a Roman poet:

> *Immortales mortales si foret fas flere*
> *flerent divae Camenae Naevium poetam.*
> *Itaque postquamst Orchi traditus thesauro,*
> *obliti sunt Romae loquier lingua latina.*

If to bewail mortals were right for immortals, then should the divine Muses bewail the poet Naevius. After he was delivered to Death's treasure-house, Romans forgot how to speak the Latin tongue.

Chronology would require that we deal next with Plautus, but of Plautus a good number of complete plays are extant, and so it will be convenient to treat of him, along with Terence, in the chapter following, and to reserve the present chapter for authors whose extant works are fragmentary. Our next figure then is Quintus Ennius (239–169 B.C.), the younger contemporary of Plautus and an author with a truer claim than Livius' to be the father of Latin literature. In him the Roman tradition emerges in its full strength, and he continued to be revered in ages which disdained even his successors as crude. Ennius' birthplace was Rudiae in Calabria, and he claimed descent from King Messapus, which was hardly more than a claim to free birth. His competence in Greek, Oscan, and Latin gave him, he said (Gellius 17.17), three hearts. His Greek education, attested by his works, was probably acquired in Tarentum. He served in the Roman army, probably as a centurion and with distinction, in Sicily in 204. There he came to the notice of M. Porcius Cato, who brought him to Rome; there is irony in the circumstance, for Ennius was a prime mover in introducing the Greek culture which Cato more than any other Roman opposed. He lived on the Aventine, the seat, as we have seen, of the poetic guild, and on the death of Livius and the banishment of Naevius found a ready market for his dramatic writings. He was on terms of friendship with important figures in Rome. When Scipio Nasica called on him (Cicero tells the story in *On the Orator* 2.68.276) Ennius' maid said he was not at home. When Ennius called on Scipio, Scipio himself shouted out that he was not at home. When Ennius claimed to recognize Scipio's voice, Scipio replied: "Shame on you. When I asked for you I believed your maidservant that you weren't at home: don't you believe me in person?" This story is probably the basis for Jerome's statement that Ennius could keep only one servant. But on the better authority of Cicero (*On Old Age* 5.14) we know that he was poor at his death. But he was no ascetic. *Numquam poetor nisi si podager,* he wrote (*Satires* 21), "I never poetize unless I have the gout." "Ennius never sallied forth to sing of arms," said Horace (*Epistles* 1.19.7–8), "unless he was drunk." Besides Scipio Nasica, Ennius was also on terms of friendship with Scipio Africanus, whose campaign he celebrated in his *Scipio.* Friendship with the philhellene Scipios and his own Epicurean and Euhemeristic tendencies cost him the attachment of the Elder Cato. Marcus Fulvius Nobilior, consul in 189 B.C., took Ennius with him on his expedition to Aetolia, as Cicero (*For Archias* 11.27) says, to celebrate his achievements, and Ennius did so, in his *Ambracia* and in Book 15 of the *Annals.* Marcus' son Quintus procured full Roman citizenship for Ennius, and gave him a grant of land. There is no evidence that he was personally acquainted with Livius, Naevius, or Plautus, though he left out a detail of the Punic War because Naevius had treated of it (Cicero, *Brutus* 19.76), and Plautus (*Poenulus,* prologue) was acquainted with Ennius' plays. Ennius did know the comic poet Caecilius Statius, and presumably also the tragic poet M. Pacuvius, his own nephew. Ennius died of the gout at the age of seventy, just after he had produced his *Thyestes.* Cicero, Livy, the Elder Pliny, Suetonius, all connect Ennius' sepulture, with more or less assurance, with the tomb of the Scipios, but the story is apparently without basis. An extant portrait statue inscribed "Q. Ennius" is unfortunately headless. For his portrait Ennius composed the epigram (Cicero, *Tusculan Disputations* 1.15.34):

> *Aspicite O cives senis Enni imaginis formam.*
> *Hic vestrum pinxit maxima facta patrum.*

Behold, my countrymen, the bust of the old man Ennius: he penned the record of your fathers' mighty deeds.

And for his tomb he wrote:

> *Nemo me lacrimis decoret nec funera fletu*
> *faxit. Cur? Volito vivus per ora virum.*

Let none embellish me with tears nor weep at my funeral. And why? Living I fly from lips to lips of men.

Ennius did celebrate the grandeur of Rome, and did retain his place on the lips of men. Because of his shaping of Roman patriotism and his influence on his successors, perhaps even for his actual poetic worth, Ennius merits a place in even the briefest history of Roman writers. Ennius' works comprised eighteen books of the *Annals,* at least twenty tragedies, two *praetextae,* two comedies (probably *palliatae*), at least four books of *Satires,* and the poems *Scipio, Sota, Protrepticum, Hedyphagetica, Epicharmus, Euhemerus* or *Sacred History,* and epigrams.

In his own regard and in fact the *Annals* is his major work, and marks an epoch in Latin literature. Its composition extended over a long period and was several times resumed after a tentative ending. Some six hundred lines have been preserved in fragments ranging from a few words to twenty lines; from the scale on which comparatively unimportant matters are treated the books would appear to have been much longer than those of *Iliad* or *Aeneid.* The fragments show close familiarity with classic Greek literature, but more important, they give evidence that Ennius was the first Roman writer who collected the traditions of early Rome, united them into a single narrative, and made of them a kind of patriotic hagiographa. Book 1 covered the period from the sack of Troy to the death of Romulus. Where Vergil speaks of the infancy of Romulus and Remus (8.630 ff.), Servius remarks *Sane totus hic locus Ennianus est.* On the other hand, our fragments have nothing of Aeneas' Carthaginian adventures, which Naevius had introduced in his *Bellum Punicum.* Books 2 and 3 covered the regal period to the establishment of the Republic. Books 4 and 5 went down to the war with Pyrrhus, which was covered in Book 6. Books 7, 8, and 9 dealt with the First and Second Punic wars; Books 10 and 11, beginning with a fresh invocation, with the First Macedonian War; and Books 11 to 14 with the peace of 196 to the Aetolian war of 189. Book 15 celebrated the achievements of M. Fulvius Nobilior in that war; Ennius glorified M. Fulvius also in the

Ambracia, which was probably a *fabula praetexta.* The *Annals* originally ended at this point. Book 16 covered the period from 188 to the
end of the Istrian war; Book 17 probably that from the Istrian war to
the defeat of P. Licinius Crassus in 171 during the Third Macedonian
War; and Book 18 presented further events of that year.

What unifies Ennius' epic is not the fortunes of a single hero, as
in the *Aeneid,* but the unbroken continuity of the unfolding of the
high destiny of Rome and the pervasive faith in that destiny. It
differs from the Homeric epic in that its author is not a detached
spectator of events, but an ardent partisan of whatever is memorable
in the annals of Rome. The characters are described not merely for the
part they play in the action, but because they are Roman heroes whom
patriotic Romans ought to know. Roman concepts of law and order,
military and political organization, practical administration, and effective command are similarly glorified. As in the *Aeneid,* the subject
is an institution, not the tragedy or the victory of individuals.

The form of the *Annals* strives to reflect suitably the fortitude and
dignity and sagacity of the Rome which is its theme. There is a sonor-
ity about Ennius' lines, rough as they sometimes are, and despite the
gravity of tone a kind of Homeric rapidity. His great formal contribution to Latin poetry is the adaptation of the Greek hexameter. His
cadences are naturally not as fine as Vergil's, and about many points
which were later fixed he is still in doubt. The laws for caesura observed by the later poets are often violated; some lines have no caesura
before the fifth foot. In most cases final *s* is not sounded before a con-
sonant (this usually disappears finally only in the Augustan poets);
final *m,* on the other hand, is sometimes not elided before a vowel. A
monstrous tmesis is seen in the line *saxo cere- comminuit -brum.* Quan-
tities of syllables and inflections are not settled, and hence Ennius had
to rely heavily on sound effects. Alliteration is carried to an extreme in
O Tite tute tibi tanta tyranne tulisti, which Warmington aptly renders,
"Thyself to thyself, Titus Tatius the tyrant, thou tookest those terrible
troubles." Sound effects are even more noticeable in *At tuba terribili
sonitu taratantara dixit,* for which Warmington has, "And the trumpet
in terrible tones taratantara blared." The diction of the *Annals* is
generally fresh and forcible, sometimes vivid and imaginative; but
occasionally Ennius will use technical words and fall into prosiness.

It was due to his Roman gravity, doubtless, that in drama Ennius' bent was towards tragedy rather than comedy. It was he who raised tragedy to a pitch of popular favor which it enjoyed to the time of Cicero, and it was his divergencies from Greek models which shaped the tragedies of Seneca. None of the ancients who speak of such matters rated Ennius high for comedy, and we know of only two *palliatae* of his, the *Cupuncula* and the *Pancratiastes*. On the other hand we know of at least twenty of his tragedies, from which some four hundred lines are preserved. Known to be derived from Euripidean models are *Alexander, Andromacha* (but not from our own extant *Andromache*), *Andromeda, Erechtheus, Hecuba, Iphigenia* (in Aulis), *Medea, Melanippe, Telephus*. Others are *Achilles* (after Aristarchus), *Ajax, Alcmeo, Athamas, Cresophontes, Eumenides* (from Aeschylus' extant play), *Hectoris Lutra* (probably compressed from an Aeschylean trilogy), *Phoenix, Telamo, Thyestes*. Comparison with what we know of his originals makes it clear that Ennius translated freely, compressed, augmented, and adapted. The *Medea,* for example, is cited by Cicero (*De finibus* 1.2.4) as having been a verbatim translation from the Greek, but in fact Ennius extended the plot to include the matter of a second Euripidean play on Medea. Many of the tragedies not definitely known to be drawn from Euripides seem to derive from that author, and the others seem to come largely from Aeschylus; Ennius seems not to have been attracted by Sophocles. This may be significant of Ennius' own interests. The manifold and ranging social and religious criticism and didacticism and the melodramatic tinge in Euripides and Aeschylus touched him more nearly than Sophocles' detached art and preoccupation with character.

Ennius' pulsing vigor is manifested in many of his fragments. There is a new power over language, for example, in Achilles' oath: *Per ego deum sublimas subices umidos/unde oritur imber sonitu saevo et spiritu,* which Warmington renders, "By heaven's god-haunted under-layers [sc. clouds] on high,/whence springs the storm with savage shriek and swirl." Also in the *Achilles* Cassandra cries out: " 'Tis here, the brand wreathed in blood and fire. Many a year had it lain hidden. Citizens! Bring ye help and quench it!" Such passages as this set the tone which Roman drama through Seneca followed in the agonizing and wrenching display of emotion. The change from recitation to song within this passage is an effective use of meter. The recurrence of such themes as the feast of Thyestes and the ghostly apparitions is another indication of the melodramatic tendency in Roman tragedy. Quite Senecan in its "point" and its didacticism is a line from the *Iphigenia: Otio qui nescit uti plus negoti habet quam cum est negotium in negotio*—"He who knows not how to use leisure has more work than when he is awork at work." Gellius, who quotes this passage (19.10.12), attributes it to the chorus (of warriors); we see then that Ennius retained the chorus, but used it as Seneca later did his, and that he felt free to change its personnel from maidens to soldiers. Philosophic reflection, again characteristic also of Seneca, is shown in a speech in the *Telamo;* though there is no evidence that this play was drawn from Euripides, the rationalism of this passage is thoroughly Euripidean:

> There is a race of gods in heaven; and yet
> They take no thought, it seems, how fares mankind;
> For if they did care, it would go well with well-doers,
> And ill with ill-doers; but this, as things are, is not to be seen.
> —*E. H. Warmington*

Another aspect of Romanism in the tragedies is the fact that so many of them afforded scope for the exhibition of the soldierly character. Besides the tragedies on Greek models Ennius wrote two specifically Roman *praetextae: Sabinae,* which, as its single surviving line shows, dealt with the rape of the Sabines; and *Ambracia,* written to glorify M. Fulvius Nobilior, as was Book 15 of the *Annals.*

Next important among Ennius' works are his four (or six) books of *Satires.* The old dramatic *satura,* as we have seen from the Livy passage quoted above, having been displaced by regular drama, Ennius invented a new form which preserved some of the essential spirit of the early type and became the intermediary to the regular hexameter satires of Lucilius and Horace. For his satires Ennius used a variety of meters. He retained the dialogue of the older form, for Quintilian (9.2.36) speaks of a contention between Life and Death in one of Ennius' satires. A description of a greedy parasite (14–19 W), quoted by Donatus as from the fourth(but the true reading may be "sixth") book of Ennius' satires, occupies ground common to Roman comedy and Roman satire. Ennius also included fables; Gellius (2.29.1 f.) mentions that Aesop's fable of the crested lark and its chicks "is very skillfully and gracefully told by Ennius in his satires." Again like Lucilius and Horace Ennius communicates not only his own criticism of life and politics but also his own feelings and experiences, as in the *Numquam poetor nisi si podager* already quoted. Since satire was the main basis of the Roman claim to originality in literature, Ennius' invention of this form gives him another title to be called father of Latin literature.

The *Scipio,* in hexameters and septenarii, celebrated the African campaign of Ennius' friend Scipio Africanus which culminated in the battle of Zama in 202. The scanty fragments deal with the crossing, the encampment, the battle, and Scipio's reception in Rome on his return. There are some ten lines of epigrams, all genuine funerary inscriptions. The few lines of the *Sota* must have been translated from Sotades, a coarse poet of the third century B.C. There are three lines of the *Protrepticum,* doubtless a poem of precepts based on a Greek model of the same name. The verse enumeration of choice food fish which Apuleius (*Apology* 39) quotes from memory as being from "the *Hedyphagetica* which Q. Ennius wrote" is in part identical with fragments of a mock-heroic poem written by Archestratus of Gela in the fourth century and quoted under the title *Gastronomia* in Athenaeus. Mock gravity in dealing with weighty gastronomic questions recurs in Horace (*Satires* 2.4).

Ennius' curiosity concerning the nature of things is reflected in his *Epicharmus,* a didactic poem in trochaic septenarii based on a genuine or pseudepigraphic work of the Sicilian philosopher-poet Epicharmus (540–450 B.C.), who seems to have resolved the gods of Greek mythology into natural substances. Such, at any rate, is the substance of the longest fragment of Ennius' *Epicharmus* (10–14 W):

That is this Jupiter of whom I speak, whom the Greeks call Aer, which is wind and clouds, and afterwards moisture; out of wetness comes cold, and after that wind is formed, and air once again. That is why Jupiter is the name for all I have spoken of, since he rejuvenates all men and cities and beasts.

—*E. H. Warmington*

Rationalization of Greek mythology could go no further than it did in Euhemerus' *Sacred History,* a sort of Utopia which explained the gods as human beings who had once shown great prowess. Cicero (*On the Nature of the Gods* 1.42.119) says that "our Ennius was beyond all others a translator and follower" of Euhemerus, and Lactantius, in Book 1 of his *Divine Institutes,* gives some five pages of excerpts from Ennius' *Sacra historia,* which set forth the rationalist ideas of Euhemerism. Though these excerpts are in prose, they have been found to show traces of septenarian rhythms, and it is on other grounds likely that Ennius wrote his work in verse; it has been plausibly suggested, therefore, that Lactantius used an intermediary prose version of Ennius.

If Ennius provided no model for Latin prose, he did provide models for the major species of Latin verse, and not only in the sense of shaping literary forms, but also of informing them with a spirit and content which became canonical. The greatest names in Latin literature are patently in Ennius' debt. Vergil took from the *Annals* not only his hexameters but also his glorification of Rome's history and Rome's destiny, though he refined his expression of both. Lucilius and Horace learned the spirit and scope of satire from Ennius. Lucretius inherited curiosity concerning the nature of things and a rationalizing view of traditional orthodoxies, as well as the vigorous hexameters in which to express his curiosity and his doubts. The tragedians had in Ennius their model for the application of rhetoric to drama and the display of intense and flamboyant emotion. All learned that Latin literature must shape and serve the national ideals and aspirations of Rome. It is a noteworthy thing that the patriarch who had the largest share in introducing Greek forms and concepts into Latin literature is at the same time the truest exponent of Romanism and himself the best demonstration of what is essentially original in Latin literature. And the Romans understood this. Cicero often speaks of him as *noster Ennius,* has his words at his finger tips, and quotes him with admiration and affection. The sentiment of traditional reverence with which he inspired the Romans is expressed by Quintilian (10.1.88): "Let us venerate Ennius like the groves, sacred from their antiquity, in which the great and ancient oaks are invested not so much with beauty as with sacred associations."

Ennius' work in tragedy was carried on by his nephew Marcus Pacuvius (220–ca.130 B.C.), who was born at Brundisium and came to Rome to paint pictures and stayed to write tragedies, retired to Tarentum when he fell ill, and there died at the age of ninety. Pliny (35.19) testifies to his fame as a painter; a picture of his was still shown in the Forum Boarium in Pliny's day. His dramatic production was small: we know of some dozen tragedies including the *praetexta*

Paulus; about four hundred lines survive. Originality in choice of subject is indicated by his titles: *Antiopa, Armorum Iudicium, Atalanta, Chryses, Dulorestes* ("Orestes Enslaved"), *Hermiona, Iliona, Medus, Niptra* ("The Washing"), *Pentheus, Periboea, Teucer.* If the *Medus* is a fair example, the plots were extremely complicated. Rationalism appears in the jeer against those "who understand the speech of birds and learn more wisdom from another's liver than from their own" (*Chryses;* 104–6 W), and curiosity concerning the nature of things in a longer passage from the same play (110–14 W), which declares that what the Greeks call Aether produces, nourishes, consumes, and again begets all things. The kindred thought in Lucretius 2.991 may derive from this passage or from its original in the *Chrysippus* of Euripides. Cicero (*Tusculan Disputations* 2.21.48) points out that in the *Niptra* (280–95 W) Ulysses bears his torments with more becoming fortitude than in the corresponding passage of Sophocles. The relative merits of the artistic and the practical life seem to be debated in the *Antiopa* (7–11 W). There are pathetic scenes, notably the appeal of murdered Deiphilus' ghost to his mother Iliona (205–210 W), and pictorial power in the description of Teucer (353–360 W), part of which may be reproduced for its sound:

> *flamma inter nubes coruscat, caelum tonitru contremit,*
> *grando mixta imbri largifico subita praecipitans cadit,*
> *undique omnes venti erumpunt, saevi existunt turbines,*
> *fervit aestu pelagus.*

Similar command of meter and sound effect may be seen in Euryclea's invitation to the unrecognized Ulysses to have his feet washed (*Niptra;* 266–8 W):

> *Cedo tuum pedem mi, lymphis flavis fulvum ut pulverem*
> *manibus isdem, quibus Ulixi saepe permulsi, abluam*
> *lassitudinemque minuam manuum mollitudine.*

The *praetexta* probably celebrated L. Aemilius Paulus' victory over Perses at Pydna in 168. Of the ancient critics most competent to judge such matters, Cicero (*De optimo genere oratorum* 1.2) places Pacuvius first in tragedy as Ennius is first in epic; Horace (*Epistles* 2.1.55) praises his learning; and Quintilian his force. Varro (Gellius 6.14.6) characterizes his style as "abundant," but Cicero (*Brutus* 74.258) criticizes both his and Caecilius' Latinity. Both his merits and shortcomings, one would think, were such as might be expected of the successor of a great pioneer.

There is a charming story in Gellius (13.2) of Pacuvius' first encounter with the young poet who was to become his rival and his friend. This was L. Accius, born in 170 B.C. at Pisaurum, of parents who were, like Horace's, freedmen. When Accius was thirty and Pacuvius eighty, Cicero tells us (*Brutus* 64.229), each presented a play under the same aediles. Accius lived to become a friend of Cicero, when Cicero was old enough to discuss literary questions with him, and hence his death can be placed at about 86 B.C. His long, and with relation to other tragedians, late career and his large productivity made him the central figure in Roman tragedy. Two or three revealing anecdotes may be repeated. When the noble Julius Caesar Strabo, who also wrote tragedies, entered a meeting of the poets' guild on the Aventine, Accius refused to rise for him because he regarded his own work as superior. Accius sued a mime who mentioned him on the stage, and won a conviction. "When asked why he did not turn advocate in view of the extraordinary skill in making apt replies which his tragedies revealed, Accius answered that in his plays the characters said what he himself wanted them to say, whereas in the courts his adversaries would probably say just what he least wanted them to say" (Quintilian 5.13.43).

Accius' principal remains are some seven hundred lines from forty or fifty tragedies on Greek models, drawn from all the various cycles of myth. These are too scanty for any meaningful distinction to be drawn between him and his predecessors, of whose work his own seems to be merely a development. Intensity of emotion may be illustrated from a passage in the *Tereus* (639–42 W): "In his wild mood and savage spirit Tereus gazed upon her, maddened with burning passion, possessed; in his madness he resolves a cursed deed." Fortitude of the Roman type is frequently commended, as in a passage from the *Telephus* (625–26 W): "Though fortune could strip me of kingdom and wealth, it cannot strip me of my virtue." There are numerous *sententiae,* as is natural in fragments gathered from quotations; for example, Thyestes says in the *Atreus* (178 W): "Wide awake a man must always be; many are the ambushes laid for the good." From the *Atreus* too is the magnificent *Oderint dum metuant* (168 W), "Let them hate, so they fear," which Seneca (*On Anger* 1.20.4) says "we would know well enough was written in the time of Sulla." There is the usual distrust of divination (*Brutus* 29–31 W) and suspicion of venal seers (*Astyanax,* 134–35 W). Nature and its phenomena are vividly described in a passage from the *Oenomaus* (509–12 W): "Before the dawn, harbinger of burning rays, when the husbandmen bring forth the oxen from their rest into the fields, that they may break the red, dew-sprinkled soil with the plough, and turn up the clods from the soft glebe." From the *Philoctetes* we have (571–72 W): "Lying beneath the pole by the seven stars, whence the blustering roar of the north wind drives before it the chill snows."

Of special interest are the *praetextae: Aeneadae* or *Decius,* on the self-immolation of Decius Mus at the battle of Sentinum in 295 B.C., from which there are sixteen lines; and *Brutus,* on the downfall of the Tarquins, from which there are twenty-three continuous and a few additional scattered lines. In 44 B.C. a performance of the *Brutus* was forbidden, for obvious reasons. Accius wrote not only plays but also works on the history and techniques of his art. Of the nine books of his *Didascalica* ("Records of the Stage") in sotadic meter, the twenty-two lines which remain are of little value either for their information or as poetry. Of the *Pragmatica,* which perhaps dealt with stage diction and ran to several books, there are only two lines remaining. From his hexameter *Annales,* not of history but apparently of festivals, which also ran to several books, there are only nine lines. In addition Accius wrote *Parerga,* probably in imitation of Hesiod; *Praxidica,* on agriculture, for his friend Brutus Gallaecus; and amatory poems. No remains of these have been identified. Mention should finally be made of spelling reforms advocated by Accius; vowels should be written double when long, and *gg* should be written for *ng.*

But the esteem in which the ancients held Accius as a tragedian and the paucity of fragments from his other works make it clear that it is as the culmination of Roman tragedy that we must regard him. Indeed, he seems to have exhausted the possibilities of the genre for Rome as perhaps Euripides did for the Greeks. After him the professional writing of tragedy fell into abeyance, and the gentlemen litterateurs, like the Julius Caesar Strabo mentioned above, seem to have borne the same relationship to Accius as the Alexandrian Pleiad bore to Euripides. Almost every man of letters tried his hand at tragedy as a sort of literary exercise—Cicero's brother Quintus wrote four in sixteen days—but none seem to have been intended for production on the stage.

Yet the theater continued to flourish to the end of the republic. Such actors as Aesopus and Roscius were highly regarded as artists and as men, and every writer, Vergil and Livy no less than Cicero, expects his reader to recognize allusions to stage performances. Audiences knew their plays well enough, as we can see from a number of cases, to look for topical allusions in their performance. A measure if not a cause of decline is to be seen in the increasing elaborateness and size of spectacles. Until 55 B.C. when Pompey gave Rome its first stone theater, which accommodated many thousands of spectators, performances had been presented in temporary wooden structures. Now it was inevitable that elaborate scenic effects and spectacle should take the place of real drama. In fifth-century Athens tragedy was a popular art form, of direct concern to a large proportion of the people. Transferred to another age and climate Greek tragedies require of their audience a specially informed taste. There were not enough Romans who possessed such taste to fill the huge theaters. As the Greeks themselves had done, the Romans were grown too sophisticated to be interested in the presentation of moral problems by a cast of characters from a remote and alien mythology. Perhaps they regarded the stalwart fortitude which the Romanized plays inculcated as a little old-fashioned. The dominance of spectacle over words was seen in the presentation of Accius' *Clutemestra,* which inaugurated Pompey's theater; six hundred caparisoned mules were led across the stage as part of Agamemnon's booty—a strong company, it has been remarked, for the Romans. Mere words could not compete, and it was natural that audiences should be entertained instead with spectacle, music, and farce.

III

COMEDY AND SATIRE

THE GREAT PREPONDERANCE OF THE COMIC OVER the serious in the extant remains of the literature of the early republic might lead the unwary to suspect that the vaunted *gravitas* of the early Romans was hypocrisy or hoax. Granting that the vicissitudes which govern the survival of ancient books are notoriously erratic, it is nevertheless probably safe to assume that the ancient Italians like their descendants understood that *desipere in loco* is not tantamount to frivolity. But the simplest explanation for the preponderance of the comic is that Greek New Comedy was surely the most common as it was without doubt the most comprehensible and attractive literary form with which the veterans for whom Plautus wrote might have become acquainted in their service abroad. Because that form is the basis of Roman comedy a word must be said of its nature.

Greek New Comedy derived not from the robust exuberance and fantasy of Aristophanes but from the intrigues and familiar characters, heroic only in name, of Euripides. Its concern was not, like Aristophanes', with criticism of public institutions, but like Euripides' in such plays as *Electra, Ion, Iphigenia at Aulis,* with plots motivated by ordinary human emotions and with such commonplace concerns as arranging suitable marriages. The shift in drama corresponded precisely to the shift in philosophy after Alexander the Great; men turned from the larger investigation of truth and consideration of the *polis* to concern for the individual. Tragedies continued to be written and acted, but the paramount dramatic form, after Alexander, was New Comedy. New Comedy does not premise a specially informed taste; its bourgeois settings give it universal applicability, and hence it can be transferred in time and place without being made, as Greek tragedy must be made, a *tour de force.* New Comedy, and not tragedy, is the ancestor of European drama and the modern stage, and the transmission of New Comedy to later ages is due solely to Plautus and Terence.

As in the case of other borrowings, the Romans naturalized their adaptations; but it is remarkable that in this most popular form the alien origin is most evident. Not only are the scenes, the *dramatis per-sonae,* and the intrigues manifestly Greek, but the morality and man-ners and atmosphere of the plays are, despite Roman touches, com-pletely un-Roman. Plays written during the period of the Punic Wars, for example, can speak of war as something remote, an occupation for young men who must seek their fortune or withdraw from an unfortunate love affair.

If the fresh reader of Roman comedy finds the conventional Greek background puzzling he is apt to be more puzzled by the convention of a world which seems to be composed of seductions and unwanted children, improbable coincidences and recognitions of long-lost daughters, irate fathers, and impertinent slaves. Not only the casts of these plays but also their plots bear so close a family resemblance that it is possible to present a pattern applicable virtually to all. A young Greek gentleman is in love with a charming girl in the posses-sion of a procurer who is about to sell her to another, since the young man does not have the price. His cunning parasite defrauds the young man's father of the necessary sum. The girl is discovered to be of free birth (having been kidnaped or exposed in infancy) and a suitable match for the young man. There are explanations for the retention of the patterned plot by the Greeks. To begin with, separations of families, loss and even ultimate recovery of identity, and surely seduc-tions must actually have been common during the wars and unsettled conditions of the early Hellenistic age. All Greek art adhered to the form found appropriate for it, and achieved variety within the limita-tions of its convention: tragedy or the Doric temple illustrate the point. Limitations in New Comedy were dictated by the history of the development of the form; for all their family resemblances the *drama-tis personae* possess individual and interesting characters, displaying, in fine gradations, amiable traits of loyalty, affection, high-minded-ness. Even the slaves, for all their occasional impudence, show a normal range of emotions and are sometimes singularly generous. Nor do these plays demonstrate contemporary moral decadence, as they have been alleged to do; if we recognize that in matters of sex the double standard is the rule, then the moral atmosphere so far from being anarchic will prove to maintain a high level.

The most abundant of the Roman comic writers, in wit as in volume, is Titus Maccus Plautus. The date of his death, given by Cicero (*Brutus* 60) as 184 B.C., is the best attested fact in his biography; his birth would then fall about 255, for he is said to have been a *senex* when the *Pseudolus* was produced in 191. Jerome, claiming the authority of Varro, provides other details of his life, but these may well be based on inferences from his plays. According to the traditional account he was born in Sarsina, an Umbrian town near the border of Cisalpine Gaul, which had been conquered by the Romans only a dozen years before Plautus' birth. His native speech was therefore probably Umbrian; his mastery of Latin he acquired at Rome, to which he moved at an early age. He did work in the theater—according to the account, manual work; but the name Maccus (if Maccus it was and not Maccius) suggests that he was an actor, for one of the stock characters in the Atellan farces was so named. The money which he saved he lost in a business venture. Perhaps in the travels connected with this venture he learned his Greek. He was forced to do menial work in a flour mill, but he was delivered from this drudgery by the plays which he wrote. His success enabled him to devote himself to writing until his death.

The popularity of his work induced imitators to pass their own work off as his, so that 130 plays came to be attributed to him. Varro drew up a list of twenty-one which were universally regarded as Plautine, though he thought that others too were written by Plautus. The twenty-one plays we have, including the fragmentary *Vidularia,* are evidently those of Varro's list. Terence ascribes to Plautus a *Colax* (*Eunuch* 25) and a *Commorientes* (*Adelphi* 7), neither of which has come down. But Terence's words may imply that the *Colax* was partly the work of Naevius, and Gellius (3.3.11 f.) states that Plautus touched up plays written by others. This may be the basis for early confusion concerning Plautine authorship of plays. Not all the plays that Plautus wrote, then, have come down to us, and not all that have come down are surely his. A few that have come down can be dated. *Miles Gloriosus* (211 f.) speaks of Naevius being in prison, and since he was liberated in 206 B.C. we have an approximate date. *Stichus* is dated to 200 by its *didascalia. Trinummus* cannot be earlier than 194, for at line 990 it mentions "the new aediles." *Aulularia* assumes (498 ff.) the abrogation of the Oppian law, which occurred in 195. *Pseudolus* is dated to 191 by its *didascalia. Bacchides* refers (1072 ff.) to the four triumphs of 189. *Epidicus* must be earlier than *Bacchides,* for it is alluded to by name in that play (214).

Though Plautus' plays all follow Greek models, each of them (with the possible exception of *Mercator,* whose authorship is therefore doubtful) gives evidence of Plautus' own robust wit and of the influence of native Italian comic forms. Satura, the Fescennines, and the Atellan farces all made their contributions. Satura was a medley of song and story, performed with dance and pantomime; but it involved no impersonation and had no plot. The Fescennines were exchanges of amusing vituperation, but not dramatic. The stock characters of the Atellan farces—Maccus, Dossenus, and the like—did follow a kind of plot in the dialogue they improvised, but they relied for their effect on gesture and indecency rather than on the unfolding of a plot. Plot, characters, organization, came from the Greek, and in adapting Greek work Plautus had a model in the work of his older contemporaries, Livius Andronicus and Naevius. Neither the work of these men nor the Greek plays which Plautus adapted have survived in sufficient volume to make a precise appraisal of Plautus' fidelity or originality possible. But from comparison with fragments of Menander's plays, which now present whole scenes, and from the more careful and more subdued and more thoughtful adaptations of Terence, it is clear that the ebullience and love of fun in Plautus, as well as the tendency to sacrifice dramatic values for pure farce, are Plautus' own.

The subtler aspects of New Comedy are often ridden down. Usually Plautus' aim is to produce the greatest possible volume of immediate laughter, and he is sometimes careless of inconsistencies in plot and character. More obvious indications of the liberty taken with Greek originals are the numerous references to Roman rather than Greek life and conditions. *Miles Gloriosus* refers to a Roman gaming law (164) and to the poet Naevius (211 f.); *Captivi* (823) and *Epidicus* (25) refer to aediles and praetors; and there are similar Roman allusions in other plays. Other manifest variations are the practice (called *contaminatio*) of fusing elements from various comedies into one, and the inclusion of lengthy lyrical *cantica.* To the sound of his plays Plautus devoted great care. The six-foot iambic line of Greek drama, with slight alteration, is standard in Roman drama also; but in Plautus the more musical seven-and-a-half-foot trochaic line is at least as frequent. Plautus uses a wide variety of other meters also, and has numerous solos, duets, and trios. The course of the action is not interrupted by choral interludes, as in the Greek, but passages in lyric meters occur throughout the plays; if these were sung (which is doubtful) they gave the plays the character of musical comedy or operetta. (The divisions into acts in our texts are a Renaissance invention.) From the few plays which can be dated it is evident that Plautus increased lyric content as time went on: *Miles Gloriosus* (205 B.C.) is metrically simple, whereas *Pseudolus* (191 B.C.) is metrically ornate. Attempts have been made to construct a chronology of all the plays on the basis of their use of meters, but other considerations prove this an uncertain gauge. The subjoined listing will follow the customary alphabetical order.

Amphitryo is a version of the story of Jupiter's violation of Amphitryon's wife Alcmena to beget Hercules. It is unique among our comedies in being a mythological travesty; its source must have been Middle or Old Comedy rather than New. It is also unique in representing the adultery of a respectable married woman. In a true comedy our sympathies would be wholly with Alcmena, and we should be shocked by Jupiter's outrageous treatment of her and of Amphitryon, whom he not only cuckolds but ridicules and pulls about on the stage. But like Greek Old Comedy the play is an intellectual joke based on fantasy, with no pretense of verisimilitude and no intention to engage either sympathy or antipathy for the characters. The fact that the infant whose begetting is so prodigious an enterprise is born before the begetter has well left the premises shows the total unconcern with dramatic illusion. Other plays turn on mistakes due to identity of appearance, but, as in *Menaechmi,* there is only one identical pair; in this play we are not disturbed, as we are in the *Comedy of Errors,* at there being two. We are not meant to wince or gloat at or believe what happens on the stage, but only to be amused at the great joke. The cream of the jest is in the closing line: "Clap your hands, audience, for Jupiter Almighty's sake."

Asinaria ("The Ass Comedy") fits the comic pattern suggested above so well that nothing more need be said of it. The line *surge, amator, i domum,* "Up, lover, home with you," four times repeated at the close of the play, would be funny in any age and any climate.

The high merit of *Aulularia* ("Pot of Gold") is demonstrated by the fact that Molière's highly successful and much-imitated *L'Avare* is so close an adaptation of it. Euclio is a real study of a morbid miser, and the reactions he evokes in the remaining characters are acutely observed and wittily presented. The best fun is where Lyconides confesses that he has robbed Euclio of his treasure, referring to the miser's daughter, while Euclio naturally thinks he is referring to the gold. Awkwardness in handling intrigue is revealed by the necessity of eavesdropping on the miser's soliloquy to discover the whereabouts of the treasure. The closing scene of this play is lost. Its suggestion of a double plot, a feature developed by Terence, gives *Bacchides* ("The Two Bacchises") a special interest. There are two sets of lovers and two fathers, and their interaction increases the intrigue with unexpected reversals and sudden developments. The portrayal of character which comparison facilitates is excellent. Plautus' original for this play was Menander's *Dis Exapaton* ("Double Deceiver").

Captivi ("The Prisoners of War") is unique in Roman drama in that no women are involved; its theme is the chivalrous devotion of a slave to his master. In the prologue Plautus declares—incidentally characterizing his other plays:

It is not composed in the hackneyed style, is quite unlike other plays, nor does it contain filthy lines that one must not repeat. In this comedy you will meet no perjured pimp, or unprincipled courtesan or braggart captain.
                                                                    —*Paul Nixon*

Philocrates and his slave Tyndarus, both captives of Hegio, exchange places so that Philocrates rather than Tyndarus may be sent to arrange an exchange for Hegio's son Philopolemus, who is a captive of Philocrates' party. When the deception is discovered and Hegio is about to punish Tyndarus, Philocrates returns, bringing not only Philopolemus but also a slave who confesses that Tyndarus is actually a son of Hegio whom he had kidnaped in infancy. The sentimentality of the play never descends to the maudlin, and it engages the emotions of the reader as no other ancient comedy does. Its suitability for school use has made it probably the most widely read of Plautine plays. Lessing thought it was the best comedy ever produced, but there are contrary opinions, based on faults of structure, almost as extravagant. *Captivi* has been much imitated; mention may be made of Ben Jonson's *The Case is Altered,* which is a combination of *Captivi* and *Aulularia*.

The repeated explanation of the plot and the repeated appeals for attention in the prologue of this play afford a revealing glimpse of the tumultuous Roman audience.

Casina is the most lyrical, most farcical, most obscene, most amusing, and probably the latest of Plautus' plays. It was probably much altered from its original, the *Kleroumenoi* ("Lot Drawers") of Diphilus. The plot concerns an old reprobate who seeks an assignation with a maid of his wife, with whom his son happens to be in love; father and son try to outdo each other to gain possession of the girl. The prologue was written for a revival, and reflects the current decline of comedy:

Those be wise men, in my opinion, who take old wine and those who love to see old plays. Yes, liking as you do the works and words of ancient days, you should like old plays better than all others; for, really, the new comedies that are produced nowadays are much more worthless than our new coins.

—Paul Nixon

Cistellaria (the "Casket" which contains the tokens of the heroine's identity), the text of which is badly mutilated, has a familiar New Comedy plot. Alcesimarchus wishes to marry his mistress Selenium, believed to be the daughter of a procuress, who is deeply in love with him. His father objects and wishes him to marry a daughter of Demipho. Selenium herself is proven to be a daughter of Demipho, and all is well. Alcesimarchus is a more violent lover than is usual in our comedies, and is once on verge of suicide. There are six female characters, and all are carefully delineated. The plot is very like that of Terence's *Andria,* and like it is based on a play of Menander—here *Synaristosae* ("The Women Who Lunch Together"). *Cistellaria* appears to be much nearer translation than other Plautine plays.

In the *Curculio* (the name of the parasite in the play) a pimp is about to sell the hero's sweetheart to a soldier; by means of the soldier's ring, which the hero's parasite steals, the girl is discovered to be the soldier's sister, and the pimp is forced to release her to the hero. The slave who gives his name to the *Epidicus* is one of the craftiest of his numerous kind. Twice he diddles his master's father of money to buy a girl, and his deceit is the more satisfactory in that he makes his dupe think that *he* is the deceiver. A recognition at the end resolves a complicated plot and flurried feelings. Shakespeare's *Comedy of Errors* has made the plot of the *Menaechmi* generally familiar; but by adding identical servants (from the *Amphitryo,* where they are appropriate) to the identical masters Shakespeare has made farce of Plautus' well-constructed comedy. Here we only have to reconcile ourselves to the obtuseness of a man who takes so long to recognize the twin he has been searching for. The catechism of the doctor is surely one of the funniest scenes in all comedy.

Mercator ("Merchant") is considered by Gilbert Norwood, who loathes Plautus, as far the best of Plautus' plays, on the grounds that here Plautus merely translated his good Greek original, which was Philemon's *Emporos* ("Merchant"). A plausible explanation for its divergence from the remaining plays is that it is by another hand. A father is in love with his son's sweetheart (but not, as in *Casina,* knowing of his son's attachment) and caches her away in the house of a neighbor, whose wife returns most inopportunely. The play lacks the boisterous fun and lyrical embellishment of *Casina,* but is well and simply told. *Miles Gloriosus* ("Braggart Soldier") is our fullest treatment of a character who was a fixture in ancient comedy. His self-esteem and lechery make him an easy dupe for the hero's slave, who contrives the union of the hero and his sweetheart, first by digging a secret passage and then by fabricating an ingenious tale which could fool only a braggart soldier. The construction of this play is poor and some of its jokes labored; but its comic ingredients have made it a favorite, and it has been much imitated—as for example in Nicholas Udall's *Ralph Roister Doister,* which has elements from Terence's *Eunuch* also.

Mostellaria ("The Haunted House") merely sets forth the devices used by a slave to keep his master's father, who has unexpectedly returned from abroad, from entering his own house where the son is giving a mixed dinner party. There can be no other end than eventual discovery and forgiveness, but we are kept in suspense to see what clever ruse the irrepressible and resourceful Tranio will next bring to bear on his dupe. College dramatic coaches have found this play and the *Menaechmi* the most suitable for their purpose in the Plautine corpus. The original of this play was probably the *Phasma* ("Ghost") of Philemon, though other Greek playwrights wrote plays of the same name. *Persa* ("The 'Girl' from Persia") presents a collection of slaves aping their betters, for better and for worse, in the absence of their masters. The burlesque tone is maintained in the extravagant improbability of the plot, the use of disguises, the speeches apparently parodying more formal drama. The play is largely lyric. *Poenulus* ("The Carthaginian") is one of the longest and dullest of Plautus' plays. Like *Curculio* and *Epidicus* it involves trickery to obtain possession of a girl and her final recognition. Like *Miles Gloriosus* it is an apparent conflation of two plots not very well fused. The Carthaginian words in this play give it a special philological interest.

Pseudolus, Cicero tells us (*On Old Age* 50), was along with *Truculentus* Plautus' favorite play in his old age; in Cicero's own day the great actor Roscius played the role of the pimp Ballio. The theme is the stereotype of a slave (*Pseudolus*) using his wits to free his young master's sweetheart, to the discomfiture of the pimp, the soldier who has paid for her, and her lover's father—who, however, is reconciled in the end. But the movement is brisk and the fun unflagging. The reading of the girl's pathetic love letter, the pimp's marshalling of his crew to demand birthday gifts, and his later mistaking of the soldier's true messenger for Pseudolus' spurious one are especially effective. There are a number of references to comic poets and their work in this play.

Rudens ("Rope") is as singular as *Captivi,* but in a different direction, and some of its admirers pay it the high compliment of comparing it to *The Tempest.* Its setting on a stormy seacoast of north Africa at dawn, with the principal characters emerging severally from the sea where they have been shipwrecked, raises to genuine romance the trite story of a bilked pimp whose charge is recognized as the daughter of a gentle old man who is unknowingly called upon to adjudicate the fate of his daughter, who is thus enabled to marry the sympathetic young man who had been cheated of her. The atmosphere facilitates suspension of disbelief. The entrances and exits are well motivated and well paced. When the distraught girls emerge from the sea their pathetic duet is the more effective as the audience knows (from Arcturus' prologue) that the heroine's father lives nearby. The audience can then gloat over the mutual recriminations of the pimp and his disreputable friend, who emerge drenched and chattering. The fishermen with their quaint costume and musical plaint are a relaxing chorus but carry the action forward, like the fishermen in *Shakuntala.* The flirtation between the slaves of the heroine and of her unknown father over Venus' water jug is more than low comedy, and serves a similar purpose. The purposeful retardation of the recognition after the chest has been found is masterful; the mock judicial dispute of the slaves is exactly right for the interval. If *Rudens* had survived alone and there were not a dozen echoes of its plot to jade our taste its position in the dramatic literature of the world would be very high.

The absence of plot in *Stichus* sets it apart from Plautus' other plays. First their father tries to persuade two sisters who are loyal to their long absent husbands to give them up, then a parasite complains of his disappointments, then slaves are shown carousing; and there is only a thin connection between the episodes. But even without intrigue or recognition the play is amusing, and it has distinct value as a social document. The original was Menander's *Adelphoi* ("Brothers"), but not the *Adelphoi* which is the original of Terence's play.

Trinummus ("Threepenny Day") is like *Captivi* in having no female characters (though love and matrimony are discussed at length), and Lessing placed it second to *Captivi* among the plays of Plautus. The theme is posed by the situation of young Lesbonicus, who has dissipated his property and so cannot discharge the honorable obligation of providing a dowry for his sister. In a long monody Lysiteles decides that love is expensive and corrupting, and determines to marry instead. His father Philto reads Lysiteles a lecture on morality, with Lysiteles agreeing and then utterly disconcerting the old man by proposing to put his doctrine into effect by marrying a girl without a dowry. The remainder of the play runs along conventional lines, and it is regrettable that the serious moral problem involved is not more adequately dealt with. The problem recurs in several plays of Molière, though none is directly based on *Trinummus*. It was adapted in Italian and French in the sixteenth century, however, and is the basis for Lessing's *Der Schatz*. The original was Philemon's *Thesaurus* ("The Treasure").

The grim earnestness of the completely unfunny *Truculentus* should absolve Plautus from any charge of flippant immorality; it is significant that this was one of the two favorites of his old age. There could be no more effective warning against the loose conduct described in many of the other plays. With the starkest realism we see the ruthless courtesan, her mind single on profit, bring to ruin an Athenian gentleman, a soldier (no braggart this time), and a country youth. All can see her unscrupulousness and their own degradation, but none can free himself. Even the truculent slave (Truculentus), of whom we would not have expected it, is demoralized. The utterness of the corruption is manifested at the end when the soldier and the country youth agree to share the woman between them. In its own way *Truculentus* is a masterpiece.

The considerable fragments of *Vidularia* ("The Chest") reveal a plot similar to that of *Rudens*. A young man has lost the tokens of his identity in a shipwreck, and has taken service with his unknown father; the chest containing the tokens is found by a fisherman, and recognition follows. Titles and fragments of some two dozen additional Plautine plays are known, but they do not add significantly to our knowledge of Plautus. The twenty more or less complete plays we have reveal a dramatist of great comic force, with some of the explosive energy of Old Comedy and some of the subtlety of New. Whatever his borrowings from these and other sources may have been, the vital drive in his plays must derive from his own comic genius. His place in the dramatic literature of the world is secure, because of the vitality of his plays and because their prolific progeny constitute an important segment of European literature.

Between Plautus and Terence was Caecilius Statius, whom ancient criticism esteemed as their peer. The little we know of his life is based on the uncertain authority of Jerome. He was an Insubrian Gaul, born about 220 B.C. in Milan, brought to Rome as a slave between 200 and 194, and there manumitted by his owner Caecilius, whose name he took. He became a friend (Jerome says a *contubernalis*) of Ennius, and possibly to avoid competition with him confined his writing to *palliatae*. In the prologue to Terence's *Hecyra* the actor-manager L. Ambivius Turpio says that Caecilius' plays were damned when they were new to the stage. Perhaps this was because he had not yet mastered Latin; Cicero (*Ad Atticum* 7.3.10) calls him *malus auctor Latinitatis,* though Cicero is elsewhere (Gellius 15.24.1) said to have put Caecilius first among the Roman writers of comedy. Of his works we have forty titles (some Latin, some Greek and Latin, some Greek) and about three hundred lines. The longest fragment is a fifteen-line passage from the *Plocium* (136–50 W) which Gellius (2.23.4) cites along with its Menandrian original to show Caecilius' inferiority. The translation is indeed not very close. Some of the single-line fragments show emotional force or farcical bent not unlike

Plautus'. Two quotable lines seem to show a Roman touch: *Saepe est etiam sub palliolo sordido sapientia,* "There's often wisdom even underneath a shabby little cloak" (255 W); and *Serit arbores quae saeclo prosint alteri,* "He plants trees to profit another age" (200 W).

It was to Caecilius, according to Suetonius' *Life of Terence* (preserved in Donatus), that Terence was ordered by the aediles to submit his first play for examination. We are told that he presented himself, humbly dressed, at the poets' college, and was permitted to read, seated on a low stool; he had not gone far when he was invited to join the company at table, and his work was received with enthusiasm. It must be noted, however, that this picturesque episode, like other singularly precise details of Terence's life, may well have been invented after his death, largely on the basis of his own informative prologues. According to the accepted tradition, then, Terence was born in Carthage about 195 B.C. and was probably of dark color. He was brought to Rome as a slave, educated by his owner, the senator Terentius Lucanus, and upon manumission took the name Publius Terentius Afer ("the African"). Perhaps it was his African origin that brought him to the attention of Scipio Africanus the Younger; in any case he is said to have became a member of the Scipionic circle, which included such champions of enlightenment as Laelius, the satirist Lucilius, the Stoic philosopher Panaetius. From his apologia in the prologue of *Hauton Timorumenos* we know of the rumor that Terence's noble friends were the real authors of his plays. Courtesy to these friends forbade a vigorous denial, and Terence evades the question with a handsome compliment (*Adelphi* 15 ff.):

For as to what these envious men allege, that some of our great men assist him, and are constantly writing with him; this, which they look upon as a mighty reproach, he regards as his greatest merit, that he has it in his power to please those with whom you and the whole people of Rome are so much pleased; and whose services in war, in peace, and even in your private affairs, each one of you has used unreservedly, according to his need.

Other attacks his prologues refute more vigorously. To the charge of plagiarism he replies (*Eunuchus* 41), *Nullumst iam dictum quod non sit dictum prius,* "Nothing is ever said which has not been said before." To the charge of "contaminating" Greek plays, that is, of fusing two Greek plays into one Latin, he offers the precedent of

Naevius, Plautus, and Ennius (*Andria* 15 ff.). The charge that he was an ill-prepared Johnny-come-lately in literature he leaves to the discretion of his audience (*Hauton Timorumenos* 22 ff.). Against the charge that his dialogue was thin and his style trivial, he asserts that he avoids extravagances and improbabilities (*Phormio* 6 ff.). He calls attention to the quieter tone of his own plays (*Hauton Timorumenos* 35 ff.):

Listen now without prejudice, and give me a chance to play a quiet comedy in silence, that I may not always have to play the parts of a bustling slave, an angry old gentleman, a hungry parasite, an impudent flatterer, or a greedy slavedealer, at the top of my voice, to my great distress.

The implied comparison with the work of Plautus is a fair appraisal of Terence's own merits. His plays do not indeed have the robust and roughshod farcical quality, the incessant and sometimes reckless attacks on the risibilities of the audience which characterize many of Plautus' plays. Terence is quieter and more refined in tone, much more careful in construction, much more polished in language, much subtler in characterizations. Where Plautus descends to farce, Terence rises to the true comedy of manners; where Plautus demands a guffaw, Terence is content with a thoughtful smile. Plautus' additions to his Greek originals are sometimes shriekingly plain and always easy to sense; Terence was doubtless at least as original, but his contributions are in careful construction and in the clarity and polish of his style. His skill in construction is illustrated by his regular practice, improving from play to play, of interweaving two mutually illuminating sets of characters. The clarity of his language is illustrated (but only partially) by the neat precision of his apothegms which stud his every page and have been naturalized in every language: *Dictum sapienti sat est,* "A word to the wise"; *Fortis fortuna adiuvat,* "Fortune favors the brave"; *Modo liceat vivere est spes,* "While there's life there's hope"; *Quot homines tot sententiae,* "Many men, many minds"; *Tacent, satis laudant,* "Their silence is praise"; *Senectus ipsast morbus,* "Age is itself a disease"; *Amantium irae amoris integratiost,* "A lovers' quarrel is a renewal of love"; *Hinc illae lacrimae,* "Hence these tears"; and most characteristic of Terence himself, *Homo sum, humani nihil a me alienum puto,* "I am a man; whatever pertains to man concerns me."

All of Terence's plays survive; indeed, a Vatican manuscript is illustrated with drawings of the characters costumed and masked. All were produced by the actor-manager L. Ambivius Turpio, and the music (doubtless much less elaborate, as are the meters, than in Plautus) was performed by Flaccus, slave of Claudius. The Greek originals of all the plays are recorded, though none is extant for comparison. The chronology of the plays is somewhat confused by the fact that *Hecyra* was twice offered before it obtained a hearing; all were produced between 166 and 160.

The earliest of the plays is *Andria,* produced at the Megalensian Games in 166. *Andria* is based on two plays of Menander, *Andria* and *Perinthia.* The basis of the plot is the intrigue and recognition common in New Comedy; Terence's innovations will become apparent from a summary of it. Simo has engaged his son Pamphilus to Chremes' daughter Philumena, but Pamphilus loves the supposed orphan Glycerium, and his friend Charinus wishes to marry Philumena; Chremes, learning of Pamphilus' entanglement, wishes to break off the engagement to Philumena, and Simo, to test his son's feelings, pretends that it holds; on the advice of his slave Davus Pamphilus feigns submission, but he is cornered when Simo persuades Chremes to retract his refusal; Davus procures Chremes' definite refusal by showing the child Glycerium has borne to Pamphilus; Glycerium is proven to be a daughter of Chremes, and she marries Pamphilus and Charinus marries Philumena. We are told by Donatus that Charinus was not part of the Menandrian model; the parallel and foil for Pamphilus is then an invention of Terence. Charinus is moreover the first young man in ancient comedy seeking marriage with a respectable young woman of good family. In the same direction, we notice that the fathers are sympathetic and not butts, and that the slave Davus genuinely tries to act for the best interests of the family and is not a mere rogue. The Latin of this play is as smooth and clear as anything in the language.

In 165 b.c. Terence attempted to produce his *Hecyra,* but the audience was drawn away by rumors of more exciting entertainment, such as rope-dancing, offered elsewhere. The next play produced was the *Hauton Timorumenos* ("The Self-Tormenter"), based on a play by Menander of the same title and presented at the Megalensian Games in 163. As in *Andria* there are two love affairs in this play, but here they are more closely integrated. The plot is highly involved; the recognition comes in the middle of the play rather than at the end, and is a means of further complication rather than a solution *ex machina*. The fathers are more carefully studied than the sons, but not so clearly contrasted as in the later *Adelphi*. The lovers too are well characterized: the rather wooden young Antipho and the hardened and grasping courtesan Bacchis; the ardent but timid Clinia and his naive and virtuous Antiphila. The truth of the characterizations combined with the ingenuity of the plot make *Hauton Timorumenos* a true drama.

In 161 B.C., also at the Megalensian Games, Terence presented his *Eunuchus,* which brought him a higher fee than had ever been paid for a comedy and proved his greatest success. The model was a Menandrian play of the same name, with some elements added, as the prologue tells us, from Menander's *Kolax* ("Flatterer"). Again there are two sets of lovers, two brothers and two supposed sisters, one a courtesan and the other a pure maiden who proves to be of good citizen birth. But the soldier and parasite that were taken from *Kolax* are quite Plautine in tone, and though not strictly essential to the plot, provide a hilarious note absent from Terence's other plays. There are offensive aspects of this play, as when Chaerea is introduced in the guise of a gift eunuch into Thais' house where Pamphila is being carefully kept, and very promptly rapes the girl, and when Phaedria exploits his rival's infatuation with Thais to procure money to give her. But Terence's delicacy of treatment rather veils than underscores the grossness. The play is the liveliest of all the Terentian comedies, and we can understand why the Roman audiences, especially those brought up on Plautus, should favor it above Terence's quieter plays.

So successful was *Eunuchus* that Terence was able to present his *Phormio* at the Ludi Romani of the same year. Its model was *Epidikazomenos* ("Litigant") of Apollodorus of Carystus. Lively as *Eunuchus,* it is free of offense in language and situation. Again we have a twofold love story, Phaedria son of Chremes being in love with a music girl, and his cousin Antipho son of Demipho with Phanium, a forlorn but honest orphan. In the absence of Antipho's father the parasite Phormio engineers a lawsuit which authorizes Antipho to marry Phanium. On his return Demipho is infuriated, not only because Phanium is a penniless unknown, but because he had promised Chremes that Antipho would marry Chremes' clandestine daughter and thus keep knowledge of her origin from becoming public. In consideration of marrying Phanium himself (which he never means to do) Phormio extracts from Demipho enough money for Phaedria to obtain his music girl. Phanium is actually Chremes' clandestine daughter; the fact is made known to the persons in the play only gradually, and the mystification of those not in the know creates much amusement. Even Chremes' wife comes to know, a contingency which he has dreaded; and his crestfallen humbleness and her indignation close the play. It is remarkable how Terence's deftness, management of suspense, careful characterization, make a plot which depends for its consummation on so inherently improbable a coincidence absorbing and even edifying to follow. Tearful, dishevelled, and forsaken Phanium engages our sympathy, and we admire Antipho for having his similarly engaged. All the characterizations are perspicacious and have timeless truth. The respectable elder plagued by the need of keeping a youthful indiscretion from his rich but not unsympathetic wife, doing his best to keep everyone content, and being discovered after all, is comedy of manners at its best. The relatively high fidelity with which Molière's admirable *Les Fourberies de Scapin* follows *Phormio* is an index of *Phormio's* merit.

Hecyra again failed to hold the audience at the funeral games for Aemilius Paulus in 160 B.C., but was finally presented at the Ludi Romani that same year. The play has been condemned as the poorest in Terence, and it has also been praised, by a competent critic, as "the purest and most perfect example of classical high comedy, strictly so called, which dramatic literature can offer from any age or nation." In structure *Hecyra* is undoubtedly poor; monologues are used where dialogue would be more effective, actions are reported which might better be enacted, the pacing is hesitant and sometimes aimless. The plot, furthermore, which turns on a man leaving his wife because he finds that she was pregnant when he married her and then discovering that it was he himself who had violated her, strains credulity to the breaking point. The plot itself was apparently acceptable enough; Apollodorus of Carystus, from whom Terence took his play, was following Menander's *Arbitrants,* whose considerable papyrus fragments reveal the same coincidence. But it is not the plot which concerns Terence most in this play; he has not even followed his usual practice of making the story double. The identification by means of the ring at the end is only a device to permit a free hand within the play—just as the incredible ending of *Tartuffe* gives Molière a free hand within that play. What we have then is a completely sober discussion of marriage, and specifically of the double standard in sex, as relevant today as it was in Terence's time, or Menander's. There is no melodrama and there are no villains and no butts; all concerned, and especially the young couple, behave according to their best lights, which are very decent lights, and yet become involved, as men and women in the real world become involved, in something approaching tragedy. All the characters, and especially the women, are well and sympathetically studied, but that of the courtesan Bacchis is most admirable, as it is most revolutionary. She is not a mere instrument in the play, to be disdained because of her trade as a moral outcast, but exhibits a social sense and true charity. The Bacchises of the world as well as the Philumenas are caught up in life, and strive for what dignity may be wrested from it; none has a right to cast stones.

Adelphi, presented at the funeral games for Aemilius Paullus in 160 B.C. when *Hecyra* failed for the second time, is usually regarded as Terence's masterpiece. It is modeled on a Menandrian play of the same name, with borrowings from *Synapothneskontes* ("Suicide Pact") of Diphilus. The play is as thoughtful as *Hecyra,* but on a less touchy theme, and has the usual Terentian merits of skillful construction, rapid pacing, and brightness which *Hecyra* lacks. A puritanical rustic and an easy-going urban bachelor brother each brings up one of the rustic's sons according to his own principles. The bachelor's charge turns out to be more generous and responsible than the rustic's. But what the play recommends is respect for human nature in education, not laxity for its own sake. When the frugal brother reforms and goes to the opposite extreme he becomes only more ridiculous. *Adelphi* is neither grim nor heavy-handed; with easy and amusing grace it enforces a lesson which educators must periodically relearn.

Both in its intellectual and dramatic qualities *Adelphi* is a fitting capstone for Terence's work. In 159 B.C. he traveled to Greece to study and acquire new plays, and did not survive the journey. His plays appear to have been revived frequently, and by Cicero's day his position as a classic was firmly established. Ancient literary criticism is purer than modern in the sense that it confines its evaluations to purely literary techniques; it has nothing to say of an author's intellectual innovations or social criticism. We would not then expect Caesar's famous epigram on Terence (quoted from Suetonius in Donatus) to expatiate on the qualities which are most attractive to us. We can heartily agree that he is *puri sermonis amator,* and perhaps regard his shortcoming in *vis comica* as a merit. As for the *dimidiate Menander,* "halved Menander," not enough of Menander survives to make its implications perfectly clear.

In the half century between Plautus and Terence during which the *palliata* flourished there were naturally other comic writers besides those two and Caecilius. Five of Terence's prologues answer the criticism of a *malus vetus poeta* whom he does not deign to name. This we know was Luscius Lanuvinus, who was apparently chief of a clique opposed to Terentian freedom in the use of Greek originals. Other writers of *palliatae,* of whom we know little more than their names, are Licinius, Imbrex, Atilius, Equilius, Turpilius, Trabea, Valerius, Vatronicus, and Juventius. *Fabulae palliatae* gave way to *fabulae togatae,* or plays in Roman dress, with Italian background and *dramatis personae.* Because the characters were usually humble tradesmen this type of play was also called *fabula tabernaria.* Naevius had indeed attempted the form, but it was apparently submerged during the reign of the *palliatae.* The technique and the action of the *togatae* seem, like the *palliatae,* to have followed the New Comedy pattern, but the Roman background necessitated certain characteristic changes; impertinent slaves and proud courtesans could not be tolerated in a Roman society, nor could respectable ladies and gentlemen be made ludicrous.

Of the three writers associated with *togatae* we know most of Lucius Afranius (born ca. 150 B.C.), of whom three hundred scattered lines and forty-four titles survive. His *Simulans,* in which a father-in-law outwits and reforms an errant son-in-law, was revived in 57 B.C. His *Incendium,* in which a fire is shown on the stage, was revived, significantly, under Nero. Other titles show the domestic character of his drama: *Stepson, Aunts, Divorce, Letter, Feast of Compitalia,* and *Extravagant. Bucco Adoptatus,* if genuine, shows that Afranius borrowed from the Atellan farces also. We should suppose that the relative independence of the *togatae* would give their authors greater scope for originality; but Afranius' avowed admiration for Menander and Terence may mean that the deviations from the *palliatae* were only superficial. Titinius was the eldest of the three writers of *togatae*, though his dates are not known. There are about a hundred and eighty lines and fifteen titles, which again reflect a domestic and workaday world. Nine of the titles are names of women. In *Fullonia* fullers are quarreling with weavers. In *Barbatus* an embroiderer remarks that he has abandoned his trade. *Quintus* has a scornful reference to people who speak Oscan and Volscian and know no Latin. In *Setina* ("Girl of Setia") a timid suitor for an heiress is encouraged by a friend. Of the third writer of *togatae*, T. Quinctius Atta (died 77 B.C.), we have only twenty lines and eleven titles. Besides such titles as *Aunt* and *Mother-in-Law*, we have *Aediles' Games, Megalensian Games,* and *Aquae Caldae*, in which the gay ladies of a watering place infuriate their respectable sisters by imitating their dress.

About the turn of the second and first centuries the improvisation of the Atellan farces was given literary form. The Atellan farce may have originated in Etruria or have been developed from the Doric farce of Magna Graecia. Its characters were fixed—Maccus the clown; Pappus, the simpleton; Bucco, the fat boy; and Dossennus the hunchback. The Atellan, then, was a Punch and Judy show or *commedia dell' arte,* with a permanent cast presenting their various adventures. We know of two writers of *fabulae Atellanae,* Novius and L. Pomponius. Of Pomponius (fl. 100–85 B.C.) we have seventy titles and of Novius (fl. 95–80) forty-three, with about three hundred verses in all. These reflect numerous comic situations, involving the stock butts of farce, coarse language and coarser jokes, probably accompanied by violent gesticulation. It is unlikely, but not impossible, that they involved serious satire on society.

This hasty survey of dramatic forms may fittingly close with mime, or *fabula riciniata,* which was kindred to the Atellan farce and supplanted it. Here the performers wore no masks and the parts of women were played by women—at the Floralia by nude women. Gesticulation degenerated into acrobatic ballet (*planipes saltans*) and lewd posturings, and words grew less than secondary in importance. These performers enjoyed huge popularity from the time of Sulla, who patronized them generously, to that of the Empress Theodora, who herself was a *mima.* As mime evolves to pantomime it departs from the purview of literature, but two writers of mimes, the equestrian Laberius and Publilius Syrus, are associated with the name of Julius Caesar.

The forty-three titles and 155 lines we have of Decimus Laberius (115–43 B.C.) are not a sufficient index to the value of his work or of the literary mime. A prologue complains of humiliation he had suffered at the hands of Caesar. In a competition which Caesar ordered Laberius was defeated by his junior Publilius Syrus, a manumitted Antiochene. Only two of his titles are recorded: *Putatores* and *Myrmidon,* but he continued in vogue at least to the time of Nero, and his aptness and terseness are praised by the elder Seneca, Petronius, and Gellius. Among the Hellenistic Greeks at least, certain forms of the mime (the *biologoi*) were valued for ethical teaching, and certainly apophthegms drawn from them would make excellent copybook material. A collection of single-line apophthegms in iambic trimeter drawn from the works of Publilius Syrus and arranged alphabetically was made in the first century A.D., but scarcely a tithe of the seven hundred lines now current under Publilius' name can be genuine. No great originality or indeed consistency can be expected in a collection of proverbs; all that can be said of Publilius' is that they are neat and terse. We turn from this excursion into a later century and return to the early republic to consider the beginnings of another form.

Satura tota nostra est, says the critic Quintilian (10.1.93), "satire is wholly Roman," or perhaps, "Rome is supreme throughout satire." Certainly there were Greek influences in satire also—Cynic-Stoic diatribes, the parabases of Old Comedy, the Menippean satire naturalized by Varro—but Roman satire is not so completely indebted to these, in form or content, as is the *palliata,* for example, to New Comedy, and the characteristically Roman note is more evident in satire than in most genres of Latin literature. The species may be defined, with Professor Gilbert Highet, "as a piece of verse, or prose mingled with verse, intended to improve society by mocking its anomalies, and marked by spontaneity, topicality, ironic wit, indecent humor, colloquial language, frequent use of dialogue, constant intrusion of the author's personality, and incessant variety of tone and style." The Italic legacy of Latin literature doubtless contained the germs of satire, in such things as Fescennine verses and Atellan farces, but literary form was given to it, as to other species of Latin literature, by Ennius. We have seen above that Ennius' satires contained dialogue, characterization, and the subjective element, but that their meter was still a medley. The author who gave satire its permanent shape, in form and in content, was Lucilius.

Gaius Lucilius was born about 180 B.C. at Suessa Aurunca of a rich and prominent family (his brother was a Roman senator and his sister the grandmother of Pompey the Great), and was thus one of the few Latin authors not of humble birth. He was one of the best educated men of his time; his acquaintance with Greek philosophy was rare in the Rome of his day. When he came to Rome after 160 he lived in a fine house, enjoyed the income of extensive estates, was a member of the Scipionic circle, and had friends and enemies among the most prominent figures in Rome. He served in Spain with Scipio Aemilianus in 134–133, and began to publish his works in 131. The order of his satires, as they appear in our editions of the fragments, is almost the exact reverse of their chronological order. Apparently Lucilius himself published three separate collections of his work. Books 26–30 (in the current numbering) are Lucilius' earliest work, and are in various meters; Books 1–21 are his mature work, all in hexameters; Books 22–25 are occasional poems, in elegiacs. When a single collection was formed, before the period of the empire, it was natural that the superior work, which was in greater demand, should come first. Within the groups the order of the satires is chronological.

Books 26, 27, and 28, the first two wholly in septenarii and the third in septenarii, senarii, and some hexameters, were completed in 131. Each book contained several satires. The same three meters occur in Book 29, which was published some time later, but probably before the death of Scipio in 129. Henceforward Lucilius gave up the meters of the stage and, except for occasional poems in elegiacs, confined himself to hexameter, which became the sole meter for satire. It may be that at this time Lucilius suffered from the measures taken against non-citizens as result of the Italian demands for Roman citizenship, and from the redistribution of land as result of the agrarian measures of Tiberius Gracchus. Book 30, in hexameter exclusively, seems to have been written after 125. In this book he apparently alludes to the popularity of his earlier poems. The first book of the new series (Books 1–21) appeared probably in 123 and the second about 119. Lucilius then went on a journey to Rhegium, and probably to Sicily and Sardinia also; the journey was described in Book 3 (the model for Horace, *Satires* 1.5). This and the fourth book appeared in 118. Book

5 attacks Gaius Metellus Caprarius, who was praetor designate in 117. The chronology of the remaining books is very uncertain. Book 11 falls between 116 and 110, and there is some evidence that Book 17 was written in 108 and Book 20 in 106. We know from Cicero (*Brutus* 160–61) that Lucilius was still writing after 107, but in 105 he retired to Naples for his health's sake. There he probably wrote the little elegiac poems on his own slaves and freedmen, later added as Books 22–25. He died at Naples between 103 and 101 and was honored by a public funeral. His career had covered a most eventful period in Roman history, the spread of Roman power east and west, social agitation in Italy, the hostile movement of the Cimbri and Teutones in the north. The ferment of the charged atmosphere is reflected in the full-bloodedness of Lucilius; at any rate a keen observer living in so stirring a time had no need to resort to Greek books to apprehend pullulating life and its absurdities.

To find and follow a thread in the fragments of Lucilius is more difficult than in the fragments of the lost tragedies. The fragments are mostly single lines chosen for the odd words they contain, and probably corrupt textually, and since we do not know how many satires were in a book nor the plot of the satires (as we frequently know the plot of tragedy) it is virtually impossible to combine lines into a meaningful pattern. The most satisfactory reconstruction is of Book 3, because we have an imitation in Horace's description of his journey to Brundisium. Yet Lucilius is too important a figure in Latin literature to dismiss without some effort to discover at least the range of his work. Great editorial ingenuity has been expended in establishing contexts for individual lines, dividing groups of lines into satires, and enucleating their subjects. For want of something more tangible a table of contents, drawn from the work of his editors and especially from the edition of E. H. Warmington in the Loeb Classical Library, will be subjoined here.

Persius' opening line, *O curas hominum, O quantum est in rebus inane!*—"Oh, the vanity of mankind!" we are told by the scholiast, was taken from Lucilius' first book, and so probably from the introductory satire. Also in the first book, we are told by Servius, who remarks that *Aeneid* 10.104 ff. was taken from it, there was a council of the gods to try L. Cornelius Lentulus Lupus for his extravagant luxury; this was probably the second satire in Book 1, of which there are about forty lines. A possible third satire in Book 1 criticized contemporary life. Book 2 probably contained a single satire—a parody of the trial of Quintus Mucius Scaevola, who was charged in 119 B.C. with extortion in Asia. The single satire of Book 3 describes the journey to Rhegium; the incidents suggested by the fragments are like those in Horace's rival piece. Some lines in Book 4 seem to contrast urban luxury with rustic simplicity: a scholiast says that Persius took his third satire, against the luxury of the rich, from Lucilius' fourth book; and some lines describe a gladiatorial combat. Book 5 is in the form of a letter to a friend who had omitted to visit Lucilius during his sickness. Book 6 probably contained the model for Horace's satire on the bore (1.9), and another satire on the politics, the luxurious nobility, and the genteel poor of Rome. Horace's reference to a town which could not be named in hexameters, *oppidulo quod versu dicere non est* (Satires 1.5.87) is adapted from Fragment 252–53 W in Book 6: *Hexametro versu non dicere possis*. The first part of Book 7 deals with sexual matters; the second with changes of fortune. Book 8 deals with physical love and other forms of luxury. The first part of Book 9 deals apparently with sights seen during a walk in Rome in March; the second part with rules of spelling. The first part of Book 10 carries on with matters of literary composition; the second part apparently has a stormy landing from a fleet during a war. According to the *Life* of Persius it was Lucilius, Book 10 which inspired that poet to write satire. Book 11 contains six anecdotes concerning well-known contemporaries. Book 12 has too few lines for comment. Book 13 attacks table luxury, like the fourth satire of Horace's second book. Book 14 seems to advocate simple living. Book 15 starts with horses and has lines showing that philosophy cures superstition and miserliness. Book 16 again speaks of luxury and the simple life. Book 17 seems to parody incidents in the *Odyssey*. Very little remains of Books 18 and 19. Book 20 contains a satire on a banquet. Porphyrio on Lalage in Horace says that Lucilius' Book 21 (emended from 16, which does not fit) was "called Collyra because its theme was his mistress Collyra"; there are no fragments of this book. Books 22–25, in elegiacs, contained little poems or epitaphs for Lucilius' freedmen and slaves, some (for example 623 W) in their own dialect. As many fragments from the last four books, which contained Lucilius' early work, survive as from the preceding twenty-five, possibly because the books were longer; it is fairly clear that they contained more separate satires per book. But though there are quotable lines, the substance of the whole cannot be profitably characterized.

We can perceive that Lucilius was a ruthless and plain-spoken critic of social life. Extremes and shams and chicanery seem to be the special objects of his attack. He censures both conspicuous consumption and miserliness, hypocrisy and crudeness. He echoes Cynic-Stoic doctrines of simplicity and advocates attaching their true value to things. He is concerned with questions of spelling and diction. He uses himself as a text. Later writers valued him next to Ennius among the ancients, but where Ennius was revered as an ancient monument Lucilius continued to be read for his own sake. Where that excellent critic Quintilian speaks of Ennius as a venerable oak, he deals with Lucilius as with a living author: *Eruditio in eo mira,* he says (10.1.93), *et libertas atque inde acerbitas et abundantia salis,* "There is remarkable learning in him, and he is outspoken and hence astringent, and he has an overflowing wit." His vitality is made manifest in his demonstrable influence on Lucretius and Catullus and Vergil. Upon the satirists, particularly Horace but also Persius and Juvenal, his influence is naturally more marked. Indeed, it is hard to think that Horace could have written satires at all without Lucilius' models, and Horace is in fact Lucilius' best monument. Horace's first mention of Lucilius (*Satires* 1.4.1–12) seems unkind: Lucilius derived wholly from Old Comedy, was keen and witty but inelegant and hasty, so that his composition was muddy; further, Lucilius' satire was, like Horace's own, essentially prosaic (1.4.57). At the beginning of 2.10 Horace reverts to the carelessness of Lucilius' composition but admires him for having "rubbed the town down with salt," *Sale multo urbem defricuit.* Pioneers, even Homer and Ennius, are apt to be unpolished; if Lucilius had lived in "modern" times he would doubtless have pruned more carefully (48–71). In the first satire of the first book he acknowledges that Lucilius is the better man. Lucilius communicated his whole life in his writings, so that it is as open to view as if painted on a votive tablet (2.1.29–34). Lucilius pulled off the mask which people wore to present a fair exterior to their inward vileness; he spared none but virtue and the friends of virtue (2.1.62–75). This, combined with Horace's close imitation of Lucilius in his two most famous satires, the Journey to Brundisium and the Bore, is handsome enough acknowledgment from the most competent, and because of rivalry, the most trustworthy critic of Roman satire. The disappearance of all of Lucilius except disjointed fragments and reputation is probably the most serious loss in Latin literature.

Besides Lucilius and the dramatists there were other poets between Ennius and Lucretius, but neither their reputation nor their remains suggest that their loss is very grievous. The Istrian war of 129 B.C. was the subject of an epic by Hostius; the meter was hexameter, and divine machinery after the Homeric manner was employed. Gellius (18.11) cites six hexameter lines from an epic poem by Furius of Antias; the subject is evidently some war, but there is no indication which. Perhaps the verses which Macrobius cites at various passages as from Furius, one from the eleventh book, come from the same poem. The Furius Alpinus whom Horace (*Satires* 2.5.40) ridicules is a later poet. Quintus Valerius of Sora (tribune in 82 B.C.), whom Cicero (*On the Orator* 3.11.43) calls *litteratissimus togatorum omnium*, wrote several works in prose and poetry, one addressed to a P. Scipio, one called *Epoptides*. Stoic pantheism is suggested by two hexameter lines quoted by St. Augustine (*City of God* 7.9):

> *Juppiter omnipotens rerum regumque repertor*
> *progenitor genetrixque deum, deus unus et idem,*

> Jupiter omnipotent, of things and of kings the contriver,
> Begetter and bearer of gods, one god he and the same.

A poem on literary criticism was the *De poetis* of Volcacius Sedigitus, which formulated the canon of ten writers of *palliatae* in order of merit: Caecilius Statius, Plautus, Naevius, Licinius, Atilius, Terence, Turpilius, Trabea, Luscius, and Ennius. The elegiac epigram was put to its proper use for tomb inscriptions, but erotic epigrams also were written by Porcius Licinus, Valerius Aeditus, Q. Lutatius Catulus. We leave these names and fragments of poets to look at the early writers of prose; poetry will emerge in a blaze of power in the persons of Lucretius and Catullus.

IV

PRE-CICERONIAN PROSE

ROME'S SPECIAL DISTINCTION, FROM EARLIEST TIMES, lay in the fields of government and administration, and it is natural that Latin prose literature should be dominated by oratory and history, forms essential to republican government. Persuasive speech must have been cultivated from the beginning of the Roman polity, but the harangues of the early centuries as reported in the pages of Livy and others are naturally fictive. In the summary history of Roman oratory at the beginning of his *Brutus* Cicero alludes (53-60) to such early figures in Roman history as Brutus, Marcus Valerius, Appius Claudius, Manius Curius, Marcus Popilius, Gaius Fannius, and others whose achievements as well as reputation imply that they must have been skillful orators. The first orator whose eloquence is attested in extant records, specifically a passage in Ennius' *Annals,* he says, (57 f.), is Marcus Cornelius Cethegus, who held a consulship in the First Punic War. But, continues Cicero, "I am unable to name a single writer earlier than Cato whose orations I deem worthy of attention."

In history as well as oratory Cato is a pioneer. Various priestly and other chronicles must have been kept from the earliest organization of the state, but it was only when Rome entered the main stream of Mediterranean history in the Second Punic War that awareness of self and of other peoples provided impulse to historiography of the Greek type. It was natural, in the absence of Latin models and with knowledge of Greek general in the selected audience whom the aristocratic early historians addressed, that the first works of this category should be written in Greek. But the nationalist note which characterizes all Roman historiography and constitutes its principal divergence from the Greek becomes apparent at once. Indeed, a collateral motive for the use of Greek was probably a desire to impress upon Greek readers the high dignity of the Roman state and the irresistible prowess of Roman arms. So Fabius Pictor, the earliest literary historian of Rome, is criticized by Polybius for his Roman bias, though Polybius respects him sufficiently to use him. He is also cited with respect by Livy and Dionysius of Halicarnassus. Fabius fought in the Second

Punic War, and was a member of the embassy to Delphi after the disaster at Cannae. It was not only Rome that Fabius favored, but his own senatorial class, and the same was doubtless true of the other senatorial writers of Roman history in Greek—L. Cincius Alimentus, P. Cornelius Scipio, A. Postumius Albinus, and C. Acilius. Cincius Alimentus also fought in the Second Punic War, and was captured by Hannibal in Sicily in 209 B.C. Scipio was the elder son of Scipio Africanus and adoptive father of the Africanus who destroyed Carthage. Postumius Albinus was consul in 151 B.C. Polybius and Cicero speak well of him, but Cato ridiculed his modest deprecation of his inadequate Greek: apology for awkward use of a language not one's own, said Cato, (Gellius 11.8.2), is appropriate only if a man had been compelled by the Amphictyons to write in that language. C. Acilius was interpreter for the three Greek philosophers who came to Rome as ambassadors in 155 B.C. Both his Roman and his senatorial bias are seen in the anecdote reported from him in Livy 35.14.5. In conversation with his conqueror Scipio, Hannibal rated the three greatest generals of the world, in order, as Alexander, Pyrrhus, and himself. When Scipio asked what Hannibal would have said if he had beaten him, Hannibal replied that he would then have put himself ahead of both Alexander and Pyrrhus. The reaction against these noble writers of Greek, and against the rising tide of Hellenism in general, was led by Cato, who is our earliest writer of Latin prose.

Marcus Porcius Cato, called "the Elder" or "the Censor" to distinguish him from his great-grandson Marcus Porcius Cato "of Utica," was born of an old plebeian family at Tusculum, about ten miles from Rome, in 234 B.C. He too fought in the Second Punic War, and thereafter in Thrace, in Greece, and in Spain. He was quaestor in Sicily and Africa in 204, aedile in 199, praetor in Sardinia in 198, consul in 195, and censor in 184. His strictness in the latter office gives "censorious" its connotation. In politics he was the leader of the opposition to the aristocratic group headed by the Scipios, and he defended his nationalist and "popular" position with ruthlessness, scathing wit, constant glorification of ancient Roman austerity and dignity, no little personal pride, and a measure of theatricality. A decree ordering the expulsion of Greek philosophers and rhetoricians from Rome in 161 B.C. testifies to the political strength of Cato's party. When, in 155 B.C. the Greeks sent to the senate an embassy composed of Carneades the Academic, Diogenes the Stoic, and Critolaus the Peripatetic, it was Cato who insisted that their business be dispatched at once, so that they should not linger in Rome to corrupt the youth. He insisted that Greek physicians were in a conspiracy to kill their Roman patients. When the question of releasing the thousand Achaean hostages (of whom Polybius was one) was brought up, Cato said it little suited the senate's dignity to debate whether Greek or Roman undertakers should bury the derelicts. He struck a senator from the roll for kissing his wife in broad daylight, and he left behind the horse that had carried him through his campaign in Spain because he refused to put Rome to the charge of transporting the animal. After a mission to Carthage in 157 he concluded his every speech in the senate, regardless of the occasion, with *delenda est Carthago*. When he died in 149 B.C. he was already a legend.

Actually the conflict between Cato and his noble adversaries was not a struggle between liberal and conservative views, but rather a rivalry within conservative ranks, with rather more enlightenment on the side of the nobles. For all their philhellenism Scipio's friends too cherished Roman values, and they too were concerned over moral deterioration. Cato's assumed monopoly of morality, like his scorn of Hellenism, had more than a touch of demagoguery. But his eminent merits and his striking personality made him, in succeeding generations, the Jefferson or Jackson or Lincoln of his party. Pamphlets doubtless embellished his known proclivities to make political capital. Hence, though we have *Lives* of Cato by Nepos and Plutarch, as well as the *Cato Maior* of Cicero and numerous other characterizations, the total picture which emerges is something of a caricature. He cannot have been ignorant of Greek until he was an octogenarian, for we know that he negotiated with Greeks in his prime. Whether his hatred of Greek was genuine or a sham, Cato's sponsorship of Ennius, who did more than any other man to introduce Hellenism to Latin literature, is a wry joke on the leading opponent of Hellenism in Rome.

In any case it was not education that Cato opposed, but Greek education, and to supply the place of Greek treatises he wrote practical handbooks on all the subjects of the curriculum except philosophy. We know that he dealt with medicine, rhetoric, and agriculture, and it seems likely that he included military science and law also. Apparently these works were combined into a kind of encyclopedia, entitled *Ad filium*. When his son was still a child he wrote for him a history of Rome "in large letters" with his own hand, and when the boy grew older he dedicated to him these various treatises. All were imbued with Roman ideals and traditions; the fragments reveal an oracular manner. An orator is *vir bonus dicendi peritus,* "a good man skilled in speech"; and in rhetoric the main principle is *Rem tene, verba sequentur,* "Hold fast to the matter, the words will come." Gellius (11.2) also ascribes to Cato a *Carmen de moribus,* from which he cites characteristic moralizing saws, but in prose.

Besides the encyclopedia for his son Cato also wrote independent treatises on various subjects. The surviving *De agricultura* or *De re rustica* is the oldest extant prose work in Latin; the language of his treatise underwent modernization in antiquity, but the tone remains authentically archaic. Beginning with a statement of the advantages of agriculture over commerce and banking, Cato proceeds to describe the best location for a farm, the duties of the owner and of his steward, and various principles of farm management. Interspersed with instructions on farm economy are prescriptions for medicaments, recipes for cooking, religious formulae, and other matters. The disorder of the book is further confused by interpolations and repetitions. Throughout the tone is a hard and cheerless drive for profit; there is nothing about the compensations of the rural life, nothing of the joys of living and cooperating with nature, or of sentimental attachment between master and slaves and livestock. "Sell worn-out oxen, blemished cattle, blemished sheep, wool, hides, an old wagon, old tools, an old slave, a sickly slave, and whatever else is superfluous. The master should have the selling habit, not the buying habit" (2.7). "The overseer must lend to no one seed grain, fodder, spelt, wine, or oil. He must have two or three households, no more, from whom he borrows and to whom he lends" (5.3). "When you issue the tunic or blanket [every second year] first take up the old one and have patchwork made of it" (59). We are told where equipment of various sorts may be bought, and the proper prices: "Lucius Tunnius of Casinum and Gaius Mennius, son of Lucius Mennius of Venafrum, make the best press ropes" (135.3). The recipes seem generous enough; the veterinary medicine has a strong admixture of superstition. "Both the sick ox and he who administers the [prescribed] medicine must stand, and both be fasting" (71). For mending a dislocated limb the split reeds to serve as splints must be joined to the accompaniment of a chant: *Motas uaeta daries dardares astataries dissunapiter;* and after they are applied the officiant must duly pronounce the charm: *Huat haut haut istasis tarsis ordannabou dannaustra* (160).

But the proper vehicle for communicating the gospel of Rome was history; and the fact that Roman history had already been written by senatorial historians and in Greek made it inevitable that Cato should turn his hand to the history. Nepos (*Cato* 3.3) tells us:

When he was an old man Cato began to write history, of which he left seven books. The first contains an account of the kings of the Roman people; the second and the third, the origin of all the states of Italy—and this seems the reason he called the whole *Origines.* Then in the fourth book we have the first Punic war, and in the fifth the second. All this is told in summary fashion, and he treated the other wars in the same manner down to the praetorship of Servius Galba, who plundered the Lusitanians. In his account of all these wars he did not name the leaders, but related the events without mentioning names. In the same work he gave an account of the noteworthy occurrences and sights in Italy and the Spains; and in it he showed great industry and carefulness, but no learning.

—*J. C. Rolfe*

The latter four books seem to have been joined on to the first three after Cato's death and the title *Origines* then applied to the whole.

But it was in his speeches that Cato gave fullest expression to his national Roman program and most effectively influenced the course of Roman literature. He spoke his mind vigorously on every political issue, and participated in numerous judicial trials; Cicero (*Brutus* 17.65) knew a hundred and fifty speeches of Cato, and the titles of some eighty have come down. Ancient critics find fault with his roughness, but all admit his torrential vigor. Many terse apophthegms drawn from his speeches testify to his scathing wit and his gift for epigram. One specimen must suffice: "Thieves who steal from individuals spend their lives in prison and chains; thieves who steal from the commonweal, in purple and gold." Cicero and Plutarch refer to Cato's letters to his son Marcus; perhaps letters addressed to others were also collected. Ennius had pioneered in various forms of verse and endowed each with a distinctive Roman color; Cato pioneered in various forms of prose, and his Roman coloring was much more vivid. In subsequent Latin prose the Roman note regularly rings clearer than in poetry.

Succeeding Roman historians followed Cato's example in writing Latin and in including social and religious items, but the series of historians we now encounter followed the annalistic form of the priestly chronicles. It was doubtless their artistic shortcomings and the great superiority in this respect of such writers as Sallust and Livy that caused their disappearance. L. Cassius Hemina, a contemporary of Cato, wrote four books of *Annals,* beginning with Aeneas. L. Calpurnius Piso Frugi, consul in 133 B.C. and opponent of the Gracchi, wrote seven books of *Annals,* from the beginnings to 146 B.C. Cn. Gellius dealt with the same period but on apparently a more generous scale, for he wrote over thirty books. C. Sempronius Tuditanus, consul in 129, wrote *Libri magistratuum,* on constitutional antiquities, and perhaps an annalistic historical work also. C. Fannius, consul in 122, also wrote *Annals* which were well spoken of by Cicero and Sallust. The most important of the early group of historians appears to be L. Coelius Antipater who devoted seven books to the single subject of the Hannibalic war. He used his sources, written and oral, critically, and was regarded by his successors as thoroughly reliable. Specialization was carried a step further by Sempronius Asellio, also a contemporary of the Gracchi, who wrote a history of his own time.

A number of historians of the Sullan period are somewhat better known because of use made of them by Livy and others. The *Annals* of Quintus Claudius Quadrigarius, in at least twenty-three books, preserved the annalistic arrangement but had greater literary and artistic pretensions. Instead of beginning with the foundation of the city, Claudius Quadrigarius began with the sack of Rome by the Gauls and continued down to his own times. This suggests a respect for fact and a desire to enlarge on the knowable. Livy cites him ten times. But Livy cites Claudius Quadrigarius' contemporary Valerius Antias at least thirty-five times and follows him for long stretches; a more unreliable source it is hard to imagine. Valerius is completely indifferent to truth and concerned solely with effect. When sources fail he resorts to imagination and provides explicit details of matters of which he can have had no knowledge. In numbers his exaggerations are unconscionable (*Si Valerio quis credat, omnium rerum immodice numerum augenti:* Livy 33.10.8), and he lends his exaggerations an air of verisimilitude by specifying soldiers engaged or slain or captured to the man and booty to the last item. He gave free play to his own family and political loyalties and antipathies: the prowess of any man named Valerius is prodigious. A goodly portion of Roman heroic legend is doubtless to be ascribed to Valerius' invention. Only later in his own work did Livy realize what an undependable witness he had trusted; and not Livy alone but Dionysius of Halicarnassus and Plutarch use him.

C. Licinius Macer, father of the orator and poet Calvus and tribune in 73 B.C., was prosecuted for extortion by Cicero and took his own life in consequence. His *Annals,* in at least sixteen books, began with the founding of the city but covered the early period rapidly, for the war with Pyrrhus was dealt with in the second book. He too is used by Dionysius and Livy, who several times mentions Licinius' use of the *Libri lintei.* It is not clear whether we are to take this as evidence of a conscientious workman or the reverse, for the *Libri lintei* were surely spurious. Just as glorification of the Valerii is to be ascribed to Valerius Antias, so is that of the Licinii to Licinius Macer. The most highly regarded historian of the period was L. Cornelius Sisenna, praetor in 78 B.C. Cicero (*Laws* 1.7) says that "Sisenna has easily surpassed all our other historians up to the present time,"and Sallust (*Jugurtha* 95.2) that he was "the best and most careful of the writers who dealt with the history of Sulla." Sisenna's history extended to at least twelve and perhaps twenty-three books. The work dealt with contemporary history, possibly in continuation of Asellio's work; fragments from the first book dealing with the mythical period apparently come from a digression or excursus. Sisenna was concerned to make his work readable. His literary bent is indicated by his translation of the scabrous *Milesian Tales* of Aristides. The presence of these in the baggage of Roman officers slain at Carrhae in 53 B.C. shocked the Parthian victors.

In addition to historical works proper we know of a number of autobiographies and political apologias. M. Aemilius Scaurus, consul in 115 B.C., wrote an autobiography in three books to justify his policies. Q. Lutatius Catulus, who, with Marius, annihilated the Cimbri in 101, wrote a memorial of his consulship. P. Rutilius Rufus, consul in 105, a disciple of the Stoic Panaetius and called by Velleius Paterculus (13)

"one of the best men not only of his age but of all time," was an exemplary provincial administrator in Asia, and as a result exiled for extortion by the machinations of the greedy moneyed class. In his exile he
wrote an autobiography in Latin, in at least five books, and a history in
Greek. Historically the most important work of this class was the autobiography of Sulla himself (138–78 B.C.); he was working on Book
22 of this work when he died. The principal tendency of the autobiography was to set forth all of Sulla's deeds as the working out of
destiny.

The single literary form most characteristic of the Romans is surely
oratory. Oratory most adequately reflects Roman ideals and aspirations, and it was most highly esteemed by the Romans themselves
for its practical effectiveness in law and politics, the only respectable
civil careers open to Romans. Oratory, says Tacitus (*Dialogue on
Orators* 5 f.), is

a pursuit than which it is impossible to imagine one in our state richer in
advantages, more splendid in its prospects, more attractive in fame at home,
more illustrious in celebrity throughout our whole empire and all the world.
If, indeed, what is useful in life should be the aim of all our plans and actions, what can be safer than to practise an art armed with which a man can
always bring aid to friends, succor to strangers, deliverance to the im-
perilled, while to malignant foes he is an actual fear and terror, himself the
while secure and intrenched, so to say, within a power and a position of lasting strength? . . . Whose name does the father din into his children's ears
before that of the orator? Whom, as he passes by, do . . . men oftener
speak of by name and point out with the finger?
                                        —*A. J. Church and W. J. Brodribb*

It is significant that this *Dialogue* of Tacitus, Quintilian's *Institutio
oratoria,* and Cicero's *Brutus,* are the most competent critical treatises
we have in Latin. The latter work must always remain the best history
of Roman oratory; modern scholars can only eke out Cicero's judicious
remarks with parallels, themselves chiefly drawn from Cicero's other
writings on the subject. Some two hundred and fifty orators are introduced in the *Brutus,* but, as has been noted above, to Cicero himself
Cato is the first tangible figure among them. This implies, what we
should in any case surmise, that famous speeches attributed to heroes
of the early republic, like Appius Claudius' rejection of negotiations
with Pyrrhus, are later fictions. Here we need only name the out-

standing orators between Cato and Cicero himself whom Cicero thought worthy of special approbation. Publius Cornelius Scipio and his intimate friend Laelius are revered by Cicero as men as well as orators. Of the Gracchan policies he could not approve, but he gave the Gracchi their due as orators, and of the younger Gaius said (33.125) that no one was ever more completely or more richly endowed for a career of eloquence. Plutarch (*Tiberius Gracchus* 2.2) contrasts Gaius' vehemence with Tiberius' gentle composure, but the speech he quotes from Tiberius (9) is telling enough:

The savage beasts in Italy have their particular dens, they have their places of repose and refuge; but the men who bear arms and expose their lives for the safety of their country enjoy nothing more in it than the air and light, and without houses or settlements of their own must wander from place to place with their wives and children. Falsely do the generals tell their soldiers, when they encourage them to battle, that they fight the enemy to protect their sepulchres and their sanctuaries; for none among so many Romans possesses either ancestral altar or monument. They fight and they die—for others' luxuries. They are styled masters of the world: no single clod can they call their own.

Of Gaius, Plutarch tells us (*Tiberius Gracchus* 2.4) that he was the first to walk back and forth on the hustings and in his ardor pull his toga from his shoulders. When vehemence carried his voice to the upper registers, a friend with a pitch pipe brought it down again. In the generation preceding Cicero's the greatest orators were C. Licinius Crassus (140–91 B.C.) and his contemporary and friend M. Antonius. Cicero's *On the Orator* is a magnificent monument to both. And finally mention must be made of Cicero's older contemporary and greatest rival, Q. Hortensius (114–50 B.C.), whom Cicero emulated, often opposed, finally outstripped, and always admired.

Compared to the output in these two major and eminently Roman fields of history and oratory, special treatises in succession to Cato's are barely worth mention. The two categories to be noticed are jurisprudence and literary scholarship. The code of the Twelve Tables had to be expounded, bases for new legislation found in it, and judicial procedures systematized. L. Acilius, a contemporary of Cato, wrote an exegetical commentary on the Twelve Tables. The *Responsa* of Ti. Coruncianus (consul 280 B.C.) first connected fresh legislation to the prescriptions of the Twelve Tables. The *Tripertita* of Sextus Aelius

Paetus (consul 198 b.c.) appears to have been a systematic derivation of current law from interpretation of the Twelve Tables. Juridical controversies gave rise to treatises on special aspects of law. M. Porcius Cato Licinianus, son of Cato the Censor, wrote a work of this character, apparently under the title *De iuris disciplina*. P. Mucius Scaevola, famed for his legalistic severity, wrote ten books of juristic formulations. Cicero ascribes three books on civil law to M. Junius Brutus; these have literary interest as presenting the earliest use of the dialogue form in Latin prose. Each day's discussion was given a different locale. M'. Manilius (consul 149 b.c.), an interlocutor in Cicero's *Republic,* wrote *Monumenta,* an account of the alleged legislation of Numa, and *Actiones,* containing sales formulae and similar practical matters. The greatest single achievement in the systematization of the law was the reduction of all scattered juristic material in eighteen books by Q. Mucius Scaevola (consul 95 b.c.), son of Publius Scaevola and Cicero's teacher in the law. In another work entitled *Horoi* ("Definitions") Scaevola dealt with the principles and the rules of law.

Literature no less than law requires commentary almost as soon as it is written down. When Crates of Mallos, ambassador from Pergamum, broke his leg in a fall into a Roman cloaca, he used his convalescence to lecture on the science of philology and so introduced critical literary scholarship to Rome. The first Roman philologer was L. Aelius Stilo Praeconinus, who taught his science to both Cicero and Varro, the latter of whom industriously carried his work forward. Stilo edited texts, determined the genuineness of plays ascribed to Plautus, commented on the language of the Salian songs, and wrote on lexicography. Patriotism, constitutional and religious requirements, and political partisanship gave the impulse to antiquarian study generally. Some half dozen treatises on religious and constitutional antiquities are ascribed to authors of the second and the early first centuries b.c. Finally we have works on agriculture. Among the books of fallen Carthage Rome preserved only Mago's twenty-eight-book treatise on agriculture, and commissioned a Latin version of it—the sole instance of state sponsorship of a book in Rome. This work was subsequently added to and then epitomized. Cato's successors the Sasernae, father and son, also wrote on agriculture. Even astronomy found its Roman devotee. C. Sulpicius Gallus (consul 166 b.c.) foretold a lunar eclipse at Pydna (168 b.c.) and wrote on astronomical subjects. Of none of the authors mentioned in this chapter do we have more than few and scattered fragments, and indeed many are scarcely more than names. We turn now to two great poets whose work we can read substantially as they left them.

V

LUCRETIUS AND CATULLUS

IF LUCRETIUS IS NOT, AS HIS PARTICULAR DEVOTEES maintain, the greatest of the Roman poets, surely he is the most eminent Roman in the intellectual galaxy of Europe. No poet could manifest more vehement compulsion to communicate truths of the highest urgency. In none could the urgency and an untarnished sense of wonder, which is the fountain spring of poetry, so transform the intractable matter of physics and sociology and charge it with the palpitating emotion which is poetry's essence. Lucretius' vision was a mission to liberate men from fear of gods, from fear of death. He would do this by demonstrating that the world and all that is in it are material, the result of a fortuitous concatenation of atoms utterly without design, and that the gods, themselves material, are utterly indifferent to mankind. Man need not crouch nor cringe before tyrant gods or the fate they would visit upon him after death. He is free to stand upright and with eyes unclouded, to shape his life according to his highest pleasure and not to walk in constant dread of capricious external powers.

Elimination of the supernatural so thoroughgoing, in the composition of the universe, in its governance, and in retribution to man for his conduct, must be abhorrent to any orthodoxy. In Christianity "Epicurean" became synonymous with "infidel," and in pagan Rome too Epicureanism was suspected of being subversive of established order. Hence, though Lucretius lived in a period illuminated by the light of history and wrote in an age sensitive to literary values and appreciative of literary figures, very little is known of Lucretius' life, and his work is almost ignored in literature. From the fact that his poem is addressed to a patron of wealth and position but of no literary or philosophic distinction it has been inferred that Lucretius was of humble birth, and his cognomen Carus has been taken to point to Celtic associations. On the other hand, the Lucretii were a family of good standing in Rome, and Lucretius may well have been Memmius' social equal. Our principal and virtually sole information on Lucretius' life is in Jerome's entry for 94 B.C. (one manuscript gives 96): *T.*

Lucretius poeta nascitur. Postea amatorio poculo in furorem versus, cum aliquot libros per intervalla insaniae conscripsisset, quos postea Cicero emendavit, propria se manu interfecit anno aetatis XLIIII. "Birth of T. Lucretius the poet. Later he was made insane by a love philter, in his lucid intervals wrote several books, which Cicero later emended, and died by his own hand in his forty-fourth year." On the basis of other notes and calculations the year of his death is fixed with some probability at 55 B.C. There is nothing inherently improbable in the insanity and suicide, but the love philter weakens the credit of the whole. By Cicero Jerome must surely mean the orator, though some have held that the reference is to his brother Quintus. Nor is it clear what "emended" means; it clearly does not mean excision of repeated lines, alteration of awkwardly repeated phrases, or deletion of passages objectionable on doctrinal grounds.

That both Cicero and his brother had read the poem by 54 B.C. and communicated their opinion on it to each other is clear from a letter of Cicero to his brother (*Ad Quintum fratrem* 2.9.3): *Lucretii poemata ut scribis ita sunt multis luminibus ingenii multae tamen artis; sed cum veneris virum te putabo si Sallustii Empedoclea legeris hominem non putabo,* "Lucretius' poems have, as you write, many flashes of genius, but also much craftsmanship. When you come I shall reckon you a hero, but not human, if you shall have read Sallust's *Empedoclea.*" Faint and qualified as this praise is, it is very meaningful from the pen of Cicero, for oddly enough, ten years later, introducing his *Tusculan Disputations,* Cicero declares that no light had hitherto been shed upon philosophy by any Latin writing. In *Tusculan Disputations* 1.3 he says, "There are *said* to be many works on this subject [Epicurean philosophy] in Latin, carelessly written"—which plainly implies that he had not read them, and in 2.3, referring to Latin works on Epicureanism he says directly, "These I have not read." The only explanation of Cicero's dissimulation is that to the political class to which Cicero adhered Epicureanism had come to be regarded as a subversive doctrine, and its most gifted exponent as dangerous to the established order. The religion of the state, which few can have believed in in a religious sense, was always a potent instrument of the nobility in retaining political control. In his famous account of the Roman constitution the completely rational Polybius gives the Romans high praise for instituting the ingenious device (6.56.9):

My own opinion at least is that the Romans have adopted this course of propagating religious awe for the sake of the common people. It is a course which perhaps would not have been necessary had it been possible to form a state composed of wise men, but as every multitude is fickle, full of lawless desires, unreasoned passion, and violent anger, the multitude must be held in by invisible terrors and suchlike pageantry. For this reason I think, not that the ancients acted rashly and at haphazard in introducing among the people notions concerning the gods and beliefs in the terrors of hell, but that the moderns are most rash and foolish in banishing such beliefs.

—W. R. Paton

For appreciating the significance of Lucretius in the Rome of his day we must look at a passage in Cicero himself (*Laws* 2.7.15, written perhaps in 45 B.C.):

So in the very beginning we must persuade our citizens that the gods are the lords and rulers of all things, and that what is done, is done by their will and authority; that they are likewise great benefactors of man, observing the character of every individual, what he does, of what wrong he is guilty, and with what intentions and with what piety he fulfils his religious duties; and that they take note of the pious and the impious. For surely minds which are imbued with such ideas will not fail to form true and useful opinions.

—C. W. Keyes

Superstition was deliberately used for political control—as Ovid put it, *expedit esse deos*—and Lucretius was dangerous because his book was above all else a solvent of superstition. Rebels and reformers occupy a large space in Greek literature, and their restless questionings give that literature much of its vitality; by contrast Roman literature is a principal organ of conformity to the established order and its ideals. Not the least among Lucretius' merits is that his earnest preachment is virtually the sole dissenting voice.

De rerum natura ("On the Nature of Things") is a hexameter poem in six books of some twelve hundred lines each, whose main purpose is to discredit belief in divine agency in human affairs. It endeavors to do this by constructing a physics which explains the genesis and the functioning of the world without divine intervention, and by showing that social and psychological phenomena as well can be explained by material and evolutionary processes in the course of nature and require no hypothesis of divine origin. Book 1, after an invocation to

Venus (here an allegory of Epicurean pleasure and ataraxy) and an appeal to Memmius, deals with the ultimate constitution of the universe, which consists solely of solid and eternal atoms and the void. The motion and forms of these atoms and their combination in objects is dealt with in Book 2, which opens with a fine proem on the blessings of philosophy. The opening of Book 3 praises Epicurus, "who out of deep darkness did first avail to raise a torch so clear," and shows the evil effects of fear of punishment after death: "This terror, this darkness of the mind, must needs be dissipated, not by the rays of the sun and the gleaming shafts of day, but by the outer view and the inner law of nature." The book proceeds to show that the soul too is material, and hence mortal; since there is no existence and hence no sensation after death, notions of divine retribution are folly. Book 4 continues the mission "to free the mind from the close bondage of religion" by showing that psychological and physiological functions can be explained materially. In vision, for example, a film of atoms from the object seen strikes the eye; and so sleep and dreams are explained by the action of atoms. The teleological view of the human organism is refuted. The mystery of love is similarly exposed; the joys of love are not to be scorned, but the passion must not be allowed to perturb the lover unreasonably. Book 5 again opens with praise of Epicurus, "who first found out that principle of life which now is called wisdom, and who by his skill saved our life from high seas and thick darkness, and enclosed it in calm waters and bright light." This book deals with the formation of the world, with the phenomena of astronomy, with the origin of vegetable, animal, and human life, and with the beginnings of civilized society—all matters, it must be noted, whose grand mysteries are apt to engender superstitious awe. Book 6 provides an atomic explanation of certain celestial and terrestrial phenomena, such as thunderstorms, earthquakes, and plagues, which are similarly apt to be ascribed to direct divine action. In organization and detail this book appears to lack final revision; this circumstance and the fact that the subject of ethics, which was of prime importance to the Epicureans, is nowhere systematically treated in the work, has given rise to the suggestion that Lucretius' original plan called for twelve books, of which the latter six would be devoted to ethics.

The preponderant interest in the poem, as will be seen from the outline, is apparently in physics, and indeed, with the hypothesis of atoms

LUCRETIUS AND CATULLUS

and the void as constituting the sole components of the universe, even
psychology and theology are reduced to a kind of physics. But though
Lucretius' curiosity concerning various phenomena is all-embracing
and his perceptive eye is scientific as well as poetic, physics is not the
chief concern of the poem. Where Lucretius is unable to offer a convincing explanation of a phenomenon, as in Book 5 where alternative
and mutually exclusive explanations of thunder and of the rise of
the Nile are given, it may be legitimately objected that such procedures
are not scientific. But the procedure admirably illustrates Lucretius'
main purpose: he is not so much concerned to show *what* the explanation is as to convince his readers that there *is* a natural explanation,
and hence that the overwhelming phenomena are not really mysteries
which seem to necessitate the intervention of the gods. The scientific
concepts and arguments and perhaps many of the illustrations even are
surely taken from the Greek. Perhaps the whole is a much more faithful adaptation of the "longer catechism" of Epicurus than has been
suspected. What is surely original with Lucretius, besides his poetic
excitement, is the thoroughly Roman practicality of the work, directed, paradoxically, against the thoroughly Roman concept of the
mos majorum, "the ancestral usages." The sixth-century atomists and
the Epicureans who adapted their theories were concerned with intellectual emancipation; Lucretius' object was of more immediate
utility. He wished not merely to instruct his fellow countrymen in
physics, to introduce them to philosophic speculation, not even merely
to liberate them intellectually from the incubus of superstition that
straitened their lives, but by freeing them from a superstition which
had been devised and exploited as a means of political control to
enable them to shake off the trammels of political constraint. Surely
the missionary zeal of *De rerum natura* is Lucretius' own. His on-
slaught on religion—*tantum religio potuit suadere malorum*—is surely
itself religious. He has been presented as an earlier Leonardo; he is
also a Savonarola. He is unique as a prophet in a nation given to
priests.

But readers oblivious or indifferent to its prophetic element must
find *De rerum natura* a great poem. It is characteristically Roman in
its dependence on Greek sources, not only for philosophic and scientific matter but for literary treatment. Lucretius has obviously read not
only the Greek philosophers and scientific writers but also the trage-

dians and Homer, whom he praises as the chief of the poets (3.1037). The description of the plague at Athens in the sixth book is taken from Thucydides. For the Latin form of his poem he owes most to Ennius, whom he credits with introducing poetry to Italy; the *noster* which he applies to Ennius (1.117) may imply kinship in rationalism as well as Roman pride. In the mechanics of the hexameter Lucretius stands midway between Ennius and Vergil. In mood, where Vergil is suggestive and allusive Lucretius is insistent and specific. His descriptions are sharp and detailed, rather like diagrams to illustrate the text than literary ornament. But the descriptions, as well as scientific points they illustrate, are unforgettable: sheep grazing on a distant hill, evolutions of an army at drill, purple color fading as threads are drawn from the cloth, the dance of the motes in the sunbeam, the apparent movement of objects on the shore seen from a passing boat, a square tower appearing round in the distance, the wearing away of a ring by use. There is deep sympathy, like Vergil's, not only for oppressed mankind as a whole but for the individual maiden sacrificed upon the altar and for the cow bereft of its calf. But where Vergil's *lacrimae rerum* has an elegiac tone and his hope the tinge of otherworldliness, Lucretius is indignant and is confident that the spread of enlightenment can put an end to unhappiness.

There is a restless intensity in Lucretius' efforts to explain, to clarify, to convince; where *Aeneid* can lull and dissolve as well as exalt, *De rerum natura* requires close and full attention. The theme and its treatment were new to Latin; Lucretius is fully aware that his enterprise requires strenuous struggle, and knows that the result cannot be easy for the reader (1.136, 2.1024). Ideas had to be expressed in a language whose scope had been limited to things, and the poetry of ideas reduced to a verse form which had never been made malleable to such use. His success in the technical aspects of his work would alone testify to Lucretius' stature. His vocabulary is still rugged, and his syntax sometimes careless. Even in poetry literary Latin was not yet so completely divorced from ordinary speech as it later became. Lucretius uses such antique forms as the passive infinitive ending in *-ier;* the genitive in *-ai;* contractions like *abstraxe* or *-at* for *-avit;* the forms *cimus, tuimur, pereit* instead of the usual conjugation forms; ablatives in *-i* for *-e; -om* for *-um;* and other deviations from classical norms. The elision (more properly apocope) of final *s,* which is frequent in Lucretius, Cicero (*Orator* 48.161) calls *subrusticus*. There are similar deviations in metrical usage.

Of the three poets who with Lucretius are most highly regarded in Latin literature, none mentions Lucretius by name. His contemporary Catullus seems to be totally unaware of him. Horace clearly is aware of him, but he finds doctrinaire intensity uncomfortable (see *Epistles* 1.1.13–19) and does not list his name where he might appropriately have done so (for example, *Satires* 1.10, *Epistles* 2.1, 3). But on Vergil his influence is deep and unmistakable. Not only did Lucretius' achievement prepare the Latin hexameter for his use, but he also absorbed much of the substance and spirit of *De rerum natura*. After speaking of the awesome phenomena of nature Vergil says (*Georgics* 2.490–92):

> *Felix qui potuit rerum cognoscere causas,*
> *atque metus omnis et inexorabile fatum*
> *subiecit pedibus strepitumque Acherontis avari.*

Blessed is he who has been able to win knowledge of the causes of things, and has cast beneath his feet all fear and unyielding Fate, and the howls of hungry Acheron.

—H. R. Fairclough

The man thus blessed is surely Lucretius, and Lucretius', just as surely, is the song which Silenus sings in *Eclogues* 6.31–40:

For he sang how, through the great void, were brought together the seeds of earth, and air, and sea, and streaming fire withal; how, from these elements came all beginnings and even the young globe of the world grew into a mass; how then it began to harden the ground, to shut Nereus apart in the deep, and, little by little, to assume the forms of things; how next the earth is awed at the new sun shining and from the uplifted clouds fall showers; when first woods begin to arise, and living things roam here and there over mountains that know them not.

—H. R. Fairclough

Aulus Gellius (1.21.7) remarked that "Vergil not only adopted single words of Lucretius but also closely followed very many verses and passages almost in their entirety"; modern scholars have pointed to hundreds of individual passages in Vergil which show Lucretius' influence. Though authors like Nepos and Velleius Paterculus mention Lucretius as a great poet, there is no tangible evidence that he exerted any considerable influence until the Renaissance. Upon the rationalist thought of the sixteenth century and after Lucretius was a great seminal influence.

Just as the lofty earnestness of *Paradise Lost* is rendered more impressive in its solitude by the frivolity of the Restoration poets, so does *De rerum natura* tower in lonely grandeur above the modernist coterie whom Cicero contemptuously styled "singers of Euphorion." Lucretius' poem leans upon a Greek model as heavily as does anything in Latin, but his sense of mission to the Romans gives his work a somber public character. The Greek influence on his more frivolous contemporaries of the first century B.C. is of a different quality. The earlier Hellenizing movement had sought its models and was guided in its aims by the Greek classics in epic and in drama. Just as among the Greeks themselves the profound and original work of the classic age was followed by self-conscious Alexandrianism, in which scholarship was paramount and poets produced polished trifles for each other's delectation, oblivious to the generality of readers and to the poet's responsibility as a moral guide, so among the Romans, when the stirring and formative period of the Punic wars was past and the Gracchan agitation initiated an era of internal political strife, poets turned away from grand and universal themes and addressed themselves to technical perfection and the subjective expression of their private concerns. For such writing the Greek works of the Alexandrian age were the natural models, and their characteristics are reproduced by the Romans. Epyllion, elegy, and epigram, all polished miniature genres, displaced the more spacious epic and drama. Erudition (the regular epithet for a poet is *doctus*) appears in mythological allusion, didactic verse, virtuosity in the niceties of language and meter. A new individualism appears in the subjectivity of lyric and the sentimentality of elegiac. But whereas the Alexandrians were, in Timon's gibe, "pedants endlessly quarreling in the bird cage of the Muses," themselves isolated from the world and their efforts betraying the exhaustion of original impulses, the Roman writers did in some degree participate in public life, and their brand of Alexandrianism was an expression of experimentation and revolt.

The work of the pioneers in the movement is extremely fragmentary. Porcius Licinus, who lived in the latter half of the second century B.C., wrote a didactic poem dealing with literary history in trochaic septenarii; eleven lines sharply critical of Terence's sycophancy are preserved in Suetonius' *Life* of Terence. Gellius (17.21.45) ascribes an erotic epigram to Porcius, and also the lines

> *Poenico bello secundo Musa pinnato gradu*
> *intulit se bellicosam in Romuli gentem feram.*

In the second Punic war the Muse with winged flight betook herself to the warlike and unpolished race of Romulus.

Pompilius (ca. 100 B.C.) is cited as an epigrammatist by Varro. The aristocratic and cultured Lutatius Catulus, consul in 102 B.C., wrote Callimachean epigrams as well as distinguished works in prose. Laevius wrote his curiously artful *Erotopaegnia* (*"Fantaisies galantes"*) early in the first century B.C. The prolific Varro of Atax (82–36 B.C.) addressed elegiacs to a pseudonymous Leucadia, besides producing adaptations of Apollonius of Rhodes' *Argonautica,* Aratus' *Phaenomena,* a geographical poem called *Chorographia,* a *Bellum Sequanicum* on Caesar's campaign of 58 B.C., and a satire.

The leader of the coterie of *neoterici* in the generation which followed the pioneers was Valerius Cato, born about 100 B.C. in Cisalpine Gaul, whence most of the coterie derived. Suetonius (*De grammaticis* 11) tells us that he was a poet and a teacher of poets and cites the couplet

> *Cato grammaticus, Latina Siren,*
> *qui solus legit ac facit poetas.*

As a *grammaticus* he edited Lucilius and wrote grammatical works. Of his poetry Suetonius mentions the *Lydia* and the *Diana,* and he cites a line of Ticidas celebrating the former, and a line of Cinna celebrating the latter (which Cinna calls *Dictynna*). Suetonius tells us also that Valerius wrote a *libellus* (probably in prose) entitled *Indignatio,* in which he asserts his free birth and complains that he was orphaned and deprived of his patrimony in the Sullan disturbances. Now the poem in the *Appendix Vergiliana* called *Dirae* complains of loss of property and speaks of a beloved Lydia, and this led Scaliger to attribute *Dirae* to Valerius Cato. Subsequently it was recognized that *Dirae* is two separate poems. The title is appropriate only to the first part (1–103), which is a series of imprecations, accompanied on a flute by the poet's friend Battarus, upon a farm which had been taken from him for a veteran's bonus; Lydia, who remains at the farm, is bidden farewell. The curses are linked by a refrain, "Thus I pray, and in our prayers may these strains abound." In the second part (lines 104-184, but usually printed separately under the title *Lydia*) the poet enviously longs for the happy farm where his beloved Lydia abides. Both parts are thoroughly in the manner of Theocritean bucolic, and the theme of the confiscated farm recurs in the first and the ninth *Eclogues* of Vergil. The preponderance of modern scholarly opinion assigns *Lydia* to Valerius Cato, and some authorities would give him the *Dirae* also. But many first-class authorities vindicate the Vergilian authorship of *Dirae;* both Donatus and Servius list a *Dirae* among Vergil's minor poems.

Horace, Propertius, and Ovid bracket Catullus with C. Licinius Calvus (82-47 B.C.), son of the annalist C. Licinius Macer. The two were friends and their poetic productions were closely parallel. Like Catullus, Calvus wrote short playful pieces, lampoons, elegies (including a lament for a Quintilia), an epithalamium and an epyllion entitled *Io*. Calvus was also a distinguished orator; the titles of five of the twenty-one carefully wrought speeches he left are preserved. The remains of both his speeches and his poetry are extremely slight. Also coupled with Catullus as a lampooner is Marcus Furius Bibaculus. Cremutius Cordus, defending himself against the charge of having written a history with republican bias, is reported by Tacitus (*Annals* 4.34) to have said: "The poems of Bibaculus and Catullus which we read are crammed with invective on the Caesars. Yet the Divine Julius, the Divine Augustus themselves bore all this and let it pass, whether in forbearance or in wisdom I cannot easily say." Some fifteen neat and humorous Phalaecian lines of Bibaculus are cited by Suetonius (*De grammaticis* 11); Horace (*Satires* 2.5.40) ridicules him for bathos: "Furius, stuffed with rich tripe, [writes] 'With hoary snow bespew the wintry Alps.' " Scholiasts refer the line to an epic on Caesar's Gallic war. It is odd that the lampooner of Caesar should celebrate him in an epic, odd too that a man born in 103 B.C. (as Bibaculus was, according to Jerome) should be bracketed with Catullus. Scholars have therefore suggested that the lampooner may be a second Bibaculus, born about 82 B.C.

Catullus himself speaks (No. 95) of the enduring fame of his friend Cinna's *Zmyrna*, which had cost nine years of labor. The poem was a treatment, in the Alexandrian manner, of Myrrha's unnatural passion for her father Cinyras. Cinna was the poet who was lynched by mistake after the funeral of Julius Caesar. The biographer Cornelius Nepos (who will be dealt with in a subsequent chapter) to whom Catullus dedicated his book, was also the author of love poems. In Number 35 Catullus addresses the "gentle poet" Caecilius, and in 38 he reproaches Cornificius, obviously also a poet, for sending him no word of comfort in his illness. In Number 36 he assigns to the flames the *Annales Volusi, cacata charta*. Catullus and Cinna too were in the train of Memmius (to whom Lucretius addressed the *De rerum natura*) when he went to Bithynia as propraetor in 57 B.C.; we might infer that Memmius too wrote poetry. The Ticidas whose line on Valerius Cato has been mentioned wrote erotic poems to Perilla, whose real name was Metella. The Alexandrian impulse continued strong in the *Culex* and *Ciris* of the *Vergilian Appendix,* in the *Eclogues* and to a lesser degree the *Georgics* of Vergil, in the work of Propertius and of Ovid. Through these writers it left its permanent impress on the literature of Europe.

There can be little doubt, happily, that the sole extant representative was the best of the school. The most obviously Alexandrian of Catullus' productions are the long poems at the center of the collection, and these, despite certain criticisms of which they are susceptible, are indeed of high poetic merit. But in true lyric Catullus is absolutely without peer in extant Latin literature; the only poet of whom we may suspect that he shared something of Catullus' quality is Catullus' boon companion Calvus. The genius of Catullus is wholly lyric in his lightning perception of an emotion, his surrender to it and mastery of it, his refraction of its sparkling fragments in exuberant but controlled language, and most of all in his unpuritanical acceptance of the emotion. The latter quality in particular was a thing un-Roman, and this explains why the Augustans were made uncomfortable by Catullus and ignored him. Professor E. A. Havelock has put the case of Catullus' un-Romanism well:

Catullus paid the price to Roman posterity of defying the unromantic Roman temper. He wrote love lyrics which his countrymen proved incompetent to classify and enjoy as modern taste may enjoy them. We have cleared a dignified space in literature for sexual passion; that is the difference. Virgil's treatment of the same theme illustrates from another side the same Roman limitations. With a temper equally sensitive, but much more cautious, his literary instincts seem early to have recognized the limits on feeling set by his audience. So he took care to treat love with a certain detachment, either playful or tragic.

Catullus was aware that his romantic absorption in his own mood must seem a frivolous thing to the Romans. When he dedicated his book to Cornelius Nepos he speaks of his poetry as *nugae*, "trifles," and when he addresses Cicero as the best of lawyers he acknowledges himself the worst of poets. Nevertheless with poetic if not puritanic austerity he went his romantic and lyric way. There is no incongruity in mentioning Catullus in the same breath as Lucretius. Their common denominator is not only authentic poetic endowment and a manifest compulsion to communicate, but also a transparent candor; each embraces his reader, neither fences with him. Lucretius was an ardent devotee of the religion of unreligion; Catullus was equally a devotee, and of a religion equally unconventional. On this too Professor Havelock's words are illuminating:

In his love for Lesbia all this religion of personal affection crystallized, and without it his love's expression cannot be understood. Hungry desire, passionate embrace, torturing jealousy—his verse has all these, the common attributes of Aphrodite Pandemos, but it also has something more, a touch of the ideal. Thus inspired, he can express an almost impersonal surrender, a joy in giving without return . . . till at the end, as the edifice of love crumbles, he is moved to open confession that such affection was his personal religion, the faith by which he lived—

> O di, reddite mi hoc pro pietate mea.

Pietas for Virgil's Aeneas meant the desertion of Dido in the cause of country; for Catullus it meant the world well lost for Lesbia. The contrast illustrates the deep division in temper which separates him from the official literature of Rome. Dido stands in Latin literature as the classic embodiment of passionate love, yet in the supreme crisis of her affection she remains faithful to the Roman type and reveals its limitations—

> At least, if but a child were born
> Of me to thee, ere thou wert gone,
> At very least, a little son
> Still to recall thy face to me . . .
>
> [*Aeneid* 4. 327–30]

Many generations have felt the beauty and pathos of the passage. Yet she speaks as a Roman matron, a potential mother, not as a mistress. Only Catullus was capable of thinking of a woman not as a means to an end, but as worth everything in herself.

Since Catullus' best work is in subjective lyric his candor makes it easy to apprehend his volatile personality and to trace the course of the love which is, for us at least, the central fact of his life. So much do we know, indeed, that scholars have been tempted to gauge and date his every shift in mood. We know that he was Gaius Valerius Catullus and that he was born in Verona. Jerome gives his birth year as 87 B.C. and says that he lived thirty years, but as he was alive in 55 when Caesar invaded Britain his dates are more probably 84–54 B.C. His family was wealthy (allusions to spiderwebs in his purse are playful); his work gives evidence of elaborate education, and when he came to Rome he had immediate access to the best society. His father was an important enough man to be on terms of friendship with Julius Caesar; in this connection Suetonius (*Julius* 73) provides an interesting note:

Valerius Catullus, as Caesar himself did not hesitate to say, inflicted a lasting stain on his name, by the verses about Mamurra [29 and 57]; yet when he apologized, Caesar invited the poet to dinner that very same day, and continued his usual friendly relations with Catullus' father.

—*J. C. Rolfe*

Catullus came to Rome in 62 B.C., the year following the excitement of the Catilinarian conspiracy. Among the people of wealth and fashion who received him was the urban praetor Q. Caecilius Metellus, a noble of ancient family, and his wife Clodia, some ten years Catullus' senior, of an even prouder family, notorious for its wilfulness. Catullus became infatuated with Clodia at once, and the series of poems which reflect the course of his love, from bliss to despair to disillusionment to resignation, make this affair one of the most memorable of its kind in literary history. First in the series, doubtless, is the imitation of Sappho's rapturous lyric (51):

> God, or more than God he seemeth
> In whose eyes thy bright glance beameth
> In whose ears thy laughter trilleth
> Sitting near to thee.

—*J. C. Rollo*

It was the reminiscence of Sappho which suggested the name of Lesbia; all the poets of the Alexandrian school chose a Greek name metrically equivalent to their lady love's true name by which to address them. It is significant that Catullus uses the Sapphic meter only once again, in the bitter poem in which he takes leave of Clodia (11):

> Tell her: God speed you, lady, to your bed,
> Where thwarted lovers lie there lay your head,
> Promising love to them give lust instead,
>   False to the core:
>
> Tell her how love, that in my heart one day
> Blossomed unbidden as a wildflower may,
> The scythe has caught, and she can throw away
>   What blooms no more.
>
> *—E. A. Havelock*

But before the disillusionment the carefree rapture of love untarnished is expressed in a handful of blissful utterances, of which the *Vivamus mea Lesbia atque amemus* (5) sets the keynote:

> Let's live and love, O Lesbia mine,
> And value at a single copper
> Chatter of greybeards too too proper!
> The setting sun again will shine;
> But once has set our little light
> We sleep forever one unbroken Night.
> Give a thousand kisses then,
> And now a hundred, and again
> A thousand, and a hundred yet,
> And this and that reiterate:
> When these to many thousands mount,
> Jumble them up—for fear we count,
> Or malice look with envious eye
> On kisses mounting up so high!
>
> *—J. H. A. Tremenheere*

Clodia's husband seems to have been no bar to the amour (83):

> When her husband is by, Lesbia rails at me sore;
>   And he chuckles to think how she scolds me.
> The dull ass! not to see that her silence would more
>   Prove how little she thinks of, or holds me.
>
> *—John Nott*

But Clodia could be unfaithful to her lover as well as to her husband. When the latter died in 59 B.C. (gossip said by Clodia's dosing) Catullus thought she would marry him, but he was soon disillusioned (70):

> Lesbia declares she'd marry none but me,
> Not even Jove, should he her wooer be;
> She says so: but on wind and rapid wave
> A woman's troth to her fond swain engrave.
>
> —*James Cranstoun*

Distraught at the realization of Clodia's fickleness, Catullus retired to Verona for a while, and upon his return to Rome found his place usurped by M. Caelius Rufus, the friend and correspondent of Cicero. Agonized pleas for the restoration of his former felicity were futile, and he sought to reconcile himself to the situation: *Miser Catulle desine ineptire* (8)—

> Catullus, hapless one, be schooled at last,
> Believe your eyes, confess the past is past.
>
> —*Hugh Macnaghten*

In Number 76 he achieves a measure of calm (10-16):

> Then what avails you still should agonise?
> Nay, steel your heart, retrace your steps again,
> And cease in Heaven's despite to suffer pain.
> 'Tis hard to end a year long love today;
> 'Tis hard, achieve it then as best you may:
> This victory win, this only safety trust,
> Say not you cannot or you can—you must.
>
> —*Hugh Macnaghten*

The final farewell is the second Sapphic poem cited above. The pulsing warmth of Catullus' affections was more than merely erotic; his attachment to his friends, his brother, his native place, his yacht, was tender and generous. While on Memmius' staff in the east he visited his brother's tomb near Troy and composed a heartfelt elegy (101):

> Over many a land, and over many an ocean
>   Here to thy desolate grave, brother, oh brother, I come!
> Only on thee to bestow death's last forlornest bestrewments,
>   Only in vain to conjure thy unanswering dust.
> Woe is me for the doom that of thee so untimely bereft me,
>   Hapless brother, when thou wert so relentlessly ta'en!

Now meanwhile the tribute our fathers from ages primeval
   Gave in their sorrow to those whom in life they had loved,
Take, all drenched with the tears of brotherly anguish; and, brother,
   Ever be blessings on thee—fare thee well evermore!

—Theodore Martin

The apostrophe to the yacht in which he returned to Italy with his
fellow poet Cinna is as affectionate as it is playful (4). The joy of his
homecoming to a beloved spot (in 56 B.C.) is expressed in an address
to Sirmio (31):

Dear Sirmio, that art the very eye
Of islands and peninsulas that lie
Deeply embosomed in calm inland lake,
Or where the waves of the vast ocean break;
Joy of all joys, to gaze on thee once more!
I scarce believe that I have left the shore
Of Thynia, and Bithynia's parching plain,
And gaze on thee in safety once again!
Oh, what more sweet than when, from care set free,
The spirit lays its burden down, and we,
With distant travel spent, come home and spread
Our limbs to rest along the wished-for bed!
This, this alone, repays such toils as these!
Smile, then, fair Sirmio, and thy master please—
And you, ye dancing waters of the lake,
Rejoice, and every smile of home awake!

—Theodore Martin

The remaining year or two of his life Catullus spent in Rome, in
literary composition and with literary friends. Dissatisfaction of his
circle at the turn Roman political life was taking is indicated by his
lampoons of Caesar and Caesar's creature Mamurra.

Though Catullus doubtless published a collection of his poems, as
the dedication of his *lepidus libellus* to Cornelius Nepos (1) shows,
the collection of 116 poems which has come down (including Numbers 18–20, which are spurious) can hardly have been Catullus' own
arrangement. Its twenty-three hundred lines make up twice the size
of the conventional Roman book, and the order bears no relationship
to chronology or subject matter, but is purely architectonic. Poems
1–60 (842 lines) are short and in various meters; 61–64 (797 lines)
are long, and also in different meters; 65–116 (645 lines) are long and

short but all in elegiac meter. The lyrics in the first group are on a variety of subjects—erotic (including the Lesbia pieces), playful, satiric—and in a variety of meters, with the eleven-syllable Phalaecian (hendecasyllables) and to a less extent the scazon predominating. All are lyric in form as well as feeling.

But even in his longer pieces Catullus remains the lyric poet. The first of the four long poems (No. 61; 231 lines) is a nuptial ode for the highborn Vinia Aurunculeia and Manlius Torquatus, friends of Catullus, in gay glyconics. Though there were Greek epithalamia to suggest the theme, the setting is thoroughly Roman. The song begins with felicitations before the bride steps out to lead the procession, continues with good wishes for her and sly comments on the groom, until the bride is lifted over the groom's threshold; the rites of the nuptial couch are then mentioned, and blessings are invoked for offspring and continued happiness. The poem is rich in color, in melody, and in exuberant spirits. The other epithalamium (No. 62; 66 lines) is in hexameter strophes for antiphonal choruses of boys and girls. In the first four strophes the leaders give instructions to their respective groups; then the choruses sing alternately, the boys greeting the rise of the evening star with joy, the maidens with feigned fright. The form resembles that of the song contests in Theocritus, and its use for a marriage is an innovation. The *Attis* (No. 63; 93 lines) in the orgiastic galliambic rhythm is the most striking of Catullus' productions. A young convert to the frenzied worship of Cybele goes to her shrine on Mount Ida in the Troad, undergoes the rites of initiation, which entail emasculation, and leads his companions in the riotous and steamy worship. When he awakens to the realization of what he has done, he stands wistfully on the seashore, longing for home and friends. Cybele sends her lions to drive him back to his rash commitments. Penetration and sympathy as well as fire and energy fill this poem. The moral closes with a prayer:

Goddess, great goddess, Cybele, goddess, lady of Dindymus, far from my house be all thy fury, O my queen; others drive thou in frenzy, others drive thou to madness.

—F. W. Cornish

The *Marriage of Peleus and Thetis* (No. 64; 408 lines) is a miniature epic, or epyllion, naturally in hexameters, and Catullus' longest poem. Even this most objective of forms is romanticized by Catullus' lyricism. The narrative is presented in a series of descriptive scenes—Peleus sailing on the Argo, his falling in love with Thetis, the wedding. The coverlet on the nuptial couch bears a design showing Ariadne on the seashore looking after Theseus, who has deserted her in her sleep. The whole moving story of Ariadne and Theseus, which occupies half the poem, is worked in as one of the several designs in the larger tapestry of the poem. The wedding proper is resumed, with divine guests bringing their gifts. The Fates sing the birth and death of Achilles in strophes with the refrain, "Run, drawing the woof-threads, ye spindles, run." At the close of this ornate and carefully worked piece we are brought up with a jolt at the picture of contemporary degeneration:

But when the earth was dyed with hideous crime, and all men banished justice from their greedy souls, and brothers sprinkled their hands with brothers' blood, the son left off to mourn his parents' death, the father wished for the death of his young son, that he might without hindrance enjoy the flower of a young bride, the unnatural mother impiously coupling with her unconscious son did not fear to sin against parental gods:—then all right and wrong, confounded in impious madness, turned from us the righteous will of the gods. Wherefore they deign not to visit such companies, nor endure the touch of clear daylight.

—F. W. Cornish

Of the third group, written in the elegiac meter, the first five poems are full-scale elegies. Number 65 is a response to Hortalus (the orator Hortensius) who had encouraged Catullus to write a poem. Catullus replies that his brother's death had so distracted him that he can only send a translation from Battiades (Callimachus). This is *The Lock of Berenice* (No. 66; 94 lines), which, as the discovery of twenty lines of Callimachus' original shows, is a fairly faithful version. The *Lock* in question is a newly discovered constellation which is identified with a lock of hair which Queen Berenice had offered for the safe return of her husband from a military expedition. The poem is an erotic narrative elegy, full of learned allusions. A piece of Veronese gossip is presented in a dialogue between the poet and a house door in Number 67 (48 lines). Manlius had written Catullus at Verona asking him to write a poem. In number 68 Catullus excuses himself on grounds of grief at his brother's death; 68A (usually numbered consecutively with 68) is a fuller reply. The three themes of his friendship for Allius, his grief for his brother's death, and love for Lesbia are interlaced in an intricate but regular pattern, the arrangement of the lines being *a b c b a.* To achieve this correspondence Catullus had to resort to padding, and the poem has many difficult allusions. "Allius" is Manlius himself, and Afer (emended from *aufert* in line 117) is probably Caelius. Of the remaining poems in the elegiac meter Number 76, protesting the sincerity of his love for Lesbia and petitioning requital of his piety, should be counted our finest example of the Roman love elegy.

The other poems of this group fall into the broad category of the epigram, with the same diversity of subject as is to be found in the *Greek Anthology,* and with anticipations of the pointed wit of the epigrams of Martial. In theme and treatment these little poems are not really different from the short poems in the first section, nor are they set apart chronologically: here too there are poems on Lesbia and on his brother's death, lampoons on Caesar and his creatures, as well as recurrent barbs against breaches of good taste and against pretensions of all sorts. Catullus' fastidiousness is, in fact, one of his most marked traits. He excoriates immoralities, one feels, not because they are sinful but because they violate good form. Political upstarts he loathes not so much out of doctrinaire convictions as because they are upstarts and therefore crude. The Arrius who said "*h*onors" for "honors," "*h*intrigue" for "intrigue," and "*h*ambush" for "ambush" (84) would have done well enough if he had not "thought he spoke marvellous well." Fastidiousness rather than political conviction seems to be the motive of the famous couplet directed against Caesar (93):

> Whether or no I please you I hardly care,
> Much less to know whether you are dark or fair.
> —*Tenney Frank*

Catullus' mercurial quality, his intensity, and his candor, as well as his verbal felicity all find expression in his lapidary *Odi et amo* (85):

> I loathe her and I love her. "Can I show
> How both should be?"
> I loathe and love, and nothing else I know
> But agony.
> —*E. A. Havelock*

VI

CAESAR, SALLUST, AND OTHERS

CAESARISM WE MAY ABHOR, AND WE MAY DESPISE the deviousness and ruthlessness by which men like Julius mount to the eminence which permits them to give that word its meaning, but so demoralized had the Roman state become under the greedy and selfish sway of a moneyed oligarchy that centralization of authority in the hands of a man with the will and energy to grasp it was inevitable. It was as leader of the popular party that Caesar rose to power, and when he was secure in his authority he at least took steps to initiate long-needed reforms. When Octavian had "avenged" his assassinated predecessor and "restored the republic" he turned his back on Caesar's program and preserved their privileges to the oligarchy.

No account of any aspect of ancient Rome could omit the name of Caesar; literature, like other expressions of life, was conditioned by the change from republic to empire, and we shall see some of the effects of the change as the history of the empire unfolds and authoritarianism grows less qualified. But Caesar claims a place in literature in his own right as a man of letters. His lines in criticism of Terence have been cited above. We know also that he wrote a treatise on astronomy, one on grammar, and a collection of apophthegms. His *Anticato,* published in the last year or so of his life, was a political pamphlet intended to counteract the continuing influence of the Stoic martyr for republicanism. He wrote poetry all through his life. Early in his career he wrote a tragedy of Oedipus, and in 45 B.C. he wrote a verse account of his journey to Spain, whither he was going to fight his last battle (Munda) against the sons of Pompey. He also wrote a number of love poems. All Caesar's poetry was suppressed by order of Augustus. His prose work which has survived, the unique and remarkable *Commentaries* on the Gallic and Civil wars, have introduced untold thousands of schoolboys to Latin in its most muscular and efficient manifestation.

The life of Julius Caesar, which can be written with fullness on the

basis of these *Commentaries,* of the ancient "lives," and most particularly of the contemporary letters of Cicero, must be at the same
time an account of the culmination of the Roman revolution—a juncture of history as meaningful and dramatic as any in the annals of
Europe, and of particular relevance to our own times. Here we need
touch only on the *fastigia rerum.* Julius was born in 102 (or 100) B.C.
He was the nephew of the wife of Marius, the leader of the popular
party, and as quaestor in 68 he used the occasion of her funeral to
deliver a public eulogy of the Julian *gens.* In 63 he advocated leniency
to those involved in the Catilinarian conspiracy. With the help of
wholesale bribery he became pontifex maximus that same year and
praetor the year following. The governorship of Farther Spain which
followed upon his praetorship first made him aware of his military
talents. In 60 he entered upon an informal triumvirate with Pompey
and Crassus which was designed to promote the political designs of
each. This gave him the consulship in 59 (his colleague being the
patrician nonentity M. Calpurnius Bibulus) and the governorship
of Gaul for the five years following. The assignment in Gaul afforded
him wealth and an army devoted to himself, as well as opportunity
to keep in close touch with the situation in Rome. The arrangement of
the triumvirs was renewed at Luca in 56, but the death of Crassus in
the battle of Carrhae in 53 left the two survivors confronting one another, the death of Julia, who was the daughter of Caesar and the wife
of Pompey, having already ruptured the personal bond between the
two men. Caesar's request that he be permitted to stand for the consulship of 49 *in absentia* (which would alone afford him protection
from his enemies) having been refused, he took the revolutionary step
of crossing the Rubicon, that is, of appearing under arms in territory
where he had no official authority to do so, in January, 49. Pompey
withdrew the senatorial forces to Greece, whither Caesar followed him
after a campaign to defeat Pompey's legates in Spain, and won a
complete victory over the Pompeian forces in the battle of Pharsalus
in August, 48. In 48/47 Caesar fought a war in Alexandria (where
Cleopatra became his mistress), and after a short sojourn in Rome
he sailed for Africa, where he defeated Cato and the remnants of the
senatorial army at the battle of Thapsus. After another short stay in
Rome he was called to Spain by the armed resistance of the sons of
Pompey, whom he defeated at the battle of Munda in 45. The few

months remaining to him before the Ides of March of 44 he spent in reorganizing the state and preparing for an expedition against the Parthians.

The picture of the shrewd and resolute and efficient politician and soldier which the testimony of other ancient writers supplies is amply confirmed by Caesar himself in his *Commentaries,* which is our principal concern here. The title, like the Greek *hypomnemata* of which it is a version, signifies notes or reports, such as might be rendered to the home authorities by a commander in the field and then be used as the basis of a formal history. Cicero (*Brutus* 75.262) and Hirtius (Preface to *Bellum Gallicum* 8) both imply that this was the design of Caesar's *Commentaries* when they declare that their high excellence has left no scope to future historians. Caesar's achievement went so far beyond his professed aim that he has remained the historian of his own wars. It is very plain, moreover, that while his professed aim may have been genuine it was not his most important motive for writing; he was far less concerned to provide information for future historians than he was to vindicate himself in the eyes of immediate contemporaries. Such classic modern historians of antiquity as Gibbon or Grote or Mommsen show that a propagandist bias need not wholly vitiate the trustworthiness of a history, and surely not its readability. Just as Julius Caesar was the most competent conceivable authority to set forth the details of his campaigns, so was he the most nearly concerned to justify his course of action. If then his *Commentaries* are pamphlets in the guise of history, his restraint is as admirable˙as it is effective; he never raises his voice in partisan recriminations or self-justification, but always maintains his third-personal objectivity. The conviction of the author's prowess and patriotism grows not out of explicit avowals but out of the total impression of what is implicit in the whole work. To the reader, at least, his posture is that desiderated of the historian by Lucian—"like Zeus' in Homer, surveying now the Mysians', now the Thracian horsemen's land" (*How to Write History* 49).

Each of Caesar's own seven books of the *Gallic War* covers the campaigns of a single year, from 58 to 52. Some scholars have thought that each book was published at the end of the year with which it dealt, but the more probable view is that the whole was written at a single stroke, naturally on the basis of contemporary notes, and published as a whole in 51. By then it was plain to all who had eyes to see, and surely to Caesar, that a breach with Pompey was inevitable, though the two men were still friends outwardly. Caesar's proconsulship was drawing to a close and he might soon have to answer for his acts in Rome. In Rome he had many bitter enemies, and if he could influence public opinion he might more easily obtain the second consulship which he needed. He could naturally not avow that his aim was to refute his political enemies. His sources were of the best, and it is unlikely that he falsified where his statements might be disproven —to do so would have defeated his purpose. Where he grinds his own ax is in distribution of emphasis and in ascription of motives. In his account the Gauls virtually force him to conquer them; the Gauls did in fact seem to offer ample provocation, but we cannot avoid a suspicion that personal ambition had something to do with the conquest. From his account of his dealings with the Usipetes and the Tencteri no one would suspect that Cato had denounced him vehemently for treacherously violating the truce with those unfortunate tribes. Caesar merely gives his version of the facts, with apparently perfect candor and with no hint that he is refuting a different view.

Caesar's credibility, and his claim to genius, is enhanced by a style at once lucid and precise and elegant, which he writes with the sovereign ease and the purity of diction characteristic of the literary aristocrat. Cicero has characterized his work acutely and justly (*Brutus* 75.262):

[The *Commentaries*] are naked and straightforward and graceful, stripped of all finery as of a garment. In supplying material for the use of others who might wish to write history Caesar may have obliged those silly men who would frill what he has left with their curling irons; but sane people he has deterred from writing, for in history nothing is more agreeable than simple and lucid brevity.

—*H. M. Poteat*

Caesar's adjutant Hirtius uses much the same terms of his master's work, and supplies an interesting addition (Preface to *Gallic War* 8):

Yet herein is our own admiration greater than all other men's; the world knows how excellently, how faultlessly, but we know also how easily, how speedily he completed his Commentaries. Caesar possessed not only the greatest facility and refinement of style, but also the surest skill in explaining his own plans.

—*H. J. Edwards*

Modern critics are at one with ancient in praising the perfection of Caesar's style. Exception is taken only to the geographical disquisitions, which certain editions go so far as to bracket as interpolations. Such an account as that of the Germans at 6.21–28 and especially of the fantastic fauna of the Hercynian forest does seem unworthy of Caesar's intelligence and shows minor stylistic differences from the rest of his work. But such descriptions of exotic peoples and places are characteristic of all ancient historiography, and Caesar wished to answer a natural and legitimate curiosity on the part of his readers. The passages in question were doubtless adapted from Greek travel books by secretaries at Caesar's order. Sometimes, as in the passage mentioned, they serve to distract attention from a military failure.

A minor school of critics has also questioned the authenticity of large sections of the *Civil War* on the grounds of slight divergencies from the usage of the *Gallic War,* but the differences are too slight to invalidate the tradition and can be explained by Caesar's different attitude in composing the book and by the circumstance that he never lived to complete and revise it. The *Civil War* starts with an account of the difficulty of procuring a reading of Caesar's "ultimatum" to the senate in January, 49, continues with the campaigns of 49 and 48, the death of Pompey, and the first part of the Alexandrine war, and stops abruptly in November, 48, with no indication of how the war would end. The whole covers a period of less than two years. The apologetic and polemic character of the book, much more pronounced than in the *Gallic War,* would itself suggest that it was published posthumously and in unrevised state; after his complete victory and in the midst of efforts to conciliate Caesar would not have needed to pamphleteer. Surely the greater part of the book was written before Thapsus and never received its author's final revision. The present division into three books is probably wrong; there is evidence that originally the material was divided into two books, one for each year as in the *Gallic War.*

Asinius Pollio, who was in position to know, said that the book lacked revision and also impugned its veracity (Suetonius, *Julius* 56.4):

Asinius Pollio thinks they [sc. the books of the *Civil War*] were put together somewhat carelessly and without strict regard for truth; since in many cases Caesar was too ready to believe the accounts which others gave of their actions, and gave a perverted account of his own, either designedly or perhaps from forgetfulness; and he thinks that he intended to rewrite and revise them.

                                                                    —*J. C. Rolfe*

It is even less likely that Caesar would venture to distort generally familiar facts in the *Civil* than in the *Gallic War,* and careful researches have proven him generally trustworthy. But in his distribution of emphasis, his attribution of motives both to himself and to his opponents, in aggrandizing his own merits and depreciating those of his opponents and making them the butts of his sarcasm, Caesar's bias is given much more outspoken expression in the *Civil* than in the *Gallic War;* such passages as 1.1–11, 3.31–33, and 3.82–83 are open propaganda. The third person and the ostensible objectivity as well as the terse elegance of style reappear in the *Civil War,* but it is a more personal book nevertheless. The satirical thumbnail sketches of the Pompeian leaders, the picture of their brawling rivalry at Pompey's headquarters concerning their shares of Caesar's offices, even the repeated exhibitions of Caesar's military genius and his generous clemency and of Pompey's fecklessness, give the work a psychologic interest which the *Gallic War* does not possess. Throughout, even when he is haranguing his troops before battle, Caesar represents himself as a devoted lover of peace who is being forced to take up arms. He is sparing of blood, even his enemies', and repeated examples of his conciliatory disposition and his clemency are given. One editor suggests as a subtitle to *Bellum Civile, Sive de Caesaris clementia.*

The *Civil War* was not designed as a continuation of the *Gallic War,* and we have no account from Caesar's own hand of the events of 51 and 50 B.C., when the Gallic revolt was liquidated and Caesar's relations with the senate exacerbated. Nor, as we have seen, is the *Civil War* itself completed. These gaps were filled by four supplementary works: *Bellum Gallicum* 8, which relates the events of 51 and 50 and in its closing chapter makes a transition to the *Civil War; Bellum Alexandrinum,* which goes beyond its title and includes the campaigns against Pharnaces, the Illyrian war, and the disturbances in Spain; *Bellum Africanum,* which describes the defeat of the Pompeians at Thapsus; and *Bellum Hispaniense,* which deals with the final defeat of the Pompeian remnants at Munda. Suetonius (*Julius* 56.1) tells us that *Bellum Gallicum* 8 was written by Hirtius and that the other three were written by either Hirtius or Oppius. In his Preface to *Bellum Gallicum* 8 Hirtius declares his intention to carry the story down to the death of Caesar. *Bellum Alexandrinum* is sufficiently like *Bellum Gallicum* 8 in style and treatment to have been written by Hirtius (who died in April, 43), but the other two treatises diverge so sharply that it is impossible to believe that Hirtius wrote them. They were obviously written by officers who participated in the campaigns they describe (which excludes Oppius, who did not), but their writing is extremely inept, alternating between infantile baldness and sophomoric turgidity. The *Bellum Hispaniense* is actually ungrammatical.

The difference between these books and Caesar's own *Commentaries* is the difference between a soldier wielding a refractory pen and a literary artist, and we should expect that the artist indulged in writing other than pamphleteering military reports. His six hexameters on Terence demonstrate his literary interests and perceptions. Suetonius (*Julius* 56.7) tells us that Caesar wrote *Praises of Hercules,* an *Oedipus,* and collected *Dicta* (Cicero refers to these as *Apophthegmata*), which Augustus forbade to be published. He also tells us (56.5) that Caesar wrote two books *De analogia,* two of *Anticatones,* and a poem called *Iter. De analogia* he wrote while crossing the Alps to join his army in Gaul. The book dealt with the correct use of grammatical forms and the correct choice of words; it contained the famous prescription that "a far-fetched word should be shunned like a rock." It was addressed to Cicero, perhaps in reply to Cicero's *De oratore.* The *Anticatones* was written amidst similar military preoccupations, in the camp at Munda, and was likewise a reply to a work of Cicero's. After Cato's suicide in 46, Cicero (as well as Brutus and M. Fadius Gallus) wrote panegyrics upon him and the republican ideals he espoused. Caesar first asked Hirtius to write a reply, and then himself wrote one in which he dealt courteously with

Cicero but exposed Cato's quixotic failings mercilessly. The *Iter* was
a verse account of his journey to Spain before Munda; his model,
like Horace's in his "Journey to Brundisium," was probably the
third book of Lucilius. Caesar's oratory is praised in the highest terms
by such competent critics as Cicero, Quintilian, and Tacitus, and
quotations in Gellius show that his speeches were collected and preserved. Quotations in Gellius, and more particularly in Suetonius,
show that collections of Caesar's letters, addressed to Cicero, to the
senate, and to sundry friends, were also made. After the Ides of
March, as after the death of Cato, Caesarians and anti-Caesarians
gave vigorous expression to their views of the dictator, but the surviving precipitate of this literature is negligible.

A figure of first-class eminence among the Caesarians, original in
style, thoughtful in historical approach, perceptive in the evaluation
of men and movements, is C. Sallustius Crispus (86–ca.34), the only
Roman historian whom we may set beside Thucydides. Sallust was
born in the Sabine town of Amiternum and settled in Rome early in
life. He was tribune in 52 and apparently *legatus pro quaestore* in 50.
That year he was expelled from the senate by the censor Appius
Claudius because of a scandal involving the wife of Annius Milo,
but in 49 Caesar restored his senatorial dignity by making him
quaestor. He served Caesar in military capacities in Illyria and in
Campania, commanded his navy in the African campaign of 46,
and after Thapsus continued as proconsul of Africa. The wealth there
accumulated enabled him to acquire Caesar's villa at Tivoli and the
magnificent Pincian gardens, which continued to be called Sallustian when Nero, Vespasian, Nerva, and Aurelian lived there.
After the assassination of Caesar, Sallust retired to private life and
literary pursuits. In any consideration of Sallust's career it must be
remembered that as an adherent of Caesar he was a natural object
of slander to the opposition. If he used his proconsulship to enrich
himself, so did many provincial administrators, especially on the
heels of a war. If the scandal which Varro painted in lurid colors
was more than a youthful peccadillo, alone it would hardly have
caused his expulsion from the senate. Caesar's prompt reinstatement
suggests that the expulsion was politically motivated, nor is it likely
that Caesar would continue to repose confidence in a reckless liber-

tine. The Sallust we know from his works, in any case, is a highly intelligent and conscientious and responsible writer, with a keen sense of ethical propriety.

The program which he adopted for his retirement Sallust sets forth in the introductory paragraphs of his *Catiline* (3.3–4.5):

> When I myself was a young man, my inclinations at first led me, like many another, into public life, and there I encountered many obstacles; for instead of modesty, incorruptibility and honesty, shamelessness, bribery and rapacity held sway. . . . Accordingly, when my mind found peace after many troubles and perils and I had determined that I must pass what was left of my life aloof from public affairs, it was not my intention to waste my precious leisure in indolence and sloth, nor yet by turning to farming or the chase, to lead a life devoted to slavish employments. On the contrary, I resolved to return to a cherished purpose from which ill-starred ambition had diverted me, and write a history of the Roman people, selecting such portions as seemed to me worthy of record. . . . The conspiracy of Catiline I regard as worthy of special notice because of the extraordinary nature of the crime and of the danger arising from it.
>
> —*J. C. Rolfe*

Not only did the conspiracy mark a high point in the evolution of the Roman polity about which his convictions (as we shall observe) were based not merely on political expediency but on a philosophy, but the episode was recent enough for him to remember it and to be able to make inquiries of eyewitnesses. He was more interested in interpretation than in historical research, and would naturally choose for his first effort a theme which required no extensive preliminary investigations. The notion of a monograph on a single historical phenomenon whose interpretation should serve to illuminate general truths concerning political behavior Sallust derived from Thucydides, who also makes it plain that his subject is a single war, not a general history, and who also expects that the truths he sets forth will have general validity and not merely record events as they occurred. Like all historians subsequent to Thucydides, Sallust introduces fictive speeches into his account; but Sallust's speeches are closest to Thucydides' own, in that they are not merely ornamental but set forth, at relevant points, the disparate ideologies and motivations of the contending parties. The best examples, perhaps, are the opposing speeches of Marius and Memmius in the *Jugurtha*.

As we should expect, the position of the *Catiline* is consistently antioptimate, and partisans of Ciceronian policies, ancient and modern, are quick to brand divergencies from Cicero's own view of the conspiracy as biased fabrications and to see the purposeful distortions as an effort to malign Cicero and glorify Caesar. No one could be expected to be as fulsome as was Cicero himself in expatiating on his own merits in suppressing the subversive movement; if Sallust omits to write a speech for Cicero like the brilliant speeches he wrote for Caesar and Cato, it is because Cicero's own speeches on the subject were too familiar for a suppositious speech to be acceptable. Considering that personal as well as party passions were still fresh when he wrote, it is remarkable that there is so little of individual inculpation in Sallust. It is not so much individual aristocrats that he blames for political demoralization as the rottenness of the aristocratic class, for which not individual worthlessness but a wrong polity, based upon a wrong philosophy of human nature, is at fault.

Why, men might ask, were present-day politicians so unlike the sterling heroes of the early republic, selfless in their patriotism, scrupulous in money matters, willing to sink private ambition for the public good? At what point did unprincipled self-seeking displace the old ideals, and how did human nature suffer so radical a change? The answer, devised possibly by the Stoic Posidonius, was that human nature had suffered no change but was always potentially what dispirited contemporaries saw it to be. What had kept Roman society puritanically sober in the early republic was the common danger from without (*metus hostilis* or *metus Punicus* takes on the character of a technical term), men realizing that if they did not submerge their private interests they would all be lost. The change came with the end of the Second Punic War, when all fear of the foreigner was eliminated, and hence all human impulses to self-seeking released. Only a compelling external force could constrain men to patriotic virtue, and such a force no longer existed. Our own century is familiar enough with the consequences of such assumptions and such reasoning: some danger, arising from a minority or a foreign power, must be conjured up, and some highly endowed individual must by his individual authority exercise the constraint which the generality is incapable of exercising for itself. Sallust's

Caesarism is logically consistent and has its rationale, wrong-headed as an Athenian or American democrat might believe that rationale to be.

If the Catilinarian conspiracy was the most obvious first choice for a man of Sallust's views and circumstances, the Jugurthine war, at least as Sallust has set it forth, is as obviously the second. Nowhere is unscrupulous venality and unredeemed corruption so absolute. Elsewhere we feel that individual cases of dishonest rapacity are exceptional and meet with general as well as judicial reprobation. But the corruption of the aristocrats in the *Jugurtha* is not due to personal wickedness and brings no personal opprobrium; it is the accepted conduct of a class. Nor is the egalitarian harangue of Marius an answer. It does show the measure of the degeneration of the aristocrats, and it discredits their claim to privilege, but it is the envy of the late-comer, not the idealist's quest for justice, that motivates Marius; as soon as he had made his way, with the help of other underprivileged men, he would likely become (as he did in fact become) as unscrupulously self-seeking as the men he attacked (85. 13–16):

Compare me now, fellow citizens, a "new man," with those haughty nobles. What they know from hearsay and reading, I have either seen with my own eyes or done with my own hands. What they have learned from books I have learned by service in the field; think now for yourselves whether words or deeds are worth more. They scorn my humble birth, I their worthlessness; I am taunted with my lot in life, they with their infamies. For my part, I believe that all men have one and the same nature, but that the bravest is the best born; and if the fathers of Albinus and Bestia could now be asked whether they would prefer to have me or those men for their descendants, what do you suppose they would reply, if not that they desired to have the best possible children?

—*J. C. Rolfe*

Even to the reader with little concern for the facts of the story or their political implications the *Jugurtha* (and the *Catiline* to a lesser degree) makes absorbing reading. The characterization of the leading figures—Jugurtha and Bocchus, Marius and Metellus—is subtle and acute, and events are presented with dramatic vividness. Sallust has no need to underscore his record of corruption; it exudes from the whole like an electric miasma and communicates a sense of pregnant tenseness to the reader. The interlarded digressions, like the speeches, are relevant and carry the story forward; they do not distract but enhance the reader's interest. Like Thucydides from whom he learned the art, and like Tacitus who learned from him, Sallust contrives his archaic Catonian vocabulary and his ingenious but terse syntax to keep his reader's attention alert. In conception and execution the *Jugurtha* is a masterpiece.

It is therefore the more regrettable that the *History,* which antiquity pronounced Sallust's masterpiece, has all but perished. The *History* was written in five books, and again was confined to a limited segment, from 78 to 67 B.C., including the wars against Sertorius, against the slaves, and part of the war against Mithridates of Pontus. The last does not seem sufficiently significant to serve as conclusion, and it has been generally held that death prevented Sallust from reaching a more appropriate close; perhaps he was simply unwilling to perpetuate the memory of Pompey's triumphs. Aside from insignificant fragments, some on palimpsests of the eighth century, all that remains of the *History* are four speeches, attributed to M. Aemilius Lepidus, L. Marcius Philippus, C. Licinius Macer, and C. Aurelius Cotta, and a letter to Arsaces attributed to Mithridates; these were preserved in a Sallustian anthology compiled as a textbook in rhetoric and are fine specimens of Sallust's style. The fragments of the history show that it was written in the same style and with the same political orientation as the monographs. Here is a characteristic passage (1.12, Maurenbrecher):

A powerful oligarchy to whom the generality has yielded has usurped dominance under the honorable title of patrician or plebeian. All being equally corrupt, they are styled good citizens or bad not for their merits to the commonwealth but in the measure that their wealth makes them too powerful to be called to account; and because they defend the *status quo* they are accounted good men.

In the Augustan reaction Sallust's reputation suffered, but he soon came into his own, as historian and stylist. Velleius Paterculus (2. 36.2) and Quintilian (10.1.101) regard him as the equal of Thucydides; his muscular style and archaizing vocabulary continued to be admired, and served as the supreme model to the classicizing age of Hadrian.

In addition to these indubitably Sallustian works there are three smaller items of which the authorship has been questioned: an invective against Cicero, and two pamphlets addressed to Caesar. The invective is accompanied by a reply attributed to Cicero—surely a pseudepigraphon composed by some defender of Cicero of unknown date. But the invective itself shows perfect knowledge of the historical situation, is written with evident sincerity, and contains nothing which Sallust might not have said; there seems to be no valid reason for denying his authorship. Of the pamphlets addressed to Caesar the chronological order is reversed; the first presumes that the civil war has been won, whereas the second envisages a date at the outbreak of the war. The first admonishes Caesar to use his victory to introduce reforms into the national economy. Money must be deprived of its power, free enterprise and wealth must both be limited; this would effect a moral improvement in the populace, which had been corrupted by the dole system. Obligations for military service should be equalized. The second pamphlet similarly condemns the policy of the oligarchs and urges a program of reform to rejuvenate the polity. Specific reforms suggested have to do with colonization, greater accessibility to public office, regularization of the jury system, senatorial elections, the franchise. The pamphlet closes with a passionately patriotic apostrophe to Caesar. Again, there is nothing in the matter of these *Suasoriae* (as they are generally called) which precludes Sallustian authorship; on the contrary, they show expert familiarity with the contemporary scene and its urgent problems, and we know of no one else to whom they might be better ascribed. The one objection that may be offered is that their style is unlike that of Sallust's other work; but these pamphlets would have been composed before Sallust turned seriously to a career of writing, and we have a precise parallel in Tacitus, whose early *Dialogue on Orators* shows no trace of the developed Tacitean style.

Cornelius Nepos, who was Sallust's senior by a dozen years and to whom Catullus dedicated his poems as "the only Italian courageous enough to set forth the whole history of the world in three learned and laboriously wrought volumes," was a much more conventional writer. His innovations were not in style or outlook but in the introduction of literary genres new to Latin. He was born about 100 B.C. in the Po country and possessed equestrian means. He did not attempt a political career but devoted himself exclusively to literature and was on terms of intimacy with Cicero and Atticus as well as other literary figures. He survived Atticus, who died in 32, and wrote a eulogistic biography of him.

Nepos' literary interests were historical and antiquarian, but he was a collector rather than a critical scholar. For his readers' entertainment he offered such fare as he himself found entertaining— collections of facts, biographies with a conventional moralizing turn, anecdotes; there is nothing in his writings to induce hard thought or social criticism or a sense of wonder. His concern with the non-Roman world, as evidenced by his universal history and his biographies of "barbarian" generals, is rather a symptom of the burgeoning ecumenical ideal than a considered incentive to its realization. His three-volume universal history, entitled *Chronica,* was, as Catullus said, the first Roman attempt to write universal history. For this compilation Nepos used the Greek work of Apollodorus, himself supplying the Roman data wanting in his model. The *Chronica,* as the allusion in Catullus proves, must have been written before 54. Another extensive work of Nepos, which was probably written some ten years later, and which has similarly disappeared, is his *Exempla,* a heterogeneous collection of curiosities and anecdotes, scientific, historical, or merely odd, accumulated in the course of wide reading. Like the *Chronica,* the *Exempla* was much used by later writers, especially in the kindred work of the Elder Pliny. The third category of Nepos' writing, and the only one besides his poetry (which the Younger Pliny once alludes to) in which a measure of creativity was possible, is biography; only of the biographies is a considerable representation extant.

Nepos' *De viris illustribus* originally comprised sixteen books in eight pairs, each pair containing one book on Roman and one on non-Roman personalities. Each of the pairs was apparently devoted to a separate category; the usual listing is Kings, Generals, Statesmen, Historians, Orators, Poets, Rhetoricians, and Grammarians— though the order and even the categories are doubtful. In a second edition Nepos added the lives of the "barbarian" generals Hamilcar, Hannibal, and Datames, and subjoined certain requisite paragraphs to the life of Atticus, who had died in the interval. The first edition, as the unrevised life of Atticus shows, was published in 35; the second edition was published after 32, the year of Atticus' death, and before 27, for the emperor is referred to as Caesar and not Augustus, as he was called after 27. What we have remaining from this encyclopedic work are the lives of twenty-three non-Roman generals from the period of the Persian wars to that of the Hellenistic age, a short life of the Elder Cato, and a long and fulsome life of Atticus.

Both as history and as biography the *Lives* leave much to be desired. Nepos relied on previous writers perforce, and he names a long list of authorities, but as is the way of ancient compilers who name long lists of authorities he probably derived them all from a single intermediary. In the nature of the case his scope was confined to selection and presentation. If the manifold errors in historical fact, chronology, and geography are not due to his own carelessness his selection must have been very bad. His presentation is no better. He lacks the insight necessary for apprehending the mainsprings of a character and conceiving it as a whole and the literary skill necessary for communicating a speaking likeness to the reader. Instead of leaving it to his story to demonstrate wherein the greatness of his subject lay, he must resort to merely asserting its greatness and exaggerating its merits, as if he were crying up his own merchandise. Lacking discernment for subtler distinctions, he can only vary his pattern and eke out his story with anecdotes, which may be piquant in themselves but do little to illuminate the character of his subject. The moralizations which he introduces are also meager in scope and variety. The result is a sameness; all the generals are cut from the same pattern, and might readily interchange their names and dates. In style as well as composition he can be equally immature. He is guilty of faults of taste in his occasional purple patches, and his sentence structure is sometimes awkward. Generally, however, his vocabulary is simple and his sentences short and easy to understand; this and the brevity of the individual pieces have made him a favorite schoolbook. Nor does Nepos consciously distort facts in the interest of a conviction, either about politics or human nature or even Roman patriotism, as biographers have always been tempted to do; but his restraint is rather to be credited to his superficiality than to historical integrity. The results of the restraint are sometimes admirable nevertheless; the extant brief paragraphs on Cato show a detachment unusual in literary treatments of that storm center, and the *Hannibal* is fairer to that great general than Romans were wont to be.

The warmest feeling as well as the greatest care Nepos naturally bestows on the *Life* of his friend Atticus, and he obviously thinks that Atticus' career as he describes it fully justifies his conviction of Atticus' greatness. But the Atticus who takes form before the modern reader from the pages of Nepos, whether or not he is the genuine Atticus, is a strangely unsatisfactory figure. Devotion so single-minded to the cause of maintaining one's ataraxy, indulging generous impulses only to the degree that the pleasure of such indulgence overbalances the pain, and limiting all participation in the concerns of one's fellow men by the measure of one's own comfort is hard to distinguish from selfishness. It may be significant of Nepos' own character, or of the times in which both men lived, that he found Atticus' course of life so admirable.

Aside from the fact that Nepos devoted a biography to him and Cicero addressed sixteen books of letters to him, Atticus claims a modest place of his own in Latin literature. He was not only a publisher and a sponsor of books but himself an author. His most important work was a one volume *Annalis,* which was a successful rival to Nepos' *Chronica.* Atticus' work seems to have been more systematic as well as briefer. Its central concern was with Roman data, and it covered the period from the founding of Rome to Atticus' own day. Under each year were listed significant events at home and abroad, not only wars and treaties but also important laws and even publications. Atticus also wrote a number of genealogical monographs and a Greek treatise on Cicero's consulship. His place, like Nepos', is with the scholars rather than with creative writers, and in scholarship both were sciolists.

Scholarship more professional in quality, more universal in scope, and nothing short of prodigious in quantity is associated with the name of M. Terentius Varro (116–27 B.C.), called Reatinus from his native Reate in the Sabine country to distinguish him from Varro of Atax. He was a pupil of L. Aelius Stilo, the first Roman philologist, and studied philosophy at Athens under the Academic Antiochus of Ascalon. In politics he was a Pompeian; but after he was

taken prisoner in Spain in 49 he was reconciled to Caesar, who put
him in charge of the public library. He was put on Antony's proscription lists along with Cicero but was saved by Fufius Calenus.
After the civil war he was able to continue his studies to the age of
ninety, with faculties unimpaired. Varro is indubitably the greatest
scholar and most productive writer of Rome; St. Augustine said of
him (*City of God* 6.2) that he read so much it was a wonder he
had time to write, and wrote so much it was a wonder he had time
to read. St. Jerome gave a list of his works (unfortunately extant
only in fragments) along with a list of Origen's to show that Origen,
surely the most copious writer of antiquity, had written even more
than Varro. Varro's total output has been calculated to comprise
seventy-four separate works in 620 books; only the *Res rusticae* and
five incomplete books of the twenty-five-book *De lingua Latina* are
extant. Far the greater part of his work was in the field of scholarship
and has naturally been incorporated in the works of his successors;
the greatest number of fragments comes from his principal work in
belles-lettres, the *Menippean Satires*.

Varro's chief interest was in antiquities, and in this department
his principal work was the *Antiquitates rerum humanarum et di-
vinarum* in forty-one books. Of the *Antiquitates* the first twenty-five
books dealt with *res humanae* and the last sixteen with *res divinae*,
all systematically arranged. Through St. Augustine's use of this work
in Book 6 of the *City of God*, Varro is still a prime source for Roman
religion. The *Disciplinae* in nine books was an encyclopedia of the
artes liberales, the probable order being grammar, dialectic, rhetoric,
geometry, arithmetic, astrology, music, medicine, and architecture.
The *De ora maritima* was a separate work on geography. Varro was
much interested in the history of literature; among a dozen works
in this department we may mention *De comoediis Plautinis* and *De
scaenicis originibus* in three books. He wrote fifteen books *De iure
civili*. A novel presentation of biography was the *Hebdomades vel
de imaginibus* in fifteen books. This contained seven hundred portraits of famous Romans and Greeks, each with a verse elogium and
a prose text. The subjects were arranged according to their professions—kings, poets, and the like—and constructed in an elaborate
system of sevens, whence the title. The seventy-six books of *Logis-*

torica, philosophic-historical essays in dialogue form, were more original. Each bore in its title an appropriate proper name as well as its subject, as for example, *Catus on Education, Curio on Worship, Marius on Fortune, Orestes on Madness, Pius on Peace,* and the like. From the point of view of creative literature Varro's most important work was in satire. His *Saturae Menippeae* were named for Menippus of Gadara, a Syrian Greek of the third century B.C. who adapted the Semitic form in which verse is intermingled with prose (*maqama*) in a *causerie* light in tone but serious in aim (*spoudogeloion*). The *Apocolocyntosis* of Seneca and the *Satyrica* of Petronius reflect this form. There are some six hundred fragments of the *Saturae Menippeae* extant, from some ninety titles out of an original hundred and fifty. Some of the titles themselves suggest the tone of the work. There are such things as *Cave canem,* " 'Ware the dog"; *Nescis quid vesper serus vehat,* "You Don't Know What Late Evening Will Bring"; *Idem Atti quod Titi,* "Sauce for the Goose Is Sauce for the Gander"; *Est modus matulae,* "The Jordan Has Its Measure"; *Cras credo hodie nihil,* "Tomorrow I Believe, Today No." Some show the Cynic affiliations of the form: "The Cynic as Preacher," "The Funeral of Menippus." Many bear the names of figures from mythology: "Prometheus," "Eumenides," "Meleager," "Endymion," "Tithonus." The scraps of these satires which survive make their loss appear one of the most regrettable in Latin literature.

We turn now to the extant works. The *Res rusticae,* preserved complete, Varro wrote for his wife Fundania when "my eightieth year admonishes me to gather up my pack before I set forth from life." The three books are devoted, respectively, to agriculture proper, cattle, and smaller stock such as poultry and bees. The work starts with an invocation to the appropriate deities, a full bibliography of previous writers on the subject, and a prospectus of arrangement; it is part of Varro's reference book style to construct elaborate divisions and subdivisions. The prefaces and some of the exchanges in the dialogue make agreeable reading and show some wit; the body of the work is in an abrupt and unadorned textbook style, and shows the author's competence in his subject. He takes occasion to smile at such incantations as Cato recommended (1.2.27), and he has an interesting anticipation of the notion of bacilli (1.12.2):

In the neighborhood of swamps . . . there are bred certain minute creatures which cannot be seen by the eyes, which float in the air and enter the body through the mouth and nose and there cause serious diseases.

—*W. D. Hooper and H. B. Ash*

Varro praises agriculture over urban employments, and Italian agriculture over all other; it was part of his purpose to reawaken interest in country life, and in this he anticipates Vergil of the *Georgics*.

The *De lingua Latina* in twenty-five books was dedicated to Cicero and published before Cicero's death in 43. As in Varro's other works, the arrangement was elaborate: the first book was an introduction and the remainder was divided into four groups of six books each, each group being subdivided by its subject matter into two halves of three books each. Books 5–10 survive, and even of these only Books 5 and 6 are complete. Books 2–7 dealt with the origin of words and their application to things and ideas. Books 8–13 dealt with the derivations of words from other words, including declensions and conjugations. Arguments for the opposing principles of Anomaly ("Irregularity") based on popular usage, and Analogy ("Regularity") based on relation of form to form are set forth. Varro favors Analogy, as did Caesar in his treatise on the subject. Books 14–25 treated of syntax, the latter books with special attention to stylistic and rhetorical embellishment. Varro makes no effort to make the reading of this book delightful. It is written in a lumpy textbook style, and the pleasure it gives is the pleasure derived from leafing through a dictionary. There is much etymologizing, some correct and some wrong, and much incidental information on the objects and usages of private life, on the topography of Rome, and on other matters. The remarkable thing is not that professional moderns have found so many errors in Varro's linguistic science but that they have found so few; it must be remembered that linguistics was but one branch of our polymath's interests and that he was equally competent in many other branches.

In the scope and quality of his work Varro was unique, but there were others of similar interests. Another author of comprehensive works on grammar, theology, and various branches of natural science was Nigidius Figulus, a Pompeian in politics and a Pythagorean in philosophy, who reached the praetorship in 58. His abstruseness and love for the paradoxical are said to have militated against his influ-

ence, and he was superseded by Varro. Some dozen or two philolo-
gians of the first century B.C. are known by name. Mention may be
made of M. Antonius Gnipho, who was teacher of both Caesar and
Cicero, L. Ateius Praetextatus, surnamed Philologus, who assisted both
Sallust and Asinius Pollio; M. Epidius, who was teacher of Antony,
Augustus, and Vergil; Santra, whose biographies St. Jerome used.
Preserved among Cicero's works and bearing a close relationship to
Cicero's *De inventione* is the *Rhetorica ad Herennium* in four books.
It was written about 85 B.C. by an unknown author upon the request
of Herennius and is our oldest work on Latin style. The work starts
with a discussion of the five familiar divisions of rhetoric—invention,
arrangement, delivery, memory, style—as applied to the judicial,
deliberative, and demonstrative modes of speech. The entire fourth
book is devoted to delivery. The doctrine is a fusion of Greek systems; the illustrations, terminology, and spirit are Roman. We have
record of a number of writers on science, agriculture, domestic economy, augury, and law. In law the great name is that of Servius
Sulpicius Rufus, friend and correspondent of Cicero, a distinguished
orator, who is said to have written no fewer than 180 learned books
on the law.

VII

CICERO

FOR NO NATIONAL GROUP IS IT SO EASY TO CHOOSE
a single representative author as it is for Rome. Not only in the
volume and scope of his work but in its form and spirit, in its
strength and its weakness, Cicero is the perfect embodiment of Latin
literature. He was a public figure, and the central interest of his life
was the state and his position in the state. His chief literary function
and his greatest success was in the public capacity of orator, and
the most competent of his essays deal with oratory. When he deigned
to regard philosophy and poetry in his retirement from public employment he felt constrained to justify such un-Roman pursuits by
their political usefulness and made them strictly utilitarian. His literary as well as his political career (for a Cicero the distinction is
virtually meaningless) was devoted to the service of the idea of Rome.
Nor does he seek to refine or enlarge that idea, for he is a conformist,
not a rebel. If Vergil's famous *Tu Romane memento* lines at the
end of the sixth *Aeneid* strike the keynote of Rome's function in
civilization, Cicero is the perfect example of that function in operation. The heart of his creed was traditional order and administration,
and he is the single greatest conserver and transmitter of cultural
values to European posterity. His was the language which gave
shape to civilized discourse in the countries of Europe, and his popu-
larizations transmitted so much of the philosophic thought of the
ancients as the Middle Ages were prepared to receive. For the centuries during which Europe was a cultural unit, its unifying force,
so far as an individual could provide one, was Cicero.

Marcus Tullius Cicero was born in 106 B.C. in Arpinum, from
which Marius, Rome's other great "new man," had derived. His
father took him and his younger brother Quintus to Rome to provide
them with a good education. He became acquainted with the doctrines of the three leading philosophical schools, preferred the Stoic
to the Epicurean, and the Academic to both. He listened to the
eminent orators M. Antonius (grandfather of the triumvir) and L.
Crassus and heard Apollonius Molon's lectures on rhetoric. He

attended the consultations of Q. Mucius Scaevola, the venerable augur, and of his younger kinsman, the pontifex maximus C. Mucius Scaevola. His first important legal case was the defense of Sextus Roscius of Ameria in 80 (he had tried several lesser cases the preceding year), and whether for reasons of health or because his defense of Roscius had offended Sulla, he went abroad for two years in 79 and heard lectures in philosophy and rhetoric at Athens and in Rhodes. On his return he pleaded in important cases and started his political career, becoming quaestor in 75. His defeat of his principal rival Hortensius in the prosecution of Verres in 70 left him the recognized leader of the Roman bar. In 69 he was curule aedile and in 66 praetor. He was elected to the consulship for 63 because as an *eques* (and so a defender of the banking interests) he was a safe man, whereas his opponent Catiline openly advocated cancellation of debts. As consul he suppressed the Catilinarian conspiracy, but the execution without the sanction of the people of certain conspirators who were Roman citizens antagonized the *populares.* Cicero's political ideal of maintaining harmony among the orders by the cooperation of all optimates was unrealistic in view of the ruthless party and personal rivalries. To gain their individual ends Caesar, Pompey, and Crassus formed a coalition (the First Triumvirate). Cicero finally rejected an invitation to cooperate with the triumvirs at the end of 60, and was left without their or the senate's protection. Clodius as tribune effected Cicero's exile in 58, but he was recalled in 57 and resumed his practice at the bar. When Caesar and Pompey were estranged after the deaths of Julia (Caesar's daughter and Pompey's wife) and Crassus, Pompey veered to the senate. Cicero was proconsul of Cilicia in 51/50; he returned from his proconsulship on the verge of the outbreak of civil war and joined Pompey. Caesar permitted him to return to Rome in 47, but he remained in political retirement. He had no part in the assassination of Caesar in March, 44, but he applauded it and reentered public life to attack Antony. He was proscribed by the Triumvirate (Octavian yielding him to Antony) and was put to death in December 43.

About 76 Cicero married Terentia, a wealthy and strong-minded woman, who bore him a daughter, Tullia, and a son, Marcus. His work brought him considerable wealth (in the form of legacies and the like; Roman lawyers did not receive direct fees), and he possessed a number of villas and a fine city house. In 47 he divorced Terentia and married his young ward Publilia; after the death of Tullia in 45 he sent her away and devoted himself to writing until the Ides. The personality of Cicero as well as the facts of his public career are easy to read from the extensive body of private correspondence which he has left behind; no other figure of antiquity, and few of modern times, stands so clearly revealed. If we find him a good deal of a trimmer and inordinately vain, we might well ask how many comparable figures in history would better pass scrutiny under such merciless light. If his views of politics and society were limited, we must recognize that it was inevitable for a man of his background to identify the interests of the state and of civilization with those views. For his faltering and his compromises there is one sufficient answer: he suffered death for his views. He is the shining example of the lawyer and politician in a republic making of his lawyership an art and of his politics statesmanship. And he transcended the ordinary measure of lawyer and politician by his concern for the cultural values of the race; he was not merely a patron of learning but set his own hand to propagating the wisdom of the past and making it accessible to all.

From Cicero's public career the student of politics has much to learn of the ways of men in political crises, and his ethical essays have educated generation upon generation of young gentlemen. But it was to oratory that he devoted his most strenuous and most continuous efforts, and it is in his quality as orator that he was preeminent in his own sight and in that of his contemporaries. We turn next, therefore, to Cicero's work as orator; but first a word must be said of the state of Roman oratory when he appeared on the scene. As the principal key to a public career no accomplishment was so important in republican Rome as oratory, and by Cicero's school days the Greek conception of oratory as an art had been established in Rome. The dominant style, in Cicero's youth, was the so-called Asianic, in which Cicero himself (*Brutus* 95.325) distinguishes two directions:

There are two types of oratorical technique which may be denominated Asianic, of which one is epigrammatic, euphuistic, and marked more by artful and charming structure than by weight or profundity of content. . . .

The other type is not so notable for the abundance of aphorisms as for a swift and passionate torrent of speech . . . and yet that oratorical flood is characterized by a careful and elegant choice of words.

—*H. M. Poteat*

His great rival Q. Hortensius Hortalus (114–50), Cicero tells us, combined both aspects of Asianism. Hortensius' oratory gained him the consulship in 69; his speeches were collected, and he also left a handbook of rhetorical commonplaces and other literary works. The reaction to the Asianic style was the Attic, modeled upon the unadorned simplicity of Lysias; the principal representative of the Attic style about 60 B.C. was C. Licinius Calvus, of whom mention has been made as a poet of the Alexandrian school. A collection of twenty-one of his speeches was highly regarded. Cicero found the one style as bare as the other was ornate, and upon his return from Rhodes in 77 he came forward as the representative of a combination of Asianism and Atticism which has been described as Rhodian eclecticism. Cicero's style has a richness of vocabulary, great beauty of phrasing, an amplitude verging on the redundant, and extraordinary attention to cadence at the close of periods. He does not have the passion of a Demosthenes but he is effective in pathos, and when his side was represented by several speakers he was always chosen to give the summation. In lawsuits he was almost always on the side of the defendant. Most of his political speeches were delivered in the senate, where his own party held the majority, but he could be effective with the multitude also, as when he persuaded them to relinquish a land law which was put forward ostensibly for their advantage.

Cicero's extant speeches number fifty-eight, some incomplete; forty-eight others are known to be lost. The earliest extant speech (in it he refers to previous appearances in court) is *Pro Quinctio* (81 B.C.), which involves highly complicated litigation arising out of a partnership. The case itself is interesting for its illumination of certain intricacies of Roman private law. Though he was only twenty-five, Cicero was able to hold his own against the formidable Hortensius. His real debut was the *Pro Sexto Roscio Amerino* (80 B.C.), in which he defended Roscius from a trumped-up charge of murder and in doing so offended Chrysogonus, a powerful freedman of Sulla. Roscius' father had been murdered, and two of his kinsmen had connived with Chrysogonus to put his name on the proscription list so that his property should be confiscated and Chrysogonus could buy it for a song. To rest secure in their ill-gotten gains the conspirators then charged the defendant with murdering his father. Cicero is careful to praise Sulla himself in the highest terms, but his vehemence against Chrysogonus is unmitigated. In later years Cicero himself acknowledged that this speech is ornate and redundant (*Orator* 107). *Pro Roscio Comoedo* (77 B.C.?) is again an interesting bit of private litigation. The famous actor Roscius (who had been Cicero's own teacher in gesticulation) had received half the ownership of a gifted slave named Panurgus in consideration of making an accomplished actor, and hence a lucrative property, of him. But Panurgus was slain, and the slayer had satisfied Roscius' civil claim (there was no other for a slave) with a piece of land, and Roscius' partner with a cash payment. The land which Roscius received had appreciated greatly in value, and the partner brings suit for a share of the increment. The style of *Pro Roscio Comoedo* is the terser of the Asianic styles. The alternative dating of 66 B.C. is rendered unlikely by Cicero's reference (44) to his own youth.

The foundation of Cicero's reputation was his brilliant impeachment (70 B.C.) of Verres for maladministration in Sicily. He undertook the prosecution at the prompting of Pompey; the defense was represented by Hortensius. The first of Cicero's seven speeches on the subject is the *Divinatio in Caecilium,* in which he successfully claimed the right to appear as prosecutor. He chides Hortensius for having accepted so unworthy a client and asserts that Hortensius has now found an opponent worthy of him. Cicero's efficiency and despatch forestalled a scheme of the opposition to postpone trial until a more favorable judge should come into office. The evidence in his *Actio prima* was so devastating that Verres, foreseeing the result, went into exile. The five speeches which followed, comprising the *Actio secunda,* were never delivered but were carefully elaborated for publication. Their liveliness and clarity and the wide variety of interests they treat give them high rank among Cicero's efforts. They are incidentally among our most important sources for provincial government, the history of Sicily, and the masterpieces of art in that island. The fiction of actual delivery is carried out skillfully (4.5):

"The statues themselves are called Canephoroe, but I can't think who the artist was. Who, did you say? Ah yes, quite right; it was Polyclitus." *Pro Tullio,* perhaps anterior to the Verrines, is in prosecution of a veteran of Sulla who had destroyed the country house of the plaintiff. The fragmentary *Pro Fonteio* (69 B.C.) was in defense of a charge of maladministration in Gaul, of the same category as Cicero had prosecuted in the case of Verres. The *Pro Caecina* of the same year turns on the point whether illegal force had been used in opposing Caecina's taking possession of a plot of land of which Caecina's late wife had been a life tenant.

The year of his praetorship (66) marks a stage in Cicero's oratorical progress. The *De imperio Cn. Pompeii* in support of the Manilian law which gave Pompey the command in the war against Mithridates and Tigranes is Cicero's first political speech. It is a brilliant and eloquent rhetorical piece but superficial with regard to basic questions of policy, and it casts a dubious light on Cicero's political integrity. His motive was simply to secure his own political future by attaching himself to the most powerful figure on the political stage, who was at the moment using the people, and would presently use the senate, to make himself supreme. In another three years Cicero would be on the conservative side, where his natural inclinations belonged; and Pompey, also a conservative, would leave Cicero in the lurch and come to terms with Caesar, who would then sweep them both away. The *Pro Cluentio,* of the same year, a defense on a charge of poisoning, is equally eloquent and more dramatic; the speech is the nearest thing to a detective thriller bequeathed by antiquity. The web of murder, incest, abortion, forgery, bribery is so tangled that a student of the case requires genealogical and chronological tables to keep the lurid events in order. The level of morality, not only among the principals but among the judicial officials, is shockingly low, and supplies an obverse of the coin of which political demoralization is the reverse. The speech had a great vogue in antiquity; Quintilian cites it almost fifty times and quotes Cicero's own boast that "he had thrown dust in the eyes of the jury" (2.17.21).

In 63 Cicero attained the consulship with the support of the senatorial party and was obliged to oppose the moves of the *populares*. Rullus, acting for Caesar, had introduced an agrarian bill whose ostensible aim was to relieve poverty and provide for the surplus population of Rome. In three speeches *Contra Rullum* (the first in the senate, the others before the people) Cicero attacks the bill as being a wholly impractical and dishonest demagogic device. Most scholars agree that the motive for the bill was purely political, but there are significant dissents. "The measure," writes Dr. E. G. Hardy, "was a singularly cool and adroit piece of statecraft, providing the popular leaders with not one but several *points d'appui* against the threatened predominance of Pompey and at the same time containing schemes for the improvement of agrarian conditions." Cicero was successful in blocking the Rullan bill, but he failed, with the *Pro C. Rabirio,* in the defense of an aged senator who was charged, at the instigation of Caesar, with having murdered a popular leader 37 years before. Cicero went so far as to say that he wished he could claim for Rabirius the honor of having killed the enemy of the Roman people.

The same political alignment governs the prosecution of the Catilinarian conspiracy, which fell in the last two months of Cicero's consulship and marked the crisis of his career. Catiline was undoubtedly guilty of an anarchic conspiracy, for even Sallust makes no defense of him; but though Catiline himself was criminal, the movement itself could not have arisen without a large measure of popular discontent with senatorial rule. The first of Cicero's four speeches *In Catilinam,* delivered in the senate on November 8, charges Catiline with his guilty project; the second, delivered to the people on the following day, reports the proceedings in the senate and the flight of Catiline. The third, delivered to the people on December 3, reports the arrest of the conspirators who had remained in Rome and the evidence found in the hands of the Allobroges. The fourth, delivered in the senate on December 5, declares that no punishment is too great for the crime and that the consul is ready to execute whatever penalty might be pronounced. When it appeared likely that life imprisonment would be voted Cato delivered a slashing speech in favor of capital punishment and carried the day. The best that Caesar could do was to prevent the confiscation of the culprits' estates.

While the Catilinarian affair was in progress Cicero delivered the *Pro Murena* in defense of the consul-elect for 62 against a charge of bribery. Associated with Cicero in the defense were Hortensius and

Crassus; the prosecutors were Cato and the defeated candidate Sulpicius. Cicero touches but lightly on the merits of the case, for Murena was doubtless guilty; he contents himself with saying that it is better to have a Murena than a Catiline as consul, and with satirizing the quibbles of the legal profession, represented by Sulpicius, and quirks of the Stoic philosophy, represented by Cato. Immediately after his consulship Cicero delivered the *Pro Sulla,* in defense against a charge of complicity in the Catilinarian conspiracy. Cicero offers an alibi for Sulla and declares that none of the investigations had indicated Sulla's complicity. At least a collateral motive for Cicero's interest was a desire to win the support of Sulla's powerful friends (Sulla was probably a nephew of the dictator) for the struggle with Clodius which he saw looming. Also in 62 falls the *Pro Archia,* in defense of the status of the Greek poet whose citizenship had been impugned. The legal points are passed over very lightly, and the speech turns to a panegyric of literature. Even those who insist that literature must be functional may find the arguments here presented somewhat banausic: Cicero finds poetry useful because it offers respite and refreshment for serious occupations, because it affords examples useful in oratory, and because it provides an incentive to distinction by its promise of making great deeds immortal. It is pleasant nevertheless to find that such a delightfully irrelevant discourse could be delivered in a Roman court of law. The Catilinarian conspiracy comes up again in the *Pro Flacco* (59), a defense in a charge of extortion against a proconsul of Asia, when Cicero acknowledges the aid he had received from Flaccus in suppressing the conspiracy. Again the charge was probably impossible to refute, and Cicero resorts to impugning the character of the witnesses—mere Asiatic Greeks and Jews. His paragraph on the latter has a familiar ring (28):

There follows the odium that is attached to Jewish gold. This is no doubt the reason why this case is being tried not far from the Aurelian Steps [where Jews congregated]. You desired this place and that crowd, Laelius, for this trial. You know what a big crowd it is, how they stick together, how influential they are in assemblies. So I will speak in a low voice so that only the jurors may hear; for those are not wanting who would incite them against me and against every respectable man. . . . Even while Jerusalem was standing and the Jews were at peace with us, the practice of their sacred rites was at variance with the glory of our empire, the dignity of our name, the customs of our ancestors. But now it is even more so, when that

nation by its armed resistance has shown what it thinks of our rule; how
dear it was to the immortal gods is shown by the fact that it has been conquered, reduced to a subject province, made a slave.

—*Louis E. Lord*

In 58 Cicero was exiled, and after his recall in 57 he delivered four
speeches which relate to the exile. In the first, *Post reditum in senatu,*
he thanks the senate for promoting his recall; in the second, *Post
reditum ad quirites,* he thanks the people at large; in the third, *De
domo sua,* he claims restitution of his house on the Palatine, which
had been illegally "consecrated" by Clodius; and in the fourth, *De
haruspicum responsis* (56), he argues that reported omens indicating
profanation of sacred places referred not to his violations but to
Clodius'. These speeches are puerile in their swagger, malignity, and
forced rhetoric, and in the eighteenth and early nineteenth centuries
they were believed spurious; today all scholars accept them as genuine.
Several other speeches of 56 grow out of the enmity of Clodius. *Pro
Sestio* defends a tribune of 57 in a suit *de vi* brought at the instance
of Clodius. *In Vatinium* is the prosecution of a witness who had
given evidence against Sestius. *Pro Caelio* is another document illus-
trative of moral degeneration. The defendant was charged with having borrowed money from Clodia (Clodius' sister) to bribe slaves to
murder an Alexandrian envoy, and with having attempted to poison
Clodia when she demanded repayment.

Caesar and Pompey were now collaborating in their coalition, and
in an attempt to initiate an independent senatorial program Cicero
gave notice that he would move to reconsider Caesar's agrarian legislation. He was promptly told both directly and through his brother
that he must submit or suffer, and he came to heel with one of his
finest efforts, the *De provinciis consularibus,* advocating the prolonga-
tion of Caesar's assignment in Gaul. Cicero eulogizes Caesar, but
vents his animosity on Piso and Gabinius, the consuls of 58 who
had helped to exile him, by proposing their recall from Macedonia
and Syria. When Piso complained, Cicero delivered a virulent reply
in the *In Pisonem.* This speech contains interesting remarks on the
Epicurean philosopher and poet Philodemus. Cicero served the triumvirs again in defending the citizenship of their friend in the *Pro
Balbo.* The *Pro Plancio* (54) defends an aedile (who had befriended

Cicero when he was in exile) on the charge of procuring his election by bribery. The speech throws much light on electioneering methods in Rome and in particular on the part played by voting clubs. In the *Pro C. Rabirio Postumo* (54) Cicero is forced to defend a creature of Caesar on an apparently well-founded accusation of extorting money from Ptolemy Auletes, though he had protested to his brother (*Ad Quintum fratrem* 3.1.5) that he would never defend Gabinius, a creature of Pompey and Rabirius' senior partner in the extortion. The Clodian affair is wound up in the *Pro Milone* (52), which argues that the murder of Clodius was in self defense. Partisans of Clodius in the court room are said to have so frightened Cicero that he was unable to deliver his speech; the beautifully constructed plea we have was specially prepared for publication. When he received a copy of it at Massilia, whither he had retired in exile after his condemnation, Milo is said to have remarked: "It is as well that Cicero did not deliver it, for had he done so I should never have known the excellent flavor of these Massilian mullets."

In 51/50 Cicero was proconsul in Cilicia, and in 49 he joined Pompey in Greece. When Caesar permitted him to return to Rome after the civil war, he naturally retired from the Forum. He did deliver a group of three so-called Caesarian speeches, all pleas for clemency, and all in a tone at which Caesar could not possibly take offense. *Pro Marcello* (46) is an eloquent plea for the pardon of a former Pompeian. The flattery amounting to adulation bestowed on Caesar would seem to be either insincere time-serving or proof of a very rapid and complete conversion. Cicero may well have come to believe that the salvation of Rome lay in Caesar; but in that case it is hard to take his gloating cry of triumph when he heard of the assassination. One of the assassins proved to be Q. Ligarius, the subject of the *Pro Ligario,* a similarly eloquent and successful plea for pardon. The third of the Caesarian speeches, *Pro rege Deiotaro* (45), is a defense of the Galatian king on the charge of an attempt to murder Caesar, brought by the king's grandson. It is not unlikely that Caesar himself promoted the charge, out of a desire to be rid of the king; in any event he postponed decision in this case. In a letter to his son-in-law Dolabella Cicero speaks slightingly of this speech (*Ad familiares* 9.12):

Read it, if you like, but please remember that it was a slight and insignificant affair, scarcely worth writing out. I wanted to pay a tribute to an old
time host and friend—coarse home-spun, like his own gifts.

—N. H. Watts

Cicero had not been privy to the plot of the Ides, but news of its
success galvanized him into an active campaign against the relicts
of Caesarism. The oratorical precipitate of this campaign are the
fourteen *Philippic* orations directed against Antony, who presumed to
the succession, during the last four months of 44 and the first four of
43. The title is derived from the speeches of Demosthenes against the
father of Alexander the Great, and its literary ring is perhaps an echo
of the ultimate futility of words amidst the active passions of revolution. The *First Philippic* is moderate in tone; only Antony's public
acts, not his private life, are criticized, and an appeal is made to his
patriotism. Antony replied with a heated invective against Cicero, to
which the *Second Philippic,* never actually delivered, purports to be
the answer. Cicero first refutes Antony's charges against himself and
then proceeds to a scathing invective of Antony's life and works since
childhood. The speech is Cicero's masterpiece in its kind. Now only
blood could settle the bitterness between the two men. The *Third
Philippic* denounces Antony in the senate as a public enemy, and the
Fourth repeats the charge to the people, who shouted (so he says in
the *Sixth Philippic*) that he had for a second time saved the state.
The *Fifth Philippic* advocates that Antony be officially bidden to de-
sist from besieging Brutus in Mutina; the *Sixth* reports his action to
the people and exhorts them to exert themselves for liberty. "Other
nations can endure slavery," he closes, "the assured possession of the
Roman people is liberty." In the *Sixth Philippic* Cicero complains of
the half-hearted measures of the senate: Antony is a public enemy,
and there can be no compromise. To the proposals of the senate Antony made counterproposals which Cicero called intolerable. It was
proposed that the disturbance be called a "tumult" rather than a
"war," and Antony an *inimicus* rather than a *hostis;* in the *Seventh
Philippic* Cicero insisted there was a state of war and proposed that
those who laid down their arms by a given date should be amnestied
and the others treated as traitors. The *Ninth Philippic* proposes a
public statue in honor of Servius Sulpicius Rufus, who had died on
the embassy to Antony; it had been objected that statues were erected

only to ambassadors who were killed in performance of their duty, and Cicero insists that Sulpicius' case fell under the rule and that his statue would moreover serve as a monument to Antony's infamy. Sulpicius was the author of the 180 treatises on law, mentioned above at the end of Chapter VI, and had written Cicero a very beautiful letter of consolation on the death of Tullia (*Ad familiares* 4.5). The *Tenth Philippic* urges that Brutus' *de facto* tenure of Greece be made *de jure;* the *Eleventh* urges that Cassius be recognized as governor of Syria and ordered to oppose Antony's partisan Dolabella. The *Twelfth Philippic* opposes the despatch of a second mission to Antony, for which it had been proposed that Cicero himself be a member. Feelers for peace were disturbed by a letter in which Antony reiterated his determination to persist in his position and to avenge Caesar. The *Thirteenth Philippic* is a minute criticism of this letter, showing the futility of hopes for peace. The last *Philippic* proposes a public thanksgiving for the defeat of Antony at Mutina, showing by historical examples that such action was tantamount to branding Antony a public enemy; Cicero also urges the erection of a monument in honor of those who had fallen in the fight. The last words of the eulogy to the fallen soldiers are *qui morte vicerunt,* "who have become victors by death." These are Cicero's last public words, and might be appropriately applied to himself. Antony formed a triumvirate with Octavian and Lepidus, and at least for the fate of Cicero had his way; Cicero was proscribed and met his death at the end of 43.

In our world rhetoric has fallen upon hard times. We seldom use the word except in a disparaging sense, and usually with the prefix "mere," to denote turgid artificiality in vocabulary and syntax. But the word and the thing have their legitimate uses; discourse is a human product. and therefore susceptible to the refinements of art, and the rules of the art are capable of being set down. Like other arts which are practiced socially and continuously—the art of table manners, for example—we learn the art of discourse by imitation, but handbooks of etiquette have their place nevertheless. Orators may unconsciously follow the rules of the handbooks, as poets may lisp in numbers; but somewhere in the consciousness of the lisping poet are the examples of predecessors who labored over the art, and orators who would be offended if the word "rhetoric" were applied to their efforts have assimilated the end product of classical theory and practice. Mr. Winston Churchill's periods are unmistakably Ciceronian, whether or not he conned Cicero's treatises, which they would not have been if Cicero's treatises had not served as Europe's textbooks in the art of discourse through the centuries. Cicero himself was doubtless magnificently endowed by nature, but he composed his speeches strictly according to theory, as the studious elaboration of the rhythmic clausulae at the ends of his periods demonstrates. He considered himself an artist in words, and from his earliest youth and throughout his life occupied himself with the theory of his art and its history.

His earliest product in this kind, written when he was not beyond twenty, is the *De inventione,* in two long books. This is a stiff and formal textbook defining the parts of a speech, the various species of speeches, and the treatment appropriate to each; subsequently Cicero prefixed a general defense of eloquence as an introduction. The relationship of this work to the *Rhetorica ad Herennium* offers a nice philological problem. It can be proven with equal plausibility that each borrowed from the other, and the only solution is the likely one that both drew from the same antecedent Greek handbooks on the subject. There were many such; Aristotle himself had not disdained to write one. A far more masterly work, and one worthy of the high opinion which Cicero himself entertained of it (*Ad Atticum* 13.19.4; compare *Ad familiares* 1.9.23), are the three books *De oratore,* written in 55 when Cicero was at the height of his artistic power but had been forced to withdraw from public life by the renewed coalition of Caesar and Pompey. The book is a serious effort by a responsible expert to put the fruit of his own experience on record for the benefit of future statesmen. He tells his brother Quintus, to whom the book is addressed, that it is intended to replace his youthful essays in the subject, and points out the great difficulty, as well as the great usefulness, of the orator's art. The book is in dialogue form; the fictive date of the dialogue is 91 B.C., and the participants are the greatest orators of the day, L. Licinius Crassus and M. Antonius (grandfather of the triumvir), P. Sulpicius Rufus, and C. Aurelius Cotta, besides others who appear intermittently. In Book 1 Mucius Scaevola the augur appears, and in Books 2 and 3 Q. Lutatius Catulus, the co-conqueror of the Cimbri, and C. Julius Caesar Strabo; both were interested in oratory and both were writers. The dialogue is not of the Platonic type, where ideas take shape through the combined efforts of the interlocutors by means of dialectic, but rather an eliciting of conclusions already formed by means of catechism. Nevertheless Cicero is careful to attribute the proper dramatic character and the proper range of information and interests to the appropriate speaker. Thus the five familiar divisions of rhetoric are not treated in order; Antonius appropriately deals with *inventio, dispositio,* and *memoria* in the second book, Crassus with *elocutio* and *pronuntiatio* in the third. Remarks on wit and the ludicrous are appropriately assigned to Caesar (2.219 ff.); this and the sections on the study of the law (1.162–200) and on historiography (2.51 ff.) serve as a relief to the technical passages. Cicero's aim, indeed, is to harmonize rhetoric with philosophy, to advance the craft to the status of a science. This is the substance of the first book, in which Crassus maintains the necessity of universal education for the orator and Antonius denies it. The range and versatility of Cicero's own interests is remarkable. The evaluation of Greek historians from Herodotus and Thucydides to Callisthenes and Timaeus was something new in Latin. There are remarks on the value of the study of philosophy, on the need of a convenient codification of the law, on many other subjects. The responsibility of the orator is very great; he must be expert in all other subjects as well as in oratory, and he must be able to lead men to true judgment against their own nature (2.178):

Nothing in oratory is more important than to win for the orator the favor of his hearer, and to have the latter so affected as to be swayed by something resembling a mental impulse or emotion, rather than by judgment or deliberation. For men decide far more problems by hate, or love, or lust, or rage, or sorrow, or joy, or hope, or fear, or illusion, or some other inward emotion, than by reality, or authority, or any legal standard, or judicial precedent or statute.

—*E. W. Sutton and H. Rackham*

Such was the fruit of Cicero's own experience. The *De oratore* itself, like all Cicero's mature treatises, is a piece of oratory. The ease and grace of its own style, its beautiful language and harmonious periods, its flashes of wit and drama, lull the reader into obliviousness to an essential weakness in the argument; with all his persuasive eloquence

Cicero merely juxtaposes the craft and the science, but sets up no philosophical principle to establish a necessary connection between them.

The artistry of the *De oratore* is entirely wanting in the *Partitiones oratoriae,* written for the instruction of Cicero's son. In the opening paragraph Cicero speaks of having leisure to go out of town. This may refer to his first withdrawal from public life in 55 B.C. or to his second in 46; the first is the more likely date, despite the son's extreme youth at that time. Here the dialogue is an unadorned catechism, Marcus Junior putting direct questions in order and Marcus Senior answering. The three sections deal, respectively, with the functions of the orator, the structure of an oration, the species of themes. In the final chapter Cicero states that his matter is derived from the teachings of the Middle Academy, and urges his son to pursue the study of logic and moral science as taught by the Academy. Cicero himself never mentions this treatise elsewhere, and it may not have been intended for publication; its genuineness is attested by frequent mention of it in Quintilian.

The most useful single book for the student of ancient oratory is the *Brutus,* written in Cicero's enforced leisure of 46, before the issue of Thapsus was decided. The time of the dialogue is the present, and Cicero himself is the chief interlocutor, the others being Brutus and Atticus. After a useful introductory section on the Greek orators Cicero proceeds to give a critical history of Roman oratory from its beginnings to its culmination in his own person. His chronological framework he derives from Atticus' *Annalis;* his own and his teachers' experience embraced virtually the entire range of historical Roman oratory, and his list is very full. He speaks not only of his subjects' endowments and training but of the historical circumstances which conditioned their work. His gauge of criticism is the established categories of rhetorical techniques. In the matter of style his judgments are not unprejudiced; his own eclecticism he regards as the standard, and he depreciates the Atticizers. The climax of the work is the remarkable autobiographical account of Cicero's own training and development; he leaves no doubt that he regarded himself as the embodiment of Roman oratory in its perfection. The opening paragraphs speak of the recent death of Hortensius as being the incentive to the work, and Hortensius himself, who is very fairly dealt with, is the last orator discussed. "The voice of Quintus Hortensius," Cicero says, "was silenced by his own death; mine, by the death of the republic." The death of the republic did in fact mean the death of oratory. The *Brutus*, then, is remarkable in being a complete history of the most characteristic genre in Roman literature, written by the acknowledged master of that genre.

Cicero's third major work on oratory, written shortly after the *Brutus* and in a manner supplementing it and similarly addressed to Brutus, is the *Orator*. The title *De optimo genere dicendi*, by which Cicero himself several times refers to the work, indicates its nature. The subject is the delineation of the ideal orator. The efficacy of the plain, intermediate, and grand styles as applied to the various divisions of rhetoric in performing the orator's functions of instructing, pleasing, and swaying (*docere, delectare, flectere*) is dealt with. The orator must assume the appropriate tone for every contingency; this the Atticist doctrinaires are unable to do. Two incidental points are worth noting. At *Orator* 33-35 Cicero says he ventured to write the treatise only upon the insistence of Brutus (it is strange that he should be so coy about his own specialty) and he praises Brutus' remarkable success in his current administration of Gaul; he also speaks of his own *Laus Catonis*, written at this time. Apparently Cicero would have the *Laus Catonis* snuggle with the *Orator* under the shelter of Caesar's own man. Almost the whole of the last third of the book is a discussion and defense of the use of rhythm in oratory; no opposition is named, but there can be little doubt that this is a reply to an expression of pronounced views to the contrary.

The short and unpolished *De optimo genere oratorum* is another refutation of Atticism and was written at about the same time as the *Brutus* and the *Orator*. It purports to be a preface to translations of Demosthenes' *On the Crown* and Aeschines' reply, *Against Ctesiphon*, but there is no indication that these translations were ever made. The last of Cicero's rhetorical works is the *Topica*, written for C. Trebatius in July, 44. Trebatius had found a copy of Aristotle's *Topica* in Cicero's Tusculan villa and had asked Cicero to expound it: Cicero composed the present treatise, entirely from memory, on a voyage from Velia to Rhegium. But whereas the book purports to be a translation or adaptation of Aristotle's *Topica*, actually it bears little resemblance to Aristotle's work; the explanation is that Cicero was confused and remembered some Hellenistic book of similar title instead. The subject is the invention or choice of arguments, which are of two types, intrinsic and extrinsic. Extrinsic arguments are based on authority; it is the intrinsic type which concerns the orator. Intrinsic arguments are discussed with reference to fact (*sitne*), definition (*quid sit*) and quality (*quale sit*). The organization of the book is somewhat confused, and it makes no pretensions to style. In the technical aspects of rhetorical theory nothing could be added to what the Greeks had done, and Cicero's three technical treatises—*De Inventione, Partitiones, Topica*—are cramped by their dependence on the Greek. It is in the works on finished oratory—*De oratore, Brutus, Orator*—that Cicero's own achievement in the art gives him scope for his own full and polished style.

Rhetoric is caviar to the general, and only amateurs of antiquity or of forensic oratory are likely to be much concerned with Cicero's orations. Like the technical treatises on rhetoric, they have done their work, and whatever contributions they have to make have been assimilated into our own culture. The works of Cicero which may still be read not as a record of antiquity but for their relevance as a guide to our modes of thinking and the substance of our thought are his philosophical essays. No one could maintain that Cicero is a giant in speculative philosophy or that he created systems of thought. He is the first to admit that his essays are merely adaptations from the Greek: "they are mere drafts, produced with little labor: I contribute only the words, of which I have a great abundance" (*Ad Atticum* 12.52). And the Greeks from whom he borrowed were themselves not "first philosophers" but adherents of the Hellenistic schools then in vogue—Stoics, Epicureans, Academics—who were concerned not with explaining the universe but with helping men adjust themselves to it. It is in his selection and presentation that Cicero performs his great service. Not only did he transform the dry and knotty treatises of the Greeks into lucid and delightful and witty essays, but by his very selection and distribution of emphasis he informed the whole of his work with his own characteristic outlook. It is the Ciceronian element in Cicero's philosophic treatises which gives them peculiar relevance to ourselves. That relevance has been admirably pointed out by Professor Richard McKeon:

We, too, have a profound respect for culture and ideas; but we read philosophy as Cicero read the Greeks, discarding subtleties, reducing differences and distinctions, and justifying contemplation by its uses. Our philosophies and our systems of criticism are based on simple distinctions —between words and things, style and content, formal language and material language, feeling and thought, action and knowledge; and the arguments by which doctrines are established or opponents are refuted frequently depend on asserting the inseparable connections between the members of such pairs. We emphasize the practical, are dubious of certainties, seek methods of discovery, and think of action in terms of utilities and ends. Cicero's distinctions are again prevalent, not because he was a profound philosopher, nor again because he was shallow and obvious, but rather because the problems to which his distinctions are applied today, after the vast variety of their uses, interpretations and judgments in the intellectual and practical history of the West, are similar to the problems with which Cicero was concerned—the problems of a world-wide commonwealth embracing all gods and men, founded upon justice and the pursuit of common aspirations, and embodying a constitutional form and applying a rule of law, in which cultural, philosophic, and religious values will have consequences in determining practical action without the prior imposition of a common doctrine and in which communication will be adequate to keep the people aware of problems and alert in the defense of rights and freedom. The study of the philosophy of Cicero turns on the statement of problems and the development of means for their solution. In Cicero's view of philosophy the problems were those of a great practical civilization and a powerful constitutional government threatened by revolution and destroyed by dictatorship; and the means which he recommended to solve them are philosophic distinctions which can be learned by practical men as well as by technical philosophers and can be applied in the course of a busy life, in which as Crassus suggested, "what cannot be learned quickly, will never be learned at all" (*De oratore* 3.23.89). They are problems which are in desperate need of reformulation today, and they are solutions which deserve reexamination.

If Cicero were a closet philosopher his work would hardly have the relevance which Mr. McKeon points out; and if political vicissitudes had not interrupted his public career he would not have written philosophy at all. He wrote the essays only in periods of enforced retirement from public life and as an inadequate surrogate, as he himself says, for the more important contributions to the Roman state which his retirement prevented him from making. The writing of philosophy was the second best service he could perform for Roman patriotism. The Romans, he explains in the introduction to the *Tusculans* and elsewhere, had no philosophic literature, though they were fully the peers of the Greeks in intellectual capacity and their superiors in morality, because they had been preoccupied with more important matters. But it would be becoming for Rome to have the ornament of a philosophic literature also, and since no other avenue of service was open and his achievements in oratory suggested his fitness for the task, he would now undertake to supply the want. The essays have patriotic aspects besides that of supplying a becoming ornament. For one thing, the Roman constitution and Roman institutions are justified, as in the *Republic;* for another, the Epicureans, who were become associated with political subversiveness, are constantly refuted. In Cicero's first period of retirement, after the renewal of the coalition between Caesar, Pompey, and Crassus, he wrote the *Republic* and started the *Laws.* In his second retirement, after Caesar won the civil war and after the death of his beloved Tullia, Cicero wrote the large mass of his essays, and at an astonishing rate of speed.

The *De republica,* begun in 54 and published in 51, may well be regarded as Cicero's best work. This was his second large treatise after the *De oratore;* like the *De oratore* it deals with a subject in which Cicero possessed peculiar competence, but consideration of society and the state involves a good deal more of philosophy and is of more immediate concern to readers ancient and modern. Both in form and content Cicero's own contribution is greater than in the ethical treatises, though here too Cicero had the Stoic theorists, probably Panaetius, to lean upon for content and Plato's *Republic* to suggest many details of treatment. As in Plato, a large number of persons are present, though only a few carry the argument; discussions of justice and injustice, of the forms of government, the ideal statesman, the influence of the drama, are introduced; and the dialogue ends with an account of a mystical experience which carries the reader beyond the bounds of present life. Until 1820, when Cardinal Mai discovered about a third of the *De republica* in a Vatican palimpsest containing St. Augustine's commentary on the Psalms, the spiritually inspiring *Dream of Scipio* from the sixth book, which was preserved independently and with a commentary by Macrobius, was the only part of the *De republica* known. The portion now available enables us to follow the design of the whole. After preliminary conversations the question of the best form of the state is introduced. The state is defined as "an assemblage of people in large numbers associated in an agreement with respect to justice and a partnership for the common good." The three simple forms of government—kingship, aristocracy, and democracy— tend to degenerate into tyranny, oligarchy, and mob rule; the best form is a balance of the three, and of this the Roman state is the ideal example. A summary of Roman history demonstrates the excellence of the slowly builded Roman constitution. Practical statesmanship of the Roman type is a higher function than philosophy. Carneades' defense of injustice as being more expedient for individuals and states alike than justice is cited and refuted. States, like men, must follow universal law, which is "right reason in agreement with nature." As the defender and exemplar of justice the state is entitled to the devoted loyalty of its citizens, all of whose activities must be guided by the interests of the commonwealth. Even the Dream of Scipio, which directs the mind away from the immediate and transitory to the idea of abiding virtue pursued for its own sake, closes with the admonition that "the best tasks are those undertaken in defense of one's native land." Cicero found this book difficult to write (*Ad Quintum fratrem* 2.12.1) and twice changed his plan of composition. The fictive date of 129 B.C. was chosen in order to avoid giving offense to powerful contemporaries at a delicate juncture in Cicero's own affairs.

The *De legibus,* begun before the *De republica* was published, laid aside and continued in 46, and never finally completed, is conceived of as a sequel to the *Republic.* The laws described are those which would prevail in Cicero's state. The work was surely in five and possibly in eight books; three are extant. The first states as a foundation for the whole treatment of laws the thesis that all law is derived from God through our inborn sense of justice. In the second and third books codes of law concerning religion and the magistrates, respectively, are set down and commented upon. Here we have what amounts to an actual constitution of an ideal state, based in general upon the law and custom of Rome but containing much original material and a rationale. Unlike the *Republic,* the date of the *Laws* is the present, and Cicero himself is the chief speaker. The treatise provides our fullest and most explicit view of Cicero's own political ideals.

During his proconsulship in Cilicia and the civil war Cicero wrote nothing, though in 48 he was urged by Matius (*Ad familiares* 11. 27.5) to write on philosophy. He actually turned to writing only in his deep grief for the death of Tullia, and produced the lost *De consolatione* in 45. After Munda he wrote an exhortation to the study of philosophy in the lost *Hortensius,* which St. Augustine four hundred years later declared effected the great change in his own life (*Confessions* 3.4.8). He had been reading Cicero to help his speaking; he now turned to this book for its content.

For Cicero political science was the natural beginning for a kind of encyclopedia of philosophy, which was, in effect, what he had set about constructing; the next logical step was a treatise on epistemology, which he produced in the *Academica.* This work has come down to us in a peculiar condition. The first edition was in two books, named *Catulus* and *Lucullus* after the principal interlocutor in each. Of this edition the second book (sometimes called *Academica posteriora*) is extant except for the loss of a considerable portion at the end. But Cicero was not satisfied with the book as it stood and began at once to revise it. He improved the style, made the treatment more concise, divided the work into four books instead of two, complimented Varro by making him a speaker instead of the men of affairs who were not dramatically appropriate for an abstruse discussion. Of the four-book edition the first book (sometimes called *Academica priora*) has come down. In the theory of knowledge Cicero consistently adheres to the skeptical position of the New Academy, as it was natural for a lawyer to do. All the schools agreed that knowledge is derived from the senses. The Epicureans asserted that the senses are infallible; the Stoics said that sense impressions might be erroneous but that man's soul possesses a criterion given by God and developed by Stoic teaching by which man is able to correct sense impressions and to attain certainty. Both Stoics and Epicureans were thus dogmatists, believing, for different reasons, in the human ability to attain absolute knowledge. The New Academy agreed that the senses are fallible but denied the Stoic criterion; for them absolute knowledge was humanly unattainable, and the proper philosophic attitude was one of doubt and indecision. All that man could attain was probability, the conviction that certain things are more likely to be true than others, and this would serve as well as any alleged knowledge both for speculation and for practical life. As a philosophic discussion the *Academica* is disappointing. The Epicureans are dismissed with a single sentence, "Let them look to their assertions," and the lines are drawn between the Stoa and the Academy. The issue Cicero discusses less as a philosopher in search of truth than as a member of the Academy rehearsing the arguments (which sometimes descended to mere ridicule) current in the school. What we have is rather a series of assertions and denials relative to the effects of the skeptical attitude than a philosophically based argument of its essential validity. For Cicero himself release from dogmatism and the necessity for scholastic consistency enabled him, in his ethical treatises, to examine various views freely and to choose at each point what seemed, on the basis of probability, the best.

This attitude is exemplified in his next treatise, the *De finibus bonorum et malorum,* which is a consideration of the fundamental question of ancient philosophy, to wit, that of the chief good which is the final aim in life and to which lesser goods and pains are only means. This long work, in five books, is Cicero's most systematic treatment of ethics, and perhaps the fullest account we have of the doctrines of the various schools in vogue in Rome. The work thus falls into three divisions, each comprising a conversation between Cicero, in the role of critic, and spokesmen of the Epicurean, the Stoic, and the Old Academic schools respectively. The first book sets forth the theory of Epicurus, and the second refutes it; the third sets forth the theory of the Stoics, and the fourth controverts it; the fifth presents a version of Peripatetic doctrine, followed by brief adverse comment from Cicero. The spokesman for the Epicureans in the first conversation is L. Manlius Torquatus, and the fictive date is 50 B.C. In the second Cato is spokesman for the Stoics; the date is 52 and the scene Cicero's Tusculan villa, where he was spending the September holiday while the games were on at Rome. The scene of the third conversation is Athens in 79 B.C., when Cicero and his friends were studying philosophy there. As in his other philosophic essays Cicero's Greek authorities in the *De finibus* can be determined with fair plausibility. The Epicurean advocates the aim of living agreeably (*iucunde vivere*), but choices are to be made according to a correct calculus of hedonism; hence in such things as limiting appetites, destroying the fear of death, eliminating superstition, and commending voluntary retirement from existence the Epicurean system presents many points of resemblance to the Stoic. Cicero's refutation (Book 2) is unmistakably in the style of a pleading lawyer, and his illustrations are taken from courts of law and Roman history. Appetites cannot be limited but must be uprooted. The instincts of infants and animals to pleasure and pain cannot be held up (as the Epicureans held them up) as mirrors of nature, for man has a responsible intelligence and must behave like a god. In the Stoic system (Book 3) good is absolute and cannot be determined by utility; so is evil absolute—there are no degrees in sin, and a miss is as bad as a mile. Pleasure and pain in the ordinary sense belong to the class of things indifferent (*adiaphora*); man must live in accordance with nature (*secundum naturam vivere*), that is, in accordance with the eternal design of the universe. Good and evil are determined by a true insight into this design. To the Stoic position Cicero is not nearly as hostile as to the Epicurean. His refutation (Book 4) has rather the tone of bantering criticism of the rigor of their logic and their impractical perfectionism; surely a lawyer must make a distinction between a misdemeanor and a felony. The discourse of the fifth book is an Academic version of Peripatetic doctrine. A theory of conduct is to be constructed on the basis of motive. Pleasure or self-preservation are to be excluded from the domain of motive, which relates rather to the highest faculties and is bound up with the virtues of prudence, self-control, courage, righteousness. The power of the soul, non-existent or immature in animals and infants, is to be rated highest. The will is sovereign over mere endowments; the *summum bonum* is the attainment of the highest accomplishment within our highest powers. Similarities to this doctrine in the Stoic system are misappropriations with the terminology changed to avoid detection. The Academy alone is worthy of gentlemen and scholars and leaders.

The *De finibus* dealt with the pursuit of happiness in large terms of ethical theory; the *Tusculan Disputations,* begun in 45 before the *Academica* and the *De finibus* were completed and published before the Ides of 44, advised how certain classes of distractions which mili-

tate against happiness might be confronted. Cicero himself describes
the contents (*De divinatione* 2.1.2):

There followed the *Tusculan Disputations,* also in five books, which examined the essentials of happiness: the first book deals with the contempt
of death; the second, with the problem of enduring affliction; the third,
with the alleviation of grief; the fourth, with other disconcerting emotions;
and the fifth offers for consideration that proposition which most radiantly
illuminates the whole of philosophy, namely, that for the happy life virtue
is all-sufficient.

—*H. M. Poteat*

Here too Cicero uses Greek authorities, but the style is that of a free
and fluent discourse with numerous and apt quotations from the poets,
both Greek (in his own translations, of course) and Latin, and many
Roman examples. The most charming is the first book, which argues,
with a wealth of literary and historical allusion, that death is either
extinction, and hence not an evil because the dead have no awareness,
or else a transition to immortality, and hence a positive good. Socrates'
argument to the same effect is quoted at length from Plato's *Apology*.
Cicero does not consider the possibility of punishment in a future
existence, and indeed immortality seems rather to mean a survival
of reputation than any kind of persistence of personality. Of the
Phaedo an interlocutor says that he agrees with the book while reading
it, "yet when I have laid the book aside and begin to reflect in my own
mind upon the immortality of souls, all my previous sense of agreement slips away" (1.24). The second book teaches that pain must
be despised; if it is an evil, it is a slight one. Virtue makes it insignificant, and death is a ready refuge. The causes of distress (Book 3) are
due to our own mistaken opinion and hence voluntary; the sage
is capable of freeing himself from false opinions which cause distress. So are all other disconcerting emotions due to false judgments
(Book 4), the error of which can be rooted out by philosophy. In the
fifth book the teaching of the various schools is examined to show
that virtue is itself sufficient for leading a happy life; if Epicurus thinks
that the wise man is always happy then surely the philosophers who
go back to Plato must think so.

The transition to theology was natural, and it was at about this time
that Cicero executed his free version of Plato's *Timaeus,* of which con-

siderable fragments are extant. Before the Ides of March also Cicero completed his major work in theology, the three books of *De natura deorum,* which sets forth the views of the Epicureans, Stoics, and Academics on this subject. The scene is laid at the house of Cotta during the Latin festival of 77 or 76. After preliminary remarks by Cicero praising philosophy as an anodyne and justifying his own preference for the Academics, Velleius, with something of the arrogance of Epicurean certainty, reviews and ridicules the doctrines of Plato and the Stoics, and incidentally the crude anthropomorphism of the poets, and sets forth the Epicurean belief in material gods completely untroubled by concern for mankind. Cotta then refutes the Epicurean structure point by point, and declares that Epicureanism is fatal to religion. In Book 2 Balbus expounds the Stoic belief in a consistent design in the constitution of the universe; the universe is itself providence. This book is of special value in presenting the views of leading Stoic teachers which are otherwise dimly known. The detailed review of the wonders of nature and the proof of the care bestowed on man by an overruling providence are very fine. Cotta presents the Academic critique of the Stoic doctrine in Book 3. The perfection of the universe does not prove that it is animated, nor is human intelligence a portion of the divine. The last part of Cotta's discourse is lost.

The natural sequel to the *De natura deorum* is supplied by the two books *De divinatione,* the first written before the Ides and the second after. The interlocutors are Cicero himself and his younger brother Quintus, and the scene is Cicero's Tusculan villa. It is hard to exaggerate the part played by the mantic art in Rome throughout its history, not only in the official religion of the state but in the private lives of the citizens; it was treated as a science, and philosophers took cognizance of it in serious treatises. Cicero's *De divinatione* is our best source on the subject. Two general types were recognized (*De divinatione* 1.11 and 2.26): the natural or intuitive type, which was immediate in its applications, and the artificial or inductive type, which supplemented observation by conjecture. For the Stoics belief in divination was central: providence would not be benign (as in their system it must be) if some signification of the course of future events were not vouchsafed to men. The Stoic doctrine on the subject is set forth fully by Quintus in the first book; the objection that prophecies are sometimes erroneous he answers with the remark that experts in other fields also sometimes make mistakes. In the second book Cicero starts with a justification and a review of his own career, listing his major writings, and proceeds to retail the Academic arguments against divination, with numerous examples from his own experience of Roman history added. Not only is belief in divination scientifically and logically untenable, but it is no kindness to men to apprise them of their fate. This point Cicero proves, significantly, by the example of the triumvirs (2.9.22–23):

Do you imagine for a moment that it would have been useful for Marcus Crassus to know, during the heyday of his affluence and power, that he was doomed to die beyond the Euphrates in ignominy and disgrace, after his son had been slain and his forces annihilated? Or do you suppose that Gnaeus Pompey would have found any happiness in his three consulships, in his three triumphs, and in the glory of his illustrious achievements, if he had been forewarned that he would be murdered in an Egyptian wilderness, after losing his army, and that his death would be followed by those dreadful developments of which I am unable to speak without weeping? And what of Caesar? If he had known that in the Senate, of which he had selected the majority of the members, in Pompey's Senate-house and in front of the statue of Pompey himself, and under the eyes of so many of his own centurions, he would be assassinated by citizens of the very highest rank, some of whom had even been recipients of unnumbered favors at his hands, and that he would lie so dishonored that not even one of his friends— not even one of his slaves—would dare come near his body, in what torture of soul would he have passed his days!

—*H. M. Poteat*

But the most telling argument against divination is, as it is always likely to be, ridicule; this and the wealth of information on Latin and Etruscan superstitions and practices make the *De divinatione* one of the most interesting of the essays.

Another supplement to the *De natura deorum* is the *De fato,* dedicated (doubtless for prudential reasons) to Hirtius, who is the principal speaker. The subject is the problem of free will versus necessity; as the *De divinatione* differentiated religion from superstition, so the *De fato* differentiated determinism from fatalism. The first part of the essay, which presented the Stoic position, is lost; the extant fragment is the Academic analysis and denial of the Stoic view. In all of these disquisitions the thoroughgoing materialist position of the

Epicureans removes them from consideration. But though Cicero's profession and temperament inclined him to the Academic attitude, there was much in Stoicism which appealed to his Roman sense of discipline and duty; what he objected to was the absolutism and perfectionism of the school. His ambivalent attitude is well illustrated in the *Paradoxa Stoicorum,* begun in 46 between the *Brutus* and the *Orator,* and probably continued at different dates. Such Stoic "paradoxes" as that the moral good is the only good, that virtue is sufficient for happiness, that there are no degrees in fault or in merit, that every unwise man is insane and enslaved, that the wise man alone is free and is rich, can be criticized only for their extremism. Cicero's own moral reflections and examples show that he could only applaud the underlying Stoic quest for righteousness. As Cicero grew older his affinity with Stoicism seems to have deepened.

A Stoic substratum seems evident in the most charming and most widely read of all of Cicero's essays, the *Cato Major* or *De senectute.* The fictive date of the dialogue is 150 B.C., when Cato (who is idealized but whose gruff Puritanism is well represented nevertheless) was eighty-four years old, Scipio Africanus Minor was thirty-five, and Laelius, the third interlocutor, was about thirty-six. The essay opens with a fine address to Atticus and continues with a placid and witty encomium of old age and a refutation of the plaints usually charged against old age. "To me," Cicero writes (1.2), "the composition of this book has been so delightful that it has not only wiped away all the annoyances of old age, but has even made it an easy and happy state." The serene detachment of a well-stocked and perceptive mind looking at life can afford delight to readers of any age. The companion piece of the *De senectute,* also written in 44, is *Laelius* or *De amicitia,* also addressed to Atticus. The time is 129 B.C., a few days after the mysterious death of the Scipio of *De senectute,* and the interlocutors, besides Laelius himself, are his two sons-in-law, Q. Mucius Scaevola the augur, and Gaius Fannius the historian. The sunny ease of the essay on old age is missing in the essay on friendship, which is sterner and more scholastic. Philosophers from Plato (in the *Lysis*) and Aristotle (in the *Nicomachean Ethics*) down had dealt with friendship, and Cicero's treatment is complete and brightened with the usual literary and historical examples. The bases of friendship, its qualities and obligations and the problem of conflicting loyalties (patriotism must supersede friendship) are discussed, and with great charm. The final word is:

I exhort you both so to esteem virtue (without which friendship cannot exist), that, excepting virtue, you will think nothing more excellent than friendship.

—W. A. Falconer

The whole aim of ethical philosophy is right conduct, and it is appropriate that Cicero's last work (besides the later *Philippics*) should be the treatise on moral duties, *De officiis,* addressed to his son, who was then a student at the university of Athens and about to embark on life, and used as their prime textbook by generations of university students in England and France and Germany who were similarly about to embark upon life. Cicero's primary sources were the Stoics Panaetius and Posidonius, but his own environment, experiences, and observations are more fully reflected in this than in any other of his philosophic treatises. The demoralization of the state is as present to his mind as in the recently written *Second Philippic* and gives edge to his moralizing. The first book treats of the *honestum* or morally good under the categories of the venerable cardinal virtues of wisdom, courage, justice, and self-control. The second book deals with the *utile;* the bases of utility and its function in the inter-relations of men are dealt with, and classes of utility are balanced and compared. In the third book, where Cicero claims greater independence (3.7.34), conflicts between the *honestum* and the *utile* are discussed. For all its brilliant style, *De officiis* shows signs of the haste with which it was written. There are repetitions and illogicalities in order, and there are misplaced rhetorical flourishes. Possibly because of its haste it gives a picture of its author as untouched as that given by his letters; sane common sense appears along with conceit; noble patriotism along with partisan politics. But there is no false posturing; *De officiis* is a sincere and valuable contribution to the ethical literature of the race.

But the fullest and most intimate portrait of Cicero is that presented by the body of his correspondence—nearly eight hundred letters which he himself wrote, and about a hundred written to him. There are sixteen books *Ad familiares,* sixteen *Ad Atticum,* three *Ad Quintum fratrem,* and two (of an original nine) *Ad Brutum.* Besides the extant books, there were thirty-seven others, addressed to various personages. Nor are these by any means all the letters Cicero wrote, for he was a diligent correspondent; he might write three letters to Atticus in a single day and did not like to have a day go by without a letter. There being no regular postal service, a letter might be written elaborately at leisure to await the chance of a messenger, or one might be written hastily while a messenger waited at the door-step. Some of the longer and politically significant letters may have been carefully revised; the great bulk are untouched. Cicero himself writes to Atticus (16.5.5) about fifteen months before his death: "There is no collection of my letters, but Tiro has about seventy, and some can be got from you. Those I ought to see and correct, and then they may be published." Our collections, then, were not made or revised by Cicero himself, but after his death by his freedman-secretary Tiro, who was expert in stenography and editorial work and devoted to his master's memory, and who doubtless had the assistance of Atticus. The arrangement is not chronological but by addressees; each book of the *Ad familiares* is entitled after the name of the addressee of the first few letters in it. So plain is it that Cicero himself did not revise the letters for publication and that Tiro conscientiously refrained from tampering with their text that scholars hostile to Cicero have been able to draw up damning bills of indictment on the basis of the information they supply, and one scholar of standing has argued at length that the collections were made by an enemy of Cicero for the specific purpose of discrediting him. But though some letters were doubtless suppressed, perhaps those reflecting unfavorably on Augustus, there can be no question not only that those we have present a just picture of Cicero, but even that the picture is that of an honorable man insofar as a man could be honorable who is neither Don Quixote nor insulated monk but an active participant in a political struggle in an age when ambition was not only condoned but approved. We must remember, in appraising Cicero's inordinate self-conceit, that he was in fact a "new man" who had made headway against the entrenched exclusiveness of an aristocracy. Approbation was meat and drink to him. A concomitant of this insatiable appetite for applause, which a modern might attribute to an inferiority complex, was a dash of hero worship for those who had surely arrived and of awe for aristocracy of blood even when the individual aristocrat was contemptible. The weak mortal who wrote the letters does sometimes fail to live up to the professions of the ethical preacher; but Cicero is surely not alone in this inconsistency, and in his day such inconsistency was more venial than in subsequent ages. And if Cicero reveals himself as vacillating and opportunistic, the blame is partly on the exigencies of the political life he was leading and the accepted standards of conduct for such a life, and partly, there is no doubt, on his Academic attitude in philosophy and his training as a lawyer. He was always able to see the merit in either side of a question, and his advocate's eloquence naturally tended to heap up arguments of probability on the side which happened to be expedient. The wide and humane range of interests in these letters, in literature, in art, and most of all in people, make them appealing even to readers unconcerned with the fascinating web of contemporary politics and history. As for the latter, as Nepos said (*Ad Atticum* 16), "anyone who perused them would hardly need a finished history of those times." Seldom has a critical and pregnant juncture in the history of Europe been so fully illuminated by a participant with such expert knowledge and such quick perception.

Of the letters addressed to Cicero included in the collection mention may be made of the gentle letter of condolence on the death of Tullia by the eminent jurist Sulpicius (*Ad familiares* 4.5). Even in so essentially private a matter the stark tone of the Roman disciplined to patriotism rings out:

Not so long ago there perished at one and the same time many of our famous men; the imperial power of the Roman people has been terribly impaired; all the provinces have been shaken to their foundations; are you so profoundly moved by the loss of the spark of life in one weak woman? If she had not met her death today, she would in any event have had to die in a few years' time, seeing that she was born a human being. . . . Bethink yourself rather of what is worthy of the part you have to play, remembering that she lived as long as life was of use to her; that she and the Republic passed away together; that she saw you, her father, elected praetor, then consul, then augur; that she had been successively the bride of more than one youth of the highest rank, that she enjoyed almost every blessing in life; and it was with the fall of the Republic that she ceased to live. What reason have either you or she for quarreling with fortune on this score? Finally, never forget that you are Cicero, one who has ever been wont to instruct and advise others; and do not imitate bad physicians who, in treating the diseases of others, profess to have mastered the whole art of healing, but

themselves they cannot cure; nay, rather apply to yourself and set before
your own mind the precepts you so often seek to impress upon others.
                                                —*W. Glynn Williams*

Associated with the *Epistulae ad Quintum fratrem* is the *Commentariolum petitionis,* which Quintus addresses to Cicero on the subject
of campaigning for the consulship. A pendant to this piece is Cicero's
long letter to Quintus (1.1) on the administration of provinces. Together the two afford useful information on important aspects of
Roman political life.

It would be strange if such a conscious artist in words and such a
lover of *belles lettres* as Cicero's writings show him to be had not himself attempted to write verse. Spiritually, as we can see from the persons and settings of many of his dialogues, Cicero identified himself
with the Scipionic circle, and it was normal for Romans who professed literary interests to indulge in poetizing. "Caesar and Brutus
wrote poems," says Tacitus (*Dialogues* 21), "not better than Cicero,
but more fortunately, for fewer people know that they did it." Cicero's
real eminence in prose made the shortcomings of his verse particularly
vulnerable. Juvenal (10.122 f.) quotes the regrettable *O fortunatam
natam me consule Romam* and adds a stinging comment:

> O happy fate for the Roman State
> Was the date of my great Consulate!

Had Cicero always spoken thus, he might have laughed at the swords of
Antony.
                                                —*G. G. Ramsay*

Breaches of taste are perhaps to be expected in a poem by Cicero *On
His Own Consulship,* but the general quality, like the quantity, of
Cicero's verse must have been quite respectable; Plutarch says that
at one time he was considered the best poet as well as the best orator
of Rome. Plutarch mentions a youthful poem in tetrameters called
Glaucus, after the divinity of the sea. We know also of an *Alcyone* in
hexameters, probably an account of a metamorphosis; a *Nilus,* which
described the Nile; an *Uxorius,* probably a satire of a uxorious husband; a *Limon* or *Meadow,* which dealt in part with literary criticism;
an elegy called *Thalia Maesta;* and some playful epigrams. The best
and most original of his poems was probably the *Marius,* on his
famous fellow townsman of Arpinum. His essays, particularly the

Tusculan Disputations, contain many and some quite long translations from the Greek tragedians. We have long fragments from Cicero's translation of Aratus' astronomical poem *Phaenomena* and his meteorological *Prognostica.* These show considerable freedom in compressing or expanding (on the bases of ancient scholia) in order to make the poem more understandable. Cicero also indulged in prose works of a similar character. He wrote a work called *Admiranda,* "Things to be Wondered At," now wholly lost; we have a quotation from a geographical work of his entitled *Choragraphia.* If his verse and his "scientific" writings were extant Cicero would surely be our fullest, as he is our most characteristic, representative of the range and interests of Latin literature.

Neither in his prose nor in his poetry does Cicero rise to the rare heights which figures of comparable reputation in other literatures occupy. Perhaps the world can look more comfortably at a stature which does not require craning of the neck and shielding of the eyes. It is significant that literary revolutions have turned upon passionate acceptance or rejection of Ciceronianism, though the true giants are above the struggle. Silver Latin is a development of Ciceronianism, but the age of Hadrian turned its back upon Cicero. Jerome chided himself for being a Ciceronian rather than a Christian—and remained a Ciceronian nevertheless. The humanists of the Renaissance refused to countenance linguistic usage which had no sanction in the pages of Cicero. When the cult of Ciceronianism hardened to the point where a Christian prelate could not name the Holy Ghost in a sermon because Cicero had no word for it the cult defeated itself and doomed Latin as a vernacular. If the language of Cicero had been allowed to retain the viability which Erasmus for one tried to give it perhaps Europe would have been better able to achieve the ecumenical ideal of Rome.

VIII

VERGIL

VERGIL MAY BE A LESS AUTHENTIC REFLECTION OF the totality of Rome than is Cicero, but the Romanism he represents has proved a far more sympathetic thing to all posterity. It is not merely that he is a true artist on a grand scale: in Vergil the concept of Rome is spiritualized rather than matter-of-fact, aspiring rather than complacent, tender rather than hard. His is the soaring voice of the prophet in a nation of time-bound ritualists, but like all true prophets he would disclaim his own innovations; he sought merely to make explicit to the Romans what had always been their high spiritual destiny, to which the tearing turmoils of the civil wars had blinded them. Indeed the salient quality which sets Vergil's poetry apart from that of the Greeks whom he so faithfully followed is his Roman patriotism. Even in the *Eclogues* the universality of Theocritus' pastorals is given a Roman tone, and in the *Aeneid* that tone swells into a diapason of glory for Rome, past, present, and future. In an age which witnessed such changes as revolutionized Vergil's world it was inevitable that patriotism should be reexamined and its responsibilities and aspirations revised. After a century of bitter strife which seemed to leave all the accumulated values of civilization in ruins a sensitive spirit would perforce look with passionate eagerness at a light, however clouded, that seemed to herald a new day. The fulfilment of the destiny which was Rome's mission would justify the ruthlessness which had made the full realization of the mission possible.

Born in 70 B.C., Vergil was old enough to assume the toga of manhood before Lucretius died, yet he was only seven years older than Augustus Caesar, who became his patron and whose redintegrated Rome he celebrated. His birthplace was Andes, a small village near Mantua in Cisalpine Gaul, where his father cultivated his own small farm. He was educated at Cremona and Milan and later studied Greek at Naples under Parthenius of Bithynia; at Rome his teachers were the Epicurean Siro and the rhetorician Epidius. He retained an admiration for philosophic and scientific study, as a noble passage in the *Georgics* (2.475-92) shows:

Me indeed first and before all things may the sweet Muses, whose priest
I am and whose great love hath smitten me, take to themselves and show
me the pathways of the sky, the stars, and the diverse eclipses of the sun
and the moon's travails; whence is the earthquake; by what force the seas
swell high over their burst barriers and sink back into themselves again;
why winter suns so hasten to dip in Ocean, or what hindrance keeps back
the lingering nights. But if I may not so attain to this side of nature for the
clog of chilly blood about my heart, may the country and the streams that
water the valleys content me, and lost to fame let me love stream and
woodland. . . . Happy he who hath availed to know the causes of things,
and hath laid all fears and immitigable Fate and the roar of hungry
Acheron under his feet; yet he no less is blessed, who knows the gods of the
country, Pan and old Silvanus and the Nymphs' sisterhood.

—*J. W. Mackail*

His rhetorical training is apparent throughout the *Aeneid,* and especially in the speeches of Book 4.

On completing his education Vergil seems to have returned home.
He must have worked at farming enough to accumulate the practical
information exhibited in the *Georgics,* and he may have written, at
this period of his youth, such minor poems as *Ciris, Copa, Culex,* and
Moretum, which are attributed to him. His poetic efforts must have
been sufficient to engage the interest of such powerful friends as
Asinius Pollio and Alfenus Rufus, who interceded to save his father's
farm when the triumvirs Octavian, Antony, and Lepidus confiscated
land in his region to bestow on the victorious veterans of Philippi
(42 B.C.) as bonuses. It was Pollio who introduced him to Octavian,
and Vergil expressed his gratitude to the youthful triumvir in the
Eclogue which he placed at the head of his collection, thus dedicating
the whole work to him. From this time forward Vergil lived at Rome
or Naples, as one of the literary men gathered in the circle of Maecenas,
who was in effect the emperor's minister of propaganda. It was at the
request of Maecenas, to whom they are dedicated, that he composed
the four books of *Georgics,* written between 37 and 30 B.C. It was
Vergil who introduced Horace to Maecenas; in the famous "Journey
to Brundisium" Horace speaks of Vergil and Plotius and Varius who
joined the party as "the fairest souls and dearest friends on earth"
(*Satires* 1.5.41), and when Vergil was sailing to Greece Horace prayed
that his ship might "preserve the half of my life" (*Odes* 1.3.8). In
the opening lines of the third *Georgic* Vergil announced his intention

to write an epic of which Augustus should be the central figure, and in 26 and 25 Augustus wrote him from Spain to ask for a draft or sections of this work. Perhaps Vergil found the career of Augustus in itself unsuitable for the stately structure he had in mind, and the poem whose advent Propertius hails about 24 B.C. (2.26.65 f.)—"Yield ye, bards of Rome, yield ye, singers of Greece! Something greater than the *Iliad* now springs to birth!"—is probably a different concept. The sixth book was not completed in 23, for Marcellus, the nephew of Augustus and his destined heir, who died in that year, is mentioned in lines 860–87 of that book. Donatus tells us that when the poet recited these lines, closing with the haunting

> Bring lilies, full handfuls of lilies!
> Let me strew blossoms of purple; at least, let me offer thy spirit
> These frail tokens of love, and pay this inadequate tribute!
> —*H. H. Ballard*

in the presence of Octavia, the bereaved mother fainted away. In 19 Vergil started on a journey to Greece and Asia, expecting to devote three years to completing the *Aeneid* and then to give himself to the study of philosophy. At Athens he met Augustus and was persuaded to return with him. He fell ill en route, and died shortly after reaching Brundisium, in September of 19 B.C. His remains were taken to Naples and buried on the road to Puteoli, with an epitaph he is himself said to have written:

> *Mantua me genuit, Calabri rapuere, tenet nunc*
> *Parthenope; cecini pascua, rura, duces.*

The references are to the places of his birth, death, and burial, and to the subjects of his three great works. Before he left Italy Vergil had exacted a promise from Varius, to whom with Plotius Tucca he had left his writings, to burn the *Aeneid* if anything should happen to him. Augustus ordered the executors to disregard the injunction, and the poem was published in its unfinished state.

In every Latin author so far mentioned we have had occasion to notice the influence of Greek models. It is not otherwise with the voice of Rome incarnate, but here we can see imitation little short of servile growing to a sovereign mastery in which Greek materials are built into a structure which is wholly the builder's. Thus the *Bucolics* ("songs about herdsmen") or, as they are more commonly called, the *Eclogues* ("selections") are so closely copied from Theocritus that it is possible to charge Vergil with misunderstanding his original in one or two passages. Theocritus, who invented the genre, was a Sicilian poet of the early third century B.C. His *Idylls,* usually in the form of singing matches or improvisations such as were associated with village celebrations, reproduce the authentic flavor of the rustic countryside with its scenes and smells and its real shepherds of flesh and blood; his broad Doric dialect adds to the sense of freshness and native vigor. Vergil's pastorals idealize reality and make it artificial. His shepherds are only masqueraders, and at times put off their disguise to show themselves as Vergil himself or Gallus or Caesar. Nature is subjected to convention (as in the *Aeneid* heroism is subjected to an institution); instead of reproducing rural life with its untrammeled charms, pastoral poetry has become an art form in which stylized rusticity is a necessary convention. If we understand that the blue jeans and sunbonnets are designed in Paris and that the barn is perfumed—in a word, that there is no effort to achieve realism—then we shall not be repelled by artificiality and can admire the genuine artistic merits of the *Eclogues.*

Artistic development can be observed in the *Eclogues* more clearly than in Vergil's later works. The order in which the *Eclogues* are arranged is not the order in which they were written. The second and third are undoubtedly the earliest, and show the largest amount of literal imitation of Theocritus. Eclogue 2, in which the shepherd Corydon laments his inability to win the affections of young Alexis, is an imitation of Theocritus 11, in which the Cyclops Polyphemus laments the cruelty of the sea-nymph Galatea. Corydon protests that he is not so very ugly, offers the attractions of his rustic life, and tries to console himself for the rebuff. Eclogue 3 is a singing contest between two unfriendly shepherds, Menalcas and Damon, with Palaemon as judge. It is largely copied from Theocritus 4 and 5, which are similarly amoebean, or in dialogue. Pollio is mentioned in this poem, as are Bavius and Maevius, two poetasters whom Vergil (and Horace) loathed. Eclogue 7 is another amoebean imitation of Theocritus; Meliboeus reports a contest between the shepherd Thyrsis and the goatherd Corydon. In Eclogue 5, similarly amoebean, the shepherds Mopsus and Menalcas engage in a friendly contest of song, the one relating the death of Daphnis (the ideal shepherd of pastoral poetry) in a song of twenty-five lines, and the other, in closely paralleled song of twenty-five lines, relating his deification. The death of Daphnis is also lamented in Theocritus 1, but the deification is original with Vergil and is probably an allegorical reference to the deification of Julius Caesar; if this is so, the poem represents Vergil's first effort to deal with a subject of national interest. It would also supply a date, for in 42 B.C. the triumvirs ordered the celebration of Julius Caesar's birthday in the month Quinctilis, which was thenceforward called Julius. The names Corydon, Alexis, and Meliboeus in lines 86–88 are an allusion to Eclogues 2 and 3, which must therefore be earlier.

The mention of Pollio's consulship in line 11 of Eclogue 4 dates that "Messianic" eclogue to 40 B.C. This poem is wholly independent of Theocritus, and is marked by Vergil himself as an attempt to rise above the lowly subjects of purely pastoral verse. "Sicilian [i.e., Theocritean] Muses," he begins, "let us sing a somewhat loftier strain." This poem has been more widely discussed than any piece of similar length in classical literature. In language reminiscent of Scripture the poet prophesies the birth of a boy whose rule will usher in a golden age of peace. Since Constantine and Augustine, Christian writers have regarded the *Eclogue* as a prophecy of the Messiah. More probably the reference is to the child expected by Octavian and Scribonia, who proved to be a girl, the infamous Julia, or possibly to a child of Antony and Octavia, or to Pollio's own son. But if the prophecy cannot refer to Jesus, the notion of an expected redeemer may quite likely derive from the hopeful speculations of the Jews on the subject. The Campanian coast where Vergil sojourned had a considerable Syrian and Palestinian population, and Vergil was by nature curious concerning religious speculations of an apocalyptic character He makes large use of apocalyptic techniques in the *Aeneid,* and millenarism reappears in the sixth book. In any case the beautiful fourth *Eclogue* presents an attractive vision of an ideal future, and shows us how the sensitive spirit of Vergil was groping out of the grim hardness of contemporary reality towards loftier aspirations for Rome and the world. The tone of spiritual hopefulness strikes a new note in pagan literature.

Eclogue 8, dated by a historical allusion in lines 6–7 to 39 B.C., reverts to the Theocritean manner. It too is amoebean, and the enchantress of the second half comes from Theocritus 2. But Theocritus, from whom (11.26) the lines are imitated, has nothing as tender as lines 37-41:

Within our garden close I saw thee— I was guide for both—a little child, along with my mother, plucking dewy apples. My eleventh year finished, the next had just greeted me; from the ground I could now reach the frail boughs. As I saw, how was I lost! How a fatal frenzy swept me away!

—H. R. Fairclough

Nothing in classical literature comes so near suggesting Dante and Beatrice. It is possible that an original collection containing the *Eclogues* already mentioned (2-7) was sent to Pollio with Eclogue 8 at their head by way of dedication; this may be the implication of lines 11-13:

From thee is my beginning; in thy honour shall I end. Accept the songs essayed at thy bidding, and grant that about thy brows this ivy may creep among the victor's laurels.

—H. R. Fairclough

In that case the substance of Eclogue 8 may be quite early, the dedication only being added in 39.

In any event the remaining four pieces (1, 6, 9, 10) form a group by themselves, all being distinctly connected with the poet's personal history, and all showing greater independence from Theocritus, Eclogue 6 being wholly independent. Eclogues 1, 6, and 9 all have to do with the recovery of Vergil's farm. In Eclogue 1 a dialogue between two shepherds serves as a thin disguise for Vergil's own history; Tityrus, representing Vergil himself, reposes at his ease among his sheep, while unhappy Meliboeus must drive his weary flock on. Tityrus renders Octavian due thanks for his happiness (6-10):

O Meliboeus, it is a god who wrought for us this peace—for a god he shall ever be to me; often shall a tender lamb from our folds stain his altar. Of his grace my kine roam, as you see, and I, their master, play what I will on my rustic pipe.

—H. R. Fairclough

And again (42-45):

Here, Meliboeus, I saw that youth for whom our altars smoke twice six days a year. Here he was the first to give my plea an answer: "Feed, swains, your oxen as of old; rear your bull."

—H. R. Fairclough

Eclogue 6 is addressed to Varus, who had helped Vergil maintain his right to his farm. The poet disclaims ability to write epic, which Varus had apparently asked him to do, and asks his patron to accept the dedication of the pastoral poem which follows. Two shepherds who caught Silenus asleep forced him to sing the song which forms the main part of the poem. But pastoral is too modest a designation for the "Song of Silenus"; as the Fauns and wild creatures dance to his measures and the oaks sway their heads, he sings of creation, following the Lucretian cosmology, and then of various mythological figures associated with the primal age of the world. Eclogue 9 is very like Eclogue 1 in subject and is perhaps an appeal to Varus for assistance. The plan follows Theocritus 7, but the contents are purely personal. In a conversation between the two shepherds Lycidas is surprised to learn that Moeris has been turned out of his farm, for he had heard that Menalcas (that is, Vergil) had secured the safety of the district by his poetry. Moeris replies that Menalcas himself had barely escaped with his life, and the two proceed to recall passages of Menalcas' poetry. There is another reference to the star of Caesar in line 47. Eclogue 10, expressly stated in its first line to be the last, is a consolation to Gallus for the loss of his mistress. This is the most artificial and at the same time the most polished of all the *Eclogues*. Gallus had distinguished himself in the war against Antony and Cleopatra and was the first governor of Egypt, where he fell into disgrace in 26 B.C. and committed suicide. But Gallus also had the highest reputation as an elegiac poet; it was he who transferred the theme of wounded love from mythological or bucolic settings to the actual sufferings of a deserted lover. It is this new approach which forms the background for Eclogue 10, which must contain many echoes of Gallus' own poetry. A passage in Eclogue 6 (64–73) handsomely acknowledges Gallus' eminence in pastoral poetry.

Vergil's close adherence to his Sicilian model and the Alexandrian flavor of his epithets and mythological allusions sometimes make the contemporary and local references we have noticed seem incongruous. The astonishing thing is that in spite of the overwhelming pervasiveness of the Greek the *Eclogues* are an unmistakably Vergilian work, with Vergil's own music and wistfulness. But in all respects the *Eclogues* are only a stage in the growing independence of Vergil. The *Georgics* show a much greater awareness of his own powers on the part of the poet; he is master rather than servant of his Greek models, master too of his materials and his attitude towards them. Where the *Eclogues* idealize reality and make it artificial, the *Georgics* describe reality and make it poetic.

The first indication of the greater independence of the *Georgics,* written between 36 and 29 B.C., is that Vergil here combines several models. He professes, indeed, that he is imitating Hesiod—"singing the song of Ascra through the towns of Rome" (2.176)—but it is mainly the idea of a didactic poem on agriculture and the glorification of hard work that he owes to the *Works and Days.* Aside from scattered phrases or precepts there are only two passages in Book 1 which are direct imitations: the description of the plough (169-75), and the account of days favorable and unfavorable for work (276-86). At least as much use is made of three didactic poets of the Alexandrian age. Aratus' *Diosemeia* is the source for much of the weather lore at 1.204 and following (the passage at 375-87 closely follows the Latin translation of Varro Atacinus), and Aratus' *Phaenomena* is the source for the description of the *mundus* (1.244-6). The description of the zones of the sky (1.233-51) comes from Eratosthenes, and some of the bee lore from Nicander's *Melissurgica.* In similes and in such a narrative as that of Aristaeus (4.315-558) we have imitations of Homer. Vergil also uses Latin authors in the *Georgics.* Cato and Varro are drawn upon for agricultural information, Ennius is used, and there are reminiscences of Lucretius throughout the work.

But a wide gulf separates the *Georgics* from the didactic poetry of the Alexandrians. For the Alexandrians the writing of such verse was a kind of stunt. Aratus himself, for example, the best of the class, knew little of astronomy but merely put into verse the honest work of the astronomer Eudoxus. He fails even to experience or communicate the intellectual or imaginative excitement which a subject like astronomy might legitimately arouse. Insofar as there is a desire to impart information, it is information that may be used for polite display—as the author fashions his verses for display—to provide for a social need like the modern requirement that a cultivated man be able to use the clichés of music appreciation. In a real sense the work of Aratus and his peers is frivolous. Vergil's work is very different. Not only has he real knowledge and real enthusiasm for his subject to communicate, but also a high moral purpose which embraces edification as well as

information. There is not, to be sure, Lucretius' burning zeal to make
converts to a new creed, but there is a solid earnestness in his celebration of the rustic life of toil and the satisfactions of the simple life
of Roman tradition. The fine appreciations of nature, animate and inanimate, are much solider stuff than the prettiness of pastoral. In the
passages glorifying Italy there is a real patriotic ardor, no less genuine
for having been encouraged, perhaps commissioned, by Maecenas as
part of Augustus' program of patriotic regeneration. If the fragments
of shattered social life were to be reassembled to construct a unified
and happy and enduring and responsible social organism, the rural
backbone of Italy had first to be regenerated and the love of native
land and its teeming activity inculcated. The Italy which Vergil sings
is well worth men's devotion (2.136–74):

> But neither flowering groves
> Of Media's realm, nor Ganges proud,
> Nor Lydian fountains flowing thick with gold,
> Can match their glories with Italia;
> Not Bactria nor Ind, nor all the wealth
> Of wide Arabia's incense-bearing sands.
> This land by Jason's bulls with breath of flame
> Never was ploughed, nor planted with the teeth
> Of monstrous dragon, nor that harvest grew
> Of helmed warrior heads and myriad spears.
> But full-eared corn and goodly Massic wine
> Inhabit here, with olives and fat herds.
> The war-horse here with forehead high in air
> Strides o'er the plain; here roam thy spotless flocks,
> Clitumnus; and for noblest sacrifice,
> The snow-white bull, bathed oft in sacred stream,
> Leads Roman triumphs to the house of Jove.
> Here Spring is endless and the Summer glows
> In months not half her own. Twice in the year
> The herds drop young, and twice the orchard bears
> The labor of its fruit. But tigers fell
> And the fierce lion's brood are absent here.
> No deadly aconite deceives the hand
> That gathers herbs; nor in enormous folds
> Or lengthened twine the scaly snake upcoils.
> Behold the famous cities!—what vast toil
> Upreared them!—and the host of strongholds piled

By hand of man on out-hewn precipice,
While swift streams under ancient bulwarks flow.
Why tell of two salt seas that wash her shore
Above, below; her multitude of lakes—
Thee, Larius, chiefest, and Benacus, where
Are swelling floods and billows like the sea?
Why name that haven where the lofty mole
Locks in the Lucrine lake, while with loud rage
The baffled waters roar, and Julian waves
Echo from far the sea's retreating tide,
And through the channels of Avernus pours
Th' invading Tuscan main? In this rich land
Deep veins of silver show, and ores for brass,
With lavish gold. Hence sprang the warlike breed
Of Marsi, hence the proud Sabellian clans,
Ligurians to hardship seasoned well,
And Volscian spearmen; hence the Decii,
Camilli, Marii, immortal names,
The Scipios, in wars implacable,
And Caesar, thou, the last, the prince of all,
Who now victorious on far Asia's end,
Art holding back from Roman citadels
The Indian weakling. Hail O Saturn's land,
Mother of all good fruits and harvests fair,
Mother of men!

—Theodore C. Williams

Vergil's honesty of purpose in writing the *Georgics* is matched by the conscientious care with which he wrote them. If seven years were consumed in their elaboration the average comes to less than a line a day; Donatus' *Life* quotes Vergil as saying that he "licked them into shape like a she-bear its cub." Dryden called the *Georgics* "the best Poem of the best Poet"; we may remember the dramatic power of the fourth *Aeneid* or the imaginative grandeur of the sixth and demur. But the Dryden approach to criticism, though it is not in current fashion, cannot be lightly dismissed, and least of all for a Roman poet; and by that gauge Dryden's appraisal is just. In the long passage just cited, for example, the heavy load of historical and mythological allusion would hamper a free ranging and spontaneous imagination, nor can the numerous meticulous prescriptions for the proper discharge of farm chores provide scope for imaginative power on a grand scale. But even the most intractable matter of this sort shows evidence of the poetic energy with which it has been endowed by a poetic genius sensitive to poetic beauty at many levels and capable of breathing poetic life into what might have been a farmer's handbook.

"A farmer's handbook" is what *Georgics* means. Of the four books, containing 2,184 lines in all, the first deals with agriculture proper, the second with arboriculture, the third with animal husbandry, and the fourth with beekeeping. *Georgics* 1 introduces the theme, invokes the appropriate deities and Caesar, and proceeds with directions for ploughing, alternating crops, burning stubble, irrigating, pest control, selection of seed, the appropriate seasons for various tasks, and many kindred matters. The prayer at the close reflects Vergil's own motives (1.498–514):

Gods of my country . . . stay not this young prince from aiding a world uptorn! Enough has our life-blood long atoned. . . . Here are right and wrong inverted; so many wars overrun the world, so many are the shapes of sin; the plough meets not its honour due; our lands, robbed of the tillers, lie waste, and the crooked pruning hooks are forged into stiff swords. Here Euphrates, there Germany, awakes war; neighbour cities break the leagues that bound them and draw the sword; throughout the world rages the god of unholy strife. . . .

                                                        —*H. R. Fairclough*

The second book is somewhat less systematic and has several enlivening digressions. After enumerating the various natural and artificial ways of propagating trees, Vergil enlarges upon the trees native to various countries and emerges with a eulogy of Italy in which trees and vines are quite incidental to the landscape. An abrupt transition is made to aptitudes of soils, in which logical order is somewhat disturbed by the inclusion of soils adapted to grain and pasturage. Next the grapevines and the trees which support them receive an artistically intermingled treatment. The olive, which was announced in the prologue as an important topic, is dismissed in five verses as a simple matter. Fruit trees and other varieties are next summarily handled in thirty verses each, and the book closes with the famous eulogy of country life (2.513–40):

The husbandman sunders the soil with curving plough; from this is the labour of his year, from this the sustenance of his native land and his little grandchildren, of his herds of oxen and faithful bullocks; and unceasingly the year lavishes fruit or young of the flock or sheaf of the corn-blade, and loads the furrow and overflows the granary with increase. Winter is come; the Sicyonian berry is crushed in the alive presses, the swine come home sleek from their acorns, the woodland yields her arbute clusters, and autumn drops his manifold fruitage, and high up the mellow vintage ripens on the sunny rock. Meanwhile sweet children cling round his kisses, the home abides in sacred purity, the kine droop their milky udders, and on the shining grass fat kids wrestle with confronting horns. Himself keeps holiday, and stretched on the sward where the fire is in the midmost and the company wreathe the wine-bowl, calls on thee, god of the wine-press, in libation, and marks an elm for contests of the flying javelin among the keepers of the flock, or they strip their hardy limbs for the rustic wrestling match. This life the ancient Sabines kept long ago, this Remus and his brother; even thus Etruria waxed mighty, ay, and Rome grew fairest of the world and ringed her sevenfold fortresses with a single wall. Yes, before the sceptre of that Cretan king, before a guilty race slew oxen for the banquet, this life golden Saturn led on earth; nor yet withal had they heard war-trumpets blown, nor yet the hard anvil clink under the sword.

—J. W. Mackail

In the third book a division is made between large animals and small, Vergil showing his special affection for the horse. The first section is interrupted and relieved by a digression on the effect of sexual passion on animal life. The less detailed section on small animals has a number of digressions, notably pictures of a shepherd's summer in Libya and a Scythian shepherd's winter. These are exquisite genre pictures and may reflect an urge on the part of Vergil to move from plants and animals to the more vital experiences of human beings. The book closes with an account of a pestilence, in imitation of Lucretius; animals other than those of interest to the farmer are included in what is in effect an independent narrative.

In the absence of sugar, honey was a much more important element in ancient than in modern diet, and beekeeping could legitimately claim a book of the *Georgics* for itself. The fourth book starts with hives, apologizes for the omission of truck gardens, and proceeds to discuss the nature and the diseases of bees. At 67–87 there is a lively and humorous account of warfare between swarms of bees. In connection with rearing bees from the carcasses of cattle the epyllion on the story of Aristaeus is included to close the book. According to Servius this portion (4.315–558) was substituted for an original encomium of Gallus after the latter's disgrace and death. Aristaeus' bees had sickened and died because of an injury he had done to Eurydice. Upon the instruction of his nymph mother Cyrene he constrains Proteus to sing him the tale of Orpheus and Eurydice. In the carcasses of the oxen he has then sacrificed to the pair he finds that a new swarm of bees has been generated. The story of Orpheus and Eurydice set within the framework of the story of Aristaeus and Cyrene is precisely such an inset as the story of Ariadne and Theseus within the "Marriage of Peleus and Thetis" in Catullus' epyllion. Like Catullus Vergil is doubtless following a Greek model quite closely. If his own hand is to be distinguished anywhere it is in the pathetic elements of the story—such things as the picture of Orpheus' endless devotion and his still crying the name of Eurydice in the agony of his gruesome death. The thronging dead in Hades, whither Orpheus had gone to reclaim Eurydice, foreshadow the picture in the sixth *Aeneid.*

The technical perfection of the *Georgics,* their love of nature and sympathy for man, their genuine patriotic motivation, make them masterpieces indeed, but masterpieces in a limited kind. Alone or with the *Eclogues* and the poems of the *Appendix* they would not have made their author the best loved and most revered poet in Europe for at least a millennium and a half. All of the qualities of Vergil's lesser works are enlarged in the *Aeneid,* but the *Aeneid* is very much more than merely the sum of the lesser works. All of Vergil's creative poetic energy is here devoted to a deeply felt idealization of the most significant concept in the ancient world, the concept of Rome itself. All too often Roman literary artistry is merely literary and nothing else, and when a poet utters his own inward feelings his range is limited by his own subjectivity. Lucretius, indeed, is an exception in being both sincere and public, but however pure Lucretius' doctrine may be it is limited and it is negative; his philosophic level is higher, but like Juvenal he can only excoriate wrong views. If the wrong beliefs or wrong practices which a Lucretius or a Juvenal attacks were abolished, men would still have no guiding aim or aspiration, and the concept of Rome would be limited to an institution which made reasonable and decent life possible. So limited a goal may be safer; recent history has taught us to value the possibility for a reasonable and decent life as a very precious thing and to suspect apostles of national glory, whose ultimate objectives usually involve the sacrifice of the possibility of a reasonable and decent life. In a sense, and with the hindsight our generation has learned, Vergil's glorification of the *pax Romana*, or more properly the Augustan peace, may have been politically shortsighted. "They make a solitude," Tacitus has a Briton say (*Agricola* 30), "and they call it peace." But the most determined liberal would be hard put to it to conceive of a solution other than Augustus' for remedying the demoralization of his world, and no herald of a new political order has given such an exalted spiritual tone and substance to the aspirations of patriotism as did Vergil.

For the conjuncture at and for which Vergil worked we can say this with assurance, for we have the productions of his colleagues who worked on the same assignment. In his own account of his stewardship called *Res gestae divi Augusti* or *Monumentum Ancyranum* (from Ancyra or Angora, where the first copy was found inscribed on a temple of Rome and Augustus) Augustus mentions parts of his program:

By new legislation I have restored many customs of our ancestors which had now begun to fall into disuse. . . . I have restored 82 temples of the gods, passing over none which was at that time in need of repair. . . . When I had put an end to the civil wars, after having obtained complete control of affairs by universal consent, I transferred the commonwealth from my own dominion to the authority of the senate and the Roman people. In return for this favor I received by decree of the senate the title Augustus, the doorposts of my house were publicly decked with laurels, a civic crown was fixed above my door, and in the Julian Curia was placed a golden shield, which, by its inscription, bore witness that it was given me by the senate and Roman people on account of my valor, clemency, justice, and piety.

—W. Fairley

It was plainly Augustus' purpose to employ religion and pride in the national traditions to foster responsible citizenship. In the magnificent new forum he built he lined the walls with niches containing busts of Roman triumphators with inscriptions describing their prowess. Livy, whose history is a sister work to the *Aeneid,* similarly employs religion and patriotic tradition to inculcate national pride and a belief in the destiny of Rome. While Vergil was working on the *Aeneid* his colleague Horace wrote a group of Roman odes (3.1–6) which are a similar admonition to return to pristine virtue; the sixth particularly castigates the deterioration of religion. But neither Augustus nor Livy nor Horace had any genuine sentiments concerning the religion they were advocating. Vergil did; his poem is permeated with the sense of the spiritual value of things and events. The official state religion may have left him cold, and his tender affection for early Italian religious traditions may have been based on other than religious sentiments, but for the majesty and sanctity of Rome he felt nothing less than religious awe. His theology, as far as it can be systematized, is a medley of folklore and philosophic speculation, but his belief in divine providence is real, and in another respect he approaches very near Christianity. He has a profound sympathy for suffering and sorrow and a conviction that it is through suffering that man reaches the depths of religious experience. It is through sacrifice and suffering that ultimate triumph is to be achieved. In this sense, as Cyril Bailey has written, the *Aeneid* is an epic commentary on the lyric of the fourth *Eclogue*.

The apocalyptic quality of the *Aeneid* is enhanced by a remarkable and skillful use of the techniques of the actual apocalypses which were written and circulated in the inter-testamentary period. The reader is placed in the twelfth century, and prophecies from that vantage point which the reader knows to have been fulfilled create credit for other prophecies which refer to the actual future. Even the sophisticated reader is astonished at Dido's clairvoyance in the matter of the Punic Wars (though he knows well enough that these wars were fought centuries before Vergil wrote), and so ready to believe that Vergil's other prophecies, referring to the future of Rome's destiny, must be equally true. Another analogy to the religious literature of the East is the position of Aeneas himself as a national symbol, chosen as the instrument of destiny and set apart from ordinary humanity. Achilles and Odysseus may be more admirable, from a literary point of view, because they are more nearly free agents and represent poetic truth of a more universal validity. Aeneas represents a specifically Roman ideal, disciplined and institutionalized in consonance with the spirit of the Augustan age. Through Silvius he is the ancestor of the Alban kings and of Romulus; through Iulus (though the etymology is baseless), of the Julian gens. Not only as the founder of these two great lines, but as the parent of the Roman people (who are sometimes called *Aeneadae: Aeneid* 8.648), Aeneas must have within him all the institutionalized virtues which his descendants inherit.

This preoccupation with the spiritual explains much of the specific quality which distinguishes the *Aeneid* from other classical poetry, and especially from Vergil's immediate Homeric models. Not only is there gentleness and boundless compassion for the *lacrimae rerum*, the untranslatable but eloquent "tears of things," but there is a studied suggestiveness and allusiveness in the language. Mark Van Doren's eloquent essay on the *Aeneid* puts the matter well:

A political subject—in this case the great role of Rome as consolidator and pacifier of world society, and more particularly the great place of Augustus at the goal of so much progress—might seem to have demanded a forthright, confident, and masculine narrative, clearly ordered and precisely phrased. Instead of that we get in the *Aeneid* indirect lighting and misty effects. Its author's favorite adjectives are *tenuis* and *inanis*. There is continual resort to the undefined—to the unspeakable, and even to the unimaginable. The scenes are invariably "tangled" or "shadowy." The prevailing hue is grey, and the time when the poet is most at home is twilight or nightfall, when things have become difficult to see in their hard, natural outlines. The result, given Vergil's genius, is a number of passages washed over with the loveliest tones the minor lyre has ever commanded.

But if hard lights are subdued and harsh corners rounded, there is a masterful firmness in structure as a whole altogether unlike the loosely articulated *Iliad*. The poet's eye is single on his large theme, and every element of his poem contributes to its realization. We feel, as in Dante, that the poet saw his vision as a whole, with all its details, and reported it correctly; the guiding purpose is never lost sight of.

From Homer Vergil derived, first, the elements which had become canonical for epic: hexameter verse, duodecimal division of books, divine machinery, extended similes; and next, a long series of individual episodes. Like Odysseus Aeneas is shipwrecked, is directed to a palace by a gracious lady (Venus instead of Nausicaa), relates his adventures at a banquet (the story of the fall of Troy is from the Cyclic poets), remains with a charming hostess (Dido instead of Calypso; the love story itself is from Apollonius of Rhodes' *Argonautica*), visits Hades, encounters a recently deceased comrade who asks to be buried (Palinurus instead of Elpenor), meets an associate who refuses to talk to him (Dido instead of Ajax), is told by another comrade how he was murdered by the connivance of his wife (Deiphobus instead of Agamemnon), and receives a prophecy of the future (from Anchises instead of Teiresias). These are from the first six books. The last six correspond to the *Iliad,* from which come the battle scenes, the attack on the ships, the catalogues of chiefs, the divinely made armor, the funeral games, the broken truce, the midnight foray of Nisus and Euryalus (Diomedes and Odysseus), the unsuccessful embassy to Diomedes (Achilles), the quarrel of Turnus and Drances (Agamemnon and Achilles), the slaying of Pallas by Turnus (Patroclus by Hector), the final duel between Aeneas and Turnus (Achilles and Hector).

Not only Homer, the Cyclic poets, Greek tragedy, and Apollonius of Rhodes, but the great volume of local Roman tradition are laid under contribution. The more we know of the mass of legend out of which Vergil worked, the more we admire the concentration and reflection and disposition of his materials to serve his purposes. Incidents of a kindred character are gathered together and made to fit into a context, figures are fewer and more carefully studied. They may be less interesting to watch than Homer's, because, like Aeneas himself, they are less free. In a free individual Aeneas' desertion of Dido might be contemptible; but a *pius* instrument of destiny must overcome private inclination. When a Homeric hero is in mortal peril he lifts a stone that two—but only two—ordinary men can scarcely lift; at the end of the *Aeneid* Turnus lifts a stone that twelve men could scarcely lift—and so forfeits interest as a human hero. Odysseus himself shoots venison for his hungry men, carries the carcass down to the seashore, and dresses it for them; but such menial employment is unbecoming the divine ancestor of the Romans. In the parallel passage (1.184-94) Aeneas shoots seven lordly stags, which are then transported and dressed by nameless powers. So it is with the gods. Homer's deities share the failings of his men; in Vergil Jupiter is exalted to something like Stoic providence, and the lesser gods are reduced to mere agents of his will.

Vergil's transformation of the episodes taken from Homer indicates his special approach. His tenderness and compassion, for example, shine out in the Nisus and Euryalus episode, which plays on the heartstrings, where the Doloneia only reflects the unlovely realities of war.

In the actual battle scenes Vergil is gorier than Homer, but he writes as with face averted; the carnage is an unfortunate necessity. The designs on Achilles' shield represent life in all its manifestations; those on Aeneas' picture the history of Rome. Vergil's first simile is from Roman political life; here is how the storm at sea was calmed (1. 148–56):

> And, as in times of revolt, which often afflicts a great nation,
> When the ignoble throng are roused to a frenzy of passion,
> Firebrands and stones are beginning to fly, for fury finds weapons,—
> Then, if they chance to behold some man, for his faith and his virtue
> Highly revered, they are awed, and attentively listen in silence,
> While he controls their minds by his words, and quiets their passion;
> So all the roar of the sea is instantly hushed as the Father,
> Looking forth over the deep, and borne under brightening heavens,
> Wheels his flying steeds, and guides the swift chariot onward.
> —*H. H. Ballard*

We should expect that a studied effort such as the *Aeneid* would be better organized than a "natural" epic like the *Iliad,* but Vergil's mastery in this respect is beyond praise. We begin the story within three months of its end, with Aeneas and his men tossed about in a magnificent storm, from which they make their way to the African shore. Venus, who intercedes with Jupiter on behalf of her son, is given a prophecy of the future greatness of Rome and of the advent of Augustus. She appears to Aeneas in the guise of a huntress, tells him Dido's story, and directs him to Dido's palace. Dido, for her part, knows of Aeneas, as the reliefs on her temple walls show. She receives her guest hospitably and prevails upon him to tell the story of the fall of Troy and of his own travels to the present, which he does in two vivid books (2 and 3). The love of Dido and Aeneas is prepared with great psychologic insight and told with great delicacy; both are widowed exiles yearning to strike new roots, each knows the other's past; we are quite ready to believe they would fall in love without the elaborate substitution of Cupid for Ascanius, which Vergil introduces out of deference to the epic requirement of divine machinery to explain crucial events. The consummation of the love, Aeneas' divinely directed desertion, Dido's confidences to her sister Anna, and her suicide are told in the highly dramatic Book 4. In Book 5 Aeneas again touches at Sicily, to celebrate funeral games for his father

Anchises. Here the discontented women fire the ships and destroy all but four. On the voyage to Italy the helmsman Palinurus (an ancestor of Catiline, incidentally) falls asleep and is lost at sea. The descent to Hades occupies Book 6, which is supreme for its somber beauty and its noble vision. Various classes of the dead occupy different sections, as in Dante, but naturally with not nearly so detailed precision. Aeneas has moving encounters with acquaintances from the real world, notably with Dido, who turns away from him in silence, and with his father Anchises. In the Elysian fields Anchises explains the workings of reincarnation, and points out the souls of the unborn heroes, his own descendants, who will glorify the name of Rome; he formulates in words the destiny of Rome and the responsibility of Romans.

Book 7 opens with a new invocation— "A greater history opens before me, to a greater work I set my hand." Arrived at the promised land, Aeneas must assert his right to it, and the hostility of Juno (who still retains her hatred of Trojans) must be overcome. Though King Latinus receives Aeneas cordially and offers him his daughter, Lavinia, in marriage, Juno succeeds in arousing the hostility of Lavinia's suitor Turnus, and the remainder of the poem is devoted to the struggle between Aeneas and Turnus. Book 7 closes with a catalogue of the Italian forces; all are sympathetically dealt with (after all, they were eventually amalgamated with Rome), except the barbarous Etruscan Mezentius. In Book 8 the two sides seek supporting alliances, and Aeneas receives his divinely wrought armor, whose design recapitulates Roman history culminating in Augustus. In Book 9 Turnus fires the Trojan ships, which turn to nymphs and swim away. Nisus and Euryalus go on their brave but ill-starred venture. Ascanius kills his first man. Turnus fights bravely but is cornered and saves himself by leaping from the battlements into the Tiber. A general battle takes place when Aeneas returns with Etruscan reinforcements. Turnus slays Evander's son Pallas and puts on his belt; he is saved from death by Juno. Aeneas kills Mezentius' son Lausus, pitying him the while, and then Mezentius, who tries to avenge him. Book 11 begins with a truce for the funeral of Pallas and the other dead. Negotiations for peace are disrupted, and the battle rages on, the warrior-maid Camilla in particular distinguishing herself. In Book 12 Turnus offers to relieve the straits of the Latins by undertaking single combat with

Aeneas to settle the issue of the war and Lavinia's marriage. Aeneas accepts the challenge, but the truce is broken by a follower of Turnus, who, at Juno's instigation, slays a Trojan. Aeneas is wounded but recovers and decides upon an attack on Laurentum. To spare the city Turnus again offers to duel. Juno agrees not to intervene for Turnus if the name Trojan will be abandoned. Aeneas wounds Turnus and is about to spare him when he notices Pallas' belt upon his shoulder and kills him in a fury of rage.

Each detail of the *Aeneid* is drenched with symbolism and like the *Divine Comedy* it must be read at several levels. But the symbolism of the sum is simple. An inevitable civil war—all the participants were Italians, all ancestors of the Romans—had happily come to its period. All had fought well and, according to their best lights, justly. All bitterness and all passion was now laid at rest, and all could now join hands as comrades and together walk to meet the shining future.

After the exaltation of the *Aeneid* and the solemn roll of its music anything in Latin is anticlimax. Whether the anticlimax we must now glance at, the group of poems called *Appendix Vergiliana,* is Vergil's own is a moot question which scholars have debated with great warmth. Included in the group are *Culex* ("Gnat"), *Ciris, Copa* ("The Cabaret Girl"), *Moretum* ("Salad"), *Dirae* ("Curses"), *Lydia, Priapea,* and *Catalepton* ("Trifles"), *Epigrammata,* and *Aetna.* A ninth-century Vergil manuscript regarded them all as Vergilian, but its testimony cannot be accepted, for some of them are certainly not his. Suetonius, as represented by Donatus, states that Vergil wrote these poems (omitting to mention *Copa* and *Moretum*) in his extreme youth, but the genuineness of the passage has been suspected. *Copa* is added to the list by Servius and *Moretum* by a medieval manuscript. No absolute proof that Vergil did not write any of the poems can be adduced, and many eminent scholars have believed that he did. Stylistic considerations and apparent incongruities with the spirit shown in the accepted works of Vergil have led more scholars to doubt the genuineness of the poems. "If any of them are his work," Professor H. W. Prescott writes, "we are simply strengthened in the conclusion we may safely draw from the *Eclogues, Georgics,* and *Aeneid,* that he had one of the most desirable of all human qualities, perfectibility. Our chief doubt of the authenticity of the poems is due to a feeling that such a degree of perfectibility as they posit is almost superhuman."

We turn to a consideration of the poems themselves, in the order of our printed texts. *Culex* tells, in 414 hexameters, of a shepherd who killed a gnat that stung him to warn him against a snake; later the insect's ghost blames the shepherd for his ingratitude and explains the torments and blessings of the nether world. Though Lucan, Statius, and Martial speak of a Vergilian *Culex,* and the poem is addressed to Octavius (not Octavian) who is also spoken of as a *puer,* which would make its date anterior to 48 B.C., Ovidian phrases and techniques point to a later date; Vergilian echoes were probably superimposed, shortly after Ovid's time, to support attribution to Vergil.

Ciris is an epyllion of the Hellenistic type, in 541 lines. Out of love for her country's enemy Minos, Scylla, daughter of King Nisus of Megara, cuts a magic red lock from her father's head and so causes his death. She is transformed to a sea hawk called Ciris, who is always pursued by a sea eagle, into which her father has been transformed. The poem has the learned obscurity of the Alexandrians (the poet himself calls his verses *caecos*) and is at times heavy-handed, but there are some delicately etched pictures. On her way to her father's chamber in her first attempt to shear the lock Scylla is intercepted by her nurse Carme, who admonishes her to tell why she is so pale and wan, suspecting an incestuous passion (250–72):

Clad as she was in soft raiment, she casts her garb about the shivering maid, who before had stood, high-girt, in light saffron robe. Then, imprinting sweet kisses on her tear-bedewed cheeks, she earnestly seeks the cause of her wasting misery, yet suffers her not to make aught of reply, until, all trembling, she has withdrawn her marble-cold feet within. Then cries the maid: "Why, dear nurse, dost thou thus torture me? Why so eager to know my madness? 'Tis no love common to mortals that inflames me; 'tis not the faces of friends that draw toward them my eyes, 'tis not my father who is thus loved: nay more, I hate them all! This soul of mine, O nurse, loves naught that should be loved, naught wherein there lurks, albeit vain, some ghost of natural regard, but loves from midst the ranks of war, from midst our foes. Alas! Alas! What can I say? With what speech can I, sad one, launch forth upon this woe? Yet surely I will speak, since thou, O nurse, dost not permit me to be silent: this take thou as my last dying gift. Yonder foe, who, thou seest, is seated before our walls, to whom the Sire himself of the gods has given the glory of sceptre, and to whom the Fates have granted that he suffer from no wound (I must speak; vainly with my words do I travel round the whole story), 'tis he, 'tis he, that same Minos, that doth besiege my heart.

—H. R. Fairclough

There is lavish use of Vergilian phraseology, but modern opinion holds that *Ciris* is neither his nor Gallus', to whom scholars once attributed it.

Copa is a high-spirited elegiac poem of thirty-eight lines, in which a cabaret entertainer, dancing to her castanets, issues an invitation to the pleasures of conviviality. The *Copa* is the work of a real poet, but its flippancy is totally alien to the spirit of Vergil. If the *Copa* is too ebullient to be Vergil's, the *Moretum* (124 hexameters) is too realistic. The poem is a description of a farmer preparing his breakfast on a dark winter morning, acutely observed and presented with masterly skill. As the farmer grinds the ingredients of his salad (29–38),

Anon he sings rustic songs, and with rude strains solaces his toil; at times he shouts to Scybale. She was his only help, African in stock, her whole form proclaiming her country: her hair curly, her lips swollen and her hue dusky, her chest broad, her breast hanging low, her belly somewhat pinched, her legs thin, her feet broad and ample. Her rough shoes were torn with many a rent. Her he calls, and bids her place on the fire fuel to burn, and over the flame heat cold water.

—H. R. Fairclough

We have spoken of the not implausible theory which ascribes *Dirae* and *Lydia* to Valerius Cato. The theme—the confiscation of a farm— is a sufficient explanation of the attribution of these poems to Vergil. The *Priapea* are four short poems in which the garden god speaks; they do not have the obscenity usually associated with the title, and there is little basis for arguing either for or against Vergilian authorship. The best case for Vergilian authorship can be made for numbers 1, 3, 5, 7, and 8 of the fifteen short poems of *Catalepton*. These are occasional poems, of the range usually covered in epigrams, which some of them are. They vary in meter and in tone, and all show considerable grace and finish. Their allusions and viewpoints fit with what we know of Vergil and if genuine provide further information about him. Number 5, for example, shows impatience with scholastic pedantry and preference for the philosophic approach represented by Siro, who was Horace's and Varus' teacher as well as Vergil's:

Avaunt, ye vain bombastic crew,
Crickets that swill no Attic dew;
Good-bye, grammarians crass and narrow,
Selius, Tarquitius, and Varro,
A pedant tribe of fat-brained fools,
The tinkling cymbals of the schools!
Sextus, my friend of friends, good-bye,
With all our pretty company!
I'm sailing for the blissful shore,
Great Siro's high recondite lore,
That haven where my life shall be
From every tyrant passion free.
You too, sweet Muses mine, farewell!
You too, sweet Muses mine, for truth to tell,
Sweet were ye once, but now begone;
And yet, and yet, return anon.
And when I write, at whiles be seen
In visits shy and far between.

                                                —*T. H. Warren*

Aetna, a didactic poem on volcanic action in 646 hexameters, is the longest of the poems in Suetonius' list; it is not included in editions of the *Appendix*. Stylistic considerations point to the early Silver Age, and the assumption that Vesuvius was extinct proves a date before the eruption of A.D. 63. A letter of Seneca to Lucilius (79.4–5) which speaks of *Aetnam in tuo carmine* was long taken to prove that Lucilius wrote the poem; but the passage only implies that Lucilius might mention Aetna in a projected work on Sicily. Its scientific attitude and its spirited digressions make the *Aetna* a very respectable work. The author begins by expressing disdain of the hackneyed subjects of mythologizing writers and states his own theme (24–28):

More gallantly I set my spirit toiling on a task untried; what are the forces for this mighty working, how great the energy which releases in dense array the eternal flames, thrusts masses of rock from the lowest depth with gigantic noise and burns everything near in rills of fire—this is the burden of my lay.

                                                —*J. W. and A. M. Duff*

Next he rejects the explanation of the poets (29–35):

First, let none be deceived by the fiction poets tell—that Aetna is the home of a god, that the fire gushing from her swollen jaws is Vulcan's fire, and

that the echo in that cavernous prison comes from his restless work. No
task so paltry have the gods. To meanest crafts one may not rightly lower
the stars; their sway is royal, aloft in a remote heaven; they reck not to
handle the toil of artisans.

—*J. W. and A. M. Duff*

He proceeds then to a sober exposition of his own explanation that
eruptions are caused by air currents in subterranean channels, whose
friction produces fire, which is then fed by lava. One digression
(224-75) is a stirring invitation to scientific research— "This is man's
more primary task, to know the earth and mark all the many wonders
nature has yielded there" (222-23). Another (604-646) celebrates the
heroic devotion of a pair of brothers who rescue their parents from a
sea of fire during a frightful eruption. The style is terse and spare, but
metaphors and mythologic allusion are freely used. The author has
obviously studied his Lucretius and is the closest approach in Latin to
Lucretius' serious devotion to scientific investigation.

IX

HORACE

MEN ARE MORE AT EASE IN THE DRY SUNLIGHT OF
secular wit than in the dim religious awe of a cathedral, more appreciative of an artistic presentation of the familiar than of a towering
creation which dwarfs them. If Vergil has been the most revered of
Latin poets, Horace has been the best beloved. He has been the favorite
of men of all conditions and in all countries; tags from his poems have
entered the vernacular of all languages. Horace has neither Vergil's
sustained grandeur of inspiration nor the majestic organ roll of his
hexameter; his burden does not transcend the ordinary reader's scope,
nor does he open vistas for the reader's own musing. His finest, most
characteristic, and most popular work are the *Odes,* which literal
translation makes so commonplace that one might well wonder at
Horace's appeal to discriminating readers. But lyric is notoriously untranslatable. In a lyricist like Pindar the power of soaring and dazzling
language, magnificent architectural structures, refractions of blazing
symbols, can be sensed even in translation. In Catullus shattering
passion makes its effect even through the insulation of an alien language. But Horace has no seer's vision, no grand concept of form. It
is not that he is limited by common sense; he makes a cult of common
sense. Every emotion and every experience with which he deals belong to the common stock of ordinary society. What Horace does is
to articulate the commonplace—what oft was thought but ne'er so
well expressed—with an art of matchless precision. He suggests no
new aspects or interpretations of the phenomena of life, but makes
the familiar artistic. In the distrust of free-ranging imagination and
in the flawless control of form Horace is the most classic of poets.

Q. Horatius Flaccus was born in 65 B.C. at Venusia in Apulia. His
father was a freedman, and he speaks of him often, with gratitude
and affection. His mother he never mentions; it has been conjectured,
but on no evidence, that she was a Jewess. Horace speaks of his education, and his father's part in it, in an autobiographical passage at
Satires 1.6.68–92:

If, to venture on self-praise, my life is free from stain and guilt and I am loved by my friends—I owe this to my father, who, though poor with a starveling farm, would not send me to the school of Flavius, to which grand boys used to go, sons of grand centurions, with slate and satchel slung over the left arm, each carrying his eightpence on the Ides—nay, he boldly took his boy off to Rome, to be taught those studies that any knight or senator would have his own offspring taught. Anyone who saw my clothes and attendant slaves—as is the way in a great city—would have thought that such expense was met from ancestral wealth. He himself, a guardian true and tried, went with me among all my teachers. Need I say more? He kept me chaste—and that is virtue's first grace—free not only from every deed of shame, but from all scandal. He had no fear that some day, if I should follow a small trade as crier or like himself as tax-collector, somebody would count this to his discredit. Nor should I have made complaint, but as it is, for this I owe him praise and thanks the more. Never while in my senses could I be ashamed of such a father, and so I will not defend myself, as would a goodly number, who say it is no fault of theirs that they have not free-born and famous parents.

—*H. R. Fairclough*

For advanced study Horace went to Athens, as was the custom among young Romans of means. There he enrolled in the army of the tyrannicide Brutus, who was collecting forces against Octavius and Antony, and after the defeat at Philippi in 42 B.C. he returned to Rome to find his father dead and his farm confiscated. To maintain himself he purchased a secretarial post in the treasury (*scriba quaestorius*) and also began to write verses. This brought him the acquaintance of Vergil and Varius, who secured him an introduction to Maecenas. His admission to Maecenas' circle nine months later, in 38 B.C., was the turning point in his career. It gave him financial independence, a respectable position in society, and incidentally won his sympathies for the regime. In 33 he was given his beloved Sabine farm, and devoted himself to his poetry and his urbane pleasures until his death in 8 B.C.

Of his poems the earliest are *Epodes* (a grammarians' title; Horace himself called them *iambi*), seventeen poems in varieties of iambic meter, written between 41 and 31 B.C. and published contemporaneously with the second book of *Satires* in 30 B.C. The *Epodes* have little of the mellow charm of the *Odes* but are an interesting index of the origin and growth of Horace's lyric style. The form and spirit are borrowed from Archilochus, who gave iambic the meaning "invective." Horace's invective can be as bitter as Archilochus', but it is directed rather at social abuses than at individual enemies. Epode 1, among the latest in the collection, is addressed to Maecenas, who is about to accompany Octavius in the campaign of Actium (31 B.C.). Though unapt for war, says Horace, he will accompany his friend, for so his fear for him will be less; his motive is not gain, for Maecenas has already filled his cup to overflowing. Epode 2 is an idyllic eulogy of country life, converted into a satire by the surprise at the end: When usurer Alfius has so delivered himself, all agog to be a farmer, he calls in all his loans on the Ides—and puts his money out again on the Kalends. Epode 3 calls vengeance down upon the head of Maecenas for having served Horace a dish too highly seasoned with garlic; a high degree of intimacy with Maecenas is implied. Epode 4 is a quite Archilochian invective against a parvenu, still scarred with the brands of slavery, who flaunts his wealth in vulgar display. It is not clear whether Horace is criticizing a specific individual or a class which had become numerous through the proscriptions and confiscations of the civil wars. Epode 5 is a genre picture of the ugly superstitions that flourished in the cosmopolis. The witch Canidia with three gruesome hags is about to torture a young boy to death to obtain the ingredients of a love philter. The poem opens with the child's pitiful appeal, and closes with his imprecations on his torturers' heads. Epode 17 is a mock recantation of the satire against witchcraft. Epode 6 is an invective against a blackmailer; again it is not clear whether the reference is to an individual or a class. Horace declares he is a faithful sheep dog who can bite back, a second Archilochus or Hipponax who will not tamely submit to insult. Epode 7 is an appeal against the renewal of civil strife, probably evoked by the rupture of the peace between Octavius and Sextus Pompey in 38 B.C. Epodes 8 and 12 are extremely coarse rejections of loathsome and lecherous women. Epode 9 is a song of triumph for the victory of Actium, addressed to Maecenas. Epode 10 is an ironical *propempticon* ("send-off") to the "smelly" poet Maevius, whom Vergil (*Eclogues* 3.90) had also damned. In Epodes 11 and 14 the poet complains that love keeps him from writing; in the latter poem, from completing a work which Maecenas had requested. Epode 13 is an invitation to banish wintry care by wine and song and cheerful talk; this is one of the best pieces in the collection, and quite in the spirit of such odes as 1.9. In Epode 15 the poet chides Neaera for jilting him; he will find another love, and she will be sorry. This Epode is like the more playful ode on Pyrrha (1.5). Number 16 is the earliest of the Epodes as well as the best in finish and patriotic fervor. It was written shortly after Philippi, before the poet had met Maecenas or had become reconciled to the new regime. The only recourse for good men, in the midst of continued turmoil, is flight to the Blessed Isles. Subsequently Horace found Rome and his Sabine farm a tolerable surrogate for the Blessed Isles.

A much completer and fairer picture of Horace's mind, and of contemporary scenes and characters, is afforded by the *Satires* or *Sermones,* informal *causeries* on the Lucilian model in hexameter verse. Book 1 of the *Satires,* containing ten poems, was published about 35 B.C.; Book 2, containing eight poems, about 30. The poems deal, in conversational tone, with a variety of subjects—social behavior, literary criticism, the encounters of urban life. They are seldom satirical in the modern sense and show none of Juvenal's indignation. They are directed against types rather than individuals, and against foibles rather than vices. Even in his moralizing, Horace's tone is not that of a preacher, but rather of a detached and well-informed and urbane observer of the social scene. The discourses are spoken by the author himself, and the tone is frequently autobiographical. The autobiographical tone, like much else in Horace, is a legacy from Lucilius. The two best known of Horace's satires, the "Bore" and the "Journey to Brundisium," are directly modelled on Lucilius; the extremely fragmentary remains of Lucilius provide a rich hunting ground for other Horatian sources. Horace himself criticizes Lucilius' careless haste and his outspokenness; we must agree that Horace's special contribution to the genre is the avoidance of these faults. He retains his amiable good humor and is fastidious in language and meter.

In Book 1, the first satire, which serves as a dedication of the whole collection to Maecenas, is a sermon against the frantic race for wealth and position. The ant, to whose example the avaricious appeal, knows when to stop accumulating and start enjoying; the competitive avarice of men reduces them to the fate of a Tantalus. Satire 1.2, starting with advocacy of the golden mean, sets forth the advantage of purchasing amatory pleasure on the open market over the discomfort and danger of adultery. The tone of this satire is coarse and sensational, and it deals freely with personalities; according to a scholiast the Maltinus whose foppishness is ridiculed in line 25 is Maecenas himself. This would prove what is in any case probable, that 1.2 is an early work. It bears striking resemblance to a poem on love by the Cynic Cercidas (late third century B.C.) found in a papyrus. Satire 1.3 looks like a recantation of the severity of 1.2 written after the author had met Maecenas. We should overlook the faults of our friends and practice mutual forbearance. The Stoic paradoxes, that all faults are equal and that every man is potentially a king, are ridiculed, but the tone of the whole is one of genial mellowness. Satire 1.4 is apparently a defense against critics who charged Horace with being a malevolent scandal-monger. Lucilius, following the model of Old Comedy, did call names, and was also careless and verbose; but Horace merely observes behavior for his own profit, as his father had taught him to do, and has no desire to give anyone pain. Incidentally, Horace disclaims the title of poetry for his satires; if his words were rearranged they would not reveal the *disiecti membra poetae*.

Satire 1.5 is the delightful account of a journey by the Appian Way and by canal boat, over the Apennines, and down to Brundisium, in company with Maecenas, who had been sent by Octavius to negotiate the treaty of 38 B.C. As has been observed, Horace's model is Lucilius' *Iter,* but the personal observations of muleteers and inns are surely Horace's own. Satire 1.6, from which the passage on Horace's father has been cited above, is an important autobiographical document. His friendship with Maecenas had exposed Horace to envy; he disclaims snobbery, and praises Maecenas for choosing friends on the basis of worth. Satire 1.7 turns on a pun. A man called Rex ("King") is on trial before Brutus, propraetor of Asia, and Brutus is urged to follow the regicide tradition of his family. Brutus died at Philippi in 42; hence this piece must be earlier, and is probably the first of the *Satires*. Like Epodes 5 and 17, Satire 1.8 ridicules sorcery. The scene is the old potter's field which Maecenas was transforming into a park, and the joke is the terror of the witch Canidia when the buttocks of a wooden Priapus cracked with a loud report. Satire 1.9 describes the efforts of the persistent bore to cling to Horace as he is taking a morning stroll and to persuade him to introduce him to Maecenas. The humor, dramatic realism, and personal note of this satire have made it justly famous. Satire 1.10 resumes the discussion of 1.4 on the history and nature of satire and is an important document in ancient literary criticism. Horace defends his earlier strictures on Lucilius, who had great satiric power indeed, but lacked the polish he would surely have had if he had lived in the Augustan age. The requisites of good satire, says Horace, are humor, brevity, clarity, variety of diction, smoothness of composition. There are interesting remarks on a number of Latin writers.

The first satire in the second book, probably the last written, is again on a literary subject, being a defense of Horace's own satires. The form is a dialogue between Horace and the lawyer C. Trebatius Testa. Horace insists he has no gift for epic, which Trebatius urges him to write, and Trebatius reminds him that satire may be subject to libel laws; but he agrees with Horace that if the satires are good and meet with Caesar's approval the poet will not be prosecuted. The satire may reflect a real anxiety induced by Augustus' restrictions upon freedom of speech. The second satire, probably the first of the second book in order of composition, is a discourse on frugal (but not mean) living, put into the mouth of the farmer Ofellus. The advice is very like that in Epicurus' letter to Menoecus (Diogenes Laertius 10.131), and there are also striking parallels with Cicero's philosophical writings. The longest and best satire in the collection is 2.3, in the form of a dialogue between Horace, who has retired to his newly acquired Sabine farm to escape the excitement of the Saturnalia in Rome, and the bankrupt speculator Damasippus, who was saved from suicide by conversion to Stoicism. Horace ridicules the Stoic doctrine *omnem stultum insanum esse*—"everyone but the sage is mad"—and at the same time uses the text to castigate the follies of mankind, specifically avarice, ambition, self-indulgence, and superstition. Nor does Horace exempt himself; he thinks he is sane, but so did Agave when she wrenched off her son's head. Criticism of the Epicureans may be implied in 2.4, in which the exaggerated importance attached to good dining is gently chided.

The most trenchant of the *Satires* is 2.5, directed against legacy hunters who ingratiated themselves with the numerous class of wealthy persons who had no natural heirs. Horace's method is to give the legacy hunter advice on procedures, and his form is an interesting example of travesty of a heroic theme, as is the *Amphitryo* of Plautus. The burlesque is a continuation of the conversation between

Ulysses and Tiresias in Hades as told in *Odyssey* 11. Ulysses is disturbed because he has learned that he will be reduced to poverty, and Tiresias introduces him to the new techniques for acquiring a fortune. *Hoc erat in votis,* 2.6, begins:

This is what I prayed for!—a piece of land not so very large, where there would be a garden, and near the house a spring of ever-flowing water, and up above these a bit of woodland. More and better than this have the gods done for me. I am content.

                                                        —*H. R. Fairclough*

This satire combines praise of the delights of country life and a heart-felt cry against the worries of the city with a delicate expression of thanks to Maecenas for his gift of the Sabine farm, which has enabled Horace to satisfy his craving. The theme is expounded and pointed up by the ingeniously introduced fable of the city mouse and the country mouse. Pope's successful imitation of this poem has added to its fame.

As in 2.3, the theme of 2.7 is the Saturnalia, and the text a Stoic paradox—*Solum sapientem esse liberum et omnem stultum servum,* "Only the sage is free; all others are slaves." Again Horace ridicules the paradox, and again uses it to enforce a sermon. The satire is cast in the form of a dialogue between Horace and his slave Davus, who, using the freedom of the Saturnalia, points out that the fashionable pursuits of the rich are only the petty vices of the slave writ large. Horace himself is vulnerable to the charge, for though he praises the old-fashioned virtues he would not go back to them if he could. In the end the slave's indictment proves too uncomfortable for the master, and he threatens to relegate him to work on the Sabine farm. Satire 2.8 is a report by Fundanius in a conversation with Horace of a dinner party given by a parvenu millionaire to Maecenas. Of the guests Fundanius himself, Viscus, and Varius are men of letters, and the others merely types—Porcius, who eats like a pig; Balatro, the buffoon; and Nomentanus, a standing character in satire. Not only are the *gaucheries* of new wealth satirized, but also the affected erudition of the epicures. Lucilius had written a number of satires on malaprop banquets; the climax of the theme is Trimalchio's famous dinner in Petronius.

Horace's *Epodes* are experimental. His hexameter writings provide entertainment and edification with superb skill. But for the generality of readers, as for Horace himself, it is his lyrics which have builded him a monument more enduring than bronze. Always excepting Catullus, posterity must agree with Quintilian (10.1.96) that Horace is practically the only Latin lyric poet worth reading. The poems were meant to be read, not (like Sappho's or Alcaeus') to be sung, though musical accompaniment is occasionally assumed as a literary convention. Of the four books of *Odes* (*Carmina*) the first three were published together in 23 B.C., and the fourth, containing chiefly "command" poems, in 13 B.C. In all, there are 103 poems varying in length from eight to eighty lines, the number being regularly divisible by four. Among the nineteen metrical patterns used, all borrowed from the Greek, Alcaics, Sapphics, and Asclepiads are predominant. It is noteworthy that Horace turned rather to the classic than to the Alexandrian Greeks for his models. Within the books the poems are carefully arranged to present a variety of meter and subject matter. Themes and treatment exhibit an almost infinite variety, but each ode normally has an addressee (Augustus, Lydia, Apollo, the Roman people, the ship of state, a wine jar, the fountain of Bandusia) and an occasion (Vergil's departure, a banquet, a winter's day, the defeat of Cleopatra). Whether his mood is that of a gay *bon vivant* or of a sober moralizer, Horace's *Odes* always display his quick perception, his agile wit, his matchless grace and economy of language. No word in an ode of Horace can be altered without spoiling the poem.

Interesting, and to him important, things might be said of the *Odes* to a philologist, just as interesting and to him important things may be said of a sonata to a musicologist; but for both sonata and lyric there can be no substitute for reading and hearing. In the case of Horace the task of offering specimens is complicated not only by embarrassment of riches but by the necessary falseness of translations of lyric; the more presentable a version is, the more likely it is to be independent of its original. But Horace's range of interests and some notion of his manner may be conveyed through specimens. First we have a few samples of the lighter mood which has attracted most of Horace's admirers:

> What slender youth, bedew'd with liquid odours,
> Courts thee on roses in some pleasant cave,
> Pyrrha? For whom bind'st thou
> In wreaths thy golden hair,
> Plain in thy neatness? O how oft shall he

On faith and changed gods complain, and seas
Rough with black winds, and storms
Unwonted shall admire!
Who now enjoys thee credulous, all gold,
Who always vacant, always amiable,
Hopes thee, of flattering gales
Unmindful. Hapless they
T'whom thou untried seem'st fair. Me in my vow'd
Picture the sacred wall declares to have hung
  My dank and dripping weeds
    To the stern God of sea.
                        —John Milton (1.5)

      Boy, I detest the Persian pomp;
        I hate those linden-bark devices;
      And as for roses, holy Moses!
        They can't be got at living prices!
      Myrtle is good enough for us,—
        For *you,* as bearer of my flagon;
      For *me,* supine beneath this vine,
        Doing my best to get a jag on!
                —Eugene Field (1.38)

Horace While, Lydia, I was lov'd of thee,
       Nor any was preferr'd 'fore me
       To hug thy whitest neck: than I,
       The Persian King liv'd not more happily.

Lydia While thou no other didst affect,
       Nor Cloe was of more respect;
       Then Lydia, far-fam'd Lydia,
       I flourish't more than Roman Ilia.

Hor.   Now Thracian Cloe governs me,
       Skilfull i' th' Harpe, and Melodie:
       For whose affection, Lydia, I
       (So Fate spares her) am well content to die.

Lyd.   My heart now set on fire is
       By Ornithes sonne, young Calais:

For whose commutuall flames here I
(To save his life) twice am content to die.

Hor.   Say our first loves we sho'd revoke,
And sever'd, joyne in brazen yoke:
Admit I Cloe put away,
And love again love-cast-off Lydia?

Lyd.   Though mine be brighter than the Star;
Thou lighter than the Cork by far;
Rough as th' Adratick sea, yet I
Will live with thee, or else for thee will die.
                                       —*Robert Herrick* (3.9)

Bandusia, stainless mirror of the sky!
Thine is the flower-crowned bowl, for thee shall die,
       When dawns yon sun, the kid
       Whose horns, half-seen, half hid,

Challenge to dalliance or to strife—in vain.
Soon must the firstling of the wild herd be slain,
       And these cold springs of thine
       With blood incarnadine.

Fierce glows the Dog-star, but his fiery beam
Toucheth not thee: still grateful thy cool stream
       To labour-wearied ox,
       Or wanderer from the flocks:

And henceforth thou shalt be a royal fountain:
My harp shall tell how from thy cavernous mountain,
       Where the brown oak grows tallest,
       All babblingly thou fallest.
                                  —*C. S. Calverley* (3.13)

Horace's genial *Weltanschauung* is reflected in the following:

No need of Moorish archer's craft
To guard the pure and stainless liver;
He wants not, Fuscus, poison'd shaft
       To store his quiver.
Whether he traverse Libyan shoals,
Or Caucasus, forlorn and horrent,

Or lands where far Hydaspes rolls
    His fabled torrent.
A wolf, while roaming trouble-free
In Sabine wood, as fancy led me,
Unarm'd I sang my Lalage,
    Beheld, and fled me.
Dire monster! in her broad oak woods
Fierce Daunia fosters none such other,
Nor Juba's land, of lion broods
    The thirsty mother.
Place me where on the ice-bound plain
No tree is cheer'd by summer breezes,
Where Jove descends in sleety rain
    Or sullen freezes;
Place me where none can live for heat,
'Neath Phoebus' very chariot plant me,
That smile so sweet, that voice so sweet,
    Shall still enchant me.
                    —*J. Conington* (1.22)

Be tranquil, Dellius, I pray;
For though you pine your life away
    With dull complaining breath.
Or speed with song and wine each day,
    Still, still your doom is death.

Where the white poplar and the pine
In glorious arching shade combine,
    And the brook singing goes,
Bid them bring store of nard and wine
And garlands of the rose.

Let's live while chance and youth obtain;
Soon shall you quit this fair domain
    Kissed by the Tiber's gold
And all your earthly pride and gain
    Some heedless heir shall hold.
                    —*Eugene Field* (2.3)

Licinius, trust a seaman's lore:
Steer not too boldly to the deep,

Nor, fearing storms, by treacherous shore
    Too closely creep.

Who makes the golden mean his guide
Shuns miser's cabin, foul and dark,
Shuns gilded roofs, where pomp and pride
    Are envy's mark.

With fiercer blasts the pine's dim height
Is rock'd; proud towers with heavier fall
Crash to the ground; and thunders smite
    The mountains tall.

In sadness hope, in gladness fear
'Gainst coming change will fortify
Your breast. The storms that Jupiter
    Sweeps o'er the sky

He chases. Why should rain today
Bring rain tomorrow? Python's foe
Is pleased sometimes his lyre to play,
    Nor bends his bow.

Be brave in trouble; meet distress
With dauntless front; but when the gale
Too prosperous blows, be wise no less,
    And shorten sail.
        —*J. Conington* (2.10)

Postumus, Postumus, alack-a-day,
The years, how swiftly do they glide away!
No piety keeps wrinkles from the brow,
Nor makes old age his near approach delay,
Nor never-mastered Death more time allow;

If thou should'st sacrifice three hundred steers
Each morning, friend, 'twere futile hope to storm
The heart of Pluto, never touched to tears.

    .   .   .   .

Earth must thou leave, thy home and charming wife,
Nor, though thou tendest many, shall one tree,
Of all that thou didst own in this brief life,
Except the hateful cypress, follow thee;

A worthier heir that Caecuban of thine,
Which thou behind a hundred locks dost hoard,
Shall drink, and splash the floor with lordly wine,
More choice than decks a Pontiff's festal board.

—F. Coutts (2.14)

Finally there are a number of moralizing and patriotic odes, perhaps
too many for modern taste. The "Ship of State" may mark Horace's
conversion to the regime:

O Ship! new billows sweep thee out
Seaward. What wilt thou? hold the port, be stout.
   See'st not? thy mast
How rent by stiff south-western blast,

   Thy side, of rowers how forlorn?
Thine hull, with groaning yards, with rigging torn,
   Can ill sustain
The fierce, and ever fiercer main;

   Thy gods, no more than sails entire,
From whom yet once thy need might aid require,
   O Pontic pine,
The first of woodland stocks is thine,

   Yet race and name are but as dust,
Not painted sterns give storm-tost seamen trust.
   Unless thou dare
To be the sport of storms, beware.

   Of old at best a weary weight,
A yearning care and constant strain of late,
   O shun the seas
That gird those glittering Cyclades.

—W. E. Gladstone (1.14)

There is a ringing ode for the victory over Cleopatra—Antony being
passed over in discreet silence:

Drink we now, and dancing round,
Press with footsteps free the ground;
Pour we now the rosy wine,
And, in honour of the gods,

Comrades, in their own abodes
Pile we the banquet on each holy shrine.

Sin it were ere now to pour
Forth the cellar's generous store;
While the haughty queen of Nile,
With her base and scurvy crew,
Dared unbridled to pursue
Wild hopes, and drunk with Fortune's favouring smile,

Madly dreamed the Capitol
Soon should totter to its fall,
And the Empire's self should die;
But her spirit quailed awhile,
When of all the ships of Nile
From Rome's avenging fires scarce one could fly.

.　.　.　.　.

On her prostrate Citadel
Dared her dauntless eye to dwell:
Firm of purpose, calm she stood,
Holding with unflinching grasp,
To her breast applied the asp,
Whose venom dire she drank through her blood.

Sternly resolute she died;
Nor could stoop her royal pride,
That, reserved to swell a show,
She a Woman and a Queen,
Should be led like captive mean
Through streets of Rome to grace her conquering foe.
—*Earl of Derby* (1.37)

But luxury is still a present danger:

Idle the plough, since rich men's lordly piles
　　Usurped the fruitful acres; pond and stew,
Broad as the Lucrine water, miles on miles,
　　Make sights for tourists gaping at the view.

The spinster plane drives out the wedded elm;
　　Myrtle and violet, every odorous weed,
Dispense their perfumes in the olive's realm,
　　Whose erstwhile masters fed the public need,

And close-bough'd laurels weave luxurious shade—
  Not thus our bearded fathers built the State,
When Romulus or Cato were obeyed,
  And in her rugged plainness Rome was great.

Wealth for the City, not the citizen,
  Was massed; no upstart burgess felled his trees
And with nice compass plotted on the plain
  Verandahs cool to take the northern breeze.

Men roofed their homes with turves from every field,
  While at the general charge their towns grew fine
With stately buildings, and the quarry's yield
  With new-cut stone adorned each holy shrine.
                                        —*Edward Marsh* (2.15)

Horace's finest expression of patriotism are the six stately odes at the opening of Book 3. The fourth book of his *Odes* contains much of his work as the laureate of Rome. The following ode from that book summarizes Augustus' achievements:

Of battles fought I fain had told,
And conquer'd towns, when Phoebus smote
His harp-string: "Sooth, 'twere over-bold
  To tempt wide seas in that frail boat."
Thy age, great Caesar, has restored
  To squalid fields the plenteous grain,
Given back to Rome's almighty Lord
Our standards, torn from Parthian fane,
Has closed Quirinian Janus' gate,
  Wild passion's erring walk controll'd,
Heal'd the foul plague-spot of the state,
  And brought again the life of old,
Life, by whose healthful power increased
  The glorious name of Latium spread
To where our sun illumes the east
  From where he seeks his western bed.
While Caesar rules, no civil strife
  Shall break our rest, nor violence rude,
Nor rage, that whets the slaughtering knife
  And plunges wretched towns in feud.
The sons of Danube shall not scorn

The Julian edicts; no, nor they
  By Tanais' distant river born,
    Nor Persia, Scythia, or Cathay.
And we on feast and working-tide,
  While Bacchus' bounties freely flow,
Our wives and children at our side,
  First paying Heaven the prayers we owe,
Shall sing of chiefs whose deeds are done.
  As wont our sires, to flute or shell,
And Troy, Anchises, and the son
  of Venus on our tongues shall dwell.
              —*J. Conington* (4.15)

Horace makes his own claim to immortality in the last poem of the third book:

Now have I reared a monument more durable than brass,
And one that doth the royal scale of pyramids surpass,
Nor shall defeated Aquilo destroy, nor soaking rain,
Nor yet the countless tide of years, nor seasons in their train.
Not all of me shall die: my praise shall grow, and never end
While pontiff and mute vestal shall the Capitol ascend,
And so a mighty share of me shall Libitina foil.
Where bellows headstrong Aufidus, where, on his arid soil,
King Daunus ruled a rural folk, of me it shall be told
That, grown from small to great, I first of all men subtly wrought
Aeolian strains to unison with our Italian thought.
So take thine honours earned by deeds; and graciously do thou,
Melpomene, with Delphic bays adorn thy poet's brow.
              —*W. E. Gladstone* (3.30)

To the period of what may fairly be called his laureateship belongs the most obviously official of Horace's productions, the *Carmen saeculare,* written by imperial command for the celebration of the inauguration of a new century in 17 B.C. It required some juggling of dates to make the centennial fall in that year, but the final establishment of the Augustan peace at home and abroad was an appropriate occasion for a solemn celebration, and a Sibylline oracle was found to justify the date. For an occasion of national stock-taking at the very beginning of Latin literature Livius Andronicus, as we have noted, composed a hymn to be performed by maidens. Horace's hymn is in nineteen

Sapphic strophes, the first nine to be chanted by girls, the second nine by boys, and the final strophe by the combined choirs. Allusion is made to the deities whose sanctuaries would be passed in the procession from the Palatine to the Capitoline, with Augustus' particular deities, Apollo and Diana, in the foreground. As the extant inscription which reports the celebration tells us, each choir consisted of twenty-seven members; the recurrence of the number three is intentional as is the number seven in Vergil's fourth eclogue. Both poems are religious in tone, but the difference between them is a perfect index of the essential difference between the poets. The eclogue is suggestive, allusive, in a word, incantational; the *Carmen saeculare* is formal, polished, and means rather less than more than it says.

The next work to appear after the publication of Books 1–3 of the *Odes* was Book 1 of the *Epistles,* which was published in 20 B.C. This book contains twenty informal verse letters addressed to various recipients. Again the first piece is dedicated to Maecenas and serves as an introduction to the whole, and its moralizing tone is characteristic of the entire book. Horace explains that he is too old to continue with lyric poetry; he would rather turn to philosophy, not as a devotee of a single school—*nullius addictus iurare in verba magistri*—but being borne along as the wind lists. Vice and folly must be avoided; the Stoic position that only the sage can be perfect has great merit— but even a sage is subject to the common cold. Many of the other epistles of Book 1 contain familiar moral admonition: Epistle 2 offers Polonius advice to Lollius Maximus; Epistle 3 urges Julius Florus to study philosophy; Epistle 6 impresses the doctrine of *nil admirari* on Numicius; Epistle 8 warns against being elated at good fortune; Epistles 10 and 14 advocate a simple country life; Epistle 11 praises solitude; Epistle 12 criticizes discontent; Epistle 16 prefers being to seeming good; Epistles 17 and 18 encourage the maintenance of personal integrity. Others have a more personal interest: Epistle 4 invites Albius (probably the elegiac poet Tibullus) to be cheered up by a visit to Horace, who is an *Epicuri de grege porcum;* Epistle 5 invites Torquatus to a simple dinner to celebrate Augustus' birthday; in Epistle 7 Horace offers Maecenas a dignified excuse for not accepting an invitation; Epistle 9 is a letter of introduction to the future emperor Tiberius; Epistle 13 accompanies a gift copy of Horace's poems to Augustus; Epistle 15 inquires concerning the relative advantages of two sea-side resorts; in Epistle 19 Horace defends his poems against the charge of being servile imitations; Epistle 20 is a send-off to his book, warning it of the perils to be encountered in the wide world.

The second book of *Epistles,* which contains two (or three if the *Ars poetica* is added, as scholars have thought it should be) long pieces, is of the greatest interest to the student of Latin literature. These writings not only contain well-informed remarks on earlier Latin writers but also set forth a theory of literary practice. Epistle 1 starts with a graceful compliment to the Emperor who, unlike the demigods of story, receives recognition for his benefits in his life time: contemporary poets should similarly receive recognition, which should not be reserved for the ancients. Appreciation of Ennius, Naevius, and Pacuvius, of Afranius, Plautus, Caecilius, and Terence should be discriminating. Literary art came to Rome late—*Graecia capta ferum victorem capit*—but it is a valuable refining influence. No sculptor reproduces the features of heroes more faithfully than Vergil and Varius (Horace himself disclaims the faculty) portray their souls. In the second epistle Horace excuses himself to Florus for not writing. He is no longer under economic pressure to do so, and the atmosphere of Rome is not congenial to poetry. Poets must form a mutual admiration society (a presage of the "recitation" of the Silver Age) and praise each other's bad work; scholars have surmised a dig at Propertius in lines 100–101. But bad poets still cling to their illusions, like the Don Quixote of Argos. For Horace the time has come to contemplate more serious questions of moral conduct. The poem closes with an echo of Lucretius 3.938:

> *vivere si recte nescis, decede peritis.*
> *lusisti satis, edisti satis atque bibisti:*
> *tempus abire tibi est, ne potum largius aequo*
> *rideat et pulset lasciva decentius aetas.*

If you know not how to live aright, make way for those who do. You have played enough, have eaten and drunk enough. 'Tis time to quit the feast, lest, when you have drunk too freely, youth mock and jostle you, playing the wanton with better grace.

—*H. R. Fairclough*

The 476-line *Ars poetica* is the longest of Horace's poems, and appears by itself in the manuscripts. Its alternative title, *Epistle to the Pisos,* its subject matter, and its discursive and personal tone would logically associate it with Book 2 of the *Epistles.* The *Ars poetica* is a central document in ancient literary criticism and has exercised incalculable influence upon European literature, especially the drama. Its matter is drawn from technical treatises of the Greeks, as is kindred material in Quintilian and in Cicero, but the whole is informed by Horace's usual good sense. The keynote is *to prepon,* literary propriety. The poem begins by calling a painter who joined a human head to a horse's neck crazy, and closes with a sketch of a crazy poet who buttonholes his unwilling audience. Propriety demands that a poem have unity, simplicity, a subject matter within the poet's competence, carefully chosen and appropriate diction, the meter established for the genre. Stories, whether taken from tradition or invented, must be consistent. A third of the *Ars poetica* is devoted to drama; division into acts, gods out of the machine, the functions of the chorus, the musical element, diction, meter, and the history of the genre are dealt with. Horace disparages the "arty" pose of genius; his own bile he purges regularly and hence, not writing himself, he will undertake to instruct others. The main lesson is philosophic wisdom, which can be conveyed through striking passages and characters. The aim of poetry is a combination of instruction with pleasure—*omne tulit punctum qui miscuit utile dulci.* Absolute perfection is not to be expected—*bonus dormitat Homerus;* but mediocrity is intolerable in poetry, and one should not be in haste to publish—*nescit vox missa reverti.* The tradition of poetry is glorious, and none need blush for the Muse and Apollo. Natural endowment is necessary for a poet, but so is training, as in racing or flute-playing. Suspect purchased flattery; an honest man will not conceal his friend's faults from him. A crazy poet is a danger to himself and society.

The ideals of classicism, in its strength and in its limitations, are perfectly reflected in the *Ars poetica,* as they are perfectly carried out in Horace's own works. There is no better exponent of the rational and scientific as applied to the arts of expression; those who desiderate something more of the poet, vision in concept and incantation in utterance, would deny Horace the title of poet altogether. It is natural that Augustan periods in various European literature drew inspiration from Horace and revered him as the ultimate authority. In his *Essay on Criticism* Alexander Pope describes Horace's manner and the character of the authority he exercised over Englishmen:

> Horace still charms with graceful negligence,
> And without method talks us into sense;
> Will, like a friend, familiarly convey
> The truest notion in the easiest way.

X
TIBULLUS AND PROPERTIUS

ONLY "GENTLEMEN" CAN INDULGE IN THE PREOC-
cupation with their own sensibilities in the mood of studied wistfulness and self-pity called (after the Roman genre) elegiac, and all our
authors of Roman elegy were in fact (unlike Vergil and Horace)
"gentlemen" by birth. It is natural that elegy should occupy a relatively larger place in Latin literature, which is always conscious of its
own art and learning and addressed to a special class, than in the
more popular literature of classical Greece. Among the Greeks the
elegy was the earliest departure from the epic hexameter, and its history goes back to the eighth century B.C. In form it consisted of
distich, of which the first line was a hexameter and the second a
so-called pentameter, actually a hexameter curtailed by a syllable in
the middle and at the end of the line. The elegist spoke in his own
person, usually voicing admonitions on politics, warfare, and moral
conduct, but occasionally dealing with convivial subjects. The elegiac
was also the regular meter for inscriptions, whether on tombs or votive
offerings, and for the literary epigram which is a development from
inscriptions. Erotic epigrams are of course very numerous (the main
collection is in Book 5 of the *Greek Anthology*), but it is curious that
we know of no precise analogue in Greek for the developed Roman
love elegy. The Romans naturally drew on Greek sources—lyric,
pastoral, New Comedy, and of course epigram, and misdirected efforts have been made to reduce Roman elegy to epigrams; but in the
present state of our knowledge the erotic elegy seems to be a Roman
development. Catullus was the first Roman poet to use the elegiac
meter frequently and successfully, and Catullus 68 may be a greater
innovation than is commonly thought; in any case that poem is an
important landmark in the history of Latin love elegy.

The roster of Roman elegists is conveniently presented in a passage
in Ovid (*Tristia* 4.10.51–55):

> *Vergilium vidi tantum: nec avara Tibullo*
> *tempus amicitiae fata dedere meae.*

successor fuit hic tibi, Galle, Propertius illi;
quartus ab his serie temporis ipse fui.

Vergil I only saw; and greedy fate vouchsafed Tibullus no time for my friendship. It was Tibullus who succeeded you, Gallus, and Propertius succeeded Tibullus; I myself was the fourth in order of time.

Our succession then is Gallus, Tibullus, Propertius, and Ovid, and since Gallus is not likely to have had important predecessors other than Catullus, the list is complete. Gallus is the poet (and important public official) whom Vergil addressed in Eclogue 10 and mentioned elsewhere. He was obviously a figure of prime importance in the development of the love elegy, but only a single line is extant of the four books he wrote on Lycoris. Tibullus we have encountered as the probable addressee of the *Epistles* (1.4) in which Horace says: "Never were you a body without a soul. The gods gave you beauty, the gods gave you wealth, and the art of enjoyment." Tibullus' sensitive nature is also suggested in Ovid's lament for him (*Amores* 3.9.9–16):

> Behold, he comes with trailing wing forlorn
>   And smites with desperate hands his bosom bare!
> Tears rain unheeded o'er his tresses torn,
>   And many a trembling sob his soft lips bear.
>
> Thus for a brother Eros mourned of yore,
>   Aeneas, in Iulus' regal hall;
> Not less do Venus' eyes this death deplore
>   Than when she saw her slain Adonis fall.
>   —*Theodore C. Williams*

The ancient *Life* of Tibullus tells us little more than can be surmised from his works. He was born, perhaps in 48 B.C., of a well-to-do equestrian family; though his property was diminished in the civil wars, he was nevertheless able to lead the life of a country gentleman on his estate between Praeneste and Tibur. An important fact in his life is his adherence to the circle of M. Valerius Messalla, whom he accompanied on a campaign in the east and possibly against the Aquitani. Messalla fought against Octavian at Philippi, and though he later served under Octavian he retained his republican sentiments; Tibullus was thus in a manner the poet of the republican resistance. He never flatters Augustus or mentions his name. He scoffs at riches, glory and war, wanting nothing but to triumph as a lover. Ovid dares

(*Amores* 3.9.60–64) to group him with the laureled shades of Catullus and Gallus, of whom the former had lampooned the divine Julius and the latter had been exiled by Augustus. Tibullus died in 19 B.C., the year of Vergil's death.

The collection which has come down to us under the name of Tibullus originally contained three books. The first book, published in 26 B.C., and the second, published before Tibullus' death in 19, were known to antiquity under the names of Delia and Nemesis, the mistresses whom they celebrate. The third book, which has been divided by Italian humanists to make a fourth, may be called the Messalla collection; it contains pieces by different hands and was added at some later time. Among its contents may be distinguished six elegies by Lygdamus dedicated to a Neaera, a panegyric on Messalla in hexameters, five short and graceful poems on the love of Sulpicia (a kinswoman of Messalla) for Cerinthus, possibly written by Tibullus, six very short pieces by Sulpicia herself, and two poems of doubtful authorship.

The first poem, addressed to Messalla (line 53) is the first of the elegies to Delia and the poet's statement of his own views of life. He praises the simple and carefree life of the countryside, cares neither for riches nor for the glory won in war: "Sooner let all the gold and emeralds perish from the world than any maiden weep for my departings" (51–52). The characteristic elegiac notes of self-submersion in contemplation of approaching dissolution occurs (59–73):

May I look on thee when my last hour comes; may I hold thy hand, as I sink, in my dying clasp. Thou wilt weep for me, Delia, when I am laid on the bed that is to burn; thou wilt give me kisses mingled with bitter tears. Thou wilt weep: thy breast is not cased in iron mail; in thy soft heart there is no stubborn flint. From that burial none, neither youth nor maiden, will return with dry eyes home. Do thou hurt not my spirit; but spare thy loosened hair and spare thy soft cheeks, Delia.

Meantime, while Fate allows, let us be one in love. Soon will Death be here with his head cowled in dark. Soon will steal on us the inactive age, nor will it be seemly to play the lover or utter soft speeches when the head is hoar. Now let gay love be my pursuit.

—*J. P. Postgate*

The Delia series continues with 2, 3, 5, and 6. Number 2 is a variation of the type called *paraklausithyron,* or serenade before a mistress' locked door, and also speaks of a love philter which a witch had prepared for the poet to ensure that his love would be reciprocated. Again the blessings of simple country life are praised. Messalla had invited Tibullus to accompany him on an official mission to the east, but the poet fell sick at Corcyra. In the third elegy the poet laments his loneliness there (5–10):

> Spare me, dark death! I have no mother here,
>   To clasp my relics to her widowed breast;
> No sister, to pour forth with hallowing tear
>   Assyrian incense where my ashes rest.
>
> Nor Delia, who, before she said adieu,
>   Asked omens fair at every potent shrine.
> —Theodore C. Williams

The picture of dishevelled Delia's greeting when he will unexpectedly return is particularly charming (89–95):

> Some evening, after tasks too closely plied,
>   My Delia, drowsing near the harmless dame,
> All sweet surprise, will find me at her side,
>   Unheralded, as if from heaven I came.
>
> Then to my arms, in lovely disarray,
>   With welcome kiss, thy darling feet will fly!
> O happy dream and prayer! O blissful day!
>   What golden dawn, at last, shall bring thee nigh?
> —Theodore C. Williams

The inevitable happened, and Delia turned to a richer lover. In Elegy 5 Tibullus protests his faithful devotion; wine and other loves are futile as anodynes. But Tibullus never uses the harsh language which Catullus applies to Lesbia. His reproaches are for the bawd who led Delia astray. In an access of self-pity at the close he can even encourage his rival to use his good fortune. In Elegy 6 the poet's suspicions are further aroused, but Delia swears both to her lover and to her husband that there is no third. He begs the blind husband to put Delia in his charge; he knows how to manage her, but would never strike her or do her any harm. Retribution is bound to overtake the faithless sweetheart (83–87):

Venus from her throne on high Olympus looks upon her weeping, and bids us mark how sharp she is with the faithless. Upon others, Delia, let these curses fall: but let us twain still be pattern lovers when our hair is white.

—*J. P. Postgate*

Elegies 4, 8, and 9 form a similar series, the object of Tibullus' attention in these being the *puer delicatus* Marathus. Elegy 4, which introduces the series, is a discourse on the art of winning a boy love placed in the mouth of the wanton garden god Priapus. The advice on techniques anticipates Ovid's treatment in the *Ars amatoria.* Elegy 8 is similarly dramatized. The poet has come upon Marathus and Pholoe whispering together; he admonishes the boy and threatens the girl with Nemesis. There is kindliness and detached appreciation of an amusing situation in this poem; the poet's attitude is that of an urbane Roman who never forgets the difference between a Roman gentleman and a couple of irresponsible slaves from the east. Elegy 9 is the last of the Marathus cycle. The vain and silly lad has been carrying on a secret intrigue with a horrible old creature whose only possible attraction is his money. The poet becomes aware of the situation, taxes the boy with perfidy, venality, and ingratitude, and definitely casts him off. Of the two remaining elegies of Book 1, the seventh is a birthday poem for Messalla, in which his various achievements are celebrated. The closing poem (it is worth noting that Vergil's *Eclogues* and Horace's *Satires* also had ten pieces each) is an echo of Elegy 1. The poet has been called to military service, and speaks of the great advantages of country life and love over a military career. Here is the conclusion (64–69):

> Thrice happy is the wight
> Whose frown some lovely mistress weeps to see!
> But he who gives her blows!—Go, let him bear
> A sword and spear! In exile let him be
> From Venus' mild domain! Come blessed Peace!
> Come, holding forth thy blade of ripened corn!
> Fill thy large lap with mellow fruits and fair!

> —*Theodore C. Williams*

Of the six pieces in the fragmentary second book 3, 4, and 6 deal with a new light of love called Nemesis. Nemesis is a much harder and more grasping type than her predecessor. She has no illusions, is not impressed by poetry, does not enjoy sentiment, and expects the poet to gratify her expensive tastes or cease wasting her valuable time. For his part he is forever complaining of her greed, heartlessness, and infidelity, and of his own bondage. In the first elegy of the series (2.3) Nemesis has left town with her wealthy lover and is now at his country place taking part in the merriment of the vintage season. The poet complains of the degenerate age when money is preferred over love. He curses the rival who has carried her away but feels that, though uninvited, he too, like a slave, must go. The next poem (2.4) is a moving confession of abjectness and despair. It begins

> A woman's slave am I, and know it well.
> Farewell, my birthright! farewell, liberty!
> In wretched slavery and chains I dwell,
> For love's sad captives never are set free.
> —*Theodore C. Williams*

The poet prays for insensibility to suffering. He realizes how completely mercenary Nemesis is, but so enslaved is he that he must satisfy her demands by any crime rather than forego seeing her. He contrasts the inevitable eventual neglect that Nemesis must suffer with the abiding affection that an honest sweetheart retains after her death. But though Tibullus is aware of his degradation he is helpless: if Nemesis demands it he will sell his home at auction, he will drain a cup of poison. There can be little doubt that this poem is a genuine expression of the poet's feeling, not a literary exercise. As a reflection of personal experience the poem is then an interesting parallel to Catullus 76; but whereas Catullus struggles manfully with his obsession, the true elegist can only yield, and revel a little in his misery. The final poem of the Nemesis cycle is 2.6, which is addressed to Tibullus' friend Macer. Macer is off to the wars, but Tibullus' martial ardor is dissipated by the hope, which springs eternal, that Nemesis may still open her closed door to him. Again he reproaches the faithless fair but cannot abide the thought that she should drop a single tear; it is the bawd who is to blame, and upon her Tibullus utters his curses. If the addressee is the Aemilius Macer who died in Asia in 16 B.C. the poem is probably its author's last work.

Of the three other elegies in Book 2, the first is a charming description of merrymaking at a country festival, probably the Ambarvalia. The rustic piety and jollity of the lustration ceremony is represented in this passage (2.1.1–10):

Attend! and favour! as our Sires ordain;
The Fields we lustrate, and the rising Grain;
This hallow'd Day suspend each Swain his Toil,
Rest let the Plough, and rest th' uncultur'd Soil:
Unyoke the Steer, his Racks heap high with Hay,
And deck with Wreaths his honest Front today.
Let all to Heaven's Service be apply'd!
And lay, ye thrifty Fair, your Wool aside!
    See! to the Flames the Victim comes unbound!
Follows the white Procession, Olive-crown'd!
    'Today we purge the Farmer and the Field,
From Ills, O sylvan Gods, our Limits shield;
O let no Weeds destroy the rising Grain;
By no swift Wolf be the weak Lambkin slain.
Prosp'rous the Hind shall trust the teeming Earth,
And heap great Logs upon his blazing Hearth.'
    Wine in our Festival its Part must play,
The tipsy Reel causes no shame Today.
    Sport on! Night yokes her Steeds; a golden Train
Follows in playful Dance the Mother's Wane;
Then Sleep comes silent, swathed in Wings of black,
And the vain Race of Dreams flits in his Track.

—*James Grainger*

The second in Book 2 is a birthday poem for Cornutus, a member of
the Messalla group, who may be identical with Sulpicia's lover Cerinthus. The poet's best wish for his friend is the abiding love of his
wife. The fifth is Tibullus' longest piece and the only one of a national
character, and even here the occasion is personal—the appointment
of Messalla's son Messalinus as a *quindecemvir*. This poem is a fine
example of the elegiac technique of progression by zigzag, each arm
being articulated with the next, with occasional purposeful retarda-
tions to enlarge on a minor theme. Apollo is asked to accept the new
priest of the Sibyl; it was the Sibyl who prophesied Rome's greatness
to Aeneas; the prophecy is accomplished and we pray that dreadful
omens cease; if the omen is propitious let rustic merriment abound,
even to the petty quarrel of the lover and his lass; me may Nemesis
spare till I can sing the praises of Messalinus celebrating a proud triumph.

    The third book of the Tibullan corpus, in our editions, contains
six rather frigid elegies of Lygdamus, whose lady is Neaera. Both

names are pseudonymous. Unconvincing efforts have been made to identify Lygdamus with Propertius, Ovid, or Ovid's brother; Neaera's social position is superior to Delia's or Nemesis', for Lygdamus aspires to marriage. Lygdamus' ideals and his elegiac surrender to love are much like Tibullus', but he is without Tibullus' appealing gentleness. Lygdamus was certainly a member of the Messalla circle; association with Messalla is the one feature which links the whole Tibullan corpus together.

Artistically the nadir of the corpus is the tasteless and bombastic panegyric of Messalla in 211 hexameters which opens the fourth book. Only the association with Messalla is responsible for its preservation. By contrast the next eleven elegies (4.2–12) are the best and most interesting in the entire collection. They tell us the charming story of two young lovers, Sulpicia, the ward and probably the niece of Messalla himself, and the young man whom she calls Cerinthus. The first five are by some sympathetic poet and friend, quite possibly Tibullus, and are based on the second group of seven, which are indubitably by Sulpicia herself. The first group is introduced (4.2) by verses supposed to accompany a present to Sulpicia on the occasion of the Matronalia, when ladies received gifts from male relatives and friends. The poem is a charming expression of warm but disinterested regard; the pleasure which the beautifully described beauty of the lady affords is purely aesthetic (4.2.1–10):

> On thy Calends hath my Ladye robed to pay thee honour due;
> Come if thou be wise, great Mavors, come thyself her charms to view!
> Venus will excuse the treason; but do thou, rude chief, beware
> Lest thine arms fall in dishonour, whilst thou gazest on the fair.
> In her eyes, whene'er her pleasure wills the hearts of gods to fire,
> Lamps, a pretty pair, are burning, ever lit by young Desire:
> Whatsoe'er the maid be doing, wheresoe'er her step she bends,
> Perfect grace is shed around her, perfect grace in stealth attends.
> Every heart is fired to see her, walk she robed in purple bright;
> Every heart is fired to see her, come she dressed in snowy white;
> If she leave her tresses flowing, grace o'er flowing locks is pour'd;
> If she braid them, in her braidings is she meet to be adored.
>
> —A. Holmes

The next piece (4.3) presents Sulpicia's thoughts when her lover has gone on a boar hunt; she is tremulous with concern for his safety and wishes he were restored to her arms. In 4.4 Sulpicia is ill, and the poet expresses Cerinthus' ardent prayer to Apollo for her recovery and his own assurance to Cerinthus that God will not hurt faithful lovers. In 4.5 (as in 4.3) Sulpicia's thoughts are presented, this time on the occasion of her beloved's birthday. The heart's desire of both is the same; may it find fulfilment! The final poem of this group is for Sulpicia's birthday, and again the poet friend presents Cerinthus' thought. 'Tis for Juno Natalis Sulpicia says she has arrayed herself so fine, but it is really for Cerinthus; may her love and yours prosper.

Next are Sulpicia's own six short pieces, totaling only forty lines but displaying an extraordinary and unaffected simplicity. The order is based on variety rather than chronology. In the probable psychological order we have first 4.8, in which Sulpicia speaks of her "hateful old birthday." Messalla had planned as a special treat an excursion to the country; but this means that she cannot be with her beloved. Book 4.9 tells her lover that the excursion has happily been called off; 4.11 tells Cerinthus that she is sick, and cannot get well without his sympathy. In 4.12 Sulpicia apologizes for having left Cerinthus abruptly; she was trying to dissemble her ardor. Sulpicia has heard that Cerinthus has been bestowing his attention elsewhere and writes the angry 4.10, palpitating with the fury of a passionate and high-spirited girl who has been deeply offended not only in her love but in her pride. She minces no words in rebuking his apparent preference for the physical attraction of a low wench. Book 4.7, which comes first in the series should actually be last, for it breathes the exaltation of love consummated. She is proud of her surrender, and has no thought of taint or regret. The utter sincerity and full-bloodedness of this and all of Sulpicia's poems make the ordinary level of Latin love poetry seem sickly or contrived by comparison.

Two final poems in the corpus remain to be considered. Book 4.13 protests unalterable fidelity to some unnamed woman; it may well be, as line 13 indicates it is, by Tibullus. Book 4.14 is an epigram in which the author begs to be spared knowledge of his mistress' infidelities. Perhaps both pieces were rejected by Tibullus himself for the two books he published and were later found and included in the posthumous publication.

In mood certainly, if not in technique, Tibullus is the great exemplar of Latin elegy. The masterful virility of the ancients would have been an anachronism in the perfectly patterned and ordered and sophisticated society of the Augustan peace. One avenue of literary escape is the artificiality of the bucolic; in Tibullus' elegies artificiality has become native and admits of a new naturalness. It is only in a self-conscious environment that love and the gentle heart can be canonized but in such an environment the canonization can be very real. The robust and hearty type may grow very impatient with Tibullus, might even call him maudlin and with some suitable expletive adjure him "to snap out of it." But Tibullus' preoccupation with love and with the bland pleasures of the countryside and with his own sensibilities is something more than a psychologic introvert weeping in his beer; it is a gentle soul seeking a viable level of existence in a brutal world.

Readers who prize gentleness will favor Tibullus above his elegiac peers, readers who prize a restless wit will prize Ovid, but those for whom Ovid is too cynical and Tibullus too bland will choose the passionate Propertius. Most of what we know of Propertius' life is from the speech of the astrologer Horos in 4.1.121–134:

> Of well-known family, you trace
> Descent from Umbria's ancient race.
> Unless my intuitions fail
> Your birthplace marches with the pale
> Where from Mevania's misty hill
> Dews on the vale below distill;
> Where basks the sun-warmed Umbrian mere
> And where the soaring walls appear
> That form the famous fortress crown,
> More famous made by your renown;
> Orphaned although so young, you gave
> Your father's scattered bones a grave,
> And you were driven to become
> The inmate of a humble home.
> For even while your oxen toil
> In many a team to turn the soil
> The stern surveyor, pole in hand,
> Seizes upon your well-tilled land.
> And when anon your neck no more
> The golden boss of boyhood wore
> And, with your mother's prayers, began

The toga of a freeborn man,
E'en at that early age some part
Apollo taught you of his art,
Nor in the market-place allowed
To bellow to the witless crowd.

—*S. G. Tremenheere*

Sextus Propertius was born, then, near Mevania in Umbria, of equestrian family (else he could not have worn "the golden boss of boyhood"); he was orphaned in boyhood and some of his land confiscated for Octavian's and Antony's veterans in 41 or 40 ("the stern surveyor seizes your land"); he assumed the *toga virilis* in his mother's house, studied the law, but left it for poetry. Upon this evidence his birth should be placed at about 50 B.C. The central passion of his life was Cynthia, whose name recurs in all of his four books, but who is the chief subject of the first. The poems are not arranged chronologically, but the labor of many scholars enables us to present a tentative course of Propertius' love. In adolescence he loved a girl called Lycinna, but his great and fatal passion was for Cynthia, a lady of easy virtue whose real name was Hostia. At first he idealized her; but she was unfaithful and after five or six years he broke with her. Perhaps there was a reconciliation, for later poems (which may be retrospective) describe a quarrel with her and her death. Maecenas was his patron, and if Horace, *Epistles* 2.2.100 refers to Propertius, Horace knew and disliked him. Ovid, *Tristia* 4.10.45 shows that Ovid was his friend and that he was dead by A.D. 2. The latest date assignable to any poem of Propertius is 16 B.C.; his death must therefore fall between the two dates.

Propertius' elegies have come down in four books (the division into five found in some texts is without authority); these may be dated, but with no certainty, as follows: 1, 33–28 B.C.; 2, 28–25 B.C.; 3, 24–22 B.C.; 3, 21–16 B.C. The text of Propertius is in a bad condition, many lines having been lost or misplaced. This sometimes makes the thought obscure and transition abrupt. Textual difficulties as well as the vivid personality of the poet have attracted much scholarly attention to Propertius. In recent years he has been edited, commented upon, and translated more frequently than Tibullus.

The first book was known in antiquity as *Cynthia monobiblos,* for its dominant theme is Propertius' love for Cynthia. The first and last poems of this book (1 and 22) are respectively prologue and epilogue and were probably written last; one introduces Cynthia, "who first enslaved wretched me with her eyes," and the other is vaguely auto-biographical. The second celebrates Cynthia's beauty, for which artificial adornment is useless. In the third the poet returns from a late party to find Cynthia asleep; as he admires her beauty she awakens and reproaches him for his long absence. In 4 he remonstrates with Bassus for urging him to break with Cynthia, and in 5 he warns Gallus (not the poet) against making overtures to Cynthia. In 6 Propertius regretfully refuses an invitation of Tullus to join him in foreign travel: Cynthia will not let him go. This poem has an obvious similarity to Tibullus 1.1, but whereas Tibullus is heartsick at having to leave Delia, Propertius for all his protestations finds Cynthia's clinging somewhat irksome. In 7 the poet warns Ponticus, who is so proud of his epic, that he will sing a different tune if ever he is smitten by love. In 8a the poet seeks to dissuade Cynthia from following the poet's rival to Illyria; he prays for storms to prevent her sailing but wishes her a safe journey if she goes; in 8b he exults at her decision not to go. Number 9 is an "I told you so" to the Ponticus of 7. In 10 Propertius rejoices at a meeting between Gallus and his mistress; a possible rival for Cynthia's favors is thus eliminated. Cynthia has gone off to Baiae in 11; the poet fears for her good name and begs her to return soon. Number 12 answers a reproach for sloth; it is his continued attachment to estranged Cynthia that makes him spiritless. Gallus may gloat over his troubles (13); he will not retaliate but only felicitate Gallus. Number 14 either is out of order or marks a reconciliation; the pleasures of wealth are not to be compared to the joys of love. Though the poet has to face some danger (15), Cynthia shows her indifference by taking another lover. The poet protests that his own love will not alter (1.15.29-32):

> Many things sooner! Rivers upward flow
>   From the vast sea, the year reverse its changes,
> Ere from my heart the thought of thee shall go!
>   Be what thou wilt! There's nothing thee estranges.
>   —E. H. W. Meyerstein

Number 16 is, like Catullus 67, the soliloquy of the door of a house which was once but is no longer respectable. In a storm at sea (17)

the poet laments that he must perish far from Cynthia. And in the
loneliness of a forest he laments Cynthia's obduracy (18):

> Here, sure, is loneliness
> Ay, dumb to my distress!
> And Zephyr's breath commands the vacant grove!
> Here with impunity
> Speak hidden griefs may I,
> If solitary rocks but true friends prove!
>
> Say, from what cause forlorn
> Shall I trace Cynthia's scorn?
> Where, Cynthia, the first ground of weeping, where?
> I, rank among the state
> Of lovers fortunate,
> Now in thy love am forced a brand to bear.
>
> Such pangs have I deserved?
> What spells thy heart have swerved?
> Is a new girl the fount of thy distaste?
> Home hither may'st thou fare
> So surely, as I swear
> No other's white foot hath my threshold paced!
>
> Though store of bitter woe
> My grief to thee doth owe,
> So dire my indignation ne'er appears
> That I should justly seem
> Ever thy fury's theme,
> And mar thine eyes by falling flow of tears.
>
> Or is it by changed hue
> Tokens I give too few?
> Or, in my utterance shouts no loyalty?
> If trees know aught of love,
> My witnesses ye'll prove,
> Thou beech, thou pine, Pan's friend in Arcady.
>
> How oft my echoing word
> 'Neath your soft shades is heard,
> And Cynthia's inscribed upon your bark!
> How oft within my soul
> Thy wrongs yield birth to dole
> None, none but thy unanswering portals hark!

Ever endure I must
In shy faint-hearted trust
All proud commands, nor raise shrill wail of woes:
And lo! my whole reward
The haunted spring, the hard
Chill crag, and on this rude path rough repose!

All, all my plaintive cries
Have power to threnodize,
Unfriended, to shrill birds must I proclaim.
But whatsoe'er thou be,
"Cynthia" every tree
Still echo, nor these lone rocks lack thy name!
                                        —*E. H. W. Meyerstein*

In 19 the lovers are apparently reconciled. The poet contemplates his
own death, in a true elegiac vein, and draws the moral (25–27):

Wherefore, while yet we may,
In love abide we gay!
Love's never long enough, however long.
                                        —*E. H. W. Meyerstein*

In 20 on the pretext of warning Gallus that the nymphs might carry
off his boy love, the poet presents a beautiful version of the rape
of Hylas. Number 21 is the dying appeal of a certain Gallus as he was
done to death by bandits.

The prologue poem to the second book is a dedication to Maecenas.
Propertius disclaims capacity for epic; he can only write of love, for
one woman possesses his heart. Poems 2–9 deal with Cynthia's beauty,
his bondage to her, her falseness, the repeal of a law which might
have forced him to leave Cynthia (2.7). In 10 the poet tries to rise to
the epic level and sing of the triumph of Roman arms, perhaps upon
an official hint; he finds the effort beyond his strength and falls back
on love poetry. The remainder of the book deals almost entirely with
phases of Propertius' love; relations with Cynthia have perceptibly
worsened, for recriminations are more frequent and protestations of
eternal fidelity less convincing. In the longer pieces of this book
transitions are particularly difficult; whereas our texts show thirty-
four pieces, scholars have subdivided these into a much larger number
of separate poems.

In the prologue poem of Book 3 Propertius puts forward his claim

to be the first Roman to follow in the steps of Callimachus and Phi-
letas. Love is still the dominant theme and is the chief subject of 2,
5, 6, 8, 10 (for Cynthia's birthday), 11, 15 (Lycinna was a puppy
love; Cynthia swept her away), 16, 20, 21, 23. Elegies 24 and 25, the
last of the book, are the final rejection of Cynthia; here is 24:

> That beauty, woman, you so prize,
> Once over-rated by mine eyes,
> Is false: 'twas love that on you gazed
> And so extravagantly praised.
> Now, Cynthia, do I blush for shame
> That verse of mine has brought you fame.
> So often have I feigned to find
> All beauty's charms in you combined
> That love my reason could deceive
> And what you were not, that believe.
> E'en your complexion have I sworn
> Was rosier than the blush of dawn,
> Although I knew that dazzling bloom
> Was studied in your dressing-room.
> No longer knife nor cautery,
> Nor shipwreck in the open sea
> Need I to force me to confess
> I lied about your loveliness.
> Enthralled, worse torments far I bore
> In Venus' cruel athanor,
> And helpless against love's attack
> My hands were bound behind my back.
> My folly from that life of vice
> My father's friends could not entice,
> Nor magic wash away the stain
> In all the waters of the main.
> Flower-crowned my bark's in port at last,
> The Syrtes crossed, the anchor cast:
> Storm-wearied now I breathe again,
> And wounds that gaped no longer pain.
> Good Sense, if such a goddess be,
> I dedicate my life to thee.
> To Jove in vain have I appealed;
> To all my prayers his ears were sealed.
>
> —*S. G. Tremenheere*

In 3.3 and 9 Propertius again rejects his historical themes; in 4 he prophesies Roman success in the expedition against the Parthians. Number 7 is an elegy in the modern sense, being a lament for Paetus, who was drowned at sea. Number 12 asks Postumus how he had the heart to leave his wife and go soldiering in the East; but his wife (probably the sister of the poet Gallus) would surely remain as faithful as Penelope. Number 13 is a denunciation of luxury and greed. In 14 the Spartan practice of allowing boys and girls to exercise together is praised; lovers thus have access to one another. Number 17 is in praise of Bacchus, who heals the woes of lovers. Marcellus, the heir apparent, of whose death in 23 Vergil had written the beautiful lines in *Aeneid* 6.861-87, is lamented also in Propertius 3.18, but without mention of his name. Number 19 insists that women are more lustful than men. Number 20 is an exhortation to Tullus to return from the East; Italy and Roman virtue are contrasted with the legendary vices of Greece.

The first part of the opening elegy of Book 4, which has a quite different character, declares the poet's intention to celebrate Rome in a series of aetiological poems; the second part (from which the autobiographical lines have been cited) presents the deterrent advice of an astrologer named Horos. The aetiological poems, modeled upon Callimachus' *Aitiai,* actually in the book are: 2, on the god Vertumnus; 4, on Tarpeia; 6, on the anniversary of Actium; 9, on the Ara Maxima; and 10, on Jupiter Feretrius. Only two poems in this book are concerned with Cynthia: 7, a denunciation of his faithlessness by Cynthia's ghost; and 8, a description of how the poet attempted to console himself by inviting two wenches to supper, and how Cynthia suddenly appeared and fumigated him. This is Propertius' sole attempt at humor, and quite successful. Number 3 is a letter from a Roman lady to her husband who has long been absent (she is weaving a fourth cloak!) on military service; the poem is very similar to Ovid's *Heroides.* In 5 a bawd named Acanthis is cursed for corrupting the mind of his mistress. In connection with her malpractices her precepts are listed; these are imitated by Ovid in his *Ars amatoria.* The last of Propertius' poems (4.11) is by all odds the finest. It is an elegy, conceived as an epitaph but in 102 lines, for the death of Cornelia, who was the daughter of Augustus' wife Scribonia. In structure the poem is highly artificial, being addressed in part to the judges of the dead and in part to the bereaved family, who are thought of as present in court. But there is a solemn spaciousness in the treatment and a nobility in the sentiments that raise the poem to a realm far above Propertius' ordinary level.

Propertius' ordinary level, one is tempted to say, is the proper level for Roman elegiac poetry. Tibullus' softness is abnormal for a Roman, and has been plausibly explained as due to his hypochondriacal tendencies. Nor is Ovid's heroic flippancy and graceful agility normal for the *gens togata*. It is hard to think of the subject of any realistic Roman portrait in our museums, draped in toga, composing Ovidian lines; but a hard-faced togate Roman might have written Propertius' Their Latin is more strained and harder than Tibullus', bearing somewhat the same relation to Tibullus as Sallust's prose to Cicero's. There is more effort to coin striking phrases, greater Alexandrianism in learned allusions, more elaborate art in structure: in Tibullus there is a sense of the poet allowing the course of his thought free rein. But the greatest difference from Tibullus, perceptible even in translation, is that of personality. The sympathy his admirers conceive for Tibullus is affection for a hypersensitive but nerveless invalid, to whose defense our less sensitive toughness impels us to rise. Propertius stands on his own feet. He is the master rather than the helpless toy of his passions, capable of controlling both his exaltation and his depression and of enjoying the savor of both. Perhaps as many of womankind would envy Cynthia her lover as would envy Delia hers.

XI

OVID

READERS WHO DEMAND OF A POET MORAL INSTRUC-
tion or inspiration will find Ovid completely frivolous; critics who
choose to disregard the "tyranny of the subject" would regard him
as almost the only pure artist in Latin literature. In none does verse
seem so natural an idiom; none devoted his verse so singly to providing the kind of pleasure which it is the function of literature to
provide. Literary pleasure Ovid has offered with generous abundance
to the countries of Europe, whose literatures he has enriched more
potently than any other Latin poet has done. But puritan Europe
(like puritan Rome) has been a little uneasy in conscience at receiving pleasure unsalted with edification. It has looked mainly to the
Metamorphoses, which could be esteemed as a useful handbook of
ancient mythology, whose deities it was no longer blasphemous to
smile at, and there have been attempts to construe the amoral *Amores*
as an allegory recommending the pursuit of Mistress Wisdom. But
Ovid is not prurient; he aims not to titillate but to entertain, he does
not leer but smile. Nothing in him is immoral unless absence of
moralizing is immoral. Amoral he may be, but that is the proper
posture for a professed expert, and none can deny that Ovid was
indeed an expert in a realm of no small importance in our world—
the ways of the species woman. Of this subject no Roman shows
profounder understanding, and no Roman has shown greater skill in
the art of telling a story. With great finesse and great perception, and
sometimes with highly literate and agile fooling, Ovid creates a mimic
world for the delectation of readers able to refract some part of his own
mercurial wit.

With Publius Ovidius Naso's mercurial temperament a degree of
volubility is to be expected, and from his writings we know a good
deal about his life and more about his psychological reaction to its
vicissitudes. Not much can or need be added to the poet's own address to posterity (*Tristia* 4.10):

> That after times may know of me each thing,
> I was the man who tender love did sing.

My country, Sulmo, fed with fresh springs all
Miles ninety distant from the Roman wall.
Here was I born: the very year to tell,
'Twas when by one sad fate two consuls fell.
May that avail, I was a knight by blood,
Not only raised by my fortunes good.
I was no first-born child, for one son more
My father had, born just a year before.

     ·   ·   ·   ·

But I, a child, the Thespian sweets did favour
And more and more did win the Muses' favour.
"Leave, leave these fruitless studies, son," oft cried
My father. "Homer but a poor man died."
Moved at his words I left the dear delight
Of Helicon, and 'gan in prose to write.
Lo, verses of their own accord came fit;
It was a verse whate'er I spake or writ.

     ·   ·   ·   ·

My brother now had passed his twentieth year;
He died in whom I lost my soul's best share.
In youth to some preferment raised was I,
And took the office of triumviri.
Both mind and body were unapt for labour
And vexed ambition I could never favour.
And still the Muses did entice me still
To their calm sweets, which e'er had my good will.
I dearly loved the poets of the time;
Each poet was a god in my esteem.
Oft did I hear sage Macer read his birds
And serpents, and the help each herb affords;
And oft Propertius, my companion dear,
With amorous raptures did present my ear.
Heroic Ponticus, iambic Battus
With pleasing strains did often recreate us,
And tuneful Horace oft my ear delighted
With curious ditties on his harp recited.
Virgil I only saw; and hasty fate
Tibullus' friendship did anticipate.
He followed Gallus, and Propertius him;
I was the fourth man in the rank of time.
As I my elders, so my juniors me

Adored; my Muse grew famous suddenly.
Thrice and no more had I shav'n off my beard,
When first my youthful strains the people heard.
My mistress, in Corinna masked, did move
My wits; each village now could chaunt our love.
Much did I write, but what I faulty knew
Into the fault-correcting fires I threw.
And at my exile cast I in the flame,
Vexed with the Muses, many a work of fame.
My tender heart oft pierced through with love
Each light occasion instantly did move.
But when I was from Cupid's passions free,
My Muse was mute and wrote no elegy.
  A worthless, loveless wife to me but young
Was matched; with whom I led my life not long.
My second wife, though free from any crime,
Yet she continued but a little time.
My last, with whom most of my days I spent,
Endured the blemish of my banishment.
One daughter have I, which once and again
Made me a grandsire, but by husbands twain.
And now my father full of silver hairs
His days concluded just at ninety years;
As he'd have mourned for me, so did I mourn
For him. Next sorrow was my mother's urn.

            ·   ·   ·   ·   ·

Parental souls, if you have heard of me
In Styx, if there my crimes related be,
Be you assured, with whom I cannot lie,
My crime was error, not dishonesty.
Enough for them; to you I now retire,
My friends, who th' actions of my life enquire.
  The summer-tropic of my years now gone,
Declining age with hoary hairs came on.
Now since my birth ten times the horse-courser
That won the race Pisaean wreaths did wear,
When, ah! offended Caesar doth command
My doleful exile to the Tomites' land.
The cause of this, too much to most revealed,
Must be for ever by myself concealed.

                              —*John Gower (ca. 1635)*

We have, then, Ovid's birthplace as Sulmo in the Abruzzi, his birth year as 43 B.C., his equestrian census, his early inclination to tragedy, his faculty of lisping in numbers, the early death of his elder brother, his desertion of a political career for poetry, his generous appreciation of his brother poets, his own youthful poetic fame, the popularity of his poems on Corinna, his inability to write any but love poetry, his domestic affairs, the "error" which caused his banishment at the age of forty. Banishment to Tomis, modern Constanza, was the central crisis in Ovid's life. The cause may have been some implication in the affairs of Augustus' dissolute granddaughter Julia, or the fact that such poems as the *Ars amatoria* were in effect subversive of Augustus' moral reforms. To Ovid, for whom the air of the cosmopolis was the breath of life, exile was catastrophic; it crushed his spirit, but did not confound his facility with his pen. But the chief burden of his writings from Tomis is plaintive appeals for restoration. These were futile, and he died in Tomis in A.D. 18.

Of Ovid's extant works those published before his banishment are *Amores, Heroides,* and the series comprising *Ars amatoria, Remedium amoris, Medicina faciei.* The *Metamorphoses* were completed but not corrected, and the *Fasti* doubtless begun. In exile he wrote the *Tristia,* and the *Epistles from Pontus,* the *Halieuticon,* and the *Ibis.* Ovid speaks of having burnt some of his works, and he surely wrote more than the ample volume we possess, but the only non-extant work of which we have positive knowledge that it survived him is his tragedy on *Medea.* Of this Quintilian says (10.1.98): "That work seems to me to demonstrate how great Ovid's achievements might be if he had preferred to rule his genius rather than indulge it." It was Quintilian also who called Ovid "overfond of his own genius." The genius, admirable or not, appeared in full stature in Ovid's early youth and continued with force but slightly abated to his death.

Ovid's earliest elegies are included in the *Amores,* which, he tells us in the introductory epigram, were originally in five books and are now reduced to three; certain poems may have been omitted for prudential considerations. Tibullus' Delia probably was real, Propertius' Cynthia was almost as certainly a real woman though skeptics have suspected she might be a literary figment. In the case of Ovid's Corinna there can be no doubt, on the one hand, that she is synthetic, and on the other that the experiences out of which she was created were real. Such a poem as *Amores* 1.5 may be cited as evidence:

> In summer's heat and mid-time of the day,
> To rest my limbs upon a bed I lay.
> One window shut, the other open stood,
> Which gave such light as twinkles in a wood,
> Like twilight glimpse at setting of the sun,
> Or night being past, and yet not day begun;
> Such light to shamefast maidens must be shown,
> Where they may sport and seem to be unknown.
> Then came Corinna in a long loose gown,
> Her white neck hid with tresses hanging down,
> Resembling fair Semiramis going to bed,
> Or Lais of a thousand lovers sped.
> I snatched her gown, being thin, the harm was small,
> Yet strived she to be covered therewithal.
> And striving thus as one that would be chaste,
> Betrayed herself and yielded at the last.
> Stark naked as she stood before mine eye,
> No one wen in her body could I spy.
> What arms and shoulders did I touch and see!
> How apt her breasts were to be pressed by me!
> How smooth a belly under her waist saw I!
> How large a leg, and what a lusty thigh!
> To leave the rest, all liked me passing well;
> I clinged her naked body, down she fell.
> Judge you the rest; being tired, she bade me kiss,
> Jove send me more such afternoons as this.
>
> —*Christopher Marlowe*

What sets Ovid's elegies apart from his predecessors' is not only their greater ebullience and wit but their versatile variety. The others require a rather special taste or special introduction; Ovid's poems can be enjoyed by anyone who can enjoy Palgrave's *Golden Treasury*. An indication of the contents of the forty-nine elegies which comprise the three books will illustrate Ovid's variety, and at the same time both his debt to his predecessors and his anticipations of his own later work. The prologues and epilogues speak of his own work: in 1.1 he is constrained by Cupid to write of love rather than war; in 1.15 he justifies the literary career and claims immortality for men of letters; in 2.1 Cupid obliges him to give up the *Battle of the Giants* which he was writing and turn to love; in 3.1 he debates whether to continue with elegy or turn to tragedy; and in 3.15 he bids Venus and his Muse farewell. Far the greater number of the remainder, as these pieces indicate, have to do with love. He is Cupid's captive, led in triumph (1.2); he protests his devotion to a disdainful mistress (1.3); he contrives a sign language to use in the presence of his mistress' husband (1.4); he begs the porter to open his mistress' house door to him (1.6); he apologizes for having beaten his mistress (1.7); he curses a procuress who teaches his mistress too well how to exploit her charms for pleasure and profit (1.8): *Casta est quam nemo rogavit*—"Only she is chaste whom none has invited." This poem is an anticipation of the *Ars amatoria.* He tells Atticus (not Cicero's friend) that love is a species of warfare (1.9); he tells his mistress (1.10) that love must not be prostituted. He thanks a maid for delivering a *billet doux* (1.11), and curses the tablets because the answer is no (1.12). In 1.13 he prays the dawn not to hasten (lines 5–26):

> The air is cold, and sleep is sweetest now,
> And birds send forth shrill notes from every bough.
> Whither run'st thou, that men and women love not?
> Hold in thy rosy horses that they move not.
> Ere thou rise, stars teach seamen where to sail,
> But when thou comest, they of their courses fail.
> Poor travellers, though tired, rise at thy sight,
> And soldiers make them ready for the fight.
> The painful hind by thee to field is sent;
> Slow oxen early in the yoke are pent.
> Thou cozenest boys of sleep, and dost betray them
> To pedants that with cruel lashes pay them.
> Thou mak'st the surety to the lawyer run
> That with one word hath nigh himself undone.
> The lawyer and the client hate thy view,
> Both whom thou raisest up to toil anew.
> By thy means women of their rest are barred;
> Thou set'st their labouring hands to spin and card,
> All could I bear; but that the wench should rise,
> Who can endure, save him with whom none lies?
> —*Christopher Marlowe*

Number 1.14 illustrates Ovid's interest in cosmetics as well as his wit. He prescribes for a lady who has almost lost her hair through using too strong a bleach, suggesting that a new shipment of hair cut from the heads of German girls will be available for transformations. In 2.2–3 the poet addresses the eunuch chamberlain of a lady he admires. He sets forth his own catholic tastes in 2.4:

> I cannot rule myself, but where love please
> Am driven like a ship upon rough seas.
> No one face likes me best, all faces move;
> A hundred reasons make me ever love.
> If any eye me with a modest look,
> I burn, and by that blushful glance am took.
> And she that's coy I like for being no clown;
> Methinks she would be nimble when she's down.
> Though her sour looks a Sabine's brow resemble,
> I think she'll do, but deeply can dissemble.
> If she be learn'd, then for her skill I crave her;
> If not, because she's simple I would have her.
> Before Callimachus one prefers me far;
> Seeing she likes my books, why should we jar?
> Another rails at me and that I write,
> Yet would I lie with her if that I might.
> Trips she, it likes me well; plods she, what then?
> She would be nimbler lying with a man.
> And when one sweetly sings, then straight I long
> To quaver on her lips even in her song.
> Or if one touch the lute with art and cunning,
> Who would not love those hands for their swift running?
> And her I like that with a majesty
> Folds up her arms, and makes low curtsey.
> To leave myself, that am in love with all,
> Some one of these might make the chastest fall.
> If she be tall, she's like an Amazon,
> And therefore fills the bed she lies upon.
> If short, she lies the rounder; to say troth,
> Both short and long please me, for I love both.
> I think what one undecked would be, being dressed;
> Is she attired? then show her graces best.
> A white wench thralls me, so doth golden-yellow;
> And nut-brown girls in doing have no fellow.

If her white neck be shadowed with black hair,
Why, so was Leda's, yet was Leda fair.
Amber-tressed is she? then on the morn think I,
My love alludes to every history;
A young wench pleaseth, and an old is good,
This for her looks, that for her womanhood.
Nay, what is she that any Roman loves
But my ambitious ranging mind approves?
                              —*Christopher Marlowe*

Number 2.5 reproves his mistress for infidelity, 2.6, on the death of
a parrot, is patently suggested by Catullus on the sparrow. In 2.7
Ovid protests to his mistress that he has not made love to her maid
Cypassis, and in 2.8 threatens Cypassis with exposure if she withholds
further favors. Number 2.9. acknowledges the dominion of Cupid. In
2.10 he explains that he is in love, and requires to be in love, with
two women simultaneously. Number 2.11 seeks to dissuade Corinna
from sailing to Baiae, but wishes her *bon voyage* if she is determined
to go. In 2.12 he exults in his possession of Corinna; in 2.13 prays for
an easy delivery when she is in travail; and in 2.14 reproaches her for
having attempted to procure abortion. A ring, which is being sent
as a gift, is envied for the intimacies it will be privileged to witness
(2.15). In 2.16 he enlarges on the beauties of his native Sulmo; what
is missing is the presence of his beloved. He acknowledges slavery
to Corinna in 2.17, but wishes she were not so hard a mistress. In
2.18 he urges Macer, who had written didactic and epic poetry, to write
on love. In 2.19 he advises a negligent husband to keep better watch
on his wife.

    In 3.2 the poet vividly describes chariot races in the Circus Maximus,
which he attended with his mistress. Number 3.3 complains that his
mistress is foresworn. The more carefully he watches his wife, he
tells a jealous husband in 3.4, the more she will be tempted to sin.
Number 3.5 is an almost Freudian interpretation of a dream involving a cow, a bull, and a crow. In 3.6 he reproaches a wicked river
which has obstructed his path to his mistress. Number 3.7 describes
a frustrating love encounter, when he was mortified to find himself
"more languid than yesterday's rose." In 3.8 he laments his mistress'
preference for a richer rival. Number 3.9 is a beautiful dirge on the
"hallowed poet" Tibullus, from which a few lines have been cited

above. In 3.10 he complains to Ceres that her abstemious festival has separated him from his mistress. He cannot help loving her (3.11) but his verses have so advertised her that he has raised many rivals (3.12); if she will not be constant he begs her at least to conceal her intrigues (3.14). Number 3.13 describes the festival of Juno which he attended with his wife at Falisci, her native place. The inclusion of this specimen of domesticity and conventional piety should teach us something about the mood in which the amatory pieces were written and are to be read.

Next in order are the *Heroides,* a series of imaginary letters from women of the heroic or legendary age to their absent heroes. All the women grieve for the separation, but the circumstances and the character of each heroine are different, so that the letters are by no means repetitious. The *Heroides* may be regarded as Ovid's most representative work; they illustrate his very great skill as a storyteller, his intimate understanding of types of female character, his ever-present and all enveloping wit. It is just that the *Heroides* should have proved perhaps the most popular of Ovid's works. The notion of a fictitious letter had been used by Propertius (4.3); Ovid's innovation was in limiting his correspondents to the remote past, thus providing free scope for the narrative art which we see more fully presented in the *Metamorphoses.* The first letter, naturally, is from Penelope, who has no betrayal to complain of, as have some of the other heroines, but is a little depressed by the cares of her ménage, the happy reunions of other wives with their returned soldiers, and stories of Ulysses' further dangers. His son and his father as well need him; will he not return soon? Demophoon, another warrior returning from Troy, tarried at Thrace and loved its young Queen Phyllis; but when he sailed away he broke his promise to return in a month, and Phyllis writes (2) to reproach him for his ingratitude and perfidy and to express her determination to take her life. By abating his pride Achilles might have recovered Briseis from Agamemnon, and Briseis reproaches him in *Heroides* 3: "The blots you see are tear stains, but my tears speak for me." Phaedra's letter to Hippolytus (4) follows the plot of the Euripidean play; she assures her stepson that relations with her will be as justifiable as they will be safe. The abrupt opening of Oenone's letter to Paris (5) is very effective: "Are you reading this through, or is your new wife preventing you?" She recalls their youthful frolics on the slopes of Ida, and his marking the bark of trees with her name and a verse—

> When pastor Paris shall revolt and Oenon's love forego,
> The Xanthus' waters shall recoil and to their fountains flow.
> —*George Turberville* (*1567*)

But fickle as he is, she will continue to be his as long as she lives. On his way to fetch the Golden Fleece Jason was entertained at Lemnos by Queen Hypsipyle. She has now heard of his marriage to Medea, and writes (6) to reproach him for his breach of faith. Upon his departure from Carthage Dido writes to Aeneas (7). She attributes his desertion to his restlessness, and professes willingness to continue as his hostess if not his wife. As she writes she fondles a sword, and she closes with the epitaph to be inscribed on her tomb: "Cause and instrument of death Aeneas provided; the hand was Dido's own." Hermione's letter to Orestes (8) is an elaboration of a hint in Euripides' *Andromache,* Dejanira's to Hercules (9) of Sophocles' *Trachinian Women.* Ariadne, in the first agony of desertion, writes perhaps the most moving of the letters, to Theseus from Naxos (10). This theme had been used by Catullus in the *Marriage of Peleus and Thetis,* and Ovid himself reverts to it in *Ars amatoria* 1.217–564 and in *Fasti* 3. 461–516. The most vigorous and passionate of the letters is Canace's to her brother Macareus (11). When their father discovered their incestuous relationship he ordered their newborn infant exposed, and sent Canace a sword and a hint for its use. Before stabbing herself Canace writes Macareus of her anguish at the murder of her babe and bespeaks his continued remembrance of her love. Ovid's favorite Medea writes Jason (12) after his new marriage; it is interesting to note that Seneca's tragedy on the subject follows Ovid more closely than Euripides. Laodamia's letter to Protesilaus (13) is of a different type. She writes to warn him of the oracle she had heard that the first man to land at Troy would be killed, and begs him, *Si tibi cura mei, sit tibi cura tui,* "If you care for me take care of yourself." Hypermnestra was the only Danaid who failed to kill her husband on their nuptial night (the *splendide mendax* of Horace, *Odes* 3.11) and was jailed in consequence; her hands weighted with chains, she writes (14) her cousin-husband glorying in her deed. Of Ovid's authorship of these fourteen elegiac epistles there can be no doubt. The genuineness of 15, Sappho to Phaon, and of the remaining six letters (16–21) has been questioned, but on apparently insufficient grounds. The last six are in pairs—from Paris, Leander, and Acontius, with replies from Helen, Hero, and Cydippe. Ovid's friend Sabinus had composed replies to six of the *Heroides* (*Amores* 2.18.27); encouraged by the popularity of his original collection and following the suggestion of Sabinus he probably added the paired letters to complete the edition.

The great attraction in all the letters is their dramatic quality Each is a tragedy in miniature, containing all that the reader (as contrasted with the spectator) seeks. Though the pattern remains constant, actually there is at least as much variety in incident and, more important, character delineation as there is in Plautus' or Terence's adaptations of New Comedy. Ariadne, Oenone, Dejanira, Hypsipyle, and Dido have all been deserted, but each is a different woman, and their circumstances are different. Medea is burdened not only by Jason's desertion but by the weight of remorse for her own crimes. Phaedra is the victim of an illicit but irresistible passion. Penelope, Laodamia, and Hermione have suffered no wrong from their husbands but have their individual reasons for appealing to them. Briseis complains of another's violence and can charge her correspondent only with supineness. Like the dramatist too, Ovid is detached from his creatures. They, not he, speak; he stands apart with his audience, stage-managing his performance and permeating it with his wit to afford easiest comprehension and greatest delight.

The tongue-in-cheek quality of the didactic series on love is apparent in its first member, *Medicina faciei,* or "Face Lotions," of which only some hundred lines are extant. In what looks like a parody of Vergil's *Georgics* Ovid declares that cultivation improves the various sorts of agricultural produce; cultivation can similarly improve that great resource of womankind, the face—though Ovid makes decent acknowledgement of the importance of good manners and amiability. Professor F. A. Wright reproduces the Ovidian mood in a rather free but delightful version of some of the opening lines:

> It may be in the days of old,
>> When Tatius was king,
> That Sabine wives their husbands told
> They did not care for silk or gold
>> Or any costly thing.

It may be then they loved to sit
  At home on stools all day,
And some would sew and some would knit
And some do wool work, bit by bit,
  To pass the hours away.

But 'tis not so with modern girls
  Who in fine clothes delight;
They deck their hair in loops and curls,
With diamond pins, and ropes of pearls:
  And for these girls I write.

Similarly didactic and professional in tone is the *Ars amatoria:*

It is by art ships sail the sea,
  It is by art that chariots move,
If then unskilled in love you be
  Come to my school and learn to love.
In all the process of seduction
This handbook gives you full instruction.

                  —F. A. Wright

The Professor of Love (*praeceptor amoris,* 1.17) then sets forth his doctrine, in the posture of the detached expert, with measureless grace and wit. Of the three books the first two provide instruction on how to find and keep a mistress, and the third gives corresponding precepts to women. The supply is abundant (1.62–66):

Whether you like them young and green,
  Or choose instead the ripe and mellow,
Or else prefer the age between,
  There's choice of each for every fellow.
The only trouble, you'll confess,
Comes from *embarras de richesse.*

                  —F. A. Wright

Of the numerous places of resort which he enumerates Ovid recommends the theater (1.97–100, 149–52):

Thus to the theatre women flock,
  So many that 'tis hard to choose,
For each puts on her smartest frock
  And cares not if her virtue goes.

They come perhaps to see the play,
But to be seen themselves they stay.

.   .   .   .   .

If grains of dust should haply stray
    And settle on your lady's breast,
Wipe them with careful zeal away,
    Your fingers on her bosom pressed.
If there be none—well, never mind:
Wipe still and see what you can find.

—F. A. Wright

The throngs watching triumphal processions also afford opportunities; when your companion asks (1.217–22):

What is that hill and what this land?
    Which are those rivers borne in state?
Have your reply at once to hand,
    You must not let her questions wait.
She will not mind a slip or two,
If you don't know, pretend you do.

—F. A. Wright

The girl once chosen, the professor proceeds with instructions for engaging her affections; gifts, less costly promises, the connivance of ladies' maids, small attentions, entertainments, persuasive speech (but parade of learning is to be avoided), good grooming, are all judiciously treated; but the main prescription is persistent and vigorous attack, as is shown by numerous instances from legend (1.670–74):

But that, you'll say, is brutal force.
    Well, force at times is not unpleasant.
Girls often seem—and are of course
    Loath to bestow the final present.
But they'll endure a rape, poor dears,
And scarcely hate their ravishers.

—F. A. Wright

For holding the lady's love (Book 2) the sum of Ovid's unexceptionable advice is *Ut ameris amabilis esto,* "If you'd be loved be lovable." Amiability is manifested by interesting conversation, a discreet willingness to lose at games, readiness to fetch and carry, thoughtful gifts, constant praise, and general complaisance (2.197–202):

> Yield to her whims and win her love:
>   Whatever part she bids you, play.
> If she approves, do you approve,
>   Her Yes and No your Yea and Nay;
> Smile with her smile, weep with her tears,
> And model all your looks on hers.
>
> —*F. A. Wright*

By such attentions love will grow, but constant vigilance is necessary. Nevertheless appearance is more important than reality (2.387–90):

> I do not mean that you should be
>   For ever tied in bondage sure.
> Heaven forbid! such constancy
>   The best of wives can scarce secure.
> You must have change, I do not doubt it:
> But be discreet: don't boast about it.
>
> —*F. A. Wright*

Flirtation on the girl's part should similarly be overlooked (2.555–59):

> But ignorance is often bliss,
>   'Tis best to let some secrets be,
> For if you knew of every kiss
>   Perhaps she'd lose her modesty;
> Let her deceive you if she will
> And think that you are blinded still.
>
> —*F. A. Wright*

Here, as elsewhere, apt and well-told examples from legend are skillfully woven into the fabric to illustrate the professor's points. The masculine part of the work closes with hints on bedroom etiquette.

The third book addresses itself to women (3.7–11):

> I know that some poor fish will say—
>   Women are snakes: why give them stings?
> We men are lambs on whom they prey;
>   Why make more fierce their ravenings?
> But that's to give to womankind
> The guilt that in one maid you find.
>
> —*F. A. Wright*

First the professor reads the girls a long lecture on the wisdom of enjoying their prime, again with examples from mythology (3.97 ff.):

I would not have you wanton be;
    I only mean there is no fear
That you will lose, however free
    To give your favours you appear;
Treasures like yours you need not save,
The more you spend the more you have.
                                        —*F. A. Wright*

He then proceeds to give very knowledgeable advice on how, by means of design and color, to make the most of good points and conceal blemishes, on the uses of tears, a graceful gait, accomplishments in music, literature, and games, on how to make and exploit the acquaintance of men, how to rouse and retain their interest, and, lastly, on how to give and derive the greatest pleasure.

Except for the latter rubric—and the exception is due only to our different notions of propriety—Ovid's well-bred decency removes all offense from even his most questionable matter. Only a prurient or an oafish mind could degrade his charm to pruriency or oafishness. Much of the depreciation which the *Art of Love* has suffered at the hands of moralists is due to the wrong assumption that a Victorian social order obtained in ancient Rome; either, then, the women the poet envisages must be professional courtesans, or else Ovid was encouraging the seduction of respectable maids and matrons. Actually neither class is in question; what Ovid has in mind are freedwomen or women who had entered the legally recognized and respectable but less constraining form of marriage known as *usus*. It is true enough that the spirit of the book is directly contrary to the spirit of the Augustan reforms looking towards the elevation of conventional family life and the increase of population; but Ovid is not suborning crime nor advocating general debauchery. And since *das ewig Weibliche* is the exclusive domain of neither Rosie O'Grady nor the Colonel's lady, much may be learned from the shrewd and observant professor of love. So far from being a salacious book the *Art of Love* may actually be recommended to the young on some such terms as Plautus' *Truculentus* or the Book of Proverbs. The poem is a minor masterpiece.

It is not too much to call the *Metamorphoses* a major masterpiece. It has no lofty program, and none of Lucretius' intensity or Vergil's exaltation, but it is a highly artistic and thoroughly adult handling of one of the world's richest legacies of stories. Judged by the gauge of direct and seminal influence, European literature and art would be poorer for the loss of the *Metamorphoses* than for the loss of Homer. What Ovid accomplishes in the *Metamorphoses* is the linking together into one artistically harmonious whole of all the stories of classical mythology. The link is the element of transformation (which is the meaning of *metamorphoses*), and Ovid traverses the entire range, from the dawn of creation, when chaos was transformed into the orderly universe, down to his own age, when the soul of Julius Caesar was transformed to a star and set in the heavens among the immortals. Every important myth is at least touched upon, and though the stories differ widely in time and place there is no break in the sequence of the narrative. It is in his transitions that the poet shows his consummate skill. For passing from cycle to cycle every thread of connection is exploited, and where none exist some ingenious transition is adroitly contrived. The wonderland of fantasy is continuous, one magic enticement growing naturally out of another, not a series of disparate museum rooms. The closest Alexandrian model we know of are the *Aitiai* of Callimachus, but these, like Propertius' aetiological poems, were disparate pieces. The framework for other great collections of individual tales—the *Decameron, Canterbury Tales, Arabian Nights,* Don Juan—is more plausible because more naturalistic. Ovid's framework makes no concession to naturalism but is pure artifice. Artifice, indeed, is the key to the Ovidian mood. Homer presumably believed in the historicity of his tale and expected his auditors to believe it. Callimachus obviously did not believe in his, but wrote as if he expected his readers to believe in them. Ovid makes no pretense of literal belief and is addressing people on the same side of his fence. His work is pure play, seriously conceived and respected as such. But this is not to say that he is oblivious to all truth: it is only for the archaeological truth that Ovid invites to suspension of disbelief; of the perennial human truths he is an acute observer and effective expositor. Aristotle's dictum in the *Poetics* to the effect that poetry is truer than history is as perfectly applicable to the *Metamorphoses* as to Greek tragedy. Whether the actual events transpired as set forth is of no consequence; but given such events the loves and hates and ambitions of men and women would so manifest themselves. The *Metamorphoses* are truer than the handbooks from which Ovid derived his tales in the same way as Shakespeare's plays are truer than his sources.

In all respects the *Metamorphoses* present Ovid at the height of his power. It was completed when he was fifty, just before he went into exile. He says (*Tristia* 1.7) that he burned his own copy out of disgust with poetry or because the work was rough and unfinished; this may suggest his own high aims for the work. He himself had no doubts of its immortality, as his Epilogue shows; this is a modernization of Golding's version, which Shakespeare read (15.871–79):

> Now have I brought a work to end which neither Jove's fierce wrath,
> Nor sword, nor fire, nor fretting age with all the force it hath
> Are able to abolish quite. Let come that fatal hour
> Which, saving of this brittle flesh, hath over me no power,
> And at his pleasure make an end of my uncertain time;
> Yet shall the better part of me assured be to climb
> Aloft above the starry sky; and all the world shall never
> Be able for to quench my name; for look! how far so ever
> The Roman Empire by the right of conquest shall extend,
> So far shall all folk read this work; and time without all end,
> If poets as by prophecy about the truth may aim,
> My life shall everlastingly be lengthened still by fame.

The fifteen books of the *Metamorphoses,* in nearly twelve thousand hexameter lines, contain some two hundred fifty myths. Ovid's meter is rapid, his Latin easy, though he seems to have coined some two hundred words, especially compounds. These enable him to obtain clever effects, in matching sound to sense. He makes frequent and effective use of epigrams and antitheses. Translation naturally loses or cheapens the effect of such devices as *Consiliis non curribus utere nostris,* "Take my counsel, not my car" ("The Sun to Phaethon," 2.146), but they are effective in the Latin and communicate the right note of ironic playfulness. A half-ironic playfulness also eases the pantheist doctrine which underlies the book. This is reflected in the account of creation in Book 1 and reverted to in an account of the Pythagorean theory of transmigration in Book 15, which gives a kind of philosophic authority to the idea of metamorphosis. Pythagoras (an odd figure in the *dramatis personae* of the *Metamorphoses*) delivers a long discourse (15.75–478) on vegetarianism and the cycle of generation on which the system depends. Mind circulates eternally, and at what is called death passes quickly from man to beast, and beast to man (15.165–72, 178–85):

> All things do change; but nothing sure doth perish. This same sprite
> Doth fleet, and frisking here and there doth swiftly take his flight
> From one place to another place, and ent'reth every wight,
> Removing out of man to beast, and out of beast to man;
> But yet it never perisheth nor never perish can.
> And even as supple wax with ease receiveth figures strange,
> And keeps not aye one shape, nor bides assured aye from change,
> And yet continueth always wax in substance; so I say
> The soul is aye the selfsame thing it was, and yet astray
> It fleeteth into sundry shapes. . . .
> In all the world there is not that that standeth at a stay.
> Things ebb and flow, and every shape is made to pass away.
> The time itself continually is fleeting like a brook,
> For neither brook nor lightsome time can tarry still. But look!
> As every wave drives other forth, and that that comes behind
> Both thrusteth and is thrust itself, even so the times by kind
> Do fly and follow both at once, and evermore renew,
> For that that was before is left, and straight there doth ensue
> Another that was never erst.
>
> —*Arthur Golding*

Space cannot be spared for citing a more typical story from the *Metamorphoses,* nor is it necessary to do so, for every reader of English literature, though he may not be aware of it, has acquaintance with the book; all that need be said is that the copies are seldom superior to the original.

In the *Metamorphoses* the note of Roman imperial patriotism is struck at many passages besides the concluding section on Julius Caesar. Ovid's specific contribution to the institutional literature of Rome is his *Fasti,* a poetical calendar in elegiac verse. The poem is didactic, but its form and spirit are unique in Latin literature and Ovid's own. Only six of the projected twelve books were completed when Ovid was banished. The original dedication to Augustus is retained at 2.3–18. These books, partially revised by Ovid and with a new dedication to Germanicus (1.3), were published after his death. The last six books were too fragmentary to be published, though citations from them occur. The plan devoted a single book to each month

of the year; what we have covers the months from January through
June. Under each month the material is arranged in three divisions—
astronomical, historical, and religious; the risings and settings of
constellations are set forth, together with remarks on the weather;
legendary and historical events connected with specific dates are
described; and festivals and religious rites are recorded with minute
detail. Ovid's astronomy is vague and inaccurate; his technical information he derived from an astronomical calendar prepared for his
use by his friend Clodius Tuscus, but like other Roman works on
astronomy this was taken from the Greek without allowances being
made for differences of time and place and with confusion of the real
and apparent risings and settings at sunrise and sunset. It is in the
antiquarian portion of his work that Ovid is most interested and has
most to contribute. In the historical portion there is little (except the
dubious dating by month and day) that is not to be found in the first
decade of Livy, but the stories of Lucretia or of the Sabine women are
told with Ovid's usual economy and light grace. But for religious
antiquities Ovid's *Fasti* is a first-class source. Only Varro as he is
represented in St. Augustine throws the same kind of light on popular
observances and beliefs, but where Varro's interest is scholarly Ovid's
is human. If his explanation of a religious custom is not always satisfactory to the historian of religion, it is good enough for the student
of popular beliefs and practices. When Janus has introduced himself
to the poet and explained his symbols and function and why gifts of
sweetmeats are made on his day, Ovid interrogates him on why
pennies are also given as gifts on that day. This is Janus' reply, with
a bow to the Augustan program of restoring ancient ideals, and with
a touch of his own sly humor and satire (1.191–214, 221–22):

> Now why they money give, I fain would learn;
> For I no portion of your Feast would lose,
> And never yet could find how this arose.
> He smiling said, Oh! skilled in tuneful rhymes,
> More than in knowledge of these latter times,
> To fancy gold less pleasing in perfume,
> Less sweet to taste than honey from the comb;
> Even I, on earth while Saturn held his seat,
> Saw scarcely one to whom gain was not sweet.
> In time the appetite more fierce did grow,
> Till farther it can scarcely find to go.

Wealth is more valued now than ere before,
When Rome was new, and all its people poor;
When a small house a great Quirinus held,
Or some rank rush-bed gathered from the field;
Jove in his fane could scarce his height display,
And brandished thunder made of potters' clay.
Leaves decked that Capitol which gems adorn,
And flocks were fed by senators at morn,
But when her head the City's Fortune reared,
And Rome among the supreme gods appeared,
Their wealth increased, wealth still they raging crave,
And when they have too much, more still would have.

—*J. Taylor*

The *Fasti* is something of the same kind of index to the life and interests of the Romans as is a personal calendar to the life and interests of the individual; and the mythological pictures with which this calendar is adorned are far superior to those provided by beer or insurance companies.

When Evander's mother offers her son encouragement, she says (*Fasti* 1.443), *Omne solum forti patria est, ut piscibus aequor,* "To a man of stout heart any soil is his country, like the sea to fish." But in his exile at Tomis on the Black Sea Ovid himself was a fish out of water. The five books of *Tristia* and the four books of *Epistles from Pontus* are filled with complaints, sometimes descending to self-pity, and with supplications for reinstatement, sometimes descending to servility. But the brightness of the versification is untarnished and the Ovidian wit still flashes. The *Tristia* is a collection of elegies, in the form of letters, consisting chiefly of laments upon his exile. The first of the five books was written in the course of the journey but finished off at Tomis and dispatched from there. As in all the books (except the second, which is a continuous essay), the first and last poems are prologue and epilogue and were written last; the remainder seem to stand in the order of their composition. The prologue poem sends the book off to Rome, poorly bound as befits its exiled author, and apologizes for its halting inspiration as being due to suffering. The author hardly dares hope that anyone will introduce the book to the emperor's presence. The book's elder brothers, the *Ars amatoria,* are spoken of as murderers of their sire, whose altered shape might now place him in the *Metamorphoses*. The second poem, actually the first of the series, was written during a storm at sea while Ovid was en route to Tomis. He has kind thoughts for his wife, who does not know that peril of drowning has been heaped on his punishment. His sentence was deserved, but his guilt was involuntary. The third poem is a moving description of Ovid's last night in Rome:

> Ah! when I think of that last fatal eve
> When all the joys of Rome I had to leave,
> When I recall that cruel, cruel hour
> E'en now adown my cheeks the tear-drops pour
>
> .   .   .   .   .
>
> And 'twas my task to choose the serving train
> Who should attend my exile o'er the main.
> But my poor heart was numbed with long delay,
> I could not think nor count each passing day,
> No gold had I prepared, no raiment for the way.
>
> Of all my friends but one or two had come
> To say farewell ere I should leave my home.
> My loving wife with cruel grief distressed
> Clasped me still mourning to her mourning breast.
>
> .   .   .   .   .
>
> Women and men and even children weep
> And every corner seemed its tears to keep.
> In truth, if we may match the small and great
> So Troy appeared when at the open gate
> The Greeks came storming in and Ilion knew her fate.
> —*F. A. Wright*

Tristia 1.4 is a vivid description of a storm on the Ionian Sea. Number 5, the first epistle proper in the *Tristia*, is a touching letter to a friend who has proven his true loyalty. It was he who prevented Ovid from suicide; perhaps he would now venture to intercede with Caesar, for Ovid's sufferings are indescribable. Number 6 is the first of a series of eight very affectionate letters addressed to Ovid's wife (*Tristia* 1.6, 3.3, 4.3, 5.2.1–44, 5.11, 5.14; *Epistles from Pontus* 1.4, 3.1) The expressions of gratitude and devotion in these letters ring true and should again tell us something of the mood in which the amatory poems were written and are to be read. Number 7 is addressed to a friend who had a portrait of the poet on his ring; 8 to another who had deserted him; and 9 to a poet, with felicitations on his success and the hope that he might escape the fate that has befallen himself. Number 10 describes the second half of the poet's voyage to Tomis; the latter part of the journey, from the Hellespont, he traveled by land. This poem was doubtless suggested by Catullus 4, which describes a voyage in the opposite direction. Number 11 is the epilogue; it apologizes for blemishes on the ground that the poems were written during rough voyages on the Adriatic and Aegean Seas.

Book 2 is a single address to Augustus in which Ovid defends his *Ars amatoria* and extenuates his misconduct with a view to obtaining a commutation of his sentence. The address falls into the traditional divisions of forensic oratory, and its argument as well as its form is very carefully wrought. Though his *Art of Love,* he says, (343–62) is held to teach adultery, no one could charge him personally with such misconduct. His verse may be free but his life is irreproachable (*Vita verecunda est, Musa iocosa mea*). Poets must not be supposed to practice what they describe; though all the great poets have sung of love, Ovid alone has been condemned for so doing. At the close (575–79) Ovid humbly declares that he does not expect a full pardon but will be content with a more agreeable place of exile.

The opening poem in Book 3 is very like that in Book 1. The remainder, addressed to various friends in Rome, speak of the writer's discomforts, solicit their efforts on his behalf, or are simply friendly letters; 3.7, for example, encourages a young poetess and bids her seek immortality. The most vehement description of his chill and barbarous environment is 3.10; even the more cheerful spring only reminds him of springtime in Rome (3.12). Number 3.11 is a bitter attack against his Roman detractor against whom he wrote the *Ibis;* 3.13 celebrates his own birthday and expresses the hope that he may never have to spend another in Pontus. The epilogue (3.14), addressed to a literary friend who seems to have undertaken to publish the book, again asks indulgence for blemishes. It speaks of the unfinished condition of the *Metamorphoses,* and draws comfort from the thought that through his books at least a part of the poet can visit Rome.

Books 4 and 5, despatched to Rome in A.D. 11 and 12, have much the same scope and character as Book 3, with a rather larger proportion of letters to friends; these are left unnamed for their own protection, as Ovid himself indicates (*Tristia* 3.4.63–70):

You too are fast in my heart, my friends, whom I am eager to mention each
by his own name, but cautious fear restrains the duty and you yourselves do
not wish a place in my poetry, I think. Of old you wished it, for it was like a
grateful honour to have your names read in my verse. Since now 'tis dangerous, within my heart will I address each one and be cause of fear to none.
—A. L. Wheeler

As the letters proceed, the note of pessimism appears to deepen. The
concluding poem of the fourth book (4.10), addressed to posterity, is
of special interest, as has been noted, for its autobiographical details.
The last poem of all (5.15) offers his wife the consolation of the immortality which his poetry has vouchsafed her and praises her constancy.

Letters of the same sort make up the four books of the *Epistles from
Pontus,* except that here, as Ovid himself says (1.1.16–19), the recipients are addressed by name:

This work is not less sad than that which I sent before—in theme the same,
in title different, and each epistle reveals the recipient without concealing
his name.
—A. L. Wheeler

The great event upon which Ovid set his hopes was the celebration
of Tiberius' Pannonian triumph in A.D. 13, but Tiberius proved as
adamant as Augustus. Ovid apparently concluded that direct appeal
to friends might be more effective and, apparently obtaining the permission of his correspondents (3.6 seems to refer to one who refused
permission), published the collection of the first three books of the
Epistles, with prologue 1.1 and epilogue at 3.9, both addressed to
Brutus. In 3.7 he finally resigns himself, with a degree of fortitude:

Words fail me to make the same request so many times; and at last it
shames me that my idle prayers are endless. You are all weary of my
monotonous verses, and my request you have learned by heart, I think.
What message my letter bears you know already, although the wax has not
been broken from its bonds. So let me change the purport of my writing
that my course be not so often against the hurrying stream.

For my good hopes of you, pardon me, my friends: of such error now
there shall be an end. Nor will I be called a trouble to my wife who in sooth
is as true to me as she is timid and backward in her efforts. This also, Naso,
thou shalt bear, and thou hast borne worse things; no burden can affect
thee now.
—A. L. Wheeler

After the death of Augustus in A.D. 14 Ovid wrote a panegyric on the emperor (4.6.17) and even composed a glorification of Caesar in the Getic language (4.15.19–23). But Tiberius could not be swayed. The poems of the fourth and last book give evidence of the poet's despairing resignation. Here as in all the poems written in exile, the main themes are concern for the deterioration and constraint of his Muse and complaints of his barbarous environment.

In his famous literary feud with Apollonius of Rhodes Callimachus' heaviest artillery was his (lost) *Ibis,* named for a foul scavenger bird. In *Tristia* 4.9 Ovid had threatened to make some unnamed enemy immortal with his pen, and his *Ibis* (650 lines), an imitation rather than a paraphrase of Callimachus' poem, is apparently the fulfilment of the threat. In the opening verses Ovid declares that in the previous fifty years of his life (which dates the poem to the early period of his exile) he had never written a line injurious to anyone but himself. The unidentifiable culprit, we gather, was a one-time friend who calumniated the poet and his wife and tried to enrich himself by confiscating their property. Every imprecation recorded in history or legend is hurled at the enemy in a profusion that would be even more shocking if somewhat labored learning did not remove some of the sting. For the figures out of the past that he cites Ovid uses patronymics rather than their familiar names, and he alludes to their stories by obscure periphrases. At the breathless end of his catalogue of curses the poet asks the gods to multiply their number and promises that he will yet reveal the dastard's name.

The last in the list of Ovid's genuine works is the fragmentary and uncompleted *Halieutica* (132 lines), a treatise on fishing. The subject had been treated by Greek writers and was a favorite in Rome, whose epicures prized exotic fish above all dainties. Ovid's interest and information were doubtless due to his residence in the Black Sea fishing port. The first part of the poem deals with means of defense with which nature has endowed all creatures (not fish alone), and the second tells where various species of fish are to be found. Lost works of Ovid of which we have knowledge, besides the *Medea* and the panegyrics on Augustus in Latin and Getic of which mention has been made, are a *Gigantomachy* (never completed), an *Epithalamium* for Fabius Maximus, epigrams, an elegy on Messalla, and a poem on the triumph of Tiberius in A.D. 13.

Other poems printed in early editions of Ovid are spurious. Most closely akin to Ovid's own style, and hence written probably not long after his death is the *Nux,* in 182 lines. A walnut tree complains pathetically that people throw stones at it, though it is defenseless and innocent of wrong, only because it happens to be fruitful. The poem is pleasant enough but too elaborate for the slightness of the theme; the model in *Greek Anthology* 9.3 is better in the degree that it is shorter. Different from Ovid's work in style, and proven by internal evidence not to be his, but very likely written at the time of the event it describes is the *Consolation to Livia* for the death of Drusus in Germany in 9 B.C. (274 lines). After the merits of the deceased are duly praised, Livia is pictured as awaiting a joyful homecoming and receiving a corpse instead, and as giving utterance to her own grief. At the funeral Tiber himself endeavors to prevent the cremation and must be deterred by Mars. The piece closes with the traditional con- solations of the schools—even the cosmos itself is transitory, life is held only on loan, Fortune is fickle, grief is vain, and the like. The *Consolation* is a very fair example of its species, and was doubtless composed by a competent poet (but not Ovid's peer) as a tribute to Drusus and Livia. To the author of the *Consolation,* finally, belong two elegies on Maecenas, transmitted as a single continuous poem in manuscripts of the *Vergilian Appendix.* Since Maecenas died eleven years after Vergil, Vergilian authorship is impossible, and there is no compelling reason to doubt the author's first line, which says that he had recently composed a dirge for a young man. There are also marked technical similarities to the *Consolation,* though in quality the *Elegies* are inferior. The poet says that the assignment was won for him by Lollius, who was consul in 20 and died in 1 B.C., and the poems exhibit familiarity with their subject. Maecenas' war service and official duties and his intellectual interests are spoken of, and even his taste in jewels is alluded to. Up to line 145 Maecenas is thought of as already dead; in the remaining thirty-four lines, which must therefore be a separate poem, he is represented as taking affectionate leave of his wife and giving Augustus his farewell and his benedic- tion.

In *Epistles from Pontus* 4.16 Ovid gives a catalogue of poets, and from other sources we know of others also, who wrote in the Augustan age and whose works have perished. The only poet in

Ovid's list whose work has survived is Grattius, of whom Ovid says (4.16.34), *Aptaque venanti Grattius arma daret,* "Grattius presents arms suitable to the huntsman." Nothing is known of Grattius besides the *Cynegetica* to which Ovid alludes, a poem on hunting in 540 hexameters. After an address to Diana the poem deals first with the hunter's equipment, and then, in a long section (150–496), with dogs. The discussion of various breeds, their merits and distempers, is interrupted by digressions on a famous hunter, on the adverse effect of luxury on human beings as on dogs, on a grotto in Sicily, and on a sacrifice to Diana. The last portion of the book is concerned with horses. There were Greek works on kindred subjects both before Grattius (Xenophon's *Cynegeticus*) and after him (Plutarch's *On the Intelligence of Animals;* the poems of the Oppians), and Grattius' technical material on breeds and the like doubtless derives from a Greek handbook. His form clearly shows imitation of Vergil's *Georgics;* there is no clear evidence that he knew the *Aeneid*. In Grattius there is still something of the emotional excitement which can make poetry of didactic, and his work can be read with pleasure. In poetry he is, for us, the last of the Augustans, in whom the strictest classicism of form was yet vitalized by a vivid sensitiveness to the substance of poetry.

XII

LIVY AND OTHERS

THE SPECIAL QUALITY OF ROMAN PATRIOTISM, AS
has been several times remarked on previous pages, involved a profound reverence for national tradition, a conviction of being the
special object and instrument of destiny, and a sense of responsibility
to the obligations of that tradition and that destiny. If we should
seek a single book which would communicate to us the atmosphere
compounded of these elements which the Augustan Romans breathed
our choice must inevitably fall upon Livy; even an alien reader who
lends himself to Livy's history will soon learn to thrill, as the Romans
must have done, to the sonorous roll of *Senatus populusque Romanus.*
For historiography put wholly at the service of patriotism Livy is our
first example in classical antiquity. Herodotus is as respectful of barbarians as of Greeks. Thucydides writes of a war between Greeks, but
if he had not told us so we should never have suspected that he was
himself a general in that war, and presumably strongly biased in favor
of one side. Polybius and Dionysius of Halicarnassus provide instructive comparisons with Livy, because for considerable stretches
they offer parallel accounts for his third and first decades respectively.
Polybius is a great admirer of Roman achievement, to be sure, but
his purpose is to fit Rome into the scheme of general history, and he
is addressing Greeks primarily. His pragmatic history follows his own
declared principle (1.14.8): "We must disregard the actors in our
narrative and apply to the actions such terms and such criticisms as
they deserve." It is significant that even when Livy is apparently
following Polybius he leaves out the numerous political and military
observations and reflections. Dionysius of Halicarnassus, Livy's own
contemporary, had a fuller prospect of Roman achievement, and yet
the point of his whole work seems to be that such achievement re-
dounds to the credit of Greece, for as he tells us (1.89), with the air of
bestowing the supreme compliment, Rome *is* a Greek city.

Only one other ancient book communicates a conviction of the
ennobling bonds of tradition, election, and manifest destiny similar
to Livy's, and that is the Old Testament in its narrative sections.

It is interesting to observe that where Livy's techniques differ most markedly from those of his Greek predecessors they approach the techniques of the Old Testament historians. Like them Livy suppresses his own personality, which gives his book the impression of being general truth instead of a personal version of it. When he does appear it is in connection with some critical remark on his sources, or, very rarely, some moral reflection; and such remarks are never intruded into a narrative but are put at the beginning or end of some unit, as is the case with the *Praefatio* and the lesser prefaces. One instance will illustrate Livy's practice: After the account of the battle of Zama, Polybius, naturally in his own person, praises Hannibal's generalship (15.15.3); in his parallel account (30.35.5) Livy does not himself express this opinion but ascribes it to Scipio and others. The determining factor in selecting among versions of a story is frankly the extent to which the version documents the Augustan ideal of what a *vir vere Romanus* should be. In 8.38–39, for example, Livy gives a circumstantial account of a great victory over the Samnites. In 8.40 he admits in so many words the difficulty in choosing among authorities and the probability that the records have been vitiated by fictitious family traditions; but this critical skepticism had not deterred him from giving the favorable account in the preceding chapters. A kindred principle is involved in the aetiological stories so frequent in the early books of Livy. Places holy and accursed, institutions religious and secular, formulaic expressions are given authority by reference to a story in antiquity. The story of the combat of the Horatii and the Curiatii and of the trial of the surviving Horatius for slaying his sister (1.24–26) not only provides an archetypal case for a complicated legal procedure but also explains the sanctity of certain spots. Indeed, sometimes two several stories (both, therefore, probably wrong) account for the sanctity of the same spot; that is the case with the Lacus Curtius (1.13.5 and 7.6.3). Here might be mentioned the highly suspect artificial chronology which accounts for the period between the arrival of Aeneas in Italy and the traditional date of the founding of the city, and for the period between that date and the expulsion of the Tarquins. This chronology was of course not invented by Livy, but he reproduces it without question.

Livy's patriotic intent may be clearly apprehended in his treatment of the national heroes, who receive a kind of reverence which the

Greek historians do not give even a Solon or a Lycurgus, a Themistocles or a Pericles. The Roman analogues of these Greeks are represented as not merely lawgivers, statesmen, generals; their lives constitute a kind of hagiographa. Numa, Camillus, even Scipio Africanus are hedged about with a kind of sanctity. Horatius Cocles, Mucius Scaevola, Cloelia, to take characters from a single episode (2.10.13), are impossible as human beings; each is a rather lifeless embodiment of a properly lofty republican patriotism. Polybius (6.55) has Horatius die in the Tiber, and Dionysius of Halicarnassus (5.33) has Cloelia and her companions effect their escape by prevailing upon the Etruscans to turn their backs while the girls bathe. Such human possibilities as baths and drowning are somehow not to be thought of in connection with Livy's beatification of these heroes. How Roman and how Augustan was Livy's emphasis on the hagiologic character of the gallery of ancient worthies is to be seen from the precisely parallel action of Augustus himself in putting before the eyes of Livy's readers an actual gallery of all the Roman triumphators from Aeneas down, done in bronze, placed in a double row of niches in the walls of his magnificent Forum dominated by the Temple of Mars Ultor, with the name and *cursus honorum* of each general engraved in the plinth and his *res gestae* on a marble slab fixed to the wall below.

For those who are accepted as national heroes there is a tendency to exaggerate the merits and gloss over the failings in order to produce a uniformly favorable picture. This tendency may be seen, for example, in the characterizations of the three heroes of the Second Punic War, Fabius Cunctator, Marcellus, and Scipio Africanus, for each of whom, however, Livy incidentally provides enough unfavorable information to render suspect the wholly favorable picture it is his manifest intention to give. Conversely, and perhaps to underline the merits of the saints, unsuccessful generals are exaggerated into villains. In the same war Flaminius and Varro are the scapegoats. Flaminius was certainly not the rash incompetent Livy makes him out to be, and Varro was certainly not alone to blame for Cannae. Livy's treatment of Roman defeats makes very clear his unquestioning conviction of Rome's superiority and Rome's destiny. With such a conviction the defeats, as being contrary to nature, must be explained; and the explanations are almost in the nature of theodicy The Gallic invasion, for example, is explained (in Book 5) as a divine means of *proving* the Romans and serving as a rod of chastisement; Roman history is divinely directed to provide instruction to all mankind.

It is in their courage, discipline, and ability to rule that the Romans are preeminent, and they have a virtual monopoly on such moral traits as *fides, pietas, clementia*—which Augustan propaganda stressed as peculiarly Roman virtues. By corollary the lesser breeds without the law are assumed to be not only deficient in these traits but generally inferior. The Romans are, in a word, in the natural order of things children of destiny, lords of creation, fated to prevail over all other peoples. Livy cannot marvel at Roman expansion as Polybius does any more than he could marvel at water running down hill. From the beginning heaven guided Rome to its destiny (1.4.1): "The fates were resolved, I believe, upon the founding of this great city and the beginning of the mightiest of empires, next after that of heaven." Rome's first king, immediately upon his translation to heaven, sends word (1.16.7): "Go, said he, and declare to the Romans the will of Heaven that my Rome shall be the capital of the world; so let them cherish the art of war, and let them know and teach their children that no human strength can resist Roman arms." From the circumstances of its occurrence it is no exaggeration to say that this quotation is intended to serve as a sort of text for Livy's whole enterprise.

Livy's history is thus a more outspoken if less alluring sister to Vergil's *Aeneid*. Both were written to support the Augustan program, and of Livy as of Vergil it must be said that he was himself convinced before he attempted to convince others. His independence is suggested in a passage of Tacitus (*Annals* 4.34) which reports that Augustus called him a Pompeian because he had written in praise of Pompey; on the other hand, we must remember that Augustus himself turned his back on Caesar's program and reverted to that of Caesar's opposition. From 4.20.7 we see that Augustus was interested in the progress of Livy's work, and Suetonius (*Claudius* 41) tells us that he encouraged Claudius in his historical studies. We know too that he wrote philosophical dialogues historical in tendency and that he advised his son in the study of rhetoric. An amateurish comparison of Hannibal with Roman generals, incongruously inserted at 9.17–19 appears to be taken bodily from a school exercise book. Aside from these hints we know only that Livy was born in Patavium (Padua) in 59 B.C., and that he died in A.D. 17. He began his history of Rome, *Ab urbe condita libri* ("Books from the Founding of Rome") at the age of thirty, and during the next forty years he wrote 142 books. Internal evidence suggests the dating of various of the books; when at 1.19.3, for example, he tells us that the temple of Janus was last closed by Emperor Augustus after Actium, we know that the passage must have been written between 27 and 25 B.C., for Augustus did not receive that title till 27, and the temple was again closed in 25. The earlier part of the work was divided into pentads and decades and was relatively brief; as the history approached Livy's own time the scale was naturally enlarged, and the arrangement by groups of five had to be modified. Whereas the first pentad carries the history down from the origins through the sack of Rome by the Gauls, the period from Caesar's consulship to his death occupied books 103–116. The battle of Actium was dealt with in Book 133; Book 142 contained the death of Drusus (9 B.C.). Books 109–116 bore the separate title of *Belli civilis libri.* Of the 142 books only 35 are extant: 1–10, from the beginnings to the close of the Second Samnite War (287 B.C.), and 21–45, from the Second Punic War through the Macedonian and Syrian wars. For the substance of the last books we have indices in the *Periochae,* or summaries of contents. Martial 14.190 refers to such an abridgement of Livy—"These little skins contain great Livius whom my whole library would not hold." We have *Periochae* for all the books except 136–37, and two for Book 1, and there is in addition a somewhat fuller papyrus epitome of Books 37–40 and 48–55. Besides the epitomes we have the works of Florus, Aurelius Victor, Eutropius, Orosius, and Julius Obsequens, who drew largely and in some cases exclusively on Livy.

Through these excerptors and independently Livy has been Europe's principal textbook of Roman history; perhaps the reason why the ordinary student's knowledge of Roman history stops where it does is that Livy stopped where he did. It is natural that Livy should be studied mainly for his history, and natural too, in view of his motives and his concept of the historian's art, that modern historians should be extremely critical of him. He never falsifies intentionally (such things as his acceptance of Augustus' reading of an inscription on a miraculously preserved linen breastplate at 4.20 is a gesture of courtesy), and indeed he quite plainly indicates that he himself does not believe in the divine parentage of Romulus and Remus and the miraculous translation of Romulus. But he does not employ the methods of the researcher or the scientist's canons of criticism. He fails to consult easily available sources, he is ignorant in military matters and inexpert in religious and constitutional antiquities, and he is gullible in accepting the work of his predecessors without question, though he occasionally does state his basis for accepting one of two versions of an incident. He knows that family histories are unreliable but follows them nevertheless, as in his stories of Fabii or Valerii. He accepts Valerius Antias' fantastic figures without question, as we have noticed, until, in a better known period, he realizes how unreliable they are; he then remarks on their unreliability but does not mend his ways.

But all this is merely to say that he was writing not a scholarly handbook but a work of literature. He was working in a tradition which had been established by the annalists of the Sullan period—Valerius Antias and Claudius Quadrigarius, Licinius Macer and Aelius Tubero —on whom he leaned heavily for both matter and arrangement. But his power of vivid historical reconstruction, his dramatic visualization of scenes and people, his color and his vitality are surely his own. His psychological insights were doubtless developed under the influence of the "pathetic" school of Hellenistic historiographers, but what we have for comparison shows an enormous superiority in Livy. A comparison of episodes in the first decade with their parallels in Dionysius of Halicarnassus demonstrates Livy's mastery. Both men used the same materials (but not one another), but a story in Livy is a tenth as long as in Dionysius and ten times as effective. The *dramatis personae* are reduced to the leading actors, the matter of speeches is concentrated, usually into a single pair, the story is rounded and so made dramatic, with a beginning, a high point, and an end. Artistically these inlaid *emblemata,* like the story of the Horatii and Curiatii, of Mettius Fufetius, of the Faliscan schoolmaster, of Coriolanus, of Lucretia, are the high points of the history. Like all historians after Thucydides, Livy follows the practice of inserting fictive speeches, but his speeches always serve the drama or historical understanding or patriotism; they are never mere display pieces, as they frequently are in Dionysius. It is no small praise to say of Livy, in view of the motive of his writing, that his *Books from the Founding of the City* make as agreeable reading as any long prose work written in Latin.

When horizons of geography and curiosity were widened by the conquests of Alexander, and philosophers, especially the Stoics, came to teach the unity of mankind, the writing of universal, as distinguished from local, history came into fashion. In Livy's own day the Sicilian Diodorus, a professing Stoic, composed such a universal history in Greek, largely by excerpting the work of his predecessors; of Diodorus' *Bibliothece* ("Library") fifteen books are extant. Another contemporary of Livy, Pompeius Trogus, a native of Gaul whose father had served under Julius Caesar, composed the first universal history in Latin. His work, based either solely on Timagenes of Alexandria (who was a teacher in the household of Augustus) or on a series of earlier Greek historians, began with the Assyrians, Medes, and Persians, continued with the Scythians and Greeks, and ended with the early history of Rome and of Gaul and Spain down to the conquest of the Cantabri in the age of Augustus. Pompeius Trogus' forty-four books are lost, but are represented in the extremely useful synopsis and abridgement of Justin, whose date is unknown but probably fell in the second or third century A.D. As reflected in Justin, Trogus' narrative was as elaborate as Livy's (but without Livy's patriotic bias), dramatic in presentation, and with a moralizing tendency. As in Livy, speeches were generally, but not always, reported indirectly. Pompeius Trogus also wrote zoological and perhaps botanical works which were used by the Elder Pliny.

A history of the period from the outbreak of the civil war, now lost, was written by Annaeus Seneca, who was born of equestrian family at Cordova in 55 B.C. and was the father of the like-named philosopher, of Gallio of Acts 18.12, and of the father of Lucan. He came to Rome early in life and there amassed a fortune and became intimate with the rhetoricians of the day. He lived until about A.D. 39. His great work is the *Oratorum sententiae divisiones colores,* on the general subject of rhetoric, addressed to his sons. It consists of extracts cited by memory from leading rhetoricians, interspersed with digressions and comments of his own. Originally the work included ten books of *Controversiae* each with its own preface, and at least two of *Suasoriae*. Of these only one of the *Suasoriae* and five books of the *Controversiae* (1, 2, 7, 9, 10), and these mutilated, have survived. The *Suasoriae* are deliberations on alternative courses of action, for example, "Shall Agamemnon sacrifice Iphigenia?", "Shall Alexander embark on the ocean?", "Shall Cicero apologize to Antony?" When we scorn the narrowness and artificiality of the education provided by the rhetors we must remember that the *proper* handling of such a *suasoria* would involve history, politics, economics, geography, law, psychology, ethics, and other disciplines, aside from precise and effective use of language. Only when preoccupation with form supplanted thoughtful consideration of matter, when ingenious conceits took the place of logical reflection, and the speaker's goal was shifted from edification and conviction to winning applause for virtuosity in expression, did the "rhetoric" of such compositions acquire the pejorative sense it has today.

The *Controversiae,* which are in form discussions on moot points of equity, show a similar degeneration from a useful practice. The laws are frequently such as could never have appeared in any code, and the discussion of them is calculated not so much to sharpen the legal mind as to display verbal cleverness. What interest they have, aside from verbal and casuistical acrobatics, is as skeleton plots for romances, and some have indeed made their way into the *Gesta Romanorum.* A vestal convicted of violating her vow of virginity and flung down a precipice escapes without injury: should she be subjected to the ordeal a second time? Perhaps the gods wished to prolong her agony? Perhaps she had practiced falling down precipices in preparation? A man is captured by pirates but freed by the chief's daughter, whom he promises to marry; when he arrives home with his bride his father disinherits him. A loving couple vow not to survive each other; the husband sends the wife a false report of his death; the wife flings herself down a precipice but recovers; her father demands that she divorce him. These cases, from the first two books of the *Controversiae,* show how rhetoric was eating into all intellectual pursuits. Seneca's work is systematic enough. The individual books of the *Controversiae* begin with very readable prefaces, which contain thumbnail characterizations of leading rhetors, followed by the *controversia* proper under the headings: (a) *sententiae,* or opinions of the rhetoricians on the general application of the law to the case in hand; (b) *divisiones,* or detailed questions arising out of the subject; and (c) *colores,* or "colorable" representations of the act under discussion. The numerous digressions, anecdotes, and criticisms of individual orators, drawn from a wide experience and a phenomenal memory, make Seneca's book a most valuable source for the literary history of the early empire. Specimens from over a hundred rhetors dealing with some forty themes show a wide range of style and mannerism. Seneca's own style and his own views are represented most fully in the prefaces. His style is easy but terse and incisive, thus marking the transition from the periodic Ciceronian to the pointed Silver style. His views show an old-fashioned sobriety and rigor and a suspicion of novelty. He has a great admiration for Cicero but deplores his want of constancy. His own view of the famous orator agrees with the striking summation of Asinius Pollio which he preserves (*Suasoriae* 6.24):

> To speak of the talent and industry of a man whose numerous and great works are destined to abide forever is otiose. . . . Would only that he had been able to bear prosperity with greater moderation and adversity with greater fortitude.

Rhetoric subsumed all the liberal disciplines, and its authority was on the upward path which would lead it to the complete domination of intellectual life under Hadrian. But other arts and sciences had their devotees who wrote books on their specialties. For its substantive value as well as its uniqueness the *De architectura* of Vitruvius, in ten books, is the most remarkable. Vitruvius had been an engineer in charge of Augustus' artillery (if the Caesar addressed in the Preface is Augustus, as it almost certainly is), and in recognition of the emperor's generosity wrote the competent treatise which he hoped would endure. He claims authority for his work though he deprecates his own literary talents (1.1.18):

> For it is not as a lofty thinker, nor as an eloquent speaker, nor as a scholar practised in the best methods of literary criticism, but as an architect who has a mere tinge of these things, that I have striven to write the present treatise.
>
> —*F. Granger*

But he is far from minimizing the importance of the architect's craft. Besides natural endowment (1.1.3),

> he should be a man of letters, a skilful draughtsman, a mathematician, familiar with scientific inquiries, a diligent student of philosophy, acquainted with music; not ignorant of medicine, learned in the responses of jurisconsults, familiar with astronomy and astronomical calculations.
>
> —*F. Granger*

Book 1 deals with the training of the architect, with various divisions of the art, and with town planning and the proper location of buildings. Book 2 treats of the history of building and of various types of building materials. Books 3 and 4 deal with temples, and especially with the Doric, Ionic, and Corinthian orders. Book 5 continues with other public structures, such as theaters (including their acoustics), baths, and harbors. In the controversy as to whether or not the Greek theater had a raised stage Vitruvius is of course a *locus classicus;* his description envisages a raised stage, but he is obviously thinking of conditions in his own day when even ancient theaters were remodeled after the new fashion. Book 6 deals with domestic architecture, for city and country, and Book 7 with interior decoration, such as pavements, ornamental plaster work, and the use of color. Book 8 deals with water supply; Book 9, in connection with dials and clocks, with geometry, mensuration, and astronomy. The last book is concerned with mechanical and military engineering. The absence of reference to the important buildings erected under Augustus' program would suggest that Vitruvius followed some Greek source, possibly the Hermogenes whom he several times names. But there can be no question that he was himself devoted to and perfectly at home in the theory and practice of his craft. The style is what we should expect of a professional man who is not a professional writer; like the continuators of Caesar he uses the vocabulary of his trade in unadorned technical passages and then bursts forth into misplaced elegance. Plebeian usages as well as the trade vocabulary of masons, carpenters, and plumbers occur, but except for the technical terms Vitruvius is not hard to read. He has indeed been read by generations of architects, not as a curio or a chapter in the history of their profession, but for his direct applicability to their practice.

We turn again to history, and to a useful work by a nonprofessional. C. Velleius Paterculus (ca. 19 B.C.–ca. A.D. 31) was descended, as he finds room to tell us, from a long line of military men, and himself served under Tiberius for eight years; on Tiberius' recommendation he became quaestor in A.D. 6 and praetor in 15. When Velleius' friend Marcus Vincius (who married Germanicus' daughter Julia) became consul in A.D. 30, Velleius presented him with his two-book compendium of Roman history down to that date. The opening pages and the section from the founding of Rome to the war against Perses (a period of 582 years) are missing; what we have, disregarding the omission, begins with the prehistory of Greece and the Orient and continues to the fall of Carthage and Corinth in 146 B.C., in the first book, and covers the remaining 176 years in the second. The author is naturally better informed and more interested in the later period, and himself projected a fuller history of the period from the civil war onwards. As a historian Velleius has many faults. He cites Cato and Hortensius, but he is not critical of his sources; he confuses Catonian and Varronian eras; he puts incidents in the wrong context. His adulation of his emperor Tiberius and his court may be abject, but it is sincere and a wholesome antidote to the lurid pages of Tacitus and Suetonius. On the other hand he provides the only continuous account of the long stretches for which we have no Livy. His interest is largely biographical and presents concise portraits not only of such major figures as the Gracchi, Marius, Sulla, Cicero, Pompey, and Caesar, but also of secondary personages like Clodius, Curio, Lepidus, and Plancus. He is much interested in literature and mentions Homer and Hesiod, the tragic and comic poets, Isocrates, Plato, and Aristotle. He has three digressions on literary topics: on early Latin literature (2.9); on the Ciceronian and Augustan period (2.36); and on the brevity of periods of bloom in Greek and Latin literature (1.16–17). Other excursuses deal with Roman colonization (1.14–15) and Roman provinces (2.38–39). Velleius' affected and artificial style is as unprofessional as his historiography. His sentences are clumsy and loaded with parentheses; his vocabulary is meager and is eked out by redundancies and pomposity. His fondness for sententious "point" and antitheses shows the influence of the rhetorical schools and points to the Silver Age. In general his model is Sallust rather than Livy, and he himself calls Sallust an emulator of Thucydides. But with all his faults of technique and style there is something refreshing in Velleius own enthusiasm. If what we desire is not a gem of polished prose or the accuracy of a seminar report but a brief account of a fascinating history by a man eager to recount it, then Velleius will give satisfaction.

The merits of Velleius shine golden when his work is compared with the much larger work of a contemporary who is nevertheless so little regarded that nine out of ten professional scholars would not recognize his name. His name was Valerius Maximus and his work the *Factorum et dictorum memorabilium libri novem* ("Nine Books of Memorable Deeds and Sayings"), dedicated to Tiberius. All that we know of the author's life is that he accompanied Ovid's friend Sextus Pompey to his governorship of Asia about A.D. 27. Adulation is heaped upon Tiberius throughout, and the violent denunciation of Sejanus (for whom Velleius had a kind word) in the last book (9.11 Ext. 4) suggests that the work was published soon after Sejanus' fall in 31. The anecdotes for the use of speakers of which the book consists are classified under various moral or philosophical headings (omens, moderation, gratitude, chastity, cruelty, and the like), each of these being illustrated from Roman (*domestica*) and, less fully, from foreign (*externa*) examples. The chief sources are Livy and Cicero, but many other Latin writers are drawn upon. Quotations of memorable sayings are fairly close, with alterations introduced for rhetorical effect. The book's rhetorical artifices, its bombast and its sententiousness illustrate the excesses of the Silver Age. Valerius himself has nothing to say worth hearing. But he knew his market, and his work enjoyed a vogue in antiquity and the Middle Ages. It was twice epitomized, in the fourth and fifth centuries.

A much more competent and useful work than Valerius Maximus' is Quintus Curtius' *History of Alexander the Great*. Several men of the early empire named Quintus Curtius are known, but none can be identified as our author. No ancient writer mentions the work, though it enjoyed great popularity in the Middle Ages, as the abundance of manuscripts proves. It is probable that our Curtius lived and wrote under Claudius. The *History of Alexander* is our first example of a Latin prose work not directly concerned with a Roman orientation, and yet the Romans of the early empire did have a special interest in Alexander. A kind of Alexander cult took shape, to which both Caesar and Antony paid homage, and the Roman empire itself was regarded successor and heir to the short-lived empire of Alexander. Furthermore, the question as to whether Alexander was an authentic hero and civilizer or merely lucky and a tyrant was a favorite issue with philosophers and indeed still exercises historians. The disquisition in Livy (9.17–19) which has been mentioned above seems to be a school exercise on this theme. Curtius' book wavers between the two points of view; the probable explanation is that he failed to weld two disparate sources successfully. Of the ten books into which Curtius' work was divided, the first two are completely lost, and there are considerable lacunae elsewhere. Curtius makes no pretense to original scholarship but writes merely to present his Latin audience with an attractive treatment of a great theme, and his treatment is indeed attractive. His carefully elaborated speeches and battle pieces are reminiscent of Livy's. His Latin is lucid and of virtually classical purity, though there are traces of Silver Latinity. He favors pointed *sententiae,* antitheses, fanciful metaphors, and other rhetorical ·devices, and he avoids long periods. But these artifices are not presented for their own sake, as they frequently are in the rhetorical virtuosi; they are there in the service of the dramatic story and of the reader's pleasure in it. For all the inconsistency in the motivation of Alexander, the portrait of him which emerges is of a truly demonic figure.

The earliest extant Latin work on geography is the *De chorographia* of Pomponius Mela, who was born in Tingentera, near Gibraltar, and wrote under Claudius. Of the three books of his geography the first describes the earth's division into hemispheres and zones, and the relative positions of the continents and oceans; the second deals with the various countries which touch on the Mediterranean; and the third, those that touch on the outer oceans, including both Britain and India. The interior of Europe, as of the other continents, is neglected. The work is well arranged and complete; more than fifteen hundred geographical names are recorded. There are some details of topography, climate, and popular customs, but no mathematical details or distances. The Elder Pliny cites the work frequently. The style of the book is suggestive of Sallust, and there are occasional excursions into rhetoric, as in the descriptions of Egypt and of Britain. The geographical concepts are roughly those of Strabo.

Encyclopedic learning in the reign of Tiberius is represented by Aulus Cornelius Celsus. The eight books *De medicina* which are extant were only a part of an encyclopedia which embraced agriculture, medicine, war, rhetoric, and probably jurisprudence and philosophy. The treatise on agriculture is quoted thirty times in very respectful terms by Celsus' younger contemporary Columella. Quintilian (12.11.24) uses the example of Celsus, whom he calls *mediocri vir ingenio,* to prove that even a layman (specifically, an orator) can learn all these various subjects; Celsus' treatise on rhetoric Quintilian criticizes, as a specialist naturally would. Celsus was not himself a medical practitioner but had acquired experience and definite opinions as the head of a household. He knew enough to select good authorities; he shows special reverence for Hippocrates but mentions more than seventy later writers on medicine. Celsus' proem presents a judicious summary of the history of medicine and of the various schools of medical theory and practice and emphasizes the value of the study of natural science as a preparation for medicine. He then proceeds to deal with dietetics (Book 1); diagnosis, prognosis, and therapeutics (2); internal diseases (3 and 4); pharmacology (5 and 6); and surgery (7 and 9). The importance of anatomy is stressed, and the anatomical knowledge displayed is sound. Stress is laid on diagnosis and prognosis, as in Hippocrates. Drugs are prescribed more than they are by Greek writers on medicine, but general hygiene and physical exercise are also strongly recommended. A Roman touch is revealed in Celsus' preference of sport over gymnastics. Celsus' style is simple and straightforward and free from meretricious embellishment. Except for such things as prescriptions his work is as readable as we should expect a discourse on an interesting and important branch of knowledge to be in the hands of a well-informed man of taste.

A more practical interest governs Columella's twelve-book treatise on agriculture. Lucius Junius Moderatus Columella was born in Gades (he mentions a variety of lettuce as belonging to "his" Gades) and, as we infer from an inscription, served as a military tribune in Syria. He acquired land in Latium, not far from holdings of Seneca, whom he speaks of as a man of extraordinary talent and principles (3.3.3); as Seneca died in A.D. 65, Columella must have written earlier. Columella's treatise *De re rustica* is the most comprehensive and systematic Roman work on agriculture. The first book presents general precepts on choice of land, water supply, arrangement of farm buildings, and distribution of chores among the farm staff. The second deals with ploughing and fertilizing for field crops. Books 3–5 are concerned with fruit trees, vines, olive orchards. Books 6 and 7 are on animal husbandry, 8 on poultry and fish, and 9 on beekeeping. When Vergil's work had taken him to the subject of gardening he excused himself from dealing with the theme: *Aliis post me memoranda relinquo* (*Georgics* 4.148). Columella writes his tenth book, on gardening, in 436 hexameters to supplement Vergil. From the prefaces to the whole work and to Book 10 it is evident that that book was intended to be the conclusion, but at the insistence of his addressee Silvinus Columella added two further books. Book 11 discusses the duties of a farm overseer, presents a calendar for various types of farm work, and adds a long section on gardening to supplement the verse treatment. Book 12 prescribes the special duties of the overseer's wife and contains recipes for making various kinds of wine and for pickling and preserving fruits and vegetables. An earlier and briefer treatment of the subject matter of Books 3–5 is the extant *De arboribus*. Other works of Columella, such as *Adversus astrologos* and *De lustrationibus,* are lost. Columella is a practical and scientific farmer, and conscious of the dignity and importance of agriculture. He is concerned for the social and moral implications of his subject; he deplores the importation of grain from abroad, the spread of fashionable country estates, and the increase of absentee landlords. A farmer must work hard and exercise personal supervision. Besides his own experience Columella draws on the works of a dozen predecessors (including Cato, Varro, and Vergil) in Latin and Greek and on the Carthaginian Mago. His prose style is clear and appropriate to his subject, and though he has an eye for landscape and color he never indulges in fine writing.

With the writers on technical subjects in the early empire we may include without undue impropriety the enigmatic figure of Marcus Manilius, the author of the *Astronomica*. Of Manilius himself nothing is known; he mentions the defeat of Varus (A.D. 9), speaks of Augustus as still alive in Books 1 and 2 but of Tiberius as the reigning emperor in Book 4. The *Astronomica* may be described as a didactic poem on astrology; its five books contain 4,258 lines. The first book is on the creation and astronomy; the remainder are concerned with astrology; the work is not complete, whether left so or subsequently mutilated it is not determined. Manilius' attitude is that of an enthusiast eager to make and teach converts. Not the least interesting aspect of the work is its illustration of the hold of astrology on good minds in the early empire; the Pantheon itself gives architectural embodiment to its teachings. By the fourth century, as we see from Firmicus Maternus' *Mathesis,* its dominance had grown almost complete. Manilius' poem is not nearly so systematic, nor so ardent, as Firmicus' treatise, and technical errors and omissions have been pointed out in it. As poetry too, it is second-rate, though the versification is smooth and there are flashes of forceful expression in it. The technical matter is enlivened by occasional display pieces and by illustrations drawn from the figures and activities of daily life. Here and in his general approach Manilius' nearest analogue is Lucretius, but the interval between the two is unbridgeable.

XIII

SENECA

IN TREATING OF POST-AUGUSTAN WRITERS FRE-
quent reference has been made to the Silver Age and to the "pointed"
style which is its chief characteristic. The pointed style Professor W. C.
Summers defines as "a kind of writing which, without sacrificing
clearness or conciseness, regularly avoids, in thought or phrase or
both, all that is obvious, direct and natural, seeking to be ingenious
rather than true, neat rather than beautiful, exercising the wit but
not rousing the emotions or appealing to the judgment of the reader."
The Roman development is paralleled in other literatures; in English
the full-blooded genius of the Elizabethans was succeeded by the conceits of Donne and Cowley, which led in turn to the more intellectu-
alized epigrammatic style of Dryden and Pope. Pope's Homer is un-
Homeric because of Pope's predilection for pointed style; Professor
Summers cites such examples as "Be still yourselves, and Hector asks
no more"; "Achilles absent was Achilles still"; "In all my equal, but
in misery." When other avenues of achievement are blocked and literature becomes fashionable, when elegance and wit usurp the place of
vigor and independence in literature as in life, a silver age must naturally emerge; and Rome of the early empire was a perfect nursery for
such a growth.

No language falls so naturally into terse *sententiae* as does Latin; its
brevity gives apophthegms, antitheses, paradoxes, a crystalline conciseness, and the facets of the jewel receive an easy glitter from the natural
alliterations and homoioteleuta of the language. *Sententiae* occur in
every Latin author from Livius Andronicus onwards; we have had
occasion to quote a handful from Terence. But now every writer with
pretensions to style devoted all his skill to fabricating and polishing
these ornaments, and there was a tendency for the jewels to preempt
attention from the fabrics they might legitimately have set off. In this
development a factor of equal importance with the nature of the
Latin language was the regularly limited appeal of Latin literature to
the cultivated few. Because the Latin author could address himself
only to readers with sufficient education to appreciate alien forms and

grasp allusions to an alien history and mythology, artificiality was
at a premium. Artificiality in turn encouraged mediocrity: if the
gauge is conformance to certain rules, it can by corollary be assumed
that anyone who knows the rules can write. Education's share in foster-
ing the artificiality has been glanced at in connection with the elder
Seneca. Connected with the standards of excellence propagated in the
rhetorical schools was a social institution which did much to give
Silver literature its peculiar character, the practice of giving public
readings or *recitationes*. Poets had always listened to and criticized
each other's works, and among the Greeks at least readings were
recognized as a form of publication. But the Roman practice which
became such an incubus under the Flavians was instituted by Asinius
Pollio, who was the first Roman to read his works before an audience
(Seneca, *Controversiae* 4, *praef*. 2). Soon the recitation became the
only means of obtaining a public hearing, and with crowded calendars
and keen rivalries, it was natural that each performer should strive
for the most numerous rounds of applause. It was "point" that would
bring the house down, and literature was studded with points calculated to elicit applause even when it was not intended for oral delivery. Line-for-line dialogue in the tragedies of Seneca is like a game
of batting apophthegms back and forth, and the reader finds his head
oscillating from one performer to the other as at a game of ping-pong.

It is Seneca, son of the rhetor, brother of Gallio, and uncle of Lucan,
who is our best illustration of the Silver style, and at the same time one
of the half dozen most significant figures in Latin literature. His
biography is of more than common interest, both for its own sake
and as a guide to the appreciation of his works. Lucius Annaeus Seneca
was born at Cordova about 4 B.C. of a wealthy and distinguished equestrian family. He was taken to Rome in infancy by an aunt, who nursed
him through a sickly childhood and helped launch him on his official
career. He devoted himself to rhetoric and money-making; his avoca-
tions were philosophy and viticulture. About A.D. 33 he was quaestor,
and by the time of Caligula's accession (37) his reputation as an
orator and writer was great enough to arouse the emperor's jealousy.
Caligula refrained from killing him only because he was given to understand that the sickly intellectual would soon die a natural death.
Certain traits in Seneca's character and his works are undoubtedly
due to his persistent valetudinarianism. In Claudius' first year (A.D.

41) Messallina procured Seneca's banishment to Corsica on the improbable charge of adultery with Julia Livilla. His despondency during the eight years of his exile was deeper than Ovid's, and his pleas for restoration more abject. In 49 Agrippina procured his recall and made him, together with the praetorian prefect Afranius Burrus, tutor to her son Nero. Nero succeeded in 54, and the beneficent administration of the first five years of his reign is attributed to the tutelage of Burrus and Seneca, who was now of consular rank and virtually prime minister. But in 59 Nero asserted his true character; Seneca and Burrus were reluctant accessories to the murder of Agrippina in that year, and Seneca wrote Nero's exculpation to the Senate. Relations with the emperor grew strained, and when Burrus died in 62 Seneca offered his enormous fortune to the emperor and went into virtual retirement on his estates. Upon apparently dubious evidence of implication in the Pisonian conspiracy of A.D. 65 Seneca was bidden to take his own life, and he did so, with a theatrical gesture becoming to his tragic heroes, but with a fortitude of which the course of his life had given no evidence. He himself found that life exemplary (Tacitus, *Annals* 15.62):

Quite unmoved Seneca asked for tablets on which to inscribe his will, and, on the centurion's refusal, turned to his friends, protesting that as he was forbidden to requite them, he bequeathed to them the only, but still the noblest possession yet remaining to him, the pattern of his life, which, if they remembered, they would win a name for moral worth and steadfast friendship.

—A. J. Church and W. J. Brodribb

Others have found much to disapprove in the pattern. He preached a self-sufficient contentment with a humble lot, indifference to circumstances, contempt of pain and death; and he amassed an enormous fortune by questionable means, wailed aloud throughout his exile, grovelled before the freedman Polybius, deftly dodged pain and death. To curry favor he reviles a dead emperor and makes a particular butt of measures which a professing Stoic must have approved: care for the judiciary, extension of franchise, study of history. Cleavage between profession and practice is a common phenomenon, but seldom is the gap so yawning, because Seneca was an artist both in his preaching and in his malefactions. But in Seneca, it has been maintained, the flaw is not subversion of conscience but a clinical morbidity connected

with his general ill health of which his intensity in either direction
is a kind of excrescence. Actual details of style in his writing as well
as the structure of his philosophical thought have been adduced to
document his psychological state.

Wrenching and straining and tormenting of the emotions is certainly characteristic of the tragedies of Seneca, to which we first turn.
We do not know at what point in Seneca's career the plays were written; he himself never speaks of them, and indeed the only external
evidence that the Seneca of the tragedies is our Seneca is Quintilian's
attribution of a line from the *Medea* to him. Style and general outlook, however, make Senecan authorship virtually certain. The corpus
includes ten pieces: *Hercules* [*furens*], *Troades, Phoenissae, Medea,
Phaedra, Oedipus, Agamemnon, Thyestes, Hercules* [*Oetaeus*], and
Octavia. The second Hercules play is almost twice as long as the average and contains much un-Senecan material; the *Octavia* is on a contemporary subject and almost certainly not Seneca's. As the titles
indicate, Seneca's sources are Greek tragedy, and chiefly Euripides, and
this circumstance has led to much disparaging criticism of Seneca, on
the assumption that he tried to do what the Greeks did well and did
it very badly. Aside from his rhetorical excesses and a preoccupation
with horror that approaches the ghoulish, and aside from faults in
dramatic structure, his plays lack the spiritual profundity we associate with the Greek. But the different traditions of the Roman stage
(whether or not Seneca's plays were intended for presentation, he
was writing in the tradition of the Roman theater) account for his
form, including the rhetorical propensities, and the object of his
plays (as of such Elizabethans as Marlowe) was not to examine the
implications of man's conflict with destiny but to exhibit, for the
vicarious satisfaction of an audience, the intensity of emotional drives
of which his heroic figures were capable. Interest in the high emotional voltage of important personages and in their theatrical display
of their agonizing seems inherent in the character of the early empire and is the key to much in Tacitus. Tacitus' colossal figures all
stalk about on a stage, like the lurid figures in Seneca; their grandeur
and their intensity are always on parade, they are always conscious
of their public and their public's expectations. Is it natural for an
elderly woman confronted by the assassins her son has sent (*Annals*
14.8) to point to her womb and say "Strike here"? An audience

familiar with the details of Agrippina's murder would not call a typical display of Clytemnestra's agonizing bombastic (*Agamemnon* 133-44):

> Too dire my grief to wait time's healing hand.
> My very soul is scorched with flaming pains:
> I feel the goads of fear and jealous rage,
> The throbbing pulse of hate, the pangs of love,
> Base love that presses hard his heavy yoke
> Upon my heart, and holds me vanquished quite.
> And always, 'mid those flames that vex my soul,
> Though faint indeed, and downcast, all undone,
> Shame struggles on. By shifting seas I'm tossed:
> As when here wind, there tide impels the deep,
> The waves stand halting 'twixt the warring powers.
> And so I'll strive no more to guide my bark.
> Where wrath, where grief, where hope shall bear me on,
> There will I speed my course; my helmless ship
> I've giv'n to be the sport of winds and floods.
> Where reason fails 'tis best to follow chance.
>
> —*F. J. Miller*

Intensification of passion is Seneca's object in most of his divergences from the Greek. If murder is frequent it is because nothing offers so fertile a field for the display of passion, in agent or victim, in prospect or actuality, as violent death. Seneca's ghosts serve the same purpose, as comparison with Greek ghosts will show. In the *Hecuba* the ghost of Polydorus simply discharges the function of a Euripidean prologue by putting the audience in possession of certain necessary data. But in the *Thyestes* the ghost of Tantalus is driven in to supplement his own torments and to abet the Furies in their fiendish work (1-121). In the *Agamemnon* Thyestes' ghost is itself the spirit of vengeance. Nor are Seneca's characters undifferentiated in their intensity. The sameness in Seneca's characters which critics complain of, their common trait of being permanently at the top pitch of emotional excitement volubly expressed, is, as a matter of fact, just the sort of sameness which meets a foreigner in a strange country. In Seneca's country it may be the custom to wear one's heart outside instead of inside one's clothes and to shriek for attention to it by all contrivances of color and sound and gesture; but that does not mean that the hearts are identical. The contrary would seem to be indicated:

the heart is so important a human document that any peculiarity must be remarked. In other drama we observe people as they react to institutions: in Seneca institutions are of the same importance for the character as the cut of his clothes or of his hair. Like the Senecan nurses, they are foils against which the outlines of the hates or ambitions of the principals may be sharpened for the observer. The cosmic order itself is expected to subserve grand human actions: in the presence of a grand sinner the sun is expected to darken, in the presence of a grand crime, to retreat backward to its rising. The heroic characters are expected to prove their right to heroic passions by *doing*. Medea, Phaedra, Clytemnestra, Deianira have nurses so that their doing shall be emphasized by contrast with their nurses merely talking. Medea is active, aggressive, virile in her hate, Andromache in her mother love, Phaedra in her passion. Lycus' suing for her hand inflames Megara into action in *Hercules furens;* in Euripides she is only the passive sufferer, patient and saintly. To help toward an understanding of the capacity, the intensity, the course of passion, illustrated in significant individuals and writ large perhaps to be more easily understood of the people, is a high service for a dramatist to render.

Given such a purpose as Seneca's, even the rhetoric of his tirades has its uses. Exaggeration is not only appropriate to such plays as these, but effective; it amuses us only if we fortify ourselves with the critic's detached determination not to be impressed. Roman drama had always been a closer approximation to our opera than Greek drama had been, and rhetoric is no more violent a distortion of ordinary speech than is singing. Other significant aspects in which Roman drama differed from the Greek are also relevant to understanding Seneca. Roman drama was entertainment, not part of a ritual; its audience were spectators, not participants; its theater was grandiose and ornate, not a simple arrangement in the open air. If we choose to call Seneca's plays Greek tragedies, we must pronounce them debased; but they are a different thing, and for their own sake as well as their enormous influence on the Elizabethans, they are worth looking at.

Whether or not the plays were intended for presentation is a moot point; the probability is that they were not, though they were written with the conditions of presentation in mind. Perhaps they were read to audiences, by a cast of readers, without the appurtenances of a regular performance. The choruses could not have been sung and danced in the classic Greek fashion, for their arrangement is not strophic but repeats the same metrical pattern line after line or, in the case of Sapphics, stanza after stanza, continuously. As is sometimes the case in the Greek, the choral interludes seem to be the special vehicle for Seneca's own doctrine, which is the Neo-Stoicism he teaches in his essays. It has been held, indeed, that Seneca's main object in writing the plays was to propagate his doctrine, and that he deliberately arranged the plays in the order cited above (the manuscript tradition which includes the *Octavia* has a different arrangement) in order to present a systematic course, each play in its proper order illustrating some Stoic principle. According to this system the plays on Hercules (a Stoic hero) are the framework; *Troades* and *Phoenissae* center upon the problems of life, death, and destiny; *Medea* and *Phaedra* provide exemplars for a treatise on the passions; and *Agamemnon, Oedipus,* and *Thyestes* deal with free will, sin, and retribution. The ideas presented are certainly characteristic of Seneca's teaching, and a ground for maintaining Senecan authorship of the plays. Their inclusion shows that Seneca regarded his enterprise seriously and not merely as a literary exercise, such as Silver Age treatment of mythologic subject matter was apt to be.

Deviations in Seneca's plays from their extant Greek models make his different objects, both in the display of emotional intensity and in the promulgation of Stoic ideas, very plain. *Mad Hercules* is not concerned, as is its Euripidean model, with Athenian-Dorian relations and abstract justice, but with the Stoic saint who combats a tyrant and who, when in a fit of madness he has stained his hands with the blood of his own children, displays his emotional writhing at length and demonstrates emotional strength (not reason, as in Euripides) by proving willing to go on living: "Yield thee, my manhood" (1315). If the plays contain lessons for Nero, the theme of the tyrant who desires to marry in order to improve his position may be a covert allusion to Nero and his marriage to Octavia. The Herculean labors whose repeated recitals occupy so large a proportion of the play are part of the Stoic treatment of the hero who devoted his life to the amelioration of mankind. The *Trojan Women,* aside from being, like Euripides' play, a pacifist document, provides a spectacle of the mutability of fortune: "See how small a company of us remains," says

Andromache (507), "a tomb, a child, a captive woman." Psychological perceptiveness and masterly theatricality are illustrated in the scene where Andromache has hidden Astyanax in Hector's tomb, has half persuaded Ulysses that the child is dead, and is finally forced to yield him when Ulysses shrewdly threatens to destroy the tomb. *Phoenician Women* seems to be a collection of disparate scenes not yet worked into a complete tragedy.

Greek tragedy normally keeps right and wrong in balance; its conflicts are not between a virtuous white against a wicked black, but between shades of gray. Drama concerned rather with display of emotional intensity than with questions of justice tends to be melodramatic, and so in *Medea* Jason is rather ingenuous and appealing, which makes Medea herself more colossal in her exhibitions of fury; she wishes she had borne fourteen children instead of two, to make her vengeance greater. The first song of the chorus is an actual epithalamium for the marriage of Jason and Creusa—which is an effective catalyst for her fury. The scenes of incantation and witchcraft—ancestors of the witches' scenes in Macbeth—are a favorite Silver device for building up tension; there are similar scenes in Lucan. *Phaedra* too is an exhibition of a woman wholly controlled by sexual passion. Phaedra does not, in Seneca, struggle against nobler impulses, but herself solicits Hippolytus' love; she seduces the nurse, not the other way round. The use of the rejected sword, instead of Euripides' awkward tablets, to calumniate Hippolytus is a fine theatrical touch which Racine borrowed. On the other hand ghoulishness becomes ludicrous when Theseus attempts to piece Hippolytus' mangled remains together like a jigsaw puzzle. Theseus exemplifies the tyrant, who was abhorrent to Stoic ideas of kingship. *Oedipus* is a fuller portrait of the tyrant, who is an abiding curse to his people; that play suffers most by comparison with its great Greek model. The same may be said of the *Agamemnon,* though that play is superior to the *Oedipus* in construction and perhaps a better example of Seneca's theatrical intensity. The ghost of Thyestes which provided the requisite horror for this play has had a numerous Elizabethan progeny.

But the Senecan play which exerted the greatest influence on English drama is the *Thyestes*. This powerful tragedy of revenge shows Seneca at his best in technical execution and in theatrical qualities.

For psychological interest as well as spectacle nothing could surpass
the scene where Thyestes is driving himself to enjoy his luxurious
banquet and being stifled by the heavy atmosphere electric with the
presage of evil, with Atreus gloating fiendishly in the background.
The description of how Atreus slaughtered and boiled and roasted
Thyestes' sons is not only perfect in the rhetoric of horror but engages
sympathies that are essential to the effectiveness of the play. When we
are told that the sun stopped in its course we are prepared to accept it
as a poetical truth. Even the Senecan point finds effective use. When
after torturing suspense Atreus reveals the severed heads of the children and asks, "Dost recognize thy sons?" Thyestes makes the all-
sufficient answer, "I recognize my brother." *Hercules on Oeta* shows
the triumph of the Stoic saint over suffering and death. This play is
much longer than Seneca left it, and the repeated rehearsals of Hercules' labors make tedious reading, but it is an extremely interesting
document in the history of religion. The report of Hercules' last moments (1618–1757) comes to this: Hercules undergoes a *passion* on a
pyre in order to become a savior of mankind; this is to be followed
by a *resurrection* and an *apotheosis;* Alcmena waits at the foot of the
pyre; Hercules speaks to his father in heaven and hears his reply: "Lo!
my father summons me, and opens his heaven: Father, I come." To
Theseus, who next after himself was a benefactor of mankind, Hercules had said at the end of *Hercules furens* (1337), "Thou lovest the
guilty," a remarkable compliment in the mouth of a pagan.

On the long debated question of the kind and degree of influence
which Seneca has exerted on the Elizabethans T. S. Eliot has contributed some judicious remarks. Three points which he makes are
of particular interest here: (1) The Tragedy of Blood is far gorier
than can even be imagined for Seneca and wantonly so (e.g., *Titus
Andronicus*), whereas Seneca's use of the revolting is restrained and
dramatic; Seneca had nothing to do with this aberration and is
superior to it. (2) Elizabethan bombast *can* be traced to Seneca.
"Certainly it is all 'rhetorical,' but if it had not been rhetorical would
it have been anything? . . . Without bombast we should not have
had King Lear. The art of dramatic language, we must remember, is
as near to oratory as to ordinary speech or to other poetry. (3) . . .
when an Elizabethan hero or villain dies, he usually dies in the odour
of Seneca. . . . Dante had behind him an Aquinas, and Shakespeare

behind him a Seneca . . . I am not here concerned with Shakespeare's 'borrowings' (where I am inclined to agree) but with
Shakespeare the voice of his time, and this voice in poetry is in the
most serious matters of life and death, most often the voice of Seneca."

Language, style, general outlook, structure, seem to justify the inclusion of the *Octavia* among the plays of Seneca; on the other hand,
the apparent prophecy of the death of Nero (who survived Seneca
by three years) and the allusion in the burning of Rome, which
occurred only a year before Seneca's death, seem to confirm the
opinion of those who deny Senecan authorship. The special interest
of the play is that it is the only surviving specimen of the *fabula
praetexta,* or drama on a historical Roman theme. In point of fact the
play does correctly reflect the events of A.D. 62, when Nero divorced
Octavia and married Poppaea, and it is faithfulness to history, indeed,
that spoils its effectiveness as drama. The *Octavia* too reflects Stoic
egalitarianism; people are entitled to just treatment, and it is the
denial of justice to the chief character and the failure of the people to
make their protest heard that make the tragedy. An interesting echo
of this aspect of the *Octavia* is George Buchanan's *John the Baptist,*
and Buchanan's advocacy of the Stoic ideal of kingship was read by
John Milton.

The influence of Seneca's philosophical writings has not been as
spectacular as that of his tragedies, but it has been equally pervasive.
The misnamed *Dialogues* and the almost equally misnamed *Epistles*
have none of the knottiness and perfectionism we should expect of a
professing Stoic, but they are as tolerant and discursive as Montaigne's;
they are indeed antiquity's closest approach to Montaigne and were
some of Montaigne's favorite reading. The more formal of Seneca's
surviving philosophical writings are the twelve treatises grouped together in the manuscript tradition under the title *Dialogi,* two out of
an original three books of *De clementia,* and seven books of *De
beneficiis.* The chronology of the essays is generally uncertain; thus
reasons have been found for assigning the first of the group, *De
providentia,* either to the beginning of the Corsican exile or to the end
of Seneca's career. The alternative title of this piece is "Why,
Though There Is a Providence, Some Misfortunes Befall Good Men,"
and its addressee is the Lucilius to whom the *Epistles* and the *Natural*

Questions are also addressed. The answer, presented with charm and eloquence, is that the misfortunes are more apparent than real, and afflict only those who lack philosophic fortitude and detachment; in fact Providence guides all things for the good of the universe, which is referred to as *magna res publica. De constantia,* addressed to Seneca's intimate Serenus, is likewise of uncertain date; its alternative title is "The Wise Man Can Receive Neither Injury Nor Insult." Again the prescription is Stoic fortitude (7.3):

"But," someone says, "if Socrates was condemned unjustly, he received an injury." At this point it is needful for us to understand that it is possible for some one to do me an injury and for me not to receive the injury.

—*J. W. Basore*

To maintain such detachment is a service to society (19.4):

That there should be something unconquerable, some man against whom Fortune has no power, works for the good of the commonwealth of mankind.

—*J. W. Basore*

Stoic ethics depended on the equanimity of the sage, who must therefore not tolerate any emotional disturbances, and especially anger, which is apt to supplant reason. Seneca's *De ira* in three books is a discussion of the nature, futility, and cure of anger. The theme was a favorite with writers on ethics; we have a treatise of Plutarch's on the same subject. Seneca's book is not well constructed, and the fact that he addresses his brother who later became Gallio as Novatus points to a date early in the reign of Claudius.

The "consolation" was a long established genre in Greek literature. The writer who gave the genre its fixed form appears to be the Academic Crantor (early third century B.C.) whom Cicero praised highly (*Academica* 2.135); Cicero himself wrote a *Consolatio* for the death of his daughter Tullia, and we have cited above part of a consolation addressed to Cicero by Servius Sulpicius (*Ad familiares* 4.5). Three of Seneca's essays (besides such *Epistles* as 63 and 99) are formal *consolationes.* All offer the stock arguments of the form: (a) all men must die; (b) grief is futile, both to the deceased and to the mourner; (c) since time must inevitably ease the blow it is better to master it by reason. But despite its formalism and Stoic brittleness there is much that is noble and tender in the *Ad Marciam,* the first of Seneca's consolations. The end is an eloquent apocalypse in terms of Stoic eschatology, which concludes:

Then also the souls of the best, who have partaken of immortality, when it shall seem best to God to create the universe anew—we, too, amid the failing universe, shall be added as a tiny fraction to this mighty destruction, and shall be changed again into our former elements.

Happy, Marcia, is your son, who already knows these mysteries!

—*J. W. Basore*

De vita beata purports to examine the question of what the Happy Life is and how it is to be obtained. Life according to Nature is obviously the only happy life, and it may be obtained by the pursuit of Stoic philosophy. But the treatise soon digresses into a polemic against pleasure and an indictment of those who sneer at philosophy, and into an apologia for the philosophic millionaire. The apparently personal note suggests a date near Seneca's surrender of his wealth; the brother is now addressed as Gallio. Perhaps the same crisis in Seneca's life is the occasion for the fragmentary *De otio* ("On Leisure") addressed to Serenus, which justifies retirement from public life even for a Stoic. The Stoic would still be part of the larger commonwealth which is distinguished from the lesser (4.1):

Let us grasp the idea that there are two commonwealths—the one, a vast and truly common state, which embraces alike gods and men, in which we look neither to this corner of earth nor to that, but measure the bounds of our citizenship by the path of the sun; the other, the one to which we have been assigned by the accident of birth.

—*J. W. Basore*

Serenus too is the recipient of *De tranquillitate animi* ("On Tranquillity of Mind"). Even the initiate is sometimes troubled by the impingement of luxury, public affairs, and literary fame. Seneca replies with a rather random analysis of the causes of restlessness and boredom, and in a series of practical rules based generally on reason and virtue he offers guidance to inward satisfactions. *De brevitate vitae,* or "On the Shortness of Life," maintains that life is long enough if it is not wasted. Books give the philosopher access to all past ages and their wisdom. Not only parlor games but antiquarian research is a waste of time (13):

No one will have any doubt that those are laborious triflers who spend their time on useless literary problems, of whom even among the Romans there is now a great number. It was once a foible confined to the Greeks to inquire into what number of rowers Ulysses had, whether the *Iliad* or the *Odyssey* was written first, whether moreover they belong to the same author, and various other matters of this stamp, which, if you keep them to yourself, in no way pleasure your secret soul, and, if you publish them, make you seem more of a bore than a scholar. But now this vain passion for learning useless things has assailed the Romans also .   does it serve any useful purpose to know that Pompey was the first to exhibit the slaughter of eighteen elephants in the Circus, pitting criminals against them in a mimic battle?

—*J. W. Basore*

This diatribe may be directed against the antiquarian interests of Claudius, to which Seneca reverts in the *Apocolocyntosis.*

The consolation addressed to Polybius (*Ad Polybium de Consolatione*) vitiates all Seneca's admonitions to Stoic fortitude, for it is in effect a groveling appeal, larded with extravagant flattery, to a powerful freedman of Claudius, to effect Seneca's recall from his exile in Corsica. Whereas he represents himself to Polybius as a mere wreck, with hope gone and faculties impaired by long disuse, the consolation to his mother (*Ad Helviam matrem de consolatione*) takes a different tone. In consoling her for his own exile he says that he finds it tolerable despite its accompaniments of poverty and disgrace and that he occupies his mind in problems of natural science and philosophy. The manliness shown in this consolation is refreshing.

Aside from the above essays collectively known as the *Dialogues* we have the treatises *De clementia* and *De beneficiis.* The *De clementia* was addressed to the emperor Nero when he was eighteen. Nero is represented as communing with himself on his responsibilities as having "been chosen to serve on earth as vicar of the gods," and the treatise offers guidance for attaining the ideal of a merciful and popular ruler. It is interesting to observe Seneca in his role as tutor to his difficult pupil, and his shrewdness both as a pedagogue (the chief technique being flattery) and as a counselor. *De beneficiis* in seven books is the longest of the moral treatises, and the most tedious. The subject is the calculus of giving and receiving, of benefaction and gratitude. The fact that so long a treatment would be devoted to the subject is a commentary on an order where benefits granted and received were carefully balanced and served as the basis for social relationships.

The most attractive of Seneca's philosophical writings are the 124 *Epistulae morales* addressed to Lucilius. They are well-written, sensible, and useful. They read like the mid-week chats of a skillful and alert modernist preacher; no lofty spiritual heights are to be scaled, no impractically rigorous code is insisted upon, deviations from orthodoxy are tolerated with a smile and lessons drawn even from unbelievers, and the reader feels that he has been edified and uplifted. The Lucilius addressed is an earnest seeker for truth with Epicurean leanings, and Seneca is the more experienced elder who shows that philosophy need not be crabbed or intolerant. The letters were written in A.D. 63 and 64; there is no logic in their order, though certain groups can be distinguished. Thus the first twenty-nine letters seem modeled on Epicurus to Idomeneus; those after 28 show that Seneca was studying Posidonius; 49–87 seem to have been written in Campania. Some are brief notes, others run to several pages. The subjects cover a wide range, but the central theme is the importance of the study of philosophy. Philosophy offers guidance to life and life's only true pleasure. It makes old age agreeable and banishes fear of death. It not only promotes personal integrity but is socially useful: *Non sum uni angulo natus, patria mea totus hic mundus est* (28.4), "I am not born unto a single corner; my fatherland is the whole universe." It enables its devotees to perceive the true values of things and men, unswayed by external pomps, and so is truly democratic. It teaches men to make the most of each day as it passes and is a worthy object in life. "A single day of the sages is more spacious than the longest lifetime of the unschooled" (78.10).

Frequently Seneca employs the encounters of daily life either as text or illustration, and these afford intimate glimpses into the Roman scene. We have views of street crowds, of the brutality of the gladiatorial combats, of the gay life at seashore resorts, of the relation of master and slave. The personal tone of the letters gives us an insight not only into Seneca's habits of mind but also into details of his daily regimen, his valetudinarianism, his exercise, his excursions, his reading. There are many instructive and judicious remarks on matters of literary style and on the writer's responsibility: it is bad to say what one does not think; it is worse to write it. "Leisure without letters is death, the burial of a living man" (82.3). The letters are studded with such apophthegms; none is without its quotable gems, and a reader who underscores them will find half his book marked. But though Seneca's Latinity is thoroughly Silver, and Ciceronian periods are avoided in the letters, the style seems quite suited to the matter. The units are themselves small and appropriate to the terseness of the style; it is when he attempts a more spacious work which requires careful articulation and a sustained level that Seneca's shortcomings become apparent.

To Lucilius too is addressed the *Naturales quaestiones,* in seven books. Material for this work had been gathered during Seneca's exile in Corsica, but the actual composition falls late in his life; Book 3 was written after his retirement in 62, and the earthquake at Pompeii in 63 is mentioned at the opening of Book 6. The work contributed to the survival of scientific speculation in the first century, and during the Middle Ages it was the accepted authority on cosmology, but the approach is literary and ethical rather than what we should call scientific. The science of nature is divided (at the opening of Book 2) under three heads: astronomy, which deals with heavenly phenomena (*caelestia*); meteorology, which deals with phenomena between heaven and earth (*sublimia*); and geography, which deals with the phenomena of the earth (*terrestria*). But these subjects are not handled at equal length or in their order. Book 1 deals with fire and includes such topics as meteors, the rainbow, the false sun, and the like. Book 2 deals with air and includes thunder and lightning. Book 3 deals with water in various forms. Book 4 discusses the rise of the Nile and, after an abrupt transition, snow, hail, and rain. Book 5 treats of wind and atmospheric movement; Book 6 with earthquakes; and Book 7 with comets. Seneca does attempt to determine causes and to choose correctly between competing explanations, but his greatest interest (and most readable sections) are in the ethical disquisitions suggested by the scientific materials. In Book 2, for example, lightning suggests other omens and leads to a discussion of fate and religion. At the end of that book Seneca remarks that some would rather be liberated from fear of lightning than know its origin; he agrees that every study should have its moral, and proceeds to offer arguments against the fear of death. Mention of snow, similarly, becomes the occasion for a sermon against the luxury of Romans who demanded snow to cool themselves and their drinks.

We come finally to the satire on the deification of Claudius called *Apocolocyntosis* ("Pumpkinification"), which is almost surely Seneca's. One would almost prefer to think that it was not, for though it is witty and the form allowed a certain license, the criticism of the late emperor's physical failings violates decency, the ridicule of his legitimate interests is a cheap philistinism, and the tone of the whole an unworthy catering to Nero's appetites. The literary type is the Menippean satire, introduced into Latin by Varro, in which more or less colloquial prose is interlarded with bits of verse. The satire opens with the formal declaration, "I wish to place on record the proceedings in heaven October 13 last," and then describes Claudius' last hours on earth and his efforts to gain admission to the place where good emperors go. Out of regard for his kinship with Augustus a resolution, in proper form, is moved, to the effect that Claudius be enrolled as a god and that the appropriate note be added to Ovid's *Metamorphoses*. Heracles (himself the son of a mortal mother) solicits votes for Claudius, but Augustus (in a parody of his own style) finds that, apart from physical disqualifications, Claudius has murdered too many members of the imperial family, and secures his banishment from heaven. Claudius realizes he is dead only when he sees his funeral cortege descending from heaven to hell. His sentence is that he is to engage forever in his favorite game of dicing—but with a box with a perforated bottom; the result was very frustrating (15):

> For when he rattled with the box, and thought he now had got 'em,
> The little cubes would vanish thro' the perforated bottom.
> Then he would pick 'em up again, and once more set a-trying:
> The dice but served him the same trick: away they went a-flying.
> So still he tries, and still he fails; still searching long he lingers;
> And every time the tricksy things go slipping thro' his fingers.
>
> —*W. H. D. Rouse*

Next Caligula arrives and proves, by virtue of the many beatings that he had administered to him, that Claudius was his slave; he then proceeds to hand him over to a freedman to serve as a law clerk. The rich slang and the irreverence of the *Apocolocyntosis* can be paralleled in Latin only in Petronius. It is funny, but to modern feeling, at least, not quite funny enough to excuse its venom. It throws an interesting light on the range of Seneca's mind and interests and on the atmosphere of Nero's court.

To the age of Nero, doubtless, belong the *Laus Pisonis,* the seven *Eclogues* of Calpurnius (to which the four of Nemesianus are wrongly joined), and kindred material transmitted with them. The *Laus Pisonis,* in 261 respectable hexameters, celebrates the Piso whose abortive conspiracy brought death to Seneca, Lucan, and himself in A.D. 65. Piso's literary, musical, and athletic talents (including skill at backgammon), and his amiability and judicious choice of friends have so impressed the writer that he wishes Piso to be his patron. His motive, he declares, is not gain, for though poor he is of a respectable family; but he realizes that even Vergil would not have become famous but for Maecenas. The author of this piece is not known, and we are in not much better case with regard to Calpurnius.

Whether Calpurnius Siculus' name denotes a relationship (perhaps of a freedman) to Calpurnius Piso cannot be determined; "Siculus" may be literally "the Sicilian," or it may signify indebtedness for the bucolic form to the Sicilian Theocritus. Calpurnius' patron Meliboeus, mentioned in *Eclogues* 1 and 4, has been conjectured, but on no convincing grounds, to be Seneca. *Eclogues* 1, 4, and 7 are in praise of the Emperor; *Eclogues* 2, 3, 5, and 6 are of the rural type. That the order is not chronological is shown by the architectural arrangement: *Eclogues* 2, 4, and 6 are amoebean and are sandwiched in between others that are not dialogues. As one would expect, Calpurnius owes much to Vergil as well as Theocritus, and something to Ovid. The subjects are: 1, shepherds find carved on a tree a prophecy of the return of the Golden Age; 2, a singing match between a gardener and a shepherd; 3, a shepherd complains of his mistress' faithlessness; 4, a shepherd (Calpurnius himself) sings of the favors he has received from his patron Meliboeus, and this is followed by an amoebean scene in praise of the emperor; 5, an old shepherd propounds the art of sheep breeding; 6, a singing match, broken off by a violent quarrel between the contestants; and 7, a shepherd describes the spectacles in the amphitheatre at Rome, with much praise of the emperor. In all of these poems Vergil's artificiality is made more extravagant; Calpurnius' relation to Vergil's *Eclogues* is in fact equivalent to that of the Silver epic poets', whom we are about to consider, to the *Aeneid.*

XIV

SILVER EPIC

THE GREATEST LITERARY GENIUS OF THE SENECAN
clan was undoubtedly Seneca's nephew Lucan, who wrote the only
Roman epic after Vergil which was not wholly dominated by slavish
imitations of Vergil, the only epic which comes to grips with momentous political and artistic problems, and the only epic which a
nonspecialist reader can find fully rewarding. Marcus Annaeus Lucanus also was born at Cordova, in A.D. 39, and he also was brought
to Rome in infancy. He studied rhetoric, with great success, and
probably philosophy, under the Stoic Cornutus. He was recalled from
Athens, whither he had gone to continue his studies, by the Emperor
Nero, who admitted him to his inner circle and made him quaestor
and augur. At the first celebration of the Neronian games in 60 he won
a prize with a poem in praise of Nero and in 62 or 63 published the
first three books of his epic on the civil war. His relations with Nero
suddenly deteriorated, and he was barred from further publication.
He then joined the Pisonian conspiracy and was compelled to take
his life in A.D. 65.

Lucan was a prolific writer, but except for the *Civil War* (usually,
but wrongly, called *Pharsalia*) his works have perished. The *Civil
War,* in ten books, was in any case his *opus magnum.* The poem begins with the causes of war between Caesar and Pompey and carries
the story beyond the latter's death. The last book is not complete. The
distribution is as follows: 1, Invocation, characterization of Caesar and
Pompey, catalogues, panic at Rome, portents; 2, character of Cato,
Caesar's capture of Corfinium, Pompey's departure from Brundisium;
3, Caesar at Rome and Marseilles; 4, the Spanish campaign, capture of
Antony's army at Illyricum, the defeat and suicide of Curio in Africa;
5, Appius Claudius' mission to Delphi, meeting of Caesarians, the
crossing of the Adriatic, Pompey's farewell to Cornelia; 6, Dyrrha-
chium, necromancy in Thessaly; 7, the battle of Pharsalus; 8, Pompey's flight, assassination, and burial; 9, Cato's march through the
desert, the delivery of Pompey's head to Caesar; 10, Caesar at Alexandria. The poem does not attempt to present a systematic account

of the war; certain episodes which were intrinsically important or which offered scope for expatiation on a favorite topic or in a favorite manner are selected for treatment. There are certain flagrant departures from historical fact; on the other hand there are extraordinary insights into motive and significations, so that the *Civil War* becomes an illuminating commentary on a very momentous historical conjunction. But it is as a poet, not a historian, that Lucan makes his claim.

As a poet his vices are shrieking and easy to find. To all the faults that can be charged to the tragedies of Seneca he adds those which characterize his fellow writers of Silver epic, Valerius Flaccus and Papinius Statius and Silius Italicus. Like them he apostrophizes, he has numerous animal similes, his battles are described by single encounters, he has the usual episodes, expressions, and details reminiscent of Vergil. But there is a difference. In a first reading Lucan's absurd rhetoric, his ludicrous exaggeration, his ill-timed philosophizing, his ponderous misinformation, his tendency to digress, his distorted moral values are apt to distract attention from his merits. Yet even in his worst aberrations we may perceive that we are dealing with a man of spirit, with strong convictions, albeit ill-defined and possibly misguided, on morals and philosophy and art. Here is a man who has something to say and knows how he wants to say it, who is not effacing his own individuality in a purely traditional treatment of a purely traditional theme. For his subject Lucan chose a great struggle which was of real moment to all the civilized world and which has determined the course of history until our own day. Nor was the struggle so remote in time as to have only academic interest. One way of life was opposed to another, and the passions involved were still ardent enough to make partisanship dangerous. Lucan is partisan and thereby he demonstrates his vital quality. The inconsistency of his enthusiasms only proves their realness. He was barely past the age of an American undergraduate when he wrote his poem, and he has all the ardor of a new convert to a philosophic system that was really a religion, and all the eagerness and liberal politics of a newly enlightened communicant of the Social Problems Club.

The abundance of Lucan's enthusiasm is illustrated by the disagreement of critics as to who the hero of his poem is. Some have maintained that the senate is the hero; this is correct, for it is republican government that Lucan advocates. But an epic must have a personal hero. Pompey is the titular hero of the poem, for he represents the old, constitutional government. Pompey is also, so to speak, the emotional hero of the poem. His reflections before the Battle of Pharsalus, his conduct in defeat, and especially his relations with his wife Cornelia are told with sympathy and tenderness. But the story is after all one of action and battle; and Lucan's manifest admiration of Caesar's force and decision and resourcefulness makes Caesar the hero in the epic sense. On the other hand, the philosophic basis for all Lucan's liberalism was the Stoic teaching. The perfect embodiment of the Stoic ideal was Cato, and in the poem Cato alone is never discouraged, never compromising, never selfish. Certainly Cato is the moral hero of the poem. One of the most magnificent of Lucan's many excellent speeches, and one characteristic of the temper of the poem is Cato's reply to the renegade Labienus who had advised him to consult the oracle of Hammon in connection with the march through the African desert (9.563–82):

> Within his heart the silent voice divine
> Prompted an answer worthy of the shrine:
> What should I ask? "Whether I choose to fall
> Free to the end, or live a tyrant's thrall?"
> Or, "Is life nothing, be it brief or long?"
> "Can any violence work a good man wrong?"
> "Is Fortune's threat on Virtue vainly spent?"
> Or, "Does Success add nothing to the good intent?"
> All this we *know;* Ammon can do no more
> Than testify the truth we knew before.
> God is about us, and, do what we will,
> We do God's bidding, though his voice be still.
> He needs no revelation, having shown
> Once, at our birthtime, all that may be known.
> Nor has he plunged the truth in barren sand
> For a few travellers in a desert land.
> Wherever there is earth and sea and air,
> Wherever Heaven and Virtue—God is there.
> Shall we search further? Vainly shall we rove,
> When every feeling, every sight, is Jove.
> Doubters may fear, and seek prophetic aid;
> *I,* being sure of death, am unafraid.

Death waits alike the coward and the bold.
—Thus hath God said, 'tis all we need be told.

—E. E. Sikes

Here are flamboyant and untimely rhetoric, strained antitheses, irrelevant Stoic doctrine, but here are also conviction and a masterful hero who has achieved epic adequacy, not over weapons and roast beef and hostile spearmen, but over tyranny and superstition that trammel life and crush it.

The chief merit of Lucan, as compared with his fellow practitioners of Roman epic, is that he rejected the prescription of learned allusions and divine interpositions and epigrams colored by mythology. Compared to other post-Vergilian writers of epic, he wrote almost as if he had never read Vergil. His men are not puppets; he has a truly epic emphasis on the prowess of human individuals. He does not abound in allusions nor does he parade hackneyed erudition. He has learning, indeed too much learning and most of it wrong, but it is a new type of learning. He is interested in geography, though most of his geography is wildly erratic; he talks at length of astronomy, though most of his astronomy is unintelligible, and he observes no times or seasons for intruding his astronomical discourses; he is interested in snakes and lists them in one of his deplorable catalogues. But his lengthy account of the effects of their bites in the Libyan desert is infinitely more vigorous and poetical than his source Nicander. Absurdities are more absurd in a sober treatise than in an intense and vivid situation. Cato's soldiers who disappeared entirely or swelled up indefinitely as the result of snake bites do not *compel* laughter. Indeed, unless one fortifies himself with the critic's air of cynical detachment it is perfectly possible to be carried away by the episode. Despite the aberrations such a passage as Cato's march through the desert shows a genuine enthusiasm for a thoroughly heroic exploit of a perfectly adequate hero, and it speaks for Lucan's poetic imagination and sincerity that he should have seized upon the exploit and celebrated it. What if we have incidental disquisitions on the origin of serpents, their classification, and the effects of their bites? The poet makes us feel that to him the learning is fresh and compelling; it still involves the sense of wonder, which is of the essence of poetry, and is not just another exhibition of stale knowledge.

But the snakes are not the worst. Lucan seems to have a passion for dwelling on the harrowing, the revolting, the ghoulish. His witch episode in Book 6 (507–830) is a study in morbid ghoulishness, he revels in repulsive details of putrefaction of human bodies, he exercises a diabolic ingenuity in inventing horrible kinds of wounds. The lurid carnage in the sea battle off Massilia in Book 3 (538–762) is an example. The ships were prevented from coming close by the crowded corpses in the water; the wounded that fell into the sea drank their own blood mixed with brine; Catus is pierced in back and breast at the same moment, and the blood stays because it is in doubt which way to gush out, until its torrent expels both weapons simultaneously; there are gruesome details of detached members and entrails. There is the same sort of thing in Book 6 (194–95), where in the fighting about Dyrrachium Scaeva has made himself so conspicuous in the forefront that nothing protects his vitals except the spears that stick in his bones. That is rather strong, and the critics profess amusement, but it is very possible that such amusement arises from a sophisticated determination not to be horrified.

Similar consideration must govern our attitude toward another of Lucan's traits which is apt to loom as an even greater defect than his gruesomeness, his tendency toward rhetorical expression and rhetorical display. Perhaps the most clamorous instance is Volteius' speech to his men on board a raft which had been trapped by the Pompeians (4.476–520). This speech is impossible in the situation, it is artificial in its strained antitheses and epigrams, it strikes a moral falsetto, it has all the faults of the rhetorical schools. But it has the highest merit as rhetoric, and in addition ardor and glamor and lifting power. Deftness in the use of words is a legitimate attribute of any poet; in a Latin poet such deftness is almost bound to take the form of epigrams. The remarkable thing about Lucan's rhetoric is that he has been able to assimilate so much of it to the fiery torrent of his narrative and to transmute it into poetry. As Professor Mackail has written, "Pure rhetoric has perhaps never come quite so near being poetry."

Explaining Lucan's faults does not remove them, any more than insisting on his youth makes his poem great. But Lucan has written with conviction a poem of great sweep and national interest, dealing with a momentous struggle directed by heroic figures that do not transcend human stature, and informed by ideals that are more vital than literary commonplaces. Like as he is to Silius and Statius and

Valerius in a hundred superficial details, he alone gives his readers the authentic experience of epic poetry, and it is a pity to allow his work to molder with theirs.

If to preserve the purity of epic the poet must insulate himself on Parnassus and eschew involvement in questions upon which men can differ and wax ardent, Lucan's successors in epic are the purer poets. Their themes were too remote to impose a tyranny of subject, and they themselves followed the traditions of their craft scrupulously and maintained the personal detachment which epic demanded. Their aim was not to teach or edify or exalt but to produce beautiful creations according to the conventions of a strict form. This some, like Silius Italicus, did badly; others, like Valerius Flaccus, did very well indeed. Quintilian, writing near A.D. 92, refers (10.1.90) to the death of Valerius Flaccus as recent, and that is all we know of the man except what may be gathered from his poem, which is that he dedicated it to Vespasian, knew of the eruption of Vesuvius in A.D. 79, and was a *decemvir,* which implies wealth and social position. He died probably while working on his epic on the Argonautic expedition (we know of no other work of his), for the book is incomplete. Valerius Flaccus' *Argonautica* is an independent treatment of the theme of Apollonius of Rhodes' epic on the same subject; a translation of Apollonius had been made by Varro of Atax. Naturally the chief persons and episodes of Apollonius recur in Valerius, but the characterizations, the distribution, and, most important, the tone of the whole, are quite different.

Books 1 through 5 carry the story from Pelias' proposal to Jason of the quest of the Golden Fleece, to the arrival of the Argonauts at Colchis and the meeting of Jason and Medea. Among the familiar incidents are the Argonauts' stay at the manless island of Lemnos, the loss of Hylas and consequently of Hercules; the boxing match of Pollux and King Amycus; the rescue of Phineus from the Harpies by Zetes and Calais; the passage of the Argo through the Symplegades. At Colchis King Aeetes promises Jason the Fleece in return for his help against Aeetes' brother Perses, whom he had banished and who is about to attack the city. In Books 6 through 8 Perses is defeated; Medea, under the influence of Juno, falls in love with Jason and helps him by her magic to master the fiery bulls and sow the dragon's teeth. Together they carry off the Fleece and flee with it on the Argo, and

Jason and Medea are married. Medea's brother Absyrtus pursues them; as the Argonauts plan to surrender Medea in order to keep the Fleece, the poem breaks off.

The inevitable comparison with Apollonius is all to the credit of the Roman. Though Valerius' unfinished poem is a fifth longer than his model (5,593 lines to 4,835), there is much less learned padding in it. Valerius expands, contracts, improves the order. His figures, though sometimes far fetched, are apt and incisive and really illustrate the text. He is more attentive to dramatic verisimilitude, careful of motivations, and particularly good in lifelike vignettes of groups emotionally moved—the uneasy fears of the Argonauts in the night before their sailing, or in the gloomy night after the loss of Hylas and Hercules, or as they watch their steersman's funeral pyre. But it is in his masterly description of the rise and growth of Medea's love for Jason that Valerius most strikingly surpasses his model, and Vergil who used that model for his Dido episode, and perhaps every other ancient poet. Like Vergil (and because Vergil had done so) Valerius feels constrained to introduce divine machinery to explain the phenomenon. Instead of Apollonius' arrows of Cupid and Vergil's elaborate substitution of Cupid for Ascanius, Valerius has Medea absorb the poison by handling the trinkets of Venus worn by Juno in her disguise as Medea's sister Chalciope. As Medea watches the fighting her mind and heart are more and more engaged by the spectacle of Jason's bravery. She does not notice that her companion has left, and is wholly possessed by her hero's fortunes (6.683–85):

> Oft as the stalwart chiefs in serried ranks
> Beset the hero and the storm of darts
> Burst on him only, e'en so oft herself,
> By stone and javelin there is buffeted.
>
> —*W. C. Summers*

The trysting scene is particularly fine (7.400–409, 431–35, 472–77):

> Even as on flock and shepherd panic burst
> At dead of night, or in the deeps of hell
> Darkling and voiceless meet the shadow ghosts:
> So in the mingled gloom of grove and night
> They twain bewildered toward each other drew,
> Like silent pines or stirless cypresses
> That boisterous Auster hath not ruffled yet.

Then, as they rooted stood, with silent eyes,
Night speeding on, fain would Medea now
Have Jason lift his face, and speak her first.

. . . .

Thus he. She, trembling, finds the suppliant done
And her own answer due, nor sees, distraught,
How to begin her tale, how order it
And how far take it, fain would have all told
In the first word—but shame and fear forbid
E'en that first utterance.

. . . . .

Her speaking done,
Now more and more she found her fancy roam
The deep seas o'er, saw now the Greeks set sail
Without herself. 'Twas then love's fiercest pang
Smote her: she seized his hand, and spake him low:
"Remember me: I shall remember thee,
Of that be sure!"

—*W. C. Summers*

The *Argonautica* is a well-organized and well-told story, with its ornaments, precious as they sometimes are, subordinated to serve its effectiveness; it is a poem, and not, like Apollonius' *Argonautica,* a skeleton on which to hang erudition and theories of composition. But aside from his Vergilian imitations Valerius manifests the other traits of the Silver Age. His striving for conciseness and point occasionally results in strange ellipses and a capricious word order, and the reader is always aware of artifice. But Silver epic is the last place to look for naturalism.

Silius Italicus' choice of the most critical period in the history of the republic as the subject for epic treatment might suggest that he favored themes of more immediate concern to his readers, but instead of making the Second Punic War a present reality, his poem relegates it, in effect, to the realm of mythology; the resources of epic treatment are not made to illuminate Roman history, but, on the contrary, Roman history is made to serve the ends of literary epic. Silius Italicus is the type of man of affairs who is a connoisseur of the arts, fancies himself a frustrated artist, and devotes the leisure of his retirement to literary pursuits. Our main source of his life is a letter of Pliny (3.7), excerpts from which will suffice for biographical details:

I am just now informed that Silius Italicus has starved himself to death, at his villa near Naples. Having been afflicted with an imposthume, which was deemed incurable, he grew weary of life under such uneasy circumstances, and therefore put an end to it with the most determined courage. He had been extremely fortunate through the whole course of his days, excepting only the loss of his younger son. .   He lived among the nobility of Rome without power, and consequently without envy. He was highly respected and much sought after, and though he was bedridden, his chamber was always thronged with visitors, who came not merely out of regard to his rank. He spent his time in philosophical discussion, when not engaged in writing verses; these he sometimes recited, in order to try the sentiments of the public, but he discovered in them more industry than genius. Lately, owing to declining years, he entirely quitted Rome, and lived altogether in Campania, from whence even the accession of the new Emperor [Trajan, A.D. 98] did not draw him.   . He carried his taste for objects of virtù so far as to incur reprehension for greedy buying. He had several villas in the same district, and the last purchase was always the chief favourite, to the neglect of the rest. They were all furnished with large collections of books, statues and portraits, which he more than enjoyed, he even adored; above all the portrait of Virgil, whose birthday he celebrated with more solemnity than his own, especially at Naples, where he used to approach his tomb with as much reverence as if it had been a temple. In this tranquillity he lived to the seventy-sixth year of his age, with a delicate, rather than a sickly, constitution.   . . He was the last person upon whom Nero conferred the consular office.

                    —*W. Melmoth and W. M. L. Hutchinson*

Silius Italicus' *Punica* tells the story of the Second Punic War in orderly sequence from Hannibal's oath to the battle of Zama. Its seventeen books and 12,200 verses make it the longest poem in Latin, and there is nearly universal agreement that it is the worst. His main source is obviously the third decade of Livy, but the absorbing and exciting account of the prose historian is made tedious and even ludicrous by the poet. The tediousness is due to endless tautology and elaboration—Trasimene has a whole book and Cannae has two—and the ludicrousness to the incongruity of applying to familiar historical characters and events every device of the heroic saga, including the physical intervention of gods. We are not only given the mandatory

descent to Hades, a book of games, catalogues, and innumerable gruesome battle pieces, but the gods join the battle at Cannae and Minerva
saves Hannibal in a cloud. There is hardly an episode or a simile in the
entire *Aeneid* which Silius does not borrow—and spoil. Scipio, like
Aeneas, represents Rome; Hannibal, like Turnus, represents the
enemy. Hannibal, this time, has the marvelous shield, but Scipio
descends to Hades to learn the future. Asbyte, heroine of Saguntum,
is another Camilla; Euryalus' speech to Nisus is reproduced in Im-
ilce's parting speech to her husband Hannibal. With equal absurdity
the battles are made up, according to the epic rule, of single combats
described at wearisome length, with invocations, apostrophes, lin-
eages, and colloquies between the antagonists featuring names and
places. The details of the exchange of blows and their effect upon the
human anatomy are recorded in ghoulish amplitude. But in short
narrative passages and in straightforward description Silius can be
effective. His similes are too numerous, but they are clear and vivid.
Here is a pleasing specimen of what the rhetoricians called *ecphrasis,*
or description of a work of art (13.326–47):

It was Pan whom Jupiter had sent, in his desire to save the city founded
by the Trojan—Pan, who seems ever to stand on tiptoe, and whose horny
hoof leaves scarce any print upon the ground. His right hand plays with a
lash of Tegean goat-skin and deals sportive blows among the holiday
crowds at the cross-ways. Pine-needles wreathe his locks and shade his
temples, and a pair of little horns sprout from his ruddy brow. He has
pointed ears, and a rough beard hangs down from his chin. He carries a
shepherd's crook, and the soft skin of a roe-deer gives a welcome covering
to his left side. There is no cliff so steep and dangerous, but he can keep his
balance on it like a winged thing, and move his horny hoofs down the un-
trodden precipice. Sometimes he turns round and laughs at the antics of the
shaggy tail that grows behind him; or he puts up a hand to keep the sun
from scorching his brow and surveys the pasture-lands with shaded eyes.
Now, when he had duly done the bidding of Jupiter, calming the angry
passions of the soldiers and softening their hearts, he went swiftly back to
the glades of Arcadia and to Maenalus, the mountain that he loves; on that
sacred height he makes sweet music far and wide with his melodious pipe,
and all the flocks from far away follow it.

                                                    --*J. D. Duff*

Animal similes are numerous, as in all the Silver epics. The best animal story is that of a captured horse throwing his Carthaginian rider

when he sees his Roman master lying wounded, and kneeling to help the Roman, as he had been trained to do (10.454 ff.). Other good things have been noted: Hannibal flying to the assistance of his wounded brother Mago (5.344 ff.); Hannibal sleepless and anxious when he is caught in Fabius' trap (7.282 ff.); Scipio visiting Syphax' palace before dawn and finding him playing with cub lions (16.229 ff.). Though there are numerous speeches and much nonessential display of learning—the allusive epithets are sometimes hard to identify— there are only two digressions from the main story. One in the eighth book deals with Dido's sister Anna, who has become an Italian nymph; the other, occupying most of the sixth book, is the story of Regulus. This section is thought to derive from Ennius, who is mentioned as a warrior at 12.393–414. But with all that can be said for Silius' individual merits and with all allowances made for the enormous differences in literary conventions and tastes between the Flavian age and our own, Silius' poem remains a failure; he commits the unforgivable sin of making an episode of high emprise and gallantry dull, and he robs heroes of authentic stature of their lineaments by stuffing them and subjecting them to incredible gods.

The classicizing program of the Silver writers of epic, their high regard for their own work, their emulation (but not rivalry!) of Vergil are expressed in Statius' *envoi* to his *Thebais* (12.810–19):

Wilt thou endure in the time to come, O my *Thebais,* for twelve years object of my wakeful toil, wilt thou survive thy master and be read? Of a truth already present Fame hath paved thee a friendly road, and begun to hold thee up, young as thou art, to future ages. Already great-hearted Caesar deigns to know thee, and the youth of Italy eagerly learns and recounts thy verse. O live, I pray! nor rival the divine *Aeneid,* but follow afar and ever venerate its footsteps. Soon, if any envy as yet o'erclouds thee, it shall pass away, and after I am gone, thy well-won honours shall be duly paid.

—J. H. Mozley

Statius is as steeped in Vergil as are Valerius Flaccus and Silius Italicus. For his subjects he reverts to Greek legend, like Valerius; in the *Thebais* his theme is the struggle between Oedipus' sons Eteocles and Polynices, which occupies so large a proportion of Greek tragedy, and in the unfinished *Achilleid* the blazing hero of Greek saga. Except for the fact that he did undertake epics on these themes and executed them as he did, there is nothing to associate his poems with Flavian Rome; like the *Argonautica* or Quintus of Smyrna's Greek *Posthomerica,* they might have been written by any poet, and in any century. In the *Silvae* the subject matter if not the form points to a definite time and place.

Publius Papinius Statius was born about A.D. 40 or 45 in Naples, where his father had settled as schoolmaster and consultant on religious lore. In the long eulogy of his father (*Silvae* 5.3) he summarizes his father's calling as follows (172–77):

So from every side came the folk to Avernus' rocks and the dark grotto of the Sibyl, to ask their questions, while she sang of the wrath of heaven and the doings of the Fates, no vain prophet even though she foiled Apollo. Soon dost thou educate the Roman youth and the chieftains that shall be, and firmly leadest them in the footsteps of their sires.

—*J. H. Mozley*

Details of Statius' own life can be extracted from the *Silvae.* He settled in Rome, recited his works to fashionable audiences, and was admitted to the court of Domitian, who showed him marked favor. He won a prize in poetry at Domitian's festival near Alba, but, to his chagrin, was unsuccessful at the important quinquennial Capitoline contest at Rome. He married Claudia, who had a daughter; in *Silvae* 3.5 he praises her devotion to himself and her loyalty to the ashes of her dead husband. Statius had no children of his own but adopted a slave child of his household, whose early death he mourns in his last, unfinished, poem (5.5):

No chattering favourite was it, bought from a Pharian vessel, no infant skilled in the repartee of his native Nile, with over-ready tongue and impudent wit, that won my heart; mine was he, mine indeed. When he lay on the ground, a new-born babe, I saw him, and with a natal ode I welcomed his anointing, and with a tremulous wailing he claimed his new heritage of air, I set him among living souls. . . . I taught thee sounds and words, and soothed thy complainings and thy hidden hurts, and as thou didst crawl on the ground, I stooped and lifted thee to my kisses, and lovingly in my bosom lulled to sleep thy drooping eyes, and bade sweet slumber take thee. My name was thy first speech, my play thy infant happiness, and my countenance was the source of all thy joy.

—*J. H. Mozley*

Towards the end of his life Statius retired to his native place, apparently for reasons of health, and there died in 96. Statius appears to have been an amiable and easygoing man with warm attachments. The only discordant note is the inordinate flattery of Domitian, but that failing may more properly be debited to Domitian than to Statius.

Statius' *opus magnum* is his *Thebais,* whose twelve books occupied him, as we have seen, for twelve years. The contents are as follows. Book 1: Invocation to Domitian; Oedipus invokes the Fury against his unnatural sons Eteocles and Polynices, who decide to rule by turn annually; Polynices goes to Argos, where Adrastus finds him wrangling with Tydeus, and in compliance with an oracle betroths his daughters to Polynices and Tydeus. Book 2: Laius' ghost prompts Eteocles to break the compact; the marriages take place at Argos, and Tydeus goes to Thebes to represent Polynices; Eteocles sets an ambush for Tydeus, who kills all the ambushers save Maeon. Book 3: Maeon returns to reproach Eteocles and then stabs himself; at Argos the seer Amphiaraus is provoked by the atheist Capaneus to predict the issue, and foretells disaster; Polynices' wife Argia persuades Adrastus to help Polynices. Book 4: The invaders from Argos are catalogued, and at Thebes the omens transmitted to Tiresias by the ghost of Laius are recorded; at Nemea the invaders are halted by a drought which dries up all streams except one, to which they are guided by Hypsipyle, now a slave nurse to King Lycurgus' infant son Opheltes. Book 5: Hypsipyle tells the story of the Lemnian massacre; a snake bites her neglected charge, and the Argives protect Hypsipyle against Adrastus' resentment. Book 6: The boy's funeral and funeral games. Book 7: an attendant catalogues the Thebans to Antigone; the Argives arrive, and Jocasta with her daughters go to intercede with Polynices; two tame tigers attack Amphiaraus' chariot driver and precipitate a battle; Amphiaraus and his chariot disappear in a sudden opening of the earth. Book 8: Amphiaraus' reception in the underworld; his successor is appointed; a Theban sortie is unsuccessful, but Tydeus is mortally wounded, and dies gnawing his enemy's skull. Book 9: Exploits of Hippomedon, who is lured from his defense of Tydeus' body by a disguised Fury; Atalanta fears for Parthenopaeus, who is killed. Book 10: Thebans guarding the defeated Argives are themselves attacked; upon an oracle of Tiresias, Creon's son Menoeceus immolates himself by leaping from the wall; Capaneus, who has almost scaled the wall, is struck down by a thunderbolt. Book 11: Preparations for a duel between the brothers; both are killed, and Creon as king forbids the burial of the invaders' bodies: Oedipus is exiled. Book 12: Funeral rites for the Thebans; self-devotion of Antigone and Argia; the Argive women petition Theseus in Athens to recover the Argive bodies, and Theseus attacks and kills Creon.

Of the *Achilleid* only one book and the beginning of a second, totalling 1,127 lines, were written. It too begins with an invocation to Domitian. Thetis is alarmed by a vision of Paris abducting Helen, and goes to visit Achilles in the cave of his tutor, Chiron. She carries young Achilles to Scyros, disguises him as a girl, and entrusts him to King Lycomedes, to the delight of the court ladies. When Greece prepares for the Trojan war Calchas reveals Achilles' whereabouts, and Ulysses and Diomedes are despatched to fetch him. In the meantime Achilles and Princess Deidamia have fallen in love. Achilles reveals himself by picking weapons from among Ulysses' gauds. Achilles and Deidamia are married, and Deidamia begs to be allowed to accompany Achilles to Troy. In the fragment of the second book Achilles entertains his escorts by an account of Chiron's educational methods.

As will be plain from the brief summary of the *Thebais,* a major fault in Statius is his want of structure. Where Lucan follows the civil war, Silius the Punic war, Valerius the fortunes of Jason, in a straight line, Statius zigzags from Thebes to Argos and from episode to episode, lingering nowhere long enough to build up stature adequate for an epic hero. The *Thebais* is almost as episodic as a *Metamorphoses,* the link being the fortunes of the Labdacids, and with such an episode as Hypsipyle's account of the Lemnian crime even that feeble link is quite snapped. But the *Thebais* has the merits of an episodic poem; each of the disparate scenes makes a lively drama of its own. One thing Statius learned from Vergil which the other Vergilians did not, and that is a vague mysticism and a tenderness that sometimes degenerates into sentimentality. He makes the horrible more horrible, but the human relationships, especially where women are involved, are warm and soft to the extreme. Examples are Argia's relationship to her husband and father, Antigone's to her brother, Atalanta's, Ismenis', and Thetis' to their sons. Here, for example, is the baby Opheltes playing by himself in the grass (4.786-93):

The child, lying in the bosom of the vernal earth and deep in herbage, now crawls forward on his face and crushes the soft grasses, now in clamorous thirst for milk cries for his beloved nurse; again he smiles, and would fain utter words that wrestle with his infant lips, and wonders at the noise of the woods, or plucks at aught he meets, or with open mouth drinks in the day, and strays in the forest all ignorant of its dangers, in carelessness profound.

—*J. H. Mozley*

In matters of theology too Statius has a reflection of Vergil's thoughtfulness, though Statius is an even fuzzier theologian. Jupiter and Nature are both supreme, but quite apart from fate or destiny, and (at 1.696 ff.) Apollo is identified with Mithras, Osiris, and other deities. Apparently different deities are conceived of as manifestations of one ultimate power; beliefs of this nature were characteristic of Roman Stoics.

In details Statius' epics differ from the others only in degree. He is fondest of descriptions and does them well except for the usual tendency to hyperbole: a mountain is so high that the stars rest upon it (2.32 ff.); a serpent covers several acres (5.50); a centaur dams a river with his bulk (4.144). He is as fond of epigram and antitheses as the others, and in the short and telling phrase probably their superior. His versification too is more varied and more skillful, but he will sacrifice syntactical clarity to create a desired impression. Altogether Statius' merits are in miniature rather than in total effect; episodes are better than the fabric of which they are part, and flashing phrases better than their context.

We should expect then that Statius' *Silvae* would be better than his epics, and so they have generally been regarded. The *Silvae* contain thirty-two poems in five books, of which the first appeared about A.D. 91, shortly after the publication of the *Thebais*, the fourth about 95, and the fifth posthumously. *Silva*, "forest," denotes raw material, and in Latin writers a hasty draft for later polishing and elaboration. In the prose preface to Book 1 Statius speaks of hesitation about collecting and publishing "these pieces of mine, which were produced in the heat of the moment and by a kind of joyful glow of improvisation." Despite the "joyful glow" the poems appear artificial and exaggerated and much too long. Most are in forms recognized by the rhetorical schools —*epithalamion, propempticon, genethliacon, epicedion, eucharisticon, ecphrasis, soteria*—marriage song, farewell, birthday poem, eulogy, thanksgiving or compliments, descriptive piece, felicitation on recovery from illness. All are in hexameter except one each in Sapphics and Alcaics (4.7, 4.5) and four in hendecasyllables (1.6, 2.7, 4.3, 4.9). Several flatter the emperor Domitian: 1.1, an *ecphrasis* on Domitian's equestrian statue, which "will stand while earth and sky abide"; 4.1, a panegyric on his seventeenth consulship; 4.2, a thanksgiving to the emperor for a dinner invitation; 1.6, an appreciation of the emperor's entertainment at the Saturnalia; 4.3, a celebration of the paving of the Domitian Road; 2.5, on a tame lion presented to the emperor; 3.4, on the dedication of the tresses of the emperor's favorite, Flavius Earinus. There is an epithalamium for the poet's friend Stella and his bride Violentilla, containing a long account of how Venus and a Cupid engineered the match. There are celebrations of buildings: 1.3, on the villa of Manlius Vopiscus at Tibur; 1.5, on the baths of Claudius Etruscus; 2.2, on the villa of Pollius Felix at Surrentum; 3.1, on the temple of Hercules at the same place. Number 1.4 is a *soteria* for Rutilius Gallicus' convalescence. There are consolations to Melior for the loss of a favorite (2.1), a parody consolation for the death of Melior's parrot (2.4), a consolation to Flavius Ursus on the death of a favorite slave (2.6), to Claudius Etruscus for the death of a son (3.3), for the death of Priscilla (5.1), an elaborate lament for his own father (5.3), and for his adopted son (5.5). Birthdays are celebrated in 2.3, which describes a picturesque tree; in 2.7, to Polla, on the birthday of her late husband, Lucan; in 4.7, to Vibius Maximus; and in 4.8, to Julius Menecrates, felicitating him on the birth of a third child. Number 3.2 is a *propempticon* to Maecius Celer. Number 3.5 is a complimentary poem to the poet's wife Claudia, urging her to agree to the removal to Naples. There are complimentary poems to Vitorius Marcellus (4.4), and to Septimius Severus. Number 4.6 is an *ecphrasis* of a statuette of Hercules. Number 4.9 is a jibe to Plotius Grypus for having sent Statius a snide present, and 5.4 is the address to Sleep, justly the best known of Statius' poems:

> What sin was mine, sweet, silent boy-god, Sleep,
> Or what, poor sufferer, have I left undone,
> That I should lack thy guerdon, I alone?
> Quiet are the brawling streams: the shuddering deep
> Sinks, and the rounded mountains feign to sleep.

The high seas slumber pillowed on Earth's breast;
All flocks and birds and beasts are stilled in rest,
But my sad eyes their nightly vigil keep.
   O! if beneath the night some happier swain,
Entwined in loving arms, refuse thy boon
In wanton happiness,—come hither soon,
Come hither, Sleep. Let happier mortals gain
The full embrace of thy soft angel wing:
But touch me with thy wand, or hovering
Above mine eyelids sweep me with thy train.

                        —*W. H. Fyfe*

The poem must have been written early in Statius' career (the post-humous fifth book contains miscellaneous pieces from various periods) and makes one regret that Statius ever turned to epic. The hexameters run more easily, the language is simpler, the similes are less elaborate, and the mythological ornaments less cumbrous. But even the longer pieces of the *Silvae* exhibit the faults of the epic. They are overburdened with mythological allusions, often far fetched and heaped up, and even find room for elaborate divine interventions. When his temple is to be built, Hercules himself does the excavation by night (3.1.134). About half the epithalamium is concerned with Venus' part in the courtship, and in the poem on the bath (1.5) it is Venus and her fire-god husband who heat the furnaces with the torches of love. But if Statius' excesses cannot be forgiven they can be explained; he was a poet of fashionable society in an age when society demanded literature as curled as are the coiffures on the busts of Flavian ladies. Given that curling is *de rigueur,* Statius' is well done.

   Besides his extant works we know of several other compositions by Statius. Juvenal (7.82–87) tells us how eagerly Statius' readings were attended, and implies that he nevertheless had to produce libretti for mimes in order to live:

Statius has gladdened the city by promising a day, people flock to hear his pleasing voice and his loved *Thebais;* so charmed are their souls by his sweetness, with such rapture does the multitude listen to him. But when his verses have brought down the house, poor Statius will starve if he does not sell his virgin *Agave* to Paris.

                        —*G. G. Ramsay*

Paris was a popular performer of mimes, and the *Agave* was based on the Theban story of Pentheus. Statius may well have written other libretti, but hardly out of such financial stringency as Juvenal suggests. Four hexameters of an epic on Domitian's German campaign survive, and there is mention of an epistle concerning the *Thebais* addressed to Vibius Maximus.

XV

SATIRE

BUT THERE WERE ROMANS IN THE FIRST CENTURY
who found the excesses of rhetoric and mythologizing bombast tedious and inane and an artificial escape from immediate questions of burning relevance to the well-being of society. Indignation at the frivolity of such works as we have been considering in the last chapter reaches the bursting point in Juvenal's first satire (1–21):

What? Am I to be a listener only all my days? Am I never to get my word in—I that have been so often bored by the *Theseid* of the ranting Cordus? Shall this one have spouted to me his comedies, and that one his love ditties, and I be unavenged? Shall I have no revenge on one who has taken up the whole day with an interminable Telephus, or with an Orestes, which, after filling the margin at the top of the roll and the back as well, hasn't even yet come to an end? No one knows his own house so well as I know the groves of Mars, and the cave of Vulcan near the cliffs of Aeolus. What the winds are brewing; whose souls Aeacus has on the rack; from what country another worthy is carrying off that stolen golden fleece; how big are the ash trees which Monychus tosses about: these are the themes with which Fronto's plane trees and marble halls are for ever ringing until the pillars quiver and quake under the continual recitations; such is the kind of stuff you may look for from every poet, greatest or least. Well, I too have slipped my hand from under the cane; I too have counselled Sulla to retire from public life and sleep his fill; it is a foolish clemency when you jostle against poets at every corner, to spare paper that will be wasted anyhow. But if you can give me time, and will listen quietly to reason, I will tell you why I prefer to run in the same course over which the great nursling of Aurunca [Lucilius] drove his steeds.

—G. G. *Ramsay*

Juvenal then proceeds to list outrageous moral abuses which might better occupy the poet's attention, and declares his determination to deal with them: "Though nature say me nay, indignation will prompt my verse," *si natura negat, facit indignatio versum.*

Juvenal's plea amounts to an admonition to return to Roman concern for Roman morality in Roman form, and he invokes both Lucilius and Horace, who had established satire in Rome. But though Juvenal's explosive zeal sets him apart, he was in fact not Horace's first successor in the form, nor the first to scorn the new poetry and its total absorption in prettiness. In the generation before him Persius' first satire is a more inclusive and devastating indictment of the utter frivolity and un-Roman character of contemporary poetry, and a recall not only to the satire of Lucilius, which flayed social abuses, but also to the honest Romanism of Vergil. It is with Persius then, that we begin.

Aulus Persius Flaccus was born of a wealthy family in Etruria in A.D. 34 and died of a stomach ailment at the age of twenty-eight. He was orphaned at the age of six and a few years later lost his step-father. He was of a modest and retiring disposition, devoted to the women of his family, and loved by his friends. His teacher was the Stoic Cornutus, who later took charge of his literary remains. He traveled with Thrasea Paetus and was familiar with most of the Stoic "opposition" to the principate. His literary acquaintances included Seneca and Lucan, the poet Caesius Bassus, and the historian Servilius Nonianus. Of all his friends he valued most highly his teacher Cornutus, whose delight it was "to grow pale over nightly study, to tell the minds of the young, and to sow the seed of [Stoic] Cleanthes in their well-cleansed ears" (5.62-64). Here is part of his appreciation of Cornutus (5.21 ff.):

To yourself alone, Cornutus, do I speak; I now shake out my heart to you at the bidding of the Muse; it is a joy to me to show you, beloved friend, how large a portion of my soul is yours. Strike it and note carefully what part of it rings true, what is but paint and plaster of the tongue. It is for this that I would ask for a hundred voices: that I may with clear voice proclaim how deeply I have planted you in the recesses of my heart, and that my words may render up all the love that lies deep and unutterable in my inmost soul. When first as a timid youth I lost the guardianship of the purple . . . I placed myself in your hands, Cornutus; you took up my tender years in your Socratic bosom. Your rule, applied with unseen skill, straightened out the crooked ways; my soul, struggling to be mastered, was moulded by your reason, and took on its features under your plastic thumb. With you, I remember, did I pass long days, with you pluck for feasting the early hours of night. We two were one in our work; we were one in our hours of rest, and unbent together over the modest board. Of this I would not have you doubt, that there is some firm bond of concord between our lives, and that both are drawn from a single star.

—*G. G. Ramsay*

Persius' satires are what we should expect of a bookish introspective young man, not robust in health, whose contacts with the world are rich enough but derived from books and like-minded friends. His total output, except for some *juvenilia* destroyed by Cornutus, amounts to only six satires in 650 hexameters. All are sincere and all are witty, but sincerity is obscured by the distortions of his language, and the edge of his wit is dulled by private conceits (*hoc ridere meum*, 1.123). The first satire, in the form of a dialogue between Persius and a friend, is an attack on the corruption of literature and literary taste in Rome, which is a symptom and concomitant of corruption in morals. Decadent trash is applauded, heroics are attempted by poetasters incapable of describing a rustic scene, rhetoric is misapplied to what demands simplicity, there is no honest criticism (1.30–40):

> See, Rome's young bloods have dined, and o'er their wine
> Ask what the news from Poesy divine,
> And straight doth one in purple all bedight
> Snuffling and lisping some poor trash recite,
> Filtering and mincing in his foppish way
> *Phyllis, Hypsipyle*—some dolorous lay.
> Thunders applause. Is not the poet dead
> Happy that hour? No lighter on his head
> Weighs now the marble? All about his tomb
> From the blest ashes will not violets bloom?

—*W. C. Summers*

When the friend objects that such indictments are dangerous Persius appeals to the example of Lucilius' scourge and Horace's rapier. He himself will divulge his private joke: All the world's an ass—*Auriculas asini quis non habet* (121). Contemporary opinion is worthless; Persius will address himself to readers who have caught the breath of the masters of Greek Old Comedy.

The remaining satires are rather in the nature of Stoic sermons. The second is on prayer; men pray openly for worthy objects, but in secret for immoral and criminal advantages. The gods are not to be measured by our own lusts, but must be approached with clean hands and a pure heart (2.61–75):

O souls bent earthward, with no heavenly spark,
What good to take our human thoughts to prayer,
Judging God's pleasure from this sinful flesh?

.   .   .   .   .

It sins, flesh sins, yet gains by sin; but say,
Ye priests, what profits gold in holy place?
As much as maiden's dolls at Venus' shrine!
Give we the gods what from his lordly plate
Messala's blear-eyed scion could not give—
Duty to God and man in soul well blent
And stainless inmost thoughts and noble heart
In honour steeped—these let me to the shrine
Convey and humble meal will win my prayer.

—*J. W. Duff*

Moral inertia and wrong desires are arraigned in Satire 3; diagnosis and prescription are couched in terms of physical illness. Satire 4 animadverts on the unfitness of an Alcibiades, whose own ideals are immature and low, to guide others and the state; it may be that Alcibiades is put for Nero, whom the charge would better fit. Satire 5 starts with eulogy of Cornutus, part of which has been quoted above, and continues with an exposition of the Stoic paradox that all men (the Stoic sage excepted) are slaves. Men nominally free are still in bondage to avarice and superstition, from which only knowledge of the right uses of life can free them. Satire 6, from which some lines may have been removed, is a justification for spending money on reasonable objects. To a supposed heir who objects, "Then what will be left?" the poet answers (6.68–74):

"Left," do you ask? Here, boy, drench the cabbage with oil, and d—n the expense! Am I to have my holiday dinner off nettles and a smoking pig's cheek with his ear split through, in order that some day or other your young ne'er-do-weel may regale himself on a goose's liver? . . . Am I to be reduced to a thread-paper while his belly is to wag with fat like that of a priest?

—*G. G. Ramsay*

L'obscurité de Perse est célèbre, says his latest French editor, and it is a pity that it is so. His transitions are abrupt and he makes frequent digressions, he employs strained metaphors, harsh colloquialisms, enigmatic allusions. It is as if his writings were intended to be deciphered for their pleasure by a little club of Persiuses. What he has to say deserves to be heard, and might profitably be heeded, by much larger numbers.

The circumstances of the life of Juvenal (Decimus Junius Juvenalis) were very different from those of Persius. He was very poor, and seems to have known no one of importance; the only ancient who mentions him is the equally poor Martial, who speaks (12.18) of Juvenal "wandering through the clamorous Subura or treading the thresholds of the great fanned by his sweaty toga." Hence, if we disregard the late and unreliable "lives," we can know only so much of his life as we may deduce from his writings. We know that his birthplace was Aquinum (3.319), but his birth year cannot be fixed with certainty. The first of his satires has an allusion (1.49) to a trial which took place in A.D. 100, and the last complete satire (15.27) refers to an event which took place "lately (*nuper*) in the consulship of Juncus," which fell in A.D. 127. Juvenal's writing career thus covered the first thirty years of the second century. In the first satire, moreover, he speaks (1.25) of a barber who used to shave him when he was young; by A.D. 100, then, he was no longer young, and for the purposes of making an entry, we might put his birth year down as about A.D. 50. In any case he will have written most of his satires after the middle years of a life of poverty and disappointment.

The "lives," which differ in many details, and the scholia agree that Juvenal was banished for lampooning the actor Paris in 7.87–92, and at the end of the first satire Juvenal himself speaks of the danger of satirizing the living and his determination to confine himself to the dead. Some say that he was banished by Trajan to Scotland, others by Domitian to Egypt; he had certainly been to Egypt (15.45). If Number 7 was actually the cause of the banishment it must have been written long before it was published, for Domitian put Paris to death in A.D. 83. Nor could such outspoken criticism of Domitian as is found in 2 and 4 have been published before Domitian's death in 96. An inscription found at Aquinum but now lost (*Corpus inscriptionum Latinarum* 10.5382) speaks of a ——*nius Iuvenalis* as military tribune, local *duumvir*, and *flamen* of the deified Vespasian. If the reference is to the satirist and not to another member of his family the inscription would prove that Juvenal had attained a respectable position as local magistrate and officer. Perhaps the lampoon cost him these prerogatives and caused his banishment. In any case his rancor against Domitian is intense, and his whole tone is of a man made bitter by disappointment and injustice. The bitterness is mollified in the later satires, which are more philosophical in tone; because of the difference in tone, which can be explained quite easily by natural evolution, and because in some of the satires Juvenal speaks of men long dead as if they were living, some scholars have gone to the needless length of positing dual authorship. The sixteen satires were published in five groups—1–5; 6; 7–9; 10–12; and 13–16. The last satire is incomplete. None of the others is shorter than a hundred lines; 6 (a book by itself) runs to 661 lines, and 3, 10, and 14 are each over three hundred.

From the first satire, which sets forth Juvenal's program, we have cited a passage at the head of this chapter. Weary of the endless beating of the dead mythologic horse, he declares his own program (1. 85–86): *Quidquid agunt homines, votum timor ira voluptas gaudia discursus, nostri farrago libelli est,* "All the doings of mankind, their prayers, their fears, their angers and pleasures, their joys, their comings and goings, shall be the gallimaufry of my page." To the warning that his campaign might be dangerous Juvenal replies that he will attack only those who are dead.

Satire 2 starts: "I would fain flee to Sarmatia and the frozen sea when people who ape the Curii and live like Bacchanals dare talk about morals." The particular vice in high places which Juvenal here excoriates is homosexuality (126–135):

O Father of our city, whence came such wickedness among thy Latin shepherds? How did such a lust possess thy grandchildren, O Gradivus? Behold! Here you have a man of high birth and wealth being handed over in marriage to a man, and yet neither shakest thy helmet, nor smitest the earth with thy spear, nor yet protestest to thy Father? Away with thee then; begone from that broad Martial Plain which thou hast forgotten! "I have a ceremony to attend," quoth one, "at dawn to-morrow, in the Quirinal valley." "What is the occasion?" "No need to ask: a friend is taking to himself a husband; quite a small affair." Yes, and if we only live long enough, we shall see these things done openly: people will wish to see them reported among the news of the day.

—G. G. Ramsay

Roman nobles, we learn, wore clothing of almost transparent texture, and the Roman Otho used cosmetics and carried a mirror to war.

Satire 3, the model of Dr. Johnson's *London,* is, with Satire 10, Juvenal's finest. Umbricius, who has packed his belongings on a cart to move from the city, tells why it is impossible for an honest man to live in Rome, and incidentally provides a lively picture of the teeming life of the capital—its sights and sounds, dangers and annoyances, luxury and meanness, empty social observances, and especially the unfair competition of Greeks and Orientals (3.60–78):

I cannot abide, Quirites, a Rome of Greeks; and yet what fraction of our dregs comes from Greece? The Syrian Orontes has long since poured into the Tiber, bringing with it its lingo and its manners, its flutes and its slanting harp-strings; bringing too the timbrels of the breed, and the trulls who are bidden ply their trade at the Circus. . . . The hungry Greekling has brought with him any character you please; grammarian, orator, geometrician; painter, trainer, or rope-dancer; augur, doctor or astrologer:—

> "All sciences a fasting monsieur knows,
> And bid him go to Hell, to Hell he goes!"
> —*G. G. Ramsay (couplet from Johnson's* London)

The fourth satire invokes the Muse Calliope for a mock-heroic account of how a council summoned by Domitian deliberated on the proper method of cooking a huge turbot which a fisherman had presented. Satire 5 is a bitter picture of the humiliation visited upon a client when his arrogant patron at last deigns to invite him to dinner. The long sixth satire is a devastating catalogue of female depravity addressed to a man who is so mad as to contemplate marriage; suicide is a much easier way out. Chastity left earth at the end of the Golden Age. Besides gross infidelity, which is discussed in unsparing detail, there are other traps: the proud heiress, the woman too perfect, the woman who spouts Greek, the masterly woman, the litigious woman, the female athlete, the bickering woman, the music- or rather musician-lover, the gossip, the termagant, the opinionated scholar, the eternal prinker, the devotee of superstitions. Women procure abortions, murder stepchildren, make their husbands insane with potions. Doubtless Juvenal could document each of his specimens and their crimes in the life of the metropolis just as similar specimens could be culled from a file of a daily newspaper today, but either collection, in isolation, gives a distorted picture of its society.

Satire 7 starts with hopes of better times for letters and learning from the patronage of the new emperor (perhaps Hadrian) and goes on to lament the inadequate remuneration received by members of the learned profession. Singers and jockeys are the highest paid, teachers the most poorly paid of all. Poets too must eat: "How can unhappy Poverty sing songs in the Pierian cave and grasp the thyrsus when it is short of cash?" Satire 8 is directed against pride of birth and maintains the position that virtue is the only true nobility. In point of fact it is because Juvenal sets a high value on good Roman blood that he finds degeneration so reprehensible. Catiline was an aristocrat, and yet it was the new man Cicero who thwarted his machinations. Satire 9 is the lament of a repulsive creature who has lived by selling his virility and has now fallen on lean days.

Satire 10 is the peer of 3, and it too was imitated by Dr. Johnson, in his *The Vanity of Human Wishes*. Our yearning for wealth, power, glory, long life, personal beauty are all in vain; better leave our destiny to the gods (10.346–66):

> So shall men pray for naught? If you desire
> Advice, you'll trust the gods themselves to give
> What most befits us and fulfills our needs.
> The gods will grant, not joys, but what is best.
> They love man more than man loves self. Inspired
> By feelings and the power of blind desire,
> We crave for wife and offspring; but heaven alone
> Knows what the children or the wife will be.
> Yet that you may ask something, and pay vows
> At shrines with victims' inwards, offering
> Prophetic cutlets of a pigling white,
> Pray for a sound mind, in a body sound,
> Ask for a valiant heart that death defies,
> That counts life's close as Nature's final boon,
> Able to bear whate'er of travail comes,
> Stranger to wrath, free from desire, convinced
> That Hercules's woes and cruel toils
> Outrival amours, feasts, and Eastern couch.
> I show what you can give yourself. The path
> To tranquil life is Virtue's path alone.
>> Thy power, O Chance, is lost, if men be wise:
>> *We* make thee Goddess, thronèd in the skies.
>
> —*J. W. Duff*

The first part of Satire 11 scores gourmands of slender means who forget the maxim "Know thyself" and ruin themselves by their extravagance; the second part invites a friend to a simple meal simply served, where the reading of Homer and Vergil will be the only entertainment. Satire 12 expresses Juvenal's pleasure at a friend's escape from shipwreck; his thanksgiving sacrifice is not calculated, for the friend has three children, and there is no chance for a legacy hunter. This leads to a tirade against legacy hunters, who would sacrifice even a hecatomb of elephants to secure a place in a rich man's will. Satire 13 offers consolation to a man who has been defrauded by a false friend and rebukes him for taking the treachery to heart. It is foolish to expect honesty in these degenerate days. Vengeance belongs to the gods, who will exact requital; the offender's conscience will be the most merciless of torturers. Satire 14 starts with an admonition on the proper upbringing of children; precepts are useless if you set the child an example of gambling, gluttony, wantonness, and cruelty, and the child cannot be blamed when he imitates his parents' example, as he inevitably must. The only vice which the young practice unwillingly, because it has a spurious appearance of virtue, is avarice, and the remaining two-thirds of the long satire is a diatribe on the vice of avarice. What men will not do to store up "bits of silver cut up into little images and inscriptions!" And what troubles they undergo to preserve their store! Satire 15 starts with an account of rioting in Egypt which results in cannibalism. Juvenal's horror at the episode leads him to reflect on the nature of civilization. Man's distinction is his capacity to weep (15.131-42):

When Nature gave tears to man, she proclaimed that he was tender-hearted; and tenderness is the best quality in man . . . What good man believes that any human woes concern him not?

—G. G. Ramsay

But in these days there is more amity among serpents than among men; lions do not prey on lions, but man devours man. The fragmentary sixteenth satire complains of the privileges enjoyed by the military; no civilian can get justice against a soldier, and soldiers have special privileges in regard to property.

The last seven satires differ in both form and substance from the first nine. The first group present a vivid picture of life at Rome and retain the abruptness and vestiges of the dialogue and dramatization of early satire. The latter group are really epistles addressed to friends; the sentences are longer and more complicated and there is much more repetition. Their subjects are general ethical themes like Seneca's— the value of prayer, the desire for revenge, the education of children, and the like. Illustrations are drawn not from the streets of Rome but from Greek history and mythology. But even where he is following the traditions of hexameter satire Juvenal is different from his predecessors. He has none of Horace's detached urbanity, but remains at a high pitch of passion against the abuses he attacks. Lucilius too lashed the town, but he could discourse amiably on other subjects also —an agreeable journey or the peculiarities of Latin grammar. Juvenal's single note is censorious indignation. Though the letters of Pliny and the evidence of tomb inscriptions bear welcome testimony to what we should in any case assume, that Rome was not wholly devoid of decent and respectable society, we also have evidence from Martial and from Tacitus, that Juvenal's vocal indignation is not blue-nosed tub-thumping. The motives of vigilantes too eager to collect and display evidence of immorality may sometimes be questioned, and preachers are sometimes more bent on exploiting the sensationalism of their exposures than on remedying evil. Of Juvenal too some have suspected that his indignation was a pose, calculated to ensure attention. But there can be little question of Juvenal's sincerity, though his rancor may approach the morbid. Surely he regarded himself as championing a righteous cause.

To the service of that cause he brought an eloquence of denunciation unrivaled for its sustained power. No one has coined such an abundance of flashing epigrams; no one can doubt their truth, for their perfection of form gives them the air of eternal verities. His individual scenes are as perfect and as memorable as his epigrams; persons, however, are not limned in detail, for Juvenal is more concerned with types than with individuals. Like all writers of Silver verse Juvenal is better in detail than in a structural whole, but for satire the fragmented style was traditional. Juvenal's large vocabulary includes colloquialisms and foreign words as well as the clichés of epic and rhetoric; his meter is under perfect control. Juvenal has not enlarged the horizons of human knowledge and imagination, but his satires are among the most vivid productions of ancient Rome, and for posterity he remains the model for verse satire.

Juvenal declared that his subject was *quidquid agunt homines* (1.85); his friend Martial similarly disdains empty mythologizing and says (10.4.10), *Hominem pagina nostra sapit*—"Humanity is the flavor of my page." Elsewhere he admonishes himself (8.3.19): "Season your little books with pleasant wit; let life recognize in them the picture of her own manners." Martial's program, then, is mainly the program of the satirist, but in the English, not the Latin sense of the word, for what Martial wrote were not long satires in hexameter verse but short epigrams, chiefly in elegiacs. For satire in the wider sense no form could be more apt than the short poem with the sting in its tail. Martial's numerous Greek forerunners (whose epigrams are collected in the *Greek Anthology*) had sometimes employed the form for satiric effect, but when it passed into Roman hands as far back as the time of Ennius the poetic element was definitely subordinated to the satiric. We have observed that all the Roman Alexandrians employed the form; Catullus in particular used it frequently and successfully. But none among either his Greek or Roman predecessors attained Martial's mastery.

Like the Senecas and Lucan, as he tells us (1.61), Marcus Valerius Martialis was born in Spain; his birth year was about A.D. 40. He came to Rome in 64 and was befriended by Seneca and Lucan, who were, however, eliminated in the Pisonian conspiracy of the year following. At Rome his existence depended on the scant liberality of patrons; he lived on the third story of a tenement (1.117.7) until he acquired a small farm in Nomentum. His acquaintanceship was wide, and he was on friendly terms with Frontinus, Juvenal, Silius Italicus, the younger Pliny, and Quintilian; it may be significant that he never mentions Statius nor Statius him. Through the interest of his friends he was given an honorary military tribuneship and the *ius trium liberorum* ("privileges of a father of three"), but he remained poor. With the accession of Nero he realized that his type of writing would no longer be acceptable; Pliny paid for his passage back to Spain, where he settled in a house presented to him by a patroness. The following letter (3.21), in which Pliny regrets Martial's recent death, is also a characteristic appreciation:

I have just heard of the death of poor Martial, which much concerns me. He was a man of an acute and lively genius, and his writings abound in both wit and satire, combined with equal candour. When he left Rome I complimented him by a present to defray the charges of his journey, not only as a testimony of my friendship, but in return for the little poem which he had written about me. . . . You will be desirous, perhaps, to see the verses which merited this acknowledgement from me; and I believe I can, from my memory, partly satisfy your curiosity, without referring you to his works: but if you are pleased with this specimen of them, you must turn to his poems for the rest. He addresses himself to his Muse, whom he directs to seek my house upon the Esquiline, and to approach me with respect:

> "Go, wanton Muse, but go with care,
> Nor meet, ill-tim'd, my Pliny's ear.
> He, by sage Minerva taught,
> Gives the day to studious thought,
> And plans that eloquence divine,
> Which shall to future ages shine,
> And rival, wond'rous Tully! thine.
> Then, cautious, watch the vacant hour,
> When Bacchus reigns in all his power!
> When crown'd with rosy chaplets gay,
> E'en rigid Catos read my lay."

Do you not think that the poet who wrote in such terms of me, deserved some friendly marks of my bounty *then,* and that he merits my sorrow *now?* For he gave me the most he could, and it was want of power only, if his present was not more valuable. But to say truth, what higher can be conferred on man than fame, and applause, and immortality? And though it should be granted, that his poems will not be immortal, still, no doubt, he composed them upon the contrary supposition. Farewell.

—*W. Melmoth and W. M. L. Hutchinson*

Martial's first publication known to us is the *Liber spectaculorum,* which commemorates the opening of the Colosseum by Titus in A.D. 80. It contains thirty-three perfunctory pieces on the various contests, all laudatory and all salted with flattery: The lion who bit its trainer is condemned to death because "our ruler expects even beasts to be humane" (10.6). Four or five years later appeared the *Xenia* and *Apophoreta,* now Books 13 and 14, which contain, respectively, 127 mottoes for gifts sent at the Saturnalia, and 223 for gifts to be taken home from the holiday parties. The *Apophoreta* are arranged in pairs, for more and less expensive gifts. The variety of objects named, including bells, brushes, and bird cages, have an antiquarian interest.

The character and quality of the mottoes are not very different from those on our Christmas cards. The twelve books of *Epigrams* proper, which better represent Martial's talents, appeared at intervals of about a year from 86 onwards. Books 1, 2, 8, and 12 have prose prefaces of a personal or literary nature. The last tells us that Martial worked on Book 12 for three years, after he left Rome.

No past society so quickens into life on the printed page as does first-century Rome in Martial's miniatures and caricatures. His eye may have been for the playful, the ludicrous, the flippant, the indecent, but he is far from being a mere clown, and his total picture adds up to an indictment of social sham in all its manifestations. He is a more convincing witness to his age than is Juvenal or Tacitus, because he is not angry and not lurid. He is more trustworthy because he is better tempered, because as a foreigner he was not so outraged by the upsurge of aliens and the relegation of Romans, and because, not having had an official career, he did not feel the bitterness of frustrated ambition. When Martial speaks well of Domitian it may not be mere time-serving; he may have appreciated the good things in his administration, and was not himself likely to be touched by Domitian's monstrosities. The flatteries and the mendicant tone of much of his work is not as culpable as has been charged. One must eat to be a poet, and Martial's kind of poetry is hard to suppress.

Of his total of 1,561 pieces about twelve hundred are epigrams. Some are epigrams in the original meaning of the term, that is, they resemble inscriptions on tombs or works of art. Of these the most memorable is the poem on the little slave girl with whom the poet used to play (5.34):

> Thou Mother dear and thou my Father's shade,
> To you I now commit the gentle maid,
>   Erotion, my little love, my sweet;
>   Let not her shuddering spirit fear to meet
> The ghosts, but soothe her lest she be afraid.
> How should a baby heart be undismayed
> To pass the lair where Cerberus is laid?
>   The little six-year maiden gently greet.
> Dear reverend spirits, give her kindly aid
> And let her play in some Elysian glade,

Lisping my name sometimes—and I entreat
Lie softly on her, kindly earth; her feet,
Such tiny feet, on thee were lightly laid.

—J. A. Pott

A few are on spectacles, like those in the *Liber Spectaculorum*. Others are anecdotes, like that of the snob who crouched between the ordinary and reserved seats in the theater (5.14) or of the man who wished to borrow but refused to buy Martial's book (1.117):

Whene'er we meet you always say
"When may I send a servant, pray,
To fetch your book? I'll read it through
And straightway send it back to you."
Nay, trouble not your servant, friend,
To Pear-tree Court is far to send,
And one must climb an awkward stair
To reach my third-floor garret there.
No need is there so far to roam,
You'll find the book much nearer home.
You know the place where Argus died?
You often pass it—close beside
Is Caesar's forum, and a stall
By columns marked, on which they scrawl
A passer-by what books they sell.
Here seek my works. You need not stop
To tell the owner of the shop—
By name Atrectus—what you seek;
He'll find you Martial ere you speak;
His top or second pigeon-hole
Is sure to hold a handsome scroll,
Well smoothed and decked with purple dye.
It costs but half a crown to buy.
"So much," you say, "for such a thing?"
You're wise, 'tis not worth borrowing.

—J. A. Pott

Martial's epigrams may be broadly divided into those that are about or are addressed to a friend or patron (which may still have something of satire), and those that describe more or less satirically some character or incident or institution (which may of course involve a name).

Martial is at his best in dealing with perennially recognizable types —
the toady (7.76), the man to whom everything is a secret (1.89), the old
servant who acts the Cato (11.39), barbers (11.84, 7.83), doctors (1.47,
5.9, 9.94, 9.96), the antique collector (8.6), the reciter (3.45). Here is
the dilettante (2.7):

> You're a moderate reciter, you've a pretty knack of pleading,
> You're a pretty story-writer, and your verse is pretty reading,
> You've a pretty style in dancing, and your voice is rather pretty,
> If your plays are not entrancing they are moderately witty,
> Then your satire's rather comic, and of letters you've a smattering,
> While on questions astronomic you've a pretty trick of chattering,
> Your music's commonplace with no unusual ability,
> At games you show some grace with no remarkable agility.
> Tho' you're moderate at all, you've mastered not a thing of them;
> So a sciolist I call you—and the very prince and king of them.
>
> —*J. A. Pott*

And here is the finicky shopper (9.59):

> About the Saepta shops Mamurra strolled
> Where opulence may squander wealth untold,
> And first he viewed fair slaves with gloating eyes,
> Not those an open shop will advertise,
> No, but the kind reserved for private view
> Unseen by common folk like me and you;
> He then stripped table-tops of antique make
> And ivories kept aloft for safety's sake.
> That couch of tortoise-shell inlay was small
> And would not fit his citron board at all;
> He tried Corinthian bronzes by their scent,
> Thought Polycleitus' work indifferent,
> And said the crystal vase was flawed—the two
> Of agate he would mark, for they might do;
> Some bowls and ancient cups he took and weighed
> As perfect gems as Mentor ever made,
> Appraised the emeralds in enamel clear
> And pearl-drops made to deck some snow-white ear,
> Hunted for sardonyx through half the town
> And tried to beat the price of jaspers down.
> Then tired at nightfall, having ransacked Rome,
> He bought two farthing crocks and took them home.
>
> —*J. A. Pott*

Nor have the circumstances of urban life changed: there are near neighbors whom one never sees (1.86); teeming open-air markets (7.61); a house for sale tricked with fine furniture not included in the bargain (12.66); the country estate—with vegetables fresh from the city (3.47); drafty attic guest rooms (8.14). There are men who try to conceal their baldness (6.57, 10.83), and women who bleach or buy their tresses (6.12, 7.13). There is the lady who chooses her companions to set off her own beauty (8.79):

> Your friends, Fabulla, either are
> Old crones or beldames uglier far:
> These frumps you trot around with you
> To parties, plays, and galleries too:
> And so, my dear, such hags among
> You look quite pretty and quite young!
>
> —*J. W. Duff*

Perhaps a tenth of all the epigrams deal with obscenities too gamy for general publication not only today but in Nerva's age; most adults today can recall limericks not noticeably purer or funnier. Martial himself says, in imitation of Catullus 16, *Lasciva est nobis pagina, vita proba* (1.4.8), "My page is wanton, but my life is clean."

All of Martial's poems conform to Coleridge's famous definition—

> What is an epigram? A dwarfish whole,
> Its body brevity, and wit its soul.

Wit in Martial has many faces, but the basic ingredient is sudden confrontation with the unexpected. For example (1.10):

> Maronilla, Gemellus doth adore thee,
> With instant prayers and vows doth oft implore thee,
> And many a lover's gift he lays before thee;
> Since neither beauty, grace, nor charm attend thee
> What makes him seek thee so, and thus commend thee?
> *A churchyard cough that promises to end thee.*
>
> —*J. A. Pott*

Or (6.51):

> I'm annoyed, my Lupercus: for ages your friend
>   Uninvited to dinner you've kept.
> I shall take my revenge. You may beg, coax, and send—
>   'Well? And what will you do?' Why, accept.
>
> —*W. C. Summers*

A subtler form of surprise is paradox: his friends wish a man who is as stingy as he is rich to come into a legacy—so that he'll starve to death (1.99); an invitation to dine with a great crowd is turned down —on the grounds that the poet does not like to dine alone. Frequently the point is a fantastic exaggeration. Sometimes the fun is in precise definition (3.9):

> He publishes lampoons on me, 'tis said;
> How can he publish who is never read?
>
> —*J. A. Pott*

But Martial is not only a wit, who can give smart expression to urban foibles: he is also a poet, who can write affectionately and perceptively of the country, of the simple life, of his native Spain. For themes like these he is apt to turn to a meter other than the elegiac; 77 of his poems are in scazons, 238 in hendecasyllables, and there are a few in hexameters and iambics. In scazons we have the beautiful description of Faustinus' farm near Baiae (3.58), a rhapsody on a seaside villa at Formiae (3.30), an appreciation of Julius Martialis' country house (4.64), a glorification of Spain (4.55), and a second poem on little Erotion (5.37), beside whom "squirrels seemed clumsy and a phoenix stale." For these poems the model was Catullus' Sirmio; Catullus' hendecasyllables, like the Sparrow piece, were the model for poems which deal with personal emotions. Three charming poems of this type are addressed to his friend and namesake Martialis —5.20, an invitation to a country holiday; 10.47, on the simple requirements for a happy life; and the final wistful poem of farewell, written from Spain (12.34):

> We have had together now
> Four and thirty years, I trow,
> Wherein mixed are grief and glee—
> But joys in the majority.
> If coloured stones the reckoning show,
> White for mirth and black for woe,
> White will be the longer row.
> Would you some vexation flee,
> Keep from bitter heart-pangs free?
> Tie with none too close maintain:
> You'll have less gladness—and less pain.
>
> —*W. C. Summers*

And in assessing Martial's life and works too we must agree that the whites have far the longer row. He is sensitive and witty and a good poet; he is one of the most amiable phenomena in Latin literature.

On the surface Petronius' *Satyrica* (*Satyricon,* the more familiar form, is the Greek genitive plural) seems simply a picaresque novel, and in form further removed from satire than Martial. In fact the *Satyrica* is our fullest example of the alternative form of Menippean satire, blending prose and verse, which was introduced by Varro and of which another extant example is the *Apocolocyntosis* of Seneca. Varro's Menippean satires had been individual and apparently rather short pieces; the *Apocolocyntosis* dealt with a single theme at some length. The *Satyrica* was a very long work (what we have are excerpts from Books 15 and 16) with many separate episodes linked together as being the adventures of a single group of characters and by their all being the result of the wrath of Priapus. The Petronius Arbiter who is named as author must surely be Nero's *arbiter elegantiae,* Caius Petronius, of whom Tacitus (*Annals* 16.18–19) gives such a fascinating picture:

With regard to Caius Petronius, I ought to dwell a little on his antecedents. His days he passed in sleep, his nights in the business and pleasures of life. Indolence had raised him to fame, as energy raises others, and he was reckoned not a debauchee and spendthrift, like most of those who squander their substance, but a man of refined luxury. And indeed his talk and his doings, the freer they were and the more show of carelessness they exhibited, were the better liked, for their look of natural simplicity. Yet as proconsul of Bithynia and soon afterwards as consul, he showed himself a man of vigour and equal to business. Then falling back into vice or affecting vice, he was chosen by Nero to be one of his few intimate associates, as a critic in matters of taste (*arbiter elegantiae*), while the emperor thought nothing charming or elegant in luxury unless Petronius had expressed to him his approval of it. Hence jealousy on the part of Tigellinus, who looked on him as a rival and even his superior in the science of pleasure. And so he worked on the prince's cruelty, which dominated every other passion, charging Petronius with having been the friend of Scaevinus, bribing a slave to become informer, robbing him of the means of defence, and hurrying into prison the greater part of his domestics.

It happened at the time that the emperor was on his way to Campania and that Petronius, after going as far as Cumae, was there detained. He bore no longer the suspense of fear or of hope. Yet he did not fling away life with precipitate haste, but having made an incision in his veins and then, according to his humour, bound them up, he again opened them, while he conversed with his friends, not in a serious strain or on topics that might win for him the glory of courage. And he listened to them as they repeated, not thoughts on the immortality of the soul or on the theories of philosophers, but light poetry and playful verses. To some of his slaves he gave liberal presents, a flogging to others. He dined, indulged himself in sleep, that death, though forced on him, might have a natural appearance. Even in his will he did not, as did many in their last moments, flatter Nero or Tigellinus or any other of the men in power. On the contrary, he described fully the prince's shameful excesses, with the names of his male and female companions and their novelties in debauchery, and sent the account under seal to Nero. Then he broke his signet-ring, that it might not be subsequently available for imperilling others.

—A. J. Church and W. J. Brodribb

No other ancient book affords such first-class entertainment at so many levels simultaneously. Nowhere is there such gross pornography and nowhere more refined criticism of literature and art; but most of all, nowhere is there a comparable picture of the seamy side of life, seen steadily and seen whole, and reported with consummate art, the reporter never twitching an eye nor leering nor inviting a leer nor raising a voice in indignation, real or simulated. The even-voiced exposition carries a heavier impact than would outraged preachment, for those who have eyes to see; with no more explicit condemnation than Shakespeare puts in a play like *Measure for Measure* we get a similar sense of general unwholesomeness. What makes such implied criticism possible and effective is the fact that the principals of the story are educated people. The vulgar parvenus at Trimalchio's dinner are in different case; that bit of realism has very high merits of its own, but our enjoyment is not disturbed by misgivings because we say, "How like that absurd kind of people; of course none of *us* would be guilty of such lapses."

When our text begins Encolpius, who has been staying in an inn in a Campanian seaport with his friend Ascyltus and young Giton, is engaged in discussing the decline of oratory with a professor of rhetoric named Agamemnon. Encolpius blames the teachers (1–2):

In my opinion, the reason why such brainless young cubs are turned out by our colleges is that they never come into touch with the facts of every-day life. Their normal diet is pirates with clanking chains stalking along the shore—tyrants drawing up decrees bidding sons to strike off their fathers' heads—oracular replies in time of plague bidding the people sacrifice three (or more) virgins—sticky rhetorical lolly-pops! and their every word and gesture is, so to speak, smeared with poppy-juice and oil of sesame. Fellows who feed on a diet of this sort have no more chance of learning sense than a kitchen-maid has of keeping clean. With all due respect, permit me to observe that you rhetoricians were the very first to drag eloquence in the dust.

—*J. M. Mitchell*

Agamemnon's defense is that parents are too ambitious for their children to give them a proper education, and he caps his argument with a poem on the high ideals of the poet's craft (5). There is no visible connection between this scene and the next (6–11), which must be left in the decent obscurity of a learned language, nor between the latter and an amusing encounter in the market place involving a dispute concerning the ownership of a stolen coat with money hidden in its seams (12–15). Next is another licentious passage, in the course of which the marriage of a seven-year old girl is celebrated; the elder Quartilla swears she cannot remember ever having been virgin.

Next (26–78) comes the dinner of the rich upstart Trimalchio, in the course of which every conceivable breach of taste, in the food and its service, in the host's conduct, dress, and souvenir gifts, in conversation, is perpetrated in an endeavor to display affluence and respectability. The guests (except our heroes) are as vulgar, though not as rich, as the host; realism is carried so far in the reproduction of their conversation that it is possible to distinguish Syrians from Greeks by their special blunders in Latin. All are carefully characterized, and all are shrewd enough in their own ways and make sensible remarks; it is only when they try to make polite conversation and spice it with learned allusions (all fantastically wrong) that they become ridiculous. During a lull in the dinner Trimalchio explains the design of his tomb and its inscription. At the end there is a general brawl, and Trimalchio calls for a rehearsal of his funeral; the horns of the funeral march are mistaken for a fire alarm, and the arrival of the fire department puts an end to the party.

Encolpius quarrels with Ascyltus over Giton and bewails the hollowness of friendship in elegant verse. In a picture gallery Encolpius encounters a poet who deplores greed and the decay of learning and illustrates a picture by reciting a long iambic poem of his own on Laocoon and the Wooden Horse. People begin to throw stones, and the poet is eventually left spouting poetry in a bath. The three friends make up their quarrel and embark on a voyage, but aboard ship are two enemies from an earlier part of the book, Lichas and the courtesan Tryphaena. They attempt disguise but are discovered. When peace is restored Eumolpus entertains the company with the famous story of the Widow of Ephesus; during Trimalchio's dinner stories of a werewolf and of a changeling had been told. Lichas is washed over-board by a sudden storm, Encolpius and Giton are saved by wreckers; Eumolpus is subsequently found ashore, still scribbling verses. The adventurers proceed to Croton, concocting a scheme to attract and fleece legacy hunters; Eumolpus will pretend to be a rich and child-less invalid, and the others his slaves. As they proceed towards the town Eumolpus delivers an epic on the civil war, perhaps in criticism of Lucan, in 295 hexameters. At Croton the intervals of preying on legacy hunters are filled with further amorous adventures. The legacy hunters grow impatient; the fragments at the end contain a clause of a will, presumably Eumolpus', requiring that a public meal be made off the testator's body.

When Quintilian spoke of satire as being a Roman innovation he was thinking mainly of verse satire like Lucilius' or Horace's; in ac-tuality nothing in Latin literature is as original as the *Satyrica*. Petro-nius was of course a well-read man, and many things in his book besides quotations come from earlier writers. But we have only to compare the *Satyrica* with the extant ancient novels to apprehend Pe-tronius' special quality. The Greek novels are wholly romantic, their heroes more perfect, their coincidences more incredible, their deliver-ances more miraculous than the workaday world can know. They are in the fullest sense escapist. Petronius' utter realism gives truth the value it must always possess. His truth and his fun—even if it evokes a grim smile rather than an exuberant guffaw—put Petronius in the tradition of satire, whose object is *ridendo dicere verum*. Another traditional ingredient of Roman satire shows that Petronius belongs in the suc-cession of Lucilius and Varro and Horace, of Seneca and Persius and Juvenal, and that is his earnest if lightly carried concern with literary and aesthetic matters. For purpose of classification the *Satyrica* belongs with the Menippean satires; but as a work of art it stands quite by itself.

Besides literary interest and vestiges of dialogue a feature of Roman satire was the animal fable; Ennius, Lucilius, and Horace all used the example of animals to enforce morals. Beast fables are among mankind's earliest imaginative creations. Aesop, who was ancient to Herodotus, certainly did something to give artistic form to fables, but Aesop surely made large use of preexistent material. Aristophanes and Plato both mention fables of Aesop, and indeed it is exceptional that a fable is mentioned without Aesop's name being attached to it. There must surely have been a "Life of Aesop" and a collection of his fables in the fifth century B.C., but it was inevitable that both should be constantly altered. It is in the nature of the fable that the animals who speak in it are really humans (who outside the laboratory knows what goes on in a mouse's head?) with traits commonly ascribed to certain animals strongly marked. It becomes inevitable then that encounters between such "animals" should not only be amusing by reason of paradox but also that they should convey comment and criticism on human nature and society, in a word, that they should be satiric. After epic and drama and lyric and the various Alexandrian forms had been introduced, a versifier eager to claim credit for introducing a new form and one that should please a Roman audience could do no better than adopt "Aesop." That is what Phaedrus did.

In his manuscripts Phaedrus is called "freedman of Augustus"; all other details of his life must be deduced from the prologues and the epilogues of his books. He was born at Pieria in Macedonia: if it is true, as scholars calculate, that his third book was published about A.D. 40 and that he was growing old when he wrote it, his birth year may be placed about 15 B.C. His two opening books contained along with fables ascribed to Aesop similar pieces of Phaedrus' own invention and were dedicated to readers at large. Because of the interpretation put upon some of them, Phaedrus was prosecuted by Tiberius' favorite, Sejanus. The third book, which he intended to be his last, he dedicated to Eutychus, presumed to be the famous chariot racer of Caligula's time. He went on to compose a fourth and a fifth book, dedicated to persons unidentified. The books contain, respectively, thirty-one, eight, nineteen, and twenty-five fables: the unequal distribution and the absence of the talking trees which Phaedrus promises in his prologue indicate that many of his fables may be lost. Scholars have suggested that similar fables attributed to Aesop in a fifteenth-century collection are in fact Phaedrus'. From his prologues and epilogues too we get Phaedrus' sense of his own importance as a writer. Like Terence he replies to malignant critics, and he proudly asserts (Epilogue 2.8) that if Latium would favor his efforts it would have more authors to rival the Greeks.

Phaedrus is not so important as he thought. But if he is not a doctrinaire like Persius nor a mordant preacher like Juvenal nor an amiable wit like Martial, he can nevertheless not be brushed aside as a versifier of the family page in the daily newspaper. We look upon the genus fable as childish, but in Rome the Aesopian fable was a staple of secondary education, and Phaedrus, though he makes full and frequent mention of his indebtedness to Aesop, fulfils his own promise (Prologue 2) to add variety and incident, in order to correct error. He insists on the utility of his work, trivial as it may seem (4.2.1–4), and says (Prologue 3.33–37) that the fable was invented to give expression to things which could not be uttered openly. Nothing that we have shows bold political opposition, but his criticism was sharp enough to provoke Sejanus. The numerous Roman allusions and the Roman setting of many of his pieces demonstrate his originality. There is the anecdote (5.2) of the flautist named Princeps ("Prince") who returns to perform after a long absence due to a broken leg. While Prince is waiting in the wings, *the* prince enters the theater, and the chorus, amid loud shouting, sings "Rejoice! Rome is secure, her Prince is well." Prince, not knowing the song, makes a natural mistake and causes a furore when he rushes to take a bow. There is the equally Roman anecdote (3.5) of the peasant in a pig-squealing contest with a ventriloquist, who loses despite the fact that his squeals are produced by a live pig under his coat which he pinches; he shows the pig at the end, and cries out, "This is the kind of judges you are." The centumvirate court at Rome is mentioned in an anecdote (3.10) very like the theme of a *controversia*. A suspicious husband rushes into his wife's chamber and kills a man he finds sleeping there. When he finds it is his own son, whom his wife had given a bed in her room to keep him from temptation, he commits suicide. The emperor Augustus himself decided that the woman is more to be pitied than damned. The stated theme of this piece is (line 1), *Periculosum est credere et non credere;* the moral, not, to be sure, very startling, is (52–53) that people whom you least suspect are sometimes guilty, and people who are innocent are sometimes suspected.

Some fables of the traditional beast type have Roman applications. The familiar fable of the wolf and the lamb is specifically said to be directed against those *qui fictis causis innocentes opprimunt,* which means the *delatores* or professional informers. The same class is envisaged in the wolf who supported the dog's claim against the sheep (1.17). The jackdaw in peacock's feathers (1.3) may be Sejanus, and his aspiration to marriage with Livia may be the point of the protest of the frogs against the marriage of sun (1.6), who was hard enough on water as it was: *Quidnam futurum est si crearit liberos?* But even the fables which seem to mean no more than they say have their own charm and applicability. When Heine came to Paris he felt that the people in the streets were all old acquaintances, for he recognized them all from an animal picture book. Reading Phaedrus has the advantage and disadvantage accruing to an otherwise adult reader who would read Matthew or *Hamlet* for the first time: it all seems to be made up of old tags. But it can be both instructive and agreeable to find the old tags in their context, and not the least of Phaedrus' merits is his very large share in making them old tags.

XVI

LEARNING AND LETTERS IN THE FIRST CENTURY

ON THE HEELS OF THE CREATORS COME LITTERA-teurs, scholars, encyclopedists. Upon the Golden Age of Greek literature followed the Alexandrian, where literary doctrine was more important than substance and where scholarship took the place of creative impulse. And when the literary force of the late republic and the Augustan age in Rome was spent we have conscious "literary" productions like the Silver epics and society verse like Statius' and Martial's, and we have encyclopedic works like the Elder Pliny's or Quintilian's or Aulus Gellius'. Originality in conception and sincerity in execution do occur—we have had the examples of Petronius and Juvenal, and we shall have the example of Tacitus—but the general level is that of the collector and systematizer, like the Elder Pliny, or of the frank imitator, like the Younger.

The elder Gaius Plinius Secundus was born at Comum in A.D. 23 of a wealthy and respected family and had a busy career in various official posts. At Rome he studied under the poet and soldier Pomponius Secundus and at the age of twenty-three started his official career in Germany, rising to the command of cavalry squadron. After some ten years of military service he returned to Rome and practiced law, but during most of Nero's principate he devoted himself to literature. Under Vespasian, with whom he was on terms of intimacy, he held a number of important procuratorships. He was admiral of the fleet at Misenum when the eruption of Vesuvius in A.D. 79 put an end to his life. Of the circumstances of his death we have an admirable description in a letter addressed to Tacitus by the Younger Pliny (6.16):

Your request that I would send you an account of my uncle's end, so that you may transmit a more exact relation of it to posterity, deserves my acknowledgements; for if his death shall be celebrated by your pen, the glory of it, I am aware, will be rendered for ever deathless. . . . He was at that time with the fleet under his command at Misenum. On the 24th of August, about one in the afternoon, my mother desired him to observe a cloud of very unusual size and appearance. . . . My uncle, true savant that he was, deemed the phenomenon important and worth a nearer view. He ordered a light vessel to be got ready, and gave me the liberty, if I thought proper, to attend him. I replied I would rather study; and, as it happened, he had himself given me a theme for composition. . . . In the meanwhile Mount Vesuvius was blazing in several places with spreading and towering flames, whose refulgent brightness the darkness of the night set in high relief. But my uncle, in order to soothe apprehensions, kept saying that some fires had been left alight by the terrified country people, and what they saw were only deserted villas on fire in the abandoned district. . . . It was now day everywhere else, but there a deeper darkness prevailed than in the most obscure night; relieved, however, by many torches and divers illuminations. They thought proper to go down upon the shore to observe from close at hand if they could possibly put out the sea, but they found the waves still run extremely high and contrary. There my uncle having thrown himself down upon a disused sail, repeatedly called for, and drank, a draught of cold water; soon after, flames, and a strong smell of sulphur, which was the forerunner of them, dispersed the rest of the company in flight; him they only aroused. He raised himself up with the assistance of two of his slaves, but instantly fell; some unusually gross vapour, as I conjecture, having obstructed his breathing and blocked his windpipe, which was not only naturally weak and constricted, but chronically inflamed. When day dawned again (the third from that he last beheld) his body was found entire and uninjured, and still fully clothed as in life; its posture was that of a sleeping, rather than a dead man.

—*W. Melmoth and W. M. L. Hutchinson*

It was his scientific curiosity that cost Pliny his life. On his devotion to his study and his literary productivity we have another informing and entertaining letter of the Younger Pliny (3.5):

It is with much pleasure that I find you are so constant a reader of my uncle's works, as to wish to have a complete collection of them; and, for that purpose desire me to send you an account of all the treatises he wrote. I will fill the place of an index and even acquaint you with the order in which they were composed: for that, too, is a sort of information not at all unacceptable to men of letters.

The first book he published was a treatise concerning the *Art of using a javelin on horseback*: this he wrote when he commanded a troop of horse, and it is drawn up with equal accuracy and judgment. *The life of Pomponius Secundus,* in two volumes: Pomponius had a very great affection for him, and he thought he owed this tribute to his memory. *The history of the wars in Germany,* in twenty books, in which he gave an account of all the campaigns we were engaged in against the nation. . . . He has left us likewise *The Students,* in three books, divided into six volumes, owing to their length. In this work he takes the orator from his cradle, and leads him on till he has carried him up to the highest point of perfection in this art. In the last years of Nero's reign, when the tyranny of the times made it dangerous to engage in studies of a more free and elevated spirit, he published *Linguistic Queries,* in eight books; *A Continuation,* in one book, of the thirty books of Aufidius Bassus' history; and thirty-seven books of a *Natural history:* this is a work of great compass and learning, and as full of variety as nature herself.

You will wonder how a man so engaged as he was, could find time to compose such a number of books; and some of them too upon abstruse subjects. But your surprise will rise still higher, when you hear, that for some time he engaged in the profession of an advocate, that he died in his fifty-sixth year, that from the time of his quitting the bar to his death he was engaged and trammelled by the execution of the highest posts, and by the friendship of his sovereigns. But he had a quick apprehension, incredible zeal, and a wakefulness beyond compare. He always began to work at midnight when the August festival of Vulcan came round; not for the good omen's sake, but for the sake of study; in winter generally at one in the morning, but never later than two, and often at midnight. . . .

Before day-break he used to wait upon Vespasian; who likewise chose that season to transact business. When he had finished the affairs which that emperor committed to his charge, he returned home again to his studies. After a short and light repast at noon (agreeably to the good old custom of our ancestors) he would frequently in the summer, if he was disengaged from business, repose himself in the sun; during which time some author was read to him, from whence he made extracts and observations, as indeed this was his constant method whatever book he read: for it was a maxim of his, that "no book was so bad but some profit might be gleaned from it." When this basking was over, he generally went into the cold bath, and as soon as he came out of it, just took a slight refreshment, and then reposed himself for a little while. Then, as if it had been a new day, he immediately resumed his studies till dinner-time, when a book was again read to him, upon which he would make some running notes. I remember once, his reader having pronounced a word wrong, somebody at the table made him repeat it again; upon which my uncle asked his friend if he understood it? Who acknowledging that he did; "why then," said he, "would you make him go back again? We have lost by this interruption of yours above ten lines:" so chary was this great man of time! In summer he always rose from supper by day-light; and in winter as soon as it was dark: and this was a sort of binding law with him.

Such was his manner of life amidst the noise and hurry of the town; but in the country his whole time was devoted to study without intermission, excepting only while he bathed. But in this exception I include no more than the time he was actually in the bath; for all the while he was rubbed and wiped, he was employed either in hearing some book read to him, or in dictating himself. In his journeys, as though released from all other cares, he found leisure for this sole pursuit. A shorthand writer, with book and tablets, constantly attended him in his chariot, who, in the winter, wore a particular sort of warm gloves, that the sharpness of the weather might not occasion any interruption to his studies; and for the same reason my uncle always used a sedan chair in Rome. I remember he once reproved me for walking; "You might," said he, "not have lost those hours:" for he thought all was time lost that was not given to study. By this extraordinary application he found time to write so many volumes, besides 160 which he left me, consisting of a kind of common-place, written on both sides, in a very small character; so that one might fairly reckon the number considerably more. I have heard him say that when he was comptroller of the revenue in Spain, Larcius Licinus offered him 400,000 sesterces for these manuscripts: and yet they were not then quite so numerous.

—*W. Melmoth and W. M. L. Hutchinson*

Of all the works that his nephew lists the only one that has survived is the latest—the *Natural History,* in thirty-seven books. This work is dedicated to Titus in his sixth consulship, which dates its completion to A.D. 77, two years before the eruption of Vesuvius and the accession of Titus. The work is an encyclopedia of the natural sciences interspersed with essays and digressions on the handiwork of men. By his own reckoning (Preface 17) Pliny accumulated twenty thousand facts from two thousand works by a hundred selected authors. He makes a point of acknowledging his indebtedness to his authorities (Preface 21). His entire first book is devoted to a systematic table of contents and long lists of authorities for each separate book; 146 Roman and 327 foreign authors are mentioned. Many may have reached him through the mediation of Varro, who was his single most important source. What he drew from his main sources he overlaid with other material from his notebooks. The distribution of the work is as follows: 2, mathematical and physical description of the world; 3–6, geography and ethnography; 7, anthropology and human physiology; 8-11, zoology; 12-27, botany, including agriculture and *materia medica;* 28-32, medical zoology; 33-37, mineralogy, especially in its application to life and art. Sections of this last group are of major importance for the history of ancient art; thus 33.154-157 is devoted to chasing in silver, 34 to bronze statuary, 35.15-149 to painting, 36 to marble sculpture, and 37 to precious stones. His catalogue of works and artists are rather like those of an art dealer or *Kunsthistoriker* than of a lover of art, but he does occasionally express independent judgments; thus he prefers the Laocoon in Titus' palace to all the pictures and bronzes in the world (36.37).

In science, too, Pliny is rather the cataloguer than the researcher; how could a cavalry commander and provincial governor and imperial advisor and admiral find time for laboratory research in a lifetime of fifty-six years? He did have a prodigious curiosity and a genuine zeal for spreading knowledge. He is industrious, accurate, and free from prejudice. But even as a compiler he has faults, mainly a want of critical discrimination and a predilection for the marvelous. But for the nonspecialist reader the merely curious items or anecdotes may be of greater interest than the more professional parts of his book. Like his incidental remarks, they give a pleasing picture of the range of interest and the views of a high official in the first century. He has no partiality for the aristocracy, and he does not suppress facts unfavorable to Rome (34.139). The imperial power he regards as indispensable to the administration of the empire. He laments the decline of agriculture and indicates its cause—the *latifundia* (ranches worked by slave labor) have destroyed Italy. Italy itself he regards as "the fairest country in all the world" (37.201); Rome's mission is to spread civilization and to unify the world (3.39):

Divine grace has chosen Italy to make heaven itself more glorious, to unite scattered empires, to civilize manners, to draw together by interchange of speech the discordant and savage tongues of so many nations, to give to humanity humane culture, and in a word become for all peoples in the whole world their one and only country.

—*J. W. Duff*

Pliny has numerous moralizing reflections and puritanical tirades, but his philosophy is scarcely more systematic than his science; in general his tendency is Stoic. He frequently censures luxury and artificiality and advocates a life of natural simplicity. The bounties of nature are glorified in glowing terms—she has even, in her compassion, provided poisons, so that suicides need not jump into the sea to be eaten by fish (2.156)! But man abuses nature, for example, by mining: "How many hands are worn away with toil that a single knuckle may shine resplendent (2.158)!" But glorification of nature leads to an un-Stoic contempt for man; good men are only nature's antidote for the poison of the bad (36.4-5):

Some men too are born poisons. Like the black dart of the serpent's tongue, their venomous souls blight what they touch. They denounce everything, and, comparable with unhallowed birds, begrudge their own darkness, and disturb the quiet of night itself with their howls—the only utterance they have—so that their mere encounter, as much as that of ill-omened creatures, paralyses action or kind-heartedness. Universal hatred is the one known gain from their loathsome breath. But in this sphere too the majesty of nature has produced good and honest men, just as she is more fertile in plants that heal and nourish. Rejoicing in the esteem of the good, we will abandon such human scum to the bitterness that burns within them, and proceed to make life fairer, and this with firmer resolution, as our aim is the pleasure, not of reputation won, but of service rendered.

—*J. W. Duff*

Literature also comes into Pliny's purview. Homer and Cicero are his greatest names, and Vergil comes next. He was himself a conscious literary craftsman, and he employs all the mannerisms of the Silver Age—epigrammatic point, rhetorical figures, questions and exclamations. There are passages of great felicity; the account of the nightingale is justly famous (10.81-82):

Nightingales pour out a ceaseless gush of song for fifteen days and nights on end when the buds of the leaves are swelling—a bird not in the lowest rank remarkable. In the first place there is so loud a voice and so persistent a supply of breath in such a tiny little body; then there is the consummate knowledge of music in a single bird: the sound is given out with modulations, and now is drawn out into a long note with one continuous breath, now varied by managing the breath, now made staccato by checking it, or linked together by prolonging it, or carried on by holding it back; or it is suddenly lowered, and at times sinks into a mere murmur, loud, low, bass, treble, with trills, with long notes, modulated when this seems good—soprano, mezzo, baritone; and briefly all the devices in that tiny throat which human science has devised with all the elaborate mechanism of the

flute, so that there can be no doubt that this sweetness was foretold by a
convincing omen when it made music on the lips of the infant Stesichorus.

                                                              —H. Rackham

But in the midst of dry catalogues of facts Pliny's fine writing is incongruous, and makes his style as a whole extremely uneven. Pliny's
importance in the cultural history of Europe is attested by his numerous manuscripts. During the Middle Ages his authority was paramount, and though (except for the antiquarian) his information is
no longer of direct use it has provided, by its substance and example,
an important stage in the development of scientific knowledge.

The Elder Pliny was responsible for the upbringing of his nephew,
born A.D. 61 or 62, also at Comum, and adopted him by will, so that
in 79 he became Gaius Plinius Caecilius Secundus. Quintilian was his
teacher in rhetoric. At eighteen he began the practice of law, at which
he attained brilliant success. He rose rapidly in his public career also.
Under Domitian he reached the praetorship and was prefect of the
military treasury, under Nerva he was prefect of the state treasury,
and under Trajan, in A.D. 100, he received the consulship and other
honors. About 111 he was governor of Bithynia; he died before 114.
Pliny's very extensive law practice was largely, as we learn from his
letters, in the centumviral court, which dealt mainly with questions
of inheritance, but he took other cases also; in 100 he was co-counsel
with Tacitus in the prosecution of Marius Priscus for malfeasance in
Africa. His court speeches, as he himself tells us (7.17) he touched up
carefully and delivered as *recitationes;* these were doubtless published,
but the only specimen of his oratory extant is the *Panegyric on Trajan,*
to which reference will be made below.

Aside from the *Panegyric* Pliny is represented by nine books of letters to various friends and a tenth book, preserved separately, containing his correspondence with the Emperor Trajan when he was
governor of Bithynia. The first nine books, containing 247 letters to
105 recipients, were published, possibly in groups of three, between
the years 97 and 109. In his first letter Pliny indicates that the selection
is random, but it is clear that the letters were carefully arranged to
secure variety; the order, however, is mainly chronological. The tenth
book contains 71 official communications from Pliny to Trajan, together with 51 replies. The collection breaks off suddenly. This, and

the different pictures of Pliny himself which the letters convey, may suggest that Pliny himself was not the editor. The great value of Pliny's letters is their refreshing testimony that the seamy side of life pictured by the satirists and Tacitus also had a respectable and amiable side. Pliny may not have been the paragon of benevolence and talent that he believed and would have us believe he was, but even discounting a somewhat exaggerated self-esteem, only too natural for a Roman and a professed imitator of Cicero, he still appears a very kindly, conscientious, and upright citizen such as would be an ornament to any community.

Pliny's letters differ from Seneca's in that they are not general homilies but genuine written communications dealing with the various subjects about which people write to one another. But they differ too from Cicero's because each was written, or at least carefully revised, with a view to publication. Cicero's letters give us a candid camera's snapshot, or rather reel of snapshots; Pliny's, a series of posed photographs of a man of distinction. So present was the reading public to Pliny's mind that even in an affectionate letter to his wife (6.11) he takes pains to make it clear why she is away from home. We must remember then that our general impression is the one Pliny designed for us, and its subject is Pliny himself. What we have then is in effect autobiography, conveyed in the shape of individual *causeries;* Montaigne did much the same thing, but his essays are frankly addressed to the public, and the autobiography is subservient to the general matter, not the other way round. Pliny takes naïve pleasure in any evidence of his fame—the young man so eager to hear him declaim (4.16) or the stranger who knows him by reputation (9.23)—and he thirsts for the approbation of posterity. A large proportion of the letters is calculated to show his virtue (which is by no means to deny that he possessed it) in one or another aspect of social intercourse. He is a fond husband and in his wife's absence writes that he is disconsolate (6.4, 6.7, 7.5); she for her part sits behind a curtain when her husband gives a *recitatio,* to enjoy the applause (4.19). He is kind to his slaves, looks out for them when they are sick (5.19), provides for their old age (6.3), and carries out their wills (8.16). He is a considerate landlord (5.15, 9.37, 8.2). He is very obliging to his friends. One he gives a large sum of money to make up the equestrian census (1.19), another a lesser sum for his daughter's dowry (2.4). He gives a dowry for Quintilian's daughter also (6.32), pays Martial's passage to Spain (3.21), and helps the philosopher Artemidorus satisfy his clamorous creditors (3.11). His influence as well as his purse was at his friends' disposal. For one or another of them he asks and obtains a centurion's commission (6.25), a military tribuneship (3.8, 4.4, 7.22), the *latus clavus* (2.9, 10.4), the *ius trium liberorum* (2.13, 10.94). He electioneered for his friends, and was generous with help and encouragement for young lawyers (6.12, 23). His benefactions to his native place throw an interesting light on Pliny and his society. He was the moving spirit and chief contributor for the establishment of a children's home (1.8, 7.7, *Corpus inscriptionum Latinarum* 5.5262), a public library (1.8), and a school (4.13.5). His style of life is also interesting as a specimen of his class. Though he was rich and came into money not only from his uncle but also from his father and mother (2.15, 4.6, 9.7), he sometimes complains of hard times or poor vintages and hesitates about a desired purchase (2.15, 3.19, 8.2). He had two villas overlooking Lake Como, playfully called Tragedy and Comedy (9.7), and a Tuscan estate near Tifernum (where he built a temple) which yielded a large income. He had country houses at Tusculum, Tibur, and Praeneste, and a very splendid villa on the seashore at Laurentum, seventeen miles from Rome. The elaborate description of this estate in one of the longest of his letters (2.17) is a *locus classicus* for Roman domestic architecture.

Pliny naturally had literary interests and himself essayed various forms, as the following letter shows (7.4):

You have read, you tell me, my hendecasyllabic poems, and are desirous to know how it happened that a man of my gravity (as you are pleased to call me, as I will say for myself, not a trifler) could fall into this way of composition. To take the account then a good way backwards, I must acquaint you that I had always an inclination to poetry, insomuch that, when I was fourteen years of age, I composed a Tragedy in Greek. If you should ask me what sort of one, I protest I don't know; all I can say is, that it was called a Tragedy. Some time afterwards, on my return from the army, being detained in the Island of Icaria by contrary winds, I composed some Latin elegiac verses upon that island and its sea. I have sometimes tried my hand at Epic poetry; but these are the first hendecasyllabic poems I ever composed; to which the following accident gave birth.

The treatise of Asinius Gallus was read to me one day at my Laurentine villa, wherein he draws a comparison between his father and Cicero; and there I met with an epigram of Tully's on his favorite Tiro. Upon retiring to take my afternoon's nap (for it was summer time), and not being visited by sleep, I began to reflect that the greatest orators have been fond of this kind of composition, and valued themselves upon it. I tried therefore what I could do in this way; and though I had long disused myself to things of this nature, I jotted down in almost no time the following lines upon the subject which had prompted me to compose. [13 hendecasyllabic lines follow.]

From this I turned to an elegiac poem which I finished as rapidly; and yielding to the temptation of facility, I added other verses. At my return to Rome I read my performances to some of my friends, who were pleased to approve of them. Afterwards whenever I had leisure, and particularly when I travelled, I made attempts in several metres. At length I determined, after the example of many others, to complete for publication a separate volume of erotic poems; and I have no reason to repent of my resolution. They are much the mode, copies are in everybody's hands; they are even sung to harp or lyre accompaniments, and by the Greeks, too, who have been learning Latin out of fondness for my little book.

—W. Melmoth and W. M. L. Hutchinson

He took the institution of *recitationes* seriously, and advised a friend to applaud them always (6.17):

In fine, be your talent greater or equal, or less than the performer's, you should still praise him; if less, because if one of more exalted abilities does not meet with applause, neither possibly can you: if greater or equal, because the higher his glory rises whom you equal or excel, the more considerable yours must necessarily be. For my own part, I honour and revere all who discover any talent for oratory; for the Muse of Eloquence is a coy and haughty dame, who scorns to reside with those that despise her.

—W. Melmoth and W. M. L. Hutchinson

Other letters illustrate other aspects of Pliny's taste. He is a genuine admirer of nature, not only its curiosities (8.20, 4.3) but also the beauty of its picturesque aspects—the source of the Clitumnus (8.8) or the seaside at Centumcellae (6.31). There are shrewd insights into types of humanity—the countryman who resents the condescension implied in a conversation about crops and insists on talking literature (7.25), or the young man who fled to his study when his grandmother was about to give a party (7.24). Many letters naturally deal with Pliny's own professional and public career. Chief among these and of prime importance for the student of imperial administration, of the rise of

Christianity, and of the reign of Trajan (for which we have very few sources) is the official correspondence of the separately transmitted tenth book. Here we have petitions on behalf of Pliny or others, reports on his struggles with the chaotic finances of the province (it was probably because of his experience as prefect of the treasury that Pliny was sent to Bithynia), problems in constructing theaters, temples, baths, aqueducts, and requests for engineers from Rome, questions of civil or criminal or religious law. Of greatest general interest is the query on the proper treatment of Christians and Trajan's reply. Though it is the longest of the collection, the letter merits reproduction in full (10.96):

It is a rule, Sir, which I inviolably observe, to refer myself to you in all my doubts; for who is more capable of guiding my uncertainty or informing my ignorance? Having never been present at any trials of the Christians, I am unacquainted with the method and limits to be observed either in examining or punishing them. Whether any difference is to be made on account of age, or no distinction allowed between the youngest and the adult; whether repentance admits to a pardon, or if a man has been once a Christian it avails him nothing to recant; whether the mere profession of Christianity, albeit without crimes, or only the crimes associated therewith are punishable—in all these points I am greatly doubtful.

In the meanwhile, the method I have observed towards those who have been denounced to me as Christians is this: I interrogated them whether they were Christians; if they confessed it I repeated the question twice again, adding the threat of capital punishment; if they still persevered, I ordered them to be executed. For whatever the nature of their creed might be, I could at least feel no doubt that contumacy and inflexible obstinacy deserved chastisement. There were others also possessed with the same infatuation, but being citizens of Rome, I directed them to be carried thither.

These accusations spread (as is usually the case) from the mere fact of the matter being investigated and several forms of the mischief came to light. A placard was put up, without any signature, accusing a large number of persons by name. Those who denied they were, or had ever been, Christians, who repeated after me an invocation to the Gods, and offered adoration, with wine and frankincense, to your image, which I had ordered to be brought for that purpose, together with those of the Gods, and who finally cursed Christ—none of which acts, it is said, those who are really Christians can be forced into performing—these I thought it proper to discharge. Others who were named by that informer at first confessed themselves Christians, and then denied it; true, they had been of that persuasion but they had quitted it, some three years, others many years, and a few as much as twenty-five years ago. They all worshipped your statue and the images of the Gods, and cursed Christ.

They affirmed, however, the whole of their guilt, or their error, was, that they were in the habit of meeting on a certain fixed day before it was light, when they sang in alternate verses a hymn to Christ, as to a god, and bound themselves by a solemn oath, not to any wicked deeds, but never to commit any fraud, theft or adultery, never to falsify their word, nor deny a trust when they should be called upon to deliver it up; after which it was their custom to separate, and then reassemble to partake of food—but food of an ordinary and innocent kind. Even this practice, however, they had abandoned, after the publication of my edict, by which, according to your orders, I had forbidden political associations. I judged it so much the more necessary to extract the real truth, with the assistance of torture, from two female slaves, who were styled *deaconesses:* but I could discover nothing more than depraved and excessive superstition.

I therefore adjourned the proceedings, and betook myself at once to your counsel. For the matter seemed to me well worth referring to you—especially considering the numbers endangered. Persons of all ranks and ages, and of both sexes are, and will be, involved in the prosecution. For this contagious superstition is not confined to the cities only, but has spread through the villages and rural districts; it seems possible, however, to check and cure it. 'Tis certain at least that the temples, which had been almost deserted, begin now to be frequented; and the sacred festivals, after a long intermission, are again revived; while there is a general demand for sacrificial animals, which for some time past have met with but few purchasers. From hence it is easy to imagine what multitudes may be reclaimed from this error, if a door be left open to repentance.

—*W. Melmoth and W. M. L. Hutchinson*

Trajan's characteristic reply, which follows, speaks well for his administration:

The method you have pursued, my dear Pliny, in sifting the cases of those denounced to you as Christians is extremely proper. It is not possible to lay down any general rule which can be applied as the fixed standard in all cases of this nature. No search should be made for these people; when they are denounced and found guilty they must be punished; with the restriction, however, that when the party denies himself to be a Christian, and shall give proof that he is not (that is, by adoring our Gods) he shall be pardoned on the ground of repentance, even though he may have formerly incurred suspicion. Informations without the accuser's name subscribed

must not be admitted in evidence against anyone, as it is introducing a very dangerous precedent, and by no means agreeable to the spirit of the age.
—*W. Melmoth and W. M. L. Hutchinson*

At times Trajan grows impatient with Pliny's niggling questions and suggests that he use his own discretion more (10.117):

But I made choice of your prudence, expressly that you might take your own measures for regulating the manner and settling the peace of this province.
—*W. Melmoth and W. M. L. Hutchinson*

Additional light on Trajan's administration is supplied by the *Panegyric* which Pliny pronounced in the senate on entering upon the consulate in A.D. 100. The speech is a most carefully wrought encomium of Trajan's public acts and personal character, but beneath its fulsome flattery is a genuine design to sketch a mirror of princes. It was by divine favor, Pliny begins, that Rome acquired such an emperor; to praise him is no flattery. He is an ideal for future ages. He is generous to the people, provides for poor children, protects commerce, assures the grain supply, exhibits manly games; he has abolished espionage, repressed informers, discouraged treason trials, stabilized finance, guaranteed wills, embarked on a sensible program of public building. He devotes anxious thought to the provinces. His private life, as shown by his relationship with his wife and sister and friends, and by his curtailing the officiousness of freedmen, is no less admirable. Modern readers must be repelled by the preciosity of the rhetoric and by flattery which verges on adulation, but if we discount these objectionable elements, as we should, as being due to a different notion of appropriate style and of court etiquette, we find an intelligently conceived and well-stated program of imperial administration. Later emperors who consciously emulated Trajan were in fact good emperors. Pliny's *Panegyric* is not only a mirror of princes but was a model for similar productions in the later empire. It is the first of the twelve pieces in the collection called *Panegyrici,* of which the others belong to the late third and early fourth century, and far the best of the collection, though some of the others follow Pliny in weaving admonition into their adulation.

A word must be said of Pliny's style, whose peculiarity is that it is at once Ciceronian and Silver. In his smooth copiousness and fluency he is like his avowed master and model, Cicero. In diction, forms of expression, syntax, he shows a striking affinity with his teacher Quintilian and his friend Tacitus. His vocabulary is more classical than that of his contemporaries, but he does have neologisms, somewhat excessive antitheses, somewhat artificial conceits. But on the whole Pliny's style is clear and interesting, sometimes beautiful, and occasionally exhibits the nervous vigor of Tacitus.

The name of Quintilian occurs frequently in these pages because Quintilian is *the* Roman classic for literary criticism. For his own and the succeeding centuries which worshiped rhetoric he was the paramount authority on rhetoric, and for an educational system that required its classics to be catalogued and labeled his evaluations were standard. He was, happily, an honest man, with sound learning and sound taste. His work, with the possible exception of the tenth book of his *Institutio Oratoria* which deals with literary criticism, is not exhilarating reading, but it is an essential document for the appreciation of education and letters in the first century.

Marcus Fabius Quintilianus was born at Calagurris in Spain about A.D. 35 or 40. He was educated in the theory and practice of rhetoric at Rome, went back to Spain some time after 57, and returned to Rome with Galba in 68. Jerome tells us that Vespasian appointed him the first salaried professor of rhetoric at Rome. After twenty years of teaching and practicing at the bar he retired to write but was recalled to be tutor to Domitian's grandnephews and received the extraordinary distinction of consular rank. He married late in life, but his young wife and both her sons predeceased him. His lament for his bereavement, in the Preface to Book 6 of the *Institutio,* strikes the most personal note in Quintilian and is a good specimen of his own style.

I thought that this work would be the most precious part of the inheritance that would fall to my son, whose ability was so remarkable that it called for the most anxious cultivation on the part of his father. Thus if, as would have been but just and devoutly to be wished, the fates had torn me from his side, he would still have been able to enjoy the benefit of his father's instruction. Night and day I pursued this design, and strove to hasten its completion in the fear that death might cut me off with my task unfinished, when misfortune overwhelmed me with such suddenness, that the success of my labours now interests no one less than myself. A second bereavement has fallen upon me, and I have lost him of whom I had formed the highest expectations, and in whom I reposed all the hopes that should solace my old age. What is there left for me to do? Or what further use can I hope to be on earth, when heaven thus frowns upon me? For it so chances that just at the moment when I began my book on the causes of the decline of eloquence, I was stricken by a like affliction. Better had I thrown that ill-omened work and all my ill-starred learning upon the flames of that untimely pyre that was to consume the darling of my heart, and had not sought to burden my unnatural persistence in this wicked world with the fatigue of fresh labours! . . . But I still live, and must find something to make life tolerable, and must needs put faith in the verdict of the wise, who held that literature alone can provide true solace in adversity.

—*H. E. Butler*

In his *Institutio* Quintilian speaks of an earlier work, *De causis corruptae eloquentiae,* of which we have no other trace. The work upon which his reputation rests is the twelve-book *Institutio oratoria,* or "Education of the Orator," published about A.D. 95, of which the contents are as follows. Book 1, after a long prefatory letter to the publisher, starts with the pupil as infant and goes through his elementary education. There is nothing in this section to which the lover of children or the educator can take exception; on the contrary, respect for the personality of the child which permeates the book is a principle which educators must periodically rediscover. The latter part of Book 1 is a careful treatment of grammar and language. Book 2 deals with rhetoric as a discipline and contains advice on the choice of a teacher and of exercises, defines aims, and justifies rhetoric as a science. Books 3–9 are a technical analysis of oratory, covering types of subjects, the formal structure of speeches according to their parts— exordium, narrative, proof, refutation, and peroration—arrangement, points of law, syllogistic arguments, style, diction, ornament, tropes of various kinds, rhythm. The latter part of Book 6 has interesting sections on emotional appeal and on wit and humor. Book 10 is the most familiar part of the *Institutio*. Its subject is the value of reading in the education of an orator; though the motive for reading may be questionable, Quintilian's remarks on the Greek and Latin authors whom he reviews are shrewd and just and constitute a concise and valuable critique of the whole of classical literature. Book 11 discusses memory, delivery, gesture, and dress. Book 12 deals with the ethics of the profession. Quintilian accepts Cato's definition of an orator as *vir bonus dicendi peritus,* "a good man, skilled in speaking," and discusses the moral and intellectual equipment requisite for the orator, the age at which his career should begin, the types of cases which he should accept or refuse, his obligations to study his cases thoroughly, the age at which he should retire from practice. Quintilian's conviction that rhetoric is a fine art appears in the illuminating parallels he draws with the arts of painting and sculpture.

The *Institutio* is a sound book, produced by a scholarly and competent and experienced professor. It leans heavily, as a professor's book should, on the work of his numerous predecessors, but its unity and individuality show that it is Quintilian's own book. He sets his face (3.6.2) against the abiding fault of pseudo-scientists who think they have explained a thing by giving it a technical name, as Molière's candidate in medicine "explained" the effect of opium by saying it had a *virtus dormitiva.* Native talent has its place in oratory as in other arts, but as in other arts hard exertion is essential and there is room for the teacher (7.10.14). Children naturally desire to learn, and it is a mistaken kindness not to give them hard lessons (1.12.8 ff.). Quintilian's sense of humor and breadth of view save him from the endemic occupational diseases of the professor. One feels that he expatiates on his subject because he thought it mattered, not because he had a vested interest in it. In style Quintilian follows his precepts (as his pupil Pliny had done) and produces what may be called Silvered Ciceronianism. He himself says that one should not make his chief model his only model (10.2.24), and though his own model is Cicero, his grammar, vocabulary, and rhetorical decoration are those of the Silver Age, but used with discretion.

Transmitted under Quintilian's name but of dubious authorship are two declamatory collections (*Declamationes Pseudo-Quintilianeae*). One collection consisting of nineteen complete declamations is generally agreed to be spurious, though Jerome and others quote passages from it as Quintilian's work. The other collection containing 145 shorter pieces (the latter part of a collection once numbering 388) is an anthology somewhat like the Elder Seneca's. It may actually derive from Quintilian's teaching, for he mentions (1, Preface 7) that without his authorization pupils of his published notes which they had taken at his lectures. On the other hand, Quintilian himself spoke out (2.10.5) against the type of sensational subject in which this collection abounds.

Besides oratory the only public career open to a Roman gentleman was the army, and on military science too we have an efficient, straightforward, and practical book. Its author was Sextus Julius Frontinus (ca. A.D. 30–104), who was consul in 74, 98, and 100, and of whom Martial, Pliny, and Tacitus speak with respect, the latter (in his *Agricola*) of his command in Britain. Frontinus' two-volume work on land surveying, published under Domitian, is lost, as is his theoretical treatise on military science (*De re militari*). What we have are four books of *Strategemata* and two *De aquis urbis Romae*. The former work lists instances of the application of the principles which had presumably been set forth in the *De re militari*. In his Preface Frontinus says:

I still feel under obligation, in order to complete the task I have begun, to summarize in convenient sketches the adroit operations of generals, which the Greeks embrace under the one name *strategemata*. For in this way commanders will be furnished with specimens of wisdom and foresight, which will serve to foster their own power of conceiving and executing like deeds.
—*C. E. Bennett*

The first book embraces matters to be attended to before battle; the second, the battle itself; and the third, ruses that deal with the siege and defense of towns. The rubrics of the individual books show their scope. In the first book they are: on concealing one's plans; on finding out the enemy's plans; on determining the character of the war; on leading an army through places infested by the enemy; on escaping from difficult situations; on laying and meeting ambushes while on the march; how to conceal the absence of the things we lack, or to supply substitutes for them; on distracting the attention of the enemy; on quelling a mutiny of soldiers; how to check an unseasonable demand for battle; how to arouse an army's enthusiasm for battle; on dispelling the fears inspired in soldiers by adverse omens. In the second book the rubrics are: on choosing the time for battle; on choosing the place for battle; on the disposition of troops for battle; on creating panic in the enemy's ranks; on ambushes; on letting the enemy escape, lest, brought to bay, he renew the battle in desperation; on concealing reverses; on restoring morale by firmness; on bringing the war to a close after a successful engagement; on repairing one's losses after a reverse; on ensuring the loyalty of those whom one mistrusts; what to do for the defense of the camp, in case a commander lacks confidence in his present forces; on retreating.

In Book 3 the rubrics on offense are: on surprise attacks; on deceiving the besieged; on inducing treachery; by what means the enemy may be reduced to want; how to persuade the enemy that the siege will be maintained; on distracting the attention of a hostile garrison; on diverting streams and contaminating waters; on terrorizing the besieged; on attacks from an unexpected quarter; on setting traps to draw out the besieged; on pretended retirements. And for defense: on stimulating the vigilance of one's own troops; on sending and receiving messages; on introducing reinforcements and supplying provisions; how to produce the impression of abundance of what is lacking; how to meet the menace of treason and desertion; on sorties; concerning steadfastness on the part of the besieged.

Under each rubric a short paragraph is devoted to each of a good number of examples, drawn from Greek history and the history of the republic; there are few genuine examples from more recent Roman history. By reason of their brevity and conciseness these anecdotes make very good reading, even for one who recognizes many of them from fuller treatment in the professed historians. They are excellent for one who wishes to read a few short paragraphs periodically to keep his Latin in working order and the same time be reminded of interesting episodes in ancient history. The stories are well told and meaty—for example, the military uses of superstition (1.11) or of symbolic action (1.10). But they are all practical, and conceivably of quite direct use to a commander in action; they are not collected for anecdotal value, as one suspects were the examples in the parallel Greek work of Polyaenus (second century A.D.). The civilian harried by alarms of atom bombs may smile at the traditional rigidity of the military mind when he reads (in the Preface to Book 3) that "the invention of works and engines of war has long since reached its limit."

The fourth book of the *Strategemata* has presented a battle ground for scholarly defense and attack, and the question of its genuineness cannot yet be said to be settled. It differs from the preceding three in details of style, it repeats material from the first three, and it is differ-

ent in tone and plan. Whereas the first three books list actual stratagems, the fourth contains material that might be headed "morale,"
with the rather awkward explanation (4, Preface):

I have given them separate treatment, for fear that if any persons should
happen in reading to run across some of them, they might be led by the resemblance to imagine that these examples had been overlooked by me.

—C. E. Bennett

The seven rubrics of this book are: on discipline; on the effect of
discipline; on restraint and disinterestedness; on justice; on determination ("the will to victory"); on good will and moderation; on
sundry maxims and devices.

One of the most competent and at the same time most unreadable
books in Latin is Frontinus' treatise on aqueducts (*De aquis*); despite
its unmitigated technicality and utter want of stylistic attraction, it
depicts a *vir vere Romanus,* a public servant of great competence, pure
motives, and high ideals. In the course of Nerva's and Trajan's program of municipal reform Frontinus was called upon to take on the
important but altogether unglamorous job of water commissioner,
which had been a wretchedly mismanaged sinecure. Believing that
"there is nothing so disgraceful for a decent man as to conduct an
office delegated to him according to the instructions of assistants"
(1.1), he set about collecting all the information that had a bearing
on his duties, for his own instruction and guidance as well as for the
use of his successors. His stated program his manual carries out faithfully. On the basis of personal investigation, and by the use of specially
made plans and charts, he records the aqueducts existing in his time,
who built them and when, where each originates, how far they are
carried underground and how far on arches, the height and size of
each, the number of outlets, the amounts supplied to public reservoirs,
amusements, state use, and private persons, the laws governing the
construction and maintenance of aqueducts, the penalties enforced by
these laws, and whether these were senatorial acts or imperial decrees.
Of many Roman writers we cannot avoid the suspicion that the poised
pen is a false posture; of many whose pens have a natural agility we
may suspect that they were the froth rather than the essence of Roman
life, and that Roman greatness was achieved by men of a different
stamp. Writers who help us understand how Rome became Rome
are men like Julius Caesar and Frontinus.

XVII

TACITUS AND SUETONIUS

THE APPARENT INSENSITIVITY OF THE ROMANS TO
their greatest historian is an exasperating accident of our faulty tradition or a melancholy commentary upon their judgment. Until the
end of the fourth century, when Ammianus Marcellinus, an Antiochene Greek, undertook to write a continuation of Tacitus' histories,
no writer other than his own friend Pliny makes mention of him. It
is true that the emperor Tacitus (A.D. 275–76) is reported, not im-
probably though the authority is dubious, to have ordered that ten
copies of his putative ancestor's works be made annually and that
these be deposited in various libraries. In any case the story would indicate that Tacitus had fallen into oblivion; and it is in fact only
through a single mutilated manuscript that Tacitus' greatest work has
survived the Middle Ages.

The Younger Pliny was associated with Tacitus in important legal
pleading and has left us eleven letters addressed to him. These and a
single inscription from Asia Minor are the only evidence for Tacitus'
life and works we possess outside those works themselves. We know
neither the place nor the date of his birth, though it has been suggested that he came from the North of Italy, and Pliny, who was
born in 62 A.D., addresses him as somewhat his senior. This, combined
with the calculation of the probable age at which he held certain
offices, would give 55 A.D. or somewhat later for Tacitus' birth year.
The best manuscript gives his name as *Publius* Cornelius Tacitus, but
we cannot be sure of his given name, for other manuscripts give it
as *Gaius* Cornelius Tacitus. The decidedly aristocratic bias in his
works and the fashionable rhetorical education of which he speaks
in his *Dialogue on Oratory* would suggest that his family possessed
means and position; his marriage in 78 to the daughter of Agricola,
governor of Britain, would point in the same direction. When Agricola died in 93 Tacitus tells us he had been absent from Rome for
four years; the natural assumption is that he was engaged in some
form of provincial administration, perhaps in Germany. This would
suit what he tells us at the beginning of his *Histories:* "I would not

deny that my elevation was begun by Vespasian, augmented by Titus, and still further advanced by Domitian." From Pliny again we learn that Tacitus as consul under Nerva in 97 pronounced the funeral oration for Verginius Rufus, one of the most admirable characters of his day. Three years later, in association with Pliny, Tacitus won an important case for the Africans against their oppressive governor, Marius Priscus. The inscription mentioned above indicates that Tacitus was governor of Asia Minor under Trajan, probably in 112. The latest event alluded to in Tacitus' extant writings is a reference in the second book of the *Annals* to the extension of the empire to the Persian Gulf. This took place in 116, and Tacitus may have died at any subsequent date that will allow time for the completion of the remaining books of the *Annals*.

Of his works the oldest is probably the *Dialogue on Oratory*. The authenticity of this treatise has been doubted from time to time, chiefly on the ground of its stylistic divergence from the other writings. Its neo-Ciceronian style, markedly unlike that of his other works, has led some to date it not long after the dramatic date of the *Dialogue,* which is A.D. 75. But at the beginning of the *Dialogue* Tacitus states that he is reporting a conversation he overheard as a young man, and at the beginning of the *Agricola,* written in 98, he deprecates his inexperience in writing; and these considerations have led some scholars to move the date far forward. No other Latin dialogue (and we have many, from Cicero and Seneca) approaches Tacitus' in dramatic verisimilitude, and it would seem reasonable to suppose that even after Tacitus had developed his own unique style he could still represent older rhetoricians in a medium appropriate to them.

This golden booklet, as it has been styled since the Renascence, deals with much of perennial interest: with vocational and humanistic education, with dilettantism and scholarship, with philosophy as a guide in life, with the loss of individual responsibility as the price of good government. The subject of the inquiry is the change in oratory since Cicero's day. The change in educational ideals and in the conditions of life are mentioned as contributory causes; but the factor which overshadows all others is the change in political life. Only the republic could make oratory vital, for only in the republic did oratory serve a necessary function in the body politic.

The *Agricola,* written in 98, is a laudatory biography of the author's father-in-law, who had had a successful military and administrative career in Britain and had then fallen under the displeasure of Domitian. The early chapters tell of Agricola's career to his appointment as governor, and then give an account of Britain and its relations to Rome. The two strands are then combined, until Agricola's recall by the emperor Domitian. Much is made of Agricola's exemplary conduct while he was the object of the emperor's jealousy. The biography continues with an account of its hero's last illness and death and closes with an address to the survivors. This epilogue is one of the finest passages in Latin and one of the best condolences in any literature:

> If there is any dwelling-place for the spirits of the just; if, as the wise believe, noble souls do not perish with the body, rest thou in peace; and call us, thy family, from weak regrets and womanish laments to the contemplation of thy virtues, for which we must not weep nor beat the breast. Let us honour thee not so much with transitory praises as with our reverence, and, if our powers permit us, with our emulation. That will be true respect, that the true affection of thy nearest kin. This, too, is what I would enjoin on daughter and wife, to honour the memory of that father, that husband, by pondering in their hearts all his words and acts, by cherishing the features and lineaments of his character rather than those of his person. It is not that I would forbid the likenesses which are wrought in marble or in bronze; but as the faces of men, so all similitudes of the face are weak and perishable things, while the fashion of the soul is everlasting, such as may be expressed not in some foreign substance, or by the help of art, but in our own lives. Whatever we loved, whatever we admired in Agricola, survives, and will survive in the hearts of men, in the succession of the ages, in the fame that waits on noble deeds. Over many indeed, of those who have gone before, as over the inglorious and ignoble, the waves of oblivion will roll; Agricola, made known to posterity by history and tradition, will live for ever.
>
> —*A. J. Church and W. J. Brodribb*

It is true that the life is eulogy rather than history, and that the eulogy might be applicable not to its subject alone but to any virtuous Roman. But for us, as for Tacitus' first readers, it is important to know that a good Roman could live through Domitian's Terror without becoming either an accessory to the emperor's crimes or his compliant tool, "that great men can exist even under evil rulers" (*posse etiam sub malis principibus magnos viros esse*).

The fullest form of the title of the *Germania*, also written in 98, is

On the Origin, Geography, Institutions, and Tribes of the Germans, and this indicates the book's character. It is a geographic and ethnologic treatise, artistic in form and scientific by contemporary standards. It has become a sort of ethnologic Bible for the Germans and has been studied in modern Germany more than any other ancient book. The early chapters deal with the public and private usages of the Germans in general, and then we have a more or less systematic account of the various tribes, with individual characteristics and other information given incidentally. The twenty-odd pages of this treatise constitute the most exhaustive and valuable work of its type preserved to us from antiquity. More than six hundred items of information are here recorded, of a credibility, to be sure, varying with that of Tacitus' sources. The sources were undoubtedly the best available, and included eyewitness accounts as well as written material, and Tacitus was a conscientious workman; but it is as absurd to credit Tacitus with the ideals of nineteenth-century scholarship as it is to despise the work as uninformed journalism. The latter was the view of the great Mommsen, and is certainly as wide of the mark as is Gibbon's praise of the work as the result of "accurate observation and diligent inquiries." It is a temptation to which many have succumbed to look upon the *Germania* as a sort of Utopia, a conscious idealization of a primitive and unspoiled people calculated to chasten and reform the decadent Romans. This view is justified in the degree that a strong moralizing strain runs through all Tacitus' work. It has been wittily remarked that no one in Tacitus is good except Agricola and the Germans. But the fact is that too many unlovely traits are reported of the Germans along with the idealization to justify making moral improvement the main end of the book.

We come now to the specifically historical works. Of these we know there were thirty books, and it is now generally assumed that there were twelve of the *Histories* and eighteen of the *Annals*. Mention should be made of the alternative theory current until recently which gave the *Histories* and the *Annals* fourteen and sixteen books, respectively The *Histories* covered the period from 69, the year of the four emperors, to the death of Domitian in 96. Only the first four books and a fragment of the fifth have been preserved. The extant portion includes the melodramatic events of 69 and most of 70. The work was written and published during the reign of Trajan; more precise dating is impossible. The only title given in the manuscript of Tacitus' greatest work is *From the Death of Deified Augustus,* but the customary *Annals* is justified on other grounds. This work covered the period from the death of Augustus in 14 A.D. to that of Nero in 68. The extant portion includes the first four books, a fragment of the fifth, most of the sixth (the first part is missing), and Books 11 to 16, with the beginning of the eleventh and the end of the sixteenth missing. These extant books cover the reign of Tiberius (A.D. 14–37), the latter seven years of Claudius (A.D. 47–54), and the first twelve years of Nero (A.D. 54–66). We have noted above that a passage in the second book indicates that it was written about 116. The *Annals* and *Histories* together covered the period from 14 to 96. In *Annals* 3.24 Tacitus promises a work on the reign of Augustus if life should permit, and in *Histories* 1.1 he reserves for his old age a study of the reigns of Nerva and Trajan. It may be significant of Tacitus' interests that the eighty-two years which his history covers included the frightful half of the period he proposed to deal with (and for this half it is, indeed, our best source), and that he did not find time for the happy reigns at either end of the span; the usual assumption is, of course, that Tacitus did not live to complete these projected works.

An account of Tacitus' career must be meager, but fuller knowledge would, after all, be useful only insofar as it might contribute to a fuller understanding of his work; and here we are not so badly off, for his books show vividly what manner of man he was. No other ancient author has so impregnated his works with his own personality. It is easy enough to see what Tacitus thought of the world in which he lived, what his convictions and his prejudices were. The illustration and enforcement of certain convictions seem to him to be, in fact, the prime purpose in the writing of history. "This I regard as history's highest function," he writes (*Annals* 3.65), "to let no worthy action be uncommemorated, and to hold out the reprobation of posterity as a terror to evil words and deeds." His moralizing intent is made even clearer in another passage (*Annals* 4.33): "There must be good in carefully noting and recording this period, for it is but few who have the foresight to distinguish right from wrong or what is sound from what is hurtful, while most men learn virtue from the fortunes of others. Still, though this is instructive, it gives very little pleasure."

But no desire to give pleasure will persuade Tacitus to lower the dignity of his work. At several points he expresses regret that his incidents are so mean and his personalities so petty compared with the grander events and figures of the republic, and he refuses to compromise what dignity his theme possesses by spicing his account with what is merely titillating. "I think it unbecoming the task I have undertaken," he writes (*Histories* 2.50), "to collect fabulous marvels and to entertain with fiction the tastes of my readers." A form such entertainment might take is glanced at in *Annals* 13.31: "One might fill volumes with the praise of the foundations and timber work on which Nero piled the immense amphitheater in the Field of Mars. But we have learned that it suits the dignity of the Roman people to reserve history for great achievements, and to leave such details to the city's daily register."

It is the moralizing intent which explains and is served by Tacitus' interest in people. Broad principles, large movements, even great achievements move him not for their own sake but because they tell us about the people who were responsible for them. "Tacite a introduit l'homme dans l'histoire," writes a French critic, "c'est l'homme, c'est l'humanité qu'il raconte en racontant Rome et les Romains." And not humanity in general but individual humans. Always Tacitus strives to penetrate into the thoughts and motives of the actors in his drama. It is Tacitus' skill in delineating characters, particularly intense and theatrical Roman characters, that is apt to strike the reader as his outstanding achievement. Macaulay has put the case well:

In the delineation of character Tacitus is unrivalled among historians and has very few superiors among dramatists and novelists. By the delineation of character we do not mean the practice of drawing up epigrammatic catalogues of good and bad qualities, and appending them to the names of eminent men. No writer, indeed, has done this more skilfully than Tacitus; but this is not his peculiar glory. All the persons who occupy a large space in his works have an individuality of character which seems to pervade all their words and actions. We know them as if we had lived with them.

If Tacitus is artist as well as historian, it remains to glance at some of his artistic devices. The masterly characterizations of which we have spoken are achieved with remarkable economy of detail. He never indulges, as Suetonius appears to do, in scandalous gossip for its own sake. His sketches are rendered in bold strokes, his effects are obtained by the use of light and shadow which bring out the essentials. If this technique results in theatricality it is but the characteristic of the age. The grand Romans all stalk about on a stage, like the lurid figures in Seneca's tragedies; their grandeur and their intensity are always on parade, they are always conscious of their public and their public's expectations. Theatrical to the highest degree and to the highest degree effective are such sequences (and they are many in number) as those which tell of Messalina's mock marriage in the eleventh book of the *Annals,* or of the events leading to Nero's murder of his mother in the fourteenth. Their effect is stunning, as theater if not as life; no ancient dramatist approaches the decor and the direction.

Such scenes are not the only things in Tacitus which suggest the dramatist's art. Using identical materials different authors achieve the most diverse effects by selecting and grouping their details. In Tacitus the details chosen are frequently such as will produce horror; then occasionally amusing episodes or instances of ordinary humanity are inserted, very like the relaxing interludes with which Shakespeare relieves and points up tragic tension. After the storm and stress of the Piso conspiracy at the end of *Annals* 15, for example, we have the hoax of Dido's buried treasure at the beginning of Book 16. Ostensibly the annalistic form is followed, but the apparently chronological order conceals a subtle art of arrangement. Traditional and obvious connections are disregarded, and fresh and illuminating associations are substituted. Again the criterion is not political clarification but dramatic effectiveness. Because of his own dramatic quality Tacitus has been easy for later dramatists and novelists to quarry from. Corneille has an *Otho,* Racine a *Britannicus,* Ben Jonson a *Sejanus,* Alfieri an *Octavia,* and Chénier a *Tiberius;* there are a dozen plays on Nero. Sienkiewicz' *Quo Vadis* and such contemporary novelists as Feuchtwanger in his Josephus stories and Robert Graves in his Claudius series have long sections which are but adaptations of Tacitus.

Effective scenes are one requirement of the dramatic art, another is effective lines. In Seneca characters exchange single-line tags for pages, each compact and pointed, each eminently quotable. No paragraph in Tacitus is without its pregnant epigram embodying some acute observation or comment. Here the English reader is put at a serious disadvantage, for only rarely does the sharp point carry over in translation. Of one of the best known, *Solitudinem faciunt pacem appellant,* only half the effectiveness is lost, for the translation requires only double the number of Latin words, "They make a wilderness and call it peace." It is to be expected that the loss in effectiveness is usually greater. In the case of the concise epigrams at least explanation is possible, but for Tacitus' style as a whole description to one who has not read the Latin is as difficult as describing peppermint to a man who has never tasted it. The style is unique and unmistakable. The ordinary word, the ordinary construction, the ordinary arrangement are studiously avoided. The balance, the parallelism, the flow characteristic of Cicero or Livy are eschewed. The only rule is that Tacitus will say a thing differently from what you expected and more concisely. The effect is frequently that of sombre and full-toned organ music played staccato. By modern standards of style Tacitus is labored, even precious; but Latin style, and particularly the Latin style of the Silver Age, must be judged by a different standard, for it never attempted to approximate the spoken language. Yet in his straining to avoid the commonplace in diction Tacitus goes far even for Silver Latin. He not only avoids "brothels" by saying (*Histories* 2.93) *inhonesta dictu,* "places unseemly to mention," but he calls spades "implements for digging earth and cutting turf" (*Annals* 1.65). For death fifty different circumlocutions have been counted in Tacitus.

If Tacitus is a dramatist he belongs to the Roman, not the Greek stage. He does not wrestle with problems of cosmic justice or attempt to explain the ways of God to man. It is impossible to extract a philosophy of history from his writings. His *Weltanschauung* has been criticized as immature and full of irreconcilable contradictions. Following the traditions of Polybius, he explains events by natural causes, and when natural causes fail he invokes accident or Fortune. But Tacitus refers events to transcendent causes also; he speaks of the gods, their grace and their wrath. He speaks of Inexorable Fate and Absolute Necessity, and then of chance, which makes a jest of prosperity and doubles the tragedy of suffering. It may be only a rhetorical striving for point that results in such odd combinations of the immanent and transcendent in explaining events: Varus succumbs to destiny and the strength of Arminius (*Annals* 1.55); a famine is averted by the grace of God and a mild winter (*Annals* 12.43). The fact of the matter is that Tacitus is no more a closet philosopher than a research historian. He is a practical man, really less confused in relating life to theory than such Stoics as Seneca and even the Younger Cato; he is interested in events and not in speculation. It may be significant that he eschews the word *philosophia* and uses the homelier Latin term *sapientia* instead. Those expressions in his works which may be combined to prove his philosophic naïveté are part of a cultured vocabulary, and they show only that Tacitus was neither a misologist nor interested in creating a neat and necessarily impracticable system.

Two other characteristics of Tacitus' work which are likely to distress the modern historian may be mentioned. One is the attribution to his characters of speeches which they cannot have delivered (an inscription discovered at Lyons in 1528 gives part of an actual speech of Claudius which Tacitus reports only in brief outline but quite differently in *Annals* 11.24), and the other is the manifest inaccuracy of his battle accounts. As for the speeches, they had become a fixture in history since Thucydides, and as in Thucydides they are frequently the most convenient way of setting forth a situation or a point of view. A discourse dramatically suited to events is more effective than exposition, and if effectiveness and intelligibility are desiderata, why reproduce a speech which is less effective and intelligible than one the writer can supply? Ancient historians are always more artists than scientists and could regard only as a fetish the sanctity we attach to inverted commas. Such a fictive speech as the British chieftain is made to deliver in the *Agricola,* for example, almost certainly sets forth the grounds for native opposition much better than any native could set them forth.

As for the battle description which follows this speech, it seems to have been lifted almost bodily from Sallust's description of a battle which had been fought in Africa two centuries before. Mommsen called Tacitus the most unmilitary of historians (which is unfair to Livy), and even Gibbon says his military history is more remarkable for elegance than perspicuity. When Tacitus describes a battle we are made to feel at least that strenuous and significant action took place; as for details, he follows the practice of the later historians generally, who seem to have resorted to commonplace books for such embellishments. All the naval battles in the later historians, for example, bear so pronounced a family resemblance that one is almost forced to the conclusion that Dio Cassius and the others resorted to the same file, under the folder marked "Sea Battles." Indeed, contemporary criticism would have condemned as eccentric a writer who refused to borrow from his predecessor and was prepared to tolerate a much larger volume of borrowing than can be charged to Tacitus.

If descriptions of battles are mere rhetoric, if speeches are fanciful, if motives are ascribed to characters when it cannot be known what their motives were, one may well ask how trustworthy the resultant history is. A modern historian guilty of such faults would surely lose all credit. But in the Roman concept the historian was never thought of as a researcher but primarily as a literary man, and his function not as the propagation of sound learning so much as the inculcation of salutary doctrine. The most highly regarded historian in Tacitus' day was Livy, and Livy's attitude to fact was much more cavalier than Tacitus'.

Tacitus appears to have been a single flash in Roman imperial historiography. For a continuator of his work he had to wait till the fourth century, when Ammianus Marcellinus (the first part of whose work is lost) took up the thread where Tacitus left off. Even in Tacitus the Roman people and their affairs are submerged almost to the vanishing point and attention is centered on the personages of the imperial court. The next logical step was to focus exclusively on the great imperial figures who subsumed history in their own persons. The history of the dynasty is all that matters, and until Ammianus, indeed, historiography takes the form of imperial biography. Biographical interest had always been strong at Rome, just as realistic portraiture had been. In Greece the study of biography developed late, as a Peripatetic specialty. The arrangement of Tacitus' *Agricola* follows the Peripatetic formula for biography. But the first Roman who took upon himself the task of composing a set of biographies of imperial personages, and so set the pattern for successors whose work is incorporated in the *Scriptores historiae Augustae,* was Suetonius.

As is the case with Tacitus, the best thing we know of Gaius Suetonius Tranquillus (ca.69–ca.140), aside from his writings, is that the Younger Pliny esteemed him highly. When Pliny solicited the *ius trium liberorum* for Suetonius he wrote Trajan (10.94, 95) that the longer he knew him the more highly he prized him. It was through Pliny's influence that the military tribunate was offered to Suetonius and that he was enabled to transfer the honor to a friend when he himself did not want it (3.8). When Pliny intercedes for Suetonius in the purchase of a piece of property he calls him *contubernalis meus* (1.24). When Suetonius was about to plead a case and was much perturbed by a dream, Pliny consoled and calmed him and even promised to secure a postponement of the trial (1.18). It was Pliny, finally, who encouraged him to put the finishing touches to some of his writings and publish them (5.10). It was through Pliny's friend and successor as his patron that Suetonius was appointed secretary to Hadrian; he lost the emperor's favor by a breach of etiquette involving the empress (*Scriptores historiae Augustae: Hadrian* 1.3). One or two additional facts may be deduced from Suetonius' writings. He mentions, for example (*Otho* 10), that his father participated in the battle of Bedriacum in A.D. 69. The last contemporary mention of him is in a letter of Fronto to Marcus Aurelius, written during the early years of Antoninus Pius.

Scholarship appears not to have been an avocation to Suetonius but his chief interest. He did practice law for a time but took no part in politics. His writings were numerous. Suidas' lexicon credits him with a long list of works (perhaps parts of a smaller number of works) which are lost: *On Famous Courtesans, On the Kings, On Public Offices, Roma, The Games of the Greeks, On Cicero's De Republica, Pratum, On Terms of Abuse in Greek, On Various Matters, On Critical Marks in Books, Historia.* But Suetonius' chief interest was in biography, and from 106 to 113 he published *De viris illustribus*, on various categories of literary men, of which parts are preserved. *De grammaticis et rhetoribus* is extant, as are a few *Lives* of Roman writers, all more or less abridged and interpolated. Jerome has thirty-three from *De poetis;* most scholars accept *Terence, Horace,* and *Lucan* as genuine, and some also accept *Vergil, Tibullus,* and *Persius.* Jerome lists fifteen lives from *De oratoribus* and six from *De historicis;* of the former a brief abstract of the *Life of Passienus Crispus* is extant, and of the latter the *Life of Pliny the Elder.* The work of Suetonius which is extant in its entirety (except for a few chapters at the beginning of the *Julius*) and upon which Suetonius' reputation is based is the *De vita Caesarum, On the Life of the Caesars,* published A.D. 121.

Of others who deal with historical subjects we have noticed that they grow fuller as they approach their own times. The fact that the reverse is true of Suetonius explains his approach and extenuates what have been called weaknesses in his work. Suetonius was the type of writer who is more at ease with written sources than with oral inquiry; where a reporter or feature writer would exploit the recollections of living witnesses of recent reigns, the scholar is at a loss for recent history and can deal more fully with the better documented reigns of the early emperors. This circumstance explains such scabrous passages as disfigure the pages of the *Tiberius*. That titillating gossip had been written down, and Suetonius therefore included it in the section where his formula called for details of private life; though a conscientious scholar, he was not sufficiently critical to discern sensationalism or malice in his sources. On the other hand, in such matters as official acts of senate and people and imperial edicts he is a valuable source, for he made conscientious use of the access to official archives which his official post gave him. From such a passage as *Caligula* 8 we see that he examined conflicting statements with care and intelligence, and that he strove for impartiality. He very seldom intrudes his own personality into his story; examples like his eulogy of Titus at the opening of that *Life* and a passage like *Tiberius* 21.3, "I cannot be led to believe that an emperor of the utmost prudence and foresight acted without con-sideration, especially in a matter of so great moment," are very rare. But though Suetonius himself may be impartial, his uncritical use of biased sources frequently gives his *Lives* a bias. His pattern called for an arrangement somewhat as follows: ancestry; birth; years before accession to power, public life and private life including reports of praise and blame, portents presaging death, death. It is neither malice nor prurience, then, that makes Suetonius' pages so often scandalous. Though Suetonius treats his subjects as individuals and not merely in their official aspects, he himself does not draw the appropriate moral lessons but leaves reflections and deductions to his thoughtful reader. It is the emphasis on the individual which makes Suetonius readable and has ensured his continuing popularity, and which, at the same time, makes him an unsatisfactory biographer of great men. He provides materials for a biography, but not a complete picture of a whole man. It is interesting to know that Augustus wore long under-wear, for example, but from Suetonius' pages no heroic or indeed com-plete figure emerges of whom we might believe that he transformed the world's politics. Nor do Suetonius' well-ordered facts reflect a development or change in character. Whatever drama incidents in the *Lives* possess is due to the incidents themselves, not to Suetonius' manipulation. His writing is direct and efficient, never ornate. His words are carefully chosen and well arranged; his occasional Tacitean conciseness grows out of his matter, and is not sought for its own sake. Not only the proper but the favorite study of mankind is man, and for that study Suetonius provides ample materials. In him we can see Tacitus' stalking figures in familiar undress.

XVIII

THE AGE OF HADRIAN

HADRIAN WAS THE FIRST OF THE ROMAN EMPERORS
to wear a beard, and the neatly trimmed archaism is a sign manifest
of the first full-blown classicizing renascence in European literature,
which Hadrian introduced. The sculptors of his age produced the
pretty copies of Greek classics which fill our museums, and the pretty
productions of the littérateurs are their exact counterpart. Silver Latin
was enslaved to rhetorical embellishment and point, as we have seen,
but the ornate dress was still a dress, calculated to make the most of
its wearers' good features. Now it becomes an end in itself, with the
idea that the dress might have contents almost obscene. In Greek the
so-called Second Sophistic was in full flower. Most exquisite care was
taken of assonance, alliteration, balance, and similar niceties, certain
"classics" of the fourth century B.C. serving as a canon; not only was
the how more important than the what, but the devotees of Second
Sophistic studied to eliminate the what entirely. This was a classicism
of imitation, not emulation, and it is significant that Roman writers
not only copied the Greek but themselves wrote in Greek, some in
part (Suetonius, Hadrian, Fronto, Apuleius, Papinian), and some exclusively (Favorinus, Appian, Marcus Aurelius, Julian). In Latin as
in Greek there was a cult of archaism; authors of the early Republic
whom cultivated taste had long disdained were scrutinized, not for
their substance, but for archaic words that might be borrowed from
them. Hadrian himself preferred Cato, Ennius, and Caelius Antipater
to Cicero, Vergil, and Sallust; even in Tacitus' day there had been
those who preferred Lucilius to Horace, Lucretius to Vergil, Sisenna
and Varro to contemporary historians. But from euphuism and
archaism of such a sort not much of abiding worth can be expected;
yet an Apuleius or a Claudian can rise to utterances of real and timeless validity, as can a Dio Chrysostom or a Philostratus. There is as
much feeling as an artistic emperor in a classicizing age can summon
in Hadrian's own familiar lines:

Animula vagula blandula
hospes comesque corporis,

quae nunc abibis in loca
pallidula rigida nudula?
nec ut soles dabis iocos!

O blithe little soul, thou, flitting away,
Guest and comrade of this my clay,
Whither now goest thou, to what place
Bare and ghostly and without grace?
Nor, as thy wont was, joke and play.
                    —*Ainsworth O'Brien-Moore*

A somewhat similar elegiac strain characterizes the *Pervigilium Veneris*, which is surely one of the loveliest pieces in all Latin literature. Of its authorship nothing is known. On the basis of affinity in style and spirit with the *Eclogues* of Nemesianus (ca. 285) and the fragments of Tiberianus (ca. 350), and of possible traces of accentual prosody, many scholars would date the poem between the end of the third and the middle of the fourth centuries. On the other hand, it was Hadrian who revived the worship of Venus on a scale of great magnificence. The amalgamation of the nationalist Roman factor and the cult aspects of Venus in the poem is exactly reflected in Hadrian's magnificent temple across from the Colosseum, in which the apses of Venus and of Rome stand back to back in the center of the one structure. With so little left to show what Hadrianic poetry was like we may therefore well accept Hadrianic dating for the *Pervigilium*. The poem consists of some ninety-two trochaic tetrameter lines, exquisite and melodious, punctuated by the refrain *Cras amet qui numquam amavit, quique amavit cras amet*—"Tomorrow shall be love for the loveless, and for the lover tomorrow shall be love." The refrain is not the formal beat of an official ode but sounds like a spontaneous and subjective interjection, uttered as the mood strikes the singer's fancy. As little is the *Pervigilium* a folk song. The *trinoctium* of Venus, which is the occasion for the piece, became, under the empire, an organized observance in the state cult. Both aspects of the festival are perfectly blended, and the sentiment expressed by the devotee is as genuine as Sappho's invocation to Aphrodite. In Latin literature it is almost unique in its release of imaginative fancy, in its evocations and blendings of nature and love and life and patriotism. What is depicted is the spring tide of the goddess of love in Sicily, with the Graces and nymphs, Ceres, Bacchus, and Apollo, and Cupid sans bow and arrows, participating in the festival. Everywhere nature awakens from winter's torpor, flowers bloom, birds chatter, and garlanded choirs chant through the glades. By the power of the benign goddess all creatures mate and ensure increase. Rome in particular is grateful to the foam-born goddess for her manifold blessings. But the note of personal elegy emerges at the close: *Illa cantat, nos tacemus: quando ver venit meum?* "The nightingale sings, but we are mute: when is *my* spring coming?"

L. Annaeus Florus (if that was his name; one manuscript calls him Julius) wrote an epitome of Roman history in two books, from the beginnings to the deification of Augustus. From Augustus to his own day, he says (1.8), almost two centuries had elapsed. If, as is more likely, the two centuries are reckoned to Augustus' *floruit* or his assumption of the title of Augustus in 27 b.c., Florus would have written in the Principate of Marcus Aurelius. But if we begin the two centuries with the birth of Augustus in 63 b.c., then our book would be written in the second half of the principate of Hadrian, and Florus would be identified as Hadrian's literary friend of that name. From a Florus of the age of Hadrian we have the fragment of the proem of a dialogue entitled *Vergilius orator an poeta,* reminiscent of the proems to Tacitus' *Dialogue On Orators* and to the *Octavius* of Minucius Felix. The proem seems adult and competent, and it is a pity that the bulk of the composition has gone. To an Annius Florus of the Hadrianic period too are attributed a number of short dactylic and trochaic poems in the *Anthologia Latina.* The subjects are literary commonplaces, mostly love and wine. One motif familiar from Ovid (and Shakespeare) is that of a lover inscribing the name of his beloved on the bark of trees. There are five charming hexameters on the rose which blooms and fades. There is nothing to prove, and nothing to disprove, the identity of the three men. The most considerable remains are of course the epitomes of the history, and these enjoyed great vogue as a textbook as late as the end of the eighteenth century. Their popularity is easy to understand. The books present all the memorable stories of Roman history, and yet are very short, because everything else which pertains to history is eliminated. The style is rhetorical and elegant, but not too turgid or difficult. And most of all, the approach to history was sympathetic to readers whose only other experience of history was the early books of the Bible. The tendency to make Roman history a hagiographa, which first comes to plain view in Livy, is here the main object of the book. Rome is the special object and agent of destiny in operating through history, and "those who read of Roman exploits are learning the history not of a single people but of the human race" (1.1). It is axiomatic that Roman policy and Roman arms must always be successful; even their failures are part of a divine plan, either as rods of chastisement, or means of discipline, or as a trial: "I can only think that the Gallic invasion was inflicted on the Roman people by heaven as a test, because the immortal gods wished to know whether Roman valor deserved the empire of the world."

Dramatic demonstration of the thinness of second-century Latin literature is afforded by the correspondence of Marcus Cornelius Fronto (ca.100–ca.167). Until 1815 Fronto was known only by reputation (Dio 69.8; Lucian, *On Writing History* 21; Aulus Gellius 2.26, 13.23, 19.8, 10, 13), and it was supposed that his merits were sufficient to lend distinction to the whole age. But the body of his writings discovered in that and the following years in Vatican and Ambrosian palimpsests show how vacuous form devoid of content can be. Most of what we know of Fronto's life derives from these remains. He was born in the Roman colony of Cirta, now Constantine, in Numidia. He probably studied at Alexandria, for he later had many friends there, and he tells us that he came late to the study of Latin literature. As teachers he mentions the philosopher Athenodotus, from whom he learned the generous use of similes (*eikones*), and the rhetor Dionysius, whose fable on the Vine and the Holm Oak he quotes. In 143 he was raised to consular rank by Antoninus Pius, the *consul ordinarius* for that year being the eminent Herodes Atticus. With Herodes he was made tutor to the heirs apparent, Marcus Aurelius and Lucius Verus. He remained on terms of intimacy with these two princes for the rest of his life, and his correspondence with them forms the bulk of his literary remains. The correspondence covers some two hundred printed pages and contains letters of Marcus Aurelius, Lucius Verus, and others as well as Fronto's own, and in Greek as well as Latin. The best thing we know about Fronto, indeed, is that so pure a character as Marcus esteemed him so highly, and it is clear that Fronto on his part did not abuse the friendship. There is a certain amount of flattery on either side—Fronto makes Marcus the peer of Julius Caesar and gives Lucius the military genius of a Marius or a Vespasian, and Marcus sets Fronto beside Cato and Gracchus, Sallust, and Cicero. The warmth of the greetings on either side seems effusive, and the jejune contents of the letters makes it difficult to surmise what significant common interests could have held the correspondents together. As his proconsular province, probably ten years after the consulship, the lot gave Fronto Asia, but the gout, of which he frequently complains, supervened, and put a period to his political career. He continued his professions as orator, advocate, and teacher and led a happy family life, though five of his six daughters and the son of the surviving daughter died in infancy. Nothing in the extant correspondence can be dated later than A.D. 166, and it is probable that Fronto died in that or the following year. Marcus set his statue up in the senate and kept his bust among his household gods.

Fronto's reputation as an orator was enormous, but the few sentences and titles we have hardly suffice to show how far his reputation was merited, or how far his practice corresponded to his theory. His theory is plain from the evidence, explicit and implicit, in his letters. Only on the question of placing the appropriate word in the appropriate position does Fronto show any deep conviction. The art of words not only mattered deeply to him, but it was the only thing in the universe that mattered at all. With his peers of the Second Sophistic Fronto sinned not so much in the deification of rhetoric but in studied Philistinism to all other intellectual pursuits. Nothing distressed him more deeply than Marcus Aurelius' decision to prefer philosophy to rhetoric. Fronto did deliver in the senate the attack on Christianity, the only such of which we have record, which evoked Minucius Felix' defense in the *Octavius*. The oration is lost, but from Fronto's general point of view and from the defense of paganism by later humanists like Symmachus we can surmise that Fronto's objections to Christianity were based upon the injury it might work to the traditional forms of classical life and letters.

By his own design and definition, therefore, Fronto's claim is solely as an expert in Latin. In his hands the language is indeed a supple and exact instrument, much easier to follow as it is much less individualized than the language of Apuleius. But an instrument is not an end.

Distaste for philosophy may be excusable, but neither has history or any other serious discipline any meaning for Fronto except as a source for ornamental anecdotes and figures. Frivolities like the *Praise of Smoke and Dust* (211 Naber) or the *Praise of Negligence* (214 Naber) may be acceptable as the pastime of a man who has serious interests elsewhere; but to Fronto such things seem to be central. From the craftsman in words who is impatient of intellectual problems we might expect at least skillful composition, but here Fronto fails us. His *Arion* (237 Naber) is an utterly flattened-out transcript from Herodotus, without Herodotus' freshness and sense of wonder. Equally flat is Fronto's other borrowing from Herodotus, the story of the Ring of Polycrates (217 Naber), which he recounts in a letter consoling Marcus for a military disaster in Parthia. Plato is challenged in the *Eroticus* (in Greek; 255 Naber), which resumes the arguments of Socrates and Lysias in the *Phaedrus* on whether it is more expedient for a beautiful youth to bestow his favors on a lover or a non-lover. There is nothing at all of the lofty moral implications of the *Phaedrus,* nor, on the other hand, is there any unphilosophical erotic heartiness. There are only phrases.

These pieces illustrate the impotence of rhetoric made paramount and the intellectual abnegation involved in the cult of archaism. Scarcely fifty years before, Quintilian had been no less concerned for correct literary usage, but with Quintilian the instrument is still an instrument. He assumes that the writers he recommends will serve his pupils not only as patterns of form but as points of departure for new intellectual achievement. But to prefer remote to immediate predecessors on principle is willfully to ignore progress in thought, indeed, to deny the validity of thought. So far from justifying his period in literature, Fronto condemns it. Latin prose was lifeless and had to await the passionate conviction of Christian writers for vitality to be breathed into it. But the second century still had one vigorous spirit and consummate artist to show.

In Apuleius we encounter the pulsing life, the wit and fantasy and prying curiosity, even a more than amateur interest in philosophy and religion, which we miss in Fronto. His *Metamorphoses,* and especially the story of Cupid and Psyche embedded in it like a jewel, assure Apuleius' position as one of the handful of Latin authors with a legitimate and perennial claim on the attention of lovers of literature. Apuleius' writing, even in fiction, reveals his personality to a special degree, and to a special degree, therefore, the background of his life clarifies his letters. For the life our main sources are the *Apology,* the *Florida,* and the eleventh book of the *Metamorphoses;* the first book of the *Metamorphoses,* which professes to be autobiographical, can scarcely be regarded as such. Apuleius was born in the African colony of Madaura, about eighty miles east of Fronto's Cirta. Madaura was rich, populous, and highly Romanized. Tagaste, about twenty miles north of Madaura, was St. Augustine's native place, and Augustine went to Madaura for his secondary education. Apuleius' father was an important local official and left his sons the considerable fortune of two million sesterces. The date of Apuleius' birth is fixed by allusions to datable officials in his works as A.D. 124 or 125. The praenomen Lucius commonly given him is probably due to identification with the hero of the *Metamorphoses.* From Madaura Apuleius went to Carthage for more advanced education, and thence, probably in 143, to Athens, where he studied philosophy, rhetoric, geometry, music, and poetry. From Athens he traveled widely; he speaks (*Apology* 23) of the expenses of his long study and distant travels and alludes casually to visits in Samos and in Hieropolis in Phrygia. At Athens he became intimate with a younger fellow student named Pontianus, son of the rich widow Pudentilla, of Oea (modern Tripoli), whom Apuleius eventually married. At the end of his student period in Greece he was initiated into the mysteries of Isis at Cenchreae and then went to Rome, probably in 150. There he was initiated into the mysteries of Osiris also and was so diligent in his religious duties that he attained an important position in the cult of Isis and Osiris in Rome. At the same time he prospered as a rhetor and perhaps also as a pleader in Roman courts. Possibly he wrote the *Metamorphoses* in Rome (though this is disputed) and published the book anonymously.

After four or five years Apuleius returned to Africa, apparently with the purpose of taking up the profession of rhetor, which was at the time very rich in profit and prestige, but he was soon seized by wanderlust and decided to go to Alexandria. He fell ill at Oea en route and was there detained; by the manoeuvres of Pontianus, who was afraid his mother would marry a fortune-hunter and he and his brother be cut off, Apuleius went to live in Pudentilla's house, and after a year or so, during which time he gave a number of public lectures with brilliant success, he agreed to marry the opulent widow, who was his senior by some ten years. But Pontianus, who had himself been married in the interval, was instigated by his uncle and his wife's family to prevent his mother's remarriage. Apuleius behaved very handsomely in securing their rights to Pontianus and his brother; Pontianus repented his conduct but died shortly after his mother was married. Pudentilla's relatives continued bitter, and when Apuleius was at the assizes in Sabrata, some forty miles west of Oea, in connection with a suit involving his wife, he was suddenly accused not only of using magic to win Pudentilla but also of having murdered his stepson Pontianus to obtain his fortune. The charge of murder was dropped, but within a few days Apuleius was indicted for the practice of magic and was incidentally accused of being a fop and a debauchee who had married his elderly wife solely for the sake of her money. Of the *Apology,* the remarkable and able defense which Apuleius offered and which is the only forensic speech surviving from imperial times, we shall say more presently. There can be no doubt that Apuleius was acquitted, but he could no longer be comfortable in Oea, and the remainder of his career was spent, as far as we can tell, at Carthage. There he delivered many of the fancy declamations of which fragments are preserved in the *Florida,* and he became the most honored and popular literary figure in the whole province. Carthage decreed a statue in his honor, and the proconsul Aemilianus Strabo promised to erect another. He was appointed to the chief priesthood in the province, the highest honor it could bestow. Sidonius Apollinaris tells us that Pudentilla proved a model wife and took a passionate interest in his work; it is even possible that she bore him a son, if the *Faustine fili* to whom the second book of *De dogmate Platonis* is dedicated refers to a son of the body. The portrait of Apuleius on a contorniate in Paris (reproduced in L. C. Purser's learned and witty *Cupid and Psyche*) is probably imaginary. His opponents called him a *philosophum formosum* (*Apology* 4), and we should expect as much of a successful declaimer, but he retorts that his body is emaciated with study and his hair matted like a lump of tow. There is no evidence for the date of his death, which must have occurred between 170 and 180.

It is from the *Apology* that the details sketched above (except for the Roman interlude, which comes from *Metamorphoses* 11, and the last phase, from the *Florida*) derive, and since that work is a practical pleading rather than a display piece, the *Apology* (it is called *Pro se de magia liber* in the manuscripts) is our best introduction to second-century Latinity as well as very valuable for the abundant light it throws on the private life and intellectual atmosphere of the time. The speech as we have it is too long to have been delivered, but it was probably enlarged for publication, like Cicero's *Pro Milone* or the Younger Pliny's *Panegyric to Trajan*. But the main part of the speech was surely delivered; it is not a wholly fictive speech like Cicero's *Against Verres* or *Second Philippic*. The first portion of the speech (1–65) disposes of the charge of wizardry. With a flamboyant display of learning Apuleius overwhelms his puny adversaries and makes them ludicrous. The second portion (66–end) defends his marriage with Pudentilla and justifies his dealings with his stepsons. The only parallel to the detailed and merciless portraiture of the villainous turpitude of his accusers and the base ingratitude of his stepsons and their unlovely domestic life is Cicero's *Pro Cluentio*. Nor, despite its extravagant Asianism, is the style of the *Apology* as different as we should expect, on the basis of the *Metamorphoses* and the *Florida,* from the classic norm. Here is genuine indignation and the practical necessity of securing acquittal from a serious charge. In prose employed as an instrument for practical ends, then, divagations from the classical norm were only such as might be expected from the natural course of development, remembering the dominant influence of rhetorical education. The display pieces would then fall into a distinct and separate category, where virtuosity in language was an end in itself.

Renascence scholars regarded the peculiarities of Apuleius' style as being due to his African origin and spoke of his *tumor Africus*. Modern scholarship has shown that there is nothing distinctly African either in Apuleius or in other African writers, though each province may have retained words which had fallen into disuse in the capital. Apuleius' style is the style of the second century. Unlike Fronto, who was a conscious archaizer, Apuleius used all available resources, ancient and contemporary, to make his style effective. The noticeable characteristics of that style are balance and symmetry, attained by devices of structure and sound; diffuseness and redundancy, by the use of synonyms, periphrases, and rhetorical repetitions; variety, by conscious syntactical alternations; alliteration and assonance, in many forms; diminutives, Grecisms, neologisms. Walter Pater (*Marius the Epicurean,* Chapter 5) aptly describes Apuleius' style as "full of archaisms and curious felicities in which that generation delighted, quaint terms and images picked from the early dramatists, the life-like phrases of some lost poet preserved by an old grammarian, racy morsels of the vernacular and studied prettinesses."

But it is rather to the *Florida* that "his rococo, very African, and, as it were, perfumed personality" (Pater, Chapter 20) applies. These are excerpts from his epideictic declamations, which Apuleius himself had probably published in four books under some such title as *Orationes.* At a later period some admirer selected an anthology (which is the meaning of *florida*) of choice bits, retaining the book division of the original, which is very unsystematic, for the selected pieces. The excerpts are elaborately polished and have an ornate kind of stateliness, though all are essentially trivial and some grotesque. Some are from speeches on public occasions, some contain moralizations, legends, or picturesque stories. There are, for example, a detailed description of the flight of an eagle (2); the contest of Apollo and Marsyas (3); a note on the flautist Antigenidas (4); remarks on India and the gymnosophists (6); the artistic taste of Alexander the Great (7); a comparison of his own versatility with that of the sophist Hippias (9, cf. 20); on the parrot (12); on the Cynic Crates (14, 22); on Samos, Polycrates, and Pythagoras (15); on the comic poet Philemon (16); on the familiar dispute of the sophist Protagoras and his disciple Euathlos concerning tuition charges (18). The inordinate care lavished on the artistic structure of these pieces and the mesmerizing effect their chanting must have had on their auditors may be apprehended from a passage taken from the first selection:

> *ara floribus redimita*
> *aut spelunca frondibus inumbrata*
> *aut quercus cornibus onerata*
> *aut fagus pellibus coronata*
> *vel enim colliculus sepimine consecratus*
> *vel truncus dolamine effigiatus*
> *vel caespes libamine umigatus*
> *vel lapis unguine delibutus.*

The piece on Philemon is quite attractive for its descriptive power and its artful simplicity; it may be presented here for its own sake, and because Dr. Purser's version succeeds to a degree in reproducing its alliterations, assonances, and other artificialities:

Philemon was a poet of the Middle Comedy, and composed plays for the stage at the same time as Menander. He competed with him, possibly as an inferior, but certainly as a rival, for he often defeated him—one is ashamed to say. You may find in him many sallies of wit, clever complications in his plots, admirably contrived recognitions, characters suited to the subject, maxims applicable to real life, the gay portions not sinking below comedy, the grave portions not soaring into tragedy. We rarely find seductions in his plays: the failings of his human characters are venial, their loves congenial. In him, too, as in the other playwrights, we have the lying procurer, the sighing lover, the sly slave-boy; the cajoling mistress, the coercing wife, the indulging mother; the uncle to scold, the friend to uphold, the soldier bold; gorging parasites, grasping parents, saucy street-girls. By these merits he had long held an eminent position in comedy.

On one occasion he had given a reading of part of a play which he had recently composed; and it happened that he had already come to the third act, wherein, as is usual in comedies, he had delightfully quickened the interest of his hearers, when a sudden shower of rain, just as occurred lately in my case with you, compelled an adjournment of the collected audience and the projected reading. However, he promised, at the request of many present, that without making any break he would finish the recitation on the ensuing day. Accordingly, next day an immense crowd gathers with the greatest eagerness: each one tries to get as near the front as possible: the late comer signs to his friends to keep a seat for him: those at the extremity complain that they are pushed out of the sitting accommodation altogether: the whole theatre is packed and there is a great crush. When quiet was attained, the people begin, those who had not been present to ask about the previous portion of the play, those that had been present to go over what they had heard, and all, when they had the beginning in mind, to wait the sequel. Meanwhile the day went on, and Philemon did not come as had been arranged; some grumbled at the poet for being late, the greater number made excuses for him. But when the delay became unreasonable, and there was no sign of Philemon, some of the more energetic members of the audience were sent to summon him; and they found him lying dead on his couch. He had ceased to breathe and had just become stiff. There he was reposing on his reading-couch in the attitude of thought: he had his fingers still in the fold of the manuscript, his face down on the book he had been reading; but he had no breath of life in him; he was forgetful of his book, and thought not of his audience. Those who had come in stood still for a space, moved by the marvel of such an unexpected event and such a beautiful death. Then they returned to the people, and announced that Philemon, the poet, who was being expected to finish in the theatre an unreal narrative, had at his house completed the real drama of life: his words to the world were, "be happy" and "your hands," to his friends, "be sorry" and "your tears": yesterday's shower was a premonition of their weeping: his play had reached the funeral knell before it reached the marriage bell: and thus, as a most excellent poet had ceased to tread the stage of life, they should go straight from the theatre to his burying, and lay now his ashes in the grave, thereafter his poems in their hearts.

—*L. C. Purser*

Of the same class as the declamations of which we have excerpts in the *Florida* is *On the God of Socrates*. The *daimonion* of which Socrates speaks as directing his conduct in Plato's *Apology*, Apuleius says, was one of the spirits intermediary between God and man who are "in nature animal, in intellect rational, in mind subject to emotion, in material airy, in duration eternal. The first three characteristics they have in common with men; the fourth is peculiar to themselves; the fifth they share with the immortal gods; but they differ from them in being subject to emotion." They are intermediaries in both directions: they execute divine behests for mankind, and they convey to the gods the prayers and offerings of men. The doctrine is ancient; it is found in Hesiod, and in the account of the birth of Eros in Plato's *Symposium*. Plutarch found it extremely useful in reconciling a perfect deity with an imperfectly administered universe, and his writings on the subject, especially *On the Obsolescence of Oracles* and *On the Face in the Moon,* were very influential. Apuleius' treatise certainly follows, if it does not translate, a Greek original. Because it was the first work in Latin on a subject important equally to pagans and Christians, Apuleius' treatise enjoyed a vogue out of all proportion to its merit.

Apuleius has been praised as a *Platonicus* (St. Augustine, *City of God* 8.12), but his *De Platone et eius dogmate* is such a summary as an undergraduate might write. The book begins with a brief biography of Plato and continues with an account of the Platonic theories of the world and the soul, based mostly on the *Timaeus*. The second book, addressed to *Faustine fili,* summarizes Plato's views on ethics and politics, drawing largely on *Gorgias, Republic,* and *Laws.* These

books show no real knowledge of Plato, but are the heaped-up learning of the rhetorician, with no judgment or critical faculty. It has
been suggested that Apuleius' immediate authority for his Platonic
writings was his contemporary Albinus. The *Peri hermeneias* on
formal logic which used to be regarded as the third book of *De
Platone* is Aristotelian and Stoic rather than Platonic, and is a separate work, if indeed it is Apuleius' If the *fili* in the dedication of the
second book is literal, the work must derive from Apuleius' last years;
if it is metaphorical, the book may have been written at any period
in Apuleius' career. *De mundo* ("On the Universe") is a free and often
inaccurate translation of an extant Greek treatise entitled *Peri kosmou,*
falsely ascribed to Aristotle and dedicated to one Alexander, probably
the apostate nephew of Philo Judaeus. This dedication Apuleius alters
to *Faustine fili,* leaving the impression that the work was his own.
Efforts to save Apuleius' honor by making him author of both the
Greek and Latin are misguided. The treatise strikes a note of lofty
monotheism almost Christian in character. Other philosophical translations by Apuleius will be listed among his lost works at the end of
the present section.

We come now to the *Metamorphoses,* upon which Apuleius' reputation in literature rests, for without the *Metamorphoses* he would
have been forgotten by all but professional scholars. Apuleius himself
does not speak of the book, and it is difficult to know at what point in
his career he wrote it. His accusers at Oea did not mention the work,
as they might well have done, if they had known of it, to prove
Apuleius' interest in magic, nor does Apuleius himself allude to it in
the passages in the *Florida* (9 and 20) in which he lists the categories
of his numerous writings. Furthermore, the nephew of Plutarch
named Sextus, with whom Lucius claims kinship in the opening chapter of the *Metamorphoses,* was still alive in 160, and it is thought unlikely that he would be mentioned in such a connection if he were.
These considerations point to a date late in Apuleius' life. On the
other hand, it is held that the ebullience of the writing implies youth
and that the accounts of the initiations and other biographical details
in the eleventh book reflect recent experience, and hence that the
Metamorphoses must have been written in Apuleius' Roman period.
It would then have been published anonymously, and even if the authorship were known in Rome it would not be known in Africa for

Apuleius' detractors to make use of the argument; nor would Apuleius himself, in view of his position of dignity in Africa, have subsequently cared to advertise his authorship of such an undignified work. On neither side are the arguments completely cogent. The genius of the work is timeless, and perhaps it is not essential that we date it to a definite year in its author's life.

More tantalizing is the question of the relationship of our *Metamorphoses* to the lost *Metamorphoses* which Photius attributes to Lucius of Patras, and to the brief *Lucius; or Ass* extant in the corpus of Lucian. This *Lucius; or Ass* is held to be an epitome, by another hand, of the *Metamorphoses* of which Lucian was the author. As in his *True History,* Lucian's aim was satire, the objects here being magicians, corrupt priests, frail women. Lucian's basis was doubtless a folk tale, but his *Lucius* represents the credulity, gullibility, and bestiality of all mankind. The main outline of Apuleius' plot is identical with that of the Greek *Lucius; or Ass,* but Apuleius' story is clearly the later because of the additions in matter and tone which can only be Apuleius' own. In matter there are the Milesian tales, the story of Cupid and Psyche, and the great eleventh book portraying the worship of Isis who redeemed Lucius from ass to human. And though Apuleius retains some of the earthiness of the original and reveals glimpses of Lucian's wit and satire, the tone of the whole is very different. Apuleius' *Metamorphoses* is neither a comic romance nor a satire, as Lucian's clearly was, but a serious novel. It is, as Miss Haight has written,

a sort of Pilgrim's Progress of the Ass-Man in quest for knowledge of marvels. . . . Apuleius exalted the tale by making the journeyings of Lucius a search for the spiritual meaning of life. His hero walks alone. The love romance in his story, the Cupid and Psyche tale, starts with the Platonic conception of the relation of Eros and Psyche, Love and the Soul, and therefrom is lifted to the realm of the Olympian gods. And finally the transformation of Lucius is no chance event, but a salvation wrought out by his mystic worship of Isis.

Apuleius' story is told in the first person by its hero Lucius. Riding over the mountains in Thessaly, Lucius encounters two other travelers and is told the story of a horrible murder by a witch in Hypata, the town to which Lucius is going. There he is entertained by Milo, whose wife Pamphile turns out to be a witch. At a party given by his kinswoman Byrrhaena he hears another horrible story of mutilation by a witch, and on his way home he kills three robbers who prove to have been animated wineskins. He makes love to the maid Fotis, who permits him to see Pamphile transform herself into an owl. He too wishes to transform himself but by a mistake in the unguent is turned into an ass (retaining his human faculties, except for voice). He need only eat roses to regain his human shape, but before Fotis can bring any, robbers attack the house and carry him off. At the robbers' hideout he hears three fine stories of robber chiefs and sees the robbers bring in the beautiful Charite, who was kidnaped for ransom on her wedding night. To console the girl, the old woman who cooked for the robbers tells her the story of Cupid and Psyche (4.28–6.24), which is a brilliant masterpiece of narrative. The beautiful maiden and her invisible lover and jealous sisters recur in fairy stories the world over, and the domesticated Venus and her unruly son bear unmistakable affinities to the middle-class Olympians in Apollonius of Rhodes; surely the story is not forced to make allegory obvious, and most scholars have denied it any such implication. But with Apuleius' interest in initiations and mysteries and with the whole of the *Metamorphoses* having the character of a quest, it seems impossible that the fortunes of a Psyche (= "Soul") who finally attains peace and gives birth to Voluptas (= "Delight") can have had no allegorical meaning for Apuleius, though it may be difficult to spell the meaning out consistently. Charite is rescued by her lover, disguised as a robber, but he is subsequently murdered by a rival and avenged by Charite. In his asinine form Lucius then witnesses the obscene orgies of lewd Syrian priests and hears four naughty Milesian tales—"The Tale of the Tub," "The Baker's Wife," "The Lost Slippers," "The Fuller's Wife." These are of the type that the Parthian Surena was shocked at finding (doubtless in the Latin translation of Cornelius Sisenna) in the baggage of a Roman officer at Carrhae in 53 B.C. Next is a story of the oppression of a poor family by an arrogant nobleman and the death of three brothers who came to the family's aid. There follows the story of an amorous stepmother who tries to poison her unresponsive stepson, and then the story of five murders committed by a sadistic woman. As part of her punishment it is proposed to display her publicly in sexual union with Lucius, who finds the prospect so abhorrent that he runs away from Corinth to Cenchreae, and there exhausted falls asleep on the seashore.

This brings us to Book 11, which is a moving religious document and affords us a glimpse of the beauty of holiness in a cult elsewhere described as compounded of superstition and chicanery. As Lucius sleeps, Isis in her refulgent beauty appears to him and promises her aid. Amidst the brilliant pageantry of the spring festival for the launching of her sacred vessel the priest of Isis offers Lucius a garland of roses, and he resumes his human shape. Determined to devote himself to the service of his savior, he undergoes the arduous preparations for initiation, receiving new visions, and finally, alone in her temple at night, being vouchsafed the experience of death, rebirth, and revelation which only the elect may attain (11.23):

I approached the borderland of death, trod the threshold of Proserpina, was borne through all the elements and returned; at midnight I saw the sun shining with a brilliant light; I approached the gods of the nether and upper world and adored them in person near at hand.

—*Elizabeth H. Haight*

Lucius then went to Rome for the service of Isis, was by her direction twice initiated into the mysteries of Osiris, and finally attained the dignity of becoming a *pastophorus* of the cult. So far from being an ill-assorted appendage to a series of picaresque and scabrous stories, Book 11 gives unity and direction to the whole and makes of it a spiritual quest. It is only northerly latitudes that find ribaldry in church or a flash of spirit in the smoking room incongruous.

It remains to say a word of the works of Apuleius no longer extant, which were probably greater in volume than those we have preserved. He himself claims to have written in virtually all forms and on virtually all subjects (*Florida* 20): "Empedocles composed [scientific] poems, Plato dialogues, Socrates hymns, Epicharmus mimes [reading *mimos* for *modos*], Xenophon researches, Xenocrates satires. Your Apuleius has cultivated all of these and all nine of the Muses." A number of lost works are mentioned by Apuleius himself or attributed to him by other writers. At *Apology* 6 Apuleius cites an eight-line poem to Calpurnianus from his *Ludicra,* which was a volume of miscellaneous light verse. At *Florida* 17 he speaks of a *carmen de virtutibus Orfiti,* and at 18, of hymns to Aesculapius written in both

Greek and Latin. There is also extant a verse translation of an obscene passage from the *Anekhomenos* of Menander. His prose works are more numerous. Short fragments from a second novel, called *Hermagoras,* are quoted by Priscian and Fulgentius. Priscian also mentions an *Epitome historiarum,* and John Lydus an *Eroticus,* presumably a collection of love adventures. Many of his speeches must have been lost: he mentions one (*Apology* 55) on the majesty of Aesculapius delivered at Oea, and in *Florida* 16 he promises to write an oration of thanks to Aemilianus Strabo. St. Augustine refers to a speech against citizens of Oea who objected to the erection of a statue in his honor. He appears to have written much on natural history. He himself mentions his *Quaestiones naturales,* written in both Greek and Latin, and speaks particularly of a treatise *De piscibus* (*Apology* 36, 38, 40). Various later writers also mention *De arboribus, De re rustica, Medicinalia, Astronomica, De musica,* and a translation of the *Arithmetica* of Nicomachus. There is also mention of a *De republica,* a translation of Plato's *Phaedo,* a work *De proverbiis,* and *Quaestiones conviviales.* On the other hand, a number of works not Apuleius' have come down under his name: a number of fragments on medicines and the *Asclepius,* a dialogue between Hermes Trismegistus and Asclepius conducted in an Egyptian temple and dealing solemnly with questions of the gods, the universe, and fate. Though of no original value, this dialogue has importance as one of the latest documents of a paganism aware of its imminent dissolution.

Apuleius is a more characteristic phenomenon in Latin literature than might at first glance seem likely. Latin literature was from its beginnings consciously "literary," and Apuleius succeeds in making his very "literary" Latin to the highest degree effective. Latin literature from the beginning set itself the task of harvesting, broadcasting, and perpetuating the artistic achievements of its predecessors; Apuleius' harvest was rich and varied, and he did broadcast and perpetuate it, with his special cachet. And from the beginning Latin literature at its best endowed its borrowings with a gravity and seriousness of purpose. Such gravity and seriousness are not wanting in Apuleius.

In earlier pages we have encountered retailers of anecdotes—the Elder Seneca in rhetoric, the Elder Pliny in natural science, Frontinus in stratagems—but these were men with a mature interest in a scholarly specialty, which their anecdotes were calculated to illustrate. It is significant of the literary temper of the second and third centuries that littérateurs now made collections of piquant anecdotes for their own sake. Among the Greeks we have Athenaeus' *Doctors at Dinner* and Aelian's *Various Stories;* even respectable thinkers like Plutarch and Clement of Alexandria were attracted by the habit. Among the Romans we have Aulus Gellius (ca. A.D. 123–ca. 165), whose *Attic Nights* is a well-stuffed rag bag. Of his life little is known; he practiced law and held a minor judgeship, he knew Fronto and was entertained in Athens, where he studied philosophy, by Herodes Atticus, and he made extracts from a large number of Greek and Latin writers which he published in twenty books. Of his procedure in the latter enterprises he tells us in his preface:

In the arrangement of my material I have adopted the same haphazard order that I had previously followed in collecting it. For whenever I had taken in hand any Greek or Latin book, or had heard anything worth remembering, I used to jot down whatever took my fancy, of any and every kind, without any definite plan or order; and such notes I would lay away as an aid to my memory, like a kind of literary storehouse, so that when the need arose of a word or a subject which I chanced for the moment to have forgotten, and the books from which I had taken it were not at hand, I could readily find and produce it. It therefore follows, that in these notes there is the same variety of subject that there was in those former brief jottings which I had made without order or arrangement, as the fruit of instruction of reading in various lines. And since, as I have said, I began to amuse myself by assembling these notes during the long winter nights which I spent on a country-place in the land of Attica, I have therefore given them the title of *Attic Nights*.

—*J. C. Rolfe*

It is hence as difficult to characterize the literary structure of the *Attic Nights* as it is to find a plot in the telephone directory or dramatic interest in a mail-order catalogue. But in much the same way as a mail-order catalogue may be, the *Attic Nights* are instructive and entertaining. No fewer than 275 authors are mentioned by name, and Gellius is on the whole accurate and conscientious. If he borrowed from predecessors like himself instead of drawing exclusively from original sources, so have all anthologizers before Gellius and after him done. His range is wide, but his chief concern is with literature—criticism, textual matters, grammar, biographical notes—yet his antiquarian interests include law, religion, history, and many other matters. Scholars complain that he had no professional competence in any of these fields, but a modern whose interest in classical antiquity is humanistic rather than scientific will find in Gellius a kindred spirit who had the advantage of being the immediate heir of the full tradition. His eye is caught by the right things, and his extracts and comments answer many questions that rise to the mind of modern readers of ancient books; without him our picture of the background to our ancient books would have many gaps now filled. He is interested, it is true, in the foliage rather than the fruit of ancient literature and philosophy; but the foliage is essential to the fruit and in itself a pleasing thing, as Boswell well remarked at the outset of his *Johnson*.

XIX

THE THIRD CENTURY

WE HAVE NO SUCH REFRESHING OASES AS APULEIUS
or the *Pervigilium Veneris* to enliven the arid third century. The most
competent writing of the age, aside from the Christian works which
will be treated separately, was in the field of jurisprudence, where we
encounter such significant names as Salvius Julianus, Gaius, Pomponius, Papinian, Ulpian, and Paulus; but these hardly fall in the
purview of such a work as this. What is left is mostly to be classed,
for better or worse, as history. The most imposing single monument,
and the most exasperating by reason of its insoluble critical difficulties,
is the *Scriptores historiae Augustae*. In the *Scriptores* no fewer than
thirty-five biographers of emperors are cited, and though most of
these are imaginary, to lend spurious authority to invented details,
there must in fact have been a great deal of biographical writing, in
imitation and continuation of the work of Suetonius. Of two of the
biographers cited in the *Scriptores* we have independent record, and
these two, Marius Maximus and Aelius Junius Cordus, are worth
mention.

Of Marius Maximus we are told by Ammianus Marcellinus (28.
4.14) that people who avoided other reading like poison eagerly de-
voured the books of Juvenal and Maximus. In the piquant gossip
which was the basis of his vogue he outdid his model Suetonius, of
whose work his own was an avowed continuation. His twelve *Lives*
began with Nerva (A.D. 97), where Suetonius stops, and continued
to Elagabalus (A.D. 218-22). He is not only more garrulous but less
critical than Suetonius. His merit is that he appended what purported
to be accurate transcripts of official documents. Maximus was continued and supplemented by Aelius Junius Cordus, who seems to
have paid special attention to the lives of Alexander Severus (A.D.
222-35) and Gordian III (A.D. 238-44). His insatiable curiosity concerning petty details of dress and food and scandals descends to the
ludicrous, but he was doubtless a diligent collector of such things and
so might be of value to a judicious historian. Of the *Scriptores* Capito-

linus alone mentions him, and always in derogation, but he doubtless used him far more than he admits.

Beginning with Tacitus himself, Roman history came increasingly to be written around the lives of the emperors, and as the imperial office overshadowed and subsumed all lesser aspects of national life, it was natural that historical curiosity should center upon the lives of the emperors. For us the precipitate of this diligent curiosity is crystallized in the biographies of the collection entitled in its principal manuscript *Vitae diversorum principum et tyrannorum a divo Hadriano usque ad Numerianum diversis compositae,* and after Casaubon generally called *Historia Augusta.* The collection comprises thirty biographies, most of a single emperor, some of a group brought together because they were kin or contemporary. Not only the reigning *Augusti* but also the *Caesares,* or heirs presumptive, and various pretenders are included. The biographies are attributed to six different authors, and are addressed to Diocletian, Constantine, and other important personages. The authors and the *Lives* attributed to them are as follows:

1. Aelius Spartianus: *Hadrian, Aelius, Didius Julianus, Severus, Pescennius Niger, Caracalla,* and *Geta.* The last is addressed to Constantine; the others, except *Hadrian* and *Caracalla,* are addressed to Diocletian. The preface of the *Aelius* mentions the Caesars Galerius Maximianus and Constantius Chlorus, who were nominated in 293; this would imply that they were written between that year and 305, when Diocletian retired.

2. Julius Capitolinus: *Pius, Marcus Aurelius, Verus, Pertinax, Clodius Albinus, Macrinus, The Maximini, The Gordiani,* and *Maximus and Balbinus. Marcus, Verus,* and *Macrinus* are addressed to Diocletian; *Albinus, Maximini,* and *Gordiani* to Constantine, evidently after the fall of Licinius in 324.

3. Vulcacius Gallicanus: *Avidius Cassius,* addressed to Diocletian.

4. Aelius Lampridius: *Commodus, Diadumenianus, Elagabalus,* and *Severus Alexander.* The last two are addressed to Constantine, being composed, the author says, at Constantine's request.

5. Trebellius Pollio wrote the *Lives* from *Philip* to *Claudius,* but those from *Philip* to *Valerian* are lost, and we have left only the *Valeriani* (in part), the *Gallieni,* the *Thirty Tyrants,* and *Claudius.* These biographies were addressed not to the emperor but to some high offi-

cial whose name has been lost. They were finished, according to Vopiscus (*Aurelian* 2.1), in 303.

6. Flavius Vopiscus: *Aurelian, Tacitus, Probus, Firmus* and his three fellow tyrants, and *Carus* and his sons. These are dedicated to various friends. The city prefect Junius Tiberianus, at whose request he says he wrote, held office in 303–4, and this date is confirmed as marking the approximate beginning of his work by the reference to Constantine as *imperator* (305–6) and to Diocletian as *iam privatus* (after 305). Internal evidence shows that this collection was completed before the death of Diocletian in 316, perhaps even before the death of Galerius in 311.

Until the end of the nineteenth century the document was accepted at its face value, though perceptive critics like Gibbon were aware of many of its historical inaccuracies. But in the 1890s critics began to ask questions concerning the *Historia Augusta* which have not yet received, and seem unlikely ever to receive, satisfactory answers. Why, for example, does the same author write *Lives* widely separated in time, and why, on the other hand, do the separate authors of the earlier *Lives* show such close similarity in construction and language? Why do the minor biographies virtually repeat the material of the major biographies, and why does Spartianus in the *Niger* refer to the *Albinus* as his work when our *Albinus* is attributed to Capitolinus? Numerous other inconsistencies and anachronisms were noticed, and it was then maintained that the whole *Historia Augusta* is not, as it professes to be, the work of a group of writers writing early in the fourth century, but the product of a single forger of the end of the fourth or early fifth century, who fabricated the purported date and authorship as a literary device to enhance the value of his work. The extreme skepticism of this position has proven untenable, but it has become evident that the biographies as they stand cannot have been written by the six authors as they are traditionally distributed. Differences in method, presentation, purpose, and stylistic traits make it impossible to believe that all are the work of a single writer. On the other hand, the whole collection must have been worked over by a single hand, for almost every biography has interpolated material, sometimes at inopportune places, and similar rhetorical passages and stock phrases recur in all the biographies. On the basis of contents, manner, and purported date it has been found possible to divide the *Lives* into groups, as it happens six in number, though by no means identical with the grouping assigned in the manuscript. Four belong to the time of Diocletian, and two to that of Constantine. Then some rather ignorant and incompetent writer, probably at the end of the fourth century, combined and worked over the whole, adding much new material, some from Eutropius and Victor or their common source. This later editor, whose identity cannot be established, also added most of the hundred and fifty "documents" cited in the work.

The general scheme for all the biographies is the same, all being modeled on the *Lives* of Suetonius. The scheme, sometimes obscured by expansion, compression, or digression, is: (a) ancestry; (b) career previous to accession; (c) policy and events of reign; (d) personal traits and habits; ( ) death; (f) personal appearance; (g) reputation after death. Suetonius had flavored his *Lives* generously with gossip, scandalous anecdotes, and documents, and the *Historia Augusta* outdid him in all these particulars. The sources of much of this material were Marius Maximus and Aelius Junius Cordus, and it seems most ample in the lives of the men who never attained to empire and whose lives therefore had to be padded out. Many of these minutiae doubtless rested on good authority, and though historians properly scorn them as trivial and frivolous, a reader may still relish them for their own sake—and justify his discreditable appetite by imagining himself edified by sociological data and deterrent examples. The proem to the *Elagabalus,* for example, is like the lurid jacket which promises that both titillation and moral uplift are to be found in the novel within:

The life of Elagabalus Antoninus, also called Varius, I should never have put into writing—hoping that it might not be known that he was emperor of the Romans—were it not that before him this same imperial office had had a Caligula, a Nero, and a Vitellius. But, just as the selfsame earth bears not only poisons but also grain and other helpful things, not only serpents but flocks as well, so the thoughtful reader may find himself some consolation for these monstrous tyrants.

—*David Magie*

A more pernicious practice, imitated from Suetonius, is the inclusion of alleged documents. Suetonius actually had access to the imperial archives, but there is no reason to suppose that Maximus and Cordus or the authors of the *Historia Augusta* had, and the letters, speeches, decrees, and acclamations found in that work are highly suspicious. It has been shown that letters purporting to have been written by different persons not only contain historical errors but show identical tricks of expression. On the other hand, the comments made upon the letters are inconsistent with their contents, and hence it is clear that the compiler inserted the documents himself, with or without knowledge of their spuriousness. Of countless other obvious interpolations, varying from a sentence to several pages, many were doubtless introduced by the compiler and others by later users of the book. These factors produce a very uneven and badly organized book. The book is nevertheless far from being the dullest in Latin, and a reader who is warned against accepting everything in the *Historia Augusta* as literal truth—and is willing to confess low tastes otherwise—will find the book interesting not only for its picture of the strange habits of a marked group of men, but also for lights upon the history of the empire which a more judicious book would deny him.

A similar cross-illumination, but far less lurid, is afforded by the corpus of twelve cloyingly fulsome orations addressed to various emperors on special occasions. Pliny the Younger's *Panegyric* of Trajan is the model for the rest, and its inclusion doubtless assured the preservation of the entire group. The others, indubitably genuine and, cautiously used, a valuable historical source are: 2, to Maximian, on April 21 (the birthday of Rome) 289, in some northerly city of the Empire; 3, to Maximian for his birthday; 4, a petition, probably by Eumenius, to rebuild the schools of Autun; 5, to Constantius, March 1, 297, on the subjugation of Britain; 6, for the marriage of Constantine and Fausta, 307; 7, for Constantius, on the birthday of Treves, 310; 8, thanksgiving to Constantine in the name of Treves; 9, felicitation to Constantine for his victory over Maxentius, at Treves, 313; 10, Nazarius on Constantine for the fifth year of his accession, 321; 11, Mamertinus on Julian, 362; 12, Pacatus Drepanius on Theodosius, 389. Names of their authors are attached only to the last three, but there is a sameness about all, so that determination of individual authorship signifies but little. All seem to follow a fixed scheme. The actual merits of their subjects are lauded in the most extravagant terms, even neutral actions are made to seem miracles of wisdom and beneficence, and derelictions are exculpated until they seem merits. No abuse is too vile for those who opposed the subject's plans or policy.

Christianity is not mentioned. The style of these orations is remarkably classical, without either the archaism of Fronto or the preciosity of Apuleius. Pliny and indirectly Cicero are their models, and they follow them faithfully. The study of eloquence was diligently and widely pursued in Gaul, and perhaps the Gallic school was not affected by the fashions of the capital.

The only poet the century has to show is M. Aurelius Olympius Nemesianus, who is praised highly in the *Historia Augusta* (*Carinus* 11.2) as an author of *Halieutica, Cynegetica,* and *Nautica* (perhaps for *Ixieutica*), didactic poems (like those of the Oppians in Greek) on fishing, hunting, and perhaps fowling. The 325 hexameters of the *Cynegetica* which survive, and Nemesianus' *Eclogues* (which were long credited to Calpurnius) do not justify this praise. The *Cynegetica* opens with a long-winded introduction (1–103), in which the poet justifies his choice of subject on the grounds that mythological material has been exhausted and promises that his next work will be a glorification of the warlike prowess of Carus' sons, Numerianus and Carinus. The poem must therefore have been written between the deaths of Carus and Numerianus, that is, between September, 283 and September, 284. There follows a long section on dogs, a shorter one on horses, and a fragmentary section on nets and other hunting gear. The framework of the *Eclogues* follows Vergil closely, and whole lines are borrowed from Calpurnius. The Bacchanal of the third *Eclogue* has charm but is certainly a rendering of a Hellenistic original. The fourth *Eclogue* is a singing match between two shepherds and contains a refrain, reminiscent of the *cras amet* of the *Pervigilium Veneris,* repeated ten times: *Cantet amat quod quisque, levant et carmina curas,* "Let each sing his love, songs too lighten cares." Nemesianus' verse exhibits correct technique; what is lacking is poetic inspiration.

Altogether without inspiration are the so-called *Dicta Catonis,* 142 apophthegms in hexameter distichs divided into four books, which enjoyed a vogue out of all proportion to their merit throughout the Middle Ages. Every dialect of Europe had its own translation of these *dicta;* many clichés of daily speech derive from them. To seek out the sources for such a snowball conglomerate is a futile pastime. Some of the apophthegms are like those elsewhere attributed to such ancient worthies as Pythagoras, Phocylides, or Chilon; some resemble apophthegms in Publilius Syrus, and some may actually derive from an early collection ascribed to Cato. The collection underwent many alterations after it was made, chiefly in the direction of Christianization. The form of the *Dicta* is as infantile as the matter. In the last lines the author explains that he could not use elegant words and still get his sayings into two lines.

XX

PAGANISM AT BAY: FOURTH-CENTURY PROSE

NO DISPARAGEMENT OF THE MIRACULOUS ELEMENT
in the conversion of Constantine to Christianity need be involved in
the observation that his recognition of Christianity as the religion
of the empire was at the same time politically expedient. Gibbon
makes the barbarian invasions and the rise of Christianity responsible
for the decline of the Roman Empire and speaks of the great fabric
falling by its own weight. In terms of history the latter expression is
meaningless, and Gibbon's causes are rather symptoms. Economic
deterioration, social tensions, and administrative inequalities aggra-
vated one another in a vicious circle. The gulf between the haughty
and ostentatious rich and the poor they exploited grew so great that
the latter sometimes welcomed barbarian invaders as liberators. The
third and fourth centuries saw a great upsurge of otherworldly cults,
with Christianity only one of a number of salvationist faiths. Mithra-
ism was for a time, and Neoplatonism continued to be, a serious rival
to Christianity. Indeed, when the latter became politically secure and
stepped out of its humble conventicles, Neoplatonism assumed the
complexion of an otherworldly communion devoted only to things of
the spirit. Efficient and ruthless Diocletian's formal division of the
empire is a plain sign that its organization was breaking down, and
by Constantine's day, as that gifted ruler saw, the only institution
sufficiently catholic and disciplined to unite the empire and preserve
the state was the Church with its episcopal organization. Constantine's
revolutionary measure transformed a fractious opposition into a pillar
of strength.

Rome had assimilated the bearers of many exotic cults into its body
politic, but the Christians posed a new problem in that their possession of exclusive truth involved the denial of all other forms of belief and hence of the prerogatives of the state. The Christians owed
complete allegiance to a power which transcended Rome, and hence
there could be no other issue of the conflict between them and Rome

save that one or the other must eventually yield. But the opposition
to the increasing power of Christianity, at least as reflected in our
literature, was motivated not so much by political as by cultural considerations. Other innovations could be assimilated into the stream
of Roman tradition, or at least would not endanger its existence. The
early Christians in Rome were outside the pale of Roman culture,
but when men like Tertullian and Cyprian came to use good Latin
for their propaganda they vehemently rejected the old culture as being
shot through with paganism. (It is for this reason that these authors
must be treated separately, as will be explained more fully in the last
chapter.) Noble Romans like Symmachus and his friends were moved
not by loyalty to the hapless Olympians (whom no one longer took
seriously) but by urgent concern for the survival of the accumulated
values of culture which had been elaborated and made precious by
a millennium of cherished devotion and which alone made civilized
life possible. Defenders of paganism at first paid little heed to the
culturally and socially despised group, whom they inclined to consider as Jewish sectaries, and when they awoke to what they regarded
a real peril it was already unsafe to speak freely. We have no such
outspoken polemic on the pagan as on the Christian side.

But on the lips of a contemporary of Ambrose, Jerome, Augustine,
Chrysostom, and Theodosius such an expression as Macrobius' *Vetustas quidem nobis semper, si sapimus, adoranda est* (*Saturnalia* 3.14.2)
—"Antiquity we must always venerate, if we are wise"—has special
significance. Though not the most impressive writer of the fourth
century, Macrobius supplies our most faithful mirror of its intellectual
climate. Aside from his name, Ambrosius Theodosius Macrobius, and
his title, *vir clarissimus et illustris,* which implies some official preferment, we know nothing of the man except what may be inferred from
his *Saturnalia* and *Commentary on Scipio's Dream.* He is obviously
a man of great culture, in the sense of knowing the best that has been
thought and said in the world, and also of sound independent judgment. The *Saturnalia* belongs to the same category as the *Attic Nights*
or the *Doctors at Dinner,* but Macrobius' own personality is much
more evident in his work than Aulus Gellius' or Athenaeus' in theirs.
His dedication of the *Saturnalia* to his son Eustachius says candidly
that the book is a medley from writers of all ages, Greek and Latin,
sometimes in their actual words, yet with a new quality as having

been digested and assimilated by a single mind. We are introduced to
a little group of gentlemen who meet to celebrate the Saturnalia by a
friendly discussion of literary, antiquarian, and philosophic subjects.
Most are known to us from the history of the day or from their own
writings, which express opinions like those Macrobius assigns to them.
Praetextatus, at whose house the company first assembles to keep the
Saturnalia, is a scholar and antiquary, a statesman and philosopher,
the hierophant of a half dozen cults, formerly prefect of Rome and
proconsul of Achaea. His dignity, urbanity, piety, grave humor, abundant erudition, and skill in drawing out his friends make him in all
respects the proper president for the feast of reason. Flavian the
Younger, more active in the affairs of the world than Praetextatus,
has only a small share in the conversation. Q. Aurelius Symmachus
is the noble champion of conservatism and the patron of literature
whose own writings we shall presently discuss. Two members of the
house of Albinus are chiefly remarkable for their worship of Vergil.
Servius, who remains our indispensable commentator on Vergil,
carries his erudition with grace and modesty. The rough manners
and uncouth opinions of Evangelus (the name is not necessarily significant) supply a foil to the correct deportment of the rest. The
physician Disarius was a friend of Ambrose; Horus, as his name
shows, was a foreigner. Of Praetextatus and Symmachus it may be
said that they had no small part in preserving classical culture to
Europe. The ages of Macrobius' characters are left vague, and the
conversational form is sometimes forgotten, as when a definite reference to an author is given as in a written treatise.

The astonishing range of the conversation covers everything that
a Roman gentleman needed to know. There are antiquarian matters,
such as the origin of the Saturnalia, of the calendar, of the *toga
praetexta;* derivations and etymologies of words; much literary history
and criticism, especially of Cicero and Vergil; discussions of medicine,
physiology, and astronomy; of religion and philosophy, reflecting the
Neoplatonist syncretism of all cults; of the ethics of slavery and suicide
(only Evangelus is contemptuous of slaves); of table manners and the
witticisms of famous men; on whether the egg or the hen came first.
The heterogeneous conversation does nevertheless set forth an organic
body of thought and a distinctive philosophical approach. There is
no hint of Christianity, and the silence cannot be accidental; one of

the Albini had a Christian wife, and the other was very probably himself a Christian. Apparently a policy of silence was conventional among writers of the pagan party, as we shall see in other cases.

The Neoplatonist faith, involving a cult of the sun, to which Macrobius and his friends adhered, is set forth clearly in his *Commentary on Scipio's Dream*. As has been remarked in the pages on Cicero, the *Dream* as presented in Macrobius was the only portion of the *Republic* known until the discovery of other sections in a palimpsest during the last century. Macrobius remarks on the successors of Plato, putting Plotinus on an equality with the master, and speaks of the propriety of the use of fiction and of dreams. The doctrine he presents is as follows. The universe is the temple of God, like him eternal and filled with his presence. He is the first cause, the source and origin of all that is and seems to be. By the overflowing fertility of his majesty he created from himself Mind (*mens*), which retains its author's image as long as it looks towards him; when it looks backwards it creates Soul (*anima*). Soul in turn keeps the likeness of Mind while it looks towards Mind, but when it turns its gaze away it degenerates, and though itself incorporeal it gives rise to bodies celestial (stars) and terrestrial (men, beasts, vegetables). There is a real kinship between man and the stars and between man and God. Thus all things from the highest to lowest are held together in an intimate and unbroken chain, which is what Homer meant by the golden chain let down by God from heaven to earth. When the soul is tempted by desire for body it falls from its abiding place with its brethren the stars, passes through the seven spheres that separate heaven from earth, and in its passage acquires component qualities of the nature of man, shedding its attributes, in various degrees, and forgetting its heavenly home in a kind of intoxication. The music of the spheres is very real (2.3.11): "Everything that lives therefore falls under the power of music, since the heavenly soul by which the universe is animated took its origin from music." Descent into the body is a kind of death, for body (*soma*) is also tomb (*sema*), from which the soul can rise only at the body's death. The real man is the soul which dominates the things of sense and is immortal. But though death of the body means life to the soul, the soul may not anticipate its bliss by a voluntary act but must purify itself as long as there is a possibility for improvement; heaven is open only to those who win purity. The body is not only a

tomb; it is a hell (*infera*). Cicero had made patriotism the highest
virtue; Macrobius knows of a higher, to wit, contemplation of the
divine, for the earth is but a point in the universe, and glory but a
transient thing. The wise man is he who does his duty upon earth,
with his eyes fixed upon heaven.

Such was the doctrine which animated enlightened pagans and
many nominal Christians, including Boethius himself. Macrobius
was not so successful as Boethius in writing a piece of literature that
can be read with pleasure simply as such and not for its reflection of
the thought and knowledge of his time, but he is responsible for communicating to the Middle Ages a mass of information and a point of
view. It has been conjectured that the heliocentric theory as recorded
in Macrobius made Columbus' adventure possible. Chaucer's account
of his own dream in the *Parlement of Foules* starts from his reading
of *Scipio's Dream* with the commentary of Macrobius.

Much more obvious to the contemporary Roman than the religious
revolution was the peril arising from the ominous stirring of the barbarians beyond and soon within the borders of the empire. It was this
more dramatic confrontation that awakened a sense of history. Ammianus Marcellinus tells us (31.5.11) that many persons thought
Rome "was never before overspread by such a dark cloud of misfortune" as that initiated by the disaster at Adrianople in 378. He calls
such persons "historical ignoramuses" (*antiquitatum ignari*), and
cites as proof that Rome would weather the storm the long series of
earlier barbarian threats, beginning with the invasion of the Cimbri
and the Teutons, which Rome had happily survived. This was a common conviction with a certain class of writers and recurs in Claudian
and in Rutilius Namatianus. The optimism of Ammianus and his
fellows was, we know, ill founded, and the ignoramuses proved to be
right. But the division of opinion shows that historical discussion
was active and that the fourth century had a special interest in history.

In Ammianus Marcellinus the fourth century can in fact boast of
a third writer of history to stand beside Livy and Tacitus. In Latinity
Ammianus is inferior to the classic historians—he learned Latin late
in life—but in maturity of historical grasp and in devotion to historical
truth he may well be regarded as superior. It is natural that the writers
of Rome's Golden Age should have preempted the interest of European readers, and natural too, when nationalisms were rising in

Europe and expanding to empires, that the formative period of Rome should occupy the center of attention. But the fourth century was also a highly critical juncture for the history of Europe, and in significant ways it offers a closer analogy to our own time; the continued neglect of the great historian of the age is therefore unfortunate.

Ammianus was an active participant in much of the history he relates, and his biography is therefore more fully known than are those of Livy or Tacitus. He was born about A.D. 325–30 in Syrian Antioch, "the fair crown of the east" (22.9.14), which was famous for its luxury and high culture as well as its impressive situation. Ammianus was of well-to-do, semi-noble birth; he probably belonged to the class of curials, the provincial aristocracy, and his affiliation colors his sympathies. He is scornful of the lower strata, and somewhat awed by the Roman aristocracy, though indignant at their arrogance. He goes out of his way to defend the interests of the upper middle class. As a young man he was enrolled in the *protectores domestici,* a regiment of high social standing. In 353 he was attached to the staff of Ursicinus, commander in the east with headquarters at Nisibis, serving with him for seven eventful years, and maintained a strong personal loyalty to his chief. After the fall of Amida in 359 (magnificently described in Book 19) Ursicinus was dismissed. The accuracy of Ammianus' defense of Ursicinus' course of action during the period when Ursicinus' loyalty to the emperor was under suspicion has been questioned on the grounds of the historian's affection for his commander. Ammianus apparently continued in military service and probably participated in the Persian expedition in which Julian lost his life in 363. He now returned to Antioch, where he may have held office or attempted a legal career. During this period he traveled to Egypt, where he learned much of Egyptian history and antiquities but found the Egyptians repulsive. He also traveled to Greece, shortly after the undersea earthquake of 366, and saw a ship which had been hurled two miles inland by the tidal wave. During the sixteen years of his stay at Antioch he read very widely. He shows his bookish predilection by his tendency to judge people by the extent of their reading: "If in a circle of learned men the name of an ancient writer happens to be mentioned," he writes of the lawyers of Antioch (30.4.17), "they think it is a foreign word for some fish or other tidbit."

After the disastrous defeat of Valens by the Goths at Adrianople in A.D. 378—which is the terminus of his history—Ammianus went to Rome. His overland journey through Thrace provided additional topographical details for his history. At Rome he was disgusted by the arrogance of the aristocrats and the vulgar display of their fantastic wealth. In the famine of 383 Ammianus, along with all other foreigners, was expelled for the duration of the shortage, but an exception was made of three thousand dancing girls with their choruses and teachers. His indignation was roused to some degree by the disdain with which he himself was regarded despite the high position he had held. But it is the failure of the aristocrats to live up to their dignity, not the institution of aristocracy, to which he takes exception. Of the senatorial class in general he speaks with bated breath. For example, when Constantius was approaching Rome (16.10.5),

as he beheld with calm countenance the dutiful attendance of the senate and the august likenesses of the patrician stock, he thought, not like Cineas, the famous envoy of Pyrrhus, that a throng of kings was assembled together, but that the sanctuary of the whole world was present before him.

—*J. C. Rolfe*

His snobbery operates in both directions: *Non omnia narratu sunt digna quae per squalidas transiere personas*—"Everything done by the great unwashed is not worthy of record." With some Romans of position Ammianus seems to have been on terms of friendship. Among these were Hypatius, brother-in-law of Constantinus and prefect of Rome in 379 and of Italy in 382/3, and Symmachus, whose place in literature we shall discuss presently. Ammianus is indignant at a show of popular ingratitude to Symmachus after he had presented a bridge to the community (27.3.4):

For after some years had passed they set fire to Symmachus' beautiful house in the Transtiberine district, spurred on by the fact that a common fellow among the plebeians (*vilis quidam plebeius*) had alleged, without any evidence or witness, that the prefect had said that he would rather use his own wine for quenching lime-kilns than sell it at the price which the people hoped for.

—*J. C. Rolfe*

It was at Rome, and from the point of view of the ancient capital, that Ammianus wrote his history. While the work was still in progress instalments of it were presented in public recitations, as appears from the prefatory remarks to Books 5 and 26, and brought their author much attention. From Antioch his old friend, the eminent orator Libanius, wrote (*Epistles* 1063) to felicitate him upon his success in 392. This is the last definite date in Ammianus' life. Internal evidence shows that the last five books of the history can scarcely have been published before September, 394, and must surely have been published before 397.

In a brief epilogue to his history Ammianus speaks of its scope and quality (31.16.9):

These events, from the principate of the emperor Nerva to the death of Valens, I, a former soldier and a Greek, have set forth to the measure of my ability, without ever (I believe) consciously venturing to debase through silence or through falsehood a work whose aim was the truth.

—*J. C. Rolfe*

Clearly Ammianus' aim was to write a continuation of Tacitus, and his work might have been entitled *Res gestae a fine Corneli Taciti* (as the Elder Pliny wrote an *A fine Aufidii Bassi*); Priscian cites it simply as *Res gestae*. Of the thirty-one books into which the history was divided the first thirteen, covering the period from the accession of Nerva in 96 to the seventeenth year of Constantius II in 353, are lost. The eighteen surviving books carry the story down to the death of Valens in 378. This great disparity—257 years in thirteen books, 25 years in eighteen—indicates that Ammianus dealt with the earlier period very briefly and enlarged on the period of which he had direct knowledge. He plainly made use of his wide reading, but attempts to account for large sections of his work as little more than transcriptions from his predecessors are surely misguided. Careful examination has shown that Ammianus speaks with assurance only of details of which he might himself have had direct knowledge. The devotion to truth which he professes in each of his prefaces and in his epilogue is a just claim. No ancient historian would appear to have been more scrupulous.

But if Ammianus' history is accepted as the conscientious product of an honest workman, allowance must be made for his honest prejudices, and, especially in the last five books, for compelling considerations of personal safety. His tenderness for his sometime chief Ursicinus has already been mentioned. A much more serious flaw, from the point of view of the student who wishes to understand the social forces operative in the fourth century, are the distortions resulting from Ammianus' class prejudices. Gallus, for example, is written down as a bloodthirsty and reckless tyrant. Ammianus has not only suppressed Gallus' great capacities as a general but has obscured his popularity with the lower classes and has not brought out the fact that the important men done to death under Gallus were actually a noble clique with conspiratorial designs. Julian is Ammianus' special hero, and he praises his achievements in the most extravagant terms; yet he is bitter at Julian's harshness to the curial class, and especially at his efforts to curb their economic exploitation of the Antiochenes. In the last six books in particular Ammianus' disclaimer of purposeful omissions seems disingenuous. At the opening of Book 26 he says that he had determined to discontinue his work (with the death of Jovian in 364, recounted at the end of Book 25), "partly to avoid the dangers which are always connected with the truth, and partly to escape unreasonable critics of the work which I am composing, who cry out as if wronged if one has failed to mention" some trivial detail. The details which Ammianus fails to mention are not trivial, but we may well believe that the reasons for their omission are "the dangers which are connected with the truth." It appears very likely that the elder Theodosius was executed for complicity in a conspiracy, and that it was out of simple fear of the emperor Theodosius that Ammianus gives a favorable account of the elder Theodosius' career and is silent on the circumstances of his death, and that he paints Maximinus more harshly than he would otherwise have done. A similar constraint probably governed Ammianus' expressions on Christianity. Ammianus himself was a pagan, and his antiquarian Roman sympathies would put him at the side of such stalwart defenders of the old order as his friend Symmachus. In Books 14–25 Ammianus speaks freely of Christianity. "No wild beasts are such enemies to mankind," he can write (22.5.4), "as are most of the Christians in their deadly hatred of one another." He is even capable of criticizing the Christian emperors' policy of prosecuting as treasonable the practice of foretelling the future. But in Books 26–31 Ammianus eschews all discussion of religious questions and nowhere reveals his own paganism. It cannot be mere coincidence that in 392, when Ammianus began the composition of these books, the emperor Theodosius dismissed important pagan functionaries and showed marked favor to Christians. The vehemence with which the religious tolerance of Valentinian is praised is tantamount to bitter criticism of a different policy (30.9.5):

His reign was distinguished by toleration, in that he remained neutral in religious differences, neither troubling anyone on that ground or ordering him to reverence this or that. He did not bend the necks of his subjects to his own belief by threatening edicts, but left such matters undisturbed as he found them.

—*J. C. Rolfe*

There can be little doubt that religious as well as political questions would have taken on a different aspect in Ammianus' last six books if he were not in present danger of imperial displeasure.

With so centralized and personal a government as that of the Roman empire it is natural that the historian's glance should be directed mainly at the dynasty, but Ammianus does not fill his pages with the inconsequential gossip of the school of imperial biographers. Indeed, he criticizes the frivolity of the biographers and is much nearer his model Tacitus, whom he surpasses in scope and in his grasp of the problems of government. He follows Thucydides in dating by summers and winters where it is convenient to do so (not because he is there using a "Thucydidean" source). He follows Thucydides also in including fictive speeches, but these are brief and relatively few, and are given only to emperors. His battle descriptions far surpass those of Livy or Tacitus, for they are the work of a seasoned professional soldier and usually based on autopsy. A marked feature are the scholarly digressions, of which there are twenty-six in the extant books. Many of these are geographic or ethnographic and so directly relevant, but others seem merely to parade information on natural science; such are the disquisitions on earthquakes (17.7.9–14), eclipses (20.3.1–12), rainbows (20.11.26–30), prophecy (21.1.8–14), artillery (23.4.1–15), pearls (23.6.85–88), the calendar (26.1.8–14).

It is probably for the shortcomings in his Latin style that Ammianus is apologizing when he avows himself (in his epilogue) a Greek and a soldier. He worked hard at his Latin; his diction shows that he had read the classics from Plautus onwards and that he had conned the handbooks of the rhetoricians. But his capricious word order suggests that he did not think in Latin, and occasionally he can only transliterate a Greek word. But if his choice and arrangement of words leave much to be desired, his style in the larger sense is always vigorous and often rises to greatness. Episodes in which Ammianus himself figured communicate the sense of adventure to the reader; this is particularly true of the masterly Book 19, which describes the siege of Amida. But Ammianus' particular excellence is his acute summation of his principal characters. His epilogues (as he himself calls them: 30.7.1) of deceased emperors are the best brief characterizations in antiquity; such are the sketches of Constantius (21.16), Julian (25.4), Valentinian I (30.7-9), and Valens (31.14).

From the safe vantage of a millennium and a half we may criticize Ammianus for not realizing the decline in the empire's fortune, for not perceiving that the barbarian invasions would prove irresistible, even for not sensing that the great economic inequalities of which he himself speaks bore within themselves the seeds of destruction for the existing social order. It is probably unreasonable to demand such clairvoyance of any contemporary. Ammianus' overriding sympathy was with the class who profited from the economic inequality; like every Roman historian he looked back on Rome's great past not only for precept and example for the present but as a guarantee for the future destiny of Rome, and like all Roman moralists he thought that moral decadence was the cause rather than the symptom of political degeneration and that only a moral regeneration was needed to restore its pristine vigor to the state. All that was wanted after Valens' disastrous defeat by the Goths was a renewal of the qualities which had restored the state after Marcus Aurelius' defeat by the Marcomanni. At that time (31.5.14),

After calamitous losses the state was presently restored to its former condition, because the temperance of old times was not yet infected by the effeminacy of a more licentious mode of life, and did not crave extravagant feasts or shameful gains; but high and low alike with united ardor and in agreement hastened to a noble death for their country, as if to some quiet and peaceful haven.

—*J. C. Rolfe*

In Ammianus' time, apparently, high and low did *not* unite to repel the invader.

Ammianus Marcellinus speaks well of his contemporary historians, Aurelius Victor and Eutropius, but their commonplace productions

serve only to put Ammianus' merits into higher relief. Sextus Aurelius
Victor was a pagan African who was governor of Pannonia Secunda
in 361 and prefect of Rome in 389. His brief history of the emperors
from Augustus to Constantius (died 361) is entitled *Caesares*. The
Caesares follows Suetonius' biographical approach, and draws from
Suetonius and similar writers. Aurelius essays an elegant style and
indulges in moralizing reflections after the manner of Sallust and
Tacitus, but his rhetoric is tasteless and tedious. The work is preserved
as the third part of a *Historia tripertita*, of which the first part, *Origo
gentis Romanae*, deals with the Aeneas legend, and the second, *De
viris illustribus*, deals with the regal period and the early republic.
Neither these nor the *Epitome de Caesaribus*, which is usually presented with them and is sometimes cited as the *Second Victor*, are by
Aurelius. The *Epitome*, of which the first eleven chapters follow
Aurelius closely, goes down to Theodosius I (A.D. 395). Aurelius'
preservation is doubtless due to the circumstance that his work was
chosen as the concluding section of the convenient *Tripertita*, which
thus covered the whole of Roman history.

A more successful work is Eutropius' *Breviarium ab urbe condita*,
whose ten books cover Roman history from Romulus to the death of
Jovian in A.D. 364. Eutropius participated in Julian's Persian campaign
(363) and was *magister memoriae* to Valens (364–78), at whose request he composed his work. The first six books go down to the
assassination of Julius Caesar and are in the succinct style of a chronicle, following the manner as well as the matter of the epitome of
Livy. For the empire Eutropius used Suetonius, and he presents brief
and just characterizations of the emperors. He was quite aware that
his style is unpretentious and efficient rather than elegant, and he
closes with the courtly remark that an account of Valens must be
loftier and more carefully wrought. But the simplicity which enabled
so vast a stretch of history to be reduced to an easily read compendium
was calculated to give the work great popularity. It is one of the very
few Latin books which was translated into Greek; a fourth-century
version by Paionios is extant, and there are specimens also of a sixth-
century version by Capito. A continuation was added by the Lombard
historian Paul the Deacon, and it was used as a school text until
modern times. As historian Eutropius is of little value, for he tells us
nothing which is not more dependably told elsewhere, but no Latin

book better presents the whole of Roman history in such brief compass.

From neither Aurelius Victor nor Eutropius would a casual reader learn that the fourth was essentially different from any other century in Roman history, and even in Ammianus Marcellinus only the discerning reader can perceive currents beyond those of the usual military campaigns and the political intrigues surrounding imperial successions. Ammianus himself, we have observed, was blind to the implications of the economic factors he himself noticed. We have observed also that Ammianus was aware of, and indeed himself constrained by, the religious tensions of his day, and we know from other sources, and particularly from the career of Julian called the Apostate, of the struggle to the death between burgeoning Christianity and senile paganism. But paganism itself experienced a remarkable upsurge of spirituality in its opposition to Christianity. The professors of Neoplatonism filled it with a spiritual content, lofty and unworldly in choice spirits like Plotinus and Porphyry, descending to charlatanry in astrologers and thaumaturgists who exploited the mood of otherworldliness. For these matters our prime source is Firmicus Maternus of Syracuse, who wrote an ardent eight-book tract for astrologers under the title of *Mathesis,* was then converted to Christianity, and wrote an even more ardent tract *On the Error of Profane Religions* (*De errore profanarum religionum*).

The *Mathesis* was written about A.D. 336. The first book defends astrology as a science, especially against the objections of the Academic Carneades (second century B.C.) and asserts its author's claim to have introduced the science to the Romans—a claim which the existence of Manilius' *Astronomica* proves unfounded. The remaining books are an exhaustive treatment of the system. Firmicus' protestations of inadequacy to his great subject are merely *pro forma*. He is in fact well informed, doubtless leaning heavily on the many predecessors in the field whom he mentions, and the ornateness of his style is obviously intended to charm his readers. His eighth book is very like Manilius' fifth, both probably following the same Greek source, perhaps Nechepso or Petosiris, whom he frequently cites. Flattery to the emperor takes the form of excluding him from the influence which the stars exert on ordinary mortals because the emperor is himself a god. Firmicus' lofty concept of the astrologer's calling is illustrated by the rigorous ethical code of conduct which he demands of practitioners in a long and solemn admonition to the *mathematicus* (as the astrologer was called) at the end of the second book. The *mathematicus* must lead a godly life because his converse is with the gods. He must be accessible, righteous, and not greedy, he must not receive immoral questions, must have wife and children and respectable friends, must eschew clandestine associations, not be a party to hate or vengeance, not practice usury, neither give nor exact oaths. He must endeavor to exert a beneficial influence and to guide passionate persons to moderation not only by formal responses from the stars but by friendly counsel. He should avoid nocturnal sacrifices and ceremonies, public or private, and should also avoid the circus, so that none should think that the victory of the Blues or Greens was connected with his presence. He should hesitate to answer questions concerning paternity or the horoscopes of third parties. The system begins by distributing individual temperaments and bodily members among the seven planets, and complexions, tastes, climates, regions, positions in life, and illnesses among the signs of the Zodiac. The Crab, for example, signifies sharp salty taste, light or whitish color, water animals and creeping things, the seventh zone, still or flowing water, mediocrity, and all diseases of the heart and diaphragm. The secrets of the system, contained in the last two books, are indices of constellations which determine whether a man is to be a murderer, commit incest, be a cripple, or become a gladiator, lawyer, slave, foundling, and so forth. In strict logic predestination so specific would banish all moral considerations, but Firmicus asserts (1.3) that even the most fearful decrees of the stars may be countered by much prayer and diligent worship of the gods. Socrates, for example, was doomed by the stars to endure all passions and bore his fate visibly in his countenance, yet by his virtues he mastered them all. "That which we suffer and which pricks us with burning torches [that is, the passions], belongs to the stars; but our own powers of resistance belong to godliness of the spirit." A number of lesser treatises on astrology, supplementing his main work, have not survived.

Between his writing of the *Mathesis* and of the *On the Error of Profane Religions* Firmicus turned Christian. His convert's zeal is like Arnobius' or Tertullian's. Not content with excoriating the ancient cults and the mysteries as the handiwork of the devil, he demands that the emperors extirpate the mischief root and branch. His condemnation of the mysteries supplies much useful information on their cult which we should otherwise not have. Firmicus' zeal, whether in behalf of paganism or of Christianity, and the earnest quest for a spiritual and ethical religion which his writings reveal, are informing indices of the pullulating religious currents of the fourth century.

Another aspect of the struggle between Christianity and paganism is illustrated by the life and works of Quintus Aurelius Symmachus, the highly cultured and aristocratic friend of Ammianus Marcellinus, who was proconsul of Africa in 373, prefect of Rome in 384/5, and consul in 391. In 403 the Christian Prudentius calls him the greatest living orator, and his death probably fell shortly after that date. Symmachus is our best representative of the adherents of ancient Roman ideals and traditions who resisted the inroads of Christianity not out of considerations of religion, in the ordinary use of the word, but because western Christianity (to a far greater degree than eastern) was hostile to all traditional cultural as well as social and political values. It is an index to the quality of Symmachus' loyalty to the old order that he was as concerned to procure Spanish horses and bears for the public spectacles as his correspondence shows him to have been. Symmachus was of those who believed that "good blood tells and never fails to recognize itself" (*impulsu boni sanguinis, qui se semper agnoscit: Orations* 8.3). To the conservative guardians of ancient Rome the victory of Christianity portended the end of civilization. The quality as well as the course of the conflict can be illustrated by the fate of the statue of Victory, in fact little more than a symbol of empire, which had always had its place in the Roman senate house. The statue was removed by Constantine in 357, restored by Julian, and again removed by Gratian in 382. St. Ambrose procured that the pagan senators who petitioned for restoration were denied an audience. They petitioned again to Valentinian II in 384, their spokesman being Symmachus. Urbane, benevolent, shaping his life like his letters with exquisite care to avoid excess, Symmachus yet rises to impassioned eloquence in his plea on behalf of Rome. He acknowledges that Victory might be looked upon as a *nomen* rather than a *numen,* but the *nomen* is itself sacred. Rome herself is represented as crying out against the death sentence of the values of which she was guardian and symbol. It required the energetic intervention of the powerful Ambrose to avert a pagan victory. The statue was restored during the rebellion of Arbogast and Eugenius in 393 and finally removed by Theodosius in 394. But so effective had Symmachus' eloquence proved that Prudentius still felt constrained to offer a reply twenty years after the speech was made.

Aside from this effort, the fragments of eight speeches of Symmachus which we possess hardly justify his enormous reputation as an orator. As a writer Symmachus is adequately portrayed for us by the ten books of his *Letters,* edited by his son, one of the largest collections of correspondence which has come down from antiquity. There are some nine hundred letters, mostly short; they were so highly prized in their own day as to encourage forgeries. Like those of the Younger Pliny, Symmachus' letters were written for publication and were therefore composed with great care. Like Pliny's too they show us that even in times of turmoil and demoralization kindly and courteous gentlemen were to be found. Like a good Roman he is always aware of his obligation to his audience: *Ubique vitam agimus consularem* (*Epistles* 8.23), "Everywhere I comported myself as befits a consul." The contents comprise recommendations, felicitations, condolences, invitations, solicitous inquiries concerning ailments, and similar private concerns. Though Symmachus himself held high offices of state and participated in the determination of critical political and religious questions, and though he obviously valued himself as a thinker and writer, the letters are confined to petty banalities. There are no ideas which might engage the interest of posterity; for posterity Symmachus' most meaningful achievement was probably his recommendation of Augustine to be teacher of rhetoric in Milan. "The luxuriancy of Symmachus," Gibbon wrote, "consists in barren leaves without fruit and even without flowers. Few facts and few sentiments can be extracted from his verbose correspondence." Dainty and melodious expression, the repetition of a single jejune conceit in several forms, are an end in themselves. Were it not for their superscription and the fact that some of the addressees are such well-known personages as Stilicho the letters would be undatable. In letters and oratory alike the phenomena are reminiscent of Fronto. The only value of the corpus for the historian is in the forty-nine so-called *Relations,* which were added to the tenth book at a later date. These deal with administrative practice and provide some light on procedures; with the exception of the defense of paganism (*Relation* 3) they had not been published in Symmachus' lifetime.

For Symmachus' contribution to the perpetuation of the classical tradition there is tangible evidence in his concern for the preservation of ancient texts, and in particular of the text of Livy. In 401 he presented his friend Valerianus with a complete transcript of the historian (*Epistles* 9.13). The interest in Livy shown by Symmachus and his family is attested by the subscriptions to all the books of the first decade: *Victorianus v. c. emendabam domnis Symmachis.* Three of them bear the further subscription of one of the Nicomachi, and three that of the other, both these revisers being connections of Symmachus by marriage. Preservation of other manuscripts is due to the same scholarly circle. A great-grandson of Symmachus revised the text of Macrobius, and Boethius and Cassiodorus were connected with the Symmachus of the generation following.

A fellow guest with Symmachus in Macrobius' *Saturnalia* was the youthful Vergilian scholar Servius, whose commentary is still a useful tool of scholarship. Servius' chief concern is with matters of grammar, rhetoric, and style, but he has much useful information on subject matter also. He quotes freely from a large number of classical authors and makes large use of the work of his predecessor Aelius Donatus, who lived earlier in the fourth century. Servius' commentary has come down in both a shorter and an expanded form; the latter includes material from Donatus which was not used in the shorter form. Aelius Donatus himself was the most distinguished teacher of his age and numbered Jerome among his pupils. Beside his material on Vergil, which is embodied in Servius (the preface and *Life* are extant), Donatus wrote a commentary on Terence, which was transcribed from margins of manuscripts, and two short textbooks: *Ars minor,* in the form of questions and answers on parts of speech; and *Ars major,* of the vices and virtues of discourse. Aelius Donatus is to be distinguished from the inferior Tiberius Claudius Donatus, who lived late in the fourth century and wrote *Interpretationes Vergilianae* in twelve books. These deal with Vergil's thought, style, rhetoric, and learning, and are not highly regarded.

Another author in Macrobius' *Saturnalia* was an Avienus. This Avienus is probably not identical with the Avianus who wrote a collection of *Fables,* but the *Fables* are dedicated to Macrobius, and Avianus therefore belonged to the same humanist circle. Like other members of the circle Avianus gives no hint of Christianity in his work, though its aim appears to be moral instruction. The dedication describes the work well enough:

I was in doubt, most excellent Theodosius, to what class of literature I should entrust the memory of my name, when the narration of fables occurred to my mind; because in these, fiction, if gracefully conceived, is not out of place, and one is not oppressed by the necessity of adhering to the truth. . . . My pioneer in this subject, you must know, is Aesop, who on the advice of the Delphic Apollo started droll stories in order to establish moral maxims. Such fables by way of examples have been introduced by Socrates into his inspired works and fitted by Horace into his poetry, because under the guise of jests of general application they contain illustrations of life. They were taken up by Babrius in Greek choliambics and abridged into two volumes. A considerable portion also was expanded by Phaedrus to a length of five books. I have compressed 42 of these into one book for publication—writing in unembellished Latin and attempting to set them forth in elegiacs. You have, therefore, a work to delight the mind, to exercise the brain, to relieve anxiety—one that will give you a wary knowledge of the whole course of life. I have made trees talk, beasts growl in conversation with men, birds engage in wordy disputes, and animals laugh, so that to meet the needs of each individual a maxim may be proffered even by inanimate things.

—*J. W. and A. M. Duff*

It seems strange that Phaedrus should be mentioned as a source, for the *Fables* follow Babrius (ca. A.D. 150) more closely. Changes from Babrius are in the direction of expansion and poetic elaboration by means of Vergilian or Ovidian echoes, yet even so the single pieces do not run beyond sixteen lines. Here is the fable of the Crab (No. 3):

A crab once tried to turn and bumped instead
on washing rocks his rugged carapace.
His mother, who desired to go ahead,
admonished thus her son with moral face:
"Come, leave these crooked ways and mend your gait;
don't dodge aside on any weak pretense:

with ready effort take the road that's straight;
and tread the unwinding path of innocence."
The son replied: "Then go in front of me
and show me what is right. I'll do it then."
A man, defaulting, is a fool if he
accuses faults revealed by other men.

—Jack Lindsay

Both the Latinity and the prosody are fairly classical, though there
are signs of degeneration in both. Avianus' hope that his work should
preserve his fame was fulfilled; the *Fables* were very widely read in
the Middle Ages.

There was a contemporary Avienus who also versified and expanded earlier work, but his interests were chiefly in astronomy,
geography, and Roman legend. This Festus Avienus was born of a
respectable family at Vulsinii; an inscription to the Etruscan goddess
Nortia who was worshipped there bears his name and testifies to his
pagan associations. Avienus was a man of high standing and held a
proconsulship. Of his paraphrases two are extant in their entirety, a
third in part, and two others we know of only from Servius. Avienus'
language and meter are even closer to classical norms than Avianus',
but his rhetoric, as we should expect in longer works, is more objectionable. Avienus' first work was an expanded translation of Aratus'
Phainomena. The expansion (1,878 lines as against 1,154 of the original) is due to the inclusion of material from ancient commentators.
Avienus apparently wished to produce a more up-to-date book than
the older versions of Cicero or Germanicus, in keeping with the astro-
logical interests of the humanist circle. His *Orbis terrae* in 1,393 good
hexameters is a closer translation of the 1,185 lines of Dionysius Perie-
getes (ca. A.D. 300), "describing noteworthy things in physical and
political geography and reproducing in vigorous style much ancient
ignorance which learned contemporaries could have corrected" (E.
H. Warmington). Of the *Ora maritima* only 703 iambic lines are extant; this also contains many errors but is valuable as the earliest description of the coast from the islands of Britain to Marseilles and for
its preservation of historical material from Pytheas and Eratosthenes.
The current interest in geography which Avienus catered to is illustrated also in the geographical excursuses of Ammianus Marcellinus.
Servius tells us that Avienus put Livy (probably only the epitomes)

into iambics and also made a poem of the Roman legends of the *Aeneid*. These enterprises would reflect the current interest of the Symmachi and Nicomachi in propagating Livy's history and Roman legend in accordance with their humanist program.

In the progeny of books as in that of princely houses genealogies are sometimes to be reckoned not in the descent of classic to classic but through barely mentionable by-blows. It was out of Dares and Dictys (who are not, as the casual reader is tempted to think, inventions of Chaucer) and not from Homer and other respectables that the Middle Ages received its knowledge of the heroic conflicts and characters of the Greeks, and from Dares and Dictys that they quarried names and episodes for their own creations. The authors of the Greek originals of their works (papyrus fragments prove that there were Greek originals) cannot have intended that readers take them as other than romance, and it is hardly likely that the fourth-century Latin adapter expected that readers would accept his fantastic account of the origin and discovery of Dictys (the elder and fuller book) as a fact. It is a mark of medieval gullibility that such an explanation as the following could be accepted without question. The Cretan Dictys (we are told) was taken to the Trojan war by Idomeneus and Meriones in order to celebrate their exploits. He wrote his account in the Phoenician language on linden bark, and procured that his work should be buried with him in Crete. In the thirteenth year of Nero the grave was laid open by an earthquake; shepherds who found the chest containing the book handed it to their master, who brought it to the governor of Crete, who sent it to the emperor, who had it translated into Greek for his library. Septimius (the author of the introductory epistle) then translated the first five books of the work into Latin and combined the remaining four, which dealt with the homecomings of the heroes, into a single book. The work is a journal of the entire war, from the abduction of Helen to the murder of Odysseus by his own son through Circe. What the "author" had not himself witnessed he presents on the voucher of some informant like Odysseus or Neoptolemus. Miraculous elements in the epic are glossed over or rationalized, and there are many minor alterations of the saga. It was not a wild deer but a goat that Agamemnon slew in Artemis' grove, and a plague, not a storm, hindered the sailing of the fleet. Ajax died *after* the fall of Troy; without him the Greeks might not have won. Polyxena is given a large and romantic role. She offers herself to Achilles as a redemption for the body of Hector, and Achilles generously refuses. Other episodes are similarly romanticized. But the episodes themselves were not invented; the Greek author took them from some handbook of mythology. The Latin style of the translation is modeled on Sallust, and there are borrowings from Vergil and Livy and Apuleius.

A sister work, perhaps a century later in date, is Dares Phrygius' *Historia de excidio Troiae*. The prefatory epistle to this work declares that Cornelius Nepos discovered it in Athens, translated it into Latin at once, and sent it to Sallust. The letter points out that Dares is a better source than Homer, having been a contemporary of the events and a participant on the Trojan side; and Homer is criticized for representing the gods as fighting with men. The story begins with the voyage of the Argonauts and closes with a summary of casualties in the Trojan war. Episodes are numerous, but the style is bald and suggests an abridgement. Here too we find romanticization, Alexandrian learning, and a tendency to rationalism. To strengthen the impression that he was an eyewitness the author offers (Chapters 12–13) an absurdly minute description of the appearance and character of thirty heroes and heroines of Homer. An equally absurd pretense of accuracy is the summary of casualties at the end: "There fell on the Greek side, as the daily reports written by Dares indicate, 886,000 men."

Dictys and Dares were surely not isolated phenomena, but these two survived to leave a deeper impress upon Europe than the more serious artistic efforts of their age. We turn now to consider writers of *belles lettres* who took their art more seriously.

XXI

HUMANIST SURVIVAL IN POETRY

IN THE DARK DAYS OF THE CHURCH THE INTEGRITY of the faithful could not be questioned, but in the Church triumphant even tepid spirits found shelter convenient and rendered Christianity devotion as perfunctory as the kisses they had blown to heathen idols. When such men were poets the new faith made little difference in the character of their work but rather enabled them to cultivate, without incurring disabilities, the aspect of pagan culture which alone had meaning for them. The Christian poets who wrote non-Christian poetry may be said to have invented secular literature, for their productions were as innocent of the antique devotion to the cult of Rome as of the evangelical warmth of Christianity. It is emptiness of any positive spiritual content that makes much fourth-century poetry so dreary and sterile despite astonishing technical virtuosity. Eventually, when tensions were allayed, a Prudentius would reinvigorate classical forms and classical imagery with dynamic Christian subject matter. But the fact that Prudentius could write "classical" poetry that was Christian and his readers appreciate it shows that the secular poets succeeded. If their work was not aimed at this particular kind of success, it was a symptom of an impulse that made the success possible—the impulse to preserve as much as possible of the precious legacy of antiquity which motivated Macrobius and Symmachus and which was to motivate Boethius and Cassiodorus to provide for the further transmission of the legacy. When we see that Rutilius Namatianus is quite plainly prevented by prudential considerations from giving more outspoken expression to his distaste for the new and attachment to the old, it may not be too much to surmise that Claudianus' mere adherence to classic forms and Macrobius-like avoidance of the mention of Christianity is a manner of resistance to the new by loyalty to the old.

Yet for writers like Ausonius, who is after all *the* poet of the fourth century, it is too generous to attribute their classicizing emptiness to anything but rampant rhetoric. The age was even more addicted to rhetoric than was Fronto's, as we have noticed in the case of Symmachus' prose. Unless their cloudcuckooland is an artificial and sophisticated insulation against the turbulent world, one might wonder that poets could be so little cognizant of clamant reality in an age which had to come to terms with Gothic invaders, and be a little tempted to feel that a society so determined upon insulation from reality was ripe for the attention of Gothic invaders. To be sure, Latin poetry had always tended, to a degree more marked than other literatures, to emanate from and address itself to a limited class. But within their limitations the classic poets were capable of reaching authentic poetic heights and of touching chords of the imagination whose vibrations might be felt far beyond their own class and their own age. Their cloistered *epigoni* were incapable of the spiritual excitement and the suggestiveness of true poetry and would likely have been suspicious of these qualities. The chorus of enthusiastic praise which greeted the work of Ausonius is evidence; as Gibbon truly said, "The poetical fame of Ausonius condemns the taste of his age." Symmachus holds the *Mosella* to be the equal of Vergil's poems, and Paulinus of Nola doubts that Vergil and Cicero could equal Ausonius. These curious judgments show that the perversion of taste emanated not from a classicizing clique, like the predilection for archaism of the Frontonians; Ausonius is actually a fit spokesman for his age, tells us much of its homely details, and is himself perfectly, even smugly, content with it. What is lacking is the vision without which the people perish.

The biography of Ausonius is easy to write, for he supplies a complete inventory of all his relations, teachers, friends, movements, employments, and patrons, and he shows the complete range of his tastes and interests; we may be sure that there are no subtleties for a prying eye to discover. He was born at Bordeaux about 310, his father being a reputable physician. From 320 he studied under his uncle Aemilius Magnus Arborius, who was professor at Toulouse, until 328, when Arborius was called to Constantinople to be tutor to a son of Constantine. He continued his studies at Bordeaux and entered upon his own career as *grammaticus* and in due time as professor of rhetoric at the university of Bordeaux. He married the daughter of a leading citizen who died after bearing him three children, of whom two survived. He remained a widower, and more than thirty years later still lamented his wife's death (*Parentalia* 40). About 364, after thirty years of teaching, he was called to be tutor to Gratian and continued in this post until Gratian became emperor in 375. He was advanced very rapidly, and his family soared with him. His father, nearly ninety, received the honorary rank of prefect of Illyricum; his son was proconsul of Africa and then *praefectus pretorio* of Italy, Illyrium, and Africa, his son-in-law succeeding to the proconsulship of Africa; a nephew was made prefect of Rome. Ausonius himself was made *praefectus Galliarum,* one of the most important posts in the empire, and by a special arrangement his office was combined with that of his son, so that the labors and the rewards of the administration of all western Europe might be shared between them. In 379 Ausonius attained the crowning honor of the consulship. In 383 the family fortunes were shattered by the usurper Maximus. When Theodosius overthrew Maximus in 388 Ausonius was too old for public employment and retired to his estates near Bordeaux. His latest work is to be dated to 393 or 394, and he presumably died about that time, past the age of eighty.

As may be seen from this resumé of his career, Ausonius was in direct touch with the leading political and intellectual personages of his time, and it is therefore the more disappointing that he affords no insight into the social and economic fabric of his important century. Some things about the organization of society we can learn incidentally—the importance of family relationships, the prestige of the teaching profession, the management of an estate, conditions of travel; of these the most important for our purposes is the attitude towards Christianity of such a man as Ausonius. We have noticed Ammianus' mild hostility to Christianity and then his discreet silence, we have observed Symmachus' opposition and its grounds, and we have seen Firmicus defending first paganism and then Christianity with equal vehemence. The Christian writers who use Latin literary forms are naturally concerned with apologetics and polemics or with specifically doctrinal matters. Ausonius is our first professing Christian to write *belles lettres,* the first Christian writer, that is, whose writings do not center on Christianity, and as such he is the ancestor of the secular literature of Christian Europe; and it is of some interest to see how he carried his Christianity. The answer would seem to be that he carried it lightly, and that it affected his life, his spirit, his verses, no more and no less than did his pagan intellectual legacy. Two poems, the Easter verses for Theodosius (*Domestica* 2) and the morning prayer (*Ephemeris* 3) do show considerable knowledge of Scripture and might suggest devout piety. But in these poems, as H. G. Evelyn White remarks, Ausonius "is deliberately airing his Christianity; he has, so to speak, dressed himself for church. His everyday attitude was clearly very different."

In dealing with Ausonius' works it is more convenient to follow the arrangement of the standard Teubner edition of Rudolf Peiper (adopted, but with misgivings, in H. G. Evelyn White's Loeb edition) than to attempt chronological precision. In general it may be said that Ausonius produced little before he became tutor to Gratian, the bulk of his work during the tutorship, comparatively little during his public employment, and more when he was relieved of his duties. Book 1 contains *Prefatory Pieces:* an autobiographical introduction in forty elegiacs, a short dedication to Syagrius, a prose letter of the emperor Theodosius asking for Ausonius' poems, and a reply from Ausonius in elegiacs. *Non habeo ingenium, Caesar sed iussit, habebo,* Ausonius writes, "I have no skill, but Caesar has bidden: I shall have it." Book 2 is the "Daily Round" (*Ephemeris*), perhaps intended as a mime. The speaker awakens in Sapphics, summons his valet in glyconics, prays at length in hexameters, dresses to go out, invites luncheon guests, instructs the cook (here there is a large lacuna), dictates to a stenographer, and retires to his dreams—all in various meters. The *Domestica* or "Personal Poems" of Book 3 date from Ausonius' consulship. The opening piece is a greeting to his patrimony on his retirement. Next are pretty and seemingly devout Easter verses written for the emperor; but the prayer in rhopalic verse which follows cannot have been very spontaneous. In each verse the first word is a monosyllable, the second a disyllable, the third a trisyllable, and so on—*Spes deus aeternae stationis conciliator.* Number 4 is an elegy (*epicedion*) on Ausonius' father, in which the deceased is represented as himself reviewing his life. The two concluding poems are New Year's prayers which contain no hint of Christianity. In Number 5 there is a refrain, "Come, Janus; come, New Year; come, Sun, with strength renewed!" The title of Book 4, *Parentalia,* is the name of an ancient pagan festival upon which offerings were made to the dead. Ausonius commemorates thirty of his relatives, some of whom he has never seen, in poems chiefly elegiac; nothing is said of a Christian after life. Book 5 similarly commemorates some twenty-five professors of Bordeaux. Connected with these is Book 6, which contains some twenty-five fictitious epitaphs of heroes of the Trojan war and a few added by the first editor of Ausonius' work. Several of the *Eclogues* of Book 7 are mnemonics for fixing the facts of the calendar; the others are not much loftier as poetry. In the *Cupid Crucified* of Book 8 Ausonius is inspired by a painting at Treves; Ausonius (as he says) "translates his amazed admiration into insipid versification." Prose *ecphraseis* of this sort occur in the contemporary Greek novelists. The Bissula celebrated in the poems of Book 9 was a fair-haired, blue-eyed German girl who fell to Ausonius' lot when he and Gratian accompanied Valentinian I on his campaign against the Germans in 368/9.

The *Mosella* (Book 10), Ausonius' masterpiece, was written at the same time. This 483-line hexameter poem does express an appreciation of natural beauties rare in earlier poetry; here are some lines describing the appearance of the river's water (56–67, 192–95):

> Through your light levels you show the depth of crystal:
> river without a secret. As the air
> in stillness, open, spreads across our eyes
> and the winds, becalmed, draw all the veils of space,
> deep in your gulf we gaze, and spy below
> wealth of whelmed things, your hidden rooms revealed.
> The stream runs gently and with a limpid lapse
> shows in an azure light the scattered shapes:
> the furrowed sand which the slight movement ripples,
> bowed water-grasses in your green bed trembling.
> Under the stream that bred them, the tossing weeds
> endure the buffets of water. Pebbles glint
> and fade, and gravel frames green drifts of moss.
>
> .   .   .   .
>
> Yon sight's for free delight. The stream, with blue,
> mirrors the shady hill. Vine shoots and leaves
> show tangled growing in the water. Look,
> what river-hues, when eve drives lazy shadows
> and spreads the green of the reflected light.
> Whole hills float in the ripples. Distant tendrils
> shake here, and here the clusters ripely-glassed.
>
> —*Jack Lindsay*

Not only the stream itself but the excellent wine produced on its hills, the delicious fish (of which we are given an exhaustive inventory) which teem in its waters, the aquatic sports of which it is the scene, the stately buildings which line its banks, the numerous tributaries which feed it, are celebrated. For all its exaggerations and arid lists and Vergilian reminiscences, there is greater integrity in this poem than there would be in a treatment of a mythological theme for which the motive could only be display of virtuosity in versification and erudition. And yet we should have expected the finest poem of the best poet of his age to show more significant perception of man and the world. It has been found strange that a poet so devoted to his own native heath should have chosen to celebrate a river as remote as the Moselle. The probable explanation is that the poem was written at the suggestion of Valentinian, to advertise the attractions of the region of his capital Treves to prospective settlers. At the time, the region was threatened by barbarian invasions, and in a few years Treves actually fell; perhaps there was depopulation, and new settlers were loath to commit themselves to the dangerous situation.

Twenty cities of the empire are celebrated in the *Order of Famous Cities* (Book 11), which is exceedingly dull, except for the piece on Bordeaux, which shows the author's local patriotism, and that on Aquileia, which is praised as the scene of Maximus' defeat. The *Technopaegnion* (Book 12) is mainly a classified list of the monosyllabic nouns in Latin arranged so as to form the endings of hexameters. This puerility is relieved by a touch of wit in the *Masque of the Seven Sages* (Book 13), in which each sage steps forward to recite and expound in verse the saying attributed to him. The *Caesars* (Book 14) presents schoolbook facts about the emperors treated in Suetonius (but the collection was several times enlarged) in mnemonic verses. Book 15 contains the concluding poems of the *Fasti*, a list of kings and consuls of Rome no longer extant. The *Griphus* (Book 16) celebrates the mystic number three, with a wide variety of examples and extremely skillful versification. It is to be noted, in connection with Ausonius' religious convictions, that the Trinity is cited in the same tone as triune pagan personages to enforce the maxim "Drink thrice." The *Nuptial Cento* (Book 17) is condemned as shocking by all commentators and is inevitably the first poem of Ausonius which the student reads. It is an ingenious patchwork of parts of Vergilian lines which, thus rearranged, give a satisfactorily obscene sense. What is shocking is not immorality—unless Vergil's words are sacrosanct—but the childish delight in the scabrous.

Most informing of all, but disappointing nevertheless, is the long book of *Epistles* (17), mostly in verse. The exchanges with Symmachus have been highly esteemed, for the two chief literary figures of the day should have something to say to one another; but their highest purpose seems to be, as Symmachus hints in the first letter, *mutuum scabere*, "mutual back-scratching." Even the letter to his father on the birth of his son and the letters to his own grandson conceal whatever emotions Ausonius may have felt in a cloud of verbiage. The exchanges with Paulinus are an intriguing parallel with the exchanges between Fronto and Marcus Aurelius. Marcus Aurelius wearied of his teacher Fronto's emptiness and found reality in Stoicism, to Fronto's genuine puzzlement. Paulinus wearied of his teacher Ausonius' emptiness and found reality in Christianity, to Ausonius' equally genuine puzzlement. Like Fronto, Ausonius repeatedly admonishes his former pupil to return to sanity, but like Marcus Aurelius, Paulinus is polite and respectful but firm. Paulinus writes (18. 31.29–46, 330–31):

Now 'tis another force governs my heart, a greater God, who demands another mode of life, claiming for himself from man the gift he gave, that we may live for the Father of life. To spend time on empty things, whether in pastime or pursuit, and on literature full of idle tales, he forbids; that we may obey his laws and behold his light which sophists' cunning skill, the art of rhetoric, and poets' feignings overcloud. For these steep our hearts in things false and vain, and train our tongues alone imparting naught which can reveal the truth. For what good thing or true can they hold who hold not the head of all, God, the enkindler and source of the good and true, whom no man seeth save in Christ. . . . If this thou dost approve, rejoice in thy friend's rich hope: if otherwise, leave me to be approved by Christ alone.

—H. G. Evelyn White

The 112 *Epigrams* of Book 19, mostly in elegiacs, deal with a wide variety of subjects. There are some on his wife, some on friends, a number of lampoons, some macaronic combinations of Greek and Latin, many translations from the *Greek Anthology*, eight pieces on Myron's realistic heifer, and some untranslatable obscenities. Ausonius' longest prose piece is his *Thanksgiving* to Gratian for his consulship (Book 20). Flattery is laid on with a shovel, and the shovel is gilt and inlaid with rhinestones. No sensible emperor could countenance such panegyric except for its value in public relations. As a versifier with almost Ovidian facility, as an amateur of the classics who had Vergil at his finger tips, as an epicure, a loyal family man, and an affectionate friend, Ausonius is a pleasing phenomenon in his age; as a thinker he is a cipher, and as a poet little beyond the journeyman stage.

That such things as Ausonius' *Cento* and *Technopaegnia* are not sports is demonstrated by the curious work of Publilius Optatianus Porfyrius, whose only claim to attention is as an index to the deplorable taste of his age. Porfyrius had been exiled by Emperor Constantine, and to regain imperial favor he composed, about 325, a collection of twenty poems (to which additional pieces were added in a later edition) entitled *Panegyricus*. To the fulsome flattery of an emperor we are by now hardened, nor do we longer expect authentic poetic imagination; but the acrobatics of Porfyrius' versification are literally stunning. The hexameter lines contain the same number of letters, and the initial and final letter of the lines, as well as diagonals from the initial to the final letter, spell out words. Certain individual letters, written in red, produced some figure, a monogram, a XP, or a flourish, and when read continuously spelled out separate apophthegms. At the end there are four hexameters whose words could be arranged in eighteen different ways, each of which produced a kind of sense and meter. The contents of the whole are naturally trivial, but the *artiste* knew his emperor. Porfyrius won his recall and a gracious letter of thanks from His Majesty, who accepted the surmounting of the technical difficulties as a genuine advance in art: "He who writes and composes in my century is followed by my favoring attention as by a gentle zephyr."

Claudius Claudianus (ca.A.D. 370–ca.405), who may fairly be called the last poet of classical Rome, is happily free of such silliness; he is as imitative as the other *epigoni,* with very numerous reminiscences from Vergil, virtual centos from Ovid and sometimes from Catullus in mythological sections, echoes from Lucretius in philosophical passages and of Lucan in describing political virtue, and finally of

Juvenal in satire and invective; but he is nevertheless not only a man of strong personal convictions but a true artist. The high points of Claudianus' career can be deduced from his datable official poems, but he speaks of himself rarely. He seems intentionally to avoid naming his birthplace, perhaps out of the natural embarrassment of the newcomer from a despised country who has gone far in the capital. Sidonius Apollinaris (9.274) and Hesychius in Suidas' lexicon say that he was born in Egypt, and his interest in and knowledge of things Egyptian are corroborative. He himself tells us (*Shorter Poems* 41) that it was in Probinus' consulship (A.D. 395) "that I first drank the stream of Latin song and that my Muse, deserting Hellas, assumed the Roman toga." There are indeed Greek writings attributed to him, a *Gigantomachia* in 77 lines and seven epigrams, but their genuineness has been questioned. It is probable that Claudianus' change of literary language was more or less contemporary with his change of country.

Shortly after his arrival in Rome Claudianus seems to have gone to the imperial court at Milan, where he became a kind of poet laureate. It is customary to assign the *De raptu Proserpinae* to the beginning of his Milan period, but, as we shall see, there may be better grounds for dating it to the end of his career. But his public poems are datable by the events with which they are associated, and the greater portion were written in Milan: the *Panegyric on the Third Consulship of Honorius* in 396; the two books *Against Rufinus, 395–97*; the *Panegyric on the Fourth Consulship of Honorius,* the *Epithalamium of Honorius and Maria,* and the *War Against Gildo,* 398; the *Panegyric on the Consulship of Fl. Manlius Theodorus* and the *War Against Eutropius,* 399. About 400 Claudianus returned to Rome, where he recited the poem on the consulship of his special hero Stilicho. In 402, when Stilicho defeated Alaric at Pollentia, Claudianus recited his poem *On the Gothic War.* The last of his datable public poems is the *Panegyric on the Sixth Consulship of Honorius,* written towards the end of 403. In 404 Claudianus seems to have married a protégée of Serena, niece and adopted daughter of Theodosius and wife of Stilicho, and in acknowledgement of her interest he wrote the *Praise of Serena.* The *Letter to Serena* appears to have been written on his honeymoon. If he survived the honeymoon (it has been suggested that he did not) and if the *De raptu Proserpinae* is not in fact an early work, he may have written that poem during the years following, but certainly be-

fore 408, which is the latest possible date for his death. The question
of Claudianus' religion has been much debated. St. Augustine and
Orosius call him a pagan, and with the exception of *Shorter Poems* 32,
On the Savior (which may be spurious) there is nothing in the poems
to demonstrate his Christianity. The attack on James Commander of
the Cavalry (*Shorter Poems* 50) invokes the saints, but the tone is
ironical. Even in the marriage of Maria, who was at least nominally
Christian, there is no mention of Christian usages. But there can be
no question that a man so devoted to Stilicho and Honorius, who
were devout Christians, was a formal Christian. Like Ausonius he
carried his Christianity lightly, and his writing followed the groove
of the classics so closely that the introduction of an alien element
would have appeared incongruous. Literature, except for the specifically Christian writers, was a thing apart. So much is indicated in the
inscription on the statue which the senate erected in his honor.
Claudianus himself tells us (*Gothic War* 7) that such a statue was
set up in the Forum of Trajan, and its base, happily preserved in the
Naples Museum, bears the following legend (*Corpus inscriptionum
Latinarum* 6, 1710):

To Claudius Claudianus *vir clarissimus,* son of Claudius Claudianus, v.c.,
tribune and notary (i.e. Permanent Secretary), master of the ennobling
arts but above all a poet and most famous of poets, though his own poems
are enough to ensure his immortality, yet, in thankful memory of his discretion and loyalty, their serene and learned majesties, the Emperors
Arcadius and Honorius have, at the instance of the senate, bidden this
statue to be raised and set up in the Forum of the Emperor Trajan of
blessed memory.

> Rome and her kings—to one who has combined
> A Homer's music with a Vergil's mind.
> —*M. Platnauer*

Some of the most momentous events in the history of Rome took
place during Claudianus' brief span, and it is with the drama's leading actors (and with a strong partisan bias) that his work chiefly
deals. Aside from the mythological works and the so-called *Shorter
Poems,* his remaining works consist of panegyrics (the *Epithalamia*
and the *Praise of Serena,* which is included in the *Shorter Poems,* belong in that category also) and invectives. Verse panegyric was no
novelty in ancient literature, and verse invective was not unexampled.

What distinguishes Claudianus' work in this respect is his thoroughly historical background and political tendenciousness. We have not general praise of an admirable character artistically presented nor reprobation of a repulsive character personally offensive to the author, but an argument and a viewpoint growing out of and specifically applicable to a *political* situation. Lucan, as the nearest analogue of a poet dealing with momentous political questions in which he was himself passionately concerned, writes a self-contained work of general validity; Claudianus cannot be appreciated without knowledge of the intricate political situation of which he was a partisan. But Claudianus' devotion to the masterful Stilicho is much more than hero worship; to Claudianus Stilicho seemed, as he very likely was, an indispensable factor for the salvation of Rome—which Claudianus reveres and personifies quite in the spirit of Symmachus.

So, in the first of the *Panegyrics* (275 lines), on the youthful brothers *Probinus and Olybrius,* who attained the consulship in 395, Rome herself applies to the emperor on behalf of her wards. When her slaves Shock and Fear have harnessed her chariot (83–99)—

Rome herself in the guise of the virgin goddess Minerva soars aloft on the road by which she takes possession of the sky after triumphing over the realms of earth. She will not have her hair bound with a comb nor her neck made effeminate with a twisted necklace. Her right side is bare; her snowy shoulder exposed; her brooch fastens her flowing garments but loosely and boldly shows her breast: the belt that supports her sword throws a strip of scarlet across her fair skin. She looks as good as she is fair, chaste beauty armed with awe; her threatening helm of blood-red plumes casts a dark shadow and her shield challenges the sun in its fearful brilliance, that shield which Vulcan forged with all the subtlety of his skill. In it are depicted the children Romulus and Remus, and their loving father Mars, Tiber's reverent stream, and the wolf that was their nurse; Tiber is embossed in electrum, the children in pure gold, brazen is the wolf, and Mars fashioned of flashing steel.

—*M. Platnauer*

Her appeal is not for favorites but for Italy. So Tiber personified invites the rivers of Italy to a feast to celebrate the occasion. Here, as elsewhere in Claudianus, exuberance and enthusiasm make poetry of fantastic flattery and exaggeration which in lesser hands would be merely grotesque.

When Theodosius died in 395 he left his sons Arcadius and

Honorius emperors of the east and west respectively. But it was the energetic Stilicho who was the mainstay of power in the west, and in his *Panegyrics on the Third* (A.D. 396; 211 lines), the *Fourth* (398; 656 lines), and the *Sixth* (404; 660 lines) *Consulship of Honorius* Claudianus shows his honesty by refusing to attribute to Honorius military prowess of which he was incapable. His distinguished birth, character, and appearance are handsomely dealt with, and appreciation of Theodosius is skillfully introduced by the device of having him deliver to Honorius a long admonition (*Fourth Consulship* 214–351) on the duties of a ruler. The *Epithalamium of Honorius and Maria* (598; 341 lines) is a very attractive piece. We are first introduced to the love-smitten prince, and then taken to Venus' palace on Cyprus, where Cupid reports his success in kindling Honorius' love for Stilicho's beautiful daughter and asks Venus' aid for the consummation of the marriage. Attended by a choir of Nereids and Graces who bear gifts for the bride, Venus rides the waves upon a Triton's back, asks the attendants to insure peace in the world, and makes her way to Maria, whom she finds conning Greek and Latin classics with her mother. Venus has no difficulty in obtaining her desire, and the poem closes with fine praise of Stilicho. Earlier literature and the doctrine of the rhetors naturally provided models for epithalamia as for other standard forms, but Claudianus unmistakably shows the individual hand of the master. Preceding the *Epithalamium* are four short pieces in various meters entitled *Fescennine Verses for the Marriage of Emperor Honorius*. They contain the usual felicitations and good wishes; only the fourth has any suggestion of the frankness associated with the title Fescennine.

The Manlius Theodorus whose consulship in 399 is celebrated in a *Panegyric* (340 lines) was apparently a lawyer who had retired after a career of office-holding. Justice herself asks him to return to the service of the state; Manlius regretfully agrees, to everyone's great satisfaction, and sets about preparing the customary entertainments— animal hunts, tragedy, acrobatics. Far the longest of the *Panegyrics* is that *On the Consulship of Stilicho* (400; 1,230 lines in three books). The first book treats of Stilicho's military prowess, which rivals that of the Romans of old; the second tells "by what virtue he governs the world, tempering fear with love"; the third describes Rome's enthusiastic and lavish welcome of Stilicho, and the magnificent games he presented. The elegiac preface to the third book makes Stilicho greater than the Elder Scipio who conquered Hannibal; as Scipio had Ennius to sing his achievements, so Stilicho has Claudianus. The unfinished poem on the *War against Gildo* (398; 526 lines) tells of the defeat of Gildo, who had rebelled in Africa and threatened to starve Rome by withholding the grain supply. Actually, the victory was won by Gildo's brother Mascezel, whom Stilicho sent against Gildo; but Mascezel himself was executed by Stilicho in the same year, and this may be the reason why Claudianus did not write or suppressed a second book of the poem. Even if we discount the vivid description of famine at Rome in the beginning of the poem, we still have evidence of Rome's dependence on imported grain. The *Gothic War* (401; 647 lines) is wholly devoted to praise of Stilicho, the occasion being the defeat at Pollentia of Alaric, who had been reconciled to Rome and had then rebelled. Stilicho's achievement is likened to that of the Roman commanders of old who turned back barbarian hordes, and the fact that it is so based on patriotic considerations of Roman survival makes the flattery unobjectionable.

When Stilicho was marching southward into Greece in 397 to fight against the Goths he was forbidden to proceed by Rufinus, Arcadius' powerful minister. Rufinus was shortly murdered, surely by Stilicho's design. Upon his return from this campaign Claudianus presented Stilicho with the *Against Rufinus* (two books; 387, 527 lines). Claudianus starts by declaring that his doubts of Providence have been allayed by the fate of Rufinus. Allecto, presiding over a pandemonium of furies, proposes resistance to the gods who seemed to be inaugurating a new golden age, but Megaera declares that it is more feasible to operate through her private monster Rufinus. She proceeds to entice him to her service through his prodigious greed. The political implications of his monstrous misdemeanors are dealt with in the second book, skillfully interwoven with eulogy of Stilicho for frustrating his machinations.

As Arcadius' most influential minister Rufinus was succeeded by Eutropius, a eunuch of the basest antecedents. This is what Claudianus says of them (*Against Eutropius* 1.24-44):

Fortune, is thy power so all-embracing? What is this savage humour of thine? To what lengths wilt thou sport with us poor mortals? If it was thy will to disgrace the consul's chair with a servile occupant let some "consul" come forward with broken chains, let an escaped jail-bird don the robes of Quirinus—but at least give us a man. There are grades even among slaves and a certain dignity; that slave who has served but one master holds a position of less infamy. Canst thou count the waves of the sea, the grains of Africa's sands, if so thou canst number Eutropius' masters. How many owners has he had, in how many sale-catalogues has he appeared, how often has he changed his name! How often has he been stripped while buyer consulted doctor whether there lurked any flaw by reason of some hidden disease! All repented having bought him and he always returned to the slave-market while he could yet fetch a price. When he became but a foul corpse-like body, a mass of senile pendulous flesh, his masters were anxious to rid their houses of him by giving him away as a present and made haste to foist the loathsome gift on an unsuspecting friend. To so many different yokes did he submit his neck, this slave, old in years but ever new to the house; there was no end to his servitude though many beginnings.

—M. Platnauer

The two books *Against Eutropius* (A.D. 399; 513, 602 lines) maintain this tone of unmitigated savagery throughout. Each of his menial and disgusting occupations is described. When he was attired in consular dress (1.303–307),

'Twas as though an ape, man's imitator, had been decked out in sport with precious silken garments by a boy who had left his back and quarters uncovered to amuse the guests at supper. Thus richly dressed he walks upright and seems the more loathsome by reason of his brilliant trappings.

—M. Platnauer

The second book deals with his frightful administration of power and his eventual discomfiture. Insofar as such satirical invective had a model it was Juvenal 4; but Claudianus' is an independent work, conceived in a blaze of indignation and refined in the fire of his individual genius, not a literary exercise.

All the works so far mentioned are historical *epyllia;* all (with the exception of elegiac prefaces and of the Fescennines) are in hexameter. Next we have a collection of some fifty poems in hexameter or elegiac verse on various subjects; most are short, and they are accordingly called *Carmina minora* or *Shorter Poems.* There are personal addresses, descriptions of works of art or animals or localities, moral anecdotes, and occasional poems of several sorts. The skill of a sculptor in modeling a chariot with horses and charioteers out of a single block of marble is admired (7). There is a forty-eight-line poem on the porcupine (9). The story of the devoted brothers who saved their father from Etna's flame is told in forty-eight lines (17). The docility of French mules is praised (18). The story of an old man of Verona who never left home affords a lesson in contentment (20):

> Happy the man who all his life has kept
> His father's homestead, from the world aloof,
> And hobbling now, where as a child he crept,
> Tells the long history of a single roof.
>
> Not this, to follow Fortune's varied lure,
> —To drink, a hurried traveller, streams afar;
> —To brave the storm, for traffic, to endure
> The battle, or the clamouring of the Bar.
>
> Unskilled to mingle in the affairs of men,
> Strange to the neighbouring town that meets his eye,
> He finds a joy, denied a citizen,
> In the free vision of an ampler sky.
>
> Seasons, not consuls, set his annual mark
> —The fruit, for autumn, for the spring, the flowers;
> And in one field, from daybreak to the dark,
> His labour registers the passing hours.
>
> He views the tall oak, where he sowed the seed,
> And ages with his own coeval trees,
> Still hale and vigorous, with a sturdy breed
> Of children's children gathered at his knees.
>
> To him lake Garda seems the Arabian sand,
> Verona, distant as the darkest Moor;
> —Travel, then, if you will, from land to land;
> *He* knows that Life is knocking at his door.
>
> —*E. E. Sikes*

There is an epithalamium for a friend in 145 lines (25), and an appreciation of the salubrious hot springs of Aponus (near Padua) in 100 (26). The attractive poem on the *Phoenix* (27; 110 lines) tells that bird's intriguing life history, as Herodotus and Tacitus (*Annals* 6.28) had done. Of a kindred poem, attributed to Lactantius, there is a much expanded translation in Anglo-Saxon. It is plain that one of the *Phoenix* poems borrowed from the other, and if the poem ascribed to Lactantius is actually his, Claudianus is the copyist; but Claudianus' is far the better and more spirited poem, and the other may be falsely ascribed to Lactantius.

Number 28 again deals with an Egyptian subject—the inundation of the Nile. Number 29 deals with the power of the magnet, whose force of attraction is like Venus'. The longest poem in the collection is the *Praise of Serena* (30) in 236 lines; despite the courtliness of the language we sense a real admiration for a gentle and learned lady. The *Letter to Serena* which follows (31) expresses the poet's thanks. Number 32, *Of the Savior,* celebrates the virgin birth and invokes blessing upon the emperor. Numbers 33–39 are seven variations on the familiar theme of a drop of water enclosed in a crystal. Numbers 40 and 41 are letters to Olybrius and Probinus. The conclusion of the *Shorter Poems* is the 128-line fragment of a *gigantomachia* (52). The poem may have been interrupted by the author's death, or a loss of a number of pages may be due to the position of the poem at the end of the collection. The *Rape of Proserpina,* to which we now turn, has a separate manuscript tradition.

Whatever the merits of Claudianus' other long poems may be, their audience must be limited to the curious who have either a special interest in the politics of the period or who, themselves remaining emotionally impervious, wish to see how well politics can be forged into poetry. Claudianus gives ample satisfaction to both groups. He is a prime historical source, and comparison with parallel sources, where such are available, has demonstrated his general accuracy. Political poetry is notoriously stiff and stilted, characterized by frigid conceits and a general sense of weary perfunctoriness. In Claudianus the strict formalism of the classicist, paradoxically, effects the release of a genuine ardor, which gives new warmth to frigid conceits and never seems to flag. But for the ordinary reader the *Rape of Proserpina,* which is happily Claudianus' finest work in other respects, is also the most accessible. It does not ask the reader to transport himself to the alien country of fourth-century *Realpolitik* but carries him easily to the nearer realm of mythological fancy to experience anew and more fully one of its most charming creations.

The story in brief is as follows. Pluto complains of his unwedded state and petitions Jupiter for a helpmeet. Proserpina, whose mother, Ceres, has kept her carefully secluded from suitors in a secret spot in

Sicily, is chosen, and Venus is dispatched to release the maiden. Henna, mother of blossoms, together with gentle Zephyr, causes the meadow to bloom with beautiful spring flowers, and while Proserpina is busily plucking flowers Pluto appears amid fearful clamor and carries the unsuspecting maiden off in his chariot. The god attempts to assuage her grief, and she is magnificently welcomed in Hades by the rejoicing shades. At an assembly of the gods Jupiter announces that the golden age of Saturn must now end and that henceforward men must labor for livelihood. Thereupon Nature (personified, as is Claudianus' habit) complains that earth has fallen barren and that mankind must therefore be reduced to a bestial existence. Returning from a visit to Cybele in Phrygia Ceres is anguished to find her daughter gone and can discover no hint of her whereabouts. In order to avert the peril to mankind Jupiter resolves that Ceres should traverse the countries of the world in her search and introduce agriculture everywhere. The poem breaks off with the preparations for Ceres' journey. Here are a few specimen lines from the account of the marriage in hell (3.326–334):

> The land of greyness laughs. The buried rush
> to take their festal seats; the ghosts are gay;
> garlanded Manes drink in holiday.
> With song the gloom of silence strangely breaks;
> throughout the murk of hell no wailing wakes;
> even the night of ages seems to thin;
> no more the dreadful urn is judging sin;
> lashes no longer hiss; each prison-cell
> is quiet, for the pain has ceased in hell.
>
> —*Jack Lindsay*

But no outline and no specimen can communicate the rich tapestry of the *Rape of Proserpina.* There is lavish but elegant richness in description, in imagery, in the full-throated and dramatic encounter of the divine *dramatis personae,* in the sombre elegiac tone which pervades the whole—a richness not of meretricious tinsel but of pure gold, and gold never made tawdry, as abundance of gold sometimes is, by faulty taste. It is remarkable that Claudianus' late-learned Latin is so completely adequate to the far reaches of his imagination. Though he must have worked at high speed—the ten thousand verses we have were written within nine years—his Latinity is fully equal to that of the best Silver Age writers, and in vital poetic energy he surpasses such writers as Valerius Flaccus, Statius, and Silius Italicus.

Claudianus was the best but not the only poet of his kind. A poet from Spain, at the other end of the empire, also received the honor of a statue erected in the Forum of Trajan, and the inscription from this statue, set up in A.D. 435, has also been preserved (*Corpus inscriptionum Latinarum* 6.1724). This poet was Merobaudes, for whom the general and statesman Aetius occupied the place Stilicho occupied for Claudianus. But Merobaudes' poems have perished, except for five fragmentary pieces discovered in palimpsest in 1823, and a *Laus Christi* in thirty hexameters, which was long thought to be Claudianus' but was found to be Merobaudes' in a manuscript discovered in 1546 which has since disappeared.

If the sun of classical poetry sets with Claudianus there is still an afterglow, and its chief light is Claudius Rutilius Namatianus, born late in the fourth century of a Gallo-Roman family, probably at Toulouse. Rutilius himself held high office under Honorius, who reigned A.D. 395–423. His poem shows that he possessed literary taste and learning and that he was a pagan with an inclination towards Stoicism. Six years after the sack of Rome in 410 Rutilius undertook a journey from Rome to his estates in Gaul, and because the overland route was unsafe he decided to go by sea. His poem *De reditu suo,* "The Voyage Home," is an account of this journey, in elegiac meter, in one book of 644 lines and the beginning of a second which ends abruptly at line 68. A few lines before the end the poet says, "Let us now resume the voyage"—clearly indicating that more was to come; whether the remainder was lost or never written it is impossible to say. The poem is in the form of a journal, from September 22 to November 21, 416. In his proem the poet explains the occasion of his work and apologizes for leaving Rome, to which he proceeds to address an eloquent eulogy (47–164) in praise of its physical and spiritual qualities. Here Rutilius has a verse (66) reminiscent of both Marcus Aurelius and the *City of God: Urbem fecisti quod prius orbis erat,* "Thou hast made a city of what was erstwhile a world." The poet makes his farewells and proceeds to Ostia, whence he can still see Rome and fancy he hears her sounds. The stages of the journey are Centumcellae, Portus Herculis, and a bivouac past the mouth of the Umbro. The sight of Elba suggests some lines in praise of iron. At Faleria the travelers chance upon an Osiris festival and are annoyed by an extortionate Jewish landlord. The poet takes the occasion to revile Jewish ritual practices and beliefs. "Each seventh day is condemned to ignoble sloth, as 'twere an effeminate picture of god fatigued" (391-92). At Populonia they receive news from Rome. On the fifth day Corsica comes into view, and the sight of Capraria provokes an attack on the monks there: "What silly fanaticism of a distorted brain is it to be unable to endure even blessings because of your terror of ills?" (445-46). At Volaterrana Vada the poet visits his friend Albinus and describes the operation of neighboring salt pans. A delay caused by a gale is beguiled by the visit of a friend from Toulouse. On Gorgon island there lives a hermit: "Surely, I ask, this sect is not less powerful than the drugs of Circe? In her days men's bodies were transformed, now 'tis their minds" (525-26). During a long stop at a port near Pisa the poet visits a friend, eulogizes him and Pisa, and inspects a statue erected by the Pisans to his own father; when weather is adverse for sailing the poet indulges in a boar hunt. Book 1 closes with the description of the storm. The sixty-eight lines of Book 2 carry the traveler only as far as Luna, but it contains a description of Italy, an invective against the dead Stilicho, and an account of the marble quarries at Luna.

Our poet is a full-blooded man with a keen eye and a consuming interest in things and men, with strong likes, as for his friends, and strong dislikes, as for Jews, monks, or Stilicho. For all its rhetoric, his encomium of Rome is a deeply felt hymn to the glory and the majesty of the eternal city. His meter admits some unclassical usages, but it is agile, graceful, and forceful. In the vivid personality it reflects, in the greater variety and interest of its subject matter, and in its deeper sincerity, the *Voyage Home* is a better poem than the *Mosella* with which it must inevitably be compared.

The troubled state of Rutilius' world is illustrated by the autobiographical *Eucharisticon* of Ausonius' grandson Paulinus of Pella (in Macedonia), which he wrote in 459, when he was past the age of eighty. Cicero, Propertius, Horace, and Ovid had written of their own lives in verse, and in Greek Gregory of Nazianz had written *On His Own Life, On His Own Matters,* and *On the Suffering of His Own Soul,* in iambics, hexameters, and elegiacs respectively. Paulinus' poem in 616 hexameters tells of his comfortable and virtuous youth—he takes credit for satisfying himself with his mother's maids rather than yielding to the charms of ladies of position—of the penetration of the barbarians "into the very entrails of the empire," of his elevation under the Goths and then his despoliation at their hands. At the age of forty-six he was converted to Christianity, and the remainder of his life was spent in poverty. Beyond its rather awkward versification there is nothing in Paulinus' piece to suggest poetry. The reader's sympathy may be engaged by a once happy and highly esteemed man fallen upon hard times in his old age, but Paulinus' stature is not sufficient to give his story tragic interest. Neither as man nor poet does he rise above mediocrity.

Reconciliation of the cultural values of Rome with professed Christianity and churchly preferment is best illustrated by Sidonius Apollinaris, the chief literary figure of the fifth century, who could be bishop of Clermont and call Rome (*Epistles* 1.6) "domicile of law, school of literature, senate house of merit, apex of the universe, fatherland of liberty, sole polity of the whole world." Sidonius Apollinaris was born in 431 at Lyon, of a family with important political connections. His father-in-law Avitus was made emperor in 455, and Sidonius delivered a *Panegyric* upon him in some six hundred hexameter lines which won him the honor of a statue in the Forum of Trajan. Of this *Panegyric* Gibbon wrote that "it seems to contain a very moderate proportion either of genius or of truth." With Majorian and then Anthemius who succeeded to the purple Sidonius made his peace with similar panegyrics. About 470 Sidonius became bishop of Clermont under unknown circumstances; his imperial father-in-law had found refuge from the disaffected Roman aristocracy in the episcopacy of Plaisance. In 474 Sidonius organized resistance against the Arian Euric and his Visigoths, but after Euric's success Sidonius won Euric over by the poem included in *Epistles* 8.3. It was as the subject of a Visigothic king that Sidonius died, in 487, as his surviving epitaph shows.

Until his episcopacy Sidonius wrote in verse. He then feared (*Epistles* 9.12) "that a reputation as a poet might sully the strictness requisite to a priest," and the remainder of his literary work took the form of letters. Apparently Christianity did not possess Sidonius as pro-

foundly as it did Paulinus of Nola and others who were able to re-
direct their poetic efforts to Christian themes. He could set a Christian
poet like Prudentius on a level with Horace (*Epistles* 2.9.4), but,
convinced though he was of his own talents, could not emulate him.
Sidonius' poetry comprises twenty-four pieces on various subjects
and in various meters. A number have detached prologues, like Claudianus', some in prose. The content is preponderantly courtly, though
there are some more frivolous pieces. Besides the three *Panegyrics*
mentioned above, there are two *Epithalamia* (10 and 15), modeled
upon those of Statius and Claudianus but with an even greater ap-
paratus of mythological, philosophical, and literary scholarship. Similarly learned is 9, in 346 hendecasyllabic lines. Number 23, in 512
hendecasyllables, is devoted to the praise of the Consentii, father and
son, and of their native Narbo. The example of Statius is expressly invoked in 22, which is a detailed description of the castle of Leontios,
in 235 hexameters. The closing poem (24) is the author's *propempticon* to his book. Scattered among Sidonius' letters are thirteen additional poems. Except for two in the last book (9.13, 16), these are all
short; 9.16 is in forty-one Sapphic strophes. Sidonius' versification is
facile and correct, and his poetic style is simple. Many lines in his
longer poems are simply versified prose; unadorned lists of names
fitted into the metrical scheme (as at 5.475 ff.) are reminiscent of the
early efforts of Ennius or Naevius. One value of Sidonius' poems is
in the light they throw on the social and political history of Gaul;
particularly memorable are the portraits of the Huns in the *Panegyric
on Anthemius* and of the Franks in the *Panegyric on Majorian*. Another value is in the curious literary information drawn from Sidonius'
astonishingly wide reading; Numbers 2, 9, 15, and 23 are especially
useful to the literary historian. Some seventy ancient authors are cited
either directly or by circumlocution or by reference to familiar content. But literary judgments are purely conventional: Cicero is praised
for his eloquence, Sallust for his brevity, Varro for his learning,
Plautus for his wit. Sidonius' use of literature, and other facets of his
mind, may be illustrated from his acknowledgement to Claudianus
Mamertus for the latter's *De statu animae* (*Epistles* 4.3):

When your book unfolds its scholarship against what it is opposing, it
proves itself equal to authors in both languages in point of morals and
learned attainments. It thinks like Pythagoras, it distinguishes like Socrates,

it explains like Plato, it drapes its meaning like Aristotle, it flatters like Aeschines, it is impassioned like Demosthenes, it is flowery like Hortensius, it inflames like Cethegus, it incites like Curio, it temporizes like Fabius, it feigns like Crassus, it dissimulates like Caesar, it counsels like Cato, it dissuades like Appius, it persuades like Tullius. . . .

There follow comparisons with the Christian writers Jerome, Lactantius, Augustine, Hilary, John Chrysostom, Basil, Gregory, Orosius, Rufinus, Eusebius, Eucherius, Paulinus, and Ambrose. Such passages as these bespeak the emptiness not only of the writer but also of the addressees who valued Sidonius' effusions and to whom qualities of imagination and invention and critical judgment were equally alien.

The high esteem in which his letters were held compensated Sidonius for the poetic fame which he resigned. His models were Symmachus and, to a greater extent, the Younger Pliny. So closely does Sidonius follow Pliny that the division of his 147 letters into nine books is sufficient proof that Pliny's tenth book, containing the Trajan correspondence, was separately transmitted. Inferior as Sidonius' letters are, yet their reflection of the current social scene and of the character of their author makes them much more like Pliny's than like the quite empty verbiage of Symmachus'. Sidonius resembles Pliny not only in his range of interests and in his style, but also in his vanity, his yearning for applause, his exaggerated praise of his friends, and his amiable traits of generosity, sympathy, helpfulness. Among the letters mention may be made of 1.2, a characterization of Theodoric; 1.7, on Avandus' trial for treason; 1.11, on a satire falsely ascribed to Sidonius; 2.2, a description of Sidonius' villa; 4.3, from which a specimen is cited above; 8.6 and 11 and 9.13 and 16, which contain autobiographical details. Thirty-five letters (6.1–12, 7.1–11, 8.13–15, 9.2–11) are addressed to bishops and close with *memor nostri esse dignare domine papa,* "Deign to be mindful of us, Lord Father," instead of the customary *Vale.* One (7.4) contains a long address which Sidonius states he composed in six hours during two summer nights but which is nevertheless adorned with all the luxuriance of traditional rhetoric. In flattery to the prelates he addresses Sidonius exhibits the fulsomeness of the panegyrist. But aside from formal expressions, Sidonius' letters show no particular Christian coloring; despite his episcopacy Christianity seems to have affected him no more deeply than it did Ausonius. Perhaps exaggerated self-esteem and pride of learning combined with intellectual poverty rendered Sidonius incapable of profound conversion; in any case spiritual emptiness makes the curled artificiality and the turgid rhetoric of his style more objectionable. Side by side with learned archaisms we have usages which show Latin in disintegration: comparatives in two words (*plus celsos*); inflections replaced by prepositions (*nebula de pulvere*); infinitives replaced by *quod* or *quia* with indicative or subjunctive; new formations like *cervicositas, saeculiloquus, familiarescere, phthisiscere, crepusculasceus*. In terms of taste, as of language, the interval between Sidonius' letters and Pliny's is very great.

The ultimate bankruptcy of the classical tradition artificially maintained in insulation and divorced from fresh currents of life and thought is illustrated by the work of Magnus Felix Ennodius (437–521), another Gallic littérateur who attained the episcopacy. Ennodius was born at Arles of a prominent family but was orphaned early and educated under the care of an aunt in Liguria. At her death in 489 he was received into a rich family, and when his engagement to the daughter of the family was broken he took holy orders (about 494) and removed to Milan, where his uncle Laurentius was bishop. He was secretary to Laurentius when Laurentius participated in the council (under the Arian Theodoric) which upheld the claim of Symmachus and rejected that of another Laurentius to the papacy to which both had been elected. In 515 Ennodius became bishop of Pavia, and in 515 and 517 he headed embassies from Pope Hormisdas to Emperor Anastasius looking towards union of the eastern and western churches. Ennodius was a prolific writer in prose and verse, and the variety of his works affords a conspectus of the literary interests of his age. Devotion to Christianity no longer needed to be militant, and in literature as in architecture the Church could tolerate ornaments drawn from paganism; but the remarkable thing about writers like Ennodius is that their secular writings tend to be not merely non-Christian but actually pagan. There is naturally no systematic program for restoring the values of paganism, but there is also no true amalgam of the disparate strands to form a harmonious whole.

Ennodius' literary remains fall into four categories: *Opuscula*, or prose miscellanies; *Dictiones*, or discourses; *Letters;* and verse compositions. Among the miscellanies far the longest and the best piece is the *Life of Epiphanius,* bishop of Pavia (438–96), who had consecrated Ennodius into the priesthood and had continued to befriend him. Epiphanius was an admirable character and devoted to the cause of peace. A far less attractive *Life* is that of *St. Anthony of Lerins,* which Ennodius wrote to order. The meager data of the monk's life are padded with bombast and descriptions as irrelevant as they are grotesque. Ennodius' *Anthony* may serve as an extreme example of the rhetorical excesses of the fifth century. A style similarly tortured characterizes Ennodius' *Panegyric on Theodoric,* thanking the emperor for tolerating Catholicism and for supporting Pope Symmachus. The *Panegyric* possesses considerable interest as a historical document. The *Parainesis didascalica* or "Educational Admonition" sets forth Ennodius' ideals of ethics and culture, in prose and in verse. The work begins with an exhortation to cultivate true love of God, and then the virtues of Shamefastness, Faith, and Modesty personified speak their own praises in verse. There follows a transition to the cultural disciplines of grammar and rhetoric. Rhetoric is praised in most extravagant terms as the culmination of the educational process: *Qui nostris servit studiis mox imperat orbi*—rhetoric rules the world. Aside from the glorification of rhetoric nothing in the *Admonition* seems to emanate from profound conviction or to be vivified by missionary enthusiasm. The superficial moral doctrine is what one would expect of a conventional cleric in the discharge of his functions. Ennodius' own short autobiography, *Eucharisticon de vita sua,* is imitated from St. Augustine's *Confessions* but is altogether without Augustine's burning conviction and zeal and indeed at several points demonstrably disingenuous. Another of the *Miscellanies* that deserves mention describes the enfranchisement of a slave in the presence of a bishop.

Ennodius' twenty-eight *Dictiones* take us back to the age of the Elder Seneca. Thetis expresses her grief upon viewing the body of Achilles; Menelaus contemplates the ruin of Troy; Dido laments her desertion by Aeneas. One man is denounced for placing a statue of Minerva in an unseemly place, and another for gambling away a field in which his parents were buried. There are *controversiae* from the Elder Seneca, and ethical harangues by mythical personages. There are scholastic discourses, eulogizing professors and pupils. Perhaps the best is the discourse for the anniversary of Laurentius of Milan. Three out of the six discourses which deal with churchly matters or are addressed to prelates were composed for delivery by others, and their inclusion in Ennodius' works is remarkable. His 297 letters comprise about half the bulk of Ennodius' prose remains. The letters are revisions of actual communications to such important contemporaries as the popes Symmachus and Hormisda, the orators Faustus and Avienus, and the writers Boethius, Olibrius, and Arator, but they are as empty as those of Symmachus, who was Ennodius' model, and so heavy with rhetorical embellishment as to be frequently unintelligible. They do provide some historical information, but far less than one would expect of a man of Ennodius' position and connections.

His poems make the picture of our fifth-century literary bishop complete. As in the case of Sidonius, his versification is correct, and because of his close dependence on classic models, the style of his poetry is actually easier than his prose. But there is no spark of originality or invention or verve. Only when he verges on the indecent does Ennodius himself seem to relish his work. The first of his two books of poems contains longer pieces. An epithalamium is an inferior imitation of Claudian; it is not only disfigured by obscenity but represents Cupid as reviling the Christian ideal of chastity. Two *Itineraria* describe journeys from Milan to Briançon and on the Po. There are *Panegyrics* on Epiphaenius, on Faustus, and on Olybrius, and a begging epistle for Dentorius, a teacher in Milan. There are twelve hymns, each in eight strophes, like those of Ambrose, but incomparably inferior to their model. The second book contains 151 epigrams, some actual inscriptions and others on persons or things. Many refer to the author himself and his works. Many are in questionable taste; for example, a series on Pasiphae and her erotic aberration.

Except in his defense of Pope Symmachus against the partisans of Laurentius, Ennodius avoids doctrinal matters and very rarely cites Scripture. As a writer his mind is so steeped in the pagan tradition that he can speak of the Christian heaven as Olympus. But whereas a somewhat kindred Greek figure like Synesius of Cyrene, who was also a bishop and also a classicizing writer, was able to combine two vital traditions to make a mutually supporting harmony, in a writer like Ennodius the factors remain in suspense, incapable of combination, it may be, because neither, to men of Ennodius' stamp, was truly vital.

The loss of such writers as Sidonius Apollinaris or Ennodius would be regrettable but no great calamity. The loss of Martianus Capella, Boethius, or Cassiodorus Senator would have dealt the intellectual life of the Middle Ages a very severe blow. Of the three, Martianus Capella is negligible as an intellect or an artist, but his *Nine Books on the Marriage of Philology and Mercury and on the Seven Liberal Arts* was among the half dozen most widely circulated books in the Middle Ages and literally shaped European education. Capella was a lawyer in Madaura in Africa and wrote his book in the first quarter of the fifth century. The work is an awkward allegory, in prose and verse, and thus in form a Menippean satire, as is Boethius' *Consolation of Philosophy*. Varro, who introduced the Menippean form to Latin literature, is Capella's chief source, and he credits Satire personified with having dictated this book to him. The style is consciously modeled on Apuleius but is more involved and verbose and fuller of metaphor; the verse is simpler. The allegory itself falls little short of the ludicrous. The first two books present the allegory proper, the marriage of Mercury to a nymph called Philology. Capella's son is concerned for his elderly father's sanity when he hears him singing a wedding song to himself and is relieved by the explanation that the song refers to a marriage which is the subject of a book Satire dictated to him. Mercury, distressed at remaining a bachelor so long, fails in attempts to win Sophia, Mantice, or Psyche, and is advised by Virtus to obtain the help of Apollo, who suggests Philology as a suitable bride. The elaborate procedures incident to obtaining the consent of Jupiter and the requisite immortality for Philology are recounted in grotesque detail. For example, Athanasia, who has been assigned the office, is unable to raise the learned maid to heaven until she has removed a load from her breast by vomiting up a parcel of miscellaneous books, which the Muses proceed to gather up. Phoebus brings forward seven damsels, who are Mercury's present to his bride, and each of the seven discourses on her specialty in the remaining seven books. The seven arts are the familiar curriculum of the schools—the *trivium* of grammar, logic, and rhetoric, and the *quadrivium* (the word is Boethius') of arithmetic, music, geometry, and astronomy; Capella did not include the disciplines of medicine and architecture, which Varro had added to the seven. Besides Varro, Capella used the Elder Pliny and other Roman encyclopedists. His own book is in fact an encyclopedia of the culture of his time and was a principal avenue for the transmission of that culture. A passage on the heliocentric theory, for example, was quoted by Copernicus. The omission of any mention of Christianity by a countryman and virtual contemporary of Augustine cannot have been other than intentional.

The theological treatises which Boethius wrote were long denied to him by modern scholars because his other scholarly writings show a similar exclusive concern for the perpetuation of the humanistic legacy, and his spirited *Consolation,* where one would soonest expect some expression of Christian hope, shows no hint of Christianity. Anicius Manlius Severinus Boethius was born about A.D. 480 of the very highest stratum of Roman nobility. His father-in-law, and possibly the guardian of his youth, was a Symmachus, great-grandson of the Symmachus who opposed Ambrose in the matter of Victory. His father had been consul, he himself was consul (in 510), and his two sons were consuls. He was high in the confidence of the Arian Theodoric until he was involved in a charge of high treason against his friend Albinus, was put into prison (where he wrote the *Consolation*), and was tortured to death in A.D. 524. From his earliest youth Boethius was devoted to learning, and he declared his purpose to translate and write commentaries upon all the writings of both Aristotle and Plato and construct a harmony of the two. Of this ambitious scheme he was able to write only on Aristotle's *On Interpretation* and *Categories,* on Porphyry's *Introduction* to Aristotle's *Categories,* and on Cicero's *Topica.* In addition to these translations and commentaries Boethius wrote a number of independent philosophical works, dealing mostly with logic, and largely derivative from Peripatetic sources. But Boethius was convinced that a necessary prerequisite to the study of philosophy was the *quadrivium.* His books on arithmetic and music have been pronounced little more than translations; the geometry under his name is probably spurious; and there is no astronomy—but it is almost certain that he did produce books on all four disciplines. The work on music was particularly influential; Chaucer mentions it in the *Nun's Priest's Tale* and reproduces its argument on sound waves in the *House of Fame* (788–822). Of four (1, 2, 3, 5) of the five *Theological Tractates* the chief interest for us is that they apply Aristotelianism to the study of theology, and so pave the way for Thomas

Aquinas and the schoolmen. The fourth treatise is a simple and easy exposition *On the Catholic Faith,* and its authenticity has been questioned by scholars who accept the other four as genuine.

But the book of Boethius which has taken its place among the spiritual treasures of the race is the *Consolation of Philosophy.* The problem of the treatise is to explain how in a world governed by *deus rector mundi* the good suffer the penalties of crime and the wicked win the rewards of virtue (*pretium sceleris—diadema*). Boethius' metaphysical explanation may fail to carry conviction, but the things he says incidentally and his general attitude reveal a gallantry of spirit which must carry its lesson. After a lifetime spent in public administration and in trying to civilize a Gothic king, he finds himself in prison, condemned to death. There, with a combination of majestic calm and sweet reasonableness he sets forth, as imperturbably as though he were still a powerful minister, the joys of contemplation, the delight in the beauty of the world, and the hopes for mankind which still did not desert him. It is the sense of responsibility to the humanistic tradition which is the more important lesson of the *Consolation,* and one may surmise that it is this aspect of his work which attracted such translators as Alfred the Great and Chaucer, and which certainly moved Gibbon to call his work "not unworthy of the leisure of Plato or Tully."

The *Consolation* too is in the form of a Menippean satire, with thirty-nine poems worked into the text, and, like the *Marriage of Philology and Mercury,* it too uses allegory, at least in the first book, where the author recounts his wrongs to Mistress Philosophy; but here a scholar and a man of taste speaks. As he sits dejected upon his couch, surrounded by the Muses of poetry who suggest accents of lamentation, there appears to him a lady at once young and of timeless age, of human stature and of a loftiness beyond human vision. The lower part of her robe bears the letter *pi,* to denote practical philosophy, and the upper part *theta,* to denote theoretical or pure philosophy. The garment shows signs of hard usage; Epicureans, Stoics, and others have torn shreds from it, fancying they had obtained the whole garment. She drives away the "theatrical strumpets" of Muses, for poetry "accustoms the minds of men to the disease but does not set them free," and begins her mission of succor.

The second book discusses the vagaries of Fortune; the man who truly knows himself cannot be disturbed by her mutability. He will have a correct understanding of the *summum bonum,* which is the subject matter of Book 3. Book 4 justifies God's government. Fate and providence are distinguished as follows (4.6.56 ff.): "Providence is the immovable and simple form of events that are to be; Fate is the movable intertwining and the order in time of the events which the Divine Simplicity has bidden come into being. Therefore all things which are under Fate are also subject to Providence, to which even Fate itself is subject. Some things, indeed, under the will of Providence rise above the ordered sequence of Fate." This introduces the subject of Book 5, which is free will.

In no specimen of the Menippean are the verses so effectively used; like the sonnets in Dante's *Vita Nuova* they "gather up in music the feelings occasioned by the narrated events." There is indeed a great deal of Boethius in Dante, not merely in his theology but in details.

> *Nessun maggior dolore*
> *Che recordarsi del tempo felice*
> *Nella miseria*

is from 2.4, and the last line of the *Divine Comedy* is from a very carefully constructed poem (2.8), which sings of the love that moves sun and stars—

> *hanc rerum seriem ligat*
> *terras ac pelagus regens*
> *et caelo imperitans amor.*

Boethius will relieve a hard discussion by a poem in which he illustrates the return of nature to itself by a caged bird which, when it again beholds the forest, spurns the sprinkled crumbs

> *silvas tantum maesta requirit*
> *silvas tantum voce susurrat,*

and then proceed at once, "You too, creatures of the earth, though in a pale image, yet dream of your origin." Greek tragedy integrates its choral interludes no more skillfully. No less effective is Boethius' skillful use of meter itself. The long labors of the siege of Troy and of Hercules are written in Sapphics, but without the short fourth line (Adonic) of the Sapphic strophe, so that the reader's mind and voice move without pause until the labors are over and heavenly rest succeeds, where the only Adonic in the poem marks its conclusion. Boethius sums up not only antiquity's erudition and acumen but also, and more remarkably, its taste; it is the latter quality which gives special point to Gibbon's judgment that "the senator Boethius is last of the Romans whom Cato or Tully could have acknowledged for their countryman."

In taste as well as learning and character Boethius' friend Magnus Aurelius Cassiodorus Senator was inferior, but he perhaps deserves even greater credit for preserving humanist culture, for he introduced the copying of manuscripts as a monastic occupation. Cassiodorus was also born about 480, and of lineage almost as proud as Boethius'. While still in his twenties he was appointed to a quaestorship in which he conducted the royal correspondence and composed state documents. At three periods he held offices which involved these duties— quaestor of the palace, 507–511; master of offices, 523–27; and praetorian prefect, 533–37. In 526 the great king Theodoric was succeeded by his daughter Amalasuntha as regent for her son Athalaric, upon whose death in 534 Theodahad usurped the throne; in 536 Theodahad was supplanted by Witigis. On the surface Cassiodorus' easy shift of loyalty from Amalasuntha to Theodahad to Witigis looks like time-serving, but Cassiodorus persisted in a sincere conviction that Italy was better off under Ostrogothic government than she would have been under Constantinople, and that it was better for Roman civilization, government and culture to survive under the Goths than to die. Upon his retirement from public life Cassiodorus withdrew to his ancestral estates at Squillace in southern Italy and founded two monasteries, a hermitage in the hills at Castellum for those who desired solitary austerity, and a less strict establishment on his own estate, called Vivarium from the nearby fishponds. Vivarium was the nursery of literary monasticism; it was in its *scriptorium* that monks set to copying manuscripts, pagan and Christian, night and day. Cassiodorus himself lived to be almost a hundred.

His retirement marks a division in the literary works of Cassiodorus. Before his retirement he wrote *Variae,* twelve books of official correspondence; a *Family History of the Cassiodori; Gothic History; Chronica;* and *Orations.* After his retirement he wrote the *Institutes of Divine and Secular Literature; On Orthography;* and various religious works. Cassiodorus' friends, the preface of the *Variae* says, insisted on his publishing his letters in order to preserve a record of his apt speeches and a mirror of his own mind. The very title shows that form rather than matter was Cassiodorus' main consideration in publishing; the collection was entitled *Variae* because good writing demands different styles for people of different degree. Nevertheless, Cassiodorus' letters are as important a source for the Ostrogothic government of Rome as are Cicero's for the end of the republic. All aspects of administration are dealt with, and there are letters on law, education, and religion; though many actual letters dealing with political matters were discarded for prudential considerations or stylistic deficiencies, on politics too Cassiodorus' letters are very informing. Books 6 and 7 of the *Variae* contain ready-made formulae for admission to various offices of state, prepared by Cassiodorus to lighten the burden of his successors. Here is the commission for the quaestorship:

We embrace the Quaestorship with our whole heart, for we regard it as the voice of our own tongue. Its holder must be privy to our own thoughts, that he may say rightly that which he knows we feel. If in aught we hesitate, we seek aid from the Quaestor, who is the treasury of the State's fair fame and the armoury of its laws. Other officials may seek the comfort of collaborators; your dignity, O Quaestor, ministers counsel to the Sovereign. Persuaded, therefore, by the repute of your prudence and eloquence, we hereby confer on you the Quaestorship: the glory of letters, the shrine of civilized living, the mother of all honours, the home of temperance, the seat of all virtues.

—*Eleanor Shipley Duckett*

In 540 Cassiodorus added his treatise *On the Soul* to the *Variae* as its thirteenth book. The treatise presents well-worn proofs of the incorporeality of the soul and ends with a vivid description of the endless material torment of the wicked and the eternal joy of the redeemed in the world to come.

Of the *Family History of the Cassiodori* we have only a fragment (called *Anecdoton Holderi*), itself made up of excerpts. The fragment contains short accounts of Cassiodorus himself, of Symmachus, and of Boethius, to whom it credits the authorship of the *Theological Tractates* which was long in dispute. Cassiodorus' *Chronica* is mostly a list of Assyrian and Latin kings and Roman consuls from Adam to A.D. 519, with particularly favorable notices of the Ostrogoths. The *Family History* says that at the bidding of Theodoric Cassiodorus wrote "the history of the Goths, of their origin, their homes, and their customs in twelve books," and in a letter (9.25) Cassiodorus claims to have shown the glory of the Gothic race and to have made the origin of the Goths part of Roman history. Just as Hellenistic writers, then, had justified Roman sway by deriving Roman descent from the Trojans, so seven hundred years later Cassiodorus sought to bestow respectability on the Goths. Cassiodorus' *Gothic History* is lost, but a good notion of it may be had from *The Origin and Deeds of the Goths* (usually cited, after Mommsen, as *Getica*) written by Cassiodorus' pupil Jordanes. The *Getica* identifies the Goths with the Getae and with the Scythians, and represents them as having fought against the Greeks at Troy and against the Persian kings Cyrus and Darius. But for the fourth and fifth centuries A.D. the *Getica* is our main source for the traditions of Gothic history.

Of all the writings of Cassiodorus' official period it may be said that their chief value is historical. It is his work at Vivarium which makes him the proper transition from Rome to the Middle Ages. In other Christian humanists Christianity and humanism had been juxtaposed indeed, but except where one was definitely made ancillary to the other each maintained its separate way Perhaps no complete fusion was ever achieved; perhaps neither could compromise without forfeiting something essential. But the pattern of Vivarium, and of Cassiodorus' *Institutes,* at least made it possible for each to survive without destroying the other. Even in his official period Cassiodorus had made an abortive attempt to found a school of Christian literature at Rome "in which the soul might gain eternal salvation, and the tongue acquire beauty by the exercise of the chaste and pure eloquence of the Christians." Martianus' *Marriage* had consciously avoided Christianity in treating of the seven liberal arts; in Cassiodorus the seven liberal arts are the second part of a treatise of which the first part is an introduction to the study of the manuscripts of the Bible. Sacred and secular learning are presented in a single survey, just as both sacred and secular books were multiplied at Vivarium. When he was ninety-three Cassiodorus wrote a treatise on spelling (*De orthographia*) for copyists. Cassiodorus was responsible for other works also. He wrote a number of Biblical commentaries, edited a translation of Josephus, entrusted the composition of a *Tripartite Ecclesi-*

astical History to his friend Epiphanius. But only the second part of the *Institutes,* in a shorter and longer version, became a popular book. The Middle Ages felt that Cassiodorus could be trusted with the direction of secular studies. Humanism had not struck a bad bargain after all, as the writing and reading of this book shows.

XXII

THE WRITERS OF CHRISTIANITY

IN ALL THE SIGNIFICANT ROMAN AUTHORS WITH whom we have had to deal, from Ennius to the humanists who preferred Christianity, the ideal of Rome was a present reality. Certainly none was consciously opposed to that ideal, and it is generally true that the greater the writer as writer, the more pronounced also was his awareness of responsibility to the Roman ideal. We must therefore deal separately with a group of writers whom logic compelled to oppose the Roman ideal and who, paradoxically, though not un-Roman were anti-Roman. Of these writers too it may be said that their eminence as writers, quite aside from their other merits, was in proportion to the intensity of their opposition.

Even after Christians recognized that the Second Coming was not immediately imminent, they still regarded themselves as strangers and pilgrims on earth. For them the rule of Rome was temporary and essentially alien; their permanent citizenship and their fundamental loyalty was in a different kingdom. As time wore on and Christians reconciled themselves to a continuing sojourn in the worldly empire their inward detachment might not be visible in their outward conduct. As Tertullian (*Apology* 42) insists to his pagan opponents, Christians behaved as other men in social and political life, using the same legal and commercial system and following the same callings. But their loyalty to Rome was basically not as undivided as Rome demanded. Rome had proven hospitable to numerous foreign cults and would easily have tolerated Christianity if its practice did not conflict with the demands of the state. But Christianity was different from other foreign religions in that it claimed a superior authority which might override the authority of the state, and hence in a strict view Christianity was potentially subversive. With Rome and the Church each claiming sovereignty, compromise was in essence impossible; logic demanded that war between the two must persist, however intermittently, until one or the other yielded. Trajan's directive to

Pliny, cited above, strikes the juridical keynote of Roman policy. Christians as such were not to be sought out; that is, their cult was tolerated. If valid accusations came before the authorities, the accused was given opportunity to affirm his loyalty to the state by offering sacrifice before the statue of the emperor. If he refused to do so, he was executed, not for his beliefs but because he violated the reverence due to the majesty of the empire and its tutelary gods. Martyrdoms were precipitated by political exploitation of popular prejudices, but the legal position continued as laid down in Trajan's rescript.

Christianity was first propagated in the Greek-speaking eastern half of the empire and was able to be integrated with cultural life with relative ease. In Italy, Gaul, and Africa too Greek was the language of the Church as late as the third century; the earliest Christian community in Rome was largely of alien origin and socially and economically depressed, and tensions between it and the dominant pagans were exacerbated by natural class hostility and suspicion. Pagans like Symmachus feared the pollution of their cultural values, and the Christians suspected literary culture as an integral element in paganism. In the Latin-speaking west the vernacular naturally had to be used, and the earliest Latin versions of Scripture are antecedent to Tertullian. With the language its education too had to be accepted, and exposure to immorality, philosophy, and sensual love of beauty to be risked. Tertullian (*On Shows* 18) might insist that "secular letters are foolishness in the eyes of God," but in practice he must admit (*On Idolatry* 10) that secular studies are essential for meeting pagans on common ground. Jerome (*Epistles* 21.13) condemned "poetry, the wisdom of the world, the pompous eloquence of the orators, this food of devils," but he prescribes (*Epistles* 70.2) that the potential snare be introduced into Christianity with "her head shaven and her nails pared" like the Gentile captive in Deuteronomy 22.12. Jerome's dream (*Epistles* 22.30) is famous. "I am a Christian," he asserted, when he was asked his faith. "Thou art a Ciceronian," was the reply, "not a Christian; where thy treasure is there is thy heart also." And Augustine, who confesses to an early passion for pagan literature, thinks (*On Christian Doctrine* 4.2) that "the Egyptians should be spoiled" for the benefit of the Church.

Tertullian, the first major Latin writer on behalf of Christianity, did spoil the Egyptians to excellent purpose. Q. Septimius Florus

Tertullianus was born a pagan about A.D. 150–60 at Carthage and was educated in the same school of rhetoric as Apuleius. He visited Athens and Rome early in life and indulged in the loose habits of the metropolis. He practiced law and rhetoric at Rome. The circumstances of his conversion to Christianity are not known. It is clear that he was repelled by the emptiness of contemporary humanism, clear too that he was impressed by the steadfastness of Christians under persecution. In any case he returned to Carthage a Christian and probably became a priest. But his zeal for righteousness caused him to shift from loyalty to Rome to Montanist sympathies and then to his own puritanism, as a chronological conspectus of his works will show. *On the Prescription of Heretics,* written about 197, is an attack on all deviations from Rome. Before 202 Tertullian wrote a series of treatises, mostly practical —*On Dress of Women, On Patience, On Prayer,* and the like. After 202 his Montanist sympathies appear, and in 207 he left the Church. Succeeding treatises find even the Montanists too latitudinarian. *On Modesty,* written about 221, is a bitter attack on Pope Calixtus for declaring that adultery and fornication could be forgiven by the Church even after baptism.

But Tertullian's most characteristic and most readable work, displaying his relentlessly mordant irony, is in his defenses of Christians against pagan persecution. In 197/98 there was an outbreak of violence against Christians, who had kept aloof from popular celebration of the accession of Septimius Severus, and Tertullian promptly came to the aid of his brethren in a series of apologetic works. For those held in prison he wrote *To the Martyrs,* to encourage them and fortify their faith. In *Against the Heathen* (two books) he protested vehemently against laws which condemned Christians as such without examination of their behavior or manner of life. In particular Tertullian refuted the calumnies that Christians practiced incest and child murder and that they were disloyal to the empire. A similar defense addressed to provincial governors is the *Apologeticus,* written in a more restrained and lawyer-like tone, though it too breathes Tertullian's savage sarcasm. The source of anti-Christian sentiment is suggested by the following refutation (*Apologeticus* 6.9):

Where is the religious awe, where is the veneration owed by you to your ancestors? In dress, habit of life, furniture, feeling, yes! and speech, you have renounced your great-grandfathers! You are forever praising antiquity, and every day you improvise some new way of life.

—*T. R. Glover*

On the legal issue of the recognition of the emperor's divinity Tertullian retorts that the Christians demonstrate their loyalty to the empire by their more meaningful prayers *for* the emperor (30.4–6):

For all our emperors we offer prayer incessantly. We pray for life prolonged; for security to the empire; for protection to the imperial house; for brave armies, a faithful senate, a virtuous people, the world at rest, whatever as a man or Caesar the emperor could wish. These things I cannot ask from any but the God from whom I know I shall obtain them, both because He alone bestows them and because I have claims upon Him for their gift, as being a servant of His, rendering homage to Him alone, persecuted for His doctrine, offering to Him at His own requirement that costly and noble sacrifice of prayer despatched from a chaste body, an unstained soul, a sanctified spirit, not a few grains of incense a farthing buys—tears of an Arabian tree—not a few drops of wine, not the blood of some worthless ox to which death is a relief, and, in addition to other offensive things, a polluted conscience, so that one wonders, when your victims are examined by these vile priests, why the examination is not rather of the sacrificers than the sacrifices.

—*S. Thelwall*

Persecution, Tertullian assures his pagan addressees, will only strengthen the Church (50): "We multiply every time we are mowed down by you; the blood of Christians is seed." In the persecutions under Caracalla in 212/13 Tertullian again spoke up, and with sharper tone; the *To Scapula* warns the proconsul of Africa to leave the Christians alone.

These apologetic works are only a fraction of Tertullian's literary output; other treatises are practical, doctrinal, and polemic. The practical treatises prescribe Christian morality or behavior in certain situations or with reference to special groups or matters. *On the Chaplet,* for example, defends a Christian soldier who refuses to wear the honorary chaplet; *On Idolatry* condemns games, shows, theatrical and gladiatorial exhibitions, as brutal, immoral, and interwoven with pagan rites. There are also treatises *On Veiling Virgins, On the Adornment of Women, On Baptism, On Patience, On Prayer, On Modesty,*

On Repentance, On Shows. Of these the last named is the best known, possibly because of Gibbon's famous criticism of the vivid description of pagan torments in the last judgment with which it closes. Here is Gibbon's version of *De spectaculis* 30 and his comment:

"You are fond of spectacles," exclaims the stern Tertullian, "expect the greatest of all spectacles, the last and eternal judgment of the universe. How shall I admire, how laugh, how rejoice, how exult, when I behold so many proud monarchs, and fancied gods, groaning in the lowest abyss of darkness; so many magistrates, who persecuted the name of the Lord, liquefying in fiercer fires than they ever kindled against the Christians; so many sage philosophers blushing in red-hot flames with their deluded scholars; so many celebrated poets trembling before the tribunal, not of Minos, but of Christ; so many tragedians, more tuneful in the expression of their own sufferings; so many dancers—" But the humanity of the reader will permit me to draw a veil over the rest of this infernal description, which the zealous African pursues in a long variety of affected and unfeeling witticisms.

It is in attack and in exhortation that Tertullian's vehemence is at its best; his doctrinal treatises are not markedly creative. These are chiefly directed against the sects of the day except that into which Tertullian himself was drifting. *On the Soul* defends the corporeality of the soul against the Gnostics; *Against Praxeas* defends the doctrine of the Trinity against the Monarchianists; *On the Flesh of Christ* and *On the Resurrection of the Flesh* are of interest in the history of science as well as religion. Tertullian's major polemic is *Against Marcion,* in five books, which were repeatedly revised in accordance with Tertullian's changing insights.

Altogether, thirty-one of Tertullian's treatises are preserved, and more than a dozen others are alluded to. In form they are philosophical essays, like those of Cicero or Seneca, but their zeal is unequaled in earlier literature and unexampled in Tertullian's own age. Tertullian is always vehement on behalf of his cause and makes no pretense of impartiality. His style is impetuous, dramatic, direct, varied, richly illustrated, with frequent apostrophe and exclamation, always driven by his overwhelming conviction. But his conviction is not the intuition of an enthusiast but informed by wide erudition. Neither is his Latinity the expression of a simple soul; his elaborate knottiness makes Tertullian one of the most difficult Latin authors to read. He has been called a "barbarizing Tacitus" and also a "Christian Juvenal."

The former designation aptly characterizes Tertullian's style, and the latter, not only his sharp invective but his little pictures of daily life, both Christian and pagan, which possess both human interest and historical importance. Such passages and Tertullian's transparent honesty and conviction merit the attention of readers whom the refutation of forgotten heresies may leave cold.

The *Martyrdom of Perpetua and Felicitas* (who were persecuted in A.D. 202/3), extant in both Greek and Latin, is much simpler than Tertullian's usual style, but its Montanist leanings suggest that he may have published it. Perpetua was a lady of position, Felicitas a slave. When her father asked Perpetua to recant she declared she could not call herself other than a Christian any more than a pitcher could be called other than a pitcher. When the beasts attacked her in the amphitheater she modestly pulled her torn garment about her, and she bound her scattered locks neatly, for she did not wish to seem to mourn at the moment of her glory.

The finest Latin apology for Christianity is the dialogue *Octavius* of Minucius Felix, written probably in the third century in refutation of a (lost) attack by M. Cornelius Fronto about A.D. 150; Fronto's was apparently the only literary attack on Christianity in Latin. Minucius, like Tertullian, was a pagan and probably an African, who was well educated in rhetoric and the law and practiced in Rome. His *Octavius* is so skillfully written that its apologetic content seems incidental. The dialogue is reported as having taken place in the past, when three friends, Caecilius Natalis, who represents paganism, Octavius Januarius who refutes him, and Minucius himself who acts as umpire, are taking a walk in Ostia. Octavius rebuked Caecilius for throwing a formal kiss to a statue of Sarapis, and Caecilius delivers the attack on Christianity. Christians are too ignorant to know what they profess to know. There is no reason or providence in the universe. Rome flourished as long as it worshiped its gods, and it is wrong for the Christians to revile them. The Christians worship a crucified man; they indulge in hideous orgies, and they are really secretive, ignorant, miserable, unequal to the demands of this life and unfitted to forecast the life to come (5–13). Octavius replies that intelligence is a natural endowment which the Christians possess even if they have no wealth. Order in the universe implies a divine ruler, who is too great even to be named. Poets and philosophers agree that he is man's father and that he is one. Against such views the fables and worship of deified men have no weight. The very birds and animals know their images are not gods; their rites are grotesque and immoral. Roman successes were due to violence, not piety. Demons, not gods, are at the bottom of oracles and slanders against Christians. God can-not be contained in a temple. The Jews admit that they forsook God before he abandoned them. Philosophers have long maintained that the universe will eventually perish. God who created man can bring back to life and reward and punish. What Christians suffer is not punishment but discipline, heroically endured. They avoid pagan shows and practices as impious, cruel, and absurd (16–38). Caecilius thereupon acknowledges defeat and accepts Christianity (39–41). The *Octavius* is highly literate; it is filled with echoes from all the chief Latin authors, but its heaviest debt is to Cicero, and particularly to the *On the Nature of the Gods*. Both sides are frank, neither appeals to revealed authority. Of all the Christian apologies the *Octavius* is least likely to irritate and most likely to persuade an unprejudiced pagan.

A third African, born a pagan and trained in rhetoric, who has a high place in Christian literature is Cyprian. The date of Cyprian's birth is not known. He was converted, after an unchaste (as he him-self says: *To Donatus* 3–4) young manhood, became a priest, and in 248 was made bishop of Carthage. During the Decian persecutions in 250 he went into hiding for the good of his flock; he suffered martyr-dom in 258. For Catholicism Cyprian is a safer and steadier guide than Tertullian; as a writer he is far inferior. Where Tertullian is passionate and independent, Cyprian is temperate, prudent, pacific. All his writings grow out of his conscientious functioning as a bishop. The pressing issue in his day was the disposition of the *lapsi* who had backslid under persecution, either *sacrificati,* who had under pressure offered incense to pagan divinities, or *libellatici,* who had committed the lesser sin of purchasing a document (*libellus*) which certified their abjuration of Christianity. Cyprian's great concern was for the solidarity of the Church and the regularization of Christian life; this is the theme of his most characteristic work, *On the Unity of the Catholic Church.*

The weaknesses of Cyprian's style are apparent in his *To Donatus,* written shortly after he became a Christian. Here Cyprian recalls his own early moral blindness and the heavy chains which his passions had riveted upon him and presents arguments, largely drawn from Minucius Felix, that should turn an educated man to the Church. The work is indubitably sincere, but it is marred by an extremely verbose and somewhat sophomoric style. The *To Demetrianus* refutes the charge (dealt with also by Tertullian, Arnobius, Lactantius, and Augustine) that Christians were responsible for the calamities which had befallen Rome. *That Idols Are Not Gods* is merely a transcription, sometimes in their actual words, from Tertullian and Minucius Felix. The three books of *Testimonies to Quirinus* and *To Fortunatus on Exhortation to Martyrdom* search the Scriptures for evidence bearing on Judaism, on the nature of Christ, and on various points in Christian practice. It is characteristic of Cyprian that arguments are drawn not from logical demonstrations or philosophic principles but only from the light of Christian revelation.

Another group of Cyprian's writings are of a homiletic character. *On the Dress of Maidens* is a eulogy of virginity and a guide to maidenly deportment. *On the Lord's Prayer* emphasizes the social character of prayer (*Our* Father, *our* daily bread, forgive *us*): "When we pray it is not for one person alone but for all the people, because all the people form but a single body." Other homilies are *On Mortality* (fortifying the Christian against suffering and death), *On Works and Alms, On the Advantage of Patience, On Envy and Jealousy.* Besides these more formal compositions we have a large volume of Cyprian's correspondence (upwards of two hundred pages in Migne, *Patrologia Latina*), concerned with questions of church policy and practice. Cyprian's prestige was great enough to attract a number of apocryphal writings; some of these are early and not unworthy of Cyprian himself.

Among Cyprian's correspondence are two letters (30 and 36) of the schismatic Novatian, the most celebrated of the Roman clergy of his day. Among the many works ascribed to Novatian his authorship of *On the Trinity* and *On the Food of the Jews* seems established. *On the Trinity* is little more than a resume of Tertullian; the interest of *On the Food of the Jews* is its thoroughgoing allegorization of the animals whose flesh the Jews refused to eat. Novatian was the first Christian author to write exclusively in Latin; this marks the decline of Greek in the western Church.

First to be recorded in the history of Christian poetry is the enigmatic Commodian, who was born a pagan and became a bishop in the third century. His two works, remarkable for their barbarous meter and syntax and careful attention to acrostic arrangement, are *Instructions through the Initial Letters of Verses* and *Poem of Apologetics.* The former comprises eighty acrostic pieces of six to 48 verses divided into two books, and the latter 1,060 verses in couplets. The *Instructions* satirizes the individual pagan gods, exhorts infidels, and describes varieties of Christians—catechumen and priest, true and hypocrite, sober and drunk, taciturn and gossiping, true martyrs and false aspirants for martyrdom. The more interesting *Carmen apologeticum* sketches the history of Israel down to the Incarnation, continues with the early church, and portrays the struggle of Christ and anti-Christ in the last days. The latter section (791-end) is the fullest record of Christian chiliastic fantasies.

The Christian authors so far dealt with, whatever their personal vagaries, must be respected for their sound grounding in the faith they espoused and promulgated. Perhaps it is a sign of the securer position of the Christians that we now come upon an apologetic work which relies upon eloquence and wit rather than logic and scholarship. Arnobius, the author of the seven-book *Against the Heathen,* had taught rhetoric in Africa until he was sixty, when about A.D. 300 he was converted to Christianity by means of a dream; he wrote his book to allay his bishop's suspicions of his *bona fides. Against the Heathen* starts with a vigorous refutation of the charge that Christianity had brought calamity upon the world; if the gods do exist it is rather with the pagans that they are angry because of the gross conceptions entertained of them and the repulsive rites by which they are worshiped. Arnobius then applies his devastating wit to dissecting the most scandalous legends associated with various pagan cults. Of these things and of ancient literature generally he knew a great deal; of Christian Scriptures and doctrine apparently very little. He can assert that the soul must win its immortality by merit and that pagan gods continue to exist though relegated to the rank of demons, and he can proscribe all forms of external worship. His ample and sonorous style ransacks the entire arsenal of the rhetorical schools. He piles up a half dozen words for the same idea, embellishes it with numerous literary reminiscences, and rounds it out with carefully constructed metrical clausulae. Rhetorical questions and exclamations are heaped up in series of dozens, and there are numerous antitheses and alliterations and homoioteleuta. His rich vocabulary contains both archaic and popular elements. In its particular kind Arnobius' *Against the Heathens* is a scintillating performance.

Like Arnobius himself his pupil Lactantius, styled the "Christian Cicero," was an African, a rhetor, and a late convert to Christianity. Diocletian made him professor of rhetoric at Nicomedia, his residence in Bithynia, and when Constantine turned Christian he appointed Lactantius, then very old, tutor to his son Crispus. Lactantius appears to have produced a series of works before his conversion; his earliest extant work, written about 304, is *On the Handiwork of God,* a vindication of Providence from the attacks of certain philosophic schools. Even man's physique illustrates the working of providence: "How appropriate is the padded flesh of the buttocks for the function of sitting!" (13.5). Lactantius' next and most important work is the *Divine Institutions* in seven books, dedicated to Constantine, which aims to justify Christianity to educated minds. Books 1 and 2 (*On False Religion* and *On the Origin of Error*) are devoted to criticism of polytheism; proof texts from Scripture are cited but are always paralleled by arguments of the "philosophers." Book 3 (*On False Philosophy*) is a systematic critique of the Roman philosophers. From Book 4 onwards Lactantius sets himself to build up rather than criticize, but without renouncing polemics altogether. Book 4 (*On True Philosophy and Religion*) demonstrates the indissoluble union of philosophy and religion and presents the doctrines of the Christian faith. Book 5 (*On Justice*) deals with personal ethics and the principles of social justice. Book 6 (*On True Worship*) deduces Christian morality from its divine origin. Book 7 (*On the Happy Life*) deals with the ends of creation and of man and the immortality of the soul and closes with an exhortation to fight the good fight. As a theologian Lactantius carries no great weight; Jerome said of him (*Epistles* 58.10), "Would that he could affirm our doctrine as readily as he destroys others'." The merit of the *Institutions* is rather as a practical guide to an ethically integrated life.

On the Wrath of God, Lactantius' next work, is a dissertation on the appropriateness of anger as a divine attribute: without it there could be no providence or divine jurisdiction. In *On the Deaths of the Persecutors* the formidable effects of divine anger are demonstrated by a long list of the gruesome deaths suffered by the instigators of Christian persecutions. The treatise begins with a thanksgiving to Providence which had at last given the Christians moral and material repose and had laid their enemies low, and closes with a hymn of gratitude:

The Lord has purged the earth of those proud names. Let us then celebrate the triumph of God with joy; day and night let us offer him our prayer and praise, that he may establish for all time this peace which has been given to us after ten years of war.

The vengeful ardor of *On the Deaths of the Persecutors,* however recent history may have exculpated it, is different from Lactantius' usually equable tone. In general Lactantius is a temperate as well as a seasoned writer. He possesses taste and talent for the oratorical style, with its copiousness, its symmetry, its harmonious balance; he invents no startling metaphors and indulges in no archaisms and popular borrowings, and his deviations from classical syntax are very slight. Perhaps such regularity is what we should expect of a writer whose works mark the reconciliation of the Church and the empire, when Christianity was not merely tolerated but had become the binding rule of government.

The Edict of Milan (A.D. 313) did not, however, put an end to all pagan sympathies, as our accounts of Ammianus Marcellinus and of Symmachus have shown. Firmicus Maternus had written his devoutly pagan *Mathesis* before he wrote his *On the Error of Profane Religions,* and we still have such figures as St. Hilary of Poitiers, who was born a pagan and (about 350) became a bishop, was a strenuous controversialist against the Arians, and composed the first Latin hymns for the church. The considerable literature evoked by the Arian controversy cannot detain us here; we proceed next to St. Ambrose, the first of the four original doctors of the Church, whom we have previously encountered as Symmachus' opponent in the matter of the statue of Victory in the Roman senate. The episode is characteristic of Ambrose's devotion to the pastoral and political functions of his office; his literary production was relatively slight and is not an adequate reflection of his real importance in the history of the Church. Ambrose was also counselor to the emperors Gratian, Valentinian, and Theodosius.

Ambrose was born between A.D. 330 and 340 of a family that was at once Christian and politically important, and in 374, while still unbaptized, he was elected bishop of Milan. He applied himself diligently to study of Scripture and of the best Greek (rather than Latin) exegetes and theologians, and his treatises, which reflect his spoken discourses, are as well informed as they are eloquent. Politically Ambrose's chief aim was to establish the secular security of the Church. "In questions affecting the faith," he wrote (*Epistles* 21.4), "it is the bishops who are judges of Christian emperors, and not the emperors who are judges of the bishops." The civil power must respect the moral law even in matters outside religion, and the state must show special and single favor to the Catholic religion and discourage all others.

Of Ambrose's literary remains the most interesting are his ninety-one letters, which afford an excellent picture of religious currents in the fourth century. Ambrose's systematic synthesis of Christian doctrine is his *On Duties of Ministers,* of which the title, the framework, and the generous borrowing of Stoic ideology is from Cicero's *On Duties.* Each of his exhortations is an amalgam of Stoicism and the teachings of the Gospels. A number of Ambrose's minor treatises deal with the ascetic life: *On Virgins, On Virginity, On Widows, On the Education of a Virgin,* and *Exhortation to Virginity. On the Mysteries* explains the significance of baptism and the eucharist. St. Augustine (*Confessions* 5.13) testifies to the extraordinary power of Ambrose's eloquence; his sermons were based on Scripture, freely interpreted by the allegorical method we have noticed in Tertullian's *On the Food of the Jews.* The *Exameron* is a series of nine such sermons preached on six consecutive days during Lent.

A number of Ambrose's dogmatic treatises are lost. Among those extant are *On Faith* and *On the Holy Spirit,* which lean heavily on Greek theologians and are addressed to Gratian; *On the Sacrament of the Incarnation,* written to refute two Arian chamberlains at the court of Gratian; and *On Penitence,* against persistent partisans of Novatian. *On the Death of Satyrus* is a touching funeral oration and sermon on Ambrose's brother and contains reflections on death and resurrection.

But the most familiar of Ambrose's works are his hymns; he has been called "the father of Church song." Augustine (*Confessions* 9.5) tells us that when the Arians were besieging Milan, Ambrose introduced the eastern practice of antiphonal singing to comfort and inspire his faithful people. Only about twenty of the nearly hundred "Ambrosian" hymns which have come down are accepted as genuine; four of these are verified by Augustine himself—*Aeterne rerum conditor, Deus creator omnium, Jam surgit hora tertia,* and *Veni redemptor gentium.* The hymns are regularly composed of eight four-line stanzas, in classical iambic dimeters. There is usually a "sense pause" at the end of the second line of each stanza and a stronger pause at the end. The hymns all expound some doctrine, but with simplicity as well as dignity and evangelical fervor. None of Ambrose's writing has the fire of Tertullian nor the ebullience of Arnobius, but he too shows his rhetorical as well as literary training. Beginning with Ambrose, Latin Christian writers no longer needed to be sensitive about their Christianity; Rome itself is Christian, and of subsequent writers it is rather the absence of Christian emphasis than its presence that is remarkable.

Such being the case, it was natural that poetry as well as prose should be cultivated by Christians, and though genuine poetic creativity asserts itself only in hymns, a number of other verse productions of the fourth century deserve mention. One whole group consists of expanded paraphrases of episodes from the Old Testament, or less often from the New, in classical meters and with classical tags, intended to edify cultivated readers. The first considerable Christian poet in the Latin tongue is the Spanish priest Gaius Vettius Aquilinus Juvencus whose *Books of the Evangelists* in 3,190 hexameters and four books were written in the reign of Constantine. Invoking the Holy Spirit instead of the Muses, Juvencus declared that he will "sing the noble deeds of Christ on earth." His epic is based chiefly on Matthew, though he occasionally uses Luke and John and more rarely Mark. The great obstacle to Juvencus' real poetic talent is his unwillingness to take liberties with the sacred text; only in such things as descriptions of nature could he use a degree of freedom—which meant for Juvencus almost as strict a constraint to the words of his favorite model Vergil. What emerges from the combined constraints is sometimes a little monstrous. For example, "May this cup pass from me" becomes

If it is right, father, may the violence of this cup pressing over me with mighty force pass me by; may your will rather than mine be done, the decree which has been determined by you in matters so momentous.

And "He stinketh" becomes

I should believe that the body, upon the flight of the motion of heat, renders a pitiful stench, the members having liquefied.

Juvencus generally follows classical prosody but with some liberties; he uses rhyme frequently and has a number of verbal coinages.

Similar treatment of scattered passages from the Old Testament by an otherwise unknown Cyprian suggest that Cyprian may have versified all of the Old Testament which lent itself to such paraphrase. A number of other poems are didactic in character. The *Phoenix* ascribed to Lactantius has been mentioned in connection with the similar poem by Claudianus. There were a number of centos from Vergil, constructed like Ausonius' *Nuptial Cento* but on Christian themes. Of these the most ambitious is the effort of the poetess Proba, granddaughter, daughter, and mother of consuls, to relate by this method the principal episodes of the Old Testament as far as the Flood and of the New as far as the Ascension.

The true creators of Christian lyrical poetry in the west, aside from writers of hymns like Ambrose, were Paulinus of Nola (A.D. 353–431) and Prudentius (A.D. 348–405). Paulinus' renunciation of his great worldly wealth and exalted position in order to devote himself to the monastic life was, as we have seen, a great puzzle and a shock to his teacher Ausonius. Technically the poetry of Paulinus, which occupies a volume in the *Corpus scriptorum ecclesiasticorum Latinorum,* is very like that of Ausonius, correct in versification and filled with reminiscences of the classics and of Ausonius himself; but Paulinus is true poet rather than an accomplished versifier because he is mastered by ideas and emotions which demand expression. The naturalization of pagan poetic elements in Paulinus may be symbolized by his own dedication of his beard to his beloved St. Felix of Nola (*Epistles* 21.377). Thus in the long and rhetorical panegyric on John the Baptist John is called *semideum virum* (6.252); of Christ enthroned in heaven Paulinus says (16.122), *Invidebat eos caelesti Christus ab arce;* in the elegiac verses on the child Celsus, *Gaudebant trepido praesagi corde parentes dum metuunt tanti muneris invidiam* (31.29). This moving poem, in which Paulinus recalls the recent death of his own child, is the first Christian elegy, and for the marriage of Julianus and Titia he composed the first Christian epithalamium (25), with "peace, modesty, and piety" taking the place usually reserved for Juno, Cupid, and Venus. Another innovation is the poem in praise of the saint and martyr. Paulinus wrote fourteen poems for the recurrent festival of St. Felix, interesting not merely for their poetical qualities but also for their vivid picture of the popular devotion of the age. One (14) describes the crowds of country folk assembling for their great festival. Inside the church the altar blazes with lights, so that "night is as bright as day, and day itself is rendered more bright by the glow of innumerable candles." The people bring their gifts in kind and ask the saint's protection for themselves and their goods through the coming year. In another (23) Paulinus begins with a description of spring and prays that he may be inspired to sing like the nightingale which pours forth an everchanging melody from its hiding place deep in the leaves of the wood. Other poems of Paulinus are a propempticon in Sapphics to Nicetas, apostle to the Dacians; three paraphrases from the Psalter; a hexameter paraphrase of the Gospel; *ecphraseis* explaining church frescoes; and the verse correspondence with Ausonius already mentioned. Paulinus' prose writings, which occupy another volume in the *Corpus,* consist of fifty-one letters. These are as rhetorical and allusive as those of Symmachus or Sidonius, except that in Paulinus the Bible also is laid under heavy contribution. Whole letters consist virtually exclusively of scriptural tags worked into the proper syntax, with only a rare *scriptum est* or *dicente apostolo* to indicate a citation. Since the letters all date after Paulinus' conversion of 393 (Number 51 is as late as 426) we get no echo of Paulinus' spiritual struggle; nevertheless the letters do illustrate contemporary intellectual currents. Letter 16, for example, discusses the proper use to be made of the pagan classics; a Christian must not allow himself to be captivated by their pernicious charm but should exploit them for "copiousness of language and elegance of expression."

But it is the Spaniard Prudentius Clemens who is usually given the title of the first great Christian poet. The preface to his collected poems, published by himself in A.D. 405 at the age of fifty-seven gives autobiographical details of education, youthful excesses, and high administrative posts, and declares his determination to devote himself henceforward to the praise of God (28–45):

> Yet what avail the prizes or the blows
> Of fortune, when the body's spark is quenched
> And death annuls whatever state I held?
> This sentence I must hear: "Whate'er thou art,
> Thy mind hath lost the world it loved: not God's
> The things thou soughtest, Whose thou now shalt be."
> Yet now, ere hence I pass, my sinning soul
> Shall doff its folly and shall praise my Lord
> If not by deeds, at least with humble lips.
> Let each day link itself with grateful hymns
> And every night re-echo songs of God:
> Yea, be it mine to fight all heresies,
> Unfold the meanings of the Catholic faith,
> Trample on Gentile rites, thy gods, O Rome,
> Dethrone, the Martyrs laud, th' Apostles sing.
> O while such themes my pen and tongue employ,
> May death strike off these fetters of the flesh
> And bear me whither my last breath shall rise!
>
> —*R. M. Pope and R. F. Davis*

Prudentius' lyrical poems are collected under the titles *Cathemerinon* and *Peristephanon*. The *Cathemerinon* is a collection of twelve hymns, but these are too long to have been intended for congregational use. Indeed, Prudentius' originality consists in his having given the Ambrosian hymn the character of a Christian ode, divorcing it from a merely liturgical aim and making it a literary product. He uses a variety of classical lyric meters with vigor and grace, but he amplifies and illustrates his subject by extracts and descriptions from the Bible. Christian poetry was learning to use a new "mythology." The *Peristephanon* is a collection of fourteen pieces in veneration of martyrs, African, Roman, but chiefly (because of Prudentius' local patriotism) Spanish. Perhaps a touch of ghoulishness in the description of torments is also a Spanish legacy from Seneca and Lucan. Romanus (10) utters no fewer than six tirades against heathen superstition, and especially against the Taurobolium of the cult of Attis—after his tongue has been cut out. Laurence, roasted on a gridiron, at least makes a grim joke (2.401 f.): "Turn me over; I'm done on this side." The cult of the martyrs was of enormous importance in Prudentius' day, and the *Peristephanon* accordingly has great historical interest. The genre is a new thing in Christian poetry. As lyrics the poems of the *Peristephanon* have the same character as those of the *Cathemerinon,* but with more grimness and less grace.

Prudentius' remaining poems are of a didactic character. The *Apotheosis,* in 1,084 hexameters with long hexameter and iambic preludes, refutes a series of errors concerning the Trinity and the divinity of Christ. One after another Patripassionists, Sabellians, Jews, Ebionites (Psilanthropists) and Docetists are taken to task. The *Hamartigenia* ("Birth of Evil"), almost as long, is an arraignment of Marcion's gnostic dualism. The object of these theological poems is to communicate correct doctrine, but Prudentius makes his abstruse doctrines intelligible by his vivid illustration; his glowing language sometimes rises to passages of distinction and elevation. The picture of Satan (*Hamartigenia* 10 ff.) is Miltonic: "proudly tall, his snake-girt head borne on ebony clouds, striding in smoke and flame," nor are the pictures of heaven and hell (824–66) unlike the style of *Paradise Lost.* The *Psychomachia* may be the weakest of Prudentius' poems aesthetically, but as the first poetical Christian allegory it has great literary and historical importance. Personified virtues such as Faith, Modesty, Patience, Humility, and the like wage a series of epic combats, with the epic tradition of speeches before or after battle, against their opposites, Worship of Ancient Gods, Lust of Sodom, Anger, Pride, and the like. The *Psychomachia* is the ultimate source for many allegorizations in medieval art. For Christian iconography (but not as poetry) the *Dittochaeon* has a special importance. This is a collection of forty-nine hexameter quatrains to explain pictures, doubtless in some church, twenty-four of Old Testament subjects and twenty-five of New.

Historically the most significant of Prudentius' poems is the *Against Symmachus,* in two books, written in refutation of Symmachus' plea of twenty years before for the retention of the altar of Victory in the Roman curia. The whole of the first book is an attack on the heathen gods, both the ancient myths (which no one longer believed) and the contemporary astrology and sun worship. There is a good passage

(1.197–211) on the heathen associations of early childhood which continue their hold on the adult. The first book closes with a fine eulogy of Symmachus; the second proceeds to refute Symmachus' plea, but on grounds as patriotic as Symmachus' own. Change does not mean the negation of the genius of Rome, for Rome has remained constant through many mutations. The *pax Romana* was a divine preparation for the advent of Christianity, and under Christianity Rome's pacifying and unifying mission will grow stronger. Prudentius' reverence for Rome, and faith in her destiny, is no less than Horace's or Vergil's and really greater than Symmachus'. He venerates Roman tradition and the outward marks of Roman greatness, insofar as they are not opposed to Christianity. The senate is "the fairest luminary of the world," the emperors are spoken of with deep respect, and even Julian, "though faithless to God was not faithless to Rome": *perfidus ille deo quamvis non perfidus urbi.* There may be an incongruity in Prudentius' amalgam of loyalties as there may be in his simultaneous devotion to classic forms and Christian content, but of all the authors who wrote while there was still an alternative for loyalty Prudentius comes nearest effecting a genuine symbiosis between the two; in his own mind, at least, he yields neither to the other.

A number of later poets may here be mentioned, in violation of chronology, to bring our summary of Christian poetry to its end. Among the Africans the greatest name is that of Dracontius, who had written a number of secular poems, had offended the Vandal King Gunthamund (484–96) by celebrating the Roman emperor, had been disgraced in consequence, and from his prison wrote a lengthy didactic poem *On the Praises of God.* The poem begins with Creation and proceeds to celebrate God's wondrous dealings with man. The poem has real beauty of detail; Adam's wonder at the spectacle of the earthly paradise and his desire for another created being with whom to share his happiness bears a striking similarity to Book 8 of Milton's *Paradise Lost.* A didactic poem which became a Christian classic is the *Carmen Paschale* of Caelius Sedulius, in five books of hexameters. The first relates the Old Testament miracles which set forth the power of God and foretold the coming of Christ, and the remaining four are devoted to the miracles of Christ, ending with the Resurrection and the Ascension. The object of the whole is to edify readers still devoted to pagan fables. Of two hymns of Sedulius one may be men-

tioned for its epanaleptic or serpentine verse, the beginning of each
hexameter being repeated at the end of the pentameter, thus

> *unius ob meritum cuncti perierunt minores:*
> *salvantur cuncti unius ob meritum.*
> *sola fuit mulier, patuit quae ianua leto:*
> *et qua vita redit, sola fuit mulier.*

Alcimus Ecdicius Avitus, bishop of Vienne in 490, wrote many
polemical works in the usual rhetorical prose, but his verse paraphrase of the Old Testament from Creation to the crossing of the Red
Sea shows a poetic talent superior to that of Juvencus and the other
writers of Biblical "epics." For all their ornamentation, his verses are
clear and strong. The last representative of Latin poetry on the
threshold of the Middle Ages was Venantius Fortunatus, who started
as a troubadour and became bishop of Poitiers about 590. Aside from
a mass of prose work Fortunatus wrote eleven books of miscellaneous
poems. These include every conceivable kind of occasional poem,
flattering anyone who might be a patron. But his magnificent hymns
—*Agnoscat omne caelum, Vexilla regis prodeunt, Pange lingua glori-
osi* (the genuineness of seven others has been questioned)—mark the
triumph of Catholic emotion and mysticism over classical form.
Pathos, whether of dejection or exaltation, overshadows even the
dogmatic intention. Regarded, therefore, as the first of the medieval
poets, Fortunatus deserves an important place; as a representative of
classical poetry he is a feeble latecomer.

From this excursus into the poetry of the sixth century we return
to the prose of the fourth and fifth, and particularly to Jerome and
Augustine, the two most prolific doctors of the western Church. The
doctor who comes nearest being the professional scholar and writer
(though he was a tremendous moral force besides) and who was
sainted for his services as such was Jerome, who was born between
A.D. 340 and 350 in Pannonia and died in 420 at Bethlehem. Jerome was
at Rome about the middle of Theodosius' reign, when Symmachus
was also there, and he received an excellent classical education under
Donatus, the commentator of Terence and Vergil. From the gayety
of student life he turned to asceticism which, with scholarship, became the great preoccupation of his life and the source of his influence.
He spent three years (from 375) in the desert of Chalcis, fifty miles

from Antioch. Of his psychological experiences there he later wrote (*Epistles* 22.7):

Though in my fear of hell I had condemned myself to this prison-house, where my only companions were scorpions and wild beasts, I often found myself surrounded by bands of dancing girls. My face was pale with fasting; but though my limbs were cold as ice my mind was burning with desire, and the fires of lust kept bubbling up before me when my flesh was as good as dead. . . . I used to dread my poor cell as though it knew my secret thoughts.

—F. A. Wright

In the desert he learned Hebrew; it is a little remarkable that none of the other doctors, who were so much concerned for the correct interpretation of Scripture, troubled to do so. Monkish pride, which made many "prefer to live in the midst of wild beasts rather than with Christians of that kind" (Epistles 17.3) drove him from his retreat but not from his ascetic ideal. He went to Constantinople, where he studied exegesis from Gregory of Nazianz and conceived a high admiration for the works of Origen, a number of which he translated. From 382 to 385 he lived at Rome as secretary and intimate friend of Pope Damasus, who himself wrote verse. In Rome Jerome became the director in study and devotion of a remarkable group of women, Paula, Lea, Asella, Marcella, and many others, whose bent towards asceticism he encouraged. These ladies followed him to Bethlehem in 386 and built convents which were very celebrated and much frequented. At Bethlehem Jerome continued, occupied with his scholarly labors and with an enormous correspondence, until his death.

Jerome's greatest work, by any gauge of measurement, is his Latin translation of the Bible called the Vulgate. Undertaking at first merely to revise existing translations of the New Testament, he was led on, in pursuit of the truest interpretation of the text, to translate the whole afresh. The labor occupied twenty years, and the result, admirable in all respects, has not only been the most widely revered work in Christendom but has given new form and spirit to European literature. The language of the Vulgate gathered up the various elements which contributed to create the appropriate medium for the expression of the new mood and outlook—the Hellenic, the vulgar tongue, the Hebraic. The latter factor in particular introduced new rhythms and a new and more romantic imagery. As F. J. E. Raby has remarked in his excellent study of Christian Latin poetry,

The mystical fervor of the prophets, the melancholy of the penitential psalms and of the Lamentations, could not be rendered into Latin without giving that severe and logical language a strange flexibility, an emotional and symbolical quality, which had been foreign to its nature. The whole literary imagination of the west was to be fed on the sonorous sentences of the Latin Bible, and Christian poetry, though true so long to its learned traditions, could not escape the spell or fail to learn the new language when it spoke in the poetical prose of lines like these (Zephaniah 1.14–16):

> *iuxta est dies domini magnus,*
> *iuxta est et velox nimis;*
> *vox diei domini amara,*
> *tribulabitur ibi fortis.*
> *dies irae, dies illa,*
> *dies tribulationis et angustiae*
> *dies calamitatis et miseriae*
> *dies tenebrarum et caliginis*
> *dies nebulae et turbinis*
> *dies tubae et clangoris*
> *super civitates munitas, et super angulos excelsos.*

Out of this music was to issue the poetry of the future, the poetry in which the Catholic emotion was to discover its final expression. It is the music of the new world, for out of it appeared at last, when its religious mission had been fulfilled, the romantic poetry of the modern world.

Jerome produced other subsidia to Biblical study and other translations also. Among the former are a number of commentaries, hastily written and rather prolix, and works on the nomenclature and topography of the Bible, based on Origen. Among the latter are thirty-seven homilies of Origen, translated between 379 and 381, fourteen each on Jeremiah and Ezekiel, and nine on Isaiah. As a translator Jerome was a conscious artist; translation, he said, should not be merely in *Latinam linguam* but *Latine,* that is, in good Latin.

Nearest to *belles lettres* among the works of Jerome are the *Lives* of a series of eremites, Paul of Thebes, Malchus, and Hilarion. He started this work early and had intended (*Malchus* 1) writing a kind of history of the Church in a series of monographs of the same kind. These *Lives* naturally contain whatever facts were available but are embellished with pious tales and read like romances: "Once upon a time," a *Life* begins, "there was an old man called Malchus." An aspect of these *Lives* which has not been sufficiently appreciated is their acute perception of the dream fancies of ascetics living in solitude. Asceticism, again, is the dominant theme of a series of letters which make Jerome Juvenal's peer in the denunciation of moral evil. The despair of ordinary female virtue, in particular, is reminiscent of the obsession in Juvenal's sixth *Satire*.

So full is the world of allurements, so weak the flesh and the devil so cunning in laying snares for the soul, that the only chance of escape lies in absolute renunciation. Avarice can be conquered only by selling all one's possessions and giving to the poor (*Epistles* 108.19). Luxury in dress and food must be replaced by sackcloth and herbs and avoidance of bathing (107.9, 10). Love is sensual and debasing; the state of marriage is inferior to intact virginity and the recovered chastity of widowhood (130.3–5, 123.11). The devotion of Demetrias to virginity exalts her family to a higher pinnacle than its long line of consuls and prefects have ever reached; it is a consolation for a Rome in ashes, Italy puts off its mourning at the news; the villages in the farthest provinces exult at the news (22.7). Jerome's pictures of worldly women are very like Juvenal's. He describes their gaudy turbans and elaborate coiffures, their costly silks and liberally applied cosmetics and blazing wealth of jewels (54.7, 108.15, 127.3). The fashionable matron moves in a litter surrounded by slaves and eunuchs and attended by a pampered domestic suspiciously familiar (54.13). A great lady attended by a crowd of eunuchs passes through St. Peter's doling out alms with equal parsimony and ostentation and repulsing the importunate widow with blows (22.32). A female toper justifies her love of wine with a blasphemous jest (22.13); a kittenish matron applies so much makeup that she cannot drop a tear without its leaving a furrow (38.3). Jerome repeatedly warns his female disciples against appearing in fashionable gatherings; dinner parties are a particular danger to female virtue (54.13). The clergy is dealt with even more harshly. The luxurious feastings of clerical epicures, who had only black bread and milk in boyhood, the dangerous intimacies of gigolo priests with rich young matrons, their scramble for wealth, the hypocritical external austerity and private sensuality of some, and the mincing foppishness of others are all vividly portrayed and vehemently chided. Among Jerome's 154 letters is some of the most effective satire ever written, and the letters would of themselves insure his place in literature. In addition, they are a most valuable document on the social and religious history of his day, and present us with a gallery of portraits of his contemporaries, with great polish and vigor.

No less vigorous are Jerome's controversial writings, which sometimes reach an extreme of truculence and personal abuse. *Against Helvidius,* the first Latin treatise on Mariology, upholds the doctrine of the perpetual virginity of Mary against a layman who had questioned it as a means of depreciating Jerome's exaltation of celibacy. Jerome calls his opponent an ignorant and nasty fool. The *Against Jovinian* is even more intemperate. It attributes to Jovinian's personal depravity the four theses he had maintained: that the merit of virgins, widows, and married women is equal; that the baptized could not be led into sin by the devil; that there is no difference between abstaining from food and partaking of it with thanksgiving; that rewards in heaven are identical for all who had maintained their baptismal faith. Here is part of Jerome's peroration:

And now for a last word to our Epicurus sweating out passion in the midst of his gardens among young men and young women. For your followers you have the plump, the well-fed, the well-washed. All the pretty boys, all the youth with curled hair that I see, their locks well kept and their cheeks painted with vermilion, form your flock, or rather all that trash that grunts among your pigs.

Against Vigilantius (whom Jerome punningly calls "Dormitantius") is a furious diatribe against criticism of the veneration of tombs of martyrs and similar liturgical practices. The *Dialogues against the Pelagians* is more temperate, since each side is given its spokesman. In his latter years Jerome's opponents sought to involve him in the disfavor into which Origen had fallen; the three books *Against Rufinus* are Jerome's vigorous exculpation.

In earlier pages of this book the *Chronicle* of Jerome is several times referred to for dating. This work is a translation and supplement of the *Chronological Canons* of Eusebius, written in 379-80, partially extant only in an Armenian version. Eusebius had set forth the chronological systems of the Chaldaeans, Assyrians, Hebrews, Egyptians, Greeks, and Romans, and had drawn up synchronous tables in which historical events, especially those pertaining to sacred history, were entered with reference to the years of Abraham (2016 B.C.), the Olympiads, the years of Rome, and the Egyptian dynasties. The first part of Eusebius' work Jerome merely translated; in the second part he added many references to Roman history and literature, on the basis of Suetonius and others, and carried the account down from the twentieth year of Constantine, where Eusebius stopped, to the death of Valens in A.D. 378. The work was done in great haste and somewhat capriciously, but it has remained a fundamental work for research in ancient history. A kindred book, devoted to recording those "who have made some contribution to the memory of sacred Scriptures" as an edifying parallel to the secular writers commemorated in Suetonius' like-named work, is Jerome's *De viris illustribus* ("On Famous Men"), written at Bethlehem in 392. The list includes 135 sections, from Simon Peter to Jerome himself. The first seventy-eight sections are so closely dependent on Eusebius' *Chronicle* and *Ecclesiastical History* as to include all of Eusebius' errors; from section 79 on Jerome continues independently, and for such figures as Tertullian, Minucius Felix, Cyprian, and Novatian he is the sole source.

Despite Jerome's rejection of Ciceronianism in favor of Christianity at the behest of his dream, his writing is fully in the tradition of Rome, and he is devoted to the ancient capital, as letters written shortly after Alaric's sack show:

I was desirous of setting to work today studying Ezekiel, but at the very moment I began to dictate I felt such anguish in thinking of the catastrophe in the west that the words ceased to come to me. For long I remained silent, bethinking me well that this was a time for weeping (126.2).

My voice left me and sobs choked my speech. The city which had conquered the whole world is herself captive. What can I say? (127.2)

That famous city, head of the Roman Empire, is laid waste by fire. There is no spot which is not receiving refugees from Rome (128.4).

Jerome even possessed the pride of literary craftsmanship and the assurance of literary immortality characteristic of the classical writers. His narration of the life of Paula (*Epistles* 108) is full of passionate sincerity and the romance of asceticism, yet at the end he records the fact that he composed it in two short sittings, without any attempt at elegance of style, and he is perfectly confident that he has left a monument which no length of time will ever efface (*quod nulla destruere possit vetustas*). Like Horace's similar confidence, Jerome's was justified. His devotion to antiquity and his unmincing forthrightness, combined with his literary scholarship and his own classical style and approach made Jerome a favorite even with the humanists of the Renascence. His ecclesiastical preoccupations do not, indeed, affect what seems to be Jerome's natural, and very high, place in the history of Latin literature.

St. Augustine, on the other hand, though a far subtler thinker, infinitely more influential in shaping subsequent theology, and a more amiable personality, and though himself thoroughly grounded in the classics and a consummate rhetorician, marks a sharper break with the classical tradition. His special talents might have effected revolutionary change in any period of literature, but because he was heir to all that was old and had himself been pagan, Manichee, and Neoplatonist before he became Christian, he was perhaps particularly suited to serve as capstone to the old world and as introduction to the new era brought on by the stunning blow of the fall of Rome. Not only does Augustine's thought initiate the new era, but he endowed language with the necessary suppleness for communicating the new realm of thought. The glowing periods of the *Confessions* finally naturalize rhetoric as an inevitable and compelling medium, and the *Psalm against the Donatists* introduces a technique which governed all subsequent European poetry. It is no accident that millions who could barely recognize the names of Augustine's fellow doctors have read with eagerness his *Confessions* and his *City of God*.

Like Tertullian, Minucius Felix, Cyprian, Lactantius, and Arnobius, Augustine was an African. He was born in A.D. 354 at Tagaste, near Carthage, of Patricius, a respectable local official, who was a pagan, and Monnica, a devout Christian. At twelve he was sent to nearby Madaura for his secondary education, and returned to Tagaste at sixteen, where his family's inability to pay for further schooling kept him in idleness for a year. His behavior at this period he recalls with sorrow (*Confessions* 2.3): "Behold with what companions I walked the streets of Babylon, in whose filth I was rolled as if in cinnamon and precious ointments." The following year a family friend enabled him to take up the study of rhetoric at Carthage. He took a mistress with whom he lived for the next thirteen years and who bore him his son Adeodatus; he was captivated by Cicero's *Hortensius;* and he was introduced to Manicheism. From A.D. 373 Augustine followed a teaching career, first in Tagaste, then in Carthage, and next in Rome. In 384 he obtained the professorship of rhetoric at Milan and removed thither with his mistress and son, his mother Monnica, who had joined him in Rome, and a few friends. His desires were to win glory in his profession, acquire wealth, marry a rich wife. In Milan St. Ambrose became a potent influence in his life; he had come to observe the famous preacher's manner but was enthralled by his matter. When Monnica found him a suitable match he dismissed his mistress: "My mistress being torn from my side as an impediment to my marriage, my heart which clove to her was wracked and wounded and bleeding. And she went back to Africa, making a vow unto Thee never to know another man, leaving with me my natural son by her" (*Confessions* 6.15). But since he had two years to wait for his bride to grow up he promptly took another mistress. In 386 Augustine decided to become a Christian, and with a group of friends retired to Cassiciacum, near Milan, where he wrote *Contra academicos, De vita beata, De ordine.* It has been found strange that these competent dialogues reflect nothing of the spiritual tumult which the *Confessions* might lead us to expect at this period. In 387 Augustine received baptism and accompanied Monnica, whose fondest hope was now realized, on her journey home. At Ostia Monnica died; Augustine and his friend remained in Rome for two years, and then returned to Tagaste, where they established a monastery. His extraordinary powers soon made themselves felt; in 391 he was ordained priest in Hippo Regius, and in 395 became bishop. His prodigious literary and pastoral activity continued for thirty-five years. He died at the age of seventy-six in A.D. 430, at the beginning of the siege of Hippo by Genseric, king of the Vandals.

Augustine's extant works occupy a dozen stout volumes, and even their titles cannot be listed here. If there is a single purpose which dominates them all it is the desire to defeat heresy, and the demands of Augustine's orthodoxy are very rigorous. In regard to the Bible, for example, he believed, and his belief was only strengthened with time, that the biblical chronology was perfectly accurate, that the events recorded were real, actually and not symbolically, that Biblical history carried so much greater authority that it could not be checked by profane history. Only through the Church, which was the sole heir of this revelation, could salvation be attained, and the Church could admit of no deviation. That man might be naturally good and require moral control only to avoid error was to Augustine tantamount to paganism; all men and their works are by nature evil—even a satiated infant will not allow its mother to feed another who is starving—and baptism and strenuous activity at the business of being a Christian are mandatory. Logically, far the greater part of humanity must be consigned to hell. It was against the Pelagians, who questioned this harsh doctrine and maintained the basic soundness of human nature and the absolute power of the will that Augustine's most vigorous and persistent polemic was directed. But there is no aspect of Christian theology and philosophy and morality which Augustine did not touch and influence. All subsequent development in Christianity, Protestant as well as Catholic, is in effect a disputation on Augustinianism.

Of all Augustine's works the *Confessions* and the *City of God*, though they are integral members of his structure, have the widest claim upon the attention of the ordinary reader, and it is to these that we must here limit our attention. The *Confessions* (the first nine books; the remaining four are mystical and philosophical) possess a unique interest as the career of a great figure, at once spiritually gifted and full-blooded, as seen through his own eyes, in respect of those experiences in particular which set him apart from ordinary men. There is nothing of vanity in Augustine's enterprise; his book is written in lyric gratitude to God and for the enlightenment of his fellow men, as a specimen passage will show (10.8-9):

But what do I love, when I love Thee? not beauty of bodies, nor the fair harmony of time, nor the brightness of the light, so gladsome to our eyes, nor sweet melodies of varied songs, nor the fragrant smell of flowers, and ointments, and spices, not manna and honey, not limbs acceptable to embracements of flesh. None of these I love, when I love my God; and yet I love a kind of light, and melody, and fragrance, and meat, and embracement, when I love my God, the light, melody, fragrance, meat, embracement of my inner man: where there shineth unto my soul, what space cannot contain, and there soundeth, what time beareth not away, and there smelleth, what breathing disperseth not, and there tasteth, what eating diminisheth not, and there clingeth, what satiety divorceth not. This is it which I love, when I love my God.

And what is this? I asked the earth, and it answered me, "I am not He;" and whatsoever are in it, confessed the same. I asked the sea and the deeps, and the living creeping things, and they answered, "We are not thy God, seek above us." I asked the moving air; and the whole air with his inhabitants answered, "Anaximenes was deceived, I am not God." I asked the heavens, sun, moon, stars, "Nor (say they) are we the God whom thou seekest." And I replied unto all the things which encompass the door of my flesh, "Ye have told me of my God, that ye are not He; tell me something of Him." And they cried out with a loud voice, "He made us."

—*E. B. Pusey*

Language like this justifies the most competent critic of ancient literary style in calling the Augustine of the *Confessions* "the greatest poet of the early Church," and in all but meter the *Confessions* is indeed a continuous lyric, charged with the author's particular emotions, recording his intimate and special perceptions, interconnected by lyric impulses of overlapping progression from emotional nucleus to emotional nucleus, and leaving the reader not merely informed but permeated with a sense of having undergone the experience vicariously. A reader who could remain untouched by the passionate earnestness of the book would find its rhetoric oppressive, but never had the rhetorical tradition been put to such sincere use. The rhetoric of the *Confessions* is completely justified in the book's lyric quality.

The *City of God* is a response to a question which had been broached as early as the third century and which had become urgent in the fifth. The question was why, with the advent of Christianity, had so many calamities befallen the empire. Cyprian had seen in the gathering catastrophe an eschatological significance, and Arnobius had pointed out that Rome throughout its history had been subject to misfortune. But why should fifth-century Rome, where godly men held the true faith concerning the Trinity, suffer at the hands of blasphemous Arian heretics? The first to offer an answer to the enigma (as we shall see, supplementary answers were offered by Orosius and by Salvian) was Augustine in his *City of God,* which is one of the greatest efforts of Christian speculation. The execution of this work falls short of its grand conception, and indeed the conception itself is not entirely original. The Manichee dichotomy of good and evil and the Platonist dream of a state whose model is in heaven are perceptible in Christianized form; and the notion of the coexistence in opposition of a heavenly and earthly city Augustine derived from his Donatist friend Tyconius. But the synthesis of doctrine which finds place for an entire history of mankind, the whole system of Christian beliefs, and the imposing drama of the struggle between the two cities to the apotheosis of the one and the abolition of the other is Augustine's own.

The twenty-two books of the *City of God* fall into two sections. Books 1–10 are a polemic against pagan religion and philosophy. Polytheism is proved unnecessary for securing happiness in this world or the next. The main argument, that contemporary misfortunes are no exception to the general experience of Roman history, is drawn from Arnobius. Earthly glory and prosperity are not necessary for true happiness. But this is not yet an answer to the problem, for its solution depends on discovering a harmony between the actual events of history and the general plan of the universe. Augustine therefore proceeds to his grand essay in the philosophy of history—yet not altogether philosophical, for its premises are derived not from reason but from revelation. The key to human history is the coexistence of a City of God, founded by the creation of angels, and an earthly city, founded by the angels who fell. Since the sin of Adam the vast majority of humanity have been citizens of the earthly city, of which the end is death; the minority who belong to the heavenly city are merely foreigners or pilgrims (*peregrini*) during their sojourn on earth. Universal history is divided, as in Eusebius, according to the epochs of Hebrew history; there is no serious consideration of the Babylonian and Roman empires, which Augustine regards as the principal embodiments of the earthly city. Our own epoch, which began with the birth of Christ, is the sixth and last, for the periods of history correspond to the days of Creation, and as God rested on the seventh day so will the seventh period witness the triumph of the heavenly city and the eternal rest of its citizens.

With reference to the book's purpose of setting forth the right view of the misfortunes which were befalling the empire, Augustine's prescription amounts to this: pagans are to regard their calamities simply as part of the heritage of their city of sin and death (in the absence of true religion even the virtues of pagans are vices); and to the Christians these things are really of no concern, for their interests could not be affected by the calamities of a city in which they are merely foreigners. As in the case of the *Confessions,* impassioned and eloquent conviction may more than compensate for the structural faults of the City of God. Critics not sympathetic to Augustine's convictions have found the eloquence diffuse and lacking in lucidity. Professor Bury, for example, contrasts the literary art and lucid exposition of Plato's ideal polity, and Plato's greater power to hold his reader enthralled. One book, he says, will hold the reader's interest— by its horror:

The book [21] in which this arch-advocate of theological materialism and vindictive punishment expends all his ingenuity in proving that the fire of hell is literal fire and spares no effort to cut off the slenderest chance that the vast majority of his fellow beings will not be tormented throughout eternity.

One minor Augustinian production must be mentioned here because of the revolution it marks in European prosody. His *Psalm against the Donatists* is the first authentic example of poetry based on rhythm, constructed on the principle of *numbering* syllables, with fixed caesura and more or less developed rhyme. The *Psalm* is made up of long strophes, each of which begins with a letter of the alphabet. Each line ends on the vowel *e* (or *ae*), and there is a refrain which possesses an internal as well as an end rime. If elision is generally observed and two adjoining vowels occasionally run together, the lines are each composed of sixteen syllables divided equally by a caesura. Beyond the rough syllabic equality the only law is accent on the penultimate syllable of each half line. The syllabic principle became standard in Christian poetry when the humanist impulse was spent, and from Christian poetry spread to the secular poetry of all Europe.

Augustine realized that his treatment of Roman history in the *City of God* was only casual, and to supply a fuller development of the historical argument in reply to the pagan charges he asked his friend Orosius, a Spanish priest (born about 390) whom Augustine had previously sent to Jerome in Bethlehem, to supply the need. Orosius' charge was (Prologue 9-10):

You bade me reply to the empty chatter and perversity of those who . . . charge that the present times are unusually beset with calamities for the sole reason that men believe in Christ and worship God while idols are increasingly neglected. You bade me, therefore, discover from all the available data of histories and annals whatever instances past ages have

WRITERS OF CHRISTIANITY

afforded of the burdens of war, the ravages of disease, the horrors of famine, of terrible earthquakes, extraordinary floods, dreadful eruptions of fire, thunderbolts and hailstorms, and also instances of the cruel miseries caused by parricides and disgusting crimes. I was to set these forth systematically and briefly in the course of my book.

—*I. W. Raymond*

His *Seven Books to Confute the Pagans* was written in little more than a year (A.D. 418). If it is the first universal history the haste and the bias with which it was written make it probably the worst. To the former factor may be attributed such howlers as assigning Caesar's *Commentaries* to Suetonius (6.7.2), and to the latter such things as the predilection for Augustine's mystic numbers—seven books, four great empires (after Daniel 7.3-27). For the historian the book has some value where Orosius is obviously using books of Livy lost to us. It is written with a certain warmth and was widely read in the Middle Ages, as more than two hundred manuscripts testify.

A third answer to the problem which Augustine attacked in the *City of God* was offered by Salvian, a priest of Marseilles, whose *On the Government of God,* in eight books, was written between 439 and 451. If Christians ask why as true believers they are more wretched than others, says Salvian, why they are conquered by barbarians, whether God is grown indifferent and has given up governing, the answer is that Christians suffer because they deserve to. If, living in such vice and wickedness as they did, they flourished and were happy, then God might indeed be accused of not governing. This argument Salvian supports by an appalling picture of administrative corruption, oppression of the poor by the rich, a frenzied appetite for pleasure. If it is objected, Salvian continues, that despite their faults Christians hold true theological beliefs whereas the conquering barbarians are heathen or heretic, the answer is that orthodoxy is the only Christian advantage; in other respects the barbarians are superior. Like Tacitus in the *Germania,* Salvian proceeds to extol barbarian virtues in order to rebuke civilized vices. Among the Germans and Huns the rich do not oppress the poor; Christians are as drunk as Alemanni, perjured and perfidious as Franks and Huns, rapacious as Alans; in sexual morality Vandals, Saxons, and Goths all put Christians to shame. Salvian is quite in the Roman tradition in associating the political fortunes of Rome with her morality, and the degradation he saw gave him no hope (4.30): "The Roman commonwealth is dead, and even where it seems still to be alive it is drawing its last breath." *Moritur et ridet,* says Salvian, "It dies and yet it smiles." The smile was wiser than Salvian knew, for the apparent death was only another of the numerous mutations in the long history of Rome, as Prudentius had seen, profounder than earlier mutations, it may be, but only a mutation nevertheless. Rome remained eternal.

BIBLIOGRAPHICAL NOTES

GENERAL

TEXTS WITH PARALLEL TRANSLATIONS OF VIRTUALLY all classical authors will be found in the volumes of the Loeb Classical Library (here abbreviated LL), published by Harvard University Press. Unless otherwise noted, translators cited in the present volume are from LL. For reference the single-volume Oxford Classical Dictionary (Oxford, 1949), here abbreviated OCD, is excellent. Both LL and OCD provide further bibliographical information.

Other standard works, particularly such as are useful to the English reader, follow.

TEXTS AND TRANSLATIONS: The standard series of classical texts are the Teubner (*Bibliotheca scriptorum Graecorum et Romanorum Teubneriana*, Leipzig), which includes almost all ancient authors, and the less full but more attractive Oxford (*Scriptorum classicorum bibliotheca Oxoniensis*). A series analogous to LL, generally superior but not so full, is the Budé (*Collection des universités de France, publiées sous le patronage de l'Association Guillaume Budé*, Paris). A key to available translations is F. S. Smith, *The Classics in Translation* (New York, 1930). There are numerous anthologies. The latest and fullest is K. Guinagh and A. P. Dorjahn, *Latin Literature in Translation* (New York, 1942); a shorter book but with fuller and more spirited introductory material is C. Bailey, *The Mind of Rome* (Oxford, 1926); a good selection of poetry is F. R. B. Godolphin, *The Latin Poets* (Modern Library).

HISTORIES OF LATIN LITERATURE: The standard work, with complete bibliographies, is M. Schanz and C. Hosius, *Geschichte der römischen Literatur* (Munich), of which the latest revisions are: Vol. I, 1927; II, 1935; III, 1922; IV, Part 1, 1914; IV, Part 2, 1920. The fullest English work are the two volumes of J. W. Duff: *A Literary History of Rome from the Origins to the Close of the Golden Age* (London, 1909), and *A Literary History of Rome in the Silver Age* (London, 1927). Among single-volume histories those by H. J. Rose, J. W. Mackail, and M. Dimsdale may be mentioned.

ENCYCLOPEDIAS AND DICTIONARIES: The fullest and most authoritative reference work for all aspects of classical antiquity is A. Pauly, G. Wissowa, and W. Kroll, *Realencyclopädie der classischen Altertumswissenschaft* (Stuttgart, 1894–). The best one-volume work is the *Oxford Classical*

448 BIBLIOGRAPHICAL NOTES

Dictionary mentioned above. The *Companion to Latin Studies,* ed. J. E. Sandys, 3d ed. (Cambridge, 1921) has succinct and authoritative summaries of public and private antiquities, literature, history, art, epigraphy, history of scholarship, etc.

HISTORY: The fullest account of the period here dealt with is in Vols. VII–XII of the *Cambridge Ancient History* (Cambridge, 1928–39) and the *Cambridge Mediaeval History,* 2d ed., Vol. I, (1936). A convenient one-volume book is A. E. R. Boak, *A History of Rome* (New York, 1943).

LEGACY: For Roman (and Greek) influences on Western literature an excellent work is G. Highet, *The Classical Tradition* (Oxford, 1949). Volumes in the series called "Our Debt to Greece and Rome" (ODGR) published by Longmans, Green in New York deal with the influence of individual authors. Contributions to various aspects of our civilization are dealt with in chapters of C. Bailey, *The Legacy of Rome* (Oxford, 1924). The actual transmission of the legacy is dealt with in J. E. Sandys, *A History of Classical Scholarship,* 3d ed., Vol. I (Cambridge, 1921).

These references are generally applicable up to Ch. XX, where other relevant works will be mentioned. Under the chapter headings which follow reference will be made only to selected works, normally in English, and to the sources of citations in the text.

I. THE NATURE OF LATIN LITERATURE

Of the many appreciations of the Roman character, mention may be made of W. Warde Fowler, *Rome,* 2d ed. (Oxford, 1947; Home University Library); G. Showerman, *Eternal Rome* (New Haven, 1925); and F. G. Moore, *The Roman's World* (New York, 1936). On the Etruscans see D. Randall-MacIver, *The Etruscans* (Oxford, 1929); R. A. L. Fell, *Etruria and Rome* (Cambridge, 1924); G. Dennis, *Cities and Cemeteries of Etruria,* 2 vols. (Everyman's Library). On the dialects, see F. D. Allen, *Remnants of Early Latin* (Boston, 1880).

II. THE BEGINNINGS

For the epigraphical material see J. C. Egbert, *Introduction to the Study of Latin Inscriptions* (New York, 1908). For Livius Andronicus, Naevius, Ennius, Pacuvius, and Accius see E. H. Warmington, *Remains of Old Latin* (LL), Vols. I and II; citations are by Warmington's numbering (W). For the early writers of comedy see W. Beare, *The Roman Stage* (London, 1950).

III. COMEDY AND SATIRE

A stimulating and informing work on the whole subject is W. Beare, *The Roman Stage* (London, 1950). Translations of all of Plautus and Terence (and Seneca's tragedies) are presented in G. E. Duckworth, *The Complete Roman Drama*, 2 vols. (New York, 1942). For stage antiquities, with copious illustrations, see M. Bieber, *The History of the Greek and Roman Theater* (Princeton, 1939). A useful guide to all ancient plays is P. W. Harsh, *A Handbook of Classical Drama* (Stanford, 1944). See also G. Norwood, *Plautus and Terence* (ODGR).

PLAUTUS: P. Nixon's LL translations (5 vols.) are sprightly. There are bright versions of *Rudens, Aulularia,* and *Pseudolus* by F. A. Wright and H. L. Rogers (London, 1925). Wright has a good chapter on Plautus in his *Three Roman Poets* (London, 1932).

CAECILIUS: Vol. I of E. H. Warmington, *Remains of Old Latin*, LL.

TERENCE: J. Sargeaunt, LL (2 vols.); among other translations those of F. Perry (Oxford, 1929), W. Ritchie (London, 1927), and the versions in Duckworth may be mentioned. A useful edition of Terence is S. Ashmore (New York, 1908). See G. Norwood, *The Art of Terence* (Oxford, 1923).

SATIRE: G. Highet on satire in OCD, *s.v. Satura.* On the whole subject see J. W. Duff, *Roman Satire* (Berkeley, 1936).

LUCILIUS: E. H. Warmington, *Remains of Old Latin,* Vol. III (LL).

IV. PRE-CICERONIAN PROSE

See T. Frank, *Life and Letters in the Roman Republic* (Berkeley, 1930). Fragments of the historians are collected in H. Peter, *Historicorum Romanorum reliquiae,* 2 vols. (Leipzig, 1906, 1914). On CATO see the forthcoming Columbia dissertation of Elsie Lewis Leeman. *On Agriculture:* W. D. Hooper and H. B. Ash, LL; E. Brehaut, *Cato the Censor on Farming* (New York, 1933). Nepos on Cato: LL. Twelve Tables: E. H. Warmington, *Remains of Old Latin,* Vol. III (LL).

V. LUCRETIUS AND CATULLUS

LUCRETIUS: Besides W. H. D. Rouse, LL, there are good prose translations by C. Bailey (Oxford, 1929) and H. A. J. Munro (e.g., in W. J. Oates, *Stoic and Epicurean Philosophers* [New York, 1940]), and verse by W. E. Leonard (Everyman's Library) and R. C. Trevelyan (Cambridge, 1937). Essays and commentaries useful for the non-Latinist also are in the editions of C. Bailey, 3 vols. (Oxford, 1947); W. E. Leonard and S. B. Smith (Madison, 1942); W. A. Merrill (New York, 1907). See also E. E. Sikes, *Lucretius, Poet and Philosopher* (Cambridge, 1936); A. P. Sinker, *Introduction to Lucretius* (Cambridge, 1937); G. D. Hadzsits (ODGR). On Lucretius as a subversive see C. Stanley, *Roots of the Tree* (Oxford, 1936), 75–90, and B. Farrington, "The Gods of Epicurus," in *Heart and Hand in Ancient Greece* (London, 1947). *Georgics* quotation from LL. Latin Alexandrianism in OCD, *s.v.*

CATULLUS: See E. A. Havelock, *The Lyric Genius of Catullus* (Oxford, 1939); T. Frank, *Catullus and Horace* (New York, 1928); A. L. Wheeler, *Catullus and the Traditions of Ancient Poetry* (Berkeley, 1934); F. A. Wright, *Three Roman Poets* (London, 1938); K. P. Harrington, *Catullus* (ODGR). The translations by Rollo, Nott, Cranstoun, and Martin are drawn from Harrington. Others are from the books of Havelock and Frank, and from J. H. A. Tremenheere, *The Lesbia of Catullus* (London, 1897); H. Macnaghten, *The Story of Catullus* (London, 1899); F. W. Cornish, LL (with Tibullus and *Pervigilium Veneris*). There are spirited translations also by Jack Lindsay (London, 1948); F. A. Wright (London, 1926); and H. Gregory (New York, 1931). Translations by various hands are presented in W. A. Aiken, *Catullus* (New York, 1950). The Suetonius quotation is from LL.

VI. CAESAR, SALLUST, AND OTHERS

CAESAR: T. Rice Holmes, *The Roman Republic and the Founder of the Empire,* 3 vols. (Oxford, 1923); J. Buchan, *Julius Caesar* (London, 1936); R. Syme, *The Roman Revolution* (Oxford, 1939); L. R. Taylor, *Party Politics in the Age of Caesar* (Berkeley, 1949). *Gallic War*: H. J. Edwards, LL, and see T. Rice Holmes, *Caesar's Conquest of Gaul,* 2d ed. (Oxford, 1911). Quotation from Cicero's *Brutus* from *M. T. Cicero, Brutus, On the Nature of the Gods, on Divination, On Duties,* translated by H. M. Poteat with introduction by R. McKeon (Chicago, 1950); Suetonius quotation from LL.

SALLUST: J. C. Rolfe, LL; Sallust's philosophy of history is well presented in W. Schur, *Sallust als Historiker* (Leipzig, 1934).

NEPOS: J. C. Rolfe, LL (with Florus); see D. R. Stuart, *Epochs of Greek and Roman Biography* (Berkeley, 1928).

ATTICUS: See G. Boissier, *Cicero and His Friends* (New York, 1897), and R. J. Leslie, *The Epicureanism of T. P. Atticus* (Philadelphia, 1950).

VARRO: *On Agriculture,* W. D. Hooper and H. B. Ash, LL (with Cato); *On the Latin Language,* R. G. Kent, 2 vols., LL. On the MENIPPEAN SATIRES see J. W. Duff, *Roman Satire* (Berkeley, 1936).

VII. CICERO

Among numerous books on Cicero mention may be made of E. G. Sihler, *Cicero of Arpinum* (New Haven, 1914); T. Petersson, *Cicero, a Biography* (Berkeley, 1920); G. C. Richards, *Cicero, a Study* (Boston, 1935); and R. McKeon's stimulating introduction to H. M. Poteat's translations of *Brutus, On the Nature of the Gods, On Divination, and On Duties* (Chicago, 1950), from which an extensive quotation is given in the text. Besides these and numerous other translations, there are 24 vols. in LL. Citations are regularly from either Poteat or LL. Good commentaries and introductions are also numerous. Mention may be made of J. S. Reid's editions of various orations, *Academica, De finibus;* J. B. Mayor's *De natura deorum;* T. W. Dougan's *Tusculanae disputationes;* A. S. Wilkins' *De oratore;* J. E. Sandys' *Orator;* H. A. Holden's *De officiis;* and R. Y. Tyrrell and L. C. Purser's *Letters.* Good selections of the letters in translation are A. P. McKinlay, *Letters of a Roman Gentleman* (Boston, 1926) and L. P. Wilkinson, *Letters of Cicero* (London, 1949). A convenient anthology is M. Hadas, *Basic Writings of Cicero* (Modern Library). The fantastic theory that the *Letters* were published by an enemy of Cicero is set forth by J. Carcopino, *Les Secrets de la correspondance de Ciceron,* 2 vols. (Paris, 1947). The quotation from E. G. Hardy on the *Contra Rullum* is from *Journal of Philology,* XXXII (1913); the Juvenal quotation is from LL.

VIII. VERGIL

Of the many books on Vergil see especially T. Frank (New York, 1922); T. R. Glover (London, 1923); W. Y. Sellar (Oxford, 1897); J. W. Mackail (ODGR). The quotation from Mark Van Doren is from the fine chapter on Vergil in his *The Noble Voice* (New York, 1946). Translations are cited from H. R. Fairclough, LL (2 vols.); J. W. Mackail (Modern Library); T. C. Williams, *Aeneid* (Boston, 1908) and *Georgics and Eclogues* (Harvard, 1915); H. H. Ballard (New York, 1930). There are good verse translations by John Dryden, J. Rhoades, J. Conington; and prose, by J. Jackson. The newest and brightest version of the *Aeneid* is Rolfe Humphries' verse (Boston, 1951). The most convenient commentary is that of T. E. Page in Macmillan's Classical Series (3 vols.). See also H. J. Rose, *The Eclogues of Vergil* (Berkeley, 1942). The *Monumentum Ancyranum* is quoted from the version of W. Fairley (Philadelphia, 1898). Cyril Bailey is quoted from his *Religion in Virgil* (Oxford, 1935); H. W. Prescott from *Classical Journal,* XXVI (1930), 62. E. E. Sikes' version of *Catalepton* 5 is from his *Ro-*

man Poetry (London, 1923). J. W. and A. M. Duff's translation of *Aetna* is from their *Minor Latin Poets*, LL.

IX. HORACE

Among books on Horace may be mentioned: T. Frank, *Catullus and Horace* (New York, 1928); L. P. Wilkinson, *Horace and His Lyric Poetry* (London, 1945); A. Y. Campbell, *Horace* (London, 1924); J. F. D'Alton, *Horace and His Age* (London, 1917); H. D. Sedgwick, *Horace, a Biography* (Harvard, 1947); Alfred Noyes, *Portrait of Horace* (London, 1947); W. Y. Sellar, *Roman Poets of the Augustan Age* (Oxford, 1892). LL *Satires and Epistles* is by H. R. Fairclough, *Odes and Epodes* by C. E. Bennett. A standard commentary is that of E. C. Wickham; Wickham also has a complete prose translation (1905). Of the versions cited that require identification, Eugene Field's are from his *Echoes of the Sabine Farm* (New York, 1897), J. Conington's and E. Marsh's from their translations of Horace (London, 1905 and 1941).

X. TIBULLUS AND PROPERTIUS

For the elegiac poets see W. Y. Sellar, *The Roman Poets of the Augustan Age* (Oxford, 1892) and K. P. Harrington, *The Roman Elegiac Poets* (New York, 1914).

Tibullus: J. P. Postgate, LL (with Catullus and *Pervigilium Veneris*). The edition of K. F. Smith (New York, 1913) is very helpful. T. C. Williams' translations are from his *The Elegies of Tibullus* (Boston, 1905); translations by Grainger and Holmes are from C. Bailey's *The Mind of Rome* (Oxford, 1926).

Propertius: H. E. Butler, LL; another good prose translation is J. S. Phillimore's (Oxford, 1906). The best commentary is H. E. Butler and E. A. Barber, *The Elegies of Propertius* (Oxford, 1933). Translations cited are from S. G. Tremenheere, *The Elegies of Propertius* (London, 1931) and E. H. W. Meyerstein, *The Elegies of Propertius* (London, 1935).

XI. OVID

On Ovid see H. Fränkel, *Ovid, a Poet between Two Worlds* (Berkeley, 1945), Sellar's *Roman Poets of the Augustan Age*, F. A. Wright's *Three Roman Poets*, and his *The Mirror of Venus*, which contains many sprightly versions. LL has *The Art of Love and Other Poems* by J. H. Mozley; *Fasti* by J. G. Frazer; *Metamorphoses* by F. J. Miller (2 vols.); and

Tristia and Ex Ponto by A. L. Wheeler. Quotations are from these, except for those from F. A. Wright's *Ovid's The Lover's Handbook* (New York, 1923) (*Ars amatoria*), and the Elizabethan versions taken from C. Bailey, *The Mind of Rome* (Oxford, 1926).

XII. LIVY AND OTHERS

LIVY: LL vols. by B. O. Foster, E. T. Sage, W. C. Schlesinger, F. G. Moore. The translation by Canon Roberts (Everyman's Library) is satisfactory. See H. Bornecque, *Tite Live* (Paris, 1933); T. Frank, *Life and Letters in the Roman Republic* (Berkeley, 1930), pp. 169 ff.; M. L. W. Laistner, *The Greater Roman Historians* (Berkeley, 1947), Ch. 5.

SENECA RHETOR: ed. with translation and commentary by W. A. Edward (New York, 1928); see W. C. Summers, *The Silver Age of Latin Literature* (London, 1920), Ch. 1.

VITRUVIUS: F. Granger, 2 vols., LL. The translation of J. H. Morgan (Harvard, 1914) has illustrations.

VELLEIUS PATERCULUS: F. W. Shipley, LL (with *Res gestae divi Augusti*).

VALERIUS MAXIMUS: The only English version is that of W. Speed (1678).

QUINTUS CURTIUS: J. C. Rolfe, 2 vols., LL.

CELSUS: W. G. Spencer, 2 vols., LL.

COLUMELLA: H. B. Ash, 1 vol. of eventual 3, LL.

MANILIUS: A. E. Housman's 5-vol. ed. (1903–1930) is famous.

XIII. SENECA

W. C. Summers' remarks on the pointed style are from the introduction to his *Select Letters of Seneca* (London, 1910); see also his *The Silver Age of Latin Literature* (London, 1920). LL has *Tragedies*, 2 vols., by F. J. Miller; *Moral Essays*, 3 vols., by J. W. Basore; *Epistulae morales*, 3 vols., by R. M. Gummere; *Apocolocyntosis* (with Petronius), by M. Heseltine. Verse translations of the tragedies by F. J. Miller and by Ella Isabel Harris are given in G. E. Duckworth, *The Complete Roman Drama*, 2 vols. (New York, 1942); see also P. W. Harsh, *A Handbook of Classical Drama* (Stanford, 1944). On the tragedies see C. W. Mendell, *Our Seneca* (New Haven, 1941); on their Stoic content, Berthe Marti, *Transactions of the American Philological Association*, LXXVI (1945), 216–45; on their influence, F. L. Lucas, *Seneca and Elizabethan Tragedy* (Cambridge, 1922). T. S. Eliot is quoted from his introduction to *Seneca His Tenne Tragedies* in the Tudor series, edited by T. Newton (London and New York, 1927). There are good remarks on Seneca's neuroses in E. P. Barker's OCD article. Aside from the introductions of Summers' edition of selected letters and J. D. Duff's of three dialogues (Cambridge, 1915), only F. Holland, *Seneca* (London, 1920) need be mentioned.

XIV. SILVER EPIC

The best treatment of the subject is Ch. 2 of W. C. Summers, *The Silver Age of Latin Literature* (London, 1920); quotations from the *Argonautica* are from this book. LL has a *Lucan* by J. D. Duff (there is a verse translation by E. Ridley [London, 1919]; Christopher Marlowe translated Book 1); a *Valerius Flaccus* by J. H. Mozley; a *Silius Italicus,* 2 vols., by J. D. Duff; and a *Statius,* 2 vols., by J. H. Mozley. The *Silvae* are also translated by D. A. Slater (Oxford, 1909). E. E. Sikes' version of the Lucan passage is from his *Roman Poetry* (London, 1923). The Pliny passage is from LL; Fyfe's version of the address to Sleep is taken from C. Bailey, *The Mind of Rome* (Oxford, 1926).

XV. SATIRE

On the whole subject see J. W. Duff, *Roman Satire* (Berkeley, 1936), and G. Highet in OCD, s.v. *Satura*. Juvenal and Persius are in a single LL volume by G. G. Ramsay; other quotations from these authors are from W. C. Summers, *The Silver Age of Latin Literature* or Duff's *Satire* or his *A Literary History of Rome in the Silver Age* (London, 1927). The standard English commentary of JUVENAL is that of J. E. B. Mayor (New York, 1901); of PERSIUS, that of J. Conington and H. Nettleship (Oxford, 1893). The French editor of Persius referred to is A. Cartault (Paris, 1920). Pliny on MARTIAL is quoted from LL. LL has a *Martial,* 2 vols., by W. C. A. Ker. Most of the translations are quoted from J. A. Pott and F. A. Wright, *Martial, The Twelve Books of Epigrams* (London, 1926); others are from Summers and Duff, as above. Tacitus on PETRONIUS is quoted from the Modern Library edition. The Petronius quotation is from the translation of J. M. Mitchell (London, 1922). There is a LL by M. Heseltine, and W. Burnaby's 1694 version is in the Modern Library with an introduction by C. K. Scott-Moncrieff. See also E. H. Haight, *Essays on Ancient Fiction* (New York, 1936). There is a good Budé *Phaedrus* by A. Brenot (1924).

XVI. LEARNING AND LETTERS IN THE FIRST CENTURY

PLINY THE ELDER: See H. N. Wethered, *The Mind of the Ancient World; a Consideration of Pliny's Natural History* (London, 1937). Four of projected ten LL volumes by H. Rackham have appeared; quotations are from this and from J. W. Duff, *A Literary History of Rome in the Silver Age* (London, 1927).

PLINY THE YOUNGER: The letters are all from LL.

QUINTILIAN: H. E. Butler, 4 vols., LL; see F. H. Colson's ed. of Book 1 (Cambridge, 1924) and W. Peterson's of Book 10 (Oxford, 1891). See also W. M. Smail, *Quintilian on Education* (Oxford, 1938).

FRONTINUS: C. E. Bennett, LL.

XVII. TACITUS AND SUETONIUS

TACITUS: Several paragraphs are taken, with the kind permission of the publishers, from M. Hadas' Modern Library edition. LL has good translations, by several hands; and there are translations of all except the *Annals* by W. H. Fyfe (Oxford, 1908 and 1912). The introductions to editions of the text by H. Furneaux are useful; see also M. L. W. Laistner, *Greater Roman Historians* (Berkeley, 1947), Chs. 6 and 7, and G. Boissier, *Tacitus and Other Roman Studies* (London, 1906); the French quotation is from the original of this work.

SUETONIUS: J. C. Rolfe, 2 vols., LL; see D. H. Stuart, *Epochs of Greek and Roman Biography* (Berkeley, 1928).

XVIII. THE AGE OF HADRIAN

O'Brien-Moore's translation of *Animula blandula* is from David Magie's excellent LL *Scriptores historiae Augustae*. The *Pervigilium Veneris* is translated in the Catullus and Tibullus vol. of LL. and also in Jack Lindsay, *Song of a Falling World* (London, 1948). The best commentary is C. Clementi's (Oxford, 1936).

FLORUS: E. S. Forster in LL with Rolfe's Nepos; the poems of Florus are in J. W. and A. M. Duff's LL *Minor Latin Poets*.

FRONTO: C. R. Haines' 2-vol. LL is especially valuable; see also M. D. Brock, *Studies in Fronto and His Age* (Cambridge, 1911).

APULEIUS: LL has Adlington's 1566 translation, revised by S. Gaselee, and there is a spirited modern translation by Robert Graves (Penguin, 1950); there are translations of *Metamorphoses* (1910) and of *Apology and Florida* (1909) by H. E. Butler. The Budé *Metamorphoses,* 3 vols., by D. S. Robertson and P. Valette (Paris, 1940–46) is excellent. There is a full commentary on the *Apology* by H. E. Butler and A. S. Owen (Oxford, 1914) and a charming edition of *Cupid and Psyche* by L. C. Purser (London, 1910); the Philemon selection from the *Florida* is taken from this book. Miss

Haight's translation from the *Metamorphoses* is from her *Essays on the Greek Romances* (New York, 1943), p. 191. See also her *Apuleius* (ODGR).

GELLIUS: J. C. Rolfe, 3 vols., LL.

XIX. THE THIRD CENTURY

SCRIPTORES HISTORIAE AUGUSTAE: D. Magie, 3 vols., LL; the excellent introduction is the best summary of the *Scriptores* problem. For the PANEGYRICI see OCD. NEMESIANUS and DICTA CATONIS: J. W. and A. M. Duff, *Minor Latin Poets*, LL.

XX. PAGANISM AT BAY: FOURTH-CENTURY PROSE

On the remaining period as a whole see G. Boissier, *La Fin du paganisme*, 2d ed., 2 vols. (Paris, 1913); J. B. Bury, *History of the Later Roman Empire*, 2 vols. (London, 1923); S. Dill, *Roman Society in the Last Century of the Roman Empire* (London, 1908); M. L. W. Laistner, *Thought and Letters in Western Europe* (London, 1931); J. Burckhardt, *The Age of Constantine*, translated by M. Hadas (New York, 1949); E. K. Rand, *The Founders of the Middle Ages* (Cambridge, 1941); E. G. Sihler, *From Augustus to Augustine* (Cambridge, 1923). T. R. Glover, *Life and Letters in the Fourth Century* (Cambridge, 1901) has fine essays on Ammianus Marcellinus, Ausonius, Symmachus, Macrobius, St. Augustine, Claudian, Prudentius, and others. E. S. Duckett, *Latin Writers of the Fifth Century* (New York, 1931) and *Gateway to the Middle Ages* (New York, 1938) are both learned and sprightly. J. E. Sandys, *A History of Classical Scholarship*, vol. 1, ed. 3 (Cambridge, 1921), is important for the transmission of humanism.

MACROBIUS: See T. Whittaker, *Macrobius, or Philosophy, Science, and Letters in the Year 400* (Cambridge, 1923); H. F. Stewart in *Cambridge Mediaeval History* 1.571 ff.; and D. Comparetti, *Vergil in the Middle Ages*, translated by E. F. M. Benecke (London, 1908).

AMMIANUS MARCELLINUS: J. C. Rolfe, 3 vols., LL; see E. A. Thompson, *The Historical Work of Ammianus Marcellinus* (Cambridge, 1947); W. M. L. Laistner, *The Greater Roman Historians* (Berkeley, 1947).

On FIRMICUS, Burckhardt has some good remarks. On SYMMACHUS, SERVIUS, and DONATUS, see Sandys, *A History of Classical Scholarship;* on DICTYS and DARES, see G. Highet, *The Classical Tradition* (Oxford, 1949).

XXI. HUMANIST SURVIVAL IN POETRY

Basic studies are F. J. E. Raby, *A History of Secular Latin Poetry in the Middle Ages*, 2 vols. (Oxford, 1934), and *A History of Christian-Latin Poetry from the Beginnings to the Close of the Middle Ages* (Oxford, 1927); these volumes contain ample bibliographies. Jack Lindsay, *Song of a Falling World* (London, 1948), has perceptive criticisms and generous translations of all the poets dealt with in this section.

AUSONIUS: H. G. Evelyn White, 2 vols., LL.

CLAUDIANUS: M. Platnauer, 2 vols., LL. There is a verse translation of the *Rape of Proserpine* by R. M. Pope (London, 1934), and by Jack Lindsay. Harry L. Levy, *The Invective in Rufinum of Claudius Claudianus* (New York, 1935) has a full introduction, commentary, and bibliography.

RUTILIUS NAMATIANUS: J. W. and A. M. Duff in *Minor Latin Poets*, LL. The edition of C. H. Keene (London, 1907) has a verse translation by C. F. Savage-Armstrong. See also E. S. Duckett, *Latin Writers of the Fifth Century* (New York, 1931).

SIDONIUS APOLLINARIS: W. B. Anderson, LL, so far only 1 vol., but with very full introduction. The *Letters* alone are translated by O. M. Dalton, 2 vols. (Oxford, 1915). See C. E. Stevens, *Sidonius Apollinaris and His Age* (Oxford, 1933). On Ennodius see E. S. Duckett, *Gateway to the Middle Ages* (New York, 1938), pp. 118-41.

BOETHIUS: The *Consolation* and the *Treatises*, H. F. Stewart and E. K. Rand in LL. There are translations of the *Consolation* by H. R. James (London, 1897) and by W. V. Cooper (Modern Library). The *Introduction to Porphyry* is translated by R. McKeon in his *Selections from Medieval Philosophers* (New York, 1929).

CASSIODORUS: The *Institutes* are edited by R. A. B. Mynors (London, 1937). The translation of the quaestorship passage is from Miss Duckett's *Gateway*.

XXII. THE WRITERS OF CHRISTIANITY

The best single book on the subject is P. de Labriolle, *Histoire de la littérature latine chrétien*, 3d ed., 2 vols. (Paris, 1947); there is an inferior translation of an earlier edition by H. Wilson, *History of the Literature of Christianity from Tertullian to Boethius* (London, 1924). A fuller work, treating Greek patristic literature also, is O. Bardenhewer, *Geschichte der altchristlichen Literatur*, 5 vols. (Freiburg, 1913-32). See also C. T. Cruttwell, *A Literary History of Early Christianity*, 2 vols. (London, 1893);

F. A. Wright, *Fathers of the Church* (London, 1928); E. J. Goodspeed, *A History of Early Christian Literature* (Chicago, 1942). Texts of all the authors are to be found in the 221 vols. of J. P. Migne's *Patrologia Latina* (Paris, 1844–80). A more scientific series, but still incomplete, is the Viennese *Corpus scriptorum ecclesiasticorum*. There are three great series of English translations: *The Ante-Nicene Christian Library,* 24 vols., edited by A. Roberts and J. Donaldson (Edinburgh, 1867–72); *The Select Library of Nicene and Post-Nicene Fathers,* 28 vols., edited by P. Schaff (Edinburgh, 1890–1908); and the older collection of E. B. Pusey, *The Fathers Anterior to the Division of East and West,* 50 vols. (Oxford, 1839 ff.).

TERTULLIAN: The *Apologeticus* and the *De spectaculis* are translated by T. R. Glover in the same LL vol. with G. H. Rendall's *Minucius Felix;* Thelwall's versions are from the *Ante-Nicene Fathers,* ed. by Allan Menzies, Vol. III. Tertullian a "barbarizing Tacitus," G. A. Simcox, *A History of Latin Literature* (New York, 1885) II, 275; "a Christian Juvenal," E. K. Rand, *Cambridge Ancient History,* XII, 593.

CYPRIAN: E. W. Benson, *Cyprian, His Life, His Time, His Work* (London, 1897).

ARNOBIUS: Translation with full introduction and commentary in G. E. McCracken, *Arnobius of Sicca, The Case against the Pagans,* 2 vols. (Westminster, Md., 1949).

LACTANTIUS: R. Pichon, *Lactance* (Paris, 1901).

AMBROSE: See T. Thompson, *St. Ambrose On the Sacraments and On the Mysteries* (New York, 1950). On Ambrose's hymns (and all poetry mentioned in this chapter) see F. J. E. Raby, *A History of Christian-Latin Poetry* (Oxford, 1927). A standard work on hymnology is G. M. Dreves and C. Blume, *Ein Jahrtausend lateinischer Hymendichtung* (Freiburg, 1909). Texts may be found in A. S. Walpole, *Early Latin Hymns* (Cambridge, 1922) or J. S. Phillimore's *The Hundred Best Latin Hymns* (London, 1926); S. A. Hurlbut's charming *Hortus conclusus* (Washington, 1936) has selected texts and translations of Ambrose, Prudentius, and Venantius Fortunatus.

PRUDENTIUS: H. J. Thompson, LL.

JEROME: F. A. Wright, *Select Letters,* LL; W. H. Fremantle, *The Principal Works of St. Jerome* (Oxford, 1893).

AUGUSTINE: A convenient collection (including the essentials of the *Confessions* and the *City of God*) is W. J. Oates, *The Basic Writings of St. Augustine,* 2 vols. (New York, 1948). *A Monument to St. Augustine* (London, 1930) is a fine collection of special studies. A modern text of the *Confessions* with full introduction and commentary is J. Gibbs and W. Montgomery (Cambridge, 1927); see also J. N. Figgis, *The Political Aspects of St. Augustine's City of God* (London, 1921) and J. B. Bury, *History of the Later Roman Empire* (London, 1923), I, 301–8. On the *Confessions* as lyric, see E. Norden, "Die lateinische Literatur im Uebergang vom Altertum zum Mittelalter," in *Die Kultur der Gegenwart* (Leipzig, 1912), I, 8, 501. On the importance of Augustine's metrical innovation, see Raby, *Christian-Latin Poetry.*

OROSIUS: The translation of I. W. Raymond, *Seven Books of History against the Pagans: The Apology of Paulus Orosius* (New York, 1936), has a good bibliography.

SALVIAN: Translation of E. M. Sanford, *On the Government of God* (New York, 1930); J. F. O'Sullivan, *The Writings of Salvian the Presbyter* (New York, 1947).

CHRONOLOGICAL TABLE

MANY OF THESE DATES ARE DOUBTFUL, SOME MERELY an arbitrary approximation. They are intended chiefly to present a sequence, inasmuch as the text, particularly in the last two chapters, does not follow chronological order.

284–204 B.C.	Livius Andronicus	116– 27 B.C.	Varro
270–201	Naevius	114– 50	Hortensius
255–184	Plautus	109– 32	Atticus
239–169	Ennius	106– 43	Cicero
168	Caecilius Statius	102– 44	Caesar
234–149	Cato	94– 55	Lucretius
220–130	Pacuvius	86– 34	Sallust
195–159	Terence	84– 54	Catullus
180–102	Lucilius	82– 47	Calvus
170– 85	Accius	70– 19	Vergil
150	Afranius	65– 8	Horace

63 B.C.–A.D. 14 Augustus
59 B.C.–A.D. 17 Livy
55 B.C.–A.D. 40 Seneca Rhetor
50 B.C.–A.D. 16 Propertius
48 B.C.–A.D. 19 Tibullus
43 B.C.–A.D. 17 Ovid
    Vitruvius
19 B.C.–A.D. 35 Velleius Paterculus
    Manilius
    Valerius Maximus
    Celsus
    Quintus Curtius
    Pomponius Mela
15 B.C.–A.D. 50 Phaedrus

A.D. 4– 65	Seneca	A.D. 66	Petronius
	Columella	40–104	Martial
	Calpurnius Siculus	45– 96	Statius
23– 79	Pliny the Elder	50–127	Juvenal
26–101	Silius Italicus	92	Valerius Flaccus
30–104	Frontinus	55–116	Tacitus
34– 62	Persius	61–113	Pliny the Younger
37– 95	Quintilian	69–140	Suetonius
39– 65	Lucan	76–138	Hadrian

A.D. 100–166 Fronto
 123–165 Aulus Gellius
 123–161 Apuleius
 160–225 Tertullian
 200–258 Cyprian
        Minucius Felix
        Arnobius
        Nemesianus
 250–317 Lactantius
        Firmicus Maternus
        Juvencus
 310–395 Ausonius
        Optatianus Porfyrianus
 330–395 Ammianus Marcellinus
 337–397 Ambrose
 340–402 Symmachus
 340–420 Jerome
 348–405 Prudentius
     408 Claudianus
        Rutilius Namatianus

        Aurelius Victor
        Eutropius
A.D. 353–451 Paulinus of Nola
        Sedulius
 354–430 Augustine
        Orosius
        Macrobius
        Aelius Donatus
        Avianus
        Avienus
        Servius
        Tiberius Claudius Dona-
          tus
        Martianus Capella
     482 Salvianus
 431–482 Sidonius Apollinaris
        Merobaudes
        Ennodius
 480–524 Boethius
 480–575 Cassiodorus

INDEX

NAMES AND TITLES ARE HERE LISTED ACCORDING TO
their more familiar form, whether *nomen* or *cognomen,* English or Latin.
Material within quoted or summarized material is not indexed, nor, as a
rule, are titles which are merely listed in the text. Figures in italics indicate
the principal passage for a rubric.